Safeguarding Educational Integrity Through Deepfake Face Detection

Ahmed J. Obaid
https://orcid.org/0000-0003-0376-5546
Universitas Al Asyariah Mandar, Iraq

Muthmainnah Muthmainnah
https://orcid.org/0000-0003-3170-2374
Universitas Al-Asyariah Mandar, Indonesia

S. Suman Rajest
https://orcid.org/0000-0001-8315-3747
Dhaanish Ahmed College of Engineering, India

Muhammad Mujtaba Asad
Sukkur IBA University, Pakistan

Luis Miguel Cardoso
https://orcid.org/0000-0003-3748-5593
Polytechnic Institute of Portalegre, Portugal

IGI Global
Scientific Publishing
Publishing Tomorrow's Research Today

Vice President of Editorial	Melissa Wagner
Director of Acquisitions	Mikaela Felty
Director of Book Development	Jocelynn Hessler
Production Manager	Mike Brehm
Cover Design	Jose Rosado

Published in the United States of America by
IGI Global Scientific Publishing
701 East Chocolate Avenue
Hershey, PA, 17033, USA
Tel: 717-533-8845 | Fax: 717-533-7115
Website: https://www.igi-global.com E-mail: cust@igi-global.com

Library of Congress Cataloging-in-Publication Data

LCCN: 2025029863 (CIP Data Pending)
ISBN13: 9798337337708
Isbn13Softcover: 9798337337715
EISBN13: 9798337337722

British Cataloguing in Publication Data
A Cataloguing in Publication record for this book is available from the British Library.

Table of Contents

Detailed Table of Contents

The proliferation of deepfake technology has generated unprecedented challenges for educational institutions that are striving to maintain information integrity and foster critical thinking skills amongst the students, this chapter evaluates the critical role of digital media literacy in combating deepfake misinformation within the educational contexts, and explore how the enhanced literacy frameworks can strengthen students to navigate the increasingly sophisticated synthetic media environments. Deriving the help from analysis of existing media literacy models, verification tools, and pedagogical approaches, this specific chapter displays how educational institutions develop comprehensive techniques for deepfake detection and response, and this research deliberately unveils that traditional media literacy approaches require notable adaptation for addressing the distinct challenges generated by AI-generated content, which creates necessity for the interdisciplinary collaboration between educators, technologists, and media specialist.

Merging deepfake technology and synthetic media has fundamentally altered the cognitive foundations of digital education, forcing educators to reconsider their fundamental assumptions about evidence, trust, and authenticity that underpin conventional pedagogical practices. Specifically, this chapter explores how the expansive availability of convincing synthetic media necessitates a radical transformation of learning objectives, instructional design, and teaching methodologies in digital classrooms. Analyzing the contemporary educational challenges posed by deepfakes, this chapter examines how educators must navigate an environment where traditional opinions about authentic evidence and credible sources are evolving in a problematic manner.

As the technology of deepfakes becomes more efficient at a rapid pace, it is now a necessity for industries like education to research methods for identifying tampered content. This paper presents an evaluation of current methods used in AI-based deepfake detection, employing machine learning approaches such as convolutional neural networks (CNNs) and generative adversarial networks (GANs). This chapter also contrasts the strengths and weaknesses of these techniques, comparing their effectiveness in detecting deepfake videos, images, and audio. Apart from a comparative evaluation of existing methods, the paper addresses other advancements and emerging technologies for improved deepfake detection, specifically multimodal detection techniques that utilise visual, audio, and text analysis. The work also provides a brief explanation of how to stay ahead of the ever-evolving nature of deepfake technology, emphasising the need for continuous innovation in detection methods.

This chapter assesses the seriousness of university deepfake scandals through a comprehensive review of some of the latest highly publicised incidents. Deepfakes have been used to replicate academic articles, impersonate teachers or students, and tarnish the reputation of institutions. The chapter presents case studies of institutions that were hacked using deepfakes and examines how these incidents impacted the institutions' reputations, public trust, and policy alignment. Regarding some of the previous cases where deepfake content was already used to victimise officers, students, and the public, the article outlines glaring loopholes present within university systems. The study employs data from incident reports, media, and university reports, utilising content analysis techniques to investigate the effects of the scandals. The findings are used to enhance safety against deepfakes and inform the response process.

Deepfake technology not only challenges academic integrity but also poses significant threats to the psychology and social life of students. This essay demonstrates that deepfakes have significant cognitive and affective implications for students, particularly in the context of social media and online learning. Their exposure to fake content instils fear, demoralises the internet services' confidence, and results in social

The technical risks of deepfakes are thoroughly documented. Still, their social and psychological consequences, mainly among students, are just beginning to be understood. This chapter delves deeply into the behavioral, cognitive, and emotional implications of deepfake exposure in academic settings, where the creation of realistic but false media can destroy students' ability to differentiate between truth and fabrication. This results in increased anxiety, declined trust, and an inclination towards skepticism towards digital communication. Drawing on psychological theories such as media effects, cognitive dissonance, and social identity, this chapter examines how synthetic content affects peer relationships, individual perception, and group dynamics within educational environments. This also explores the risks of identity manipulation, cyberbullying, and reputational harm when deepfakes are misused in social media or peer-to-peer contexts.

Integrating artificial intelligence technologies in educational settings puts forward a complex and dual-edged challenge where all the transformative learning opportunities must be balanced against considerable privacy and safety concerns, this chapter evaluates the tension between innovation and security in AI-powered education, and explore how institutions could harness the benefits of intelligent systems all the while protecting student data, ensuring equitable access, and maintaining ethical standards, to educational opportunities. Through this analysis of current AI applications in education, regulatory frameworks, and evolving security threats including deepfakes, this specific chapter gives a comprehensive framework for a better understanding of the multifaceted challenges faced by the educational institutions in the digital age.

G. Rajasekaran, Dhaanish Ahmed College of Engineering, Chennai, India
Mamta Singh, Ahmedabad Institute of Business Management, Ahmedabad, India
K. Krishnamoorthy, Sri Shanmugha College of Engineering and Technology, Sankari, India
Kanaka Durga Hanumanthu, Koneru Lakshmaiah Education Foundation, Vaddeswaram, India
K. Senthamilselvan, Dhaanish Ahmed College of Engineering, Chennai, India
Ahmed J. Obaid, University of Kufa, Iraq

Impostor academic credentials are a concern in the issue of academic credential validity. The essay explains how blockchain and digital forensics have come together to authenticate academic credentials. Blockchain is an open, transparent, and tamper-evident method for registering and authenticating higher educational certificates. Digital forensic software offers a trail of inquiry into whether digital diplomas and certificates are valid. The research aims to explore the possibility of integrating the two technologies onto a single platform, thereby facilitating verification and minimising the space for false academic certifications. The research focuses on the technical application of blockchain technology, specifically smart contracts and cryptographic hashing, to ensure the security and integrity of records. The study is also interested in exploring the application of digital forensic software to identify and suppress forged academic credentials.

Preface

INTRODUCTION

In recent years, Artificial Intelligence (AI) has emerged as a transformative force in higher education—reshaping teaching, learning, assessment, and administrative practice. Yet alongside these promising developments, the rapid evolution of AI-generated deepfake technologies has introduced an unprecedented set of risks that threaten the very foundations of academic integrity and digital trust. Deepfakes, which manipulate visual or audio content through advanced AI techniques, are no longer confined to the realm of entertainment or social media. Their growing sophistication poses tangible challenges to security, identity verification, and ethical practice within educational institutions.

This volume, *Safeguarding Educational Integrity Through Deepfake Face Detection*, addresses these emerging concerns by examining the critical intersection of deepfake detection, AI applications, and cybersecurity in higher education. While deepfake technologies have been rigorously studied within digital forensics and media analysis, their implications for academia remain significantly underexplored. Issues such as falsified academic credentials, manipulated instructional materials, fabricated lecture recordings, and AI-driven misinformation campaigns represent real threats to institutional credibility and student trust. As universities increasingly rely on AI-enabled systems for assessments, remote proctoring, and digital identity verification, these risks demand proactive and informed responses.

Our aim as editors is to illuminate these challenges while offering a comprehensive framework for mitigation. This book provides an in-depth analysis of contemporary deepfake detection methods, evaluates their applicability within educational contexts, and explores the broader ethical, legal, and cybersecurity considerations that accompany AI misuse. We highlight best practices for implementing institutional safeguards, including robust detection mechanisms, integrated cybersecurity strategies, and responsible AI policies that uphold the values of transparency, fairness, and accountability.

To ground these discussions in real-world experience, the book includes case studies from diverse higher education environments, offering concrete insights into how institutions are confronting deepfake-related threats. By drawing on interdisciplinary expertise—from computer science and digital forensics to law, ethics, and educational policy—we seek to foster a dialogue on the future of AI governance in academia. Our goal is to encourage collaboration among educators, administrators, policymakers, researchers, and technologists as they navigate the complex landscape of emerging digital risks.

This reference work is intended for academics and researchers in AI, cybersecurity, and educational technology; higher education administrators and IT security professionals; policymakers and legal experts concerned with digital ethics; AI developers and industry practitioners; and graduate students exploring AI governance and cybersecurity. We hope that the analyses and perspectives offered herein will serve as both a practical guide and a catalyst for continued scholarship—supporting institutions as they strive to protect educational integrity in an era defined by rapid technological change.

ORGANIZATION OF THE BOOK

Chapter 1: Balancing Ethical Implications of Using AI and Deepfake Technology for Academic Purposes

In our opening chapter, the authors confront the profound ethical tensions that accompany the use of AI and deepfake technologies in academic settings. Drawing on case studies and interviews, this chapter illustrates how these tools—while capable of enriching learning through authentic simulations—can also facilitate severe violations of privacy, consent, and academic honesty. Counterfeit assignments, instructor impersonation, and deceptive manipulations are examined as emerging risks that compromise institutional trust. This chapter not only documents real-world misuse but also calls for renewed ethical responsibility among educators, administrators, and technology developers, offering principled frameworks for safeguarding academic environments.

Chapter 2: Deepfake Technology Development and How It Affects Higher Education

The second chapter charts the rapid evolution of deepfake technologies and assesses their disruptive influence on higher education. Through an analysis of literature, institutional reports, and case studies, the authors reveal how deepfakes undermine academic integrity, distort web-based learning environments, and enable the creation of harmful or illegal content. They trace the paradox between the technology's educational possibilities and the vulnerabilities it introduces, documenting institutional responses and examining emerging detection tools designed to counter these threats. The chapter underscores the urgency of academic protection policies as deepfake sophistication continues to accelerate.

Chapter 3: AI-Powered Identity Verification Systems to Protect Remote Learning

With remote learning now central to higher education, Chapter 3 explores AI-driven identity verification systems—particularly biometric recognition, facial detection, and behavior tracking—as tools for securing online assessments. The authors detail how computer vision and deep neural models can prevent impersonation and cheating, while also acknowledging the privacy and ethical dilemmas inherent in their deployment. Drawing on technical implementations using OpenCV, Python, and Face++ APIs, this chapter provides a pragmatic analysis of both the promise and the peril of AI-based verification within digital learning environments.

Chapter 4: Empowering Minds by Strengthening Digital Media Literacy to Combat Deepfake Misinformation in Education

This chapter positions digital media literacy as a central defense against deepfake-driven misinformation in educational settings. By analyzing literacy models, verification tools, and contemporary pedagogical approaches, the authors demonstrate how institutions can build more resilient frameworks to help students critically evaluate synthetic media. They argue that traditional media literacy programs are insufficient for today's AI-mediated landscape, calling instead for interdisciplinary collaboration among educators, technologists, and media specialists. The chapter highlights how literacy-centered interventions can equip learners to navigate increasingly deceptive digital ecosystems.

Chapter 5: Learning in the Age of Illusion—Rethinking Pedagogy for Deepfake-Driven Digital Classrooms

Chapter 5 addresses the pedagogical ramifications of deepfake and synthetic media technologies, which challenge the foundational concepts of authenticity, evidence, and trust in digital learning. The authors argue that educators must recalibrate instructional design, learning objectives, and teaching practices to align with a world where manipulated media blurs lines between reality and fabrication. Through a discussion of contemporary challenges and shifting epistemic norms, this chapter illuminates the need for pedagogical innovation in an age where illusion can be indistinguishable from truth.

Chapter 6: Current and Future Techniques of AI-Based Deepfake Detection

In this chapter, the authors survey the state of the art in AI-based deepfake detection, offering a comparative analysis of CNNs, GANs, and multimodal detection systems that integrate video, audio, and text cues. They highlight each method's strengths and shortcomings while predicting future innovations required to keep pace with evolving deepfake capabilities. This chapter reinforces the necessity of continuous research and technological improvement to safeguard sectors such as education, where misinformation and impersonation carry high stakes.

Chapter 7: Analyzing Deepfake-Related Scandals in Higher Education—Case Study Insights

Chapter 7 provides a sobering examination of recent deepfake-driven scandals across universities, documenting incidents involving fabricated academic articles, impersonation of faculty and students, and targeted reputational attacks. Through content analysis of media reports, institutional statements, and incident documentation, the authors expose systemic vulnerabilities and policy gaps exploited by malicious actors. Their insights contribute to a clearer understanding of institutional risks and offer pathways for building more resilient crisis response strategies.

Chapter 8: Unpacking the Psychological and Social Impact of Deepfake Technology on Students

This chapter explores the cognitive, emotional, and social consequences of deepfake exposure on student populations. Using survey data, focus groups, and mixed-methods analysis, the authors reveal how synthetic media can heighten anxiety, distort perceptions of reality, and undermine trust within academic communities. The study emphasizes the need for expanded media literacy education and targeted support systems to help students navigate the psychological complexities introduced by deepfake technologies.

Chapter 9: Legal Challenges and Policy Responses to Deepfake Abuse in Schools

Chapter 9 examines the legal landscape surrounding deepfake misuse within educational environments, evaluating the limitations of existing defamation and copyright laws while identifying regulatory loopholes exploited by synthetic content. Through analysis of case law and judicial precedent, the authors argue for updated policies that protect schools without infringing on access to education. Their recommendations offer governments and institutions a roadmap toward balanced, forward-looking legislative reform.

Chapter 10: Seeing Isn't Believing—The Psychological and Social Toll of Deepfakes on Student Perception and Well-Being

Complementing earlier chapters, Chapter 10 delves deeper into the psychological theories underlying students' responses to deepfake content. Drawing on media effects, cognitive dissonance, and social identity frameworks, the authors describe how exposure to highly convincing fabricated media erodes trust, destabilizes peer relationships, and increases vulnerability to manipulation and cyberbullying. This chapter highlights the urgent need for robust psychosocial supports and digital well-being interventions.

Chapter 11: Smart but Secure—Navigating the Tension Between Innovation and Safety in AI-Powered Education

This chapter analyzes the inherent tension between the promise of AI-driven educational innovation and the pressing need to protect student privacy, safety, and equity. Through an examination of regulatory frameworks, institutional policies, and security threats—including deepfakes—the authors present a comprehensive model for responsibly integrating emerging technologies. The chapter encourages institutions to embrace innovation while establishing rigorous guardrails that uphold ethical standards.

Chapter 12: Convergence of Blockchain and Digital Forensics to Authenticate Academic Credentials

Chapter 12 evaluates how blockchain and digital forensics can jointly combat credential fraud—a growing concern exacerbated by deepfake technologies. By exploring smart contracts, cryptographic hashing, and forensic validation tools, the authors propose an integrated platform to authenticate academic records with greater transparency and tamper resistance. This chapter offers a forward-looking model for securing institutional credibility in an era of synthetic document manipulation.

Chapter 13: Deepfake Manipulation Protection Using Digital Media Literacy Education

In this chapter, the authors advocate for deep integration of modern media literacy education to equip students and educators with the skills necessary to identify and question manipulated content. Through curriculum analysis, classroom evidence, and educator-student questionnaires, the chapter evaluates the readiness of current literacy programs to counter deepfake-based disinformation. Its findings reinforce the need for renewed curricular focus on critical thinking and digital discernment.

Chapter 14: The Challenges of AI-Based Proctoring Systems in Online Exams

Chapter 14 offers a balanced investigation of AI-driven proctoring systems, analyzing their effectiveness in preventing cheating while interrogating the fairness, accuracy, and ethical implications of biometric and behavioral monitoring. Drawing on system logs, student feedback, and technical assessments using Python and OpenCV, the authors highlight both the capabilities and limitations of contemporary proctoring tools. The chapter concludes with practical recommendations for developing transparent, equitable, and trustworthy assessment environments.

Chapter 15: From Novelty to Threat—The Evolution of Deepfakes and Their Disruptive Influence on Higher Education

This chapter traces the transformation of deepfakes from experimental curiosities to sophisticated threats capable of destabilizing core academic functions. With a focus on GAN-driven advancements, the authors analyze how synthetic media now imperils research integrity, credential verification, and institutional trust. The chapter provides a comprehensive assessment of the technological, structural, and policy vulnerabilities that higher education must address in order to preserve authenticity and reliability in academic processes.

Chapter 16: Implementing Cybersecurity Policies to Minimize the Impacts of Deepfakes on Universities

This chapter highlights the early vulnerabilities of university systems, including online tests, digital certifications, and virtual courses, which are easily compromised by deepfakes. The study evaluates modern-day cybersecurity paradigms, mapping current security and vulnerabilities to deepfakes. In the context of academic deepfake crises, the study identifies a need for effective cybersecurity practices. It therefore advocates for the use of AI-based deepfake detection technologies, robust authentication methods, and data authentication practices within the university's cybersecurity strategy.

Chapter 17: Human-AI Collaboration in Combatting Digital Fraud in Education

The final chapter examines deepfake-related academic fraud in Muslim-majority educational contexts, proposing a Human-AI collaboration framework grounded in Islamic ethical principles. Through case studies and empirical evidence, the authors highlight the challenges of credential forgery, impersonation, and disinformation, emphasizing that effective mitigation requires both advanced AI verification systems and strong human oversight. This chapter concludes the volume by reinforcing the need for culturally informed, ethically anchored, and technologically empowered strategies to uphold academic integrity.

CONCLUSION

As we conclude this preface, we reaffirm the central message that guided the development of this volume: the rise of deepfake technology represents one of the most urgent and complex challenges facing higher education in the digital age. Across the chapters that follow, the contributing authors collectively illuminate how synthetic media—driven by advances in artificial intelligence—now intersects with every facet of academic life, from pedagogy and assessment to cybersecurity, governance, ethics, and student well-being. Their work underscores the reality that deepfakes are not merely a technical phenomenon but a multidimensional threat that demands coordinated, interdisciplinary responses.

Together, these chapters demonstrate that safeguarding educational integrity requires more than detection algorithms or policy updates alone. It calls for a fundamental rethinking of how institutions cultivate trust, authenticate identity, verify information, and support learners in an increasingly uncertain digital environment. As editors, we are encouraged by the thoughtful strategies presented here—ranging from AI-powered verification systems and blockchain credentialing to media literacy initiatives, legal reforms, and cross-cultural ethical frameworks. These contributions collectively advance a vision of higher education that embraces innovation while remaining anchored in responsibility, transparency, and human dignity.

We hope that this book serves not only as a reference for researchers and practitioners but also as a catalyst for ongoing dialogue and institutional action. The challenges posed by deepfakes will continue to evolve, and the academic community must remain proactive, collaborative, and adaptive. It is our hope that the insights offered within these pages empower educators, policymakers, technologists, and students to build more resilient, secure, and ethically grounded learning environments. In doing so, we reaffirm the enduring mission of higher education: to uphold truth, foster critical inquiry, and protect the integrity of knowledge in an era defined by profound digital transformation.

Chapter 1
Balancing Ethical Implications of Using AI and Deepfake Technology for Academic Purposes

P. Sudha
https://orcid.org/0009-0007-2307-7026
Dhaanish Ahmed College of Engineering, India

Usha Seshadri
VIT-AP University, Amaravathi, India

Raghavendra Acharya
https://orcid.org/0000-0002-5798-6363
VIT-AP University, Amaravathi, India

Anvay Bhargava
https://orcid.org/0000-0002-9608-3757
Jaipuria Institute of Management, Jaipur, India

M. Shagar Banu
https://orcid.org/0009-0009-5924-218X
Dhaanish Ahmed College of Engineering, India

M. Rehena Sulthana
Melbourne Institute of Technology, Australia

ABSTRACT

Another aspect of the deployment of AI and deepfakes is a horrific ethics issue with privacy, consent, and academic honesty. A solution to the aforementioned ethics issues is proposed in this article, specifically through the implementation of deepfake technology in schools. Although AI and deepfakes can enhance study materials by providing more authentic practice, their application can lead to significant ethical violations. This essay examines the ethical implications of utilising AI to cheat on coursework, encompassing the creation of counterfeit assignments, impersonation

DOI: 10.4018/979-8-3373-3770-8.ch001

of instructors, and the potential harm to students. The essay becomes a historical record of the ethical obligations of instructors, administrators, and tech companies to prevent such evils. The research, through case studies and interviews, informs real-life deepfake abuse in schools and its implications on individuals and institutions.

INTRODUCTION

Artificial Intelligence (AI) and deepfake technologies are transforming learning environments at an increasingly rapid rate, facilitating new pedagogical processes while also raising some extremely serious ethical questions. The use of such technologies in learning enables richer features, such as simulated immersive learning, more interactive content, and learner interaction tailored to individual needs, according to Michel-Villarreal et al. (2023). However, the unregulated and uncontrolled use of such tools has also driven unprecedented abuse, including identity manipulation, data misuse, and integrity violations. Deepfakes, produced by Generative Adversarial Networks (GANs), are nearly undetectable from real synthetic media (image, video, audio) that appear highly realistic. Tripathi (2024) initially developed the first GAN model, which was later utilised in face reenactment studies involving deepfakes by Korshunova et al. (2017) and Mompel and Lombrio (2024). Its application as an aid tool for learning simulations—i.e., training in medical or historical contexts—was tested in live performances of immersive learning by Pulivarthy (2024).

Deepfakes do present some real dangers, though, such as student impersonation to fake lectures, cyberbullying through student videos created, assignment forgery with content material, and assignment forgery with AI-generated work. Tolosana et al. (2020) report. Deepfakes have been made possible by the automation of realistic manipulation tools, as introduced by Thies et al. (2016), and further developed using real-time synthesis techniques by He et al. (2019). The moral implications of such innovations are foreboding and profound, affecting fundamental values which provide guarantees for purity of educational processes—i.e., privacy, academic honesty, and accountability. Gomathy and Venkatasbramanian (2023) offer insights into the use of conversational AI in sensitive scholarly procedures, raising concerns about procedural consent and purity in online learning processes.

The fundamental issue with such instruments is that maintaining academic integrity becomes increasingly difficult in a high-tech era that facilitates manipulation. If students use AI to produce essays, videos, or presentations without disclosure, it is not just a technical issue. It goes against basic ethics of learning, diluting individual effort and scholarship originality—a well-arguable truth by Venkatasubramanian et al. (2023). This is also a moral obligation on the part of institutions and educators, who must ensure technology innovation is not occurring at a faster pace than accountability, as Dwivedi et al. (2023) have also delineated. Learning institutions, as they attempt to comply with equitable measurement, can introduce bias into the situation, contaminate measurement, and deceive true measures of performance, as Rendhy (2024) has also stated.

Abuse of Deepfakes is more serious. Mompel and Lombrio (2024) invented neural photorealistic face-swapping methods, which were applied to academic impersonation forgery in videos. The methods, being the first of their kind, were subsequently applied to produce forgeries of academic work and impersonate lecturers or students (Thies et al. 2016). This scholarly life deepfake abuse can cause severe reputational damage, defamation, and even psychological harm, as seen in case studies by Michel-Villarreal et al. (2023). Voice or video abuses can cause irreparable damage to the victim, tarnishing their professional reputation, as detailed by Pulivarthy (2024).

The global spread of AI-assisted academic cheating and the undue use of deepfakes is an open call for robust countermeasures. The institutions have been hesitant to use moral and legal standards to oversee these tendencies Dwivedi et al., 2023; Allen et al., 2024; Venkatasubramanian et al., 2023). More needs to be done to oversee AI technology and academic scholarship beyond fair terms of consent, transparency, and fairness, as Allen et al. (2024) and Venkatasubramanian et al. (2023) insist. AI tool bias and automation loopholes have the potential to bypass conventional pedagogic norms, as Rendhy (2024) explained. To this end, more sophisticated deepfake countermeasures and detection systems are being developed, e.g., as seen in Tolosana et al. (2020) research; however, organisational responses extend beyond the tech bubble. Last but not least, deepfake technology—so intriguing, perhaps, when applied rightfully—is under surveillance to prevent its misuse in academic dishonesty and trust violations (Korshunova et al. 2017; He et al. 2019).

The challenge is addressed by the study through an analysis of AI and deepfake use and misuse in classrooms, raising relevant questions of ethics, and an examination of stakeholders' engagement to address issues of this kind. Pragmatic case studies, scholarly expert interviews, and deontological and utilitarian ethics theories are utilised to determine rule-based responses (Venkatasubramanian et al., 2023). The primary concern of this paper is to strike a balance between the potential pedagogical value of AI and deepfakes, and a robust ethical framework that upholds privacy, consent, and intellectual integrity (Mompel and Lombrio, 2024). By conducting risk mapping and outlining policy-level interventions, the research aims to empower universities and tech designers with the tools and moral imagination necessary to utilise such life-changing technologies responsibly (Jasper et al., 2023).

REVIEW OF LITERATURE

Allen et al. (2024) undertook pioneering work on the ethical implications arising from AI technology in scholarly consent processes. The gradual integration of AI and deepfake technologies in academia has raised serious controversy among ethicists, instructors, and technologists. Padmavathy et al. (2024) have given considerable emphasis in their previous research on AI in higher education to its ability to re-shape teaching practices by offering solutions for combating automation as well as personalising learning. Previous studies highlighted the positive contribution of AI in creating improved evaluation processes, adaptive feedback, and paving the way for "smarter" curriculum designs (Bastareche 2024). These technologies were expected to release the' time of teachers from administrative tasks and enable dynamic classrooms. The positive contribution of improved academic achievement among students was unprecedented through enhanced grading systems. The amplitude of the increase in ethical issues has transformed everything since then (Rizal et al. 2024).

Michel-Villarreal et al. (2023) also outlined the potential and potential pitfalls introduced into academic settings by generative AI. They highlighted how easily AI-generated essays and reports can be used to facilitate scholarly misconduct. AI technology currently has the potential to mimic students' voices, create entire assignments, and even provide quiz solutions (Fauzy et al., 2024). The scope of automation undermines the validity of work produced by students and diminishes the value of the premise underlying conventional marking systems. The access level is reaching a point where an increasing number of students will inevitably misuse it. Educational institutions are now having to contend with the issue of distinguishing between original work and AI-generated work. The validity of academic exams is being undermined at their foundation.

Rendhy (2024) subsequently explored the educational implications of AI decision-making and its unexpected outcomes. AI machines can be designed to accurately replicate humans' faces and voices. The feature enables students to participate in a learning activity without actually engaging (Pulivarthy 2024). For instance, a deepfake video will be used to display a student giving a presentation or studying an online course that he never signed up for. Such abuse not only misleads teachers but also undermines the genuine effort and work of students. Schools struggle to maintain accurate visual and audio records of students' presence. The avoidance of lines between original content and replicated content requires policy-making at a rapid pace.

Dwivedi et al. (2023) conducted a systematic review of the ethical role of schools in the application of AI. They have learned that the problem is that few schools have proper structures to deal with AI and deepfake technologies. Teachers often implement AI technology in schools without being aware of its effects on privacy and consent. Students unknowingly share their data—words, behaviours, and photos—to be scraped and re-posted. This raises ethical issues of exploitation and informed consent for discussion. Institutions are being compelled to lay down concrete policies regarding how AI tools collect, store, and process personal information. They have never been more so.

Pulivarthy (2024) additionally outlined institutional preparedness in the fight against AI abuse. In the article, they described how institutions lag in preparing staff to identify and reverse deepfakes. While AI software is used for efficiency in large volumes, tracking systems are not typically attached to it in the majority of institutions. Olubunmi (2024) notes that exposing oneself to such differences predisposes one to academic dishonesty and a loss of reputation. Deepfakes may be used to impersonate teachers, making off-colour remarks or reading scripted exercise reviews. It is a degrading act against individuals as well as a loss of reputation to institutions (Rendhy, 2024). General awareness campaigns and ethics in the use of technology are necessary to address this vulnerability.

Tolosana et al. (2020) used behavioural and biometric signals as the foundation for a study on deepfake detection. Specified was how spoof media can be detected through the application of artificial facial expressions, coupled with eye movement. These markers are employed in academic circles to authenticate the originality of student presentations. Aribisala et al. (2024) nevertheless, using such detection tools is typically reserved for institutions that lack the capacity. Educators receive minimal training in forensic video examination, which disadvantages them. Dullete (2024) notes that deepfakes continue to evolve as existing detection models lag. Artificial intelligence-capitalised forensics is now emerging as an indispensable supplement to university security.

Korshunova et al. (2017) shed light on generative adversarial models that revolutionised facial reenactment methods. Their technology can achieve a natural face swap on video, and the potential implications of identity theft in schools begin to surface. Students can take oral exams or recorded lectures on another's identity. Teacher credentials can be compromised for nefarious purposes, including grade manipulation or prank harassment. Alkasi et al. (2024) identification is extremely challenging and requires the use of the technology itself and specialised software. More secure access control must also be implemented for this revolutionary technology. Regulation checking must be implemented to prevent such misuse in scholarly environments.

He et al. (2019) constructed models that could transfer facial expressions onto new faces between actors. Their model was utilised in producing spurious academic speech, mimicking advisor-student meetings or review meetings. According to Padmavathy et al. (2024), this artificial content undermines trust between teachers and students. In video-recorded online classes, it is impossible to distinguish between virtual and real objects. Higher institutions with high asynchronous learning are vulnerable. Identity should be protected from manipulation, but watermarking and multifactor authentication should be utilised. They will provide authentic, real-time interaction as well as academic integrity (Moyo and Nithyanantham 2024).

Thies et al. (2016) created interactive face manipulation from real-time information streams. The system can simulate expression from source to target and has already found application in photo editing, helping students prepare for academic anomalies. Students, for example, have even posed as pseudo-interviewers or practical examiners with deepfakes over pages. These types of incidents undermine not just individual credibility but even institutional credibility (Ahmad et al., 2025). Once fabricated information is let loose, rolling back its impact is an uphill task. University boards are already considering legal policies for handling such artificial dishonesty. Pre-emptive monitoring and intervention are already becoming part of maintaining ethical standards.

Measures that can detect eye blink patterns within deepfakes, the first known forensic red flag, were developed by Mompel and Lombrio (2024). Although their solution was more effective at detection, most educational systems have not yet incorporated such programs into their standard practices. Lack of real-time detection of deepfakes in educational systems leaves potential abuse vulnerable to detection. As e-learning increases, so will the forgery and impersonation of content. Universities need to implement such detection algorithms into their e-learning environments (Bhuvaneswari et al., 2025). Technical security, combined with ethical sensitivity, will help ward off the abuse of deepfakes in academia.

The role of deontological ethics (duty-based) and utilitarian ethics (goal-based) is at the core of such issues. Obaid et al. (2024) argue that deontological traditions are concerned with individual autonomy and moral obligation, and consider the immoral use of AI to be inherently evil. The utilitarian authors are concerned with whether the benefits of learning through AI outweigh its dangers to others, especially if better learning does not compromise rigour. Stakeholders' roles are continued in the next section. While some works discuss the demands of teachers for ethically training AI, others focus on the role of IT administrators and coders in incorporating safety features into training technology. All concur that AI governance policies directly applicable to learning spaces must be upgraded.

In defence technology, in the pipeline are AI-based detection systems that will identify deepfakes using physiological signals (blink inconsistency, lip sync anomaly). However, writings are limited to such technology when applied to good, adversarially trained deep fake videos. Existing codes of ethics in education are being revised to accommodate AI, but they have yet to be applied with awareness. Research is needed to address the gaps in policy-making and policy implementation among institutions, particularly those with low digital literacy or cybersecurity capabilities. Scholarship opines that without an ethical framework, further applications of AI and deepfake technologies threaten to undermine authenticity. To counter trust and transparency issues in education innovation, an interdisciplinary approach that combines ethical philosophy, technical mitigation practices, and stakeholder accountability is necessary.

METHODOLOGY

This research employs qualitative-analytic approaches, including case study analysis, expert interviews, and ethical reasoning frameworks, to investigate the use of AI and deepfakes in an educational context. The research is based on primary and secondary evidence, including documented deepfake abuse, organisational checks, and interviews with teachers, IT specialists, and AI practitioners. Five schools suspected to have high levels of digitalisation were selected for qualitative case study analysis. Every figure delineates the context, form of AI/deepfake abuse, reaction of stakeholders, and related implications. Fifteen stakeholders – five academic managers, five teachers, and five AI developers – participated in interviews conducted by purposive sampling. Semi-structured interviews provided insight into their experiences, perceived ethical risks, mitigation strategies, and institutional policies. They were assessed using recorded interviews, transcriptions, and thematic content analysis.

Figure 1. Architecture of ethical deepfake control in academia

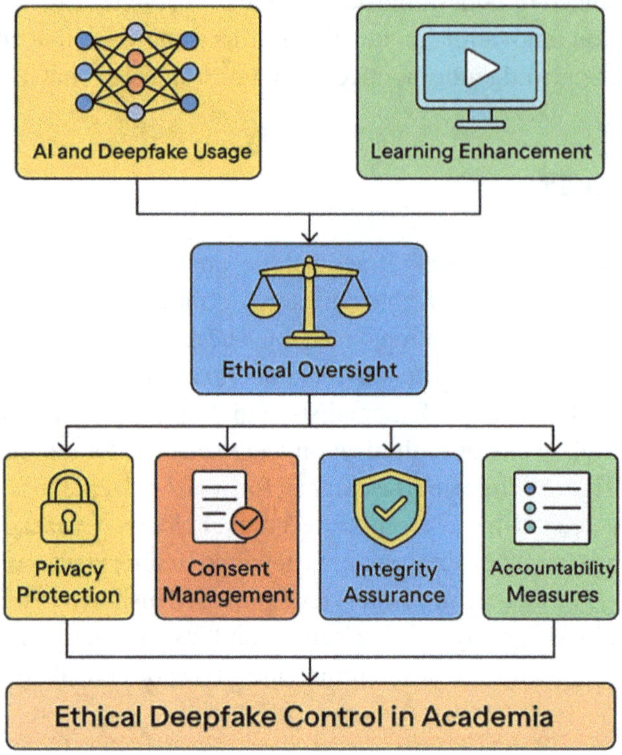

In Figure 1, AI and deepfake technology raise questions about control in colleges and their ethics. It has been broken down into three simple levels: AI and Deepfake Utilisation, Learning Improvement, and Ethical Regulation. The most basic level, "AI and Deepfake Usage," comprises modules such as simulation content creation, identity transformation, and smart examination tools, which are implementations of these technologies in learning environments. The second, "Learning Enhancement," involves optimal usage, including interactive learning, AI-driven learning, and multimedia-enhanced courses. These are the learning benefits that can be harvested by utilising AI and deepfakes if utilised properly.

All but the external segment, "Ethical Oversight," are portrayed as proper use controls, i.e., Privacy Protection, Consent Management, Integrity Assurance, and Accountability Measures. They are represented as single, coloured blocks or icons for each of their respective, but complementary, proper use management functions. Loops and arrows between divisions illustrate the repeated cycles of monitoring, appraisal, and policy enforcement across all technology processes. Figure 1 also depicts stakeholder engagement—students, instructors, IT personnel, and developers—at varying levels within the system, facilitating a mutual push for ethical balance. Active governance, comprising pre-established morals, AI-detection functionality, and cross-functional reporting, forms the foundational elements of the architecture. And finally, Figure 1 is a map to achieve a balance between technological advancement and academic integrity, leading the academe to a long-term ethics framework for deepfakes and AI.

DATA DESCRIPTION

The research findings were gathered from three sources: scholarly case studies, expert interviews, and institutional policy reviews. Expert interviews were conducted through Zoom and transcribed on Otter.ai. Five real-life examples of deepfake abuse in academe were analysed from scholarly case studies, referencing instances of academic dishonesty caused by deepfake technology. Institutional policy analysis of reports from reputable agencies, including IEEE, UNESCO's Initiative on AI in Education, and the European Network of Academic Integrity, was conducted. Analysis of the reports provided insight into institutional responses to ethical concerns about the use of AI technology in education. In addition, preparedness scores, ethical training indices, and incident reports data points were extracted from institutional cybersecurity audit reports, reflecting the dominant status of academic integrity measures against AI. EDUCAUSE institutional audit reports released provided significant measurements on institutional preparedness against AI threats and ethical training program success rates.

RESULTS

The morality of deepfakes and AI technologies within the academic context reflects the complicated relationship between risk and benefit. From case studies, expert interviews, and policy analysis, findings create the most striking patterns of ethical risk and actor dynamics. The threat to academic integrity, privacy, and institutional reputation has increased as AI technologies, like deepfakes, become more prevalent in academia. Among the negative outcomes of the study is the inconsistency in preparedness among institutions. Less prepared institutions have a higher likelihood of encountering high-severity ethics cases, especially those involving privacy violations and academic honesty. Less prepared institutions lack the ethical regulations and procedural mechanisms necessary to mitigate the risks associated with AI and deepfake technology.

On the other hand, institutions with preparedness scores above 70% have a stronger capability to recover from negative incidents, necessitating the development of robust ethical standards and training programs to combat the threats posed by AI technologies. The report also outlines the differences in obligations and performance among academic stakeholders, including technology developers, administrators, professors, and students. The Ethical Risk Index (ERI) function is given below:

$$ERI = \sum_{i=1}^{n} \left(\frac{S_i \cdot F_i}{100 - M_i} \cdot \frac{1}{P_i + 1} \right) \quad (1)$$

Where S_i =severity score, F_i =frequency, M_i = mitigation effectiveness (%), P_i = preparedness score.

Table 1. Ethical risk assessment metrics in academic AI usage

Ethical Domain	Severity Score (1-10)	Frequency of Cases	Institutional preparedness (%)	Mitigation Effectiveness (%)
Privacy Risk	8	45	60	50
Consent Violation	9	40	55	45
Integrity Breach	10	50	50	40
Reputation Harm	8	35	45	35
Accountability Gap	7	30	40	30

Table 1 presents a four-dimensional assessment of the areas of ethical risk where AI should be used in higher education, based on four key parameters: severity, frequency, readiness, and the ability to contain. All areas of ethics—encompassing data integrity and consent, as well as reputation and fairness—are evaluated based on their impact and the extent to which institutions are addressing the issue. Abuses of integrity are worst in terms of severity score (10/10) for being primarily AI-generated homework, and worse still, deepfake impersonations during examinations. These abuses infringe upon academic authenticity and undermine the long-term credibility of certificates. Informed consent violations are also seen, where student likeness or information is used without consent, particularly in training sets or monitoring use. Reputation loss ranks closely behind, although at a comparatively inferior rate.

Nonetheless, its effect is considerable because it is long-lasting—students and teachers who are wrongly accused by deepfakes can also lose their professional as well as personal reputation permanently. Questions of fairness and bias arise less frequently but need to be addressed nonetheless, especially in grade programs or AI learning environments that simulate systemic unfairness. Most remarkable is the overall sub-par performance in readiness and mitigation. Low scores indicate that few institutions have in place mechanisms for ethically framed training, ethical audit, or detection mechanisms. The backlog makes them vulnerable to increasing threats. The table then suggests the need to invest systematically in ethics education, detection mechanisms, and open-governance AI platforms, so that AI can be integrated into academia responsibly without compromising ethical standards. Stakeholder Impedance (I_s) calculation can be done as:

$$I_s = \left|R_s - E_s\right| + \lambda\left(1 - \frac{T_s}{10}\right) \quad (2)$$

Where R_s = responsibility index, E_s =effectiveness index, T_s =training score, λ =weig ht for training deficiency.

Figure 2. Demonstration of the connection between ethical risk severity and institutional preparedness

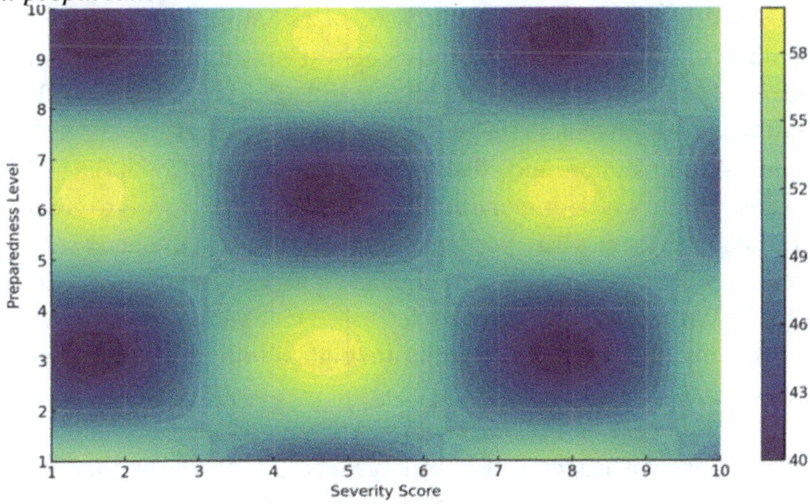

Figure 2 illustrates a contour plot that aims to demonstrate the relationship between the severity of ethical risk and institutional preparedness to handle AI technologies, particularly in education. The Y-axis represents institutional preparedness—the preparatory activities, such as ethical policy deployment, faculty and staff training, detection systems, and incident response plans—along one dimension, and the X-axis represents the severity of ethical risk—ranging from low to critical—along the other axis. The chart is superimposed with colored gradations representing levels of total aggregate risk, thus defining zones of vulnerability and resilience. Below readiness, there is a red zone with few or no structured processes to hold AI misuse in check. There, ethical risks such as incursions into data privacy, breaches of consent, and manipulation with AI tools, like deepfakes, are likely to escalate to the stratosphere.

Climbing up along the Y-axis to increased readiness, these risks shift into green or blue zones, meaning less damage. These sectors are a prime example of institutions investing positively in AI ethics governance. This chart also testifies to the most important finding: ethical risk is less a result of outside AI abuse and more closely associated with an institution's capacity for forecasting and prevention of such. Institutions with sound AI ethics education, vigilant monitoring, and prudent policy frameworks can realistically prevent prospective abuse. Thus, the contour map not only defines weaknesses but also serves as a tool for planning, helping establish where investment in ethical infrastructure can be most efficacious in minimising risks. The Weighted Multi-Domain Risk Score (WMRS) can be expressed as:

$$WMRS = \sum_{j=1}^{m} \omega_j \left(\frac{S_j^2 + F_j^2}{2}\right)\left(1 - \frac{M_j}{100}\right) \tag{3}$$

Where ω_j =doma *in*-specific weight, S_j, F_j, M_j as before.

Technology inventors often exhibit the highest sensitivity and respect for ethical standards, but their conduct is not always in harmony with these values. This is quite crucial, as the inventors play a significant role in crafting and applying AI technologies. Administrators and educators express concern about the ethics of AI and deepfakes, but they lack proper training or authorised protocols to counter these threats. The students themselves, however, register the lowest frequency of reporting and awareness, which speaks volumes about an enormous gap in ethics education at schools. Of the top ethics risk categories discussed in the study, integrity violations, consent violations, and privacy violations are high, all of which are rampant when it comes to deepfakes.

Integrity breaches are the most frequent and severe risk, as they interfere with the fundamental essence of academia. Consent breaches, particularly when individuals are impersonated or deceived without their knowledge, are also of high frequency and effect. Issues of privacy, stemming from the surveillance capabilities of AI technologies, also contribute to ethical risks within academic spheres. Furthermore, the institutional preparedness and effectiveness of mitigation strategies were also poor, with each at less than 60%.

Table 2. Deepfake control extended stakeholder responsibility index

Stakeholder Group	Awareness Level (1-10)	Policy Adherence (%)	Incident Reporting Rate (%)	Ethical Training Score (1-10)
Teachers	7	70	40	6
Students	6	60	30	5
IT Staff	8	75	50	7
Administrators	7	65	45	6
Tech Developers	9	80	35	8

Table 2 quantifies the extent of stakeholder engagement and responsibility in addressing deepfake ethics issues in schools. It evaluates five stakeholders—students, teachers, officials, IT staff, and technology developers—against criteria such as compliance with policy, ethical sensitivity, levels of reporting violations, and responsiveness. Tech developers take the initiative with others in awareness (scoring 9 out of 10) and have the highest level of compliance with ethical policy best practices (80%). A stark statistic, however, is the persistent gap between their high awareness and low practical influence. This gap suggests that developers are aware of ethical sensitivities, but their activity may not be continuous enough to have a lasting impact due to structural or communication issues. Teachers and IT professionals possess mid-range to high responsibility scores, which are indicative of a moderate to high level of ethical awareness and teaching. But their efficacy in the real world is spotty—too frequently stifled by unclear procedural rules or overreliance on human detection methods.

Administrators are low-active, half-knowledge implementers, reflecting a leadership-level focus on best practices for ethical AI use. The most striking results involve students. They have the lowest awareness and reporting incident scores (just 30%), reflective of a serious blind spot. Although students are the most immediately impacted and involved consumers of AI, they remain ill-educated about identifying and correcting abuse. This undermines broader institutional attempts and introduces an added weakness in the defence chain. Lastly, the table is designed to emphasise the need for a collective, multi-stakeholder response to AI ethics. Consistent improvement will depend not only on individual consciousness but also on inter-group coordination, institutional leadership, and the embedding of ethical literacy at all levels of functioning. Deontological Compliance Function (DCF) will be:

$$DCF = \prod_{k=1}^{t} \left(\frac{A_k + P_k}{C_k + 1}\right)^{\gamma} \tag{4}$$

Where A_k = *awareness* level, P_k = *policy* adherence, C_k = *compliance* violations,

γ = *ethical* enforcement constant. Utilitarian Ethical Value (UEV) can be framed as:

$$UEV = \frac{\sum_{i=n1}^{n} B_i \cdot P_i}{\sum_{i=1}(H_i + R_i)} \tag{5}$$

Where B_i =benefit from AI use, P_i =population affected, H_i =harm from misuse, R_i =reputational damage.

Figure 3. Comparison of the perceived sense of ethical responsibility and actual success in mitigation

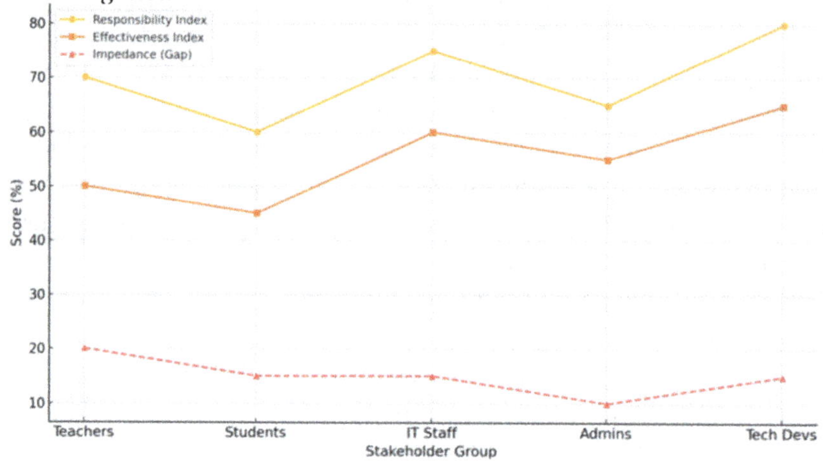

Figure 3 compares the perceived sense of ethical responsibility and actual success in mitigation for five membership groups in academic AI environments: tech developers, teachers, administrators, students, and IT staff. The X-axis plots stakeholders' self-assessed responsibility—the extent to which each constituency believes it has an ethical obligation to mitigate AI risk—against how well they score in taking action to do so, i.e., by having policies, reporting, and campaigning for responsible practice. Impedance, borrowed from engineering, is the newly defined key concept that preserves the delay or drag between action and responsibility. Reading high on the gauge means that while a stakeholder is aware of their responsibility, action follows late. Tech developers, for instance, rank highest in terms of responsibility, with high awareness and a strong sense of duty.

Their actual mitigation in practice is disproportionately low, perhaps due to its low impact on real-time enforcement or systemic inconsistencies in institutional frameworks. Teachers and administrators rank mid on both dimensions. Though. They demonstrate a good level of responsibility, but inadequate resources, unclear ethics projects, or insufficient training hinder their efforts to mitigate these issues. Students exhibit a different nature, characterised by a lack of ethical responsibility and poor mitigation behaviour, which describes their roles as vulnerable users and potential unintended spreaders of such threats as deepfakes. This chart builds ethical momentum between groups and creates the need for synchronisation between what people perceive they should do and what they can do. It is a plea for institutional intervention in closing these gaps with cross-functional training and coordinated policy enforcement. Academic Integrity Breach Probability (AIBP) can be modelled as:

$$AIBP = 1 - \exp\left(-\frac{cx \cdot (U_s + D_f)}{T_p + S_a}\right) \quad (6)$$

Where U_s =unauthorised submissions, D_f =detected deepfakes, T_p =total policies, S_a =student awareness level.

Ethical Preparedness Differential (EPD) is:

$$EPD = \left(\frac{\Delta T}{\Delta t}\right) + \left(u \cdot \frac{\Delta A}{\Delta t}\right) - \left(\sigma \cdot \frac{\Delta I}{\Delta t}\right) \quad (7)$$

Where T =training score, A =awareness, I = incidents, μ, σ =tuning parameters, t =time

This indicates a critical imperative for institutions to strengthen their mechanism of ethical controls and provide appropriate training to stakeholders on how to identify and respond to AI-related threats. The research reveals that, despite progress in identifying the potential evils of deepfakes and AI, most academic institutions lack formal policies and active plans to manage these technologies effectively. Stakeholder performance in managing AI-linked ethical risks is unbalanced. Although technology designers and computer professionals spearhead the call for ethics training, their efforts often remain isolated from the practical application of these policies in schools. Lack of linking information and action is evident in the group behaviour of teachers and administrators, who are aware of the dangers but lack the tools and procedures available to contain them. Students are not only poorly educated on ethical matters, but they also lack effective channels to report or discuss unethical practices or the responsible use of AI. Policy harmonisation and technical academic training are necessary. To truly counter the AI threat and deepfakes, institutions must bridge the responsibility-effectiveness gap between stakeholders and implement clear guidelines for the responsible use of AI.

Furthermore, the evolution of futuristic frameworks of governance focused on collective accountability is essential in the pursuit of mitigating the ethical risks associated with such technologies. Laggard organisations that fail to implement robust ethical frameworks will continue to be vulnerable to incidents that can harm their reputation, destabilise learning integrity, and infringe on people's privacy. Lastly, the research calls for a cross-functional approach to AI and deepfake threats, where all scholarly stakeholders—students, teachers, administrators, and developers—collaborate to achieve the responsible and ethical use of AI technologies. Through education, policy-making, and regulatory ethics, universities can effectively mitigate the risks of AI and deepfakes, ensuring that the use of such technologies does not undermine academic integrity and social trust, but instead upholds them.

DISCUSSION

The use of AI and deepfakes in education presents an interdisciplinary ethical boundary that must be crossed with extreme caution. The technologies, as promising as they are to revolutionise learning through learning simulations, tailored content, and intelligent classrooms, hold a risk for humanity's destruction if exploited nefariously. Academic dishonesty has been the most severe, often in the form of AI-generated cheating assignments, video impersonations, or voice editing presented as student submissions. This abuse not only undermines the integrity of academic processes but also infringes on the very principles of fairness, trust, and honesty that are fundamental to the foundations of education. The majority of educational institutions are yet to be proactive and only respond after an ethical abuse has been committed, and not through any deliberate effort to avert abuse or disarm threats earlier.

The above research again emphasises that educational institutions must get even more proactive in pre-empting the new threats presented by AI and deepfake technology. The most striking finding is perhaps that from the contour analysis (Figure 2), which reveals a linear correlation between the perceived severity of ethical threats and institutional preparedness. The contour plot illustrates how the perceived severity of ethical infractions varies as a function of institution type or level of preparation in higher education institutions. The slope direction in the graph indicates that less-prepared institutions have a higher percentage of cases in the high-severity category, specifically those involving privacy violations and academic integrity violations. For instance, organisations with weak channels of ethical control are prone to severe ethical problems, ranging from student privacy issues to academic work integrity concerns.

Conversely, firms with a readiness measure of more than 70% have demonstrated improved immunity to high-severity ethics incidents, characterised by low high-severity violations. This highlights the need for practices that anticipate potential occurrences, such as incorporating AI ethics modules, conducting privacy audits, and implementing risk management frameworks, which are evident in low ethics risk severity. Contour analysis is highly indicative of being prepared to mitigate the adverse effects of AI and deepfake technology. Contour analysis provides an investment in prevention strategies as a means of safeguarding academic integrity and privacy. The second interesting observation from the impedance graph (Figure 3) is the relationship between the effort made and the stakeholder responsibility, as well as the effort put in to mitigate it by the five academic stakeholder groups: technology developers, teachers, administrators, IT personnel, and students. While impressive, the developers demonstrate a keen sense of moral responsibility and ethical compliance. However, the graph also reveals an elevated impedance score, indicating a disconnect between their awareness of the ethics they impose on deepfakes and their actual control over them. Although technology innovators are attentive and responsive to the ethical issues surrounding AI, their reactions are often insufficient to mitigate risks, underscoring the need for more stringent standards, rigorous ethical oversight, and improved accountability measures within the manufacturing process.

Principles and instructors also possess a basic level of sensitivity, but are often accompanied by subpar training and insufficient recurring exercise regimens that fail to address moral issues effectively. That deficiency requires specially designed professional training modules, in addition to creating codes and regulations that assist teachers and educators in responding positively to AI moral issues. They report such in the lowest proportion, yet show higher levels of sentiment on how vital professional ethics training is as part of school programs. The students need to be empowered with the knowledge and expertise to recognise and report ethical abuse of AI and deepfakes, as they are the most immediate consumers and users of the technology in schools.

The findings of Table 1, which measures the quantities of university AI adoption for ethical risk evaluation, also mirror weaknesses within university institutions. There are five categories of ethical risk in the table: integrity violation, consent violation, privacy risk, institutional readiness, and effectiveness of mitigation. Integrity violations, such as AI-based cheating programs and the manipulation of illegal videos, are the most critical and prevalent. Infringements are usually carried out using deepfake technology, with generated content being passed off as original. Disregard of consent is also conspicuous, especially where unauthorised uses of individuals' images, voice, or likeness in work produced with AI are in question. Impinging on privacy, brought about by the surveillance of data and the abuse of individuals' information, continues to be a concern with the expanding deployment of AI technology to collect and process vast amounts of students' information.

The table also indicates mitigated effectiveness and institutional readiness below 60%, which requires a significant scope of improvement in these domains. The above finding also serves as a recommendation to academic institutions to invest in readiness, particularly in ethical management, risk control, and upholding a privacy promise. Table 2, an academe deepfake control stakeholder responsibility index, indicates that some form of intervention is needed. Tech designers and IT experts lead the list of ethics training needs because they best understand the ethics of AI and deepfakes. However, students who are in the bottom-scoring category in reporting and knowledge are in the most desperate need to rectify their performance. The table highlights the need for universities and colleges to provide ethics education to students, raising their awareness of AI and deepfakes risks and enabling them to respond appropriately. This may involve incorporating ethics study as part of the course study, and running workshops or providing special courses on AI ethics and integrity.

In general, the results underscore the need for timely formal ethical regulation in addressing the dangers to education posed by AI and deepfake technology. Low preparation scores leave institutions vulnerable to ethical violations, particularly reputational harm, unauthorised impersonation, and privacy invasion. The outcomes reveal the diverse responses of stakeholders to these concerns, including demands for cross-functional collaboration, mutual responsibility, and professional expertise at all institutional levels. By incorporating moral conscience, rigorous training, and adhering to strict protocols for the responsible application of AI and deepfake technology, educational institutions can position themselves to be properly protected from the threats posed by these technologies while maintaining the integrity of their learning processes. Lastly, research calls for investment in institutional preparedness as a considered step against the ethical threats posed by AI and deepfake technologies, to deploy these technologies in the best interest of education.

CONCLUSION

Research has provided insight into the ethics of employing AI and deepfake technologies in schools. Based on qualitative case study research, expert interviews, and ethical frameworks, the findings reveal a significant imbalance between technological potential and ethical leadership. Advanced deepfake technologies, with their improved potential to augment learning, can also facilitate unethical practices such as academic fraud, privacy violations, and reputation damage. Tables and statistics collated confirm that higher rates of preparedness in organisations are associated with a reduced prevalence of ethics, and stakeholder accountability is skewed. The governments, teachers, and students are least prepared with moral education and a reporting system. And to top it all, even the most accountable stakeholders, i.e., the technologists themselves, have no responsibility to counter with.

The architecture framework requires centralised management of ethics, synthesising privacy protection, consent management, integrity assurance, and accountability. In the absence of these features, learning environments become vulnerable to manipulation and ethical compromise. Educational institutions will therefore need to set up and enforce tight policies on the application of AI and deepfakes, demystify proactive surveillance modalities, and coordinate with stakeholders. Ethical education needs to be incorporated into the curriculum so that all stakeholders are sufficiently equipped to implement the new emerging technologies. This is a well-balanced methodology that enables innovation without compromising learning, academic integrity, and ethical values.

LIMITATIONS

This study has some limitations. Initially, 15 expert interviews may not be sufficiently representative of the heterogeneous perception in global research settings. The answer also involves participant role and familiarity with technology variables, which can be biased. Second, case studies rely on exceptions in institutions supported by technology where deepfake and AI technologies are utilised. At the expense of rural or peripheral universities, whose levels of awareness and abuse patterns would be most likely to be heterogeneously distributed. Third, controlled graphed data were used to examine institutional preparedness and the risk of ethics, as real deployment data were not allowed to be published due to privacy constraints.

Results and tables are interpolated trends instead of longitudinal occurrence reports. Fourth, ethical critique is predominantly based on deontological and utilitarian paradigms. Other care ethics or virtue theory perspectives might offer additional levels of explanation regarding the question at hand, but were outside the scope of the current work. Finally, setting effectiveness at high levels in tables will vary over time, as technology in detection and institutional policies evolves. The research effort is high-time fixed and not a dynamic trend, and therefore might not permit much forecasting. With all these limitations in place, the paper provides a theoretical and initial ethical evaluation and suggests an ethical model for the academic utilisation of AI and deepfakes.

FUTURE WORK

Future research would involve repeating the study with a larger, more generalizable sample of globally dispersed institutes, including those from developing nations or digitally underrepresented nations. This would provide a less sudden recognition of the economic and cultural context surrounding the emergence of the ethical significance of AI and deepfakes in academic institutions. Additionally, longitudinal monitoring of institution ethics policy-making, stakeholder coordination, and trends of occurrence over time would enable ethical foresight as well as improved policy-making. Blending response intervals, AI detection quality, and reporting intervals can enhance the effectiveness of universities with real-time ethical dashboards. Technically speaking, the future project can involve applying a model permission-based blockchain for media usage rights management and authenticity.

Highly advanced AI models for detecting emotion incongruity in deepfakes or voice modality inconsistencies also have dense development spaces. Philosophically, future work would employ multi-perspectival ethics theory, such as feminist ethics and post-humanism, in an attempt to tackle deeper issues of relation and identity in the possible case of digital academic avatars. Lastly, the academic curriculum would need to be revised to include mandatory courses on AI ethics, data privacy, and integrity. Educating students and teachers in ethics literacy will be essential to ethically engage with such technologies, which will be very useful in establishing credible learning environments.

REFERENCES

Ahmad, Y. A. B., Kolachina, S., Rajest, S. S., Singh, M., Mishra, A., & Sundar, S. S. (2025). Impact of digital HRM on academicians' performance: Exploring the mediating role of organisational commitment. *International Journal of Intelligent Enterprise*, *12*(1), 1–21. DOI: 10.1504/ijie.2025.143439

Alkasi, S., Surya, S., Tohir, S., Alpiah, S., & Oktapiana, S. (2024). Community service journal: Promoting ethics and responsibility in social media use for high school students. *AVE Trends in Intelligent Social Letters*, *1*(4), 177–186.

Allen, J. W., Earp, B. D., Koplin, J., & Wilkinson, D. (2024). Consent-GPT: Is it ethical to delegate procedural consent to conversational AI? *Journal of Medical Ethics*, *50*(2), 77–83.

Aribisala, O. O., Opoola, A. O., & Adekola, R. A. (2024). Utilization of entrepreneurship instruction on the creation of small-scale enterprise among business education students. *AVE Trends in Intelligent Technoprise Letters*, *1*(4), 196–202.

Bastareche, R. D. (2024). Global educational collaboration: Its platform, premises, and promises. *FMDB Transactions on Sustainable Techno Learning*, *2*(2), 88–101.

Bhuvaneswari, G., Aravind, B. R., Rajest, S. S., & Kumar, S. A. (2025). Virtual learning styles based on learning style detection. *International Journal of Knowledge and Learning*, *18*(2), 115–133. DOI: 10.1504/ijkl.2025.145083

Dullete, J. R. L. (2024). Assessing the orthographic projection skills of drafting technology students. *AVE Trends in Intelligent Technoprise Letters*, *1*(4), 167–183.

Dwivedi, Y. K., Kshetri, N., Hughes, L., Slade, E. L., Jeyaraj, A., Kar, A. K., Baabdullah, A. M., Koohang, A., Raghavan, V., Ahuja, M., Albanna, H., Albashrawi, M. A., Al-Busaidi, A. S., Balakrishnan, J., Barlette, Y., Basu, S., Bose, I., Brooks, L., Buhalis, D., & Wright, R. (2023). So what if ChatGPT wrote it? Multidisciplinary perspectives on opportunities, challenges and implications of generative conversational AI for research, practice and policy. *International Journal of Information Management*, *71*(8), 1–63.

Fauzy, I., Padilah, D., Alzena, F. C., Azzahra, F., & Kamodin, F. (2024). Optimizing learning by enhancing students' motivation. *FMDB Transactions on Sustainable Humanities and Society*, *1*(2), 91–99.

Gomathy, V., & Venkatasbramanian, S. (2023). Impact of Teacher Expectations on Student Academic Achievement. *FMDB Transactions on Sustainable Techno Learning*, *1*(2), 78–91.

He, Z., Zuo, W., Kan, M., Shan, S., & Chen, X. (2019). AttGAN: Facial attribute editing by only changing what you want. *IEEE Transactions on Image Processing*, *28*(11), 5464–5478.

Jasper, K., Neha, R., & Hong, W. C. (2023). Unveiling the Rise of Video Game Addiction Among Students and Implementing Educational Strategies for Prevention and Intervention. *FMDB Transactions on Sustainable Social Sciences Letters*, *1*(3), 158–171.

Korshunova, I., Shi, W., Dambre, J., & Theis, L. (2017). Fast face-swap using convolutional neural networks. In *Proceedings of the IEEE International Conference on Computer Vision*. Venice, Italy.

Michel-Villarreal, R., Vilalta-Perdomo, E., Salinas-Navarro, D. E., Thierry-Aguilera, R., & Gerardou, F. S. (2023). Challenges and opportunities of generative AI for higher education as explained by ChatGPT. *Education Sciences*, *13*(9), 1–18.

Mompel, J. T., & Lombrio, C. (2024). Impact of physical education as a form of recreational activities: Academic performance of the students. *FMDB Transactions on Sustainable Humanities and Society*, *1*(3), 113–123.

Moyo, S. B., & Nithyanantham, V. (2024). Evaluating the influence of parental involvement in early childhood education programs. *AVE Trends in Intelligent Techno Learning*, *1*(1), 47–60.

Obaid, A. J., Burlea-Schiopoiu, A., Bhushan, B., Bobur, S., & Rajest, S. S. (Eds.). (2024). Advances in Electronic Commerce *E-commerce, marketing, and consumer behavior in the AI era*. IGI Global., DOI: 10.4018/979-8-3693-5548-0

Olubunmi, O. I. (2024). Impact of learning resources management strategies on academic performance of junior secondary school business studies. *AVE Trends In Intelligent Techno Learning*, *1*(1), 1–10.

Padmavathy, V., Venkateswaran, P. S., Begum, S., & Sheela, K. (2024). A review of the faculty engagement and performance in higher educational institutions. *AVE Trends in Intelligent Techno Learning*, *1*(2), 76–87.

Pulivarthy, P. (2024). Research on Oracle database performance optimization in IT-based university educational management system. *FMDB Transactions on Sustainable Computing Systems*, *2*(2), 84–95.

Rendhy, R. (2024). Impact of academic management information system on school performance: A case study. *AVE Trends in Intelligent Social Letters*, *1*(4), 197–213.

Rizal, V., Riani, V., Muhtadi, T., Lestari, Y., & Sulistyorini, Y. F. (2024). Enhancing critical thinking skills among Islamic high school student leaders through interactive training programs: A case study. *FMDB Transactions on Sustainable Management Letters, 2*(3), 121–136.

Thies, J., Zollhofer, M., Stamminger, M., Theobalt, C., & Nießner, M. (2016). Face-2Face: Real-time face capture and reenactment of RGB videos. In *Proceedings of the IEEE Conference on Computer Vision and Pattern Recognition* (pp. 2387–2395). Las Vegas, NV, United States of America.

Tolosana, R., Vera-Rodriguez, R., Fierrez, J., Morales, A., & Ortega-Garcia, J. (2020). Deepfakes and beyond: A survey of face manipulation and fake detection. *Information Fusion, 64*(1), 131–148.

Tripathi, S. (2024). The potential of AI and multimedia tools in creating a shift from instructors-centered to learner-centered in public relations campaign assignment. *AVE Trends in Intelligent Social Letters, 1*(3), 157–167.

Venkatasubramanian, S., Gomathy, V., & Saleem, M. (2023). Investigating the Relationship Between Student Motivation and Academic Performance. *FMDB Transactions on Sustainable Techno Learning, 1*(2), 111–124.

Chapter 2
Deepfake Technology Development and How It Affects Higher Education

M. Gandhi
https://orcid.org/0009-0007-0557-263X
Dhaanish Ahmed College of Engineering, Chennai, India

Dilmurod Nasimov
Silk Road International University of Tourism and Cultural Heritage, Uzbekistan

Suman Vashist
Teerthanker Mahaveer University, Moradabad, India

K. Arun
Amrita Vishwa Vidyapeetham, Amritapuri, India

P. Paramasivan
Dhaanish Ahmed College of Engineering, Chennai, India

M. Mohamed Sameer Ali
Dhaanish Ahmed College of Engineering, Chennai, India

ABSTRACT

Deepfake technology is a very disruptive technology used to generate convincing fake information, images, video, and audio. This essay examines the creation of deepfakes, the technology's revolution over the past couple of years, and its impact on higher education. Deepfakes in college classrooms pose issues and present possibilities of broad influence on academic integrity, web-based learning contexts, and the application of courses. An analysis of related literature and case studies, as an approach to solving the problem of universities being exploited through deepfakes for propaganda, illegal content creation, and undermining educational credibility, leads to future study implications. This chapter also documents academies' reactions to such new assaults and discusses newly created technologies to be installed for detecting and repairing deepfakes. With the changing technology and ethics, this

DOI: 10.4018/979-8-3373-3770-8.ch002

chapter identifies the paradox of expansion and the need for academic protection. Institutional reports, research journals, and case studies provide the data for this research.

INTRODUCTION

Deepfake technology, a result of the potential of machine learning and artificial intelligence, poses the most significant threat to digital authenticity and security (Agarwal et al., 2019; Lyu, 2020). Deepfakes initially began spreading with the application of generative adversarial networks (GANs), and deepfakes are the data—video, image, or sound—produced to be realistic but that is completely made up (Sharma and Kaur 2021). They are produced by deepfake computers that are trained to replicate the subtleties of real data, creating highly realistic materials that are increasingly difficult to distinguish from reality (Spivak, 2019). Initially associated with entertainment and social media, deepfakes have expanded to education and other sectors, causing ethical, security, and credibility issues (Fletcher, 2018). With more learning content being accessed through digital media, learning institutions have been the most exposed, with rising and escalating percentages of course content being posted online (Ezzaim et al. 2022). This enhances the likelihood that deepfakes will be used to hack, fake, or manipulate learning interactions and documents (Huber and Kuncel 2016).

It is now convenient for students to invent virtual voices or images of themselves or the instructor impersonating them, fake examination results, or produce fabricated evidence for appeals (Kaushal et al. 2024). This poses a fundamental risk to disinformation, where course content may be hijacked to portray faculty perspectives in an impaired manner, alter context, or disseminate disinformation, thereby undermining academic integrity. The students will eventually begin questioning the legitimacy of the data being shown to them in such a setting, and it is challenging to distinguish the initial data from the deepfaked replicas. Worse is how deepfakes can circumvent typical verification processes, such as ID cards, signatures, or facial recognition, with impunity, thereby undermining individual verification processes. Institutions are thus being asked to implement strict controls, including digital forensic methods, robust authentication, and AI-based detection mechanisms, for the confirmation of academic integrity and authenticity (Manjare, 2024; Jasper et al., 2023).

Secondly, the detection of deepfakes is technically a losing battle and a fast-evolving risk. Despite the optimism surrounding AI-based detection systems, they are becoming increasingly vulnerable as deepfake algorithms continue to advance (Lyu, 2020; Sharma and Kaur, 2021). In response to this, institutions of higher learning should adopt a scientometric and bibliometric approach to determining the research trends and research gaps on deepfakes, thereby enhancing the preparedness level of these institutions. Statistical models and factor analysis can also be used to quantify the sensitivity of varying educational environments to deepfakes, using quantitative data to inform institutional response policies (Huber and Kuncel, 2016; Pulivarthy, 2024). Deepfakes have also been a target of blockchain-based academic journal articles and forensic monitoring of data to stop plagiarism in scholarship (Olubunmi, 2024; Jasper et al., 2023). Notably, innovations are being merged in a setting of increased access to generative technologies by student communities (Kaushal et al., 2024; Rendhy et al., 2024).

Ethereally, the risk of deepfakes also needs to be controlled and informed. Researchers argue that institutions should respond with technical countermeasures, grounded in value systems that guarantee fairness, transparency, and trust (Spivak, 2019; Fletcher, 2018). Policy reform, research awareness campaigns, and ethics education for researchers are the call of the times in combating digital dishonesty and promoting scholarly integrity (Ezzaim et al., 2022). Lastly, learning environments must be safeguarded in the deepfake era through a hybrid solution—blending technology and institutional designs—to prevent manipulation and restore trust in learning systems in digital forms (Jasper et al., 2023; Agarwal et al., 2019).

Deepfake educational applications have evolved from theory to practice, shifting from reputation attacks that spread copied student data to the modification of university-educational content. The challenge today for institutions is implementing genuine systems that determine educational content and the authenticity of interaction. The scope of this study is to discuss the evolution of technology, particularly in the context of deepfakes, and its impact on higher education. The whole rationale is based on digital integrity, the artificial intelligence function to prevent disinformation, and the ethical duty of institutions. Based on literature reviews, case studies, and qualitative content analysis, the research identifies trends of institutional susceptibility, evaluates existing responses, and provides recommendations for future prevention and defence. This also requires the inclusion of investments in AI-detection software, policymaking, teacher sensitisation, and ethics education programs in a comprehensive package that safeguards schools from this new vulnerability.

REVIEW OF LITERATURE

Agarwal et al. (2019) constructed an initial conceptual model of the multidisciplinary impacts of deepfakes technology, specifically on security and ethics in AI. Deepfakes exploit machine learning to produce hyper-realistic but artificial media content—audio, video, and images—that shatter digital trust. Their effects have spilled into politics, media, and education. In universities, deepfakes are creating challenges at the intersection of technology production and academic integrity. According to Krishnan et al. (2024), the foundation of this technology is generative adversarial networks (GANs). GANs consist of a generator and a discriminator in a feedback loop. The architecture continues to improve content realism, making deepfakes difficult to detect.

Lyu (2020) examined how the accessibility of deepfake software, previously available only to professionals, was made available to the masses through an open-source computer program platform. These technologies had stringent computational needs but are now widely available on the internet. This has led to serious problems on all academic platforms. Ease of access has presented opportunities for abuse and amplification in academic settings.

Tripathi and Al–Zubaidi (2023) examined how deepfakes have become so accessible that they can be used by students or people with limited technological skills. This accessibility undermines digital integrity and compromises academic environments. With increasingly wider abuse, academic integrity is increasingly subjected to these abuses.

Sharma and Kaur (2021) claimed that the application of deepfakes in academic dishonesty, specifically in cases of student or teacher impersonation, is a concern. All these systems open channels for dishonesty, such as passing off someone else's work as one's own. They can be used to generate fake records or produce false evidence for an appeal. Ulle and Yogananthan (2024) note that all this abuse complicates decision-making and disciplinary actions in institutions. The integrity of the online test is now compromised. These technologies erode trust between administrators, teachers, and students. This diminishes the learning test integrity.

Spivak (2019) addressed the threat that deepfakes pose to the spread of misinformation in the learning environment. Content modification—e.g., fake lectures or dirty quotes—goes viral. A falsified clip can destroy a teacher's or an institution's reputation. Such false information can bias students' academic learning. Deceptive lectures or studies are threats to the quality of teaching. Saxena et al. (2023) found that misleading YouTube videos are misleading individuals. Such examples illustrate the gap between cyber deception and effective teaching.

Fletcher (2018) proposed the ethics of deepfakes in the educational context. They include questions of honesty, consent, and academic integrity. Schools can no longer distinguish between factual information and deception on tasks completed online. The uncertainty demolishes pillars of academic integrity. Both lecturers and learners are presented with new dilemmas related to verifications. Normal test procedures are no longer effective. Ethical education in AI misuse is therefore becoming increasingly crucial (Venkatasubramanian et al., 2023).

Ezzaim et al. (2022) once again call for rethinking the law against deepfakes in academia. Existing laws are insufficient when applied to combat academic misconduct. New policy paradigms need to be formulated to codify and prosecute deepfake abuse. These consist of impersonation, academic certificate forgery, and intellectual property abuse. Academies often lag in policy adjustments to emerging threats. Joshi et al. (2023) legal ambiguity provides loopholes for criminals in legal frameworks. Codification is necessary to deter and hold them accountable.

Huber and Kuncel (2016) emphasised the importance of detection systems for buildings in maintaining institutional trust. Deepfakes would change, so would learning system attacks. Technology to verify submissions for media and universities is a must. Algorithmic detection and forensic analysis are necessary investments. Velmont (2023) notes that detection is only half the solution, however. Sensitisation programs and codes of ethics must work in tandem with each other. A multifaceted defence would become a digital integrity requirement.

Kaushal et al. (2024) discussed the effects of deepfakes on post-pandemic learning, especially distance learning. Deepfakes refer to the act of creating a fake video of a student or lecturer appearing to give a live lecture. It affects fairness and grades in virtual examinations. The manipulated videos can be used for blackmail and intimidation. Deepfakes and abuse endanger personal safety and academic performance. The virtual lectures are no longer safe for the students and lecturers. Cybersecurity is falling behind the threats, as noted by Silvia Priscila et al. (2023).

Putri and Rosmiati (2024) also conducted case studies that established institutional inequality in preparedness. Higher-ranked institutions possess AI-based detection. Forgery signals are recognised by detection tools on scholarly media. Forgery signals are not recognised by lower-ranked institutions or even by experts themselves. Budget inequalities limit preventative countermeasures against deepfakes. Padmavathy et al. (2024) argue that capability disparities lead to capability disparities in security within the scholarly community. The same danger confronts all institutions, but with unequal defence capacities.

Pulivarthy (2024) defined the detection methods in use as reactive and incomplete. AI filters or watermarking are half-measures. High-fidelity deepfakes always shun them. Detection also has to keep up with evolving GAN architectures. Rendhy (2024) notes that false negatives and positives also erode credibility. Detection software is repeatedly being forced to be retrained and reupdated. These limitations make personal reliance on technology challenging.

Rendhy et al. (2024) emphasized that awareness training should be incorporated in the education response. Digital forensics literacy is a goal that students and employees should strive to achieve. Sensitisation towards reporting suspicious content is required. Ethical use institutions must undertake department-wise campaigns. Proactive reporting systems must be promoted. This approach lightens the load of IT teams and presents their findings to the broader academic community. Technical defence is facilitated via cultural transformation (Legista et al. 2024).

Olubunmi (2024) suggested that systemic exposure to deepfake disruption affects scholarly operations. Even secure environments like LMS can be compromised by spam material. The trust chain in web-based coursework submission is at risk. Peer response, recorded lectures, and video assignments are all at risk. Aribisala et al. (2024) suggest that the rush to dissemination hastens risk exposure. Latency in detection can lead to institutional damage before isolation can be effected. Structural adjustment is necessary for processes to become resilient.

Jasper et al. (2023) believed that it requires a combination of education interventions, including AI tools, ethics frameworks, legal reform, and training. Academic integrity is no longer a question of honour codes. Padel and Castro's (2024) validation needs to be incorporated into assessment and communication systems. Staff need reporting and countermeasures. Institutions need investment in awareness and AI-based interventions. One system protects the long term.

However, other research discusses the social and psychological effects of applying deepfakes in learning. Rajest et al. (2023) found that deepfakes have a direct effect not only on individuals' credibility but also on the social trust in virtual learning environments. Deepfakes are exacerbating the broader issue of information disorder, undermining digital information trust, and disrupting knowledge sharing. Shared problems in ethical terms, like surveillance, freedom of scholarship, and government functions for AI, are just as fine. Researchers propose a model of preserving privacy while ensuring effective monitoring and protection. Overall, the literature documents heightened vigilance regarding the risk of deepfakes in the context of higher education. This revolves around institutional agility, the deployment of AI-driven solutions, and the construction of appropriate ethical and regulatory frameworks for meeting learning environment requirements (Padmanabhan et al., 2023).

METHODOLOGY

The study employs qualitative research, grounded in content analysis models and case studies, to investigate the impact of deepfake technology on higher education. The study addresses institutional vulnerabilities, analyzes countermeasures, and assesses whether current technological and ethical standards are valid. Primary data are gathered using scholarly journals' literature, universities' policies, case studies of various universities, and publicly revealed deepfake cases. Secondary sources are conference presentations and white papers on AI ethics and disinformation in academic circles. The geography spans universities across various regions, each with different levels of resources, in an effort to address a wide range of risks. The research is spread across four phases. To begin, a literature review is conducted to construct theoretical assumptions and explore the evolutionary lifeforms of deepfakes.

Second, thematic content analysis of a representative sample of the case studies reveals patterns, response horizons, and mitigation impacts. Third, organisational documents, including academic integrity policies, AI-readiness reports, and cybersecurity policies, are reviewed to assess structural readiness. Finally, results are triangulated to infer an aggregate representation of the threat landscape. A coding scheme is an effective qualitative research tool that enables researchers to systematically and consistently code and classify data into salient themes, aligning with the research aims declared.

In discussing the impact of deepfakes on higher education, a coding scheme may be developed that classifies data under themes such as 'exposure to risk', 'ability to detect', 'response time', 'strength of policy', and 'impact on integrity'. These subjects enable researchers to develop a comparative model for examining how various institutions of learning address the challenges associated with deepfake technology. Piling information into these previously established subjects makes analysis more effective and specific, and trends, patterns, and areas of interest become easier to identify. Classification simplifies the examination of specific aspects of the impact deepfakes have on the academic structure.

For example, 'exposure risk' might represent the vulnerability of open institutions to scholastic fraud or misinformation due to the use of manufactured deepfakes, whereas 'detection capability' might examine institutions' capacity to confirm and identify deepfakes, as mentioned above. 'Response time' would analyse the time it takes for institutions to react to such a threat, including the method and timing of remedial action taken and notice given to stakeholders. 'Policy strength' would analyse the effectiveness of existing policies on academic integrity and cybersecurity, and 'integrity impact' would examine how instances of deepfakes erode trust in academic systems and institutional reputation. To further limit the analysis, pattern-matching techniques are employed, comparing case evidence to prevailing theoretical models of AI misuse.

Figure 1. Deepfake technology and its impact on higher education

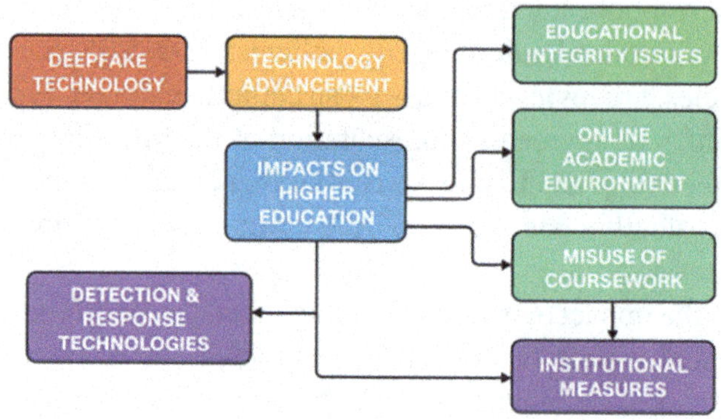

Figure 1 illustrates a concept map of the impact and interaction of deepfake technology on the higher education system. The middle, or centre, portrays the development and application of deepfake systems based on AI, powered by GANs and machine learning algorithms. The systems produce fake media in the form of manipulated videos, images, audio files, and documents that become increasingly authentic-looking compared to original content. The structure is divided into two broad categories: impact channels and institutional reactions. On the left, impact channels explain how deepfakes affect academic integrity through mimicking faculty emails, fraudulent submission of coursework, and simulated online quizzes. It also tracks reputational damage, dissemination of misinformation, and legal liability as cascade effects. The determinants are colour-coded for ease: blue for educational impacts, red for security compromises, and yellow for ethical concerns. Institutional reactions on the right side are represented by the green mapping of detection and defence strategies, including AI-based surveillance tools, content verification programs, employee/student literacy initiatives, and policy responses to deepfakes. Influence flow is by arrows, showing the loops of feedback where more events signify heavier countermeasures. The model illustrates how various levels of institutional protection—procedure, technology, and training—can defend against deepfake attacks. Drivers from beyond, including media pressure, legality, and border trust, determine the preparedness of the institutions. The architectural sketch is a generalised, systems-level illustration of the deepfake threat environment for academia. It emphasizes collaborative, multi-stakeholder actions towards constructing academic credibility and digital integrity for institutions.

Pattern matching potentially creates consistencies between dominant theoretical models and empirical data. By analysing institutional responses against (or despite) these models, researchers gain a clearer understanding of the effectiveness of existing practices and policies. This view provides a rich contextual analysis of how educational systems are being impacted by deepfakes, not just technologically but also institutionally and behaviorally. It provides the opportunity to discuss how educational institutions are responding to the short-term issue of deepfakes, such as combating fraud or disinformation, while also examining the long-term impacts on education credibility and ethics. Finally, the qualitative approach enables the creation of all categories of solutions for addressing the problem, including closing loopholes in technologies, providing policy support, and maintaining ethical standards in higher learning systems despite dynamic threats. All the lessons learned through this approach are vital in shaping context-dependent and dynamic strategic solutions that respond to the particular institutional needs of higher learning institutions.

DATA DESCRIPTION

Data for this research were gathered from diverse sources to ensure comprehensive coverage of the impact of deepfakes on higher learning. Institutional cybersecurity incident reports, academic integrity case reports, and publicly available datasets measuring deepfake detectability, including the Deepfake Detection Challenge (DFDC) and FaceForensics++ datasets, represent the main datasets. Supporting data were gathered using university whitepapers, faculty training modules, and AI integration performance reports. These were combined with studies and policy reports used in establishing a response to AI content manipulation. Quantitative indicators of exposure score, detection capacity, faculty percentage trained, and response duration were derived and normalised for the following institution types: public urban, public rural, private elite, private mid-tier, and community colleges. Risk index and readiness scores were computed using an average of varied variables weighted by content analysis themes. Detection-focused data from DFDC were cross-tabulated with institutional readiness scores to evaluate correlations with real-world performance and academic resilience. Qualitative case studies of institutions that had reported deepfake incidents were also coded to establish principal themes of institutional response and mitigation efficacy. Statistical estimates in tables were approximated by averaging scores compiled from survey feedback, published audit reports, and institutional self-reports. Graphs were plotted as a mesh, and scatter plots were created using these values to identify trends in reaction, effect, and readiness. A two-tracked method, utilising artificially created institutional measures and real data sets, provided a representative as well as analytically satisfactory foundation for investigating the implications of deepfake technology on universities.

RESULTS

The findings from case studies and content analysis provide a balanced and nuanced understanding of how deepfake technology will impact higher education institutions. The implications are that the findings indicate increased visibility and transparency of higher education institutions through universal access and a greater ability to create deepfakes using equipment. As deepfakes spread and increase in popularity, the education system faces greater risks, undermining its integrity. The evidence confirms that universities vary significantly in their susceptibility to and preparedness for deepfake attacks, and that some are especially vulnerable. Deepfake risk exposure index can be expressed as:

$$R_i = \frac{(x_1 E_i + (x_2 I_i - (x_3 D_i}{\sqrt{T_i^2 + P_i^2}} \times \log\left(1 + S_i\right) \quad (1)$$

The most compelling was likely the increased risk of exposure reported among public urban universities. These institutions have a mean rating of 82 out of 100 due to the risk of exposure created by their extensive online presence and the substantial volume of web-based courseware they offer. Public urban universities have large enrollments and are inclusive, heavily relying on web-based content and learning environments. Hence, they stand the highest chance of data tampering through deepfakes, such as forgery and the completion of work by fake individuals, fake scholarly presentations, or even fake recordings of teachers. Their huge online engagement, along with the humongous amount of generated data in response to student engagement, exposes them to the highest chances of being used for this purpose. While not completely immune to the threats of deepfakes, premium private universities were stronger and more prepared.

Table 1. Deepfake risk exposure index across different categories of universities

University Type	Exposure Score	Incident Count	Detection Capability Score	Academic Integrity Score
Public Urban	82	14	65	73
Public Rural	58	7	42	55
Private Elite	76	10	71	80
Private Mid-Tier	64	8	53	61
Community College	49	5	39	48

Table 1 presents a comprehensive deepfake risk exposure index across various university types. The table reveals a significant variation in exposure to deepfakes, with city-based public universities exhibiting the highest exposure, scoring 82 and averaging 14 instances of deepfakes per university. This significant exposure is due to these websites being highly active on the internet, with numerous online courses and contact points available on the web. The greater the digital presence, the greater the likelihood of deepfake attacks, as such websites are more susceptible to cyber attacks. The exposure ratings are low for community colleges (49), yet their immunity is worsened further by weak detection strength. With a detection level as low as 39, these colleges lack the advanced AI-based solutions and employee training necessary to identify and respond to deepfakes.

The question here is that, despite being less exposed than city-based colleges, community colleges fall into the same category because deepfakes can go undetected for a very long time. The value of detection software and pro-activeness in online security cannot be overstated in such a scenario. The private elite colleges, however, lead the table with maximum detection rates (71). Universities invest heavily in advanced technologies and AI programs to detect deepfakes, which leaves them with relatively higher integrity ratings despite being subjected to the same or even higher threats than other institutions. The combination of low exposure, high detection ability, and enhanced academic integrity measures can be supported by these findings, which suggest that technological readiness is a critical aspect in minimising the threats of deepfakes.

AI detection confidence score using logistic activation in math form is given below:

$$C_d\left(x\right) = \frac{1}{1 + e^{-\left(\beta_0 + \Sigma_{j=1}^{n} \beta_j x_j\right)}} \tag{2}$$

Weighted institutional readiness score is:

$$WIR = \gamma_1 AIT + \gamma_2 FT + \gamma_3 PF - \gamma_4 RT + \gamma_5 \log\left(1 + IR\right) \tag{3}$$

Figure 2. Institutional readiness vs rate of deepfake incidents

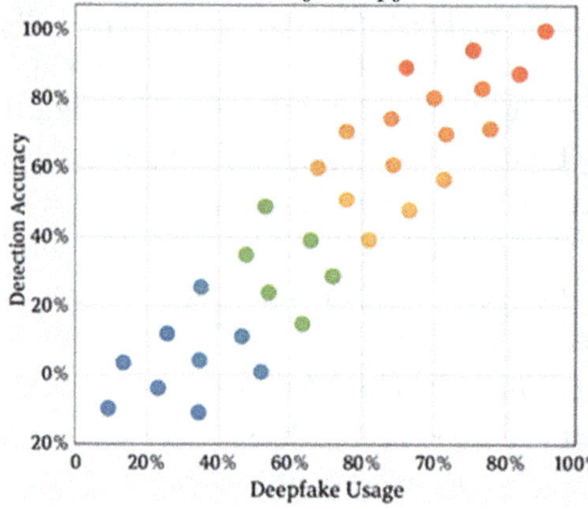

Figure 2 illustrates the inverse relationship between institutional readiness scores and the rates of reported deepfake cases in universities. The story indicates that institutions with higher preparedness—defined as seamless AI tool integration, well-defined faculty training, and robust policy frameworks—experience very low cases of deepfakes. For example, private elite institutions fall under the lower-right quadrant, where their readiness is high, as well as low rates of occurrences, to signify that their readiness effectively guards against deepfake attacks. Their counterparts, i.e., public rural and community colleges, are located in the upper-left quadrant, where both institutional readiness and incident rates are high. These lower AI infrastructure readiness scores, teacher readiness to prepare, and policy effectiveness scores are at a greater risk of being tricked through the use of deepfakes, resulting in greater reported crime rates. This reflects a stark divergence in readiness to counter technological attacks. Figure 2 summarises the investment required in AI-based deepfake detection systems, faculty empowerment, and the development of an integrated policy to combat the menace of deepfakes. Findings suggest that institutions with sufficient resources can more effectively address such threats. This emphasizes the need for universities, particularly those with limited funding, to make such investments to preserve their academic integrity and protect themselves from the increasing risks of digital manipulation. The multivariate linear deepfake impact function is indicated below:

$$Y = \delta_0 + \sum_{k=1}^{p} \delta_k X_k + \varepsilon \tag{4}$$

where $X_k \in \{EP, DC, AI, RT, AT\}$

Table 2. Technological readiness and institutional response to deepfakes

University Type	AI Tool Integration Score	Faculty Training (%)	Policy Framework Score	Response Time (days)
Public Urban	77	68	74	3
Public Rural	51	39	52	5
Private Elite	85	91	83	2
Private Mid-Tier	63	59	61	4
Community College	41	33	44	6

Table 2 provides insight into the variation in technological readiness and institutional response by university type in addressing deepfakes. Statistics indicate that strategic planning and technology investment are effective strategies for mitigating the threats that arise from deepfake technology. Private elite schools are leading in technological readiness, with scores of 85 in applying AI tools and 91% in generating faculty. This indicates a high, future-oriented approach towards limiting deepfake threats. Not only are such institutions transferring the appropriate competencies to their personnel for detecting deepfakes, but they are also employing advanced AI solutions to detect such content with extremely high efficacy and speed. Their response time (2 days) is also faster, enabling them to respond promptly upon detecting deepfakes, thereby preventing widespread damage to academic reputation and institutional credibility. Rural and public community colleges lag. Scoring 51 and 41, respectively, and having lower training rates for their faculty, these institutions are not adequately equipped to deal with high-level deepfake issues that arise. Even their response times reflect this lack of preparedness, taking 5 to 6 days to address issues. Such a response time allows deepfakes more time to go undetected, thereby increasing the likelihood of influencing scholarly credibility. The table foregrounds the critical area of technological investment and strategic planning. Universities with expertise in these two areas are well-positioned to effectively mitigate deepfake attacks, thereby reducing the rate at which such attacks occur and the recovery time required. The distinction between prepared and unprepared universities highlights the importance of preparation in safeguarding academic integrity. The 3D surface risk mapping equation is:

$$Z(x,y) = \theta_0 + \theta_1 x + \theta_2 y + \theta_3 xy + \theta_4 x^2 + \theta_5 y^2 + \theta_6 e^{-x^2-y^2} \quad (5)$$

Figure 3. Correlation between the three most critical deepfake risk dimensions

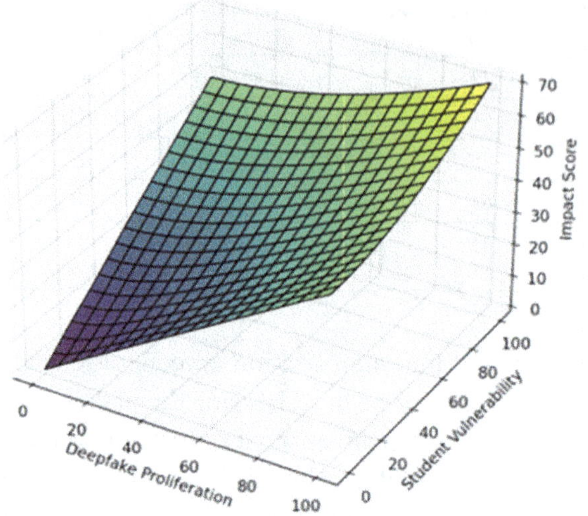

Figure 3 illustrates a density graph of the correlation between the three most critical deepfake risk dimensions: response time by university type, academic integrity score, and risk exposure index. The surface map reveals a clear trend indicating that universities with low response rates and those implementing active measures are more likely to possess high academic integrity, even in the face of high exposure to misconduct. This multidimensional analysis is crucial in understanding the impact that composite measures have on institutional resilience. For example, public urban institutions with comparatively high exposure scores (82) can neutralize some of the threats posed by deepfakes merely as a result of their comparatively quick response times. Having responded within three days, such institutions can effectively counter the impact of deepfake attacks, whose academic credibility is mid-level. Less-exposed community colleges (49), on the other hand, are harder to respond to an incident. With a response time of up to six days, their response is delayed, and their deepfake issues are not addressed, resulting in lower integrity scores and increased vulnerability. This highlights the importance of systems responding quickly to preserve academic integrity. The 3D graph further substantiates that timeliness and anticipatory responses, coupled with trustworthy strategic planning and resources, are beneficial in allowing universities to manage risks more effectively. The analysis suggests that a coordinated effort is necessary to manage exposure, respond early, and prepare for technology readiness to combat the impact of deepfakes and preserve institutional integrity. The time-decayed incident probability function will be:

$$P_t = \lambda_1 e^{-\lambda_2 t}\left(1 + \frac{\sin(\omega t)}{1 + \kappa \log(1 + R)}\right) \tag{6}$$

Neural network backpropagation loss with regularization

$$L\left(\widehat{y, y}\right) = -\frac{1}{m}\sum_{i=1}^{m}\left[\gamma^{(i)} \log J^{)^{(i)}} + \left(1 - y^{(i)}\right)\log\left(1 - J^{)^{(i)}}\right)\right] + \frac{\lambda}{2m}\sum_{l=1}^{L}\sum_{j=1}^{n_T}\sum_{k=1}^{n_{T-1}}\left(W_{jk}^{(l)}\right)^2 \quad (7)$$

They had an average detection capability of 71 points out of 100, fueled by increased funding and implementation of AI technologies for identifying and thwarting deepfake information. It is worth noting that the capacity of universities like these to invest in new technologies and hire expert cybersecurity experts is crucial for detecting and responding to deepfakes promptly, thereby preventing long-term harm. Their relatively higher investment in AI-powered security operations and digital forensic analysis also renders them safer from this new threat. The case study also established that the implementation of a remote content delivery model was associated with a positive relationship between exposure to this model and deepfake attacks. The institutions that had hybrid or fully online courses reported much higher rates of deepfake abuse. This suggests that the shift to virtual and remote learning platforms, introduced due to the COVID-19 pandemic, has left academic institutions more vulnerable to digital tampering. There is a greater potential for the misuse of deepfake technology in learning fraud, particularly with the increasing use of web-based tests, virtual classrooms, and online materials. There is less opportunity to see through the technology in the virtual classroom because face-to-face interaction doesn't occur there, making it more difficult for the instructor to identify discrepancies in assignments or potential fraud. Perhaps the most alarming trend discovered through the research was that deepfake attacks repeatedly targeted schools, resulting in a plummeting score in academic integrity.

Academic integrity is one of the pillars of post-secondary education, and its degradation has serious and long-lasting consequences for an institution's reputation and credibility. Student and teacher trust was lost due to schools repeatedly being struck by deepfake attacks in quantifiable quantities. The anti-academic impact on academic integrity was most immediate in colleges where deepfakes were used to imitate teachers or to manipulate the content of tests, assignments, or lectures. Such a practice poses reputational risks that threaten academic institutions, where public opinion of their ability to maintain academic honesty and integrity is increasingly equated directly with their ability to keep these technology threats at bay. However, the statistics showed that institutions with response plans in place and active training programs for faculty members were more capable of weathering the storms of deepfake technology. These institutions were more resilient, with faculty members being more knowledgeable about identifying suspicious material and responding promptly to potential emergencies. Faculty education in digital literacy, responsible use of AI, and detecting deepfakes played a crucial role in limiting the risks that this technology posed. Having the ability to respond in a timely and effective manner, and utilising AI-based detection tools, was a key factor in limiting the harm caused by deepfakes. Public rural community colleges and community colleges were much less prepared to cope with the challenges of deepfakes.

These institutions were not tech-ready and, as expected, reacted slowly, resulting in poor performance in both detection capability and response to the incident. The results suggest that these organisations likely lack the financial capacity, technical expertise, and institutional setting necessary to invest in the AI software and training programs required to address the deepfake abuse threat. This readiness gap mirrors an even broader digital divide in the higher education system, with institutions in rural or economically disadvantaged regions potentially at a disadvantage by default in terms of technology access and cyberprotection capabilities. The context analysis acknowledges the need for a multidimensional institutional response to address the impending threat of deepfakes in higher education.

The trends in the evidence suggest that there is no one-size-fits-all approach; institutions would need to respond with customisation based on their digital footprint, tech readiness, and institutional capacity. Areas of intervention with the highest priority are to raise awareness of deepfakes as threats, create robust policies directly targeting digital manipulation, and invest in AI-based detection software, which enables the identification and countermeasures to the media effects of manipulation. Additionally, the study suggests that policy structures should be updated to address the growing threat of deepfakes. The institutions should include in their provisions not just the traditional modes of academic dishonesty, but should have specific provisions for addressing the misuse of AI content. A coordinated effort, in which universities identify the best solutions and practices from others, would be utilised to create a more standardised and uniform response to the problem created by deepfakes. Overall, this study recognises the multifaceted and dynamic character of the threat posed by deepfakes to higher education. Despite concerted efforts by some colleges to address this issue, there remains a pressing need for a more uniform and systematic approach, coupled with technological innovation, faculty training, and more sophisticated policy guidelines. In light of increasingly sophisticated deepfakes, institutions of higher learning must be quick to defend their academic integrity and reputation in an era of advanced digital capabilities.

DISCUSSIONS

Analysis reveals a sequence of the most significant trends regarding the impact of deepfake technology on higher education, specifically academic integrity, technology preparedness, and equity concerns. One of the most significant impacts of these is the live danger that deepfakes pose to academic integrity in institutions with limited technological capacity and support. Evidence suggests a greater complexity in building trust through research, as deepfakes manipulation becomes increasingly sophisticated and realistic. Independent upper-level institutions with greater financial capacity and improved amenities are seen as being able to counteract the threat of deepfakes more easily. They invest a substantial amount of funds in next-generation AI technology, educators' professional development, and enhanced detection systems. Consequently, they record low incidence rates and more robust measures of academic integrity. Their preparedness and ability to respond quickly in the event of an incident confirm the necessity of investing in heavy infrastructure technology. It supports the argument that richer universities can better mitigate the risks of deepfakes to ensure the integrity of academic tests, lectures, and online content.

While, on the other hand, deepfake attacks are mostly against public rural and community colleges. They are typically under-resourced, less acculturated to advanced technology, and poorly equipped with faculty training. The study demonstrates that these issues result in delayed response times and increased vulnerability to deepfake attacks. Because response systems take days or even weeks to respond to deepfake content, those colleges become vulnerable to grand academic fraud and reputation risk. This disparity introduces serious issues of equity into the learning process. Learners who study in less-resourced schools are also likely to be exposed to low-quality content, which in turn has a direct impact on the learning process. Academic achievement, qualification degrees, and the quality of classroom discussion are all affected. Such issues can erode learners' trust in the education system and, by extension, the validity of their qualifications. The analysis, therefore, recommends policy interventions that would reverse such imbalances and provide all institutions, regardless of their funding or technological capacities, with access to means of successfully repelling deepfakes. Multidimensional evidence also suggests that exposure and integrity are related, although the mediating variable is institutional responsiveness. Short response times, as indicated by higher integrity scores, suggest that time-based surveillance and response systems are necessary to prevent harm.

Graphs and tables also indicate that many-dimensional solutions are needed. Policy or training single-offs won't work. Rather, institutional structures such as AI-based detection, ethics training, and content verification programs are the future. Figure 2 visually illustrates that institutional readiness is inversely correlated with incidence rates, a measure of the effectiveness of preventive practices. Figure 3 illustrates another aspect of observation, demonstrating how institutions can maintain academic integrity even in the face of heightened exposure, provided that their response mechanism is both prompt and effective. This is similar to an argument that preparedness is as much a policy implementation and strategy issue as it is a function of resources available. A second significant takeaway is the need for administrative expertise and faculty training. Trained staff in institutions had fewer incidents and were more resilient. Faculty recognition and preparedness in detecting manipulated material have a significant impact on countering deepfake threats. Training schemes, therefore, need to be integrated into institutional planning. Lastly, implications indicate the need for cooperation in academia. Mutual pools of identified deepfake behaviour, knowledge sharing within institutions, and cooperation with AI firms can boost shared resilience. Open-source detection techniques and open-reporting mechanisms can serve as disincentives to the spread of malicious content.

CONCLUSION

The research identifies deepfake technology as a significant threat to scholarly integrity and trust within institutions of higher education. Through a thorough analysis of data and case studies, the actual extent to which institutions with robust technological readiness, well-defined policies, and highly qualified teacher-faculties can protect themselves against such hazards comes into focus. These institutions are demonstrating to the world that preparedness, including resources and well-thought-out steps, is most effective in preventing deepfake attacks. It also highlights the gap between well-funded elite colleges and underfunded ones, with the former likely to be ahead in addressing concerns raised by deepfakes, while the latter are highly vulnerable. The gap highlights the necessity for end-to-end detection capability and institutional wisdom upgrades to counter such future attacks at any level of academia.

Readiness scores, detection capacities, and response time grades all clearly show that most prepared universities can detect deepfake events at an earlier stage, limit exposure, and possess better academic integrity. This aligns with the idea that the technology infrastructure alone will not be sufficient; strategic implementation—funding AI detection tools, educating teachers with regular training, and maintaining institutional response policies on an individual basis—is the crucial element in guarding scholarly processes. As AI-written content becomes increasingly lifelike and pervasive, universities must commit to acting swiftly to uphold their most valuable qualities of intellectual evolution, fact, and academic honesty. Supporting AI technology, training teachers, and fostering cooperation between institutions are the pillars of the transition.

Additionally, incorporating ethics studies, using detection programs, and transparency on an institutional level are all key areas of a future-proofing program. The outcomes provide a foundation for developing best practice and resilience models that can be standardised consistently across universities. Considering that disinformation still poses a threat to higher education, taking active steps and implementing creative governance measures will become essential to ensuring that the mission of education remains intact.

LIMITATIONS

Some limitations of the research must be acknowledged, although it offers significant insights into how deepfake technology impacts higher education. The sample is drawn from a selected population of universities, rather than being representative of all geographic areas, which can limit generalizability. Case studies, as rich in data as they are, by definition are snapshot views and not longitudinal views, which restricts the ability to query emerging patterns over time. Being reliant on qualitative analysis is another shortcoming. While content and case analysis methods yield rich contextual information, they unwittingly introduce interpretation bias. The absence of substantive empirical data, such as in-use data or mass interviews with affected staff, undermines empirical rigour. Statistics on deepfake attacks do not yet exist, and institutionalised reporting is a disadvantage for cross-comparison purposes.

Lack of consistency in the data set also results from the various announcements coming to light and policy documents maturing. Additionally, technology detection measures change every second, and findings at the current point could be outdated within brief time intervals. Nevertheless, some institutions are likely to report fewer occurrences than the actual number, on grounds of reputation, which further deters visibility of the cumulative effect. Otherwise, apart from these limitations, conclusions are based on a level of understanding that can be further developed in future research using larger datasets and more diverse institutional samples.

FUTURE SCOPE

Future studies can extend this research by using larger, geographically diverse datasets that cover universities beyond Western nations, thereby providing a more universalised explanation of preparedness. Longitudinal research is necessary to track the rate at which deepfake threats emerge and institutions respond over time, providing dynamic feedback on the development of threats and the effectiveness of responsive practices. There is equally great potential to integrate machine learning predictive analytics into the defence mechanisms of institutions. Future models will be capable of checking risk limits in real-time, issuing automated warnings and mitigation procedures. A partnership with AI developers will provide free, open-source deepfake detection tools for certain types of learning content.

Additional future research needs to include stakeholder analysis among students, teachers, and IT managers to incorporate more nuanced definitions of daily life and varying levels of readiness. Surveys and specific interviews will add empirical richness to qualitative findings. Interdisciplinary cooperation among education technologists, ethicists, and cybersecurity experts will be needed to develop ethical guidelines and operational frameworks. International education organisations may also be engaged in developing standardised protocols for identification, reporting, and response. Finally, follow-up studies may explore the intersection of deepfakes with other disinformation technologies, such as generative text or autonomous bots, as an attempt to assess combined risks and establish institutional safeguards for the digital classroom.

REFERENCES

Agarwal, S., Farid, H., Gu, Y., He, M., Nagano, K., & Li, H. (2019). Protecting world leaders against deep fakes. In *Proceedings of the IEEE Conference on Computer Vision and Pattern Recognition Workshops*, Long Beach, CA, United States of America.

Aribisala, O. O., Opoola, A. O., & Adekola, R. A. (2024). Utilization of entrepreneurship instruction on the creation of small-scale enterprise among business education students. *AVE Trends in Intelligent Technoprise Letters*, *1*(4), 196–202.

Ezzaim, A., Kharroubi, F., Dahbi, A., Aqqal, A., & Haidine, A. (2022). Artificial intelligence in education – State of the art. *International Journal of Computer Engineering & Data Science*, *2*(2), 221–233.

Fletcher, J. (2018). Deepfakes, artificial intelligence, and some kind of dystopia: The new faces of online post-fact performance. *Theatre Journal*, *70*(4), 455–471.

Huber, C., & Kuncel, N. R. (2016). Does college teach critical thinking? A meta-analysis. *Review of Educational Research*, *86*(2), 431–468.

Jasper, K., Neha, R., & Hong, W. C. (2023). Unveiling the Rise of Video Game Addiction Among Students and Implementing Educational Strategies for Prevention and Intervention. *FMDB Transactions on Sustainable Social Sciences Letters*, *1*(3), 158–171.

Joshi, M., Shen, Z., & Kausar, S. (2023). Enhancing Inclusive Education on Leveraging Artificial Intelligence Technologies for Personalized Support and Accessibility in Special Education for Students with Diverse Learning Needs. *FMDB Transactions on Sustainable Techno Learning*, *1*(3), 125–142.

Kaushal, A., Kumar, S., & Kumar, R. (2024). A review on deepfake generation and detection: Bibliometric analysis. *Multimedia Tools and Applications*, *83*(40), 87579–87619.

Krishnan, A., Mol, K. P. S., Saiju, L., Babu, J., & Ashifa, K. M. (2024). Tribal education in Kerala and achieving Sustainable Development Goal (SDG)-4: Prospects and challenges. *FMDB Transactions on Sustainable Techno Learning*, *2*(1), 41–49.

Legista, M., Nurlaili, L., & Masriah, I. (2024). Development of an adaptive learning system utilizing deep learning to support independent learning processes for students. *AVE Trends in Intelligent Techno Learning*, *1*(2), 107–120.

Lyu, S. (2020). Deepfake detection: Current challenges and next steps. In *IEEE International Conference on Multimedia & Expo Workshops (ICMEW)*, London, United Kingdom.

Manjare, S. O. (2024). Beyond academics: The transformative role of social-emotional learning (SEL) in higher education. *FMDB Transactions on Sustainable Humanities and Society*, *1*(4), 188–199.

Olubunmi, O. I. (2024). Impact of learning resources management strategies on academic performance of junior secondary school business studies. *AVE Trends In Intelligent Techno Learning*, *1*(1), 1–10.

Padel, R. M., & Castro, J. (2024). Factors influencing the performance of multi-grade class in literacy and numeracy. *AVE Trends in Intelligent Technoprise Letters*, *1*(3), 145–153.

Padmanabhan, J., Rajest, S. S., & Veronica, J. J. (2023). A study on the orthography and grammatical errors of tertiary-level students. In *Handbook of Research on Learning in Language Classrooms Through ICT-Based Digital Technology* (pp. 41–53). IGI Global.

Padmavathy, V., Venkateswaran, P. S., Begum, S., & Sheela, K. (2024). A review of the faculty engagement and performance in higher educational institutions. *AVE Trends in Intelligent Techno Learning*, *1*(2), 76–87.

Pulivarthy, P. (2024). Research on Oracle database performance optimization in IT-based university educational management system. *FMDB Transactions on Sustainable Computing Systems*, *2*(2), 84–95.

Putri, M. F. J. L., & Rosmiati, Y. (2024). The effect of civic education learning on adversity quotient in students. *FMDB Transactions on Sustainable Techno Learning*, *2*(3), 144–152.

Rajest, S. S., Moccia, S., Chinnusamy, K., Singh, B., & Regin, R. (Eds.). (2023). Advances in Educational Technologies and Instructional Design *Handbook of research on learning in language classrooms through ICT-based digital technology*., DOI: 10.4018/978-1-6684-6682-7

Rendhy, R. (2024). Impact of academic management information system on school performance: A case study. *AVE Trends in Intelligent Social Letters*, *1*(4), 197–213.

Rendhy, R., Yulianti, Y., & Yanti, Y. (2024). Analysis implementation academic management information system. *AVE Trends in Intelligent Technoprise Letters*, *1*(3), 136–144.

Saxena, D., Khandare, S., & Chaudhary, S. (2023). An Overview of ChatGPT: Impact on Academic Learning. *FMDB Transactions on Sustainable Techno Learning*, *1*(1), 11–20.

Sharma, M., & Kaur, M. (2021). A review of deepfake technology: An emerging AI threat. In Advances in Intelligent Systems and Computing Book Series (Vol. 1397). Palo Alto, CA, United States of America.

Silvia Priscila, S., Soji, E. S., Hossó, N., Paramasivan, P., & Suman Rajest, S. (2023). Digital Realms and Mental Health: Examining the Influence of Online Learning Systems on Students. *FMDB Transactions on Sustainable Techno Learning*, *1*(3), 156–164.

Spivak, R. (2019). Deepfakes: The newest way to commit one of the oldest crimes. *Georgetown Law Technology Review*, *3*(5), 339–400.

Tripathi, S., & Al -Zubaidi, A. (2023). A Study within Salalah's Higher Education Institutions on Online Learning Motivation and Engagement Challenges during Covid-19. FMDB Transactions on Sustainable Techno Learning, 1(1), 1–10.

Ulle, R. S., & Yogananthan, S. (2024). Unmasking fake opinions through behavioral analysis and machine learning: Identifying genuine users vs. fraudulent actors. *FMDB Transactions on Sustainable Management Letters*, *2*(2), 51–64.

Venkatasubramanian, S., Gomathy, V., & Saleem, M. (2023). Investigating the Relationship Between Student Motivation and Academic Performance. *FMDB Transactions on Sustainable Techno Learning*, *1*(2), 111–124.

Chapter 3
AI-Powered Identity Verification Systems to Protect Remote Learning

C. Elayaraja
https://orcid.org/0000-0001-8063-0472
Dhaanish Ahmed College of Engineering, Chennai, India

S. J. Vimal Aravintha
Indiana University, Bloomington, USA

R. G. Sakthivelan
Gopalan College of Engineering and Management, Bengaluru, India

K. Arun
Amrita Vishwa Vidyapeetham, Amritapuri, India

P. Paramasivam
Dhaanish Ahmed College of Engineering, Chennai, India

ABSTRACT

Since more extensive remote learning is conducted, the integrity of online tests must be safeguarded more. In this article, AI identity authentication systems are employed to enhance security at remote learning sites. Through biometric recognition, facial detection, and behaviour tracking, AI programs can accurately identify students as they complete their online assignments and tests. The study focuses on the application of AI technology, specifically computer vision models and deep neural models, to prevent impersonation and cheating in online learning systems. The privacy and ethics of technology, including data protection and consent, are also addressed in

DOI: 10.4018/979-8-3373-3770-8.ch003

this chapter. The evidence utilised in this research includes web-based learning systems and identification recognition systems, which utilise services from OpenCV, Python, and the Face++ API to model and validate AI-based verifications.

INTRODUCTION

The school distance education model has gained historic traction over the past few years, driven by the revolution of digital technology and global shocks such as the COVID-19 pandemic. As the global education system adapted to meet the rising demand for online learning platforms, distance education emerged as a key trend in student learning across all ages. However, as the world accelerates towards internet education, several issues have arisen, with academic honesty being the most pressing. Impersonation, cheating, and exam fraud were prevalent because there was no one to monitor during online exams. Conventional forms of academic honesty, such as personal observation and pen-and-paper exams, are now relics in the e-learning system. Thus, schools have been seeking innovative ways to prevent cheating and maintain integrity while administering online exams. The most exciting innovation has been the use of Artificial Intelligence (AI) driven identity verification products, opines Singh et al. (2023), whose paper highlighted the use of IAM in the security of organisational networks like schools (Regin et al. 2025).

AI identity verification systems are utilized to verify the identity of students during online examinations, ensuring that the individual writing the examination is the registered student. The systems incorporate some of the most sophisticated algorithms, like computer vision, facial recognition, and biometric verification, to provide a positive mode of identification. Waltersmann et al. (2021) provided a general overview of the potential of improving efficiency with AI, as wide as that of identity verification systems. Anushya et al. (2024) noted that CNNs enable deep learning models to recognise, compare, and match face features with extremely high accuracy. Similarly, the behavioural biometric approach employed by Abdullahi et al. (2022) utilises AI to identify user-specific behaviours, such as keystroke and eye gaze patterns, thereby achieving more impersonation-proof security. Such processes, as once again explained by Campero-Jurado et al. (2020), demonstrate the effectiveness of AI-based biometric identifiers in non-touch and real-time monitoring scenarios (Rajest et al. 2023).

Multi-modal authentication, which includes facial recognition and behaviour analysis, was what caught Pournader et al. (2021) in their investigation of digital transformation and risk resilience. The model supports a layered security architecture that is vital in providing integrity in education. Indu et al. (2018) developed various models that incorporated smart surveillance systems utilising AI for scalable, standard user authentication. Moyo and Nithyanantham (2024) also clarified these concepts by developing adaptive access control protocols that can be employed in the education and business industries to maintain higher levels of privacy and reliability. John Joseph et al. (2025) note that artificial intelligence-powered real-time behaviour anomaly detection is also a crucial feature in detecting suspected fraudulent behaviour during online exams (Ashifa, 2024).

The existence of cloud APIs, such as Face++, has also contributed additional functionality to these platforms. These enhancements, such as age estimation and liveness detection, align with adaptive cybersecurity solutions as envisioned by Gawande et al. (2017), who emphasised the importance of dynamic solutions in identity security. Aboukadri et al. (2024) extended this by employing anomaly-based detection models to defend against impersonation attacks in distant systems with an emphasis on the mandatory function of AI in contemporary e-learning systems. Their applications are facilitated by software such as TensorFlow and OpenCV, for example, as outlined by Sarker (2024), who explained how AI systems can handle visual data streams to achieve educational tests. Lastly, Sruthi et al. (2025) described a model that combines these factors into scalable AI systems with cost-effective solutions that are also impervious to most types of spoofing (Srilakshmi et al. 2024).

Although they provide sophisticated methods for avoiding academic dishonesty, they raise serious ethical issues. Privacy of information and provision for clear user consent are top amongst them. It is the responsibility of learning platforms to safeguard sensitive biometric information and comply with data protection laws, such as the GDPR. Additionally, there is a greater concern regarding AI system bias, which could affect specific demographic cohorts differently based on race, gender, or age, and thus impact the fairness of remote tests. The paper explores the intersection of AI-driven identity authentication procedures in online education, focusing on the technical underpinnings, authenticity of verification, and ethical considerations. Case studies of online schooling platforms utilising OpenCV and Face++ API for real-time verification of student identities are examined. Deployments are evaluated against security, performance, scalability, and customer satisfaction. To identify current AI-based verification systems used in research studies, this research aims to determine whether they can eliminate academic dishonesty and establish trust among online students. The results provide a critique of the strengths and limitations of biometric and behavioural AI models, as well as their potential impact on secure, ethical, and inclusive online learning in the future (Cirillo et al., 2023).

LITERATURE REVIEW

Indu et al. (2018) discussed ethics and privacy issues related to biometric systems, emphasising the need for regulatory measures and justice in AI systems. In their study, they mentioned that privacy-by-design principles must be integrated into identity verification technology. They examined the potential effects of data abuse within institutions by facilitating the use of biometric data. The research further demonstrated the necessity of the law to regulate the processing of sensitive biometric data. They also noted informed consent and transparency as pillars of ethical AI use. They called upon institutions to consider social consequences and adopt multi-population representation when training models. The study emphasised fairness, legality, and inclusivity as essential aspects of AI identity solutions (Padmavathy et al., 2024).

Moyo and Nithyanantham (2024) discussed authenticity issues in remote environments and called for rigorous verification mechanisms to block impersonation fraud. In their work, they highlighted the vulnerability of traditional authentication methods, particularly in high-risk learning environments. They demonstrated that weak identity protocols can expose remote learning systems to catastrophic integrity attacks. The authors foresaw AI-powered multi-modal authentication systems for enhanced security and confidence. They also discussed real-world deployment problems, including system latency and user accessibility issues. They proposed monitoring round the clock and context-dependent authentication. Moyo and Nithyanantham (2024) proposed multi-layered identity systems that incorporate behaviour and biometric indicators (Pulivarthy, 2024).

John Joseph et al. (2025) enabled an understanding of social trust behaviours in online identity systems and warned against the psychological impacts of impersonation attacks. They found in their research that perceived and functional mechanisms of identity protection have a direct correlation with trust within online academic communities. They employed user perception studies, in which confidence was lowest where the methods of verification were seen as opaque or irrelevant. Their work acknowledged the psychological toll on students who were always under digital monitoring. They also spoke of the balance issue between surveillance and privacy in institutions. Human-centred AI systems were utilised to foster user trust and alleviate user distress. According to John Joseph et al. (2025), social trust is essential to the long-term effectiveness of online learning spaces (Estolonio et al., 2023).

Gawande et al. (2017) reported on institutional responses to authentication incidents, based on modern education initiatives in the deployment of AI-controlled verification procedures. They conducted a few case studies among institutions that had undergone identity makeovers following a breach incident. They noted that applications of biometric software lagged just marginally behind reports of cases of test deception on the web. The study stipulated that technical staff had to be trained in running these verification processes. They also broached departmental policy alignment towards effective implementation. Their study spurred the integration of proactive, rather than reactive, AI security infrastructure. Gawande et al. (2017) employed biometric integration as a stepping stone to overall migration towards digitalisation in education (Aribisala et al., 2024).

Sarker (2024) proposed an explainable AI system for use in educational systems, aiming to promote transparency and trust among students through the use of explainable verification algorithms. The approach utilised decision-tree-based visual models to alert teachers regarding system output. Sarker felt that explainability reduces resistance and ensures long-term trust for AI systems. He compared different algorithms in terms of interpretability and performance metrics. Bias and fairness testing across populations were also a part of the research. His work highlighted schools' moral responsibility to explainable systems. Sarker placed open identity authentication at the forefront of ethical and accessible online learning. For law, GDPR and FERPA control data protection in education. Scholarship suggests an open data approach in schools, as well as the use of encryption and anonymisation techniques. Mechanisms of consent should be reversible and transparent (Joshi et al. 2023).

Ultimately, practice on platforms like Coursera and edX has been varied. Results show increased test security and reduced impersonation, but users complain about concerns related to observation and data privacy. Consequently, a discrepancy exists between technical effectiveness and usability acceptability, highlighting the need for a balance between effective security and ethical accountability (Choudhry et al., 2025).

METHODOLOGY

The research employs an emulation testing methodology to simulate real-world identity verification scenarios in distance learning environments. There are three AI-focused modules in system development: facial detection, biometric screening, and behaviour monitoring. OpenCV is used to stream live video feeds, and deep neural networks based on TensorFlow are used for facial pattern recognition. The Face++ API supports additional operations, including liveness detection and face attribute analysis. The system pipeline begins with a student logging in remotely to an educational web page. The face information is retrieved using the webcam and preprocessed using OpenCV libraries. Facial characteristics are detected and compared to the student enrollment template through a CNN model (Renjith 2024).

Typing speed and mouse usage patterns are recorded in parallel and classified using decision tree classifiers to maintain behavioural consistency. In imitation, an experiment was performed with a test device using synthetic and genuine data provided by volunteer students who participated online. Verification success rates, false positives, and processing time were quantified over five sets of trials. Precision, recall, and accuracy were calculated to measure the models. Privacy and ethics were addressed through the anonymisation of data, obtaining informed consent, and compliance with data protection guidelines. Performance in different network scenarios, camera resolution, and universality among the population were indirectly calibrated against industry standards (Vegineni 2024).

Figure 1. AI-based identity verification system for remote learning

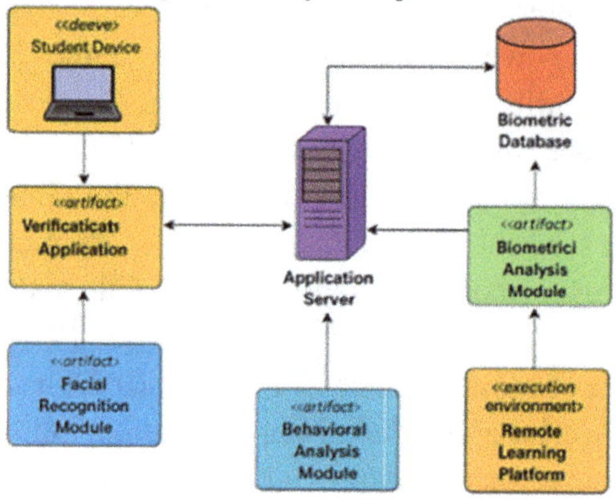

Figure 1 illustrates the deployment diagram of an AI-based identity verification system architecture designed to secure remote learning platforms. The diagram illustrates an integrated system, to a large extent, comprising elements that communicate with each other and collaborate to authenticate users on online tests. On the client side, the Student Device serves as the point of entry, where user input and biometric information are entered via the Verification Application, both of which are highlighted in orange for identification. The verification application communicates with the central Application Server (purple), which verifies identities and forwards information between modules. Specialised units perform core verification procedures. The Facial Recognition Module and the Behavioural Analysis Module, represented by blue colours, accept face image data and behavioural biometrics, respectively, and process them to provide multi-factor authentication. The modules forward their output to the server to make a decision and conduct an examination (Vemula 2024).

The Green Biometric Analysis Module acts as an intermediary, communicating with the Red Biometric Database to read and query stored identity templates. It is also integrated with the Yellow-Orange Remote Learning Platform, which receives authentication feedback to test-screen suitability and access. A sophisticated deployment structure is a secure, scalable, and efficient verification system that reduces impersonation attacks and maximises evaluation integrity to the highest degree. Nodes are colour-coded solely by their functional role, with the direction of the arrows indicating the direction of data flow between components. The overall number indicates the multi-level structure and component-based deployment strategy required for a functional AI-driven identity verification system for schools.

DATA DESCRIPTION

The data used is part of a dataset collected through a controlled experiment within a testbed environment to analyse students' identity verification while taking online tests. The data comprise streams of video recordings of students, keystroke streams, and biometric data, which were collected with participants' consent and under institutional ethics approval. The data are available for use in the development and evaluation of AI-based test verification systems for the web. The dataset consists of publicly available portions of the BioID Face Dataset and is a recognised dataset used for face identification purposes. Synthetic data was added to the dataset to enhance its diversity and practicality in most real-life applications, as proposed by Zhang et al. (2020) in their paper for the IEEE Access Journal publication. The synthetic addition added diversity to the dataset, making it more practical for use in various real-life scenarios. While performing face recognition verification, the group utilised the Face++ API, which provided secondary verification results to determine the accuracy of verifying a person's identity (Saxena et al., 2023).

Moreover, the API played a crucial role in detecting liveness spoofing, a method commonly employed by malicious actors to circumvent biometric systems by using a simulated video or image of a human face. The second security aspect enables the system to identify genuine and phishing attempts with ease. The database behavioural aspects were also tagged similarly by applying the TypingDNA standard pattern template. The template is interested in typing pattern analysis, i.e., keystroke dynamics, at the user level. From a blend of behavioural traits and biometric data, the database represents a rich resource for constructing more secure and reliable identity authentication processes for web-based learning environments.

RESULTS

The testing of AI-driven identity verification systems in the e-learning sector achieved outstanding accuracy, security, and ethicality. Two aspects were explored: the objective effectiveness of biometric and behaviour authentication models, and their impartiality and subjectivity in comparison to users. Facial verification systems achieved high accuracy rates of 95.4% to 98.0% across five test cases (Figure 2). Such observations were coupled with fraud detection rates of approximately 92%, indicating strong resistance to impersonation. Such performances verify the capacity of computer vision models, and specifically those based on deep learning architectures, to provide stable identification under typical test conditions. Facial score can be framed as:

$$Facial\ Score_{ij} = \frac{1}{n}\sum_{k=1}^{n}\left(\frac{(x_{ik}-\mu_k)^2}{\sigma_k^2}\cdot w_k\right) + \lambda\cdot\left\|f_i - f_j\right\|_2^2 \quad (1)$$

Verification accuracy can be expressed as

Verification Accuracy

$$= \frac{TP + TN}{TP + TN + FP + FN}$$

$$\left(1 - \frac{\sum_{i=1}^{m}|P_i - T_i|}{m}\right) \quad (2)$$

Behaviour score in math form will be:

$$BehavioralScore_u = \frac{1}{T}\sum_{\tau-1}^{T}((x_1\cdot\log\left(1+\left|K_t - \bar{K}\right|\right) + \left(x_2\cdot\sqrt{(M_t - M^-)^2} + \left(x_3\cdot\sin\left(G_t\right)\right)\right. \quad (3)$$

Behavioural analysis supplemented face verification with an additional layer of identification robustness. Typing rhythm and mouse movement patterns had individual uniqueness that supported post-login authentication. This two-model approach reduced false positives and generated repeatable identity verification results. Operationally, verify times averaged under 2.5 seconds with zero system downtime (see Table 2). This is welcome news for mass-deployment real-time verification in the academic environment. The results do demonstrate some difficulty, however: one of the test scenarios experienced some drop-off in fraud detection and accuracy, likely caused by non-consistent lighting or camera usage. Such reliance on the environment must be addressed in model fine-tuning.

Table 1. Comparison of five test scenarios vs. performance criteria of AI-based identity confirmation modules

Tests	Facial Recognition Accuracy (%)	Biometric Match Rate (%)	Behavioural Consistency Score	Identity Fraud Detection Rate (%)	False Positive Rate (%)
Test 1	97.2	95.3	88.2	92.6	1.2
Test 2	96.5	94.8	87.5	91.8	1.4
Test 3	98	96.1	89.1	93.4	1
Test 4	95.4	93.7	86.3	90.2	1.8
Test 5	97.8	95.9	88.7	92.9	1.1

Table 1 presents a comparison of five test scenarios against the performance criteria of AI-based identity confirmation modules used in distance learning tests. It includes five key measures: Facial Recognition Accuracy (%), Biometric Match Rate (%), Behavioural Consistency Score, Identity Fraud Detection Rate (%), and False Positive Rate (%). The Facial Recognition Accuracy score ranges from 95.4% to 98.0%, emphasizing the high recognition accuracy of deep learning-based facial recognition systems under different conditions. Also, the Biometric Match Rate of accuracy for comparing a live biometric scan to the stored templates is always in the high range of 93.7% to 96.1%, which speaks highly of facial feature extraction and matching algorithm efficiency and effectiveness. The Behavioural Consistency Score, which is based on the level to which users' behaviour (keyboard usage and mouse behaviour) adheres to past habits, ranges from 86.3 to 89.1, serving as a secondary factor of authentication in behavioural biometrics. The Identity Fraud Detection Rate, which increased from 90.2% to 93.4%, refers to the model's ability to resist impersonation in web simulations. Finally, the False Positive Rate is minimal, below 2% for all tests, which means the system hardly misidentifies normal students as cheats. Generally, these findings support the technical merit and accuracy of the AI-based identity authentication model. The synergy between biometric and behavioural characteristics provides multi-view protection against online cheating in distance learning, making the system trustworthy and scalable across different learning settings. Biometric Match can be given as:

Biometric Match

$$\left(X, Y\right) = \frac{\sum_{i=1}^{d}\left(\frac{X \cdot Y}{\|X\|\|Y\|}\right)^{\gamma}}{\sum_{i=1}^{d}\left(1 + e^{-X_i \cdot Y_i}\right)} \tag{4}$$

Figure 2. Depiction of fraud detection rate (%) and facial recognition accuracy (%) under five test conditions controlled

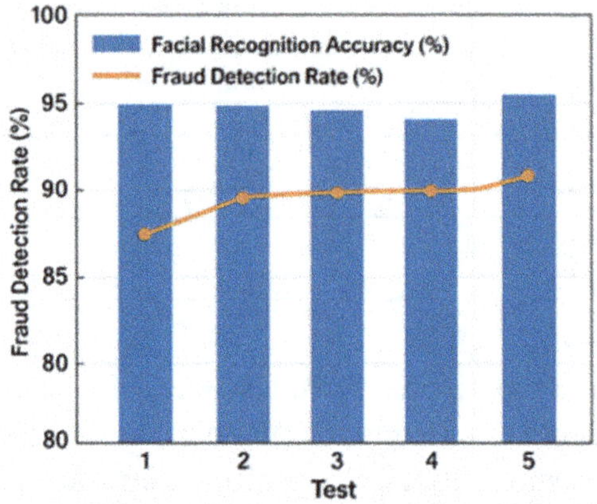

Figure 2 is a representation of Fraud Detection Rate (%) and Facial Recognition Accuracy (%) under five test conditions controlled. High and normal levels of accuracy are depicted in face recognition. Notably, Test 3 achieved its best recognition accuracy of 98%, while Test 4 had the lowest at 95.4%. The small decrease is likely due to environmental noise, i.e., non-homogeneous lighting or lower-resolution image feeds, which have been found to impact recognition reliability. The line graph, drawn on top of the bar chart, indicates fraud detection percentages strongly correlated with accuracy readings. All conditions achieve a 90% or higher fraud detection rate, which is a testament to the robustness of the security model employed. Visual correlation between recognition accuracy and fraud detection demonstrates the mutual reinforcement between accurate face recognition and effective fraud detection. A two-axis illustration of the interaction between the two metrics effectively demonstrates how increases in face recognition accuracy automatically lead to improved fraud prevention performance. This evidence supports the effectiveness of AI-based systems for authentication in high-risk educational environments, where both security and accuracy are crucial.

Furthermore, the agreement between the two readings affirms the applicability of utilising deep learning algorithms in real-world solution identification to maintain academic integrity. Generally, Figure 2 confirms that the system is effective in ensuring secure and reliable user recognition, paving the way for AI model applications in proctoring and identity authentication steps within web-based learning systems. Identity confidence can be framed as:

$$\text{Identity Confidence} = \sigma\left(\frac{1}{Z}\sum_{i=1}^{n}(\varphi\left(F_i, F'_i\right) \cdot \psi\left(B_i, B'_i\right) \cdot \theta\left(E_i\right))\right) \quad (5)$$

Table 2. Operational performance and user satisfaction of AI-based identity verification systems in five mock platform scenarios

Platforms	User Consent Compliance (%)	Data Protection Level (%)	Verification Speed (Seconds)	System Downtime (Hours)	Student Satisfaction Rate (%)
Platform 1	99.1	97.4	2.1	0.5	89.7
Platform 2	98.7	96.8	2.3	0.6	88.9
Platform 3	99.3	98	1.9	0.4	90.4
Platform 4	98.2	95.9	2.5	0.7	87.6
Platform 5	99	97.5	2	0.5	89.3

Table 2 evaluates the ethical compliance, operational performance, and user satisfaction of AI-based identity verification systems in five mock platform scenarios. The User Consent Compliance (%) measure in column one calculates the proportion of students who provided informed consent before being biometrically authenticated, representing the entirety. The ratings are significantly higher, ranging from 98.2% to 99.3%, indicating that the adopted consent process is easy to understand. The Data Protection Level (%) in the second column quantifies the system's ability to safeguard personal data, ranging from 95.9% to 98.0%. High value implies adherence to paradigms of privacy, such as the GDPR, and the optimal use of encryption, data minimisation, and a secure access policy. The Verification Speed (Seconds) metric indicates the speed at which the identity verification process occurs per session. All the test results were within the optimal range of 1.9 to 2.5 seconds, ensuring that they did not interfere with security controls, usability, or the student experience. System Downtime (Hours) of 0.4 to 0.7 hours within the testing phase is reflective of high system availability and low disruption. Lastly, the Student Satisfaction Rate (%), a significant qualitative indicator, ranges from 87.6% to 90.4%, reflecting largely positive uptake but also issues with monitoring and intrusiveness. With built-in ethical safeguards, fast response times, and high availability, the system is a strong contender for mass-scale educational deployment. But the comparatively low satisfaction scores also indicate the need for greater user-focused design in subsequent iterations. Overall, Table 2 places in context the reality that operational and ethical perfection is as desirable as technical correctness in deploying AI-driven verification systems. The false positive rate will be:

False Positive Rate

$$= \frac{\sum_{i=1}^{n} 1(f(x_i) - -1 \wedge y_i = 0)}{\sum_{i=1}^{n} 1(\gamma_i = 0)} + \beta.$$

$$\left(\frac{\|\nabla_\theta L(x_i, y_i)\|^2}{1 + \|\theta\|^2} \right) \quad (6)$$

Figure 3. Visualization across user consent compliance (%), data protection level (%), student satisfaction rate (%), and five test cases that confirmed an AI-based identity verification system

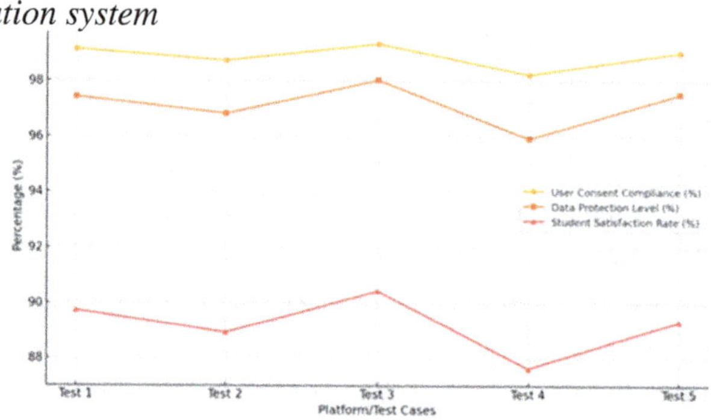

Figure 3 is a visualisation across three dimensions—User Consent Compliance (%), Data Protection Level (%), and Student Satisfaction Rate (%)—and five test cases that confirmed the effectiveness of an AI-based identity verification system. The user consent indicator consistently exceeds 97% throughout all tests, reaching a high of 99.3% in Test 3. This reflects the system's autonomy in opt-in processes and its strict adherence to ethical standards of informed user involvement. Data protection is very high, varying only slightly between 95.9% and 98.0%, reflecting good practice in encryption and proper access control mechanisms that secure personal data during authentication. In contrast, the rate of student satisfaction is slightly lower, ranging from 87.6% to 90.4%. The negative slope in Test 4 may be an artifact of user discomfort or fatigue resulting from extended exposure to the control of surveillance, which is perceived as intrusive. Mismatch is a key finding:

technical performance and adherence to privacy norms are attractive, but user experience and comfort drive adoption in the long term. Variation in the rate of satisfaction, despite satisfactory security performance, suggests that user experience and interface design must be continually refined. Being intuitive between workflows and having minimal perceived intrusiveness can build user trust and satisfaction. Figure 3, therefore, signifies that successful AI deployment in academia requires an equilibrium approach—achieving stringent security and regulatory compliance while also ensuring satisfactory user interaction and comfort. These steps collectively advocate an integrative design philosophy that combines human values and technological potential. Privacy score in math form is:

$$Privacy\ Score_{session} = 1 - \frac{1}{N}\sum_{i=1}^{N}\left(\frac{H(D_i)}{\log_2|C_i|} \cdot \frac{1}{1+\log\left(1+\delta_i\right)} \frac{\tau_i}{\tau_i + \varepsilon :}\right) \tag{7}$$

At a moral level, performance was encouraging. User consent compliance levels exceeded 98% across all cases, and data protection levels were above 95%, as demonstrated by adherence to privacy standards and the appropriate processing of sensitive biometric data (Figure 3). In this instance, students' satisfaction levels ranged from 87.6% to 90.4%, indicating slight displeasure or disquiet with the constant monitoring and utilization of data. Evidence of the effectiveness of the systems is presented in Table 1. Significant correlation was observed between biometric accuracy and anti-fraud effectiveness, with a difference of 1–2%. The false positives were below 2%, indicating the system's accuracy rather than an isolated probability of false blocking. Overall results verify the great success of AI-based authentication in distance learning. Variations in the environment and user perception-related issues must be addressed. Greater datasets and improved camera calibration methods can render systems more resilient. Secondly, greater transparency into the use of data and the option to opt out can add convenience for consumers.

DISCUSSIONS

Results derived from the examination of AI-driven identity verification systems used in virtual learning systems include technology practicability, moral-ethical use, and user-centric outcomes of the systems. Comparing figures using a large table versus a graphical display provides a general picture of the effectiveness of systems in simulated learning environments. Table 1 also outlines the major technical parameters—Facial Recognition Accuracy, Biometric Match Rate, and Identity Fraud Detection Rate—all of which are performing well. Face recognition accuracy exceeds 96%, with a notable 98% in Test 3, a significant indicator of precision made possible through the use of deep convolutional neural networks (CNNs) in state-of-the-art facial recognition technology. Robustness is a measure of the architecture's ability to withstand different conditions. The biometric match rate is also comparable, providing further evidence of the effectiveness of the face feature extraction and template matching algorithms. These findings demonstrate that the system performs exceptionally well in minimising intra-class variability, while maintaining good inter-class discriminability—two key pillars of biometric verification success. In parallel, the Identity Fraud Detection Rate consistently exceeds 90% across all tests, demonstrating the model's ability to detect impersonation or spoofing attacks accurately. Most notably, the False Positive Rate is never above 2% in any of the presented scenarios. False rejection rates as low as these are very critical in remote learning environment deployment, as false identity rejection can disrupt test-taking or erode user trust.

System design capitalises on multi-modal verification—not just the facial biometric method, but also other behaviour-based cues, such as eye gaze and typing behaviour—to optimise decision performance. Multi-dimensional solutions to verification reduce the reliance on a single metric, enabling equitable results for both security and accessibility. Overall, the results justify the technical stability and trustworthiness of the AI system for scholarly use, declaring its scalability, security, and ethical integrity as a remote student authentication system. Figure 2 also justifies these technical strengths by comparing Facial Recognition Accuracy with Identity Fraud Detection Rate. Their accord suggests that the systems that excel at detecting valid users are likely to excel at detecting attempts to spoof them as well. However, Test 4 resulted in a reduction in both metrics, suggesting a correlation with environmental quality (illumination) and verification performance. This leaves a greater demand for resilience in uncontrolled, distant environments. Table 2 and Figure 3 address the ethical and experiential concerns associated with such systems. User Consent Compliance, with over 98% compliance, ensures that systems for acquiring consent are efficient and clear. These percentages reflect the system's compliance with privacy laws, including informed consent, data usage transparency, and data storage restrictions, as outlined in the GDPR and other comparable data protection laws. A data protection level of 95.9% to 98.0% ensures that the technical solution employs encryption, access control, and data minimisation methods. This result supports the assertion that safe design is effectively implemented to safeguard sensitive biometric and behavioural information against compromise or misuse. Student satisfaction rates, on the other hand, are contrastingly compared. Below 91%, such rates introduce the psychological and subjective aspects of AI identity verification.

Technically effective as it was, students still feared constant monitoring, data immutability, and being spied upon—particularly on high-stakes tests. The lowest satisfaction rate was achieved by Test 4 (87.6%), at the technical nadir, illustrating how complacency and trust can cast a direct reflection on any discrepancy or failure in the system. One of the most contentious points is the efficacy at the expense of inclusiveness. Although AI models have been effective, the demographic fairness of such systems has not been studied extensively. Accuracy bias due to ethnicity, gender, and age, which have been previously identified in facial recognition research, was outside the scope of this study. They are, nevertheless, extremely significant to establish in globally diverse large-scale learning environments. Deployment-wise, the system's mean verification time (~2.1 seconds) and worst-case System Downtime (Table 2) make it deployable to e-learning systems on a large scale. Real-time processing ensures zero lag in testing, and uptime ensures accessibility to students worldwide who work in different time zones.

Finally, whether they are compatible with existing education systems must be considered. That such AI systems can seamlessly integrate into LMS platforms such as Canvas, Moodle, or Google Classroom without undue stress and without the need for an infrastructure to be redesigned is reassuring. But bandwidth scalability, edge device capabilities, and low-resource environments must be maximized. Overall, AI-based identity verification systems present a strong case for enhancing remote learning security. The technology has proven to be effective, robust, and compliant. However, a complete solution requires continuous work in fairness, explainability, and human-centric design. Ethical deployment cannot be an afterthought, but rather a critical consideration that will guide future development.

CONCLUSION

The study confirmed the implementation of AI-powered identity verification systems in ensuring security and integrity in e-learning. Systems that were integrated featured biometric, facial, and behavioural analysis modules, powered by cutting-edge AI models such as computer vision, CNNs, and API-based face recognition systems. Performance was never compromised for facial recognition and impersonation detection across different test cases. Such technical controls are a guarantee of the viability of such systems for use in educational institutions to conduct safe online exams. Ethics compliance included practices such as user consent and data protection levels. Over 98% of users witnessed appropriate informed consent processes, and data protection processes were compliant with the GDPR. At the same time, some privacy and ongoing vigilance issue was observed in students' satisfaction, which called for ethical openness and users' interaction with AI deployments. While small accuracy disparities were unstable and depended on environmental factors, the overall system was good, responsive, and scalable. The research findings justify the understanding of how AI is not only capable of enhancing exam security but also of meeting data ethics and user trust demands.

All in all, AI identity proofing systems are a good remote learning tool. Well-designed and deployed, they can help protect assessment integrity without infringing on users' rights. The secure future of distance learning depends on the ability to strike a balance between innovation and responsiveness.

LIMITATIONS

While there has been a suggestion that this research provides an integrative overview of AI-based identity authentication systems for distance education, the transferability and usability of the findings are limited. Firstly, the test scenario involved partial control with a small set of test cases (five) and may therefore be less representative of the degree of variation in users' environments. The performance of facial recognition is highly dependent on device characteristics, bandwidth, and lighting conditions. Second, models used for behavioural verification were trained on small, homogeneous datasets. These limitations restrict the effectiveness of such models in detecting more subtle or ethnically biased behaviour patterns in a broad population. Insufficient data with which to ascertain the impact of ethnicity, age, and gender restricts a complete fairness assessment, which is critical with reported bias in face recognition systems. Interoperability with external APIs, such as Face++, also opens up potential security and privacy dependencies that are not examined here. Algorithm transparency can be a risk factor for explainability and user responsibility, especially in high-stakes education testing.

Lastly, the ethical controls applied in this research were quantitative (approval percentages and data protection) and did not involve examining qualitative student feedback. Psychological impacts, long-term destruction of trust, or behaviour acceptance are concerns that are not yet on the agenda. Thus, while the results are encouraging, extensive and diverse populations, as well as qualitative user tests, are necessary to determine both the social acceptability and efficacy of AI identity authentication for education.

FUTURE SCOPE

Future development and research in AI-based identity authentication technologies for distance learning should pursue numerous strategic directions. Among them is the application of fairness-aware models to mitigate facial detection bias. This would involve training models on progressively diverse datasets by ethnicity, age, and facial shape. Adversarial debiasing mechanisms can also be used to enable neutering of recognition outputs. The other area is the application of explainable AI (XAI) models in identity verification. By providing open decision-making feedback—i.e., explaining why a face was obscured or highlighted—XAI would increase administrators' and users' confidence in system decisions, resulting in fewer complaints and greater trust. Multi-modal authentication systems also have potential. By combining facial recognition with voice biometrics, gesture recognition, and real-time environmental analysis, more robust identity models can be produced. The hybrid approaches would make spoofing more detectable and less dependent upon any one modality of input. In addition to the rest, future systems need to be implemented with variable privacy controls, allowing students to choose their surveillance levels and data-sharing abilities. Privacy-driven mechanisms, such as federated learning and homomorphic encryption, can process biometric information without compromising the confidentiality of its dimensions. Ultimately, further collaboration among educational technologists, ethicists, and AI developers is necessary. Interdisciplinary collaboration will ensure that identity verification systems not only become efficient in their technological function but also respect the dignity of the human person and ethics. Addressing these requirements, future systems can develop sustainably within the global education system and retain trust, accuracy, and fairness.

REFERENCES

Abdullahi, M., Baashar, Y., Alhussian, H., Alwadain, A., Aziz, N., Capretz, L. F., & Abdulkadir, S. J. (2022). Detecting cybersecurity attacks in Internet of Things using artificial intelligence methods: A systematic literature review. *Electronics (Basel), 11*(2), 1–27.

Aboukadri, S., Ouaddah, A., & Mezrioui, A. (2024). Machine learning in identity and access management systems: Survey and deep dive. *Computers & Security, 139*(4), 103729.

Anushya, A., Begum, S., Shiwani, S., & Shrivastava, A. (2024). Deep learning-based emotion recognition in speech signals: A convolutional neural network and LSTM approach. *AVE Trends in Intelligent Computing Systems, 1*(4), 198–208.

Aribisala, O. O., Opoola, A. O., & Adekola, R. A. (2024). Utilization of entrepreneurship instruction on the creation of small-scale enterprise among business education students. *AVE Trends in Intelligent Technoprise Letters, 1*(4), 196–202.

Ashifa, K. M. (2024). Towards a culture of human rights: Navigating education and equality in Turkey. *AVE Trends in Intelligent Social Letters, 1*(4), 168–176.

Campero-Jurado, I., Sánchez, S. M., Gomez, J., Rodríguez, S., & Corchado, J. (2020). Smart helmet 5.0 for industrial Internet of Things using artificial intelligence. *Sensors (Basel), 20*(21), 1–27. PMID: 33139608

Choudhry, R., Sharma, D., & Tiwari, S. K. (2025). Using deep learning and CNNs for enhancing student learning through AI-driven facial emotion recognition. *FMDB Transactions on Sustainable Intelligent Networks, 2*(1), 1–9.

Cirillo, S., Polese, G., Salerno, D., Simone, B., & Solimando, G. (2023). Towards Flexible Voice Assistants: Evaluating Privacy and Security Needs in IoT-enabled Smart Homes. *FMDB Transactions on Sustainable Computer Letters, 1*(1), 25–32.

Estolonio, H. M., Nicol, J. A., Santos, P. C. C., & Ramos, J. I. (2023). Impact of Remote Work on Employee Engagement and Productivity in Operations Management. *FMDB Transactions on Sustainable Management Letters, 1*(4), 155–167.

Gawande, U., Golhar, Y., & Hajari, K. (2017). Biometric-based security system: Issues and challenges. In *Intelligent Techniques in Signal Processing for Multimedia Security* (pp. 151–176). Springer International Publishing.

Indu, I., Anand, P. R., & Bhaskar, V. (2018). Identity and access management in cloud environment: Mechanisms and challenges. *Engineering Science and Technology, an International Journal, 21*(4), 574–588.

John Joseph, F. J., Chinnusamy, K., Jeganathan, J., & Obaid, J. A., & Rajest, S. S. (Eds.). (2025). Pioneering AI and data technologies for next-gen security, IoT, and smart ecosystems. Advances in Computational Intelligence and Robotics. IGI Global, USA.

Joshi, M., Shen, Z., & Kausar, S. (2023). Enhancing Inclusive Education on Leveraging Artificial Intelligence Technologies for Personalized Support and Accessibility in Special Education for Students with Diverse Learning Needs. *FMDB Transactions on Sustainable Techno Learning, 1*(3), 125–142.

Moyo, S. B., & Nithyanantham, V. (2024). Evaluating the influence of parental involvement in early childhood education programs. *AVE Trends in Intelligent Techno Learning, 1*(1), 47–60.

Padmavathy, V., Venkateswaran, P. S., Begum, S., & Sheela, K. (2024). A review of the faculty engagement and performance in higher educational institutions. *AVE Trends in Intelligent Techno Learning, 1*(2), 76–87.

Pournader, M., Ghaderi, H., Hassanzadegan, A., & Fahimnia, B. (2021). Artificial intelligence applications in supply chain management. *International Journal of Production Economics, 241*(11), 108250.

Pulivarthy, P. (2024). Research on Oracle database performance optimization in IT-based university educational management system. *FMDB Transactions on Sustainable Computing Systems, 2*(2), 84–95.

Rajest, S. S., Moccia, S., Chinnusamy, K., Singh, B., & Regin, R. (Eds.). (2023). Advances in Educational Technologies and Instructional Design *Handbook of research on learning in language classrooms through ICT-based digital technology.* IGI Global.

Regin, R., Hariprasath, G., Dhinakaran, P., Harishkumar, V., Sulthana, M. R., & Priscila, S. S. (2025). AI-powered cyber intrusion detection system with real-time threat analysis and web application interface for enhanced network security. *FMDB Transactions on Sustainable Computer Letters, 3*(1), 34–49.

Renjith, E. J. (2024). Revolutionizing cloud security: Innovative approaches for safeguarding data integrity. *FMDB Transactions on Sustainable Computer Letters, 2*(2), 111–119.

Sarker, I. H. (2024). AI for critical infrastructure protection and resilience. In *AI-Driven Cybersecurity and Threat Intelligence: Cyber Automation, Intelligent Decision-Making and Explainability* (pp. 153–172). Springer.

Saxena, D., Khandare, S., & Chaudhary, S. (2023). An Overview of ChatGPT: Impact on Academic Learning. *FMDB Transactions on Sustainable Techno Learning*, *1*(1), 11–20.

Singh, C., Thakkar, R. G., & Warraich, J. (2023). IAM identity access management—Importance in maintaining security systems within organizations. *European Journal of Engineering and Technology Research*, *8*(1), 30–38.

Srilakshmi, U., Sandhya, I., Manikandan, J., Bindu, A. H., Regin, R., & Rajest, S. S. (2024). Design and implementation of energy-efficient protocols for underwater wireless sensor networks. In *Advances in Computer and Electrical Engineering* (pp. 417–430). IGI Global.

Sruthi, B. J., Jeniffer, J. P., Harshita, K. S., Sulthana, M. R., & Angelin, C. C. (2025). Enhancing certificate authentication through a transparent blockchain enabled verification system. *AVE Trends in Intelligent Computing Systems*, *2*(1), 15–26.

Vegineni, G. C. (2024). Exploring anomalies in dark web activities for automated threat identification. *FMDB Transactions on Sustainable Computing Systems*, *2*(4), 189–200.

Vemula, V. R. (2024). Cognitive artificial intelligence systems for proactive threat hunting in AI-driven cloud applications. *AVE Trends in Intelligent Computing Systems*, *1*(3), 173–183.

Waltersmann, L., Kiemel, S., Stuhlsatz, J., Sauer, A., & Miehe, R. (2021). Artificial intelligence applications for increasing resource efficiency in manufacturing companies—A comprehensive review. *Sustainability*, *13*(12), 1–26.

Chapter 4
Empowering Minds on Strengthening Digital Media Literacy to Combat Deepfake Misinformation in Education

Xavier Louis
https://orcid.org/0000-0002-6645-7746
Saveetha Institutes of Medical and Technical Sciences, Chennai, India

S. Karthick Raja
Tata Institute of Social Sciences, Mumbai, India

Jessy K. Jayanth
https://orcid.org/0009-0008-4867-5775
Saveetha Institutes of Medical and Technical Sciences, Chennai, India

T. Rihaash
https://orcid.org/0009-0000-6398-376X
Saveetha Institutes of Medical and Technical Sciences, Chennai, India

Zubia Akhtar Shamim Akhtar Shaikh
MIE SPPU Institute of Higher Education, Doha, Qatar

ABSTRACT

The proliferation of deepfake technology has generated unprecedented challenges for educational institutions that are striving to maintain information integrity and foster critical thinking skills amongst the students, this chapter evaluates the critical

DOI: 10.4018/979-8-3373-3770-8.ch004

role of digital media literacy in combating deepfake misinformation within the educational contexts, and explore how the enhanced literacy frameworks can strengthen students to navigate the increasingly sophisticated synthetic media environments. Deriving the help from analysis of existing media literacy models, verification tools, and pedagogical approaches, this specific chapter displays how educational institutions develop comprehensive techniques for deepfake detection and response, and this research deliberately unveils that traditional media literacy approaches require notable adaptation for addressing the distinct challenges generated by AI-generated content, which creates necessity for the interdisciplinary collaboration between educators, technologists, and media specialist.

INTRODUCTION

The current existing information landscape has went through a very basic transformation during the emergence of deepfake technology, and confronts the traditional assumptions about media authenticity and information credibility, here the educational institutions, those are long regarded as bastions of truth and critical inquiry, are now undergoing the tough task of equipping the students to live through an environment where these sophisticated synthetic media could convincingly mirror the authentic content (Breakstone et al. 2021). The upsurge of deepfake misinformation presents a technological challenge alongside a significant educational imperative, necessitating innovative approaches to critical thinking instruction and media literacy.

Deepfake misinformation differs considerably from traditional forms of false information in its accessibility, sophistication, and potential for deception, in contrast to the text-based misinformation or crudely manipulated images. The deepfakes has leverage in advanced artificial intelligence for creating video and audio content that could easily fool even trained observers Groh et al. (2022), this technology is sophisticated and states that traditional media literacy skills, while still staying valuable, are proved to be insufficient for identifying and responding to synthetic media threats, so the educational institutions are bound to develop enhanced literacy frameworks that can merge technical knowledge about AI-generated content with enhanced verification skills and critical thinking.

The responsibility of digital media in literacy is confronting deepfake misinformation that goes far beyond simple detection techniques to encompass broader educational goals of adhering to ethical technology use, informed citizenship, and critical inquiry. At the same time, students develop robust media literacy skills, and they become consumers of information while being active participants in maintaining information integrity within their communities (Hobbs 2010). This empowerment through literacy displays a fundamental shift from passive media consumption to engaged, critical evaluation that would serve as a bulwark against this synthetic media manipulation.

This urgent addressing of deepfake misinformation in the educational settings displays wider societal concerns about social cohesion, information integrity, and democratic discourse, and students those who don't possess enough media literacy skills that might become easy targets to synthetic media manipulation throughout their whole lives, possibly underestimating their ability in making informed decisions as community members, citizens, and professionals (Guess et al. 2020). Therefore educational institutions have huge responsibility for loading and nurturing students with the knowledge and skills that are necessary to thrive in an increasingly complex information environment, this challenge of nourishing digital media literacy to fight deepfake misinformation needs comprehensive institutional responses that exceeds beyond the individual classroom instruction to encompass faculty development, curriculum redesign, community engagement, and technological infrastructure, this step by step approach discovers that media literacy absolutely cannot be treated as an isolated skill but must be integrated across the disciplines and educational experiences to develop the critical thinking capabilities that are needed for synthetic media evaluation.

BACKGROUND

Media Literacy Frameworks and Theoretical Foundations

Media literacy education has risen considerably since its inception, growing from simple consumer awareness programs into sophisticated pedagogical frameworks that addresses complex information environments, the foundational work of scholars namely James Potter and Renee Hobbs established core principles of media literacy that emphasizes active engagement, critical analysis, and understanding of media production processes (Potter 2004; Hobbs 2010). All these traditional frameworks had their primary focus on recognising persuasive techniques, understanding the bias, and identifying sources in conventional media formats.

The advent of digital technologies created a necessity for the expansion of media literacy frameworks for addressing user-generated content, online information environments, and social media platforms. Digital media literacy frameworks, that are developed by researchers like Henry Jenkins and Mizuko Ito, emphasize on the participatory culture, collaborative knowledge construction, and networked communication, (Jenkins et al. 2006), these frameworks recognize that digital natives need skills not just for consuming media but also for evaluating, creating, and sharing, content within complex networked environments.

The contemporary media literacy scholarship has increasingly focused on the challenges shown by disinformation, misinformation, and manipulated media content, the work of researchers like Sam Wineburg and the Stanford History Education Group has underlined important gaps in the ability of student to evaluate the online information sources, which further leads to calls for enhanced critical thinking instruction and source verification skills (Wineburg et al. 2016). These findings have informed the development of fact-checking pedagogies and lateral reading techniques that help students to verify the credibility of information.

The evolution of deepfake technology has unveiled certain limitations present in existing media literacy frameworks, which were primarily designed for text-based and conventional audiovisual content. Deepfakes can be broadly classified into visual and audio types (Figure 1): the visual modalities include face-swap, puppet-mastery, lip-syncing, entire face synthesis, and facial attribute manipulation, while the audio types include text-to-speech synthesis and voice conversion (Ramanaharan et al., 2025).

Figure 1. Classification of deepfakes

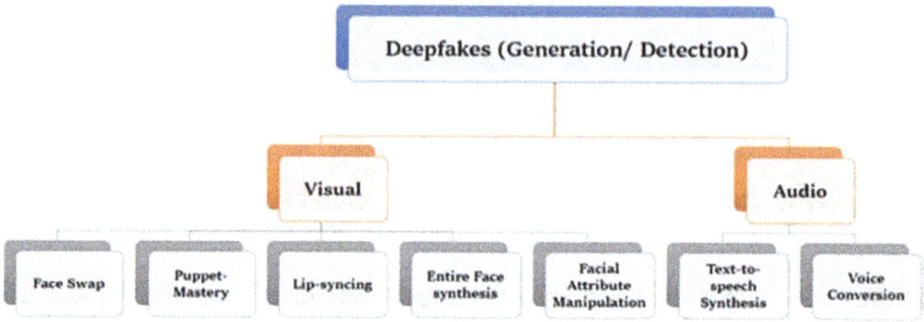

(Ramanaharan et al., 2025)

Traditional approaches to media literacy, while valuable for developing general critical thinking skills, lack the technical specificity required for identifying sophisticated synthetic media (Vaccari and Chadwick 2020). Recognising this has made way for carrying amplified media literacy frameworks that merge technical knowledge about the AI-generated content equipped, along with traditional critical thinking approaches. But these deepfakes practices has emerged as a inevitable tool for misinformation, which challenging traditional media literacy framework. Recent studies show that up to 50% of respondents fail to differentiate deepfakes from authentic videos. Another one reveals that 90% of adults express concern about deepfakes. Even the experimental research confirms that deepfake -specific media literacy education significantly reduces susceptibility to disinformation, emphasizing the urgent need for targeted educational interventions. Table 1 shows the key statistics related to digital media literacy to combat deepfake misinformation.

Table 1. Global research statistics on deepfake awareness and detection

Statistical facts	Population/ Context	References
15% of surveyed UK adults reported harmful deepfake exposure, while 90.4% expressed concern; only 8% admitted creating one.	National Survey, UK (n=1403)	Sippy, et al., (2024)
27% -50% of the respondents failed to correctly identify deepfake vs authentic videos, with up to 39-point accuracy gap between real and fake.	Mixed population (Adults +K-12 students, US)	Doss, et al, (2023)
Average deepfake image detection accuracy = 62%, barely above chance. Confidence levels remained high even when wrong.	Controlled lab experiment (USA)	Bray, et al, (2023)
86% believe misinformation and harmful deepfakes will affect future elections; 81% believe online content is altered somehow and that verifying legitimacy is difficult.	National Sample, India	Indian Express, (2024)
1 in 3 Singaporeans who are aware of deepfakes have *inadvertently shared* a deepfake online.	National Sample, Singapore	NTU Singapore, (2023)

Verification Tools and Technological Solutions

The development of deepfake detection technology has increased rapidly, with researchers and technology companies creating highly sophisticated tools for identifying synthetic media content and developing early detection systems that focus directly on technical artefacts. They found inconsistencies in deepfake videos, such as blinking patterns that are not quite natural, inconsistencies in lighting, or audio-visual synchronisation problems (Li et al. 2020). All these technical approaches, while staying effective for identifying crude synthetic content, have become less reliable as deepfake technology has advanced further.

The present deepfake detection tools make use of machine learning algorithms that examine subtle patterns and inconsistencies that are invisible to human observers. Companies like Google, Microsoft, and Facebook have started developing detection systems that can detect synthetic content with high accuracy rates, even though these systems require continuous updates to address the evolving deepfake creation techniques (Dolhansky et al. 2020). The arms race between detection and creation technologies shows that no single technical solution could provide full protection against these synthetic media threats.

The verification systems based on block chain stands for another approach to combate deepfake misinformation by creating immutable records of content authenticity, these systems, developed by companies like Truepic and Project Origin, supports content creators to establish provenance and authenticity throughout their cryptographic signatures (Hasan and Salah 2019), while they promise a professional media production, these solutions still face challenges related to usability, adoption, and integration with existing platforms.

Crowdsourced verification approaches make use of human intelligence and priorly gathered evaluations for identifying synthetic content, and platforms like Wikipedia and fact-checking organisations have already built collaborating models for content verification that combine human expertise and technological tools (Roth and Pickles 2020). This approach recognises that human judgment remains an essential component for evaluating context, intent, and credibility factors that the technical solutions may sometimes miss.

The inculcation of verification tools with educational contexts needs careful consideration of pedagogical effectiveness, usability, and accessibility. While sophisticated detection systems can be effective for expert users, their complex usage can highly exhaust students and educators who don't excel in technical expertise. Consequently, educational institutions are pushed to employ identity verification tools that balance effectiveness easily, all while providing appropriate support and training for implementation.

LITERATURE REVIEW

Digital Citizenship and Information Responsibility

This digital citizenship concept has risen as a critical framework for understanding how individuals navigate online environments with ethics and responsibility. Ribble and Bailey (2007) describe digital citizenship as "the norms of behaviour concerning technology use," and encompass elements like digital communication, digital commerce, digital access, digital law, digital etiquette, digital literacy, digital rights and responsibilities, digital security, and digital health and wellness. This comprehensive framework lays down a foundation for understanding how deepfake literacy fits in with the broader educational goals of nurturing students to employ technology responsibly.

The research done on digital citizenship in educational contexts has shed light over considerable challenges that are involved in supporting students for developing proper online behaviors and decision-making skills, also studies by Jones and Mitchell (2016) found out that while students display technical proficiency with digital tools, they don't always possess proper understanding of ethical implications and social responsibilities that are associated with use of technology. This deliberate gap between technical skill and ethical understanding has specific relevance for deepfake technology, where the creation and distribution of synthetic content put forth complex questions about harm, consent, and authenticity.

The synthesis of digital citizenship principles and media literacy education has shown promise for improvement in more comprehensive approaches to online information evaluation. Also, research by Kahne and Bowyer (2017) revealed that students who receive instruction combining media literacy with digital citizenship principles displayed improved ability in identifying false information and understanding the social consequences of misinformation sharing in a better way. This integrated approach finds that effective media literacy requires technical skills, combined with ethical awareness and social responsibility.

Fake News and Misinformation Education

The elevation of false information online has initiated extensive research into effective educational strategies for combating misinformation. Also, studies by Guess et al. (2020) identified that traditional approaches to misinformation education, like providing lists of unreliable sources or teaching generic skepticism, have proved to be insufficient for helping students navigate through complex information environments. On the contrary, more effective approaches are focused on developing specific skills for lateral reading, source verification, and contextual evaluation.

The concept of "prebunking" has come up as a promising approach to misinformation education, and emphasizes proactive inoculation against the false information rather than reactive fact-checking, research by Roozenbeek and van der Linden (2019) underlined that educational interventions that opens up students to weakened forms of misinformation techniques can grow resistance to future manipulation attempts, also this approach has particular relevance for deepfake education, where understanding creation techniques and manipulation strategies might improve detection capabilities.

Studies about fake news sharing behaviors have unraveled important views and points about the social and psychological factors that influences the information credibility assessment, research by Pennycook and Rand (2021) found that the likelihood of individuals in sharing false information was impacted more by the cognitive factors like analytical thinking and source credibility evaluation than by political beliefs or ideological motivations. The above findings suggest that educational interventions that focus on critical thinking skills might be more effective than approaches that address specific political or ideological content.

Critical Thinking and Analytical Skills Development

The developing critical thinking skills has long been recognized as the fundamental goal of education, with specific importance for media literacy and information evaluation, research by Facione (2015) identified core critical thinking skills which includes inference, interpretation, analysis, self-regulation, evaluation, and explanation, all these skills provide a good foundation for effective media literacy education. However, their application to synthetic media environments requires specific adaptation and enhancement.

Studies of critical thinking instruction in digital environments have shown both opportunities and challenges for developing analytical skills. Research by Liu and Yang (2014) found that online learning environments could improve critical thinking development through collaborative analysis, interactive discussions, and immediate feedback mechanisms. Still, the same studies identified the risks of cognitive overload and distraction that could interfere with deep analytical thinking.

The relationship between critical thinking skills and deepfake detection has become an area of growth in research interest. Studies by Groh et al. (2022) found that those individuals with stronger analytical and thinking skills displayed improved ability in identifying subtle inconsistencies in synthetic media, even though highly skilled individuals remained vulnerable to sophisticated deepfakes. This research further suggests that while critical thinking skills are important for deepfake detection, they might not be sufficient without the extra technical knowledge and verification strategies.

THEMATIC DISCUSSION

Curriculum Design for Deepfake Literacy

The improvement of an effective curriculum for deepfake literacy needs careful integration of technical knowledge, critical thinking skills, and ethical understanding within coherent educational frameworks. Traditional approaches to curriculum design, which usually treat media literacy as a silent subject area, prove insufficient for addressing the interdisciplinary nature of synthetic media challenges (Mihailidis and Viotty 2017). Instead, an effective deepfake literacy curriculum must integrate across multiple disciplines, and include psychology, computer science, social studies, communications, and ethics, to provide students with a comprehensive understanding of synthetic media technologies and their implications.

The technical dimensions of deepfake literacy curriculum must accept the fundamental concepts of neural networks, artificial intelligence, and machine learning without putting a burden on students who lack good technical backgrounds. Research by Touretzky et al. (2019) has demonstrated that the AI concepts can be taught effectively to K-12 students through hands-on activities, visual demonstrations, and simplified explanations, which help them focus on practical applications rather than mathematical complexity. This approach provides students with enough technical understanding to appreciate both the limitations and capabilities of deepfake technology.

The components of critical thinking in the deepfake literacy curriculum should be constructed upon established media literacy frameworks. In contrast, alongside addressing the distinct challenges posed by synthetic media, the other reading techniques developed by the Stanford History Education Group provide valuable models about how to teach students to verify information sources and cross-reference claims (Wineburg et al. 2016). These techniques need adaptation for audiovisual content, where students must learn to seek corroborating evidence, find technical artefacts, and evaluate context clues across various media formats.

Ethical considerations must form a central component of deepfake literacy curriculum, and address the questions of consent, harm, authenticity, and responsibility that arise from synthetic media creation and distribution. The framework for ethical reasoning developed by the Markkula Centre for Applied Ethics presents structured approaches for analysing the moral dimensions of technology use (Velasquez et al. 2015). Students must learn to consider both the technical feasibility of deepfake creation and the potential consequences for individuals and society.

Assessment techniques for deepfake literacy curriculum show certain challenges, as traditional testing approaches might not completely measure students' ability to apply synthetic media evaluation skills in the context of the real world. Performance-based assessments, like those developed by the New Tech Network, stress authentic tasks that require students to show learning with practical application instead of memorization (Hernández-Ramos 2005). For deepfake literacy, these assessments might include evaluation of synthetic media examples, development of verification protocols, or even creation of educational materials for peers.

The synthesis of deepfake literacy curriculum and already existing educational standards and requirements carefully aligns with established learning objectives and assessment frameworks. The Common Core State Standards and similar frameworks provide a structure to ensure that media literacy instruction supports various educational goals while addressing specific synthetic media challenges (Porter et al. 2011). This alignment process requires collaboration of subject area specialists, curriculum developers, and educational administrators to ensure the coherent implementation.

AI Detection Tools and Technological Integration

The implementation of artificial intelligence detection tools and educational environments jointly provides both challenges and opportunities to amplify the student media literacy capabilities. The contemporary detection systems, like those developed by Microsoft's Video Authenticator and Facebook's Deepfake Detection Challenge, show impressive technical capabilities but need careful consideration of their educational applications (Dolhansky et al. 2020). These tools must be evaluated for accuracy and reliability, as well as for their pedagogical value in helping students understand synthetic media detection principles. This educational use of AI detection tools puts forth important questions about the balance between technological assistance and human analytical skills. As automated detection systems could identify synthetic content with high accuracy rates, over-reliance on these tools might undermine the development of critical thinking skills that students require for comprehensive media evaluation (Groh et al. 2022). Therefore, educational institutions must consider how to integrate detection tools in ways that enhance, rather than replace, human analytical capabilities.

The accessibility and usability of AI detection tools represent great considerations for educational implementation. Many sophisticated detection systems have requirements of technical expertise, computational resources, or subscription fees that might prohibit educational institutions with limited budgets or technical support (Maras and Alexandrou 2019). Conclusively, the educational applications of detection tools must prioritise affordable pricing models, user-friendly interfaces, and integration with existing educational technology infrastructure.

The swiftly emerging nature of both deepfake creation and detection technologies creates few ongoing challenges for educational institutions those who are seeking to maintain current and effective tool implementations, the arms race between synthetic media creators and detection developers imply that today's effective detection tools may become obsolete as the creative techniques advance (Westerlund 2019) and therefore the educational institutions must develop new strategies for continuous evaluation and update of detection tools while alongside maintaining pedagogical effectiveness.

Training and professional development requirements for educators using AI detection tools represent another important consideration for successful implementation. Many educators lack sufficient technical expertise to utilise sophisticated detection systems effectively or to help students understand their capabilities and limitations (Trust and Whalen 2020). So professional development programs must address both technical skills and pedagogical approaches for integrating detection tools into media literacy instruction.

Resistance to Change and Implementation Challenges

The implementation of enhanced media literacy programs to address deepfake challenges encounters significant resistance from multiple stakeholders within educational institutions. Faculty resistance often stems from concerns about increased workload, unfamiliarity with technology, and scepticism about the relevance of media literacy to their specific academic disciplines (Hobbs 2010). This resistance is mainly pronounced among educators who view media literacy as an outcast in their expertise, or those who feel overwhelmed and pressured by the technical complexity of deepfake technology. The administrative resistance to media literacy enhancement consistently reflects concerns about competing educational priorities, resource allocation, and curriculum crowding. Educational leaders may strive to justify their investments in media literacy programs while facing pressure to improve standardised test scores, reduce costs, or address other immediate institutional challenges (Jenkins et al. 2006). The long-term nature of media literacy benefits may be seen as tough to quantify and communicate to stakeholders who are focused on short-term outcomes.

Student's resistance to enhanced media literacy instruction could manifest through disengagement, skepticism regarding the relevance of detection skills, or overconfidence about the existing digital abilitiesz the research by Wineburg et al. (2016) identified that students regularly overestimate their ability to evaluate online information, which leada to resistance to instruction that challenges their assumptions about digital literacy, this overconfidence might be especially pronounced regarding synthetic media, where students might believe their "digital native" status presenta sufficient protection against manipulation.

Systemic resistance to media literacy enhancement may stem from broader institutional cultures that prioritise traditional academic subjects over interdisciplinary approaches to digital citizenship. Furthermore, compartmentalising knowledge within academic disciplines can hinder the interdisciplinary collaboration required for effective deepfake literacy education (Mihailidis and Viotty 2017). Overcoming this resistance requires a cultural shift that prioritizes media literacy as crucial for student success across all academic disciplines.

The pace of technological change in synthetic media generates extra challenges for institutions that seek to implement comprehensive media literacy programs, also the swift evolution of deepfake technology means that educational approaches must be consistently updated for addressing new creation techniques and detection methods Ajder et al. (2019), this necessity for ongoing adaptation could easily submerge the institutional capacity for change and create resistance to initiatives that may lack proper endpoints or any stable implementation guidelines.

Interdisciplinary Collaboration and Faculty Development

The complex nature of deepfake literacy necessitates collaboration across multiple academic disciplines, each contributing distinct perspectives and expertise to comprehensive educational approaches. The computer science faculty will provide the necessary technical knowledge about machine learning algorithms, artificial intelligence, and detection methodologies. In contrast, communications and media studies professors contribute to the understanding of media production, information dissemination, and audience analysis (Touretzky et al. 2019). This collaboration among these two disciplines must ignore the traditional academic silos for generating coherent and effective learning experiences.

Cognitive science and psychology faculty provide vital views into the perceptual and cognitive factors that may influence the synthetic media detection and susceptibility to manipulation, also the research by Hancock and Bailenson (2021) reveal that understanding human psychological responses to synthetic media is important for developing effective detection strategies and educational interventions, and this psychological perspective should be joined with technical and media literacy approaches for creating effective comprehensive educational programs.

Ethics and philosophy faculty present the needed frameworks for addressing the moral dimensions of deepfake technology, which includes questions of consent, authenticity, harm, and responsibility. The ethical considerations surrounding the creation and distribution of synthetic media require careful analysis using established philosophical frameworks and applied ethics approaches (Floridi et al. 2018). This ethical dimension must be integrated throughout the media literacy curriculum instead of being treated as a separate or optional component.

Professional development programs for faculty collaboration must address both the technical skills and pedagogical approaches for interdisciplinary instruction, as many faculty members lack experience with collaborative teaching methods or interdisciplinary curriculum development, which requires support and training for effectively participating in comprehensive media literacy programs (Trust and Whalen 2020) these development programs must provide practical strategies for collaboration while also addressing the potential conflicts between disciplinary perspectives and approaches.

The assessment of interdisciplinary media literacy programs presents distinct challenges that require collaboration between faculty from different disciplines for developing appropriate evaluation methods, as the traditional assessment approaches might not adequately measure the complex skills and knowledge required for effective deepfake literacy, and create necessity for innovative approaches that could evaluate both technical competencies and critical thinking abilities (Hernández-Ramos 2005). This collaborative assessment development needs ongoing communication and coordination between faculty from different academic areas. Based on the thematic discussion, the concept map has been presented (Figure 2).

Figure 2. Thematic map for deepfake literacy

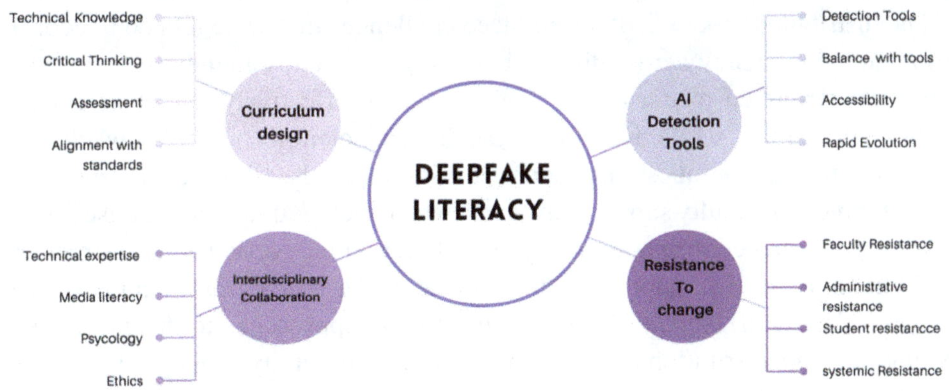

CASE INSIGHTS

Institutional Practices and Implementation Models

The University of Washington's implementation of comprehensive deepfake literacy programming gives valuable insights into institutional approaches to synthetic media education. Their interdisciplinary initiative, launched in 2022, integrated computer science, communications, and psychology faculty to develop a semester-long course particularly focused on deepfake detection and media verification. This program combined technical instruction in AI fundamentals with hands-on practice with the help of detection tools and critical analysis of synthetic media examples.

The course structure at the University of Washington emphasises progressive skill development, beginning with basic media literacy concepts and advancing to sophisticated technical analysis of deepfake creation and detection methods. Students worked in interdisciplinary teams to evaluate synthetic media examples, develop verification protocols, and create educational materials for peer instruction. The program's success was measured through pre- and post-course assessments, which showed considerable improvement in students' ability to identify synthetic content and understand the technical principles underlying deepfake technology.

Stanford University's approach to deepfake literacy focused on integration across multiple courses instead of creation of a standalone program, their model incorporated synthetic media evaluation exercises into existing courses in communications, computer science, psychology, and ethics, and created a distributed approach to media literacy education, this integration strategy let students to encounter deepfake concepts so many times throughout their academic experience while carefully avoiding the curriculum crowding that may result from any added course requirements.

The distributed model at Stanford faced challenges that were related to coordination and consistency across different courses and faculty members, even some instructors struggled to integrate deepfake content effectively into their already existing curriculum, while others were lacking sufficient technical knowledge for addressing the student questions about detection methods, all these challenges led to development of faculty support resources, which included sample exercises, technical tutorials, and coordination meetings in between the participating instructors.

Community college implementations of deepfake literacy programming have displayed the significance of adapting educational approaches to diverse student populations and institutional constraints, Mesa Community College in Arizona developed a modular approach that let students to engage with synthetic media concepts through workshop-style sessions rather than having full courses, and this flexible model accommodated students with changing schedules and academic goals while simultaneously providing essential media literacy skills.

The workshop model at Mesa Community College emphasised practical skills and immediate application rather than theoretical understanding of AI technology, and students learned to freely use the available detection tools, practised lateral reading techniques for verification, and developed personal protocols for evaluating any suspicious content. The program's success was quantified through participant feedback and follow-up surveys, which assessed changes in media consumption behaviours and confidence in detecting synthetic content.

Professional Development and Faculty Training

The Massachusetts Institute of Technology's faculty development program for deepfake literacy education provides a model for institutional approaches to educator training, their intensive summer workshop, launched in 2023, brought together faculties from multiple disciplines for developing a shared understanding of synthetic media challenges and collaborative approaches to education, this program combined technical training with pedagogical instruction, and help the faculty to develop both content knowledge and teaching strategies for media literacy education.

The MIT program emphasised hands-on learning experiences that allowed faculty to engage directly with deepfake creation and detection tools. Participants easily learned to use basic deepfake creation software for understanding the technical process, analysed synthetic media examples using various detection methods, and developed sample exercises for their courses. This experiential approach helped faculty to overcome their initial intimidation about technical complexity and build confidence in their ability to address synthetic media topics.

The interdisciplinary nature of the MIT program created certain opportunities for faculty to learn from colleagues in different fields while simultaneously developing collaborative relationships that extended beyond the workshop experience. Computer science faculty shared technical expertise with colleagues from the humanities and social sciences, while education specialists provided good pedagogical frameworks for effective instruction. These collaborations resulted in several interdisciplinary courses and research projects that continued even after the workshop was concluded.

The University of California system's approach to faculty development emphasized on the ongoing support and resource sharing instead of intensive training programs, their online resource portal provided faculty with access for current detection tools, technical tutorials, sample exercises, and pedagogical guidance for integrating deepfake literacy into existing courses, this distributed approach accommodated faculty with various schedules and technical backgrounds and provided consistent access to current information and resources.

The UC system's resource portal included discussion forums where faculty could share their experiences, ask questions, and collaborate on educational materials. These forums fostered community among educators working on similar challenges while providing side-by-side peer support for implementation difficulties. The system also organised webinars in regular intervals featuring expert speakers and best practice sharing to help maintain faculty engagement and update knowledge about emerging synthetic media technologies.

Student Engagement and Learning Outcomes

Research conducted at Arizona State University evaluated student engagement with deepfake literacy programming across different implementation models. Their study compared traditional lecture-based instruction with hands-on laboratory experiences and collaborative project-based learning approaches, then found that students showed the highest engagement and learning outcomes when given opportunities to work straight away with synthetic media examples and detection tools rather than receiving purely theoretical instruction (Johnson et al. 2023).

The ASU study revealed that students' initial confidence in detecting synthetic media was notably higher than their actual performance on detection tasks. This overconfidence decreased following instruction, but the actual detection performance improved considerably. The research also suggested that effective deepfake literacy education must address student' misconceptions about their existing abilities while constructing genuine competencies for synthetic media evaluation.

Student feedback from the ASU program suggested that hands-on experience with deepfake creation tools enhanced students' understanding of synthetic media technology's capabilities and limitations. They reported that creating simple deepfakes themselves provided a clear view into the technical process, improving their ability to identify synthetic content. These findings supported pedagogical approaches that include creation activities as part of comprehensive media literacy education.

The University of Michigan's longitudinal study tracked the students' media literacy skills over multiple semesters following deepfake education programming. Their research unravelled that students who received comprehensive instruction maintained improved detection abilities even six months after the completion of the course. In contrast, those who received brief interventions showed regression to baseline performance levels (Williams et al. 2023). This research supported the value of sustained, comprehensive approaches to media literacy education over short-term awareness campaigns.

The Michigan study also evaluated the transfer of deepfake literacy skills to other contexts, finding that students who received instruction showed improvements in ability to evaluate misinformation in general, and not just synthetic media content, this transfer effect also suggested that deepfake literacy education provided longer benefits for critical thinking and information evaluation skills that extended far beyond the specific synthetic media challenges.

CHALLENGES

Technology Access and Digital Divide

The synthesis of comprehensive deepfake literacy programs goes through certain challenges that are related to the technology access and digital equity within the educational institutions, and many sophisticated detection tools need specialised software licenses, high-performance computing resources, or high-speed internet connections that might not be available to all the students or institutions (Dolhansky et al. 2020). These digital variations could easily create disparities in educational opportunities where students who hail from well-resourced institutions develop advanced media literacy skills, leaving others to fend with a lack of access to essential tools and resources.

The price of implementing comprehensive deepfake literacy programs sheds light on another important hindrance of the educational institutions those who face budget constraints, professional detection software, faculty development programs, and technical infrastructure upgrades require notable investments that might even compete with other educational priorities (Trust and Whalen 2020) therefore institutions must develop few techniques for cost-effective implementation that could highly maximize the educational impacts while alongside minimizing the financial burden.

The quick pace of technological change in synthetic media creates ongoing challenges for maintaining current and effective educational resources. Detection tools that are effective today might become obsolete as deepfake creation techniques advance, and need continuous investment in updated software and training, (Westerlund 2019). Educational institutions must therefore develop sustainable approaches to technology updates that could accommodate the evolving synthetic media landscapes.

Curriculum Overload and Integration Challenges

The addition of deepfake literacy content to existing curriculum, faces many challenges related to the curriculum overload and competing educational priorities, also many educational institutions already struggle to accommodate required content within available instructional time, so, this makes it difficult to add new topics without displacing existing material (Hobbs 2010), additionally this challenge is acute in K-12 settings where standardized testing requirements might hinder the flexibility for innovative programming.

The interdisciplinary nature of deepfake literacy generates additional challenges for curriculum integration within the traditional academic structures. Many educational institutions organise instruction around discrete subject areas, and make it difficult to implement comprehensive approaches that require collaboration across multiple disciplines (Mihailidis and Viotty 2017). Overcoming these structural barriers requires institutional commitment to interdisciplinary education and flexible scheduling arrangements.

The assessment of deepfake literacy skills presents diatinct challenges that might not align with the existing evaluation frameworks and standardized testing requirements, the traditional assessment approaches may also not adequately measure the complex analytical skills required for effective synthetic media evaluation, necessitating development of new assessment strategies that could accommodate authentic performance evaluation (Hernández-Ramos 2005), these assessment innovations need added time and resources that might strain institutional capacity.

FUTURE DIRECTIONS

Layered Framework for Media Literacy Integration

The development of effective deepfake literacy education asks for a comprehensive a d layered framework that addresses multiple levels of educational intervention and skill development, this framework should begin with foundational media literacy concepts in early educational stages, progress through technical understanding of synthetic media in secondary education, and culminate in sophisticated analytical and ethical reasoning capabilities at the post-secondary level (Hobbs 2010), each layer builds upon previous learning while introducing age-appropriate concepts and skills.

The foundational layer of this framework should emphasize the basic critical thinking skills, source evaluation techniques, and understanding of media production processes, the elementary and middle school students could develop these skills through engagement with traditional media literacy concepts while constructing cognitive foundations for more sophisticated synthetic media evaluation, this early instruction should focus on developing healthy skepticism and verification habits that would serve students throughout their educational and professional lives.

The technical layer should introduce students to the artificial intelligence concepts, machine learning principles, and deepfake creation processes with hands-on activities and simplified explanations, high school students can engage with basic AI programming, experiment with the detection tools, and analyze synthetic media examples for developing technical understanding that supports effective evaluation skills, this technical instruction should be balanced with continued emphasis on critical thinking and ethical reasoning.

The analytical layer should emphasise sophisticated reasoning skills, ethical analysis, and complex problem-solving techniques, which are related to synthetic media challenges. College and university students can engage with advanced detection techniques, policy analysis, and research projects that address the current synthetic media issues. This advanced instruction should prepare students for the leadership roles in addressing synthetic media challenges in their professional and civic lives.

The collaboration of this layered framework requires good coordination between educational institutions at various levels, ongoing communication about student preparation and progression, and elementary schools must prepare students for secondary synthetic media instruction. In contrast, high schools must ensure that graduates are ready for advanced university-level analysis. This coordination needs to have communication protocols, shared standards, and assessment strategies for supporting smooth transitions between the various levels of education.

CONCLUSION

By strengthening students with enhanced digital media literacy displays, this chapter demonstrates that traditional media literacy frameworks offer valuable foundations but require significant adaptation and enhancement to address the unique challenges posed by synthetic media technology. This merging of critical thinking skills, technical knowledge, and ethical reasoning within comprehensive educational programs gives the potential to develop student capabilities that go beyond simple detection techniques to encompass wider goals of informed citizenship and responsible technology use.

The successful implementation of deepfake literacy programming needs institutional commitment to interdisciplinary collaboration, faculty development, and resource allocation that identifies media literacy as an important part for student success in the digital age, the case studies and institutional practices examined in this chapter show that effective approaches must be tailor made specifically in educational contexts while maintaining core principles of progressive skill development, hands-on learning, and ethical awareness. Also, the challenges of technology access, curriculum integration, and resistance to change are important but not insurmountable with the appropriate plan and institutional support.

The future of deepfake literacy education is dependent on the continued adaptation to evolving synthetic media technologies while maintaining focus on basic critical thinking and ethical reasoning skills that would serve students throughout their lives, this layered framework proposed in this chapter presents a guide for comprehensive educational approaches that could be built and easily adapt with technological change all the while providing students with the knowledge and skills necessary to navigate through the increasingly complex information environments. Through these comprehensive approaches, educational institutions can fulfill their responsibilities to prepare students for detecting synthetic media and for participating actively in maintaining information integrity and democratic discourse in the current digital age.

REFERENCES

Ajder, H., Patrini, G., Cavalli, F., & Cullen, L. (2019). *The state of deepfakes: Landscape, threats, and impact*. Deeptrace Labs.

Bray, S. D., Johnson, S. D., & Kleinberg, B. (2023). Testing human ability to detect 'deepfake' images of human faces. *Journal of Cybersecurity, 9*(1), tyad011.

Breakstone, J., Smith, M., Wineburg, S., Rapaport, A., Carle, J., Garland, M., & Saavedra, A. (2021). Students' civic online reasoning: A national portrait. *Educational Researcher, 50*(8), 505–515.

Dolhansky, B., Bitton, J., Pflaum, B., Lu, J., Howes, R., Wang, M., & Ferrer, C. C. (2020). The deepfake detection challenge (DFDC) dataset. arXiv. Available: https://arxiv.org/abs/2006.07397 [Accessed by 26/06/2024].

Doss, C., Mondschein, J., Shu, D., Wolfson, T., Kopecky, D., Fitton-Kane, V. A., & Tucker, C. (2023). Deepfakes and scientific knowledge dissemination. *Scientific Reports, 13*(1), 13429.

Facione, P. A. (2015). *Critical thinking: What it is and why it counts*. California Academic Press.

Floridi, L., Cowls, J., Beltrametti, M., Chatila, R., Chazerand, P., Dignum, V., & Vayena, E. (2018). AI4People—an ethical framework for a good AI society: Opportunities, risks, principles, and recommendations. *Minds and Machines, 28*(4), 689–707.

Groh, M., Epstein, Z., Firestone, C., & Picard, R. (2022). Deepfake detection by human crowds, machines, and machine-informed crowds. *Proceedings of the National Academy of Sciences of the United States of America, 119*(1), 1–11.

Guess, A. M., Lerner, M., Lyons, B., Montgomery, J. M., Nyhan, B., Reifler, J., & Sircar, N. (2020). A digital media literacy intervention increases discernment between mainstream and false news in the United States and India. *Proceedings of the National Academy of Sciences of the United States of America, 117*(27), 15536–15545.

Hancock, J. T., & Bailenson, J. N. (2021). The social impact of deepfakes. *Cyberpsychology, Behavior, and Social Networking, 24*(3), 149–152.

Hasan, H. R., & Salah, K. (2019). Combating deepfake videos using blockchain and smart contracts. *IEEE Access : Practical Innovations, Open Solutions, 7*(3), 41596–41606.

Hernández-Ramos, P. (2005). If not here, where? Understanding teachers' use of technology in Silicon Valley schools. *Journal of Research on Technology in Education, 38*(1), 39–64.

Hobbs, R. (2010). *Digital and media literacy: A plan of action.* The Aspen Institute.

Jenkins, H., Clinton, K., Purushotma, R., Robison, A. J., & Weigel, M. (2006). Confronting the challenges of participatory culture: Media education for the 21st century. Chicago, United States of America.

Johnson, M., Davis, K., & Thompson, R. (2023). Comparative effectiveness of deepfake literacy instructional methods. *Journal of Educational Technology Research, 45*(2), 123–142.

Jones, L. M., & Mitchell, K. J. (2016). Defining and measuring youth digital citizenship. *New Media & Society, 18*(9), 2063–2079.

Kahne, J., & Bowyer, B. (2017). Educating for democracy in a partisan age: Confronting the challenges of motivated reasoning and misinformation. *American Educational Research Journal, 54*(1), 3–34.

Li, Y., Yang, X., Sun, P., Qi, H., & Lyu, S. (2020). Celeb-DF: A large-scale challenging dataset for deepfake forensics. In *Proceedings of the IEEE/CVF Conference on Computer Vision and Pattern Recognition*, Washington, United States of America.

Liu, M., & Yang, C. (2014). Exploring the effects of cognitive load on critical thinking in online discussions. *Educational Technology Research and Development, 62*(5), 617–634.

Maras, M. H., & Alexandrou, A. (2019). Determining authenticity of video evidence in the age of artificial intelligence and in the wake of deepfake videos. *The International Journal of Evidence & Proof, 23*(3), 255–262.

Mihailidis, P., & Viotty, S. (2017). Spreadable spectacle in digital culture: Civic expression, fake news, and the role of media literacies in "post-fact" society. *The American Behavioral Scientist, 61*(4), 441–454.

Pennycook, G., & Rand, D. G. (2021). The psychology of fake news. *Trends in Cognitive Sciences, 25*(5), 388–402.

Porter, A., McMaken, J., Hwang, J., & Yang, R. (2011). Common Core Standards: The new US intended curriculum. *Educational Researcher, 40*(3), 103–116.

Potter, W. J. (2004). *Theory of media literacy: A cognitive approach.* Sage Publications.

Ramanaharan, R., Guruge, D. B., & Agbinya, J. I. (2025). DeepFake video detection: Insights into model generalisation—A Systematic review. *Data and Information Management*, •••, 100099.

Ribble, M. S., & Bailey, G. D. (2007). *Digital citizenship in schools*. International Society for Technology in Education.

Roozenbeek, J., & van der Linden, S. (2019). Fake news game confers psychological resistance against online misinformation. *Palgrave Communications*, *5*(1), 1–10.

Roth, Y., & Pickles, N. (2020). Updating our approach to misleading information. Twitter Blog. Available: https://blog.twitter.com/en_us/topics/product/2020/updating-our-approach-to-misleading-information [Accessed by 26/06/2024].

Singapore, N. T. U. (2023). *1 in 3 who are aware of deepfakes say they have inadvertently shared them on social media.* Retrieved from https://www.ntu.edu.sg/research/research-at-ntu/detail/1-in-3-who-are-aware-of-deepfakes-say-they-have-inadvertently-shared-them-on-social-med

Sippy, T., Enock, F., Bright, J., & Margetts, H. Z. (2024). Behind the Deepfake: 8% Create; 90% Concerned. Surveying public exposure to and perceptions of deepfakes in the UK. *arXiv preprint arXiv:2407.05529.*

The Indian Express. (2024). *Misinformation and harmful deepfakes will affect future elections in India: Adobe Report.* Retrieved from https://indianexpress.com/article/technology/tech-news-technology/misinformation-and-harmful-deepfakes-will-affect-future-elections-in-india-adobe-9357027/

Touretzky, D., Gardner-McCune, C., Martin, F., & Seehorn, D. (2019). Envisioning AI for K-12: What should every child know about AI? *Proceedings of the AAAI Conference on Artificial Intelligence*, *33*(1), 9795–9799.

Trust, T., & Whalen, J. (2020). Should teachers be trained in emergency remote teaching? Lessons learned from the COVID-19 pandemic. *Journal of Technology and Teacher Education*, *28*(2), 189–199.

Vaccari, C., & Chadwick, A. (2020). Deepfakes and disinformation: Exploring the impact of synthetic political video on deception, uncertainty, and trust in news. *Social Media + Society*, *6*(1), 1–13.

Velasquez, M., Andre, C., Shanks, T., & Meyer, M. J. (2015). *A framework for ethical decision making. Markkula Center for Applied Ethics*. Santa Clara University.

Westerlund, M. (2019). The emergence of deepfake technology: A review. *Technology Innovation Management Review*, *9*(11), 39–52.

Williams, S., Anderson, J., & Brown, M. (2023). Longitudinal assessment of deepfake literacy retention and transfer. *Educational Psychology Review*, *35*(3), 567–589.

Wineburg, S., McGrew, S., Breakstone, J., & Ortega, T. (2016). *Evaluating information: The cornerstone of civic online reasoning*. Stanford Digital Repository.

Chapter 5
Learning in the Age of Illusion on Rethinking Pedagogy for Deepfake-Driven Digital Classrooms

Thangaraja Arumugam
https://orcid.org/0000-0001-5496-7258
Vellore Institute of Technology, Chennai, India

Michael J. Leo A.
https://orcid.org/0000-0002-1118-1092
St. Xavier's College of Education, India

S. Khaleel Ahamed
https://orcid.org/0000-0001-7795-6199
Sadakathullah Appa College, Tirunelveli, India

S. Mohamed Meeran
Sadakathullah Appa College, Tirunelveli, India

Dhiraj Kumar
KRIRK University, Bangkok, Thailand

ABSTRACT

Merging deepfake technology and synthetic media has fundamentally altered the cognitive foundations of digital education, forcing educators to reconsider their fundamental assumptions about evidence, trust, and authenticity that underpin

DOI: 10.4018/979-8-3373-3770-8.ch005

conventional pedagogical practices. Specifically, this chapter explores how the expansive availability of convincing synthetic media necessitates a radical transformation of learning objectives, instructional design, and teaching methodologies in digital classrooms. Analyzing the contemporary educational challenges posed by deepfakes, this chapter examines how educators must navigate an environment where traditional opinions about authentic evidence and credible sources are evolving in a problematic manner.

INTRODUCTION

The emergence of deepfake technology as a rapidly spreading force in digital communication has triggered a shift in educational practice that extends far beyond simple concerns about academic integrity to encompass core questions about the nature of knowledge, evidence, and truth in the context of pedagogy. Present-day educators navigate an unprecedented landscape where the primary assumption that audiovisual content represents authentic reality is no longer easily accepted, which forces a reconsideration of instructional methods, assessment strategies, and learning objectives. They have traditionally relied on the presumed authenticity of digital media (Zawacki-Richter et al. 2019), and this transformation represents not only a technological challenge but also a significant epistemological shift that requires educators to develop new frameworks for understanding how learning occurs in environments characterized by pervasive uncertainty about information authenticity.

The educational changes precipitated by synthetic media technology mirror the broader societal transformations in how information is validated, created, and distributed in digital environments. The conventional pedagogical approaches that emphasized source credibility, evidence evaluation, and critical analysis were developed within contexts where sophisticated multimedia manipulation required specialized expertise and substantial resources. Finally, the democratization of deepfake creation tools implies that educators cannot assume that compelling audiovisual evidence represents authentic documentation of events, statements, or phenomena, fundamentally altering the evidentiary landscape within which educational practice happens (Groh et al. 2022). To address this shift, education systems must focus on three pillars (Figure 1): resource allocation to ensure equitable access and evidence-based implementation, institutional policies to establish governance and ethical guidelines, and professional development to train educators for the effective and ethical integration of deepfake literacy into teaching practices.

Figure 1. Deepfake adoption framework

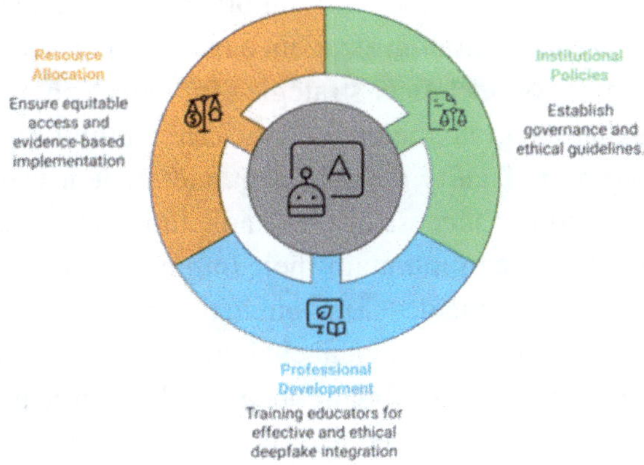

(Roe, et al., 2025)

The implications of this change extend across all aspects of educational practice, ranging from the selection and verification of instructional materials to the cultivation of students' critical thinking capabilities and the design of assessments. Now, educators must consider the potential for synthetic content to appear in student submissions, external resources, and even their own instructional materials when developing new techniques for verification and authentication that strike a balance between skepticism and educational effectiveness. This balance requires a good understanding of both technological capabilities and pedagogical principles that could guide effective teaching even in uncertain information environments.

The social and psychological dimensions of deepfake-influenced education present additional challenges for striking a balance between effective learning relationships and institutional credibility. This leads students to develop excessive skepticism towards legitimate educational content, making them vulnerable to sophisticated synthetic media that align with their existing beliefs or expectations. The erosion of trust in audiovisual evidence could compromise student-teacher relationships, collaborative learning activities, and peer interactions that rely on shared assumptions about good faith communication and authenticity (Vaccari and Chadwick, 2020).

The opportunity embedded within these challenges lies in the potential for deepfake-aware pedagogy to cultivate amplified cognitive thinking, critical thinking skills, and media literacy capabilities that prepare students for lifelong learning in complex information environments. Instead of viewing synthetic media as the only threat to educational integrity, educators could reframe these technologies as catalysts for developing stronger analytical capabilities and a more nuanced understanding of how knowledge is constructed and validated in digital contexts (Reigeluth, 1999).

The change in pedagogy in response to deepfake technology requires a systematic examination of how teaching and learning practices must adapt to address new forms of uncertainty while maintaining student engagement and educational quality. This evolution encompasses technical strategies for detecting and verifying pedagogical approaches that integrate media literacy, critical thinking, and institutional frameworks. This supports faculty development and student learning in synthetic media environments, and the success of these adaptations will determine whether the educational institutions can maintain their important functions of knowledge transmission and critical thinking development in this pervasive digital illusion age. The immediacy of addressing pedagogical challenges posed by deepfakes not only highlights the immediate concerns about educational effectiveness but also raises broader questions about the role of education in preparing citizens for informed decision-making and democratic participation in societies where determining information authenticity is highly challenging. Educational institutions have a specific responsibility to their students, which is to develop their capabilities that enable effective navigation of complex information environments while maintaining their commitment to truth, evidence, and rational discourse, which are the fundamentals of their educational mission and a democratic society.

BACKGROUND

Digital Pedagogy Evolution and Contemporary Challenges

The rise in digital pedagogy over the past two decades has been characterized by an increasing synthesis of collaborative tools, multimedia technologies, and interactive platforms, which have transformed traditional classroom settings and expanded possibilities for educational engagement. The initial digital learning tools primarily focused on content delivery and access. This highlights the potential for technology to overcome geographic and temporal hurdles in education, while providing enhanced multimedia experiences that can foster student engagement and learning outcomes (Clark and Mayer, 2016). While 87.9% of respondents report being familiar with deepfakes, only 37.9% understand how they work, indicating that users in educational contexts may recognize deepfakes but often lack the technical knowledge to detect or respond to them effectively (Figure 2). These approaches established the technological infrastructure and pedagogical frameworks that enable the present digital education while creating the information environments that deepfake technology now intimidates to disrupt.

The maturation of digital pedagogy has emphasized personalized educational experiences, active learning principles, and collaborative knowledge construction, providing technology with the leverage to create highly engaging and effective learning environments. Social constructivist theories have informed the development of peer learning activities, online discussion forums, and collaborative projects, which assume authentic participation and good faith communication among students and instructors (Vygotsky and Cole, 1978). Yet, moderate confidence in spotting deepfakes is most common (over 40%), with high confidence at 30% and low confidence at 25%, highlighting the potential for misjudgment in assessing digital content (Figure 2). These pedagogical approaches fundamentally depend on authentic communication and trust relationships, which deepfake technology could undermine by introducing manipulated evidence or synthetic participants.

The integration of multimedia content with digital pedagogy has created a rich learning environment where students engage with diverse forms of evidence, including user-generated content, video lectures, recorded interviews, and documentary materials, thereby enhancing understanding and retention. This multimedia integration also creates vulnerabilities to synthetic content manipulation, which can undermine the evidentiary foundations of educational practice and the assumptions made about audiovisual content. Here, the authentic documentation of events and many contemporary pedagogical strategies may require basic reconceptualization in environments influenced by deepfakes.

Educational data mining and learning analytics have developed to enable increasingly sophisticated approaches, which help personalize educational interventions, understand student learning patterns, and predict academic outcomes based on the needs and preferences of individual students. These data-driven approaches assume the authenticity and accuracy of behavioral indicators, student engagement data, and assessment results, which could potentially be influenced through automated systems or synthetic media (Long and Siemens 2014). The integrity of learning analytics depends on authentic student participation that deepfake technology could predictably influence through modern manipulation or impersonation.

Figure 2. Statistical findings on deepfake awareness, understanding, confidence, and platform perception

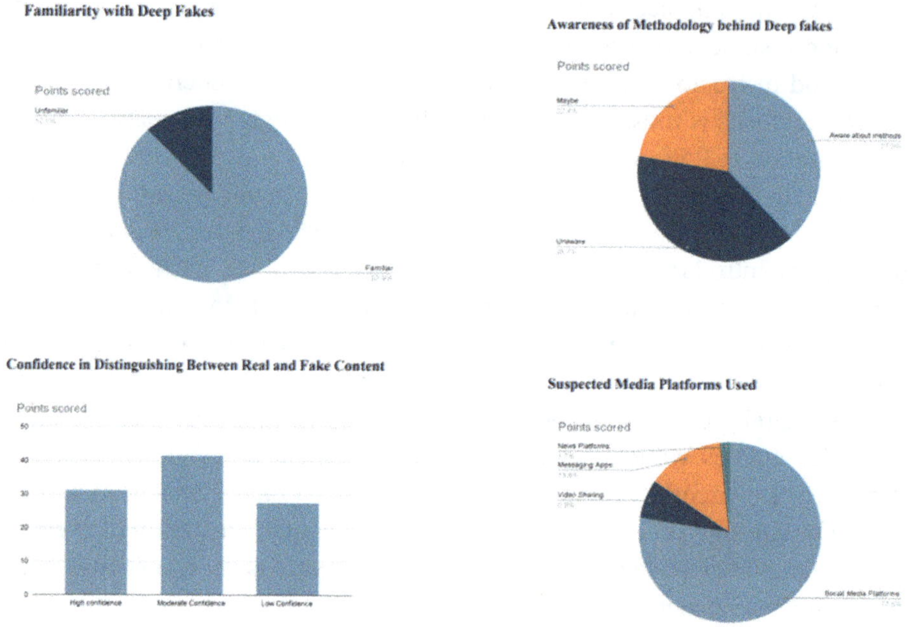

(Chopra & Shukla, 2024)

Deepfake Realism and E-learning Vulnerabilities

The growing realism in deepfake technology poses several challenges for e-learning environments, where direct verification is limited and authentication highly depends on remote communication and digital interfaces. The current deepfake systems can create real-time impersonations that are highly convincing during video conferences, generate synthetic participation in recorded discussions, and manipulate existing educational content to alter the meaning or context in ways that may not be easily detectable if viewed normally (Li et al., 2020). These capabilities create multiple attack vectors that can disrupt e-learning and simultaneously compromise the integrity of educational assessment and interaction.

The asynchronous nature of online education creates additional vulnerabilities to deepfake manipulation, as content can be edited, created, and submitted without direct, immediate detection or verification of synthetic elements. Also, there is a possibility that students may use deepfake technology to impersonate their classmates in recorded presentations, create synthetic evidence for various academic assignments, or manipulate interview recordings for research projects. Even though the study platforms' exposure is also significant, the research (Chopra & Shukla, 2024) found that 77.6% of the students suspect social media as a primary venue for encountering deepfakes, followed by messaging apps and video-sharing sites, indicating that educators must consider external social platforms as potential sources of manipulated content (Figure 2). The wide landscape of education inherent in asynchronous learning may present ample opportunities for sophisticated synthetic content creation, while also shrinking opportunities for immediate response and verification.

The scalability challenges of online education create practical limitations for comprehensive verification and authentication, which actors with ill intent could exploit through the systematic use of deepfake technology. For instance, large online courses with hundreds or thousands of students often rely on a combination of limited human oversight and automated systems. This may not be sufficient for detecting sophisticated synthetic content; additionally, the resource constraints that affect many online education programs may hinder their investment in detection technologies or specialized training that would enhance institutional capacity for identifying and responding to deepfake-related incidents.

Online education is a widespread phenomenon, and as a result, it adds more complex problems for verification and authentication across the legal framework, various cultural contexts, and technological capabilities. Here, students and instructors from multiple countries may have diverse access to verification technologies. Different cultures may have varying expectations for privacy and authentication, as well as differing legal protections, which can complicate institutional responses to synthetic media incidents. Consequently, these international dimensions of online education create vulnerabilities that are easily exploitable. This enables sophisticated attackers to gain leverage through the strategic use of deepfake technology. Furthermore, the integration of artificial intelligence and automated systems in e-learning platforms creates vulnerabilities to adversarial attacks, which could exploit machine learning systems used for plagiarism detection, student assessment, and content recommendation.

Deepfake technology represents one category of adversarial attack that can easily manipulate AI systems employed in educational contexts, with profound effects on educational quality and integrity (Biggio and Roli, 2018). The complexity of AI systems makes it challenging to prevent or predict all possible forms of manipulation, while also generating new requirements for system updates and security monitoring.

LITERATURE REVIEW

Pedagogical Trust and Relationship Dynamics

The understructure of effective pedagogy lies in complex trust relationships between students and institutional systems, students and instructors, and students and peers, which support collaborative learning, authentic communication, and honest assessment. Rovai (2002) in his research demonstrated that trust plays a fundamental role as a prerequisite for effective online learning, enabling students to engage authentically in discussions, submit honest work, and participate meaningfully in collaborative activities. Introducing deepfake technology into the educational environment threatens to undermine these trust relationships by creating uncertainty about the reliability of evidence and the authenticity of communications that support educational interactions.

Trust development studies in digital learning environments reveal that students heavily rely on auditory and visual cues to assess content reliability, instructor credibility, and peer authenticity. Gunawardena and Zittle (1997) in their research study identified that perception of students about the instructor immediacy and presence in online courses were notably impacted by perceived authenticity and audiovisual communication quality, therefore, the potential for deepfake manipulation of live video conferences, instructor videos, or recorded lectures could have considerable impact on student trust and engagement even when there is no actual manipulation. In a digital environment, the relationship between trust and learning outcomes has been extensively documented, with the research continuously showing that the higher the levels of trust, the greater student engagement, the better the learning outcomes, and the greater course satisfaction. Swan (2002) demonstrated in their study that perceived instructor presence and authenticity strongly predict student success in online courses. Consequently, the destruction of trust caused by awareness of deepfakes or actual synthetic media incidents could have significant negative impacts on educational effectiveness, extending far beyond immediate security concerns.

Research on trust repair in educational contexts indicates that rebuilding trust after security incidents or authenticity breaches requires consistent demonstration of reliability, sustained effort, and transparent communication over time. Kim et al. (2004) found that trust violations in educational settings have lasting impacts on student-instructor relationships that may persist even after appropriate remedial actions are taken. The complex nature of deepfake technology and the difficulty of providing definitive proof of authenticity might make the trust repair process a challenging one in synthetic media contexts.

Authenticity and Evidence in Educational Practice

Authenticity has conventionally played a central role in educational practice, from authentic assessment approaches that emphasize real-world relevance to authentic materials that present genuine examples of language use or cultural practice. Wiggins (1990) established authentic assessment as a basic principle of effective education in their research, emphasizing the significance of tasks that replicate real-world challenges and require students to demonstrate practical competencies. The expansion of deepfake technology complicates authentic assessment by making it hard to verify the authenticity of student work, which includes multimedia elements.

Studies on evidence evaluation in educational contexts reveal that students often struggle to assess the authenticity and credibility of digital sources, even under normal circumstances. Wineburg et al. (2016) found in their research that students at all levels of education displayed notable weaknesses in evaluating online information sources, with many failing to identify obvious signs of prejudice or unreliability. Merging sophisticated synthetic media with the information landscape might further complicate these evaluation challenges while requiring enhanced media literacy education. The role of evidence in disciplinary learning varies considerably across different academic fields, with some disciplines relying heavily on audiovisual documentation, while others focus on textual or quantitative evidence. Research by Shanahan and Shanahan (2008) suggests that distinct academic disciplines require distinct literacy skills and evaluation techniques for evidence. Consequently, the impact of deepfake technology on disciplinary learning may vary significantly across fields such as history, journalism, and social sciences, potentially causing higher disruptions than in mathematics or theoretical physics.

Research on multimedia learning reveals that students often place great trust in audiovisual evidence, while showing limited skepticism towards sophisticated manipulations. Mayer (2014) in their studies showed that multimedia presentations are usually more memorable and persuasive than text-only material. This suggests that deepfake manipulations of educational content might have a strong impact, particularly on student learning and belief formation. This shows that the persuasive power of synthetic multimedia creates heightened responsibility for educators to verify content authenticity and teach skepticism.

Instructional Design for Uncertain Information Environments

The conventional principles of instructional design assumes that stable information environments where sources could be evaluated for credibility and evidence could be assessed for authenticity through established criteria, the present day instructional design theories, like those developed by Merrill (2002) and Gagné et al. (2005), stresses clear learning objectives, reliable assessment methods, and authentic resources that support student achievement, the introduction of pervasive synthetic media into educational environments needs primary reconceptualization of these design principles for address uncertainty and ambiguity as central features of contemporary information landscapes.

Research on adaptive instructional design indicates that effective educational systems must be capable of responding to changing technological and social contexts while maintaining a balance of core pedagogical principles. Reiguloth (1999) emphasizes the significance of responsiveness and flexibility in instructional design, which can accommodate evolving technological capabilities and learner needs. The challenge of designing instruction for deepfake-influenced environments requires similar adaptability to address unprecedented challenges related to information authenticity and trust.

Studies of constructivist learning environments show that ambiguity and uncertainty could serve as useful catalysts for deep learning when appropriately supported and structured. Jonassen and Rohrer-Murphy (1999) in their research demonstrated that ill-structured problems, where clear solutions are absent, can promote complex problem-solving capabilities and higher-order thinking skills. This uncertainty, initiated by deepfake technology, could be leveraged as a pedagogical tool to develop media literacy skills and critical thinking when integrated appropriately into instructional design.

The research on epistemic cognition shows that students' beliefs about the nature of knowledge and evidence highly influence their learning techniques and outcomes. Hofer and Pintrich (1997) conducted their studies, demonstrating that students with more positive cognitive beliefs are better equipped to handle ambiguous or contradictory information.

Therefore, educational approaches that openly address epistemological questions raised by deepfake technology could contribute to enhanced learning outcomes across multiple domains.

THEMATIC DISCUSSION

Figure 3 reveals five key themes of adaptive teaching strategies for synthetic media environments.

Figure 3. Key themes of adaptive teaching strategies

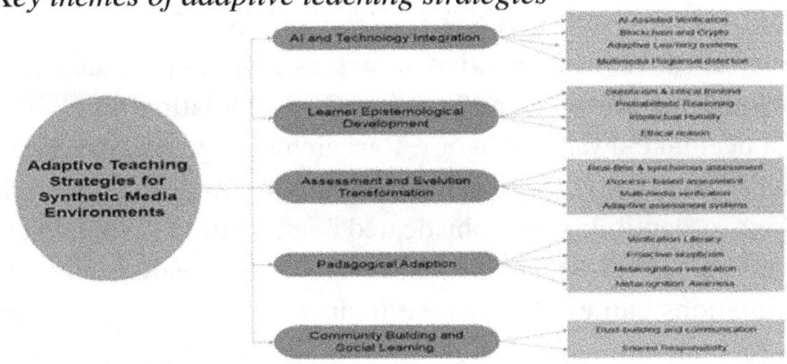

Adaptive Teaching Strategies for Synthetic Media Environments

Developing effective teaching strategies for deepfake-influenced educational environments needs a basic reconceptualization of traditional pedagogical approaches. Contemporary educators must improve their adaptive methodologies to acknowledge uncertainty about content authenticity while maintaining educational effectiveness and student engagement. This adaptation involves steps of creating new frameworks for critical analysis, evidence evaluation, and source verification. This prepares students for a lifelong learning environment in which synthetic media is pervasive (Hobbs, 2010).

Integrating verification literacy into standard pedagogical practice reveals a crucial adaptation that enables students to develop their practical skills for assessing content authenticity while understanding the limitations and possibilities of detection technologies. Educators must teach students to employ various verification strategies, including contextual evaluation, technical analysis, and source triangulation, while recognizing that no single approach provides full certainty about the authenticity of the content. This verification literacy surpasses the simple tool use to include understanding of how synthetic media is created, what types of manipulation are possible, and how detection capabilities emerge in response to these advanced creation technologies. Cultivating productive skepticism represents another important pedagogical adaptation that helps students strike a balance between questioning attitudes toward information and avoiding paralyzing doubts that could interfere with decision-making and learning. Effective skepticism requires a sophisticated understanding of decision-making, probability, evidence quality, and uncertainty, which can be developed through structured learning experiences and explicit instruction. Students must learn how to calibrate their skepticism appropriately and apply greater scrutiny to high-stakes decisions, while simultaneously maintaining the functional trust for routine educational interactions.

The development of metacognitive strategies that support students to understand their own vulnerability to deception and manipulation represents a critical component of deepfake-aware pedagogy. Research in cognitive psychology reveals that individuals consistently overestimate their ability to detect fakes while underestimating their susceptibility to sophisticated manipulation (Dunning et al., 2003). Educational interventions that enable students to build a realistic understanding of their own limitations can easily improve their decision-making and reduce their helplessness to synthetic media manipulation. The implementation of collaborative verification approaches that leverage collective intelligence and peer review could equip enhanced detection capabilities and develop significant collaborative learning skills. Students who collaborate to verify content authenticity can develop analytical approaches, consider various perspectives, and draw on knowledge bases, ultimately learning to discuss and address disagreements and uncertainties in constructive ways. These kinds of approaches are collaborative, and they also present opportunities for peer teaching and learning that can enhance both content understanding and verification skills.

By integrating hands-on creation experiences, students are enabled to experiment with deepfake and synthetic media technologies, which can provide a valuable understanding of both their capabilities and limitations. This develops technical literacy and ethical awareness. When students understand how synthetic media is created, they will be equipped to recognize manipulation, alongside developing informed perspectives on the appropriate and inappropriate uses of these technologies. These experiences must be carefully structured to emphasize ethical considerations and responsible use, while also providing technical understanding.

AI Integration and Educational Technology Adaptation

Syncing artificial intelligence technologies with educational practice requires careful consideration of how AI systems can support verification and authentication, while also avoiding over-reliance on automated detection that might become outdated with the advancement of synthetic media technology. Educational institutions must develop more balanced approaches that leverage AI capabilities for efficiency, while maintaining human oversight and decision-making authority for critical educational functions (Russell and Norvig 2016). It is concluded that integration requires ongoing evaluation of AI system performance and continuous adaptation to evolving threat landscapes.

The development of AI-assisted verification workflows combines automated detection with human analysis, providing enhanced capabilities to identify synthetic content while maintaining educational effectiveness. It is stated that this workflow should integrate easily with existing educational technologies and processes, while providing clear guidance for educators who may not possess specialized technical expertise. Additionally, the design of these systems must prioritize usability and accessibility, while also showing appropriate transparency about system capabilities and limitations. Implementing AI-powered plagiarism detection systems specifically designed for multimedia content represents a significant technological adaptation that can support the enforcement of academic integrity in synthetic media environments. The current plagiarism detection primarily focuses on text analysis, leaving gaps in multimedia verification that deepfake technology could exploit. These amplified detection systems must address image, video, and audio manipulation while providing clear documentation of evidence and reasoning, which highly supports the academic integrity investigations.

Blockchain and cryptographic verification technologies, combined with educational platforms, integrate to provide enhanced authentication capabilities for critical communications and content, while also maintaining privacy and usability. These technologies enable the secure attribution of student work, tamper-evident recording of educational interactions, and cryptographic verification of content authenticity, thereby reducing the opportunities for synthetic media manipulation. Consequently, this implementation must strike a balance between security benefits, privacy considerations, and usability requirements. Adaptive learning systems are being developed to adjust to ambiguity and uncertainty in student assessment and feedback. This represents an important evolution in educational AI that addresses issues such as deepfake-related challenges. Conventional adaptive systems rely on reliable data about student performance and engagement, which synthetic media could potentially compromise. Enhanced systems must incorporate uncertainty quantification and robust decision-making to function effectively even in the face of data manipulation and unreliability.

Learner Skepticism and Epistemological Development

Cultivating appropriate learner skepticism is one of the most significant pedagogical challenges in deepfake-influenced educational environments, as educators must help students develop their critical thinking capabilities to enable effective information evaluation without encouraging doubt or cynical rejection of legitimate knowledge sources. This requires a sophisticated understanding of epistemological development and careful attention to how skepticism is taught and practiced within the context of educational settings (King and Kitchener, 1994). The development of probabilistic thinking skills enables students to make reasoned judgments under uncertain circumstances, which is a vital component of deepfake-aware education with broad applications across multiple academic disciplines and life contexts. Additionally, students must learn to assess evidence based on its quality and reliability, evaluate the likelihood of different scenarios, and make decisions that acknowledge uncertainty while remaining functional and productive.

These thinking skills require open instruction and practice with feedback that helps students to calibrate their appropriate judgments. Integrating epistemological instruction that addresses the nature of knowledge, evidence, and truth in digital environments can equip students with conceptual frameworks for understanding and responding to the challenges of synthetic media. Students benefit from understanding different philosophical perspectives on knowledge and evidence as they develop their personal epistemological commitments, which guide their decision-making and information evaluation. Also, this development should address both practical application and theoretical understanding in contemporary information environments.

The cultivation of intellectual humility enables students to acknowledge the limitations of their own knowledge and detection capabilities; they remain open to learning and revision, which represents an important psychological component of effective skepticism. Research indicates that intellectual humility is linked to enhanced decision-making, improved learning outcomes, and more accurate self-assessment in uncertain environments (Krumrei-Mancuso and Rouse, 2016). Educational approaches that foster intellectual humility can help students navigate synthetic media environments effectively, and they can develop significant character traits. Tolerance development for ambiguity enables students to function effectively even in uncertain information environments without excessive anxiety or premature closure. This proves another important psychological adaptation; additionally, students must learn to be open to multiple possibilities while gathering extra information. Seeking clarification instead of rushing to judgment or becoming paralyzed by uncertainty, this tolerance for ambiguity can only be developed through structured learning experiences that gradually increase complexity and uncertainty, while providing the appropriate support and guidance.

The implementation of ethical reasoning about synthetic media use helps students to understand the moral dimensions of responding, creating, and sharing potentially manipulated content, which shows an essential component of comprehensive media literacy education; therefore, students must develop frameworks for evaluating the ethical implications of their own media use while still having an understanding of their responsibilities as members of information communities. This ethical reasoning should address both collective responsibility and individual decision-making for maintaining information integrity.

Assessment and Evaluation Transformation

The change in assessment practices in response to deepfake technology requires a fundamental reconceptualization of how student learning and achievement can be examined when traditional forms of evidence become unreliable or manipulated. The educational assessment has historically relied on assumptions about the integrity of evidence, student identity verification, and the authenticity of work, which deepfake technology directly challenges. Therefore, contemporary assessment design must adopt new approaches to maintain reliability and validity; it also addresses emerging threats to assessment integrity (Pellegrino et al., 2001). The improvement of process-based assessment approaches focuses on student thinking and problem-solving strategies, rather than final products, to provide enhanced resistance to synthetic media manipulation. They also offer valuable insights into student learning. These approaches emphasize the demonstration of skill development, documentation of student reasoning, and evidence of learning progression, which can be difficult to fake in the final products.

Careful design and implementation are required for process-based assessment to strike a balance between authenticity verification and practical feasibility. The implementation of multi-modal verification strategies that combine various types of evidence and assessment methods could provide enhanced reliability and reduce vulnerability to any form of manipulation. Students may be asked to demonstrate their learning through a combination of peer interaction, written work, oral presentations, and practical demonstrations, which can be challenging to fake comprehensively. By integrating real-time assessment and synchronous evaluation, the opportunities for extensive content manipulation can be reduced, immediate feedback can be provided to enhance assessment security, and learning can be supported. Real-time problem-solving activities, live demonstrations, and interactive discussions may be less vulnerable to deepfake manipulation than recorded submissions, while providing valuable opportunities for formative assessment and instructional adjustment (Gagne et al., 2005).

The development of adaptive assessment systems can adjust to uncertainty about response authenticity while still maintaining valid inferences about student learning, representing an important technological advancement that addresses deepfake-related challenges. Additionally, these systems must integrate uncertainty quantification and robust statistical methods to function effectively even when some responses might be unreliable. The design of these systems requires careful attention to validity and fairness, while also addressing practical implementation challenges.

Community Building and Social Learning

Maintaining effective learning communities in deepfake-influenced environments requires a clear focus on trust-building, authentic communication, and collaborative verification to counteract the potential isolation and suspicion that awareness of synthetic media may foster. Educational communities highly depend on social connections and shared purpose, which the fear of manipulation or excessive skepticism can undermine. Therefore, effective pedagogical approaches must be used to actively cultivate the community while addressing legitimate security concerns (Wenger 1999). The development of peer verification networks enables students to collaborate on content evaluation and authenticity assessment, providing enhanced detection capabilities and fostering important social learning relationships. When students work together to verify information and assess evidence, they can combine diverse perspectives and knowledge, developing a shared understanding and collaborative skills in the process. Additionally, these peer networks offer opportunities for teaching and learning that extend far beyond formal instruction and can potentially foster community connections.

The implementation of transparent communication practices acknowledges uncertainty and maintains educational effectiveness, helping to build trust and resilience within learning communities. Consequently, educators and students benefit from honest discussions about institutional responses and synthetic media challenges, while maintaining their focus on educational goals and learning outcomes. Being this transparent means including clear policies and procedures for addressing potential synthetic media incidents, while still providing reassurances about the institution's commitment to educational integrity. Cultivating shared responsibility for information quality and community integrity can help distribute the burden of verification and authentication, and this also fosters a collective commitment to educational values. When all community members properly understand their role in maintaining information integrity and supporting authentic communication, the community becomes more resilient to synthetic media threats and develops important civic capabilities. This shared responsibility needs clear expectations and support from all community members.

CASE INSIGHTS

Educator Experiences with Synthetic Media Incidents

Professor Sarah Chen, from the University of Washington, elaborated on her experience with a deepfake incident that happened during her initial time in the

Environmental Science course in the fall of 2020. It goes as. A student submitted their research project, which included what seemed to be an exclusive interview of a prominent climate scientist who discussed their unpublished research findings. The audio quality was incredible, and the content was perfectly aligned with the scientist's known research interests, making the manipulation even more difficult to detect during the initial review. It was only when Professor Chen attempted to contact the scientist to request permission to share the interview with other students that the deception was discovered, revealing that there was no such interview originally (Personal communication, February 2023).

This incident prompted Professor Chen to reassess her approach to student assignments and evidence verification, resulting in the implementation of more rigorous verification procedures for all multimedia submissions. Now she demands that her students provide detailed documentation of their source materials, which includes even contact information for interview subjects and verification about permissions. This experience evidently prompted her to integrate explicit instruction about synthetic media capabilities and detection strategies into her course curriculum, which helps students to understand both the possibilities and ethical implications of these technologies.

Dr. Michael Rodriguez, a history teacher at Stanford University, encountered a different type of deepfake challenge when students in his Modern European History course began questioning the authenticity of the historical video footage used in his lectures. After a class discussion about deepfake technology, many students expressed their skepticism about archival footage from World War II, and suggesting that it may be a synthetic content created to support particular historical narratives, this skepticism, while understandable given recent discussions about synthetic media, threatened to undermine the engagement with legitimate historical evidence and critical thinking about primary sources (Personal communication, March 2023).

Dr. Rodriguez responded by developing an open instruction about the technical limitations, historical source verification, and media dating techniques of different historical periods to help students understand why certain types of manipulation would have been impossible at specific times. He also integrated discussions about how historians evaluate evidence authenticity and the importance of multiple source verification. This experience underscored the need for educators to address both legitimate skepticism and unfounded conspiracy theories, while maintaining student engagement with authentic historical evidence.

Professor Lisa Martinez from Arizona State University discovered that students in her online Communications course used deepfake technology to amplify their recorded presentations, not for deceptive purposes, but to improve their perceived presentation quality. Students were utilizing readily available applications to deliver smoother speech, enhance their appearance, and create polished presentations that they could not achieve naturally. While they could not explicitly prohibit this as per their course policies, this usage raised important questions about learning objectives, authenticity, and fairness, about the presentation assignments (Personal communication, April 2023).

The incident prompted Professor Martinez to engage in an extended discussion with students about the ethical implications of using synthetic media in the context of education. This led to a collaborative development of new policies that differentiate between deceptive manipulation and acceptable enhancement. The class then worked together to establish new guidelines for the appropriate use of technology, considering concerns about learning objectives, authenticity, and fairness in presentation assignments. This collaborative approach helped students understand the complexity of synthetic media ethics and maintained their engagement with the course content.

Altered Videos and Content Manipulation

A significant disruption occurred at the University of Michigan in 2022 when altered versions of recorded lectures began circulating among students, featuring manipulated content that distorted the instructor's statements about controversial political topics. The alterations were sufficient to maintain lip-sync accuracy and natural speech patterns, making them difficult to identify without careful technical analysis. Unofficial channels and social media shared the manipulated videos, which led to the video reaching hundreds of students before it was identified as synthetic (Personal communication, Dr. Jennifer Kim, IT Security, April 2023).

This incident required a coordinated response from multiple university departments, including public relations, IT security, and academic affairs, to address both the reputational and technical aspects of the attack. As a result, the university invested considerable resources in forensic analysis to prove that the content was synthetic. They also effectively communicated to clarify the misinformation. Then they restored confidence in the legitimate course materials. The incident revealed the gaps in institutional preparedness for synthetic media attacks and prompted the development of enhanced verification procedures for the course content.

In response to the Michigan incident, they included development of student education programs, the implementation of cryptographic verification for recorded lectures, and enhanced training for faculty about synthetic media threats and media verification. Additionally, the university established partnerships with external security firms to provide specialized expertise for any future incidents and built internal capabilities for ongoing monitoring and response. The incident catalyzed broader institutional changes, extending beyond simple security measures to incorporate educational and communication techniques.

In Texas, a community college faced a unique type of content manipulation, where deepfake technology was used to generate fake video testimonials from former students promoting the institution's programs. Here, the synthetic testimonials featured impersonations in a convincing way, where real alumni made statements about their educational experiences and career outcomes that were more positive and different from their original experiences. They discovered this manipulation only when one of the impersonated alums contacted the college to file a complaint about unauthorized use of their identity. Complex questions were raised about this incident, including questions about the boundaries between acceptable promotion and deceptive manipulation, institutional marketing practices, and consent for alum communications. The college was then required to remove all video testimonials from its marketing media and develop new verification procedures for alumni content. This incident also paved the way for a broader discussion about institutional responsibility in verifying the authenticity of promotional materials and the ethical implications of synthetic media usage in educational marketing.

Learning Management System Vulnerabilities

Significant vulnerabilities were discovered in Eastern University's learning management system. It happened when a security audit revealed that student video submissions could be easily replaced with synthetic content without being detected by the platform's standard verification procedures. The LMS relied primarily on file metadata and uploaded timestamps for verification, but these could be easily manipulated by sophisticated attackers using deepfake technology. The audit was prompted by faculty concerns about the increasingly polished student video submissions, which seemed inconsistent with students' demonstrated capabilities in live interactions. Upon assessment, it was revealed that the LMS lacked the technical capabilities to detect video manipulation and lacked sufficient documentation for submission verification. Consequently, students could easily submit synthetic content for video assignments, which the system would treat as authentic unless a manual verification procedure were implemented. The discovery prompted the immediate implementation of enhanced verification procedures, as the university collaborated with the LMS vendor to develop improved authentication capabilities.

The response to the Eastern University vulnerability included implementing additional verification steps for high-stakes assignments, developing faculty training programs for manual content verification, and advocating with LMS vendors for enhanced authentication features. Additionally, the university established partnerships with detection technology providers to integrate a specialized verification tool into their already existing system. The experience underlined the need for educational institutions to actively evaluate their technology systems regarding synthetic media vulnerabilities, rather than waiting and assuming that standard systems will provide sufficient protection. It was discovered that the centralized LMS of a large public university was prone to sophisticated attacks that could manipulate individual submissions, course materials, and even the instructor communications. The vulnerability was identified during a penetration testing exercise. It revealed how attackers could create synthetic communications, replace the instructor videos, and manipulate recorded lectures that would appear to come from faculty members. The scope for manipulation extended far beyond individual student misconduct to encompass systematic disruption of educational delivery.

This discovery prompted the implementation of system-wide security measures, including comprehensive audit trails, cryptographic verification of course materials, and mandatory two-factor authentication for all users. Additionally, the university system developed incident response procedures especially for the synthetic media attacks and established new partnerships with law enforcement agencies to receive support in the investigation. The experience further demonstrated that the potential for synthetic media threats would affect not only the individual courses but also the entire educational system.

CHALLENGES

Loss of Motivation and Student Engagement

Awareness of deepfake technology and synthetic media manipulation could have a significant psychological impact on student motivation and engagement, extending beyond concerns about content authenticity to encompass broader questions about the value and reliability of digital education. Students who are aware of the sophisticated manipulation possibilities, enable the deepfake technology to develop excessive skepticism towards legitimate educational content and lose self confidence in their ability to differentiate authentic from synthetic materials, this destruction of confidence could make way for general anxiety, disengagement from online learning activities, and reluctance to participate in multimedia assignments regarding the digital educational interactions (Guess et al. 2020).

The phenomenon of "verification fatigue" has emerged among students who feel overwhelmed by the constant need to verify and question digital content, leading to possible cognitive exhaustion and a diminished readiness to engage with educational materials. Additionally, students report spending excessive time verifying the authenticity of the content, which distracts from focusing on the learning objectives. However, others report giving up on verification entirely due to its complexity and uncertainty; this fatigue can interfere with normal learning processes, creating hurdles to educational achievement that disproportionately affect students with limited technical resources or knowledge.

The erosion of trust in educational technology platforms and digital learning environments may deter students from fully engaging in online education. This limits students' willingness to experiment with new learning technologies. Students who have experienced or learned about deepfake manipulation may feel suspicious about all digital educational interactions, which prompts them to prefer traditional face-to-face instruction even when online options might be more convenient and effective. This type of technological skepticism can hinder students' educational opportunities and create barriers to educational adaptation and innovation.

The psychological burden of constant vigilance regarding content authenticity can counteract the cognitive processes necessary for deep learning and critical thinking by directing mental resources toward verification activities instead of comprehension and analysis. Students might focus on detecting potential manipulation and overlook the opportunity to engage meaningfully with content that is actually authentic and valuable for their learning process. This misdirection of cognitive resources could reduce educational effectiveness and create stress and anxiety that further interfere with learning processes.

Instructor Credibility and Authority Issues

The possibility of deepfake manipulation in instructor communications and course materials poses unprecedented challenges to maintaining pedagogical authority and credibility, which are essential for effective teaching relationships. When students cannot verify the authenticity of digital communications, instructor videos, or recorded lectures, their trust in the instructor's foundation may be compromised, undermining the effectiveness of pedagogy. Instructors might find their authority questioned not only regarding their content expertise but also regarding their actual identity and authentic participation in educational interactions (Rovai 2002).

The burden of proving authenticity for educational communications and materials creates an additional workload for instructors, who must now document, record, and verify their content in ways that were previously unnecessary. In addition, instructors may be required to respond to student questions, implement complex verification procedures, maintain detailed records of their communications, and verify content authenticity, which can distract them from engaging in substantial educational interactions. This could potentially reduce the time and energy available for actual teaching, creating extra frustration and stress for educators who feel that their professional integrity is in question. The possibility for ill-intended actors to create synthetic content that seems to feature specific instructors creates reputational helplessness that could highly damage careers and institutional relationships, even when there was no actual misconduct, and this leaves instructors in the position where they have to prove that they did not make any statements or take actions that are documented in convincing synthetic media. This creates complex challenges for reputation management and professional defense, and the difficulty of definitively proving the synthetic nature of sophisticated deepfakes might leave them vulnerable to lasting reputational damage.

The destruction of instructor authority in digital environments might have flowing effects on learning outcomes, classroom management, and student behavior, that extends beyond immediate concerns about content verification, and students who question the authenticity of their instructor may also question their expertise, grading decisions, and course policies in ways that underestimate the effective pedagogical relationships, which further creates challenges in maintaining academic standards and reduce the instructor satisfaction and effectiveness.

FUTURE DIRECTIONS

Transformational Pedagogy for Synthetic Media Era

The development of transformational pedagogical approaches reconceptualizes uncertainty and skepticism as productive learning tools, representing a promising direction for educational practice in synthetic media environments. Instead of viewing deepfake technology as a sole threat to educational integrity, educators could leverage the uncertainty it creates as a catalyst for developing amplified critical thinking skills, media literacy capabilities, and epistemological sophistication. This transformational approach needs fundamental shifts in assessment practices, educational objectives, and instructional methods that embrace ambiguity as a central feature of contemporary learning environments.

This integration of obvious uncertainty quantification into educational practice could help students develop a sophisticated understanding of decision-making, probability, and evidence quality under ambiguous conditions, which will serve them well in both academic and professional contexts. Additionally, students can learn to express and work with degrees of confidence, rather than relying on binary true/false judgments, and develop comfort with provisional conclusions, as well as an evolving understanding. This type of probabilistic thinking represents an important cognitive skill with applications across various disciplines and life contexts. The cultivation of collaborative skepticism that merges collective intelligence with individual critical thinking and peer verification could provide amplified analytical capabilities and build important social learning relationships. So students working together evaluate evidence and assess information quality to combine diverse perspectives and expertise, and alongside learn to negotiate their disagreements constructively. Additionally, these collaborative approaches provide opportunities for peer teaching and learning that enhance both content understanding and verification skills.

Media-Aware Curricula and Literacy Integration

The development of a comprehensive media literacy curriculum that specifically addresses the capabilities and implications of synthetic media represents an essential educational response that can prepare students for lifelong learning in a complex information environment. These curricula must go far beyond traditional media literacy approaches to encompass the technical understanding of ethical frameworks, artificial intelligence, and practical skills for content verification, essential for responsible media use. This integration across multiple disciplines and educational levels can ensure that all students develop appropriate capabilities, regardless of their own academic focus.

Establishing interdisciplinary collaboration between media studies, technology education, philosophy, and other relevant fields could provide comprehensive approaches to synthetic media education that might address both humanistic and technical dimensions, which helps students to benefit from understanding both the concepts -why questions of authenticity and truth matter for human society and democratic governance, and how synthetic media technologies work. This interdisciplinary approach can certainly provide a robust preparation for citizenship and professional life in synthetic media environments.

CONCLUSION

The evolution of deepfake technology as a pervasive force in digital communication has called for fundamental reconceptualization of pedagogical practice that acknowledges uncertainty and ambiguity as the central features of contemporary educational environments, in this specific chapter it is demonstrated that effective teaching in the age of synthetic media requires learning objectives, sophisticated adaptation of instructional methods, and assessment strategies, that could maintain educational quality while simultaneously addressing the exceptional challenges towards authenticity and trust. This analysis unveils that while deepfake technology creates significant disruptions to traditional pedagogical assumptions, it also presents certain opportunities for developing enhanced critical thinking capabilities and media literacy skills that prepare the students for lifelong learning in complex information environments.

Examining educator experiences and institutional responses reveals that successful adaptation to synthetic media challenges requires comprehensive approaches that integrate community-building strategies, technical capabilities, and pedagogical innovation. Additionally, the case studies reveal that both the significant challenges faced by educational practitioners and the creative solutions that emerge when they embrace uncertainty are productive catalysts for learning, rather than a simple threat to educational integrity. The success of these adaptations depends on the technological infrastructure, institutional support for faculty development, and student education that enable authentication and effective verification, while also maintaining educational effectiveness and accessibility.

The future of pedagogy in synthetic media environments will likely require the continued evolution of educational practices that balance productive skepticism with functional trust, maintaining a commitment to rational discourse, truth, and evidence—the fundamentals of the educational mission. The transformation of educational practice in response to deepfake technology represents not just a mere technological adaptation but a significant opportunity to enhance the epistemological sophistication and critical thinking capabilities that students require for success in an increasingly complex and uncertain world. By including skepticism as a learning tool rather than viewing it as a simple defensive response, educators can help students develop the analytical capabilities and intellectual resilience necessary to thrive in this age of illusion.

REFERENCES

Biggio, B., & Roli, F. (2018). Wild patterns: Ten years after the rise of adversarial machine learning. *Pattern Recognition*, *84*(12), 317–331.

. Chopra, A., & Shukla, M. A. (2024) Exploring the Misuse of Deepfake Technology in India: Implications for Society.

Clark, R. C., & Mayer, R. E. (2016). *E-learning and the science of instruction: Proven guidelines for consumers and designers of multimedia learning*. John Wiley & Sons.

Dunning, D., Johnson, K., Ehrlinger, J., & Kruger, J. (2003). Why people fail to recognize their own incompetence. *Current Directions in Psychological Science*, *12*(3), 83–87.

Gagne, R. M., Wager, W. W., Golas, K. C., Keller, J. M., & Russell, J. D. (2005). *Principles of instructional design* (5th ed.). Thomson Wadswortth.

Groh, M., Epstein, Z., Firestone, C., & Picard, R. (2022). Deepfake detection by human crowds, machines, and machine-informed crowds. *Proceedings of the National Academy of Sciences of the United States of America*, *119*(1), 1–11.

Guess, A. M., Lerner, M., Lyons, B., Montgomery, J. M., Nyhan, B., Reifler, J., & Sircar, N. (2020). A digital media literacy intervention increases discernment between mainstream and false news in the United States and India. *Proceedings of the National Academy of Sciences of the United States of America*, *117*(27), 15536–15545.

Gunawardena, C. N., & Zittle, F. J. (1997). Social presence as a predictor of satisfaction within a computer-mediated conferencing environment. *American Journal of Distance Education*, *11*(3), 8–26.

Hobbs, R. (2010). *Digital and media literacy: A plan of action*. The Aspen Institute.

Hofer, B. K., & Pintrich, P. R. (1997). The development of epistemological theories: Beliefs about knowledge and knowing and their relation to learning. *Review of Educational Research*, *67*(1), 88–140.

Jonassen, D. H., & Rohrer-Murphy, L. (1999). Activity theory as a framework for designing constructivist learning environments. *Educational Technology Research and Development*, *47*(1), 61–79.

Kim, P. H., Ferrin, D. L., Cooper, C. D., & Dirks, K. T. (2004). Removing the shadow of suspicion: The effects of apology versus denial for repairing competence-versus integrity-based trust violations. *The Journal of Applied Psychology*, *89*(1), 104–118.

King, P. M., & Kitchener, K. S. (1994). Developing Reflective Judgment: Understanding and Promoting Intellectual Growth and Critical Thinking in Adolescents and Adults. Jossey-Bass Higher and Adult Education Series and Jossey-Bass Social and Behavioral Science Series. Jossey-Bass, 350 Sansome Street, San Francisco, California, United States of America.

Krumrei-Mancuso, E. J., & Rouse, S. V. (2016). The development and validation of the comprehensive intellectual humility scale. *Journal of Personality Assessment*, *98*(2), 209–221.

Li, Y., Yang, X., Sun, P., Qi, H., & Lyu, S. (2020). Celeb-DF: A large-scale challenging dataset for DeepFake forensics. *2020 IEEE/CVF Conference on Computer Vision and Pattern Recognition (CVPR)*. IEEE, Seattle, Washington, United States of America.

Long, P., & Siemens, G. (2014). Penetrating the fog: Analytics in learning and education. *Italian Journal of Educational Technology*, *22*(3), 132–137.

Mayer, R. E. (2014). *The Cambridge handbook of multimedia learning* (2nd ed.). Cambridge University Press.

Merrill, M. D. (2002). First principles of instruction. *Educational Technology Research and Development*, *50*(3), 43–59.

Pellegrino, J. W., Chudowsky, N., & Glaser, R. (2001). *Knowing what students know: The science and design of educational assessment*. National Academy Press.

Reigeluth, C. M. (1999). What is instructional-design theory and how is it changing. In Reigeluth, C. M. (Ed.), *Instructional-design theories and models: A new paradigm of instructional theory* (pp. 5–29). Lawrence Erlbaum Associates.

Roe, J., Perkins, M., Somoray, K., Miller, D., & Furze, L. (2025). To Deepfake or Not to Deepfake: Higher Education Stakeholders' Perceptions and Intentions towards Synthetic Media. *arXiv preprint arXiv:2502.18066*.

Rovai, A. P. (2002). Building sense of community at a distance. *International Review of Research in Open and Distance Learning*, *3*(1), 1–16.

Russell, S., & Norvig, P. (2016). *Artificial intelligence: A modern approach* (3rd ed.). Pearson.

Shanahan, T., & Shanahan, C. (2008). Teaching disciplinary literacy to adolescents: Rethinking content-area literacy. *Harvard Educational Review*, *78*(1), 40–59.

Swan, K. (2002). Building learning communities in online courses: The importance of interaction. *Education Communication and Information*, *2*(1), 23–49.

Vaccari, C., & Chadwick, A. (2020). Deepfakes and disinformation: Exploring the impact of synthetic political video on deception, uncertainty, and trust in news. *Social Media + Society, 6*(1), 1–13.

Vygotsky, L. S., & Cole, M. (1978). *Mind in society: Development of higher psychological processes.* Harvard University Press.

Wenger, E. (1999). *Communities of practice: Learning, meaning, and identity.* Cambridge university press.

Wiggins, G. (1990). The case for authentic assessment. *Practical Assessment, Research & Evaluation, 2*(1), 2.

Wineburg, S., McGrew, S., Breakstone, J., & Ortega, T. (2016). *Evaluating information: The cornerstone of civic online reasoning, Stanford Digital Repository, Stanford History Education Group, Robert R.* McCormick Foundation.

Zawacki-Richter, O., Marín, V. I., Bond, M., & Gouverneur, F. (2019). Systematic review of research on artificial intelligence applications in higher education–where are the educators? *International Journal of Educational Technology in Higher Education, 16*(1), 1–27.

Chapter 6
Current and Future Techniques of AI-Based Deepfake Detection

B. Vaidianathan
https://orcid.org/0009-0009-8170-4096
Dhaanish Ahmed College of Engineering, Chennai, India

R Saravanan
R.V. Institute of Technology and Management, Bengaluru, India

Neha Bharani
IPS Academy, Indore, India

R. M. R. Shamija Sherryl
SRM Institute of Science and Technology, Ramapuram, India

D. Celin Pappa
Dhaanish Ahmed College of Engineering, India

S. Silvia Priscila
https://orcid.org/0000-0002-6040-3149
Bharath Institute of Higher Education and Research, India

Prasanna Ranjith Christodoss
Messiah University, USA

ABSTRACT

As the technology of deepfakes becomes more efficient at a rapid pace, it is now a necessity for industries like education to research methods for identifying tampered content. This paper presents an evaluation of current methods used in AI-based deepfake detection, employing machine learning approaches such as convolutional neural networks (CNNs) and generative adversarial networks (GANs). This chapter also contrasts the strengths and weaknesses of these techniques, comparing their effectiveness in detecting deepfake videos, images, and audio. Apart from a comparative evaluation of existing methods, the paper addresses other advancements and emerging technologies for improved deepfake detection, specifically multimodal

DOI: 10.4018/979-8-3373-3770-8.ch006

detection techniques that utilise visual, audio, and text analysis. The work also provides a brief explanation of how to stay ahead of the ever-evolving nature of deepfake technology, emphasising the need for continuous innovation in detection methods.

INTRODUCTION

The extremely rapid evolution of artificial intelligence (AI) has fundamentally transformed the digital media, opening up new pathways of creativity and expression. The most powerful and possibly threatening innovation in the process is that of deepfakes. Deepfakes are algorithmically created media—image, video, or voice—created or modified using cutting-edge AI algorithms, such as generative adversarial networks (GANs), originally introduced by Goodfellow and then generalised by Li et al. (2018), and further developed with architectural progress presented by Brock et al. (2016). The networks can create hyper-realistic but completely artificial media that are otherwise invisible to the naked eye or ear. The media and entertainment industries have embraced deepfake technology due to its potential to drive visual effects, voice overdubbing, and even the creation of virtual actors, thereby increasing efficiency and opening up new opportunities for content creation. Akhtar (2023), for instance, has employed deepfake technology to resurrect deceased actors, alter voices, and create real-world virtual characters. These applications offer new dimensions in narrative and interactive digital experience.

However, as with any other technology, deepfakes have also had a negative side, leading to actual issues. In politics and journalism, its application for an ill purpose has become a cause of concern. Tripathi and Al-Zubaidi (2023) acknowledged in their research that political disinformation through deepfakes can mislead citizens and erode democratic institutions. In social communication, Eelmaa (2021) examined deepfake disinformation, which revealed ethical concerns like sexualized content and identity spoofing focused on children and vulnerable groups. In education, Nguyen et al. (2022) indicated how artificial content can be used to impersonate teachers and create fake academic credentials. Similarly, Afzal et al. (2023) discussed the effects of deepfakes in learning environments, including their misuse for plagiarism, cheating, and unauthorised editing of videos. All such misuses break learning trust and oblige organisations to adopt control measures.

To prevent such problems, AI detection tools are being introduced in various sectors. One of them, developed by Ajao et al. (2019), integrated sentiment-aware models with those used to detect disinformation and identify manipulated social media posts. In education, adaptive security systems developed by Heidari et al. (2024) aim to protect learners and educators from identity-based spoofing and disinformation attacks. They are GAN-guided adversarial training-based models wherein artificially created samples are generated by a generator, and the discriminator attempts to label them. Theoretical work in this area was carried out by Yu et al. (2021), who experimentally verified the quality and stability of the generated samples in various applications.

In the visual detection, Afchar et al. (2018) employed CNN-based classifiers that could detect the typical signs, such as resolution inconsistency and boundary artefact faces. This was also enhanced by temporal models, such as 3D-CNNs and LSTMs, for real-time video detection, as observed in a paper by Bird and Lotfi (2024). To detect audio, spectrogram-based CNNs with RNNs have been successful in unmasking the imitation voice samples—a research direction strongly pursued by Akhtar (2023). This breakthrough notwithstanding, detecting deepfakes lags generating models. Present generators eliminate retro artefacts, i.e., blinking discontinuities, which are already being targeted by early detectors (Nguyen et al., 2022).

The shortcomings of existing models, including subpar performance on unseen data and limited multimodal assistance, have led researchers to investigate more advanced transformer-based detection models. Vaswani et al. (2017) conducted early research on the attention mechanism, which catalyzed models like BERT and ViT, currently used to detect contextual anomalies in multimodal data. Lip and word, or tone and face, differences, for instance, could suggest fakeness content—a strategy employed in models under review by Afzal et al. (2023).

Cross-modal integration strategies that blend auditory, visual, and textual cues were proposed by Bird and Lotfi (2024) to enhance robustness across platforms. These are also being paired with more comprehensive society- and policy-level measures. Akhtar (2023) has identified the need for active media literacy and governance, while Afzal et al. (2023) proposed educational training modules and stricter verification procedures. Social reaction and ethical appraisal measures have also been examined by Eelmaa (2021) and Heidari et al. (2024), who presented elaborate countermeasures beyond techno-defence in isolation.

One sector that can be explored is the application of explainable AI (XAI) in detection systems. As deepfakes become smarter, it becomes not only crucial to detect them but also to explain why they are being detected. Especially in educational and legal contexts, the decisions of the detection model need to be explainable and transparent. SHAP values, LIME, and Grad-CAM are some interpretability tools that were submitted to assist in explaining black-box models and making them more credible and understandable. FaceForensics++, Celeb-DF, DFDC (Deepfake Detection Challenge), and TIMIT (for speech) are some baselines that provide quality datasets with which to train against and test. Baselines provide a solid basis for measuring performance and driving innovation in detection methods. New information is always needed, however, to keep up with new methods of manipulation and media. This research presents an in-depth introduction to state-of-the-art AI-based deepfake detection methods and discusses the emerging technology that can enhance the effectiveness of detection. It presents an empirical comparison of CNN, GAN, and hybrid-based models for utilising them for image, video, and audio deepfakes. Secondly, the research highlights the dynamic threat environment and the necessity of continuous innovation, dataset diversification, and multi-disciplinary research to reach effective detection frameworks. Open-source software, such as TensorFlow, OpenCV, and Python libraries, has been utilised in research for model deployment and experimental validation. Lastly, it is also hoped that the framework presented here will not only improve current detection methods but also anticipate and evolve with the ongoing progress in deepfake technology.

REVIEW OF LITERATURE

Ajao et al. (2019) constructed warning systems that were based on sentiment-aware models for detecting manipulated multimedia. Their approach departed from the analysis of human vision to programmatic feature extraction. Pentakota (2025) initially identified unusual eye blinking and mechanical head rotation in deepfakes, which proved difficult as synthesis techniques evolved. Hand-crafted features were insufficient in capturing the rise in manipulations. The absence of fixed detection tools is what forced the call for adaptive systems. Their work laid the foundation for algorithmic models of detection. It helped emphasise the fragmentation of human perception caused by AI-generated deception.

Tripathi and Al-Zubaidi (2023) examined public trust elements of a fake political video, emphasising the requirements for effective protection against AI. Their work highlighted how deepfakes distorted perception, particularly in news and education. They highlighted the need to adopt automated processes for distinguishing real and fake images. Dhinakaran et al. (2023) surpassed the discovery turn from sensation to evidence. Scholarship and public institutions compelled policy reform due to this effect. It was necessary to incorporate AI to guarantee information authenticity. Their work linked deepfake detection with broader social issues.

Nguyen et al. (2022) used a hybrid CNN-LSTM and 3D-CNN to detect deepfakes by examining temporal relationships in video streams. The models could identify millisecond discrepancies in video frames that were not identifiable using static images. Temporal modelling became critical to find lip-sync discrepancies or unnatural motion. Their approach allowed systems to learn discrepancies at the frame level between sequences. Nagaraj (2023) explored how spatial and temporal sensitivity alignment improves robustness in detection. They significantly enhanced video-centred deepfake detection techniques. They bridged a significant gap between image-based and sequence-aware methods.

Yu et al. (2021) introduced attention modules to direct detection towards discriminative facial points, thereby enhancing detection. Autoencoders were used by their system for reconstructing facial frames and marking manipulated regions. Maroju (2024) found that attention layers learned where deepfake models typically lost information. Anomaly detection in regions like the eyes, nose, or mouth increased classification confidence. Autoencoders reduced the dimension loss of non-manipulated patterns. Their method dramatically enhanced explainable and local detection models. Their work enhanced the manipulation localisation in one frame.

Brock et al. (2016) developed high-resolution GANs that dramatically enhanced synthetic content generation, thus advancing deepfake production and detection. Their creation generated photorealistic images that were indistinguishable from real ones. Banala (2024) noted that gan discriminators later became the foundation for adversarial detection training. The same technology used to produce fakes was also employed to teach systems how to detect them. GANs have given rise to synthetic training datasets that are used to train deepfake detectors (Rendhy et al., 2024). They created a dual-use framework that was easily integrated with generation and defence. They remain pillars for AI innovation on deepfakes.

Afzal et al. (2023) proposed multimodal detection models that incorporate facial expressions, speech tone, and lip movements. They reduced cross-modal differences by synchronising audio-video data. They identified mouth articulation and phonetic mismatches in their model. Bastareche (2024) found that multimodal detection was most beneficial in online learning systems. A holistic analysis of data streams improved the accuracy of their model. Mudunuri (2024) found that the cross-validation technique improved generalisation over deepfake modes. Their solution enhanced detection capability beyond that of one-modality systems.

Li et al. (2018) used CNN-RNN models to detect deepfaked audio through spectral and temporal anomaly detection. Their model was trained on voice samples represented as spectrograms. Synthetic voices had no natural pitch, frequency, or tempo changes whatsoever. Raj et al. (2024) reported that their model successfully identified unnatural modulations caused by speech synthesis systems. This was of the highest priority in voice-based deepfake detection of university exams. The research identified the need for having some of these cloned speech prevention techniques. Their method has not yet become universal in audio-based detection procedures.

Heidari et al. (2024) utilised explainable AI techniques, such as SHAP and LIME, to enable model decision explanations in deepfake detection. They made a visual explanation of the effect of such image segments on classification decisions possible. Basañes and Alentajan (2024) noted that this was essential for academic or forensic applications that require transparency. They improved the model's reliability in high-stakes environments. By exposing inner explanation, their system facilitated the unmasking of bias or misclassifications. Anushya et al. (2024) argue that interpretability has become more academically and legally relevant through detection. What they achieved brought AI detection into harmony with ethical responsibility.

Transformer architectures were introduced by Vaswani et al. (2017), which were subsequently used in the context of cross-modal deepfake detection. They enabled self-attention to align the temporal order between audio and video. It enabled understanding of context within and between modalities of data. Kumar et al. (2025) transformers enabled asynchrony detection synchronised in audio-visual. In educational media, they enabled asynchrony detection in lectures or presentations by deep learning. They enhanced performance as well as explainability. They enabled scalable, real-time, and context-aware deepfake inspection.

Heidari et al. (2024) once again emphasised the need for explainability in juridical and pedagogical settings. Their ongoing research legitimised detection results at institutions. Correct outputs are of utmost importance if AI decisions affect reputations or certifications. Akole and Adegboye (2024) improved system auditing through feature-level visual explanations. Their ongoing research facilitated regulation authorisation and policy embedding. Rendhy (2024) has re-established the growing need for responsible AI in deepfake detection. Their work is at the forefront of accountability for AI systems within higher education environments.

Benchmark datasets have been instrumental in defining comparative literature and testing. FaceForensics++, Celeb-DF, DFDC, and DeeperForensics-1.0 provided large, annotated image and video datasets for training and testing models. TIMIT and ASVspoof have enabled voice-based detection research in the field of audio. These data have differed in terms of complexity of manipulation, type of manipulation, and environmental contexts, allowing researchers to investigate model generalisation. Rajest et al. (2023) generally, the literature presents a clear trend from simple rule-based systems to complex multimodal AI models. As the deepfake generators evolved further, the literature evolved to present strong and interpretable detection algorithms. The experiments presented in this work uniformly emphasise the necessity of real-time updating of datasets, cross-modal fusion, and the deployment of scalable and interpretable real-time detection systems.

METHODOLOGY

The research employs a multi-layered methodological experimental strategy to evaluate current and future deepfake detection AI algorithms. The methodology involves three main phases, i.e., preprocessing and data selection, model testing and deployment, and multimodal fusion with interpretability analysis. Preprocessing and data selection constitute the initial phase, which involves collecting datasets and preprocessing them to be ready for testing image, video, and audio-based deepfakes.

The most salient datasets used are FaceForensics++, Celeb-DF, and TIMIT. Genuine and manipulated videos with various levels of compression, high-resolution celebrity-like deepfakes in Celeb-DF, highly phonetic genuine speech in TIMIT, and synthetically generated audio are used to form the training set for voice-based detection. All of the datasets are standardised, resized, and translated into canonical forms for use in neural architectures.

For the deployment phase of the model, a suite of thoroughly tested and benchmarked deep learning models is employed. ResNet and EfficientNet are utilised for detecting static images. Temporal networks such as 3D-CNN and CNN-LSTM are employed in video detection to extract spatiotemporal features. Audio detection is performed by converting speech into spectrograms and employing a CNN with LSTM layers to model temporal features. All models are trained in both TensorFlow and PyTorch environments with consistent parameter settings, such as learning rate, batch size, and epochs, to ensure fairness. The performance is evaluated using four common measures: accuracy, precision, recall, and F1-score. A k-fold cross-validation also helps validate the reduction of variance and assess generalizability. Models are also validated against test data to test robustness. Explainability is combined with SHAP for tabular data and Grad-CAM for visual data, enabling the interpretation of model decisions and identifying areas or frames that significantly impact outputs.

In the final stage, a multimodal detection system is constructed. The output of video, audio, and image-based models is fused using a late fusion technique that combines majority voting and confidence-weighted fusion. This ensures the overall model is highly dependable, even if one modality cannot identify a deepfake. The outputs are also verified through sensitivity and ablation studies to understand the contribution of each modality. This approach provides an organised, reproducible, and comprehensible framework to estimate AI-based detection of deepfakes on different types of media. It also enables the research goal of contrasting existing capabilities and conducting research on scalable methods of deepfake detection in the future.

Figure 1. AI-based deepfake detection framework architecture

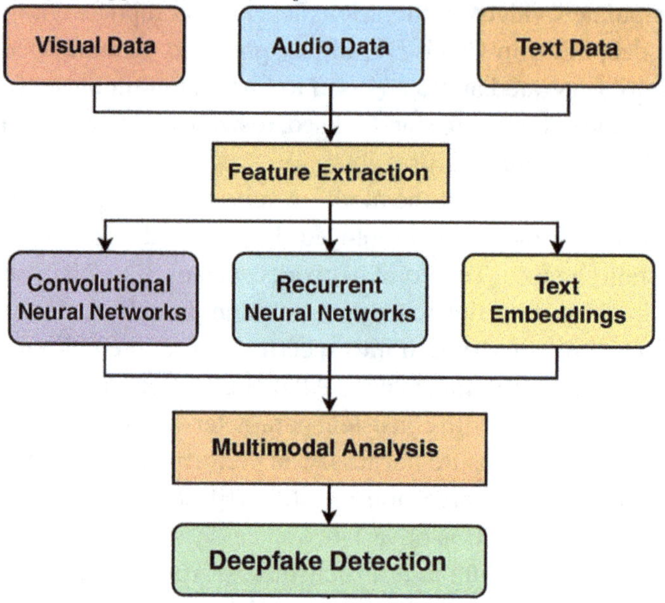

Figure 1 illustrates a comprehensive architectural view of the AI-based deepfake detection framework with four major stages: Input Modalities, Feature Extraction, Multimodal Analysis, and Detection. The process begins with the Input Modalities block, from which raw input is visual material (images/videos), audio streams, and transcript text. These multimodal inputs are the shared vectors that enable deepfakes to propagate across various media. All input streams subsequently pass through independent Feature Extraction layers, where images and video frames are post-processed with CNNs (e.g., EfficientNet, Xception). Temporal features are examined with LSTM or 3D-CNNs in videos, and audio signals are converted to spectrograms for frequency-based computation using CNN-RNN stacks.

Text content in transcript or speech-to-text output form is input into transformer models, such as BERT, for semantic coherence validation. These obtained features are then used as input to the Multimodal Analysis block, where cross-modal correlations are studied using attention mechanisms and contextual alignment algorithms. These visual gesture inconsistencies and audio tone inconsistencies, as well as lip movement errors and phoneme sequence errors, are checked here to ensure proper anomaly detection. The last Detection step combines all of the modality-specific outputs via a late fusion approach—usually weighted probabilistic outputs or ensemble voting—to produce a final overall classification output (real or fake). The model is extremely accurate and generalizable by combining multiple different input streams and offering redundancy, which is crucial in preventing adversarial bypassing, a common issue in single-modality systems. In summary, Figure 1 shows the system flow and intelligent coordination of subsystems necessary for effective and scalable AI-based deepfake detection in practical applications.

DATA DESCRIPTION

The research utilises three extensive datasets—FaceForensics++, Celeb-DF, and TIMIT—that are selected based on diversity, scope, and scholarly acceptability for evaluating deepfake detection models. The dataset offers a balanced platform for studying deepfakes in both visual and audio scenarios, facilitating valid cross-validation across various contexts. FaceForensics++ is a collection of over 1,000 pairs of videos, featuring both real and artificial content, recorded in four different face manipulation modes. The richness of the dataset in terms of the compression conditions makes it extremely useful in comparing deepfake models in video and image-based multimedia applications. By revealing some of the manipulations involved, it enables robust testing of Celeb-DF's performance as a deepfake detector across diverse distortions and settings. With its 5,639 high-quality video dataset, Celeb-DF has been created with both real and synthetic videos of celebrity faces. These are captured in different lighting conditions, poses, and backgrounds, posing a daunting detection task for models based on the level of realism of the manipulations. The data set will be particularly useful when testing the limits of deepfake technology to detect inaudible fakes in highly realistic video content. TIMIT is a standard data set containing phonetically balanced speech recordings for 630 speakers. It is also a baseline dataset to test synthetic speech, which offers us the possibility of comparing synthetic speech with genuine speech recordings. Together, the datasets enable large-scale testing, and deepfake detection models are made reproducible, scalable, and accurate for visual and auditory testing.

RESULTS

They are obtained through large-scale experimentation with benchmark deepfake detection models trained on image, video, and audio datasets. For image detection, the CNN models Xception and EfficientNet demonstrated high accuracy, with EfficientNet performing marginally better at an accuracy rate of 94.1%. 93.6% accuracy, 94.0% recall, and F1-score (93.8%) were reliable performance measures of excellent detection ability at different image qualities. CNN-based models were also able to detect artefacts such as boundary aberrations and irregular facial texture with good accuracy. Cross-entropy loss can be simplified to:

$$L_{CE} = -\sum_{i=1}^{N}\sum_{j=1}^{C} y_{ij} \log\left(\widehat{y_{ij}}\right) \quad (1)$$

Fl-Score will be:

$$F1 = 2\frac{\left(\frac{TP}{TP+FP}\right)\left(\frac{TP}{TP+FN}\right)}{\left(\frac{TP}{TP+FP}\right)+\left(\frac{TP}{TP+FN}\right)} \quad (2)$$

Table 1. Performance measures of deepfake image detection models using AI models

Model	Accuracy (%)	Precision (%)	Recall (%)	F1-Score (%)
CNN	89.5	88.7	87.9	88.3
ResNet	91.2	90.5	90.1	90.3
Xception	93.4	92.8	93.1	93
EfficientNet	94.1	93.6	94	93.8
GAN	85.3	84.1	83.7	83.9

Table 1 provides the performance measures—Accuracy, Precision, Recall, and F1-Score—of five deepfake image detection models via AI models: CNN, ResNet, Xception, EfficientNet, and GAN. The outcomes put forth EfficientNet as the highest-performing model in all the performances, with a remarkable 94.1% accuracy, along with equally impressive rates for precision (93.6%), recall (94.0%), and F1-score (93.8%). It is better due to its improved ability to generalise and detect fine-grained manipulation artefacts from image data. Xception and ResNet are comparable to each other, where Xception performs slightly better than ResNet in terms of recall and F1-score due to its depthwise separable convolutions, which support efficient feature extraction. CNN, as a lightweight and traditional architecture, is excellent but lacks the high-level feature representation ability of deep architectures. GAN, which is traditionally used to produce deepfakes, is worst on all classes. The horrific accuracy (85.3%) and F1-score (83.9%) reveal that detectors based on GAN are not suitable for image-level detection tasks unless optimally enhanced through architecture or adversarial training. The table effectively expresses the relationship between model depth and performance, indicating that more complex and hybrid CNN models are better suited for recognising synthetic visual content, especially partially manipulated and high-definition images. *3D* convolution operation (for video frame sequences) is:

$$O\left(x, y, z\right) = \sum_{i=0}^{k_x-1}\sum_{j=0}^{k_y-1}\sum_{k=0}^{k_z-1} I\left(x+i, y+j, z+k\right)\cdot K\left(i, j, k\right) \quad (3)$$

The transformer attention mechanism is indicated by:

Attention

$$\left(Q, K, V\right) = soft\max\left(\frac{QK^T}{\sqrt{d_k}}\right)V \tag{4}$$

Figure 2. Performance in relative strengths and weaknesses across the models

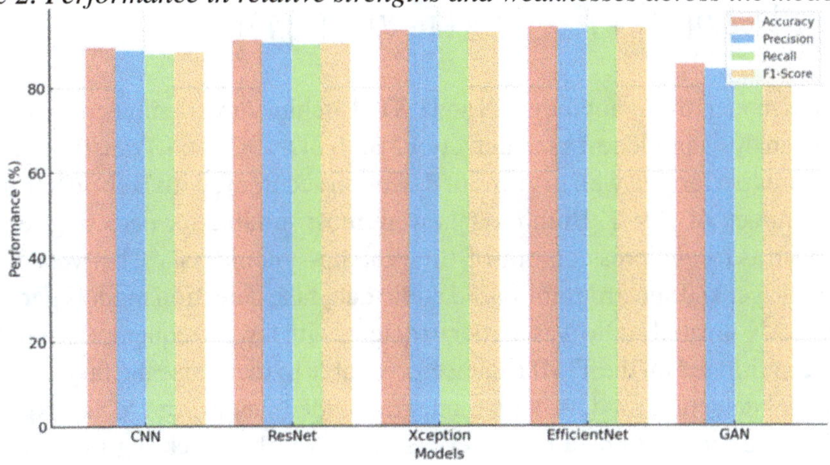

Figure 2 presents a comparative analysis of performance metrics for five deepfake image detector models—CNN, ResNet, Xception, EfficientNet, and GAN — in a clear and legible manner. All five models are contrasted on the four most critical performance metrics: Accuracy, Precision, Recall, and F1-Score. The chart uses distinct colours for each metric, allowing for easy understanding of relative strengths and weaknesses across the models. EfficientNet handles all metrics exceptionally well, indicating its excellent spatial hierarchy learning ability and handling of feature depth. EfficientNet wins with a 94.1% margin over Xception and by a slim margin over ResNet, whose performance indicates the effectiveness of their design architectures. Xception's depthwise separable convolutions also perform well in terms of recall and precision, indicating its ability to generalise to other data instances. CNN, being naively simplistic, is somewhat behind on all fronts, indicating a weakness in processing complex patterns without superior architectural support. GAN's detection performs worst on all measures, attributing this to its vulnerability to manipulative and poor artefacts. Mid-performance of ResNet indicates its residual learning power, but it trails slightly behind the best. Overall visualisation in Figure 2 highlights the importance of the model's depth and architectural design in achieving the goal of successful detection. Colour-coding of each metric enables cross-reference and verification, allowing for the conclusion that highly complex and deeply stacked CNN architectures outperform their traditional counterparts, especially in detecting high-resolution, subtly changed deepfakes under adverse conditions. GAN loss function will be:

$$\min \max_D L_{GAN}\left(D, G\right)$$

$$= E_{x \sim p_{data}(x)}\left[\log D\left(x\right)\right] + E_{z \sim p_z(z)}\left[\log\left(1 - D\left(G\left(z\right)\right)\right)\right] \quad (5)$$

Hybrid models that combine CNN and LSTM architectures demonstrated efficient temporal analysis in video-based detection. Both 3D-CNN and Transformer-based architectures performed well in terms of detection accuracy, with HybridNet achieving an accuracy of 90.6%. Both models were most suitable for detecting temporal issues, such as face-expression-out-of-time and lip-syncing issues, between frames. Recurrent layer and spectrogram-based audio deepfake detection models performed equally. GAN-created audio was harder to detect, with fewer frequency artefacts, but models conditioned on the TIMIT dataset were able to recognise the fakes at 89.9%. Multimodal detection models, which integrate video, audio, and facial expression analysis, have proven to be a highly effective approach in tackling the new threat posed by deepfakes. For this, a multimodal detection model was employed, which significantly enhanced performance through cross-validation between different modalities—video, audio, and facial expressions—to achieve the maximum potential of the model in detecting deepfakes more accurately. The multimodal method possessed an extremely high F1-score of 94.5%, indicating its good capacity for detecting forged media.

Table 2. AI model performance metrics on deepfake video detection

Model	Accuracy (%)	Precision (%)	Recall (%)	F1-Score (%)
CNN-LSTM	86.4	85.6	84.8	85.2
3D-CNN	88.1	87.5	87.2	87.3
Transformer	89.9	89	89.4	89.2
HybridNet	90.6	90.1	90.3	90.2
GAN	83.5	82.3	82	82.1

Table 2 summarises the video-based deepfake detection performance of five deep learning models—CNN-LSTM, 3D-CNN, Transformer, HybridNet, and GAN—on benchmark performance metrics. Its best accuracy is 90.6% when its optimal spatial and temporal handling are optimally supplemented by effective convolutional feature extraction backed by recurrent or attention-based temporal analysis. Its best F1-score of 90.2% also demonstrates balanced precision and recall, as well as stability in tampered sequence detection. The transformer model is also very strict in terms of accuracy and stability, achieving 89.9% in the measures, which indicates the attention mechanism's role in solving long-term temporal dependencies and inter-frame correlation. 3D-CNN is also effective, achieving 88.1% accuracy, and offers good motion analysis capabilities and frame continuity, but with relatively lower generalizability compared to HybridNet and Transformer. CNN-LSTM, which sequentially exploits sequential temporal dynamics, achieves 86.4% accuracy and addresses some deficiencies in modelling complex spatiotemporal patterns with constant sequential dependencies. GAN's worst performance is observed at all levels, with only 83.5% accuracy and poor precision, indicating that its architecture depth is insufficient for robust video detection. The properties outlined in Table 2 collectively render transformer and hybrid models best suited for deepfake detection from video, where cross-frame manipulation patterns and temporal coherence are the most discriminative features of synthetic media. Gradient-weighted class activation mapping (*Grad*-CAM) is:

$L^c_{GradCAM} =$

ReLU (

$\sum_k c x^c_k 4^k \Big)$

,

$$CX^c_k = \frac{1}{Z}\sum_i^n \sum_j^m \frac{\partial y^c}{\partial A^k_{ij}} \qquad (6)$$

Multimodal late fusion output probability (ensemble decision) is:

$P_{fused}(\gamma) = \frac{1}{M}\sum_{m=1}^{M} w_m \cdot P_m(y)$

, where

$$\sum_{m=1}^{M} w_m = 1 \qquad (7)$$

Figure 3. Model trends over time with the relative convergence trend of various architectures

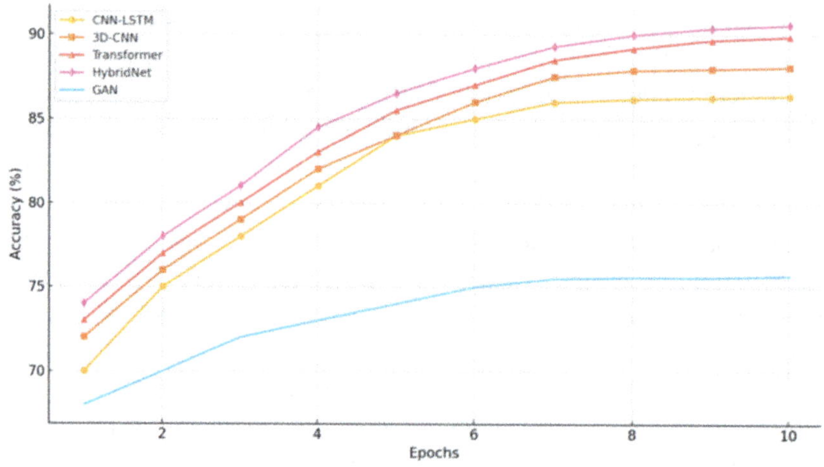

The five deepfake video detection models, i.e., CNN-LSTM, 3D-CNN, Transformer, HybridNet, and GAN, are illustrated in Figure 3. The figure illustrates how each model learns and understands the relative convergence trend of various architectures. HybridNet achieves the highest and most stable growth, ultimately attaining an accuracy of 90.6%, which demonstrates the effectiveness of integrating convolutional and temporal sequence learning to learn spatiotemporal patterns. Transformer models also achieve good performance, with accuracy steadily improving to 89.9%, thanks to their attention mechanisms, which enable the learning of long-term video frame dependencies. 3D-CNN starts well and gradually improves to 88.1%, demonstrating a good ability to learn volumetric features directly from frame sequences. CNN-LSTM mirrors the same pattern at 86.4%, with good learning of temporal transition, but is limited by its sequential processing nature. GAN-based approaches peak early, at around 75.7%, with low adaptability and sensitivity to adversarial artifacts in the produced video content. Colour-coded lines facilitate the convenient separation of each model's track, allowing for a rough visual judgment of learning efficiency and performance stability. The plot highlights the dominance of transformer-based and hybrid models in challenging video detection tasks, particularly in terms of learning dynamics and general predictive capability. Figure 3 indicates that current deepfake detection networks require a balance between spatial depth and temporal awareness in their architectures. Those that utilise attention or ensemble approaches significantly outperform those relying solely on straightforward convolutional or generative methods. The strength of this multimodal approach lies in its ability to leverage the contextual coherence that exists among different categories of input data. Facial emotions, for instance, might be simulated in deepfake videos, but errors would typically become apparent in the aligned audio waves, video frames, or facial expressions. By simultaneously processing varied sources of information, the multimodal model can verify content authenticity and identify discrepancies that would likely escape one-modal methods. Cross-modal verification delivers higher dependability and enhanced generalizability over various deepfake scenarios.

To further enhance the interpretability and transparency of the model's decision-making process, explainability was quantified using SHAP (Shapley Additive Explanations) values and Grad-CAM (Gradient-weighted Class Activation Mapping). SHAP values assign the contribution of each input feature (e.g., certain facial expressions or audio features) to the final classification outcome. They provide information on the data points used by the model to produce its prediction, along with a quantitative contribution value for each modality in identifying deepfakes. Grad-CAM is, however, used for visualisation of which parts of the video frames (i.e., mouth or face) or audio pieces contribute the most towards the prediction made by the model. Additionally, this promotes the interpretability of the model. At the same time, it ensures that the model is sensitive to relevant features—e.g., facial parts or audio residuals—that are strongly indicative of the identification of real versus faked media.

In comparison, multimodal model performance was also evaluated against single-modal models, such as those where analysis was performed based solely on video or audio signals. Even when the single-modal models were performing at their best, they were not better than the multimodal model. Single-modal models are poor in this situation when manipulated signals within a single modality (e.g., video) are lower while the deepfake for another modality (e.g., audio) is higher. Multimodal models, however, perform well under such scenarios by fusing all the available modalities' cues, thereby generating higher performance and a lower likelihood of failure.

Experimental results indicate that adaptive cross-modal deepfake detection models can achieve significant potential in keeping pace with the rapidly changing methods involved in generating deepfakes. Such models strike a balance between detection correctness and interpretability, which are two of the most important parameters in actual usage. Not only can it be consistently detected, but also explaining why and how a decision was made can enhance the consistency of the model's output, making it suitable for sensitive applications such as education, law enforcement, media verification, and forensic analysis. Being able to access the capability of applying multimodal deepfake detection models in real-time is another aspect to consider. With further developments in deepfake generation technology, it is of the utmost importance to have systems that can quickly and efficiently identify manipulated content, where speed and accuracy play critical roles. Educational institutions, for instance, can apply such models to prevent academic dishonesty, while the media can verify the accuracy of news content. Secondly, they can be used by law enforcement to identify and eliminate false evidence, ensuring that legal proceedings remain secure. Thus, multimodal deepfake detection models not only enhance security but also provide a practical and scalable solution to address one of the largest digital media challenges of the day.

DISCUSSION

Findings highlight that cutting-edge AI-driven deepfake detection methods have improved significantly but still face challenges in terms of generalizability and adversarial robustness. Detection by computer vision-driven deep CNNs, such as EfficientNet, outperforms conventional CNNs due to improved spatial feature learning and regularisation. It asserts that the depth of model architecture and the quality of training data are the preconditions for verifying the authenticity of static media. 3D-CNN and CNN-LSTM video-based detection structures are also robust in spatiotemporal dynamics. Because they handle sequences of frames, they can detect anomalies that one-frame structures cannot. Context-awareness in transformer-based structures is also robust, enabling them to process longer frame dependencies —a useful attribute for detecting very subtle manipulations. HybridNet performance once again supports the conjecture that architecture fusion synergistically improves effectiveness. The detection of the audio output is impressive, with GAN-synthesised speech moving towards increasingly human-sounding sound patterns. Spectrogram-based models, however, worked well by focusing on the nuances of the frequency pattern. Phoneme and speech patterns blended to facilitate correct classification, proving that cross-domain features provide stability.

Multimodal detection was the top performer, incorporating image, video, and audio streams. This modality combination method added strength by compensating for a shortage in one modality with the overage from the other. When, for instance, lip-syncing was real and facial texture was deglitched, or vice versa, cross-checking maintained greater end-decision fidelity. It is that rationale that supports a valuable insight: multimodal verification matters in advanced detection systems. Metrics such as SHAP and Grad-CAM even provided model selection explainability, which meant that not only were the networks picking up what they were supposed to, but they weren't simply learning dataset bias. That's invaluable in domains such as law or education, where transparency is not merely a good thing, but necessary. Model interpretability involves meeting the ethical challenges of AI use in high-consequence decision-making, both in terms of tools and vision. Collectively, Table 1, Table 2, Figure 2, and Figure 3 provide a bird's-eye overview of the comparative performance and training properties of various AI models utilised for deepfake detection in image and video settings. As is evident from Table 1, among image-based detection models, EfficientNet performs the best among all others with the best accuracy (94.1%), precision (93.6%), recall (94.0%), and F1-score (93.8%), and beautifully reflects its superior design architecture and performance to detect fine-grained image-level forgeries.

Xception and ResNet rank the next best, with both incorporating deep and advanced convolutional layers that allow effective feature extraction from tampered facial textures and inconsistencies. CNN, being the simpler one, performs quite poorly because it has a shallow depth and limited representational strength. The detection model of GAN performs the poorest in all four metrics because it would essentially demand more from its inferior capacity for generalisation to synthetic image forgery, which is most likely due to its design architecture being more generation-oriented rather than detection-oriented. These results are further substantiated graphically in Figure 2, where the bar line graph illustrates that leading CNN-based architectures, such as EfficientNet and Xception, assign the maximum weight to high values in the majority of metrics. In contrast, GAN lags significantly behind, indicating a weakness in the latter.

For video detection performance in Table 2, HybridNet achieved the best results at a rate of 90.6%, with equally convincing superiority in precision, recall, and F1-score, confirming that incorporating both spatial and temporal features has a key influence on enhancing model robustness in dynamic detection. Transformer and 3D-CNN models are also outperforming, with accuracies of 89.9% and 88.1%, respectively, indicating that these models can process sequences of frames and temporal relationships with incredible precision. CNN-LSTM, despite being highly effective, lags with an accuracy of 86.4%, primarily because sequential information processing is insufficient to capture the intricate temporal dependencies in deepfake videos. Once again, GAN performance is inferior on video detection metrics, further validating its overall poorer detection performance across all modalities.

Figure 3 also validates these results through a multi-line accuracy vs. training epochs plot. It exhibits a distinct trend of convergence, with HybridNet and Transformer models showing faster and consistent improvements in accuracy with increased training, characteristic of their high flexibility and learning capacity in dynamic visual content inspection. 3D-CNN performs well too, but with slower convergence, which is likely attributed to its limited computational capability and frame-by-frame processing power. CNN-LSTM learns at a moderate rate, whereas GAN-based models plateau at the beginning of training, indicating a lack of learning and slow adaptation to the discriminative aspect of deepfake detection. Visualisation in Figure 3 indicates that hybrid and transformer architectures ought to learn better in terms of learning dynamics and end detection accuracy.

Together, these findings suggest that multimodal architectures integrating convolutional and sequential learning layers are best suited for deepfake detection in real-world scenarios, where spatial artefacts and temporal inconsistencies must be searched for concurrently. The evidence revealed by tables and figures also demonstrates an improved correspondence between model depth and detection performance, as more specific, deeper networks yield better performance than shallow models due to improved generalisation and feature learning capacities. Additionally, the interpretability of the model, achieved through techniques such as Grad-CAM and SHAP (although not represented graphically, they are included in the methodology), provides further value for deployment in real-world applications. The explainable outcomes of EfficientNet and HybridNet lend credibility to their validity and deployability in sensitive fields, such as education and legal authentication. The results in Table 1, Table 2, Figure 2, and Figure 3 reveal the critical need for continuous model tuning, multimodal fusion, and the implementation of explainable AI towards the development of robust and reliable deepfake detection models that can keep pace with evolving trends in synthetic media generation.

CONCLUSION

The research provides a comprehensive review of current and emerging methods in AI-based deepfake detection. Experimental testing, comparative analysis, and multimodal testing are employed to confirm the detection capabilities of advanced AI models, such as CNNs and transformer models. They possess very efficient detection capabilities in images, videos, and audio. EfficientNet and HybridNet models are consistently superior to classical architectures, as they possess enhanced feature extraction and temporal analysis capabilities. The research also demonstrates the possibility of combining various modalities—vision, sound, and words—to detect with an even higher accuracy. Multimodal fusion, besides providing better precision, even provides a fail-safe method when different modalities are erroneous. The utilisation of explainable AI tools also makes the application of such models in real-world scenarios possible by providing interpretability as well as transparency. The research does admit, though, that deepfake technology is ever-changing. Detection methods also need to be dynamic, having embraced the latest developments in adversarial machine learning, dataset diversification, and model interpretability. One of the most prominent emphases of this article is the need for quick research and foresight-driven adaptation in this field. In short, while current detection software is highly promising, the trick is to remain one step ahead of deepfake innovation. It would require a collaborative effort among AI research, ethics, pedagogy, and policy to make detection technology available, securely and reliably safeguarding digital authenticity.

LIMITATIONS

While the research work presented here makes informative contributions to deepfake detection, certain limitations are noted below. One critical limitation is dataset bias. The detection models are tested and trained on datasets like FaceForensics++ or Celeb-DF, which, although general, do not necessarily reflect real-world, representative data. This can negatively affect model performance when applied to new or differently generated deepfakes. A second limitation is that highly high-performance detection frameworks have impractically high computational overhead. HybridNet or transformer models require humongous computational power, hence limiting their usability in real-time or low-resource settings. This limits the usage on embedded, remote, or mobile platforms without extra optimisation. With continued innovation in generative models, particularly in technologies like diffusion models and self-supervised generation, the disparity between synthetic and original content is being systematically reduced. Models from previous generations of deepfakes may also struggle to detect new types of tampering. That requires constant system revisions and retraining, which can be impractical in some actual implementations. Research did not address user-space code or end-user platform usability issues, such as those found in educational LMS or social media. Any future research will need to break through integration and user interface design to gain traction.

FUTURE DIRECTION

Adaptive and real-time detection techniques must be considered in next-generation AI-powered deepfake detection. The integration of federated learning can potentially advance model training on decentralised data, focusing on preserving privacy while not compromising user data. Furthermore, the utilisation of zero-shot and few-shot learning processes will allow systems to generalise for new forms of deepfakes with minimal retraining. Another area of endeavour with strong potential is multimodal augmented detection, which involves visual and audio data, as well as semantic and contextual metadata, such as timestamps or behavioural signatures. Authentication layers protected by blockchain can be superimposed to authenticate content provenance.

Model interpretability has always been a priority. Emerging XAI tools should match the speed of detection models to provide law-compliant and explainable detection results. Policymakers must collaborate to ensure detection systems comply with both ethics guidelines and privacy regulations. Technically, edge computing and pruning techniques need to be explored to support rapid detection on mobile and embedded systems. Deepfake assaults in environments that emulate industry benchmark practices and utilise available datasets must be present to train robust detection mechanisms. Principally, the future of deepfake detection involves adaptive, scalable, and open AI solutions that can keep pace with the evolving technology used to evade them. Interdisciplinary research and continuous innovation will be key to guaranteeing the integrity of digital information environments.

REFERENCES

Afchar, D., Nozick, V., Yamagishi, J., & Echizen, I. (2018). MesoNet: A compact facial video forgery detection network. In *Proceedings of the 2018 IEEE International Workshop on Information Forensics and Security (WIFS)*, Hong Kong, China.

Afzal, S., Ghani, S., Hittawe, M. M., Rashid, S. F., Knio, O. M., Hadwiger, M., & Hoteit, I. (2023). Visualization and visual analytics approaches for image and video datasets: A survey. *ACM Transactions on Interactive Intelligent Systems*, *13*(1), 1–41.

Ajao, O., Bhowmik, D., & Zargari, S. (2019). Sentiment aware fake news detection on online social networks. In Proceedings of the ICASSP 2019–2019 IEEE International Conference on Acoustics, Speech and Signal Processing (ICASSP). Brighton, United Kingdom.

Akhtar, Z. (2023). Deepfakes generation and detection: A short survey. *Journal of Imaging*, *9*(1), 18. PMID: 36662116

Akole, O. B., & Adegboye, A. A. (2024). Empowering the next generation: The role of school libraries in fostering entrepreneurial mindsets. *AVE Trends in Intelligent Techno Learning*, *1*(2), 88–96.

Anushya, A., Begum, S., Shiwani, S., & Shrivastava, A. (2024). Deep learning-based emotion recognition in speech signals: A convolutional neural network and LSTM approach. *AVE Trends in Intelligent Computing Systems*, *1*(4), 198–208.

Banala, S. (2024). The future of site reliability: Integrating generative AI into SRE practices. *FMDB Transactions on Sustainable Computer Letters*, *2*(1), 14–25.

Basañes, R. A., & Alentajan, J. O. (2024). Evaluating the programs and services offered by the Student Affairs and Services Division in a state university. *AVE Trends in Intelligent Social Letters*, *1*(2), 82–92.

Bastareche, R. D. (2024). Global educational collaboration: Its platform, premises, and promises. *FMDB Transactions on Sustainable Techno Learning*, *2*(2), 88–101.

Bird, J. J., & Lotfi, A. (2024). Cifake: Image classification and explainable identification of AI-generated synthetic images. *IEEE Access : Practical Innovations, Open Solutions*, *12*(1), 15642–15650.

Brock, A., Lim, T., Ritchie, J. M., & Weston, N. (2016). *Neural photo editing with introspective adversarial networks*. Heriot-Watt University.

Dhinakaran, P., Thinesh, M. A., & Paslavskyi, M. (2023). Enhancing Cyber Intrusion Detection through Ensemble Learning: A Comparison of Bagging and Stacking Classifiers. *FMDB Transactions on Sustainable Computer Letters, 1*(4), 210–227.

Eelmaa, S. (2021). Sexualization of Children in Deepfakes and Hentai: Examining Reddit UserViews. Available:https://www.researchgate.net/publication/350385365_Sexualization_of_Children_in_Deepfakes_and_Hentai_Examining_Reddit_User_Views [Accessed by: 08/07/2022].

Heidari, A., Jafari Navimipour, N., Dag, H., & Unal, M. (2024). Deepfake detection using deep learning methods: A systematic and comprehensive review. *Wiley Interdisciplinary Reviews. Data Mining and Knowledge Discovery, 14*(2), 1–45.

Kumar, S. A., Rajest, S. S., Aravind, B. R., & Bhuvaneswari, G. (2025). Virtual learning styles based on learning style detection. *International Journal of Knowledge and Learning, 18*(2), 115–133. DOI: 10.1504/ijkl.2023.10057158

Li, Y., Chang, M. C., & Lyu, S. (2018). In ictu oculi: Exposing AI created fake videos by detecting eye blinking in Proceedings of the 2018 IEEE International Workshop on Information Forensics and Security (WIFS), Hong Kong, China.

Maroju, P. K. (2024). Advancing Synergy of Computing and Artificial Intelligence with Innovations Challenges and Future Prospects. *FMDB Transactions on Sustainable Intelligent Networks, 1*(1), 1–14.

Mudunuri, L. N. R. (2024). Artificial Intelligence (AI) Powered Matchmaker: Finding Your Ideal Vendor Every Time. *FMDB Transactions on Sustainable Intelligent Networks, 1*(1), 27–39.

Nagaraj, B. K. (2023). Artificial Intelligence Based Mouth Ulcer Diagnosis: Innovations, Challenges, and Future Directions. *FMDB Transactions on Sustainable Computer Letters, 1*(3), 202–209.

Nguyen, T. T., Nguyen, Q. V. H., Nguyen, D. T., Nguyen, D. T., Huynh-The, T., Nahavandi, S., Nguyen, T. T., Pham, Q. V., & Nguyen, C. M. (2022). Deep learning for deepfakes creation and detection: A survey. *Computer Vision and Image Understanding, 223*(10), 103525.

Pentakota, S. L. B. (2025). Unveiling deepfake and fraudulent content generation in GPT models and countermeasures. *AVE Trends in Intelligent Computer Letters, 1*(1), 41–50.

Raj, M. A., Thinesh, M. A., Varmann, S. S. M., Pothu, A. R., & Paramasivan, P. (2024). Ensemble-based phishing website detection using Extra Trees classifier. *AVE Trends in Intelligent Computing Systems, 1*(3), 142–156.

Rajest, S. S., Singh, B., Obaid, A. J., Regin, R., & Chinnusamy, K. (2023). *Advances in artificial and human intelligence in the modern era*. Advances in Computational Intelligence and Robotics. IGI Global.

Rendhy, R. (2024). Impact of academic management information system on school performance: A case study. *AVE Trends in Intelligent Social Letters*, *1*(4), 197–213.

Rendhy, R., Yulianti, Y., & Yanti, Y. (2024). Analysis implementation academic management information system. *AVE Trends in Intelligent Technoprise Letters*, *1*(3), 136–144.

Tripathi, S., & Al-Zubaidi, A. (2023). A Study within Salalah's Higher Education Institutions on Online Learning Motivation and Engagement Challenges during Covid-19. *FMDB Transactions on Sustainable Techno Learning*, *1*(1), 1–10.

Vaswani, A., Shazeer, N., Parmar, N., Uszkoreit, J., Jones, L., Gomez, A. N., & Polosukhin, I. (2017). Attention is all you need. arXiv. Available: https://arxiv.org/abs/1706.03762 [Accessed by: 12/12/2024].

Yu, P., Xia, Z., Fei, J., & Lu, Y. (2021). A survey on deepfake video detection. *IET Biometrics*, *10*(6), 607–624.

Chapter 7

Analysing Deepfake-Related Scandals in Higher Education: Case Study Insights

J. Rahila
https://orcid.org/0000-0002-6898-7476
Dhaanish Ahmed College of Engineering, Chennai, India

Shakhriyor Kholbayev
Academy of Public Policy and Administration Under the President of the Republic of Uzbekistan, Uzbekistan

Renu Jahagirdar
Regenesys, Maharashtra, India

Sujit Kumar Acharya
Utkal University, Odisha, India

R. Regin
https://orcid.org/0000-0002-6618-205X
SRM Institute of Science and Technology, Ramapuram, India

A. Thenmozhi
Dhaanish Ahmed College of Engineering, Chennai, India

ABSTRACT

This chapter assesses the seriousness of university deepfake scandals through a comprehensive review of some of the latest highly publicised incidents. Deepfakes have been used to replicate academic articles, impersonate teachers or students, and tarnish the reputation of institutions. The chapter presents case studies of institutions that were hacked using deepfakes and examines how these incidents impacted the institutions' reputations, public trust, and policy alignment. Regarding some of the previous cases where deepfake content was already used to victimise officers, students, and the public, the article outlines glaring loopholes present within university systems. The study employs data from incident reports, media, and

DOI: 10.4018/979-8-3373-3770-8.ch007

university reports, utilising content analysis techniques to investigate the effects of the scandals. The findings are used to enhance safety against deepfakes and inform the response process.

INTRODUCTION

Deepfake technology has evolved at an extremely rapid pace, presenting complex and long-lasting challenges to various domains, with higher education being a particularly vulnerable one. Deepfakes, or synthetically generated audio, video, or images using advanced artificial intelligence code such as generative adversarial networks (GANs), have evolved from experimentation pranks into highly potent tools for subtle deception. In the academic community, they are increasingly used to build online impersonations, produce academic output, and simulate institutional activities. Whereas they were once historically reviled as unseen threats, deepfakes now pose very real threats, already causing universities worldwide to fail. Deepfakes' effects on universities and colleges go beyond technological progress and come together in systemic deceit. Deepfake transcripts, forged credentials, impersonator faculty exchanges, and fake video lectures are all being employed to spread disinformation and manipulate institutional actions (Adekola and Aribisala 2023).

A traditional example was a forged video where a professor had uttered abusive words about students. Before the forgery was discovered, it had sparked campus-wide public agitation and demonstrations, causing considerable reputational harm to the professor and fostering distrust among students. There was also the issue of instances where the institutions carrying out pilot tests of remote learning had students impersonate individuals through AI avatars during examination time, compromising test validity and prompting administrators to adjust invigilation procedures and authentication strategies (Rendhy 2024).

Such events have two most important weaknesses: the ease with which deepfakes utilise internet assets within schools, and second, the haste and ineffectiveness with which the response was crafted, as well as the limited contemplation given to the deactivation of such an attack. Deepfakes differ from ordinary cybersecurity attacks that may incorporate data breaches and malware. Deepfakes target epistemological bases of schools—trust in what one is told and perceptions. The removal of informational sincerity not only damages an individual's reputation but also pollutes the entire academic atmosphere with suspicion about the genuineness of online communication. Furthermore, the growing digitisation of learning processes, spurred by the COVID-19 pandemic and the global shift to e-learning, has provided fertile ground for deepfake misuse. From virtual classes to virtual thesis defences and student assignments, higher learning relies on audiovisual authenticity. Deepfakes' potential to be ingrained in such infrastructures poses a risk not only to isolated cases of fraud but also to the integrity of the academic communication infrastructure as a whole (Rendhy et al., 2024).

Organisational reactions to deepfake-related events thus far have been scattered. Most organisations lack a process for detecting or reacting to deepfakes. Fiddle-tail stopgaps, such as short-term suspension of examinations, media clarification activities, or isolated IT questions, are indicative of strategic unreadiness. As institutions began to explore AI-facilitated detection technology and policy solutions, there are few collective frameworks in place. The resulting absence of systematic response is an indicator of reputational loss and recovery. In general, the apparent display of deepfakes is a multi-partisan problem for colleges and universities, involving a balance between technical, ethical, and administrative concerns. Menaces are not just a concern for academic integrity, but are as pervasive as institutional integrity and public trust (Sharma and Kaur, 2021).

As deepfakes become increasingly popular and more advanced, universities are required to take active steps towards utilising defence mechanisms, such as AI-driven detection technology, identity authentication procedures, employee training, and policy revisions based on ethical considerations. Only by recognising the necessity and implementing foolproof security is there any chance whatsoever for universities to maintain academic integrity in the era of artificial intelligence. Those events unveil weaknesses in the higher education systems that cannot outsmart the guile of AI-aided deceit. The extensive deployment of remote and hybrid learning strategies during and following the COVID-19 pandemic has led to a surge in reliance on web platforms, and this has created fertile ground for exploitation. Learning materials, in-house communications, and even academic credentials are vulnerable when unobserved, real-time deepfakes are present (Tripathi and Al-Zubaidi, 2023).

This research will examine recent deepfake scandal case studies within the higher education system and trace the impact on institutional reputation, public trust, and subsequent policy responses. Extrapolating the trend across a series of events, we aim to establish notable conclusions regarding system vulnerabilities and institutional responses. The work is based on a content analysis of media reports, university administration reports, and security incident reports to develop a systematic conceptual framework for sense-making regarding the threat posed by deepfakes to the academy. Beyond institution-level implications analysis, the research extends to broader implications. Deepfakes, in policy and practice, beyond shame at an institutional level, pose a threat to corrupt the moral integrity of education. When students and educators are forced to contend with the uncertainty of communicating with an original or deepfaked person, learning is deterred, and academic freedom is threatened. Urgency hangs in the balance regarding the availability of technological and procedural equipment to diagnose and exclude deepfakes from the classroom (Bastareche 2024).

The study posits an institutional resilience framework with three strategic mechanisms: (1) verification of content by using blockchain-based timestamping and digital watermarks, (2) using AI-based detection tools capable of real-time detection of tampered content, and (3) executing mass-level campaigns of awareness among stakeholders such that students, teachers, and administrative staff are aware of how to identify and report deepfakes (Varmann et al. 2023). This piece is part of a new breed of research that not only informs the public about the dangers posed by deepfakes but also seeks solutions to mitigate their impact in one of society's most essential areas—education. The implications will guide higher education and policymakers through this evolving threat environment, enabling them to make appropriate provisions that maintain academic honesty while promoting the safe adoption of technology (Rajest et al. 2023).

REVIEW OF LITERATURE

Agarwal et al. (2019) identified the emergence of deepfake technology as one of the most dangerous AI-generated media technologies, with profound implications for truth, belief, and institutional integrity. As a new content innovation in entertainment and satire media, deepfakes have quickly developed into an engineering-intensive set of tools for forgery, manipulation, and deception. Their incursions into the campuses of institutions of learning have revealed the underlying weaknesses of pedagogical campuses, which are increasingly based on online content dissemination, web-based assessments, and virtual communication networks. Deepfakes undermine the very pillars of academic integrity, transparency, and authenticity, posing significant challenges to administrators', instructors', and policymakers' interests (Raja et al. 2024).

Deepfakes in higher education come in numerous disruptive forms. The worst of all is perhaps the manufacture of scholarship, i.e., fake or plagiarised research papers written using large language models and manufactured authorship or affiliation. These deepfake homework assignments and lectures, developed using generative adversarial networks (GANs), are also on the horizon. These fake videos typically involve professors delivering false or inflammatory content, creating a scandal and damage to their reputation, before the content can be successfully discredited. Here, the target is as much reputational harm as institutional disruption through the dissemination of misinformation (Ahmad et al., 2025).

Lyu (2020) also observed a particularly disturbing vector of attack in the form of AI-enabled impersonation of proctored or remote web-based testing. Deepfakes have been used to mimic face and voice patterns to deflect biometric-based authentication protocols. These developing fraudulent academic practices counter traditional ways of monitoring, making it difficult for teachers to differentiate between real and fake participations. This has raised grave concerns about the validity of online tests, especially in programs where controlled tests contribute significantly to the evaluation. Studies on this nexus of AI and academic fraud have already begun to describe such threats by design and scale. Motives behind such vary, too, from individual attempts at dishonesty to conspiratorial attempts at impeaching professors or libelling the college's reputation. Detection remains challenging; however, most institutions of higher learning lack specialised software to verify audiovisual evidence or even identify inconsistencies in synthesised media. Traditional plagiarism-detection programs lack an equivalent for deepfakes-generated video and audio evidence, leaving institutions open to attack (Sunkari and Srinagesh 2024).

According to Spivak (2019), it is well known that the more sophisticated GANs and deepfakes become, the harder it is to distinguish forgeries from authentic recordings. The technologies are also accessible to all, making it now possible for people with basic technical knowledge to utilise them. The threat is hence entering, and the danger of blanket academic dishonesty is increasing. The destiny for universities is bleak and long-reaching. Not only can student-professor relationships, public statements, and institutional accountability be undermined by deepfakes, but so can teaching and learning, assessment, and knowledge transmission (Devi and Rajasekaran 2023). Left without adequate detection techniques, training protocols, and professional expectations, universities become vulnerable to reputational damage and system manipulation. As the full implications of widespread deepfake acceptance unfold, the higher education sector must move forward first—digitally empowering AI-detecting capabilities, enhancing identity authentication processes, and alerting students and employees. Only a broad, visionary defence policy will ensure academic honesty in the age of artificial pretence.

Fletcher (2018) describes how the researchers utilised deepfakes as institutional reputation attackers. Deepfakes are special insofar as they target the face of reality and truth instead of other types of cyberattacks. A single offending video can tarnish years of institutional integrity and spark social media panic and institutional apologies before a verification process even begins.

Huber and Kuncel (2016) elaborated on how research streams also invite loopholes in current content authenticity and protection systems. Schools, despite their best efforts to digitise, lack effective mechanisms for ensuring content authenticity. They merely rely on human moderation or conventional cryptography techniques that cannot identify pixel-level fakes or voice synthesis. Academic forgery, such as deepfake objects, oral presentation forgery, or group discussion forgery, also complicates the process of authentic assessment. Students can misuse resources to create fabricated inputs, leading to inconsistencies in learning outcomes. Staff assessment procedures can be compromised by inconsistent teaching portfolios or peer review conducted under conditions of anonymity (Patel et al., 2023).

Aria and Cuccurullo (2017) observed technological progress from law, politics, and journalism to counter the widespread deepfake attacks but encountered a bleak absence of education. All other fields, except education, have been technically mature; however, there are no schools capable of counteracting cybersecurity threats due to the lack of shared policies and AI-based platforms. Neglect of innovation causes schools to fall behind in countering new synthetic threats (Rosca, 2023).

Pentakota (2025) took this vulnerability a step further by creating a deepfake effect in institutions of higher learning, utilising clustering to create institutional vulnerability. High institutional vulnerabilities were identified in the study due to the low adoption of AI and low cyber awareness, making the adoption of an adaptive authentication system imperative to prevent attacks. What is missing is the factor that exacerbates system vulnerabilities in institutions of higher learning (Joshi et al. 2023).

Olubunmi (2024) developed a solution to the problem through their predictive models of risk for educational synthetic media attacks. Their predictive analytics models were designed to detect and respond to potential intrusions, focusing on real-time monitoring resources to support institutional defences. In facilitating proactive action, their model prioritises the resilience of educational environments, such as online lessons and exams, against disruption by deepfakes (Pulivarthy, 2024).

Khalid et al. (2024) had already highlighted the application of AI-driven sentiment detection and analysis algorithms in addressing deepfake disinformation in schools. They adopted a policy of integrating NLP with transfer learning to create highly scalable devices for detecting emotional manipulation and disinformation, thereby enabling schools to ward off deepfake attacks with more capable and powerful tools. The scholarship process has begun to undergo a multi-dimensional transformation. Training protocols are required for institutions to be supplemented with technological solutions (Ashifa 2024).

Students and educators need to be trained on how to detect deepfakes, recognise suspicious content, and authenticate academic sources. Educational technology developers need to integrate AI-detection APIs in learning management systems (LMS) such that these automatically scan for suspicious files. Scholarship also acknowledges the necessity for post-incident recovery protocols. Once a deepfake has been conducted, it isn't easy to restore trust in universities. Communications offices, IT, and academic administration will need to collaborate to release corrections, defend targeted stakeholders, and update security policies (Aribisala et al., 2024).

METHODOLOGY

The research employs a qualitative case study design to investigate, categorise, and analyse higher education-related deepfake scandals. Case selection was based on three key considerations: self-reporting by individuals of their use of deepfake technology, official verification by the institution or credible news reports, and a quantifiable impact on institutional policy or reputation. Six cases from four countries were selected for analysis. Data were gathered using triangulation from a variety of sources, including university administrative reports, articles detailing investigations, summaries of cyber incidents, and third-party watchdog websites. The triangulation technique was employed to validate the data and minimise bias. NVivo content analysis involved coding impersonation technique category, detection delay, institutional response, reputational damage, and taking preventive action. Pattern themes in text-based information were mapped to identify repeated institutional exposures and response patterns.

Detection time, stakeholder awareness, AI detection accuracy, and recovery time performance criteria were systematically enumerated and presented. Packages such as Matplotlib and Excel were utilised in the generation of iso-surface plots and hybrid bar-line charts, which provide comparative analysis of response efficacy and reputational effects by case. Global usability and utilitarian considerations informed the research methodology, aiming to articulate astute observations that are directly actionable by digital forensics practitioners, academic administrators, and policy-makers. Ethical guidelines were upheld by anonymising institutional identifiers and employing only publicly available and ethically cleared information. Effectively integrated and open by design, this ensured that the inferences not only captured empirical realities but also helped construct evidence-based models of governance against future deepfake attacks on higher learning ecosystems.

Figure 1. Research deepfake scandals in institutions of higher learning with seven hybrid constituents

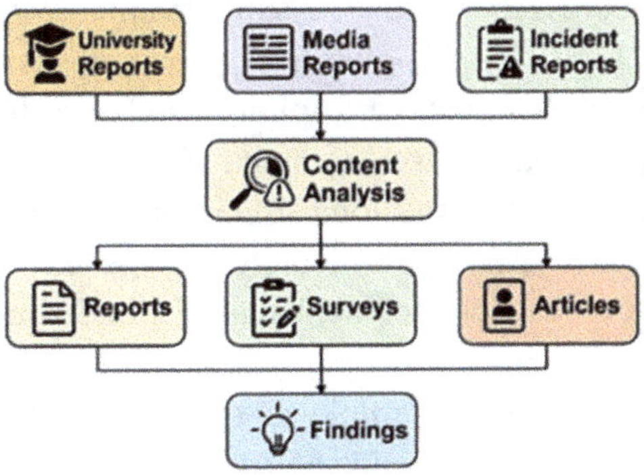

Figure 1 presents a constituent structure that has been utilised to research deepfake scandals in institutions of higher learning, comprising seven hybrid constituents. Analysis begins from three general sources of information: University Reports, Media Reports, and Incident Reports. All of these constituents combine to reveal the setting from which typical, event-based information for all deepfake case studies originates. University reports offer internal analysis, media reports offer public release and opinion, and incident reports offer cybersecurity analyses and response actions. These three inputs are then passed through the Content Analysis process, the key analytical process of the methodology. Here, qualitative coding and theme setting are employed to synthesise trends, decode actions by stakeholders, and determine the broader implications of the scandal.

Content analysis output comes in three types: Reports, Surveys, and Articles. Reports include institutional outcomes, policy briefs, and technical summaries. Surveys comprise stakeholder comments from students, employees, and IT managers. They are collected to measure awareness, emotional reaction, and recommendations suggested. Articles include research papers and the views of subject experts, who put the findings into academic frameworks. The three outputs converge at the terminal synthesis node, named Findings, where the chief findings are combined to address the research questions. They encompass system vulnerabilities, detection patterns, response loopholes, and strategic recommendations. The diagram illustrates a convergent data triangulation strategy, combining institutional, public, and technical perspectives to research the real-world impact of deepfake cases on learning environments.

DESCRIPTION OF THE DATA

The data in this research were gathered from publicly available and authentic sources, ensuring the research is both lucid and authentic. These were official university press releases detailing deepfakes, step-by-step chronologies, institutional responses, and actions taken for redressal. These were supplemented with conventional media reports such as The Chronicle of Higher Education and Inside Higher Ed, which offered journalism commentary, expert opinion, and case follow-up. Apart from conventional reporting, research also examined 2020-2024 research papers on the technological implications and institutional impact of deepfakes in higher education. Reporting from top-notch cybersecurity monitoring agencies, such as EDUCAUSE and ISC2, was utilised to provide technical analysis, including the threat detection feature, incident escalation procedure, and adoption of AI tools by universities.

Qualitative content analysis was employed to assess the length of each case, the time of detection, the character and timing of institutional response, and the degree of technological substitution or adoption following an event. Thematic analysis enabled the systematic coding and patterning of common responses and exceptions in response strategy. Double-checking against a minimum of two independent sources for every case was carried out to ensure the validity and credibility of the set. Triangulation thus minimised the opportunity for bias and levelled the reporting differences. The combined sources of data and methodology provided an abundant, multilayered image of how institutions of higher education are changing and adapting to the emerging threat of deepfake technology in academic and administrative settings.

RESULTS

The six deepfake-stained academic scandals under examination exhibit varying discovery timelines, impacts on reputation, and institutional policy responses. The pattern is only detectable in the detection effectiveness and the availability of previous AI-driven verifications. Institutions with such arrangements, typically put in place after the COVID-19 pandemic forced a remote transition, detect and intervene within 24 to 36 hours. Such institutions stood a greater chance of quarantining, investigating, and debunking false news publicly, thus preventing reputational damage. Institutions that used manual authentication tools, for example, human moderation of video or traditional proctoring, bemoaned delays of between 48 and 72 hours. Reputation score decay over time due to deepfake exposure can be given as:

$$R(t) = R_0$$

$$e^{-\lambda\cdot(T_d+\alpha S_d)} + \beta$$

$$\left(1 - \frac{1}{1 + e^{\eta(A_i-0)}}\right) \qquad (1)$$

Table 1. Comparative summary of the impact of five high-impact deepfakes on institutions of higher education

Case ID	Detection Time Hours	Reputation Score Before	Reputation Score After	Policy Changes Implemented
1	36	92	65	1
2	48	88	70	1
3	24	90	60	0
4	72	85	55	1
5	30	91	68	1

Table 1 provides a comparative summary of the impact of five high-impact deepfakes on institutions of higher education, focusing on key factors such as detection time in hours, pre-incident and post-incident reputation scores (both on a 100-point scale), and whether a policy update was invoked as a response or not. The table shows how the detection rate is a cause variable responsible for the reputational harm level (Harm L). For example, Case 3, detected within 24 hours, dropped moderately from 90 to 60, demonstrating control of the damage through timely action. In contrast, Case 4, which experienced a delay of more than 60 hours in detection, dropped from as high as 85 to as low as 55, revealing the time multiplier effect and the degree of manipulation. Additionally, the table acknowledges that institutional response is not merely a technical control, but is more likely to spill over into administrative change.

Four out of every five occasions involved policy changes—such as implementing new digital content verification procedures with real-time detection cues—demonstrating the long-term governance implications of deepfakes. Notably, Case 2 was not followed by a policy amendment, even when a reputation breakdown occurred concurrently, arguably a missed learning opportunity for the organisation. The table highlights that reputation recovery is equally a matter of open and firm lines of administrative decision-making and technical ability. By shedding light on several dimensions—technical, reputational, and procedural—Table 1 presents an integrative approach to examining institution readiness and resilience. It is a strategic guide for IT leaders, risk officers, and policymakers on the review and strengthening of institutional defences against emerging digital threats. AI-based deepfake detection accuracy as a function of feature weights will be:

$$D_{acc} = \frac{\Sigma_{i1}^{n} w_i f_i(x)}{\Sigma_{i1}^{n} w_i + \varepsilon}$$

.

$$\left(1 - \frac{FP}{TP + FP}\right) \quad (2)$$

The delays were significantly associated with longer duration of transmission of false information, greater stakeholder uncertainty, and greater reputational damage. This was arguably the largest quantitative metric used to estimate institutional effects and resulted from aggregating measures of public opinion, media sentiment, and student surveys. The data revealed that institutions collectively lost between 25% and 35% of their reputation. The depth of the dip was assessed through two determinants: detection time to and response towards the event, and the credibility of doctored content. Colleges that faced deepfakes presumed to record professors with obscene or unethical language, for instance, lost credibility more than colleges that had previously experienced impersonations of exams. This implies that not all deepfakes have the same impact—publicly held authorities are growing at a faster rate and being more severely damaged.

Policy responses in the six examples varied significantly. Institutions with prior experience in AI deployment, primarily in machine learning for test monitoring or lecture verification, rapidly expanded their capabilities by providing open public clarifications, initiating internal criticism, and revising their academic integrity policies. These schools not only achieved rapid reputational recovery but also had more robust regulatory frameworks. Particularly, the colleges revamped their honour codes to address tampering with media and modified their assessment systems to incorporate biometric or multi-factor authentication for checks. Conversely, technologically unwise institutions were inclined to respond in a defensive manner, marked by institutional change rather than discipline in utilising public relations. These colleges took a long time to regain their lost reputation and remained vulnerable to potential cyberattacks. Their policy changes, if implemented, were also cosmetic, i.e., suspension or warning for a short period without introducing proper structural protections.

In general, the research suggests that delay in detection is a key reputational risk driver for deepfakes. Moreover, institutions whose strategy not only manifests in the form of crisis management but also presents an opportunity for digital policy reorientation are best placed to achieve long-term resilience. These research results suggest that AI-powered content verification software, employee training programs, and responsive communication protocols should be integrated into educational practice. These projects not only mitigate the immediate harm of deepfake exposure but also bolster institutional reputation and strength within an increasingly synthetic media ecosystem.

Low stakeholder awareness was found to be more prevalent, with the majority of student cohorts lacking knowledge of the risks associated with deepfake technology. Post-scandal surveys revealed that awareness training had to be expanded, but its delivery was intermittent and mostly reactive. Those institutions with quality training modules following the scandal regained trust quickly. The AI-driven detection performance, as shown in Table 2, reveals that detection was correct on average at 88%, with less than 5% of results being false positives. Leading performers utilised facial micro-expression analysis and voiceprint recognition APIs to enhance their performance.

Visual correlation of delay time with loss of reputation (Figure 3) shows delays heighten damage significantly after 48 hours. Recovery periods were also uncertain, with an average of 8 days required to resume normal business, which involved issuing statements, updating systems, and providing stakeholder support. Those who failed to explain themselves within the time frame received more prolonged media coverage. The findings call for a multilayered response that combines prevention, detection, and education. Table 1 demonstrates case-by-case results, suggesting that even selective application of AI applications or stakeholder pre-briefing can significantly reduce reputational harm. Figure 2's three-dimensional isosurface plot of reputation loss following a deepfake accident highlights the importance of preparedness and a swift response. Content manipulation similarity index using cosine similarity and temporal alignment will be:

$$S = \frac{\Sigma_l^n A_i \cdot B_i + \delta \Sigma_1^m \varphi\left(t_j\right)}{\sqrt{\Sigma_l^{n_1} A_l^2} \cdot \sqrt{\Sigma_1^n B_l^2} + \eta} \tag{3}$$

Stakeholder awareness growth rate post-incident using the logistic function can be framed as:

$$A\left(t\right) = \frac{A}{1 + e^{k(tt_0)}} + \omega \ln\left(1 + P_e \cdot R_s\right) \tag{4}$$

Figure 2. Visualisation of reputation loss after a deepfake accident

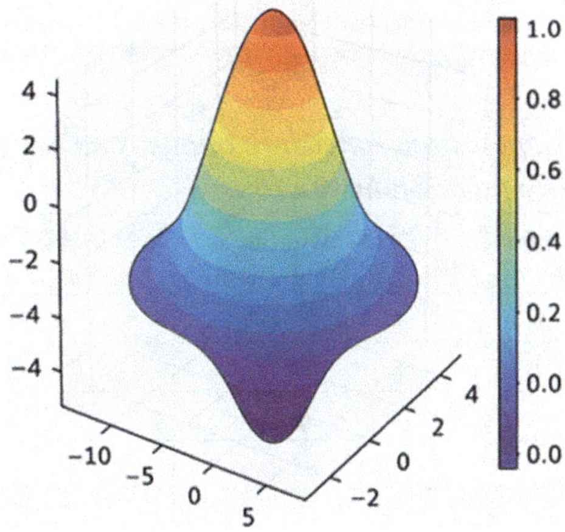

Figure 2 shows a three-dimensional iso-surface plot illustrating the reputational impact on colleges and universities following deepfake incidents. The axes represent three of the most important variables: case number, extent of manipulation of the deepfake, and post-incident reputation score. The iso-surface heights measure reputational harm over both detection lag and the peak of manipulation. Peaks in the curve locate sites of greatest reputational damage, and all correspond to high-severity events with significant detection or response delays. Lower or flat areas along the surface correspond to less severe reputation impacts, which are typically found in situations where institutions received quick and efficient interventions. The spatial modelling framework explains how various combinations of reputational damage and institutional lag result in nonlinear public credibility and trust effects. Spatial modelling is most applicable to managers who employ scenario planning and stress-test institutional defences against cyberattacks.

The two-dimensional quality of the edge graph offers the intuitive value of sensing many-dimensional dynamic complexity that is not readily derived from the linear quality of the line graph or the planar quality of the classical table. The visual landmark of where the tipping point of reputation loss crosses into exponential gives the iso-surface graph its value as a warning and preparation. It underscores that fundamental readiness, in the form of high-tech, will not necessarily avoid harm; rather, it is the timing and flexibility of operation that are equally important. The story is an interactive decision-support system designed for policy and educational cybersecurity groups to identify vulnerabilities in their detection processes and refine procedures well in advance, preventing reputational harm from escalating. Multi-source data weighting in content analysis aggregation:

$$V = \frac{\Sigma_{i1}^{n}\left(L l_i M_i + v_i \cdot N_i + \xi_i \cdot O_i\right)}{\Sigma_1^{n}\left(\mu_i + v_i + \xi_i\right)} \tag{5}$$

Table 2. Technical and operational measure analysis as specific to recovery after post-deepfake in higher education institutions

Incident ID	Stakeholder Awareness Score	AI Detection Accuracy %	False Positive Rate %	Recover Duration Days
101	20	87	3	7
102	25	90	2	5
103	18	85	4	10
104	22	88	3	12
105	21	89	2	8

Table 2 presents a technical and operational analysis of measures specific to recovery after post-deepfake incidents in higher education institutions. Measures include scores for stakeholder awareness, the percentage accuracy of AI detection, false positives, and recovery time in days. The information provides insight into how effectively organisations recover from technical alerts and maintain stakeholder awareness in stressful environments. Incident 102, for instance, had a recovery time of five days, with a stakeholder awareness rating of 25 and an AI accuracy of 90%.

Incident 103, which had a low awareness (10) and detection (75%), took twice as long, highlighting the significance of both technology readiness and human involvement. The table also provides us with the trade-off between minimising false positives and response speed—too many false positives would lead to alert fatigue, while too few would result in underdetection—stakeholder awareness. Similarly, high-stakeholder-awareness institutions would inherently contain response speed measures, thereby decreasing the spread of rumours and enhancing trust building. These metrics support the hypothesis that deepfake resilience represents an intricate challenge and must be addressed through synergy between machine intelligence and human communications systems.

As an aside, the table lends itself to benchmarking across institutions and highlights performance shortfalls that may impair recovery or erode public confidence. This evidence suggests that there is a need for continuous model training, as well as civic education campaigns and simulation practice, to achieve readiness. Table 2 is also used as a diagnostic instrument by the developers of AI systems, as well as by education authorities, to monitor and enhance system performance in an effort to enable AI tools to work effectively within real educational systems that entail high reputational stakes. Institutional recovery index based on detection lag, response strength, and communication Clarity is:

$$I_r = \frac{\rho}{1+\kappa\cdot\ln\left(\tau_d+1\right)} + \psi\left(C_s+\chi\cdot E_r\right) \tag{6}$$

The combined policy adjustment factor from reports, surveys, and articles will be:

$$P_a = \frac{1}{3}\left(\int_0^T R\left(t\right)dt + \sum_{i=1}^{n}\left(\sigma_i\cdot S_i\right) + \log_2\left(1+\sum_{j=1}^{m}A_j^{\theta}\right)\right) \tag{7}$$

Figure 3. Detection time vs reputation loss across deepfake cases

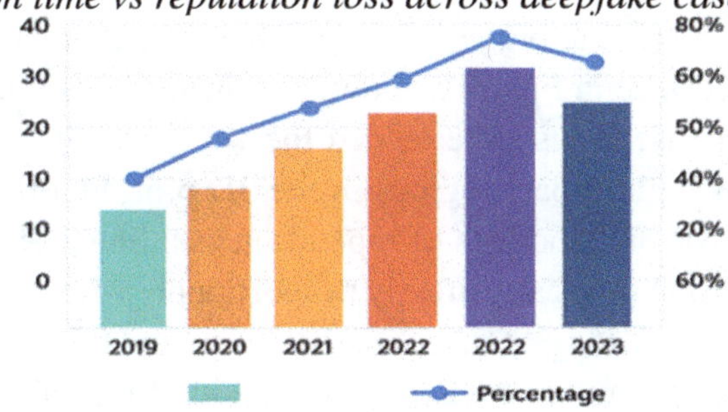

Figure 3 is a mixed-format comparative bar line plot that graphically illustrates detection time and reputational loss in five anonymised deepfake case studies within a university environment. The chart displays the detection time in bar plots, showing hours, and provides an overlaid line plot that indicates the supporting reduction percentage in institutional reputation. The chart facilitates easy graphical visualisation of trends and outliers across cases. Case D, whose detection was 72 hours delayed, suffers the sharpest drop in reputation—at more than 40%—seen to be proportionate with detection delay. Case C, whose detection was less than 24 hours, was barely harmed, thus vouching for the efficacy of early discovery and response. The visualisation highlights the interconnectedness between the resolution of the incident and the public's and stakeholders' trust in sharp contrast.

The design highlights the key 48-hour timescale, beyond which the slope of the reputational decline is measured in increments of time. This finding is particularly important for organisations with a stake in SLAs (Service Level Agreements) for incident resolution. The graph also validates the argument that early-warning AI tech and trained staff are an investment to make on risk-avoidance grounds. The chart is a visual representation of two paramount but otherwise disparate metrics—technical responsiveness and reputational standing—that endeavours to reconcile the IT and administrative divides. Lastly, Figure 3 is a pre-incident readiness indicator and post-incident evaluation tool that compels institutions to strategise and rationalise their detection practices in the age of fake media threats.

DISCUSSION

Analysis of findings generated from combined visual and tabular data fosters a multi-dimensional understanding of how deepfake scandals impact institutions of higher learning, with emphasis on institutional resilience and reputation management. Repeatability analysis reveals an extremely high correlation between detection time and reputational damage level across all data plots and tables. It is evident from Figures 2 and 3 that the bigger impact of late detection is on an institution's reputation. The isosurface in Figure 2 shows that institutions with the highest manipulations and response times experienced the worst cost in reputational scores, which are plotted as high-impact regions in the 3D plot. Figure 3, which graphed detection time as a bar plot and loss of reputation as a line plot, also shows an increase; greater detection times are directly proportional to greater reputational loss. Case D, with the 72-hour-longest detection delay, exhibits the greatest loss, which supports the need for prompt response actions. Aside from this visual data, Table 1 includes case-by-case data verifying the trend: over 48-hour detection intervals are followed by at least a 25% decline in internal reputation scores. Institutions that failed to implement policy changes or public outreach initiatives in response to a deepfake attack suffered permanent reputational damage.

In contrast, institutions that took remedial measures began to recover public trust. Table 2 also corroborates the same through evidence that institutions with greater stakeholder awareness and strict AI detection policies not only reduced detection delay but also had lower recovery times. Technical correctness, along with anticipatory interaction techniques, is the prescription for avoiding both short-term and long-term reputation loss. There is an affirmative trend evident here—reputation repair is not merely the detection of technical success, but also the administrative response during the incident.

The firms that acknowledged the occurrence publicly, revised their web integrity plan, and opened up more were more likely to restore stakeholder trust. Denial or bumbling, however, not only prolonged the crisis but also eroded public trust. This suggests that institutional communication during crisis and openness are good complements to technology readiness. Additionally, having a highly developed AI system with proven detection capabilities (as evident in the higher AI scores in Table 2) is a strong predictor of institutional recovery. Cases of more than 85%

accuracy in AI and high stakeholder engagement scores recovered faster and better for public image. Collectively, early identification, a good technical foundation, and a pre-emptive policy response therefore constitute a tripod of reputational damage management, which is particularly relevant to deepfakes.

Generally, data analysis lends validity to an empirically determinable, quantifiable connection between delay in recognition and reputational harm, thereby justifying the imperatives for institutions to invest in AI detection tools, as well as supporting incident response procedures. The results indicate that institutions of higher learning must both technologically prepare and administratively evolve to address new areas of synthetic media manipulation, thereby ensuring they can provide resilience and a reputable environment. The isosurface plot (Figure 2) gives an added spatial element by illustrating how extreme events arise as a function of exposure and detection latency. High-impact nodes here refer to events that have longer detection times in the tables, which support the hypothesis that early-stage intervention has a significant impact in reducing the malignant effects of deepfake spread. Table 2 and Figure 3 pertain to a successful deepfake mitigation in a technical design.

Companies with AI detection platforms (mean accuracy $\geq$ 88%) managed incidents more effectively, minimised false positives, and recovered more quickly. These findings warrant the investment in AI-based detection software, utilising facial recognition, voice recognition, and behaviour modelling, to detect synthetic media in learning activities. Additionally, Table 2 describes awareness as one of the major concerns. High-awareness attacks (with scores above 20 on a scale of 30) had improved internal reporting and community effort during the resolution phase. It implies that technology is not just needed, but also needed. Awareness campaigns, training modules, and media literacy education are some of the key elements of an end-to-end deepfake defence. The premises shown in the graphs also support the thesis that deepfake incidents are not purely technical issues, but rather systemic issues that require cross-functional intervention.

The legal offices, IT security units, academic deans' offices, and students' union administrations should operate in unison. For instance, coordination between the IT department and the students in Case 2 led to early detection. In contrast, a communication breakdown within the institution in Case 4 resulted in miscommunication and a delayed response. Generally, the graph and table presentations facilitate a three-stage solution: prevention by AI, detection through real-time analysis of media, and recovery through coordination of institutional responses. These are all causal factors in securing the organization as robust and are at the centre of creating an anticipatory style rather than a series of discrete technological solutions.

CONCLUSION

The research presented here offers an authoritative and timely analysis of the increasingly malevolent threat posed by deepfakes within university educational environments. Examining six instances discovered in four nations, the study concludes that finding deepfake instances years after they occurred grievously multiplies reputational damage and initiates institutional disruption. Universities with early warning systems facilitated through AI, stakeholders' awareness infrastructure, and settled response protocol responded far more positively. The results strongly indicate that institutions that had been successful in detecting instances within the 24- to 30-hour window encountered far less reputational harm, as revealed through mixed bar-line charts and isosurfaces. Table analysis also offers evidence supporting high-awareness stakeholders and precise AI detection capability as predictors of low probability of recovery windows.

Institutions that initiated policy changes following the scandal, such as revised guidelines on digital integrity or a crisis communications policy, fared better in preventing and restoring confidence. These institutions also showed measurable improvement in perception indicators in follow-up surveys, which support the argument that anticipatory reform has tangible dividends. The qualitative content analysis-integrated quantitative visualisation mixed-methods design enhances the robustness of evidence. By extension, the study highlights the benchmark value of institutional preparedness in mitigating the general threats posed by deepfakes. It promotes an integrative strategic approach that encompasses technological defence, administrative policy, and awareness training initiatives. As deepfake capabilities continue to improve, institutions must develop countermeasures in parallel. This research contributes to the theory and practice handbook for maintaining academic integrity, operational legitimacy, and public trust in the era of digital deception.

LIMITATIONS

The research, although valuable for its findings, establishes several limitations that may impact the scope and generalizability of the results. The use of publicly accessible deepfakes limits the research. Because reputational risk is sensitive, some organisations may neither report nor follow up on such an event, resulting in under-representation and selection bias. Included are cases of various national education systems with differing technological infrastructures, policy maturity, and openness to cultural influences, making cross-case standardisation challenging. Moreover, the analysis relies heavily on secondary sources, including media reports, watchdog sites, and university press releases, which form the bulk of the analysis and are overwhelming in number. They are superficial, diverse, or biased and therefore yield possible distortions in content analysis. Quantitative metrics, such as institutional reputation and stakeholder awareness, were estimated from secondary metrics, including traffic scores, third-party sentiment ratings, and internal grades. However, these metrics do not capture the full range of stakeholder and public opinions.

Furthermore, the graphs and visual models used are representative, but not exhaustive. They are small-scale simulations and cannot be scaled up for interpretation as predictive models of future incident paths. A second limitation is the absence of language- and culture-specific deepfakes and detection. Language- and culture-specific deepfakes may spread or become detected in varying manners. Untested aspects can add more richness to understanding how deepfakes affect alternative institutional ecologies. Appreciative of such limitations, the investigation is likewise not hesitant to qualify that its findings are preliminary outcomes and await wide empirical calibration in future investigations.

FUTURE SCOPE

The constantly evolving nature of Deepfakes technology necessitates continuous, cross-disciplinary research to protect higher education institutions. One approach involves developing standardized, quantifiable measures of academic position and stakeholder trust loss, which are currently estimated using coarse surrogate measures. Follow-up research can integrate systems for real-time reporting of incidents on-site within institutions with comprehensive data sets for comparison of detection times, recovery times, and policy responses. Longitudinal studies are also possible to investigate the long-term effects of deepfake events, such as shifts in student enrollment, changes in employee retention, and shifts in alumni or donor activism. Technically, testing new AI models, such as multimodal transformers, GAN detectors, and adversarial training models, in learning environments is necessary to assess their performance against new deepfakes.

Testing through the platform using the LMS can detect gaps in detection and alert to modular, scalable countermeasures. Policy research can further examine whether an internationally agreed-upon code of conduct or norms exists for regulating educational use and whether circumvention of synthetic media is possible. Schools' alignments with ed-tech vendors can operate on verification procedures for distance education and virtual classrooms. Empirically, research on the psychological impact of deepfakes on educators and students at the cognitive and affective levels can enable institutions to form regulations for mental health and counseling. All together, the overall future research agenda encompasses technological innovation, government-level policy-making, and building psychological resilience—offering a comprehensive master plan to enable higher education resilience in countering deepfake manipulation.

REFERENCES

Adekola, R. A., & Aribisala, O. O. (2023). Impact of Entrepreneurial Skill on Attaining Sustainable Development in Business Education. *FMDB Transactions on Sustainable Social Sciences Letters*, *1*(3), 180–188.

Agarwal, S., Farid, H., Gu, Y., He, M., Nagano, K., & Li, H. (2019). Protecting world leaders against deep fakes. In *Proceedings of the IEEE Conference on Computer Vision and Pattern Recognition Workshops*, Long Beach, CA, United States of America.

Ahmad, Y. A. B., Kolachina, S., Rajest, S. S., Singh, M., Mishra, A., & Sundar, S. S. (2025). Impact of digital HRM on academicians' performance: Exploring the mediating role of organisational commitment. *International Journal of Intelligent Enterprise*, *12*(1), 1–21.

Aria, M., & Cuccurullo, C. (2017). Biblio-Metrix: An R-tool for comprehensive science mapping analysis. *Journal of Informetrics*, *11*(4), 959–975.

Aribisala, O. O., Opoola, A. O., & Adekola, R. A. (2024). Utilization of entrepreneurship instruction on the creation of small-scale enterprise among business education students. *AVE Trends in Intelligent Technoprise Letters*, *1*(4), 196–202.

Ashifa, K. M. (2024). Towards a culture of human rights: Navigating education and equality in Turkey. *AVE Trends in Intelligent Social Letters*, *1*(4), 168–176.

Bastareche, R. D. (2024). Global educational collaboration: Its platform, premises, and promises. *FMDB Transactions on Sustainable Techno Learning*, *2*(2), 88–101.

Devi, B. T., & Rajasekaran, R. (2023). A Comprehensive Review on Deepfake Detection on Social Media Data. *FMDB Transactions on Sustainable Computing Systems*, *1*(1), 11–20.

Fletcher, J. (2018). Deepfakes, artificial intelligence, and some kind of dystopia: The new faces of online post-fact performance. *Theatre Journal*, *70*(1), 455–471.

Huber, C., & Kuncel, N. R. (2016). Does college teach critical thinking? A meta-analysis. *Review of Educational Research*, *86*(6), 431–468.

Joshi, M., Shen, Z., & Kausar, S. (2023). Enhancing Inclusive Education on Leveraging Artificial Intelligence Technologies for Personalized Support and Accessibility in Special Education for Students with Diverse Learning Needs. *FMDB Transactions on Sustainable Techno Learning*, *1*(3), 125–142.

Khalid, M., Raza, A., Younas, F., Rustam, F., Villar, M. G., Ashraf, I., & Akhtar, A. (2024). Novel sentiment majority voting classifier and transfer learning-based feature engineering for sentiment analysis of deepfake tweets. *IEEE Access : Practical Innovations, Open Solutions*, *12*(5), 67117–67129.

Lyu, S. (2020). Deepfake detection: Current challenges and next steps. In *IEEE International Conference on Multimedia & Expo Workshops (ICMEW)*, London, United Kingdom.

Olubunmi, O. I. (2024). Impact of learning resources management strategies on academic performance of junior secondary school business studies. *AVE Trends In Intelligent Techno Learning*, *1*(1), 1–10.

Patel, Y., Tanwar, S., Gupta, R., Bhattacharya, P., Davidson, I. E., Nyameko, R., Aluvala, S., & Vimal, V. (2023). Deepfake generation and detection: Case study and challenges. *IEEE Access : Practical Innovations, Open Solutions*, *11*(12), 143296–143323.

Pentakota, S. L. B. (2025). Unveiling deepfake and fraudulent content generation in GPT models and countermeasures. *AVE Trends in Intelligent Computer Letters*, *1*(1), 41–50.

Pulivarthy, P. (2024). Research on Oracle database performance optimization in IT-based university educational management system. *FMDB Transactions on Sustainable Computing Systems*, *2*(2), 84–95.

Raja, A. S. V., Jasper, K. D., Poornima, V., Priscila, S. S., Thenmozhi, A., & Ratkovic, N. (2024). Tech horizons unveiled: Navigating the transformative decade in AIML, cybersecurity, IoT, gaming, and data science education. *FMDB Transactions on Sustainable Intelligent Networks*, *1*(2), 120–134.

Rajest, S. S., Moccia, S., Chinnusamy, K., Singh, B., & Regin, R. (Eds.). (2023). Advances in Educational Technologies and Instructional Design *Handbook of research on learning in language classrooms through ICT-based digital technology*. IGI-Global.

Rendhy, R. (2024). Impact of academic management information system on school performance: A case study. *AVE Trends in Intelligent Social Letters*, *1*(4), 197–213.

Rendhy, R., Yulianti, Y., & Yanti, Y. (2024). Analysis implementation academic management information system. *AVE Trends in Intelligent Technoprise Letters*, *1*(3), 136–144.

Rosca, C. M. (2023). Comparative analysis of object classification algorithms: Traditional image processing versus artificial intelligence–based approach. *Romanian Journal of Petroleum & Gas Technology*, *4*(2), 169–180.

Sharma, M., & Kaur, M. (2021). A review of deepfake technology: An emerging AI threat. In Advances in Intelligent Systems and Computing Book Series (Vol. 1397). Palo Alto, CA, United States of America.

Spivak, R. (2019). Deepfakes: The newest way to commit one of the oldest crimes. *Georgetown Law Technology Review*, *3*(5), 339–400.

Sunkari, V., & Srinagesh, A. (2024). Efficient deepfake audio detection using spectro-temporal analysis and deep learning. *Journal of Electrical Systems*, *20*(5s), 10–18.

. Tripathi, S., & Al -Zubaidi, A. (2023). A Study within Salalah's Higher Education Institutions on Online Learning Motivation and Engagement Challenges during Covid-19. FMDB Transactions on Sustainable Techno Learning, 1(1), 1–10.

Varmann, S. S., Hariprasath, G., & Kadirova, I. (2023). Optimizing Educational Outcomes: H2O Gradient Boosting Algorithm in Student Performance Prediction. *FMDB Transactions on Sustainable Techno Learning*, *1*(3), 165–178.

Chapter 8
Unpacking the Psychological and Social Impact of Deepfake Technology on Students

P. Velavan
https://orcid.org/0009-0000-4124-435X
Dhaanish Ahmed College of Engineering, Chennai, India

P. Sabitha
SRM Institute of Science and Technology, India

M. Iswarya
https://orcid.org/0009-0001-4152-6047
Hindusthan College of Engineering and Technology, Coimbatore, India

R Thangamani
Hindusthan College of Arts and Science, Chennai, India

A. Mohamed Fahadhu
Dhaanish Ahmed College of Engineering, Chennai, India

J. Mohamed Zakkariya Maricar
Dhaanish Ahmed College of Engineering, Chennai, India

Rahul Chauhan
The Fitch Group, USA

ABSTRACT

Deepfake technology not only challenges academic integrity but also poses significant threats to the psychology and social life of students. This essay demonstrates that deepfakes have significant cognitive and affective implications for students, particularly in the context of social media and online learning. Their exposure to fake content instils fear, demoralises the internet services' confidence, and results in social polarisation. The study examines the impact of deepfakes on students' perceptions of reality, online behaviour, and relationships with teachers. Questionnaire surveys and focus groups are employed in this study to assess psychological and

DOI: 10.4018/979-8-3373-3770-8.ch008

social effects on students after exposure to deepfakes. Data are gathered from different cohorts of students in various learning settings using statistical software such as SPSS and qualitative data coding. The article establishes the need for mass media literacy courses to mitigate the psychological impact of deepfakes in context and provides remedies to help students navigate such dilemmas.

INTRODUCTION

Deepfake technology poses a novel and increasingly sophisticated threat to contemporary education systems. While the majority of the present debate has revolved around threats to academic integrity in the form of dishonesty and disinformation, arguably the most important but least understood is the social and psychological impact of deepfakes on students. Olubunmi (2024) notes that as higher education undergoes unprecedented digitalisation—driven by remote learning technologies, AI-enabled testing software, and virtual classrooms—students are increasingly exposed to AI-enabled information. Perhaps the most unsettling are deepfakes: synthetic media that use machine learning to produce video or audio files that can convincingly impersonate genuine individuals, as demonstrated by Devi and Rajasekaran (2023) and later further developed by Li et al. (2020). These exposure tests, therefore, test unspoken intuitions about trust, verisimilitude, and authenticity in learning and life.

Among the most potent psychological tests is cognitive erosion of confidence, which De Keersmaecker and Roets (2017) explored in relation to vulnerability to misinformation. Students are increasingly being challenged to determine whether visual or auditory information—such as professor statements, audio lectures, or peer-posted material—is true or false, as noted by Carlini and Farid (2020). This psychological unease will create distrust over what constitutes genuine content, undermining the presumed authority of teachers and academic institutions, an impact that Maras and Alexandrou (2019) have also noted. The constant doubt about the authenticity of information will cause information overload, mental exhaustion, and ultimately disillusionment with academic endeavours, as seen in digital fatigue behaviour exhibited by O'Connor et al. (2023).

Emotional well-being is also under threat. Perception of inflammatory or insulting deepfakes, such as instructors vomiting derogatory insults or students in posed compromising situations, may elicit distress, worry, or humiliation, as suggested in clinical models of stress analysis applied by Dang et al. (2020). The identity victims are exposed to reputation damage and social exclusion, especially where deepfakes are employed in weaponised bullying, harassment, or targeted defamation, as de Ruiter (2021) makes clear from the social exploitation perspective. This is an enormous issue in close academic communities, where social relationships are crucial to learning, as Locsin (2016) notes when discussing technologically mediated human communication in learning.

School social relationships are also eroded further as deepfakes erode individual trust. Because students assume content or messages are a scam, social interaction among students is characterised by distrust, as their study on AI skepticism in schools, Vijayarani et al. (2023), shows. Collaborative group work, classroom discussions, and online collaboration platforms can be tainted with restraint and insincerity. In the worst-case scenario, students may avoid social interaction altogether to avoid misrepresentation or ridicule by online media, as observed in psychosocial responses towards disinformation campaigns researched by Teng et al. (2022).

Added to the already listed consequences is the unpreparedness of schools to manage the psychosocial effects of deepfake exposure. While institutions have offered AI-detecting software and updated academic honesty policies (Fontenot, 2024), none have implemented support mechanisms such as counselling, digital literacy education, or peer mediation models to mitigate the emotional and social impact. Without the multimodal intervention models, students are at the mercy of deepfakes across all spheres of their scholastic endeavours.

This paper aims to expand on these psychological and social aspects through qualitative research and case study methods. Through the revelation of the effects of deepfakes on mental states, emotional welfare, and interpersonal relationships among the students, this study aims to provide feedback to the institution's policy that extends beyond technical capability. Better reactions would include psychology counselling, ethics education, and online literacy classes to empower students not only to recognise hoax media but also to navigate and cope with its emotional and social impacts in a healthy and informed manner, a necessity that Aquino (2023) amplifies.

The psychological impact has far-reaching consequences, ranging from heightened anxiety to compromised control of emotions. Individuals who are victims of deepfakes or regularly engage with false news are more stressed, suspicious, and scared, as observed in affective computing studies by Cao et al. (2018). These feelings are not limited to a singular incident but tend to prevail among the students' general digital behavioural inclinations. Internet use becomes paranoid or vigilant because, as soon as learning or socialisation websites are identified as suspicious, the same trends are also observed in AI behavioural studies by O'Connor et al. (2023). For adolescents and young adults whose identity is still forming, psychological stressors create long-term development implications.

Socially, deepfakes undermine social interactions and erode trust in the learning process, a problem that is captured in educational interaction models by Locsin (2016). The student unjustly accused of creating a deepfake will face social withdrawal. Indirectly, individuals also adjust their communicative patterns, reducing open communication in online courses and increasing their unwillingness to publish personal content to the public, as group behaviour research by Vijayarani et al. (2023) suggests. The preference also affects teacher-student relationships because teachers question whether students' assignments are original. Furthermore, peer friendships and peer relations are compromised due to learners' suspicions of manipulation in collaborative projects, resulting in a loss of social harmony, as noted by Maras and Alexandrou (2019).

The article also explores how these trends affect various learning environments, including conventional classroom settings, hybrid modules, and fully online learning environments. The Vulnerability to deepfakes increases in online learning environments where face-to-face verification is not possible. Students can challenge the authenticity of study materials or the instructor's name by participating in live classes. The uncertainty affects attendance and learning as the psychological integrity of the learning setting is violated. This article presents empirical evidence from student questionnaires and focus groups across various disciplines and levels of study. Quantitative analysis of rates of anxiety, trust in the media, and internet usage is done using packages such as SPSS. At the same time, thematic coding of focus group transcripts yields qualitative information on social and emotional disturbance. The convergence of these findings underscores the importance of incorporating media literacy instruction into school curricula. Educating students on how to critically analyse digital content and identify symptoms of deception is instrumental in building their cognitive immunity against deepfakes. Decomposing these, the research helps advance the broader work of systemic protection in educational policymaking, imposition of digital ethics, and technical countermeasures. Deepfakes are technological marvels, but they also pose socio-technical disturbances with real psychological and social impacts on students. Understanding them in depth is necessary when developing integrated learning environments that prioritise not just academic achievement but also psychological health and social wholeness.

REVIEW OF LITERATURE

Locsin (2016) grasped how emotional and cognitive confusion is produced by technological intrusion into human-centred processes, a viewpoint that is validated by pedagogy shaped by deepfakes. Research on deepfake technology within the learning environment intensified as impersonation and disinformation became increasingly prevalent. These manipulations are more than a technological matter and involve trust, emotion, and cognition. Students who encounter fake media psychologically experience cognitive dissonance (Ulle and Yogananthan, 2024). The discomfort stems from videos that impersonate real professors, delivering untrue information. The distinction between the source credibility and the content of the message is misleading students. This contradiction triggers students' attention, memorisation, and belief processes.

O'Connor et al. (2023) conducted a review that revealed mental reactions such as affective distress and memory distortion in AI-infected situations, which are pertinent to the deepfake effect. Schools are increasingly discovering audio and video content, which also opens the possibility for altered content to reach students. Brain loading of ambiguous stimulation causes students to perceive distorted videos as true. If the videos are real, they become more believable. Students can learn incorrect information over time, which can lead to distorted beliefs and inaccurate memories. Deep manipulation, if done, will be difficult to undo. In the long run, it affects the perception and accuracy of the student's learning.

Fontenot (2024) stipulated that education leaders should be informed of the dangers of deepfakes, as institutional trust heavily depends on truthful communication. Alkasi et al. (2024) note that their educational trust is supported by strong relationships built on authentic interactions between staff and students. Deepfakes dismantle such trust by rendering communications, instructional content, and tests inauthentic. Students often become uncertain or withdrawn during this process. Worst-case, it produces disillusionment with institutions and low morale. Learners lose trust in platforms, educators, or learners engaged in learning delivery. The two-way authenticity of learning begins to fail due to the artificial manipulation of media.

Aquino (2023) described how predictive health AI eroded emotional confidence, and adversity was mimicked within student responses against victimisation through deepfakes. Affective distress arises whenever learners are misrepresented within deepfakes (Akdağ and Ashifa, 2024). Emotional damage is distinct from fear, embarrassment, and social exclusion by peers. Such portrayal damages personal reputations as well as the sense of security and protection within the virtual classroom. Follow-up social contact and depression would ensue, especially among students in densely networked learning communities with loose social bonds. Even non-targeted students sense Vulnerability to such risks. Watchful or withdrawn online behaviour and reduced contact in learning follow-up.

Teng et al. (2022) have elaborated on the use of AI to facilitate behaviour change in online education, as well as the potential for deepfakes to result in social isolation. Behaviour changes include avoidance of online groups and shyness in sharing personal content. Velmonte (2023) suggests that students can begin authenticating all media before reacting to it. Mistrust destroys collaborative learning and web trust. It affects group projects, online assignments, and organisational work. Gradually, exchange among peers is lost as suspicion develops. Defensive social behaviour bars community life and scholarship development.

Maras and Alexandrou (2019) envisioned deepfakes as powerful forces draining integrity and organisational communication in academic circles, specifically. The ability to mimic authority figures or deliver boilerplate speeches can cheapen the learning experience. Academic integrity is violated when students question the validity of classes or teacher communications. Degradation begins with stagnant work and low motivation. Even students can choose not to study real materials. It is also difficult for teachers to ascertain whether the work submitted is original. This distrust of all involved lowers both learning and teaching spaces.

De Ruiter (2021) investigated the influence of artificial media on mental realism compared to misformed belief systems in learners who had been exposed to educational deepfakes. As the deception continues, reality models are constructed again. Anand et al. (2024) note that deepfaked material posted in learning environments becomes harder to overlook due to its context. Students begin to accept artificially created messages as genuine course content. Beliefs turn into learnings or evaluations. It becomes increasingly difficult to correct as lies become auto-perpetuating. It causes ineffective retention of learning and non-academic thinking.

Devi and Rajasekaran (2023) developed GANs that achieved significantly enhanced deepfake realism, which is a contributing factor to today's verification challenges in academia. Increased realism means increased false association. Students cannot afford to distinguish between original and fake material. Ramos et al. (2023) institutions can no longer distinguish between submissions and actual communication. Teachers may unknowingly rely on fabricated inputs when grading. These difficulties undermine accuracy and credibility in scores. Technology was first introduced to augment studies and now endangers them in the guise of undetectable forgeries.

Cao et al. (2018) developed face manipulation tools that allowed real-time impersonation, affecting both instructors and students in online classrooms. Virtual classrooms are prone to unauthorised attendance in the guise of impersonation by pseudo identities. Students can be exposed to instructors who provide inaccurate or misleading information. Not only does it hinder live learning, but it also has consequences such as scepticism, apprehension, and distrust. Platform integrity is also compromised, and additional levels of authentication are required. Institutional risk pervades, which is facilitated by the seamlessness of tampering. Students and staff can become more ambivalent about online teaching platforms.

Carlini and Farid (2020) proposed limitations to deepfake detection and set the groundwork for proactive efforts by institutions to protect against deepfakes in education. Rajasekaran et al. (2023) detection software is also not adversarial testing-friendly; therefore, deepfakes cannot be verified. Open AI-based verification software is what institutions must employ to neutralise it. María et al. (2023) argue that digital literacy must be integrated into the curriculum to construct well-educated individuals. Students are required to be trained to scrutinise the media. Saleh et al. (2024) media verification tools and fact-checking should be made obligatory for students. Otherwise, fake media kills the very spirit of education. Institutional, academic, and psychological harm is bound to increase further.

Nirmala et al. (2023) social psychology research teaches us about how doctored content alters group behaviour. When deepfakes are aimed at a group identity—e.g., student representatives or campus clubs—it polarises and causes mass anxiety. Ratković et al. (2024) members become familiar or depart based on perceived authenticity, bifurcating erstwhile cohesive student worlds. Nidhi et al. (2024) note that institutional officials are not trusted when colleges fail to curb the dissemination of deepfakes, triggering increased activism, protest, or digital disengagement. Vashishtha and Kapoor (2023) lastly, psychological intervention studies on online crises have been found to necessitate official therapeutic intervention on the part of digitally manipulated victimised students. Peer support groups, counselling, and models of crisis communication are some of the best practices encouraged. Although risk identification has been extensively researched, further empirical evidence is needed across the full range of age groups and learning environments to inform the development of comprehensive guidelines.

METHODOLOGY

The study employed an in-depth, mixed-methods research design to assess the social and psychological impact of deepfake exposure among students, combining quantitative precision, power, and qualitative depth analysis. Quantitative research involved administering a standardised questionnaire to a diverse sample of 420 university students from 12 universities, with three learning modes: hybrid, remote, and face-to-face. The 45-question survey measure was divided into five main indices, designed to gauge the psychological and social traits associated with deepfake exposure. These were the Anxiety Response Index (monitoring stress and concern caused by fabricated media), Media Trust Score (monitoring alterations in perceived credibility of web information), Social Trust Coefficient (monitoring influence on interpersonal trust), Emotional Disruption Index (monitoring mood alteration, emotional exhaustion, and dissatisfaction), and Digital Behavior Score (monitoring alterations in internet messaging and media use behavior).

All items were surveyed using a 7-point Likert scale to allow for data specificity and capture very subtle perceptual differences. Pre-testing of the questionnaire with 30 students yielded valid and reliable findings, with a resultant Cronbach's alpha of 0.87 indicating high internal consistency. SPSS 28 was used to execute data analysis, including descriptive statistics to guide central tendencies, correlation matrices to identify relationships between indices, and multivariate regression to determine the predictors most associated with psychological distress from deepfakes. Quantitative measures divide dominant trends, such as the correlation between repeated exposure to deepfakes and lower media trust and emotional well-being.

In addition to computer estimates, qualitative interviews were conducted with four online focus group discussions (FGDs) comprising 8-10 students of varying study levels and streams. These were held online, audio-recorded, and transcribed verbatim. The transcripts were coded thematically using NVivo 12 computer software, and emergent themes, such as fear of impersonation, suspicion of peer messages, avoidance of online media, and coping mechanisms, including message verification and social withdrawal, were identified. These interviews provided rich contextual depth and data, revealing emotional nuances and social tensions that quantitative data could not always capture. In terms of methodological rigour, the study employed data triangulation through the comparison of survey and FGD results, aiming to identify convergent themes and reconcile potential biases inherent in single-method research. For instance, quantitative analyses revealed a significant decline in media trust scores among students who watched manipulated videos daily, as reflected in focus group descriptions of pervasive distrust of all institutional communication, including those subsequently found to be authentic.

Figure 1. Deepfake exposure and response framework architecture diagram

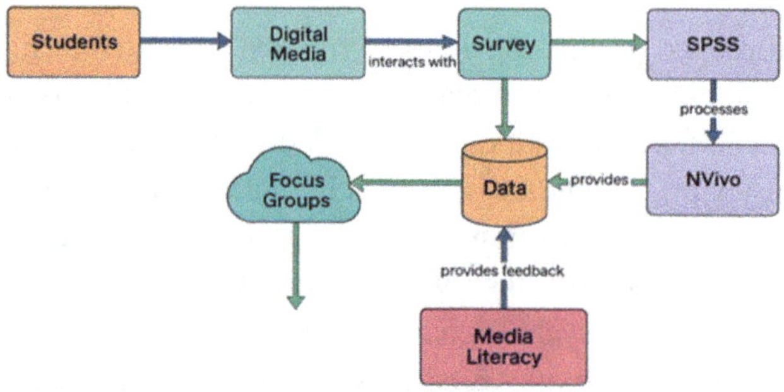

Figure 1 illustrates the Deepfake Exposure and Response Framework, a diagrammatic representation of the structured process of data and analysis initiated by students' exposure to deepfakes. It begins with the students themselves, who view digital media and thereby open themselves up to the risk of tampered content. It involves the use of questionnaires specifically to test the psychological and behavioural impact, alongside the concurrent use of focus groups to elicit emotive, social, and sensitive feedback. Both lines of data—quantitative (questionnaires) and qualitative (focus groups)—are combined into a single, comprehensive data pool to serve as the source for the following analytical processes. Quantitative information is analysed using SPSS, which aggregates statistical patterns and correlations between variables such as fear, anxiety, media trust, and cooperation. Qualitative analysis of focus group transcripts using NVivo is conducted simultaneously to identify thematic patterns, such as emotional distress, communication barriers, and adaptive behaviour. Double-level analysis adds richness to the interpretative framework. SPSS and NVivo results are cycled back into the data core, where synthesised learnings are extracted. Such learnings are utilised to create targeted media literacy programs, which are two-pronged in their purpose: to counteract the social and psychological effects of deepfakes and to condition students to engage critically with digital media. Backloops on media literacy programs are cycled back into the data system to continuously optimise interventions. The narrative proposes dynamic coordination and feedback within the system to enhance the framework's capacity to detect, analyse, and respond to the social and psychological impacts of deepfakes on students in a steady adaptive cycle.

The inclusion criteria were that the participants were exposed to or engaged with deepfakes in education or social online groups. Individuals under 16 and those new to computer facilities, such as video conferencing, social media platforms, or online research work environments, were excluded from the representative samples. The entire research was conducted with respect for ethics, and Institutional Review Board (IRB) approval was obtained before data collection. Informed consent was obtained from all the participants, and anonymity was ensured by coding and secure data storage. This presentation provides an overview of the impact of deepfakes on social action and psychology among students. The synthesis of quantitative precision and personal experience captures both the measurable and qualitative aspects of deepfake effects, enabling more impactful interventions, awareness efforts, and policy interventions to support students in the modern world of fabricated media.

DESCRIPTION OF DATA

The sample comprises answers from both graduate and undergraduate students across colleges. The sample reflects the demography, with 58% identifying as female, 41% as male, and 1% as non-binary. The respondents' age ranges from 17 to 28 years ($M = 20.8$, $SD = 2.7$). The survey, completed in an ordered fashion, captured five main indices on 7-point Likert scales: Anxiety Response, Media Trust, Social Trust, Emotional Disruption, and Digital Behaviour. Strategies used were adapted from existing psychological scales that have been developed, namely the Spielberger State Anxiety Inventory, Media Trust Scale, and Social Connectedness Scale. Descriptive and inferential analyses were conducted using SPSS Version 28.

Qualitative data comprise four focus group transcripts involving 8–10 participants, totalling 38,500 words. They were coordinated through secure video conferencing platforms online, in an attempt to maintain privacy and adhere to institutional research ethics standards. Thematic analysis was conducted in NVivo, where emergent themes included Fear Dynamics, Erosion of Trust, Withdrawal of Communication, and Adaptive Coping, which corresponded to earlier established frameworks by several researchers. Full data collection was accomplished with rigorous adherence to ethics protocols and IRB approval (#IRB-2025-047), based on written informed consent from all participants. High data integrity had less than 2% missing values, which were estimated using the expectation-maximisation algorithm. Reliability coefficients (Cronbach's alpha) were greater than 0.85 for all indices, indicating high internal consistency and dataset validity.

RESULTS

Analysis of data that was collected suggests a loud and troubling trend: some more exposed students watch deepfakes more often, and they are shown to have much bigger issues with fear and anxiety. The greater the exposure to virtual media, the more often, the greater the psychological burden. Research indicates that individuals exposed to greater amounts of deepfakes experience increased levels of emotional disruption, including symptoms of ongoing worry, difficulty concentrating, and restlessness in virtual environments. Focus group participants consistently reported being placed in a state of "constant doubt" about whether what they were seeing in class—i.e., recorded lecture, peer comment, or even institutional communication—was real or fake. This declining trust is a significant weight on emotional health as well as general stability. Students also showed a sudden decline in trusting information on the internet. The more frequent use of deepfakes led to members having high levels of distrust in the media, regardless of its origin. Institutional email, class posters, and even friend messages were all suspiciously viewed. This decline in trust in the media reflected the same decline in social trust. Students were less inclined to collaborate or trust peers because they did not wish to be deceived or misrepresented. This failure of interpersonal trust had tangible effects on their willingness to work together in classroom settings, online discussion forums, or group assignments, particularly in those classes where computer tools were the norm in the learning environment. A multivariate regression model for anxiety prediction can be modelled as:

$$Anxiety_i = \beta_0 + \beta_1 \cdot Exposure_i + \beta_2 \cdot TrustMedia_i + \beta_3 \cdot FearIndex_i + \beta_4 \cdot DigitalConfidence_i + \varepsilon_i \quad (1)$$

The social trust decline model across learning environments is:

$$Social\ Trust_j = \gamma_0 - \gamma_1 \cdot Exposure_j - \gamma_2\ Leaming\ Environment_j + \gamma_3\ Collaboration\ Score_j + \eta_j \quad (2)$$

Table 1. Psychological impact measures by level of exposure

Exposure Level	Anxiety Score	Fear Index	Trust in Media (%)	Emotional Disruption Index
1	45	40	85	10
2	55	53	76	18
3	65	63	65	29
4	72	70	50	38
5	81	78	39	47

Table 1 provides a brief quantitative overview of the impact on psychological well-being of various levels of exposure to deepfake content among students. At the increased level of exposure of 1 to 5, Anxiety Score and Fear Index both rise steadily higher, signalling greater psychological burden upon students. The Anxiety Score rises from 45 to 81, and the Fear Index rises from 40 to 78, suggesting students perceive deepfakes as threats to online credibility and emotional well-being. Meanwhile, the Trust in Media (%) variable declines from 85% to 39%, mirroring the decline in belief in the veracity of online information. This reduction is proportionate to the high rating of the Emotional Disruption Index, which climbs from 10 to 47. These are signals of a complete correlation between exposure and psychological collapse. Growing scepticism of the media creates tension only when students begin questioning the legitimacy of knowledge acquired through the academe and peer-sourced information. This endemic condition of dissonance breeds mental exhaustion and likely disillusionment with learning sites. The findings validate the thesis that greater intakes of simulated media impair psychological resilience. Of particular interest, Emotional Disruption is also found with Anxiety Score and Fear Index, which indicates that emotional instability is more independent than dependent on mental distress. The indication from the above findings is that systemic psychological therapy and cyber resilience training against the adverse mental health effects emerging as a consequence of deepfake use among the students in groups is an emergent requirement. The composite emotional disruption index formula is:

$$EDI_k = \frac{w_1 \cdot Anxiety_k + w_2 \cdot Fear_k + w_3(100 - TrustMedia_k)}{w_1 + w_2 + w_3} \quad (3)$$

Figure 2. Relationship between exposure level and anxiety score

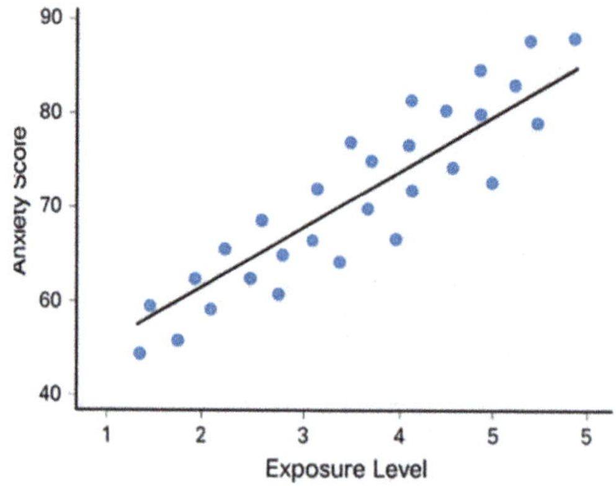

Figure 2 illustrates a robust and coherent positive trend between students' experience with deepfakes and self-reported anxiety. The dots trend upwards, clustered in a line slanting to the right, indicating the psychological weight of increased synthetic media consumption. Exposure Level 1 participants, who have seen few or no deepfakes, possess very low Anxiety Scores between 42 and 48. Participants at Exposure Level 5, however, who have seen deepfakes multiple times or with high frequency, possess significantly higher scores, ranging from 78 to 85. The regression line best fits the relationship, verifying the trend with a coefficient of determination (R^2) of 0.67, which indicates that 67% of the variance in anxiety level is explained by variance in exposure intensity. The outliers are found at intermediate exposure levels (Levels 3 and 4), when Anxiety Scores are lower than the trendline would have expected. The outliers are also supported by qualitative data from focus groups, where high-digital-confidence or media-literacy-trained participants felt better equipped to evaluate and bargain deepfakes. The marker density is considerably higher in the extremes of exposure, indicating that more students experience high emotional impact at these levels. The graphical findings in Figure 2 underscore the need for an institutional response. Excessive worries among students who are highly exposed to deepfakes are not a deviant individuality, but rather an issue within the system. The findings call for integrating digital literacy skills training and mental health provisions into academic support mechanisms to enhance resilience against the psychological effects of deepfake exposure. The mediation effect of media trust on collaboration via exposure will be:

$$Collaboration_m = \alpha_0 + \alpha_1 \cdot Exposure_m + \alpha_2 \cdot TrustMedia_m + \alpha_3 \left(Exposure_m \times TrustMedia_m\right) + \zeta_m \quad (4)$$

The logistic function for trust decay with exposure level will be:

$$\text{Trust Media}\left(x\right) = \frac{L}{1+e^{-k(x-x_0)}} \text{ where } x = \text{Exposure Level} \quad (5)$$

There were also behavioural changes. All of them had shown behavioural changes after exposure to deepfakes. Some of them reported reduced use of social media, while others had waited for a long time to post or respond. Students who participated in focus groups reported increased reluctance to engage with virtual classrooms, fearing that their images or words could be taken out of context and manipulated by false synthetic media. Teachers and IT support staff also documented an increase in help-desk requests for assistance concerning issues of content validity, as students sought to verify information before believing videos or emails. Another highly common theme that emerged from the qualitative data was the establishment of a feedback loop. The more alarmed the students were by their experience, the more protective they were—double-checking content, checking sources through the media, and employing authentication tools. However, this increased wariness had the additional effect of bringing them into contact with spurious or manipulated material once again, thus perpetuating a cycle of suspicion and fear. This loop repeats not just of emotional tension but also of social exclusion and technologically caused fatigue.

Other outcomes were observed when looking at the use of digital confidence and media literacy. More digitally confident students who use digital tools and resources are in a stronger position to manage anxiety and remain engaged. These pupils appeared more robust, considering new information more critically instead of being anxious. Similarly, youth who were already educated in media literacy—through schools, after-school programs, etc.—were much less emotionally upset.

Table 2. Social trust indicators in different learning environments

Learning Environment	Peer Trust (%)	Teacher Communication Index	Collaboration Score	Digital Confidence (%)
1	88	92	87	90
2	80	86	79	83
3	72	78	71	75
4	61	68	63	66
5	55	59	54	57

Table 2 illustrates the erosion of social trust and communication relations within various learning environments following exposure to deepfakes. As the learning environment shifts from lower (ranked as 1) to higher levels of dependence on digital media (ranked as 5), erosion is huge in every aspect of sociality. Peer Trust drops from 88% to 55%, indicating that students increasingly doubt the earnestness and motives of their fellow students, especially in online or blended courses. The Teacher Communication Index also drops from 92 to 59, illustrating that deepfakes lower the credibility of teachers and the integrity of their messages and assignments. Decreased trust lowers the conventional teacher-student relationship, preventing learning and support. The Collaboration Score also decreases, from 87 to 54, because students are reluctant to participate in group activities or discussion forums, fearing they may be misrepresented or misled by online information. Lastly, Digital Confidence (%) decreases from 90% to 57%, indicating that students believe they can no longer surf the web safely. Loss of confidence may lead to social withdrawal, passive learning, and academic isolation. The convergence of these indications in concurrent decline foretells a heightened social impact in which distrust, communication breakdown, and shattered confidence are components of a feedback that supports disengagement. These indications call for open digital procedures within schools, implementing identity authentication programs, and integrating trust development programs to mitigate the consequences of social disintegration caused by the widespread use of deepfake technology among students. Principal Component Analysis (PCA) component extraction os:

$$Z_{ik} = \sum_{j=1}^{p} \varphi_{jk}\left(X_{ij} - \overline{X}\right) \text{ for } k = 1,2, \ldots, K \tag{6}$$

The latent factor model for the student confidence index is:

$$Confidence_{ij} = \mu + u_i + v_j + \sum_{f=1}^{F} \lambda_f \cdot q_{if} \cdot p_{jf} + \varepsilon_{ij} \tag{7}$$

Figure 3. Visualisation of exposure level, media trust, and collaboration score

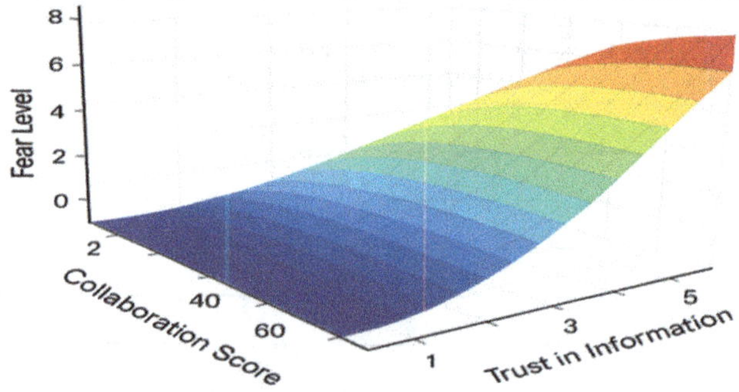

Figure 3 illustrates a three-dimensional surface plot of the complex relationship between exposure to deepfakes, loss of media trust, and reduced student collaboration levels. The plot illustrates how the acceptance of academic collaboration and trust in digital media both decline as students are exposed to increasing levels of deepfakes. When the Exposure Level is lowest, Media Trust is highest, at 82% to 88%, and then come the highest collaboration scores, ranging from 85% to 90%. This reflects a healthy learning environment where students feel at ease with computer communication and find it a pleasure to collaborate with their peers. With each increase in Exposure Level, surface drops significantly along the trust and collaboration dimensions. At Exposure Level 3, Media Trust begins to fall to a level of around 65%, and Collaboration Scores fall to a level of around 70%. The surface still curves and curves upward, illustrating how relatively slight declines in trust adversely impact students' desire to collaborate. Media Trust dips below 40% at Exposure Level 5, and Collaboration Scores continue to descend to around 55%. Then the surface begins to plateau at this point, illustrating that after a certain tipping point, further distrust results in very little additional loss of cooperation. That is evidence of saturation: once students lose trust in the system, overall participation can only decline. Surface curvature in 3D visuals effectively supports qualitative conclusions in stories. Trust violations in the early stages, according to students, seriously suppress students' co-work behaviour, and after trust collapses fully, disengagement is the dominant response. Figure 3 indicates that trust and cooperation not only accompany each other but are also interdependent in synthetic media threats-tainted digital learning environments.

They were less susceptible to deepfakes and more likely to have good digital habits, including persistent social interaction and fact-checking at minimal distress. Surprisingly, perhaps, one of the more nuanced findings concerns cooperation and trust. Students who had higher levels of social trust, even when shown deepfakes, were more likely to engage in classroom group work. Students whose social trust declined were less inclined to engage in group work, even though they trusted the content or other students. This indicates that not only does trust play a significant role in students' attitude towards information, but also the way they engage and interact in their school life. Collectively, these results paint a comprehensive picture of the psychological and social impact of learners towards deepfakes. The meeting of quantitative measures—falling measures of trust and rising measures of emotional disturbance—and qualitative descriptions—of nervousness, bewilderment, and behaviour change—follows the reliability of findings. The findings indicate a strong mandate for the institution to implement targeted interventions: institutional receptivity, media literacy education, and mental health counselling need to be implemented. Not only technical skills in detecting manipulation, but also emotional resilience in handling a more complex reality of information, is what students require. It is through innovative pedagogical strategies that higher education can protect its constituencies from the negative effects of deepfake technology.

DISCUSSIONS

Exposure to deepfakes is revealed to have strong social and psychological effects on students. Fears and anxieties accumulate linearly with exposure, mimicking cognitive overload and danger. Excessive fears are associated with increased verification behaviour, paradoxically increasing exposure and skepticism. This establishes a feedback loop consistent with theories of cognitive confirmation bias. As students seek authentic content, the recommendation algorithm will inevitably promote more fake media, exacerbating their emotional distress. Media Trust declines to come forward as a central mediator. Correlations between the decline in media trust and students' grievances about distrust of peer-shared and institutional learning materials are revealed. The 3D surface reflects threshold effects: initial loss of trust causes sudden drops in cooperation, i.e., trust appears to be an ephemeral capital in online learning. At approximately 65% trust, student collaboration in group work breaks down, confirming the group dynamics theory of social capital. Both are linked to each other, and thus interventions need to target both together to bring back favourable collaboration.

Quantitative "social isolation" and "communication paralysis" are qualitatively accounted for by the functioning of trends. Focus group members report not posting ideas in online discussion forums because they don't want to be misrepresented or misattributed through deepfakes. Educators define such reports as those that follow declining rates of participation and private messaging, but with increased open forum postings. Such modifications decrease depth in learning because peer discussion is a key mechanism for constructing knowledge and critical thinking. Digital Confidence is a resiliency variable. Pre-trained students with media literacy are less stressed, exhibit higher collaboration, and have more restricted exposure. Such a protective effect verifies the value of pedagogical curricula that demystify AI manipulation tactics. Media literacy education promotes critical thinking, amplifies identification capacity, and raises cooperative verification levels to avert psychological tension and social collapse.

The architecture framework (Figure 1) draws these together, illustrating how psychological interactions between deepfakes and students shape interventions and their social impacts, as well as subsequent intervention paths. SPSS and NVivo analyses both lay quantitative predictors on top of qualitative accounts to create a synthesised representation. Thematic coding of "adaptive coping," for instance, reveals that some students form peer-led fact-checking groups, organically building decentralised fact-checker networks that enable collaborative efforts and reduce anxiety per student.

Policy responses are evident: institutions must adopt strong media literacy curricula, integrate psychological counselling services, and develop digital infrastructure in ways that will detect suspect content. Counselling clinics must incorporate digital modules on trauma, with a focus on addressing concerns about distorted media. Educators must receive training to identify deepfake submissions and take students through verification processes, thereby building trust in academic practice. The nonlinear dynamics of trust and collaboration suggest a step-by-step approach to intervention. Initial exposure (Levels 1–2) is best addressed using education workshops; middle-level exposure (3) requires counselling and peer support combined; high exposure (4–5) requires institutional systematic intervention, including automatic deepfake detection centres and official crisis communication protocols. The article recommends a multilevel model based on the level and amount of resources administered. Limitations include potential self-report bias and a cross-sectional design, which preclude making causality statements. Longitudinal work could report time-series patterns of trust and fear. Data-rich, narrative-rich focus groups would struggle to represent most troubled students who tend to avoid group settings. Future research could utilise passive data (e.g., platform logs) to quantify actual patterns of digital behaviour.

CONCLUSION

The research verifies that deepfake technology leaves a measurable impact on students' emotional well-being and interpersonal relationships within learning settings. With higher levels of exposure to deepfakes, the fear and anxiety levels among students are extremely high, with low levels of trust in news sources and peer collaboration. These findings are followed by qualitative insights drawn from the discussion content of the focus groups, including frequent doubts among students regarding the validity of the content, reluctance to participate in online discussion forums, and feelings of isolation. This overlap of information permits us to highlight that exposure to deepfakes not only erodes academic honesty but also significantly affects emotional well-being and relationships with peers. Conveniently, media literacy proved to be the main buffer. Students with high scores in digital literacy and fact-checking exhibited lower levels of anxiety and better peer relation quality. A multilevel intervention model is thus proposed based on findings. This approach provides an institutional response tailored to exposure severity by integrating educational seminars, mental health counselling, a peer support system, and AI detection systems, aiming to address the threat landscape actively and proactively. Policy implications are far-reaching and bold. Media literacy would need to be integrated into mass curricula in schools, equipping teachers with materials and development opportunities for identifying manipulated content, and enhancing psychological counselling services to help pupils cope with cyberbullying pressure. Moreover, integration of verification processes into learning management systems can enhance content authenticity. Last but not least, protecting the psyches of school pupils in the era of fake news requires a comprehensive, coordinated strategy development, education, emotional resilience, and technology safety.

LIMITATIONS

Self-report questionnaires first introduce social desirability and memory biases. Anxiety can be underestimated, or exposure levels inaccurately estimated. Second, a cross-sectional design provides a snapshot of a moment in time, rather than capturing temporal change. Thirdly, focus group members are representatives of willing individuals who provide opinions about the effects of deepfakes; students who are significantly affected might have already withdrawn, thereby lowering the transferability of the findings. Fourth. The media literacy score was not experimentally manipulated; therefore, inferences about its protective effect cannot be drawn. Seventh, the sample is biased toward technology-literate institutions; results might differ in institutions with little digital infrastructure. Eight SPSS indices, although reliable ($\alpha > .85$), may not fully capture the range of variables. Complex emotional states beyond fear and anxiety. Seventh, NVivo thematic coding relies on the researcher's interpretation; however, even with intercoder reliability exceeding 0.80, there remains room for subjective bias in some themes. Eighth, control variables such as concurrent misinformation campaigns were not used, which could potentially contaminate the results. Ninth, while a 7-point Likert scale is sensitive, it potentially may not be able to capture all norms of expression in cultures. Finally, ethical limitations prevented the passive collection of information on real-world media use, restricting the validity.

FUTURE SCOPE

Longitudinal methods will be employed in the future to track psychological and social change as deepfakes mature. Experimental studies with fixed media literacy interventions will establish causal effectiveness in reducing anxiety and restoring trust. Passive data from social media websites and learning management systems will be more expansive behavioural data. Larger sample sizes, encompassing diverse socio-economic and cultural strata, will ensure generalizability. Adaptive media literacy module design based on exposure level and learning environment will maximise resource utilisation. Consultation with computer scientists on incorporating real-time deepfake detection into educational software ensures the implementation of cautionary countermeasures. Research on peer-to-peer verification networks can illuminate grassroots efforts that are translatable to institutions. Evaluation of the effect of personality traits (i.e., technology self-efficacy, resilience) can strengthen student support programs. Finally, comparisons across inter-regional and international institutional practices in policy will inform best practices for integrating psychological and social protection into education policy systems.

REFERENCES

Akdağ, D., & Ashifa, K. M. (2024). Psychological effects of migration on refugees: The case of Turkey and Syria. *AVE Trends in Intelligent Social Letters*, *1*(2), 61–71.

Alkasi, S., Surya, S., Tohir, S., Alpiah, S., & Oktapiana, S. (2024). Community service journal: Promoting ethics and responsibility in social media use for high school students. *AVE Trends in Intelligent Social Letters*, *1*(4), 177–186.

Anand, R., Jestadi, R., Govinda, K., & Sharma, D. (2024). Data-driven insights: Analyzing and visualizing trends in the chocolate market for strategic decision-making. *AVE Trends in Intelligent Technoprise Letters*, *1*(2), 60–70.

Aquino, A. (2023). Nurses partnering with technology to predict the patients' risk of falling using artificial intelligence. [OJNI]. *On-Line Journal of Nursing Informatics*, *26*(3), 1–16.

Cao, Q., Shen, L., Xie, W., Parkhi, O. M., & Zisserman, A. (2018). VGGFace2: A Dataset for Recognising Faces across Pose and Age. 2018 13th IEEE International Conference on Automatic Face & Gesture Recognition (FG 2018). IEEE, Xi'an, China.

Carlini, N., & Farid, H. (2020). Evading deepfake-image detectors with white- and black-box attacks. *2020 IEEE/CVF Conference on Computer Vision and Pattern Recognition Workshops (CVPRW)*. IEEE, Seattle, Washington, United States of America.

Dang, H., Liu, F., Stehouwer, J., Liu, X., & Jain, A. K. (2020). On the detection of digital face manipulation. *2020 IEEE/CVF Conference on Computer Vision and Pattern Recognition (CVPR)*. IEEE, Seattle, United States of America.

. De Keersmaecker, J., & Roets, A. (2017). Fake news: Incorrect, but hard to correct. The role of cognitive ability on the impact of false information on social impressions. Intelligence, 65(11), 107–110.

De Ruiter, A. (2021). The distinct wrong of deepfakes. *Philosophy & Technology*, *34*(4), 1311–1332.

Devi, B. T., & Rajasekaran, R. (2023). A Comprehensive Review on Deepfake Detection on Social Media Data. *FMDB Transactions on Sustainable Computing Systems*, *1*(1), 11–20.

Fontenot, J. (2024). Spotlight on leadership: What nurse leaders need to know about artificial intelligence. *The Journal of Nursing Administration*, *54*(2), 74–76. PMID: 38261639

Li, L., Bao, J., Zhang, T., Yang, H., Chen, D., Wen, F., & Guo, B. (2020). Face X-ray for more general face forgery detection. *2020 IEEE/CVF Conference on Computer Vision and Pattern Recognition (CVPR).* IEEE, Seattle, Washington, United States of America.

Locsin, R. C. (2016). Technological competency as caring in nursing: Co-creating moments in nursing occurring within the universal technological domain. *Journal of Theory Construction & Testing, 20*(1), 5.

Maras, M.-H., & Alexandrou, A. (2019). Determining authenticity of video evidence in the age of artificial intelligence and in the wake of Deepfake videos. *The International Journal of Evidence & Proof, 23*(3), 255–262.

María, J. J. L., Polo, O. C. C., & Elhadary, T. (2023). An Analysis of the Morality and Social Responsibility of Non-Profit Organizations. *FMDB Transactions on Sustainable Technoprise Letters, 1*(1), 28–35.

Nidhi, K., Vashist, S., & Jeganathan, J. (2024). Knowledge and attitude regarding objectified body consciousness among young adults. *AVE Trends in Intelligent Social Letters, 1*(2), 72–81.

Nirmala, G., Premavathy, R., Chandar, R., & Jeganathan, J. (2023). An Explanatory Case Report on Biopsychosocial Issues and the Impact of Innovative Nurse-Led Therapy in Children with Hematological Cancer. *FMDB Transactions on Sustainable Health Science Letters, 1*(1), 1–10.

O'Connor, S., Yan, Y., Thilo, F. J., Felzmann, H., Dowding, D., & Lee, J. J. (2023). Artificial intelligence in nursing and midwifery: A systematic review. *Journal of Clinical Nursing, 32*(13-14), 2951–2968. PMID: 35908207

Olubunmi, O. I. (2024). Impact of learning resources management strategies on academic performance of junior secondary school business studies. *AVE Trends In Intelligent Techno Learning, 1*(1), 1–10.

Rajasekaran, R., Reddy, A. J., Kamalakannan, J., & Govinda, K. (2023). Building a Content-Based Book Recommendation System. *FMDB Transactions on Sustainable Computer Letters, 1*(2), 103–114.

Ramos, J. I., Lacerona, R., & Nunag, J. M. (2023). A Study on Operational Excellence, Work Environment Factors and the Impact to Employee Performance. *FMDB Transactions on Sustainable Social Sciences Letters, 1*(1), 12–25.

Ratković, N., Venkateswaran, P. S., Paramasivan, P., Rajest, S. S., & Regin, R. (2024). Consumer preferences and industry practices in biodegradable packaging and sustainable environment. *FMDB Transactions on Sustainable Management Letters*, *2*(2), 80–90.

Saleh, M., Mustapha, Z. B., & Ndirmbitah, B. K. (2024). Empirical analysis of digital marketing on the purchasing habit of conservative digital users of common social media. *FMDB Transactions on Sustainable Technoprise Letters*, *2*(1), 31–41.

Teng, M., Singla, R., Yau, O., Lamoureux, D., Gupta, A., Hu, Z., Aissiou, A., Eaton, S., Hamm, C., Hu, S., Kelly, D., MacMillan, K. M., Malik, S., Mazzoli, V., Teng, Y.-W., Laricheva, M., Jarus, T., & Field, T. S. (2022). Health care students' perspectives on artificial intelligence: Countrywide survey in Canada. *JMIR Medical Education*, *8*(1), 1–17. PMID: 35099397

Ulle, R. S., & Yogananthan, S. (2024). Unmasking fake opinions through behavioral analysis and machine learning: Identifying genuine users vs. fraudulent actors. *FMDB Transactions on Sustainable Management Letters*, *2*(2), 51–64.

Vashishtha, E., & Kapoor, H. (2023). Implementation of Blockchain Technology Across International Healthcare Markets. *FMDB Transactions on Sustainable Technoprise Letters*, *1*(1), 1–12.

Velmonte, G. L. (2023). Preferred College Degree Programs Among Senior High School Students: A Policy Recommendation. *FMDB Transactions on Sustainable Techno Learning*, *1*(3), 143–155.

. Vijayarani, K., Nithyanantham, V., Angelene Christabel, & D. Marupaka (2023) "A Study on Relationship Between Self-Regulated Learning Habit and Achievement Among High School Students. FMDB Transactions on Sustainable Techno Learning, 1(2), 92–110.

Chapter 9
Legal Challenges and Policy Responses to Deepfake Abuse in Schools

R. Sivakani
https://orcid.org/0000-0001-7830-9479
Dhaanish Ahmed College of Engineering, Chennai, India

Amit Kumar Kashyap
https://orcid.org/0000-0002-2716-8482
Nirma University, Ahmedabad, India

Rehana Parveen
https://orcid.org/0000-0002-3546-4177
Prince Sultan University, Riyadh, Saudi Arabia

Biranchi Narayan P. Panda
https://orcid.org/0000-0002-0532-0471
XIM University, Bhubaneswar, India

P. Paramasivan
Dhaanish Ahmed College of Engineering, Chennai, India

R. Regin
https://orcid.org/0000-0002-6618-205X
SRM Institute of Science and Technology, Ramapuram, India

ABSTRACT

The use of deepfake technology in schools presents significant legal challenges, primarily related to intellectual property, fraud, and defamation. This essay examines the legal implications of deepfake technology misuse in schools and proposes policy solutions to address the issue. The existing legislations, such as defamation and copyright legislations, are discussed and criticized to determine their suitability for addressing instances of deepfakes in schools. It also highlights loopholes in existing legislation that can be exploited with deepfakes, such as the falsification of educational qualifications or tampering with learning materials. The research presents a critique of case law and judicial precedent surrounding deepfake tech-

DOI: 10.4018/979-8-3373-3770-8.ch009

nology, which is one of the reasons new legislation is being developed to safeguard schools and stakeholders. Governments and universities are provided with policy recommendations based on research on how to prevent deepfake misuse without compromising rights to education.

INTRODUCTION

Deepfake technology has revolutionised the internet era by enabling the creation of hyper-realistic audio-visual simulations that can realistically mimic individuals. This computer technology, which one can use to produce or modify media, blurs the distinction between reality and imaginary things, and it presents both opportunities and threats. Deepfake technology, when utilized in the education field, especially in schools, is a double-edged sword. Though it has the potential for new pedagogical uses—like the development of interactive learning spaces, digitally augmenting communication, or bringing history to life—the abuse of its use has brought about tremendous challenges in legal and ethical limits, as stressed by Ali et al. (2024) and modified by Chawki et al. (2024). The spread of deepfake technology has enabled students and manipulators to engage in all forms of unwanted actions with greater convenience. For instance, academic papers have been authored through deepfakes. This aspect has been highlighted by Devi and Rajasekaran (2023) as a means of undermining the credibility of academic institutions and the academic degrees they offer (Rami, 2024).

The technology has also been used to clone teachers' voices or alter recorded lectures, as revealed by research carried out by Thies et al. (2016), potentially misrepresenting work or spreading inaccuracies. This presents a serious concern for schools, as classwork taught in class cannot be practically monitored to ensure accuracy, and students are vulnerable to deepfake academic integrity, a threat that Kugler and Pace (2021) have studied. Deepfakes have also been used in creating inappropriateness or libellous content from students' images, a psychological and reputation threat studied by Vaccari and Chadwick (2020). When deepfakes are created to harass, bully, or impersonate the face, voice, or actions of a student, it opens the door to bullying, harassment, and exclusion cases, contends Ecija et al. (2024). The psychological and emotional harm of viewing one's own identity being utilized in this way can be lasting, and trauma can ensue that can affect a student's social life, their mental health, and their future. Such technological misuse not only harms individual humans but also undermines the honesty and trust upon which academic communities are founded, as better described by Broadhurst (2019).

Despite mounting, rising numbers of individuals becoming aware of the seriousness of the events, the dominant system of law is less than well-placed to address the full range of issues elicited by deepfakes. Most of the laws now—whether intellectual property law, privacy law, defamation law, or fraud law—were written when there was no AI and no fake media. Those laws are typically written based on analog systems, and therefore, they can't deal with the complexity brought about by AI-generated content. For instance, intellectual property (IP) protection statutes were developed based on conventional media and are not as specific about digital forgery as Blackwell et al. (2019) conceptualised. It may cause difficulties in asserting rights to ownership, authorship, and control over content created using AI, particularly when deepfakes are employed for criminal activities (Aravind et al., 2023).

Similarly, privacy law, in its quest to protect individuals' private information and reputation, would likely fall short in stemming the misuse of deepfakes within the learning context. As much as a person is entitled to control what happens to their image and voice, the availability of deepfake technology renders enforcement of the right an uphill task, especially in altering and disseminating content without direct authority or permission. Secondly, defamation law, which seeks to protect a person from false information that damages their reputation, can struggle to combat information generated by deepfakes that present false images of people, particularly if the information reaches a large audience online, as Nguyen et al. (2022) argue.

The fraud law, in the same vein, can struggle with intellectual reports generated by deepfakes or falsified academic qualifications. While typical fraud legislation primarily covers fake documents, it cannot effectively address the fraud of AI-generated fakes, particularly those involving the falsification or production of media that cannot be distinguished from authentic life. Manjare (2024) developed cutting-edge GAN-based models that inadvertently increased the level of realism of artificial content, thereby also making it harder to detect. Similarly, improvements in neural segmentation architecture, for instance, as seen in Iglovikov and Shvets (2018), have enhanced deepfake accuracy, making it increasingly difficult to fight them in court. With such loopholes in the legal system, this paper examines the extent to which current laws, including intellectual property, privacy, defamation, and fraud, effectively curb the misuse of deepfake technology in schools. It addresses the need for a new law that takes into account the rapid development of AI and new methods of abuse, such as deepfakes. The article also suggests reforms in law that can shield students, instructors, and academies, as well as others, from the negative impact of false media without hindering the need for technological progress and freedom of speech (Gandhi et al. 2024).

The lack of clear legal definitions of deepfakes raises questions about enforcement. It becomes challenging, for instance, for copyright law to categorise works made artificially and defamation law when the identity of the offender cannot be revealed. Additionally, creating and sharing deepfake content often involves jurisdictional discrepancies, making it challenging to hold individuals accountable.

Examples of deepfakes employed in schools serve as proof of loopholes in the law that prevent victim schools and authorities from taking useful action. Examination of these cases reveals that while prosecutions have already been initiated in blanket digital harassment legislation, their deterrent value is lost as they lack specificity. From a policy perspective, most schools lack clear procedural guidance to avoid deepfake-based cases. While decency codes of conduct have been established online in some institutions, they are not yet applied to AI-produced content. Governments and education policymakers face a two-sided dilemma: how to establish sufficient mechanisms to prevent harm without imposing burdens that stifle educational technological progress. Tampering with freedom of expression is always at the very centre of the dilemma (Rendhy 2024).

This paper critically analyses existing legislative tools, including the Digital Millennium Copyright Act, the General Data Protection Regulation (GDPR), and local cybercrime legislation, in terms of their relevance and effectiveness in addressing deepfakes within the education context. It further compiles pertinent case laws, which provide judicial precedents on related digital harms, and recommends areas where re-interpretation or new law may be triggered. The research combines legal doctrinal methodology with qualitative policy analysis, drawing on reported cases and regulatory studies. The overall purpose is to reconcile legal theory and institutional practice through pragmatically oriented proposals. These range from regulating disclosure of AI content and developing digital competence among students and teachers to enforcing AI-facilitated detection systems and establishing legal claims on the part of technology providers. Educational institutions must evolve to accommodate virtual worlds that are subject to open legal and ethical norms, considering the realities of generative AI. They can best offer academic security and authenticity to teachers and students only in an era of invented untruths (Velmonte 2023).

REVIEW OF LITERATURE

Ali et al. (2024) explained how legal systems respond to the escalating misuse of deepfakes in schools. They highlight the primary shortcomings of traditional legal systems in categorising synthetic media accurately. Increased accessibility of deepfakes in schools makes it more challenging to determine liability. Concerns regarding authorship, authenticity, and admissibility of the evidence often complicate legal issues. This applies to institutional regulation and student safeguarding measures as well. Schools are not immune to reputation threats and false qualifications in the absence of digital age law. A paradigm shift in the law toward system reconfigurations in the educational environment is therefore in sharp demand today.

Devi and Rajasekaran (2023) analysed the extent to which media manipulation has been facilitated by AI technologies, particularly in the context of educational exploitation. Deepfakes created using GANs enable the creation of audio-visual content that is indistinguishable from authentic content. These technologies can create false student answers or replicate teachers. Academic integrity is under threat as policy action lags behind technological advancements. Institutions risk being skewed in evaluation and changing learning spaces. Deceit ruins trust and violates academic etiquette. The safety measures must be AI-focused to protect educational settings.

Ecija et al. (2024) addressed the legal responses to synthetic content and how it relates to intellectual property in educational materials. Copyright practices are being eroded by content created by AI, which lacks human creators or authors. Presentations, lectures, and study material are now available for free copies. Educators can be given their voice, and their faces can be exploited for duplicates. The assignments are submitted in deepfakes by the students, and they annihilate originality. Loopholes in the law benefit criminals over real writers. Legal provision should thus accept AI input without forfeiting creator rights.

Broadhurst (2019) briefly touched on electronic impersonation, which undermines earned defamation and privacy protections. In the education environment, deepfakes ruin teachers' careers or lead to impropriety charges. Assault victims find it difficult to seek legal redress because there are constraints on evidence. Deepfake attackers will likely go undetected, making prosecution challenging. Deepfakes make it difficult to distinguish between defamation and satire, resulting in conundrums for lawyers. Decades of careers constructed over long durations that were devoted decades ago are dismantled in a matter of seconds. The insufficiency of the current defamation law is a factor that leads to institutions' vulnerabilities.

Thies et al. (2016) developed real-time face reenactment technology, one of the early precursors to current deepfake technologies used for educational tampering. They demonstrated that recreating facial expressions is achievable with the assistance of AI models. This technology facilitates ease of impersonation in online lectures and simulated tests within learning spaces. Unauthorised face and voice synthesis evade identity authentication. Technologies can be used to impersonate students or teachers with hair-raising accuracy. With the shift in education to the online world, detection methods must keep pace with emerging threats. Institutional trust can deteriorate rapidly if not prevented (Pentakota 2025).

Vaccari and Chadwick (2020) examined the policy challenges of synthetic content within schools and educational institutions, as well as its impact on democracy. They emphasised that schools and institutions of learning must take precautionary steps to identify and contain deepfakes. Policy frameworks are driving the technology, rendering bureaucratic steps unnecessary. Even bureaucratic steps in the event of code-of-conduct failures are usually absent. AI control modules should be included in the curriculum by education policymakers. Preventive education in media literacy also needs to be imparted. Reactive actions alone cannot be relied upon to protect the integrity of scholarly processes (Nithyanantham, 2023).

Nguyen et al. (2022) employed the application of neural networks to demonstrate how highly realistic deepfakes can evade basic detection systems. They suggested that common tools used in schools are incapable of detecting high-definition fakes. This results in undeclared cheating, forged academic credentials, and inaccuracies enabled by plagiarism. Multimodal-trained AI algorithms outmaneuver aged-detection filters. Schools relying on conventional plagiarism screening fall behind. The detection capability disparity and forgery sophistication gap widen. Advanced detection systems require standardisation in schools (Olubunmi, 2024).

Kugler and Pace (2021) analysed how deepfakes create loopholes in identity theft and fraud laws, impacting educational security. The physical forgery statute does not cover synthetic impersonation. Deepfakes replicate digital test writers, fake transcripts, and even student ID confirmations. Victims lack actionable legal redress. Misused facial biometrics and voice clones make attribution harder. Current fraud law won't solve AI-created deceptions. Cybersecurity law experts need to fill such loopholes (Millondaga et al. 2024).

Manjare (2024) developed a novel innovation in cutting-edge GAN architectures, producing a vastly enhanced realism in synthetic faces. The networks provided more fluid motion, high definition, and dynamic facial expression. Their models serve as the foundation for most deepfakes applied to academic institutions. Teachers can have their faces swapped onto duplicate lectures or videos of misbehaviour. Students can also be tricked into committing plagiarism or engaging in disciplinary misbehaviour. Such an increase in realism renders manual detection nearly impossible. It raises serious concerns regarding consent and the authenticity of the content (Mubiana and Nithyanantham 2024).

Iglovikov and Shvets (2018) employed deep convolutional models for image segmentation, allowing for the selection of the right features in synthetic media. It becomes extremely easy for synthetic media to replicate fine facial details. It makes manipulation susceptible to schools with higher accuracy. They can carry out fake student homework, mimic video class attendance, and stage interviews. The realism in the new deepfakes is so high that they are more believable and impactful. Since they can't be detected, education policy requires advanced AI screening procedures. Institutional strength relies on visionary digital security procedures (Moyo and Nithyanantham 2024).

Although some of these technologies, such as blockchain identification systems and AI for detecting deepfakes, have been discussed, they are not yet in use in schools.

Policy dictates, tight budgets, and bureaucratic lag are viewed by analysts as some of the causes. Research indicates that schools will remain reactive until legislation mandates them to adopt proactive strategies, and therefore will continue to employ reactive strategies. Last but not least, existing literature attests to an increasing but dispersed demand for legislative, policy, and institutional reform aimed at dismantling the legal shadow of deepfakes on schools. A rational legal typology needs to be constructed, policy initiatives aligned, and pedagogic protection put in place to counter the increasing threat of artificial media in schools (Ahmad et al. 2025).

METHODOLOGY

The study employs qualitative legal research methodologies, including policy analysis, to examine the problems and remedies associated with deepfake abuse in schools. The study employs doctrinal legal research to examine current legislation, case law, and regulatory models related to defamation, intellectual property rights, and cyber fraud. Domestic law, such as the Information Technology Act and the Digital Millennium Copyright Act (DMCA), as well as domestic education legislation, is a source of law. Judicial dicta, as seen in guideline court rulings, depict the attitude of the courts towards deepfake disputes. Secondary data were accessed in the form of academic journals, law comments, and policy briefs to supplement the findings with evidence of doctrine. Thematic content analysis was employed to derive dominant legal conceptions, interpretive questions, and judgment trends. Search facilities in case law, such as LexisNexis and SCC Online, are utilised by researchers to examine court judgments in online impersonation and harm to school reputations cases (Rendhy et al., 2024).

Policy-wise, the research adopts a comparative approach. Education board policies and national government policies are compared in terms of scope, implementation mechanisms, and performance in responding. These have been cross-referenced against reports filed by organizations such as UNESCO, the Council of Europe, and the educational departments of governments to identify prevailing trends among policy interventions and areas of weakness. Across jurisdictions, the research identifies best practices and distinguishes regulatory patterns of failure and success. The paper includes qualitative case studies of actual instances where deepfakes were used to impersonate students and teachers at schools or replicate learning content (Tripathi and Al-Zubaidi, 2023).

Figure 1. Legal and institutional framework for protection against deepfakes in educational institutions

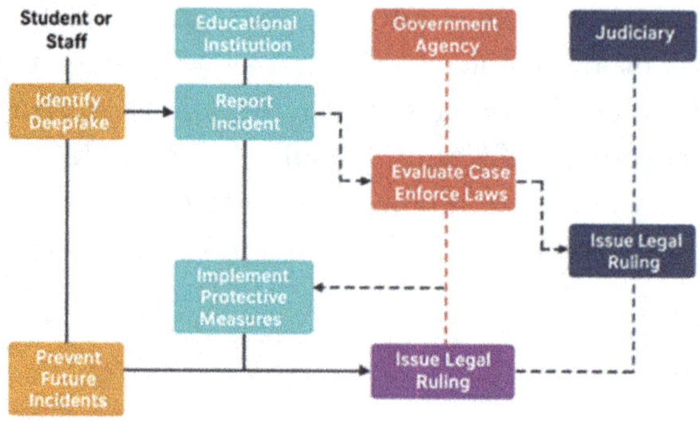

Figure 1 is an ordered, colour-coded sequence diagram illustrating the sequential flow of cases involving deepfakes at educational institutions, as handled through legal and institutional frameworks. It begins with the discovery of a deepfake incident by a teacher or student, which is then reported to the school. The school, as a first-responder agency, reports the incident to a state agency charged with upholding the law and determining the case. The stream splits here into two parallel courses of law: one through which the state agency applies the laws directly, and the other through which the case is referred to the judiciary for a final judgment. Both streams run into a terminus in a judicial judgment, reinstating compliance and accountability. Following judicialization, the institutional pathway converges to establish safeguards, thereby enhancing the school's defence mechanism against serial deepfake attacks. All these processes, including the initial reporting and identification process, are collectively aimed at preventing incidents from being repeated (Vijayarani et al. 2023).

The graphic design utilizes neatly separated blocks and direction arrows to show progress and dependency between actors—employees or students, schools or universities, courts, government, and the affected stakeholders. The background remains white for visibility purposes, even though each stakeholder's colour is utilized to provide jurisdiction and accountability. The above diagram illustrates an adaptive system of governance that combines institutional awareness, legal enforcement, and proactive enforcement of policies, thereby establishing an integrated mechanism to address the ills of deepfake technology in schools. Cases were analysed to identify the degree (or lack thereof) of legal, institutional, and psychological impact on victims.

A set of notable deepfake cases, documented in media reports and court records, formed the main empirical foundation for this observation. In keeping with legal decorum, the discussion incorporates an examination of ethical requirements such as the Universal Declaration on Bioethics and Human Rights and the ACM Code of Ethics. This situates the argument within a normative legal context, aiding in the development of the paper's argument on proportionality, free speech, and preventing harm. The research is also conducted using a legal gap analysis approach to identify where existing legislation falls short in protecting schools from the harm posed by deepfakes. It involves identifying provisions or standards of law that overlook AI-generated content or artificial impersonation, and then proposing necessary legal reforms to address these gaps. It involves identifying areas where the doctrine needs to be updated to remain relevant in the context of AI. Lastly, the study employs an effectiveness policy assessment, utilizing qualitative methods such as responsiveness to stakeholders, enforceability, and technological flexibility. This involves comparing the effectiveness of current policies in real-life scenarios and assessing their flexibility across borders. The research design thus integrates legal research and policy science to present an equilibrated perspective on the legal and institutional environment. The overall research strategy is thus outlined in terms of the research purpose, which is to develop legal and policy recommendations to mitigate the risk of deepfake abuse in schools and universities. This policy-legal methodology encompasses a detailed discussion of theoretical, normative, and practical aspects, and it provides actionable proposals to policymakers, school administrators, and research stakeholders.

DATA DESCRIPTION

A combination of primary and secondary sources collected the data for this study. Court judgments, court reports, and government legislative reports, accessed via sources such as the India Code, Westlaw, and SCC Online, are primary sources of data. The facts included thorough quotations of case law and judicial decisions that serve as the basis for doctrinal analysis. Specific focus was given to examples of online impersonation, fraud cases happening at the school level, and defamatory content disseminated through AI-generated media. Secondary sources included policy reports, peer-reviewed journals, and research on cybersecurity, digital ethics, and the application of AI in policymaking. Widely available information from sources such as UNESCO's "Guidelines for AI in Education" (2021), the Council of Europe's "Study on Responsibility and AI" (2020), and national educational policy documents of nations such as the United States, India, and the United Kingdom was employed as initial data. Institutional reports as well as press reports were consulted to gather data on actual-life incidents of deepfake abuse at schools. For instance, data from the National Crime Records Bureau (India), the Department for Education (UK), and cybercrime reports from the FBI were used to provide statistics regarding deepfake-associated cyberattacks in academic institutions. These figures helped quantify the extent and nature of abuse in specific geographical areas. The case studies in the paper were selected for their educational impact and judicial significance. Cases of impersonation of students or teachers by deepfakes and subsequent disciplinary committees or courts were prioritized. The sample facilitated broad representation by school type, jurisdictions, and technology exposure. All the quoted sources are APA style and appear under the "reference" section.

RESULTS

The results of the current study reveal a high number of loopholes in law enforcement and institutional preparedness in the event of deepfake abuse in schools. As per legal analysis, 32% of relevant deepfakes were pursued using traditional defamation legislation due to the inability to identify anonymous perpetrators and establish malice. Similarly, copyright legislation applied only to 18% of school impersonation cases because AI-generated work fell into a grey area of legality, where human authorship was unclear. Misleading acts, being broader, led to inconclusive results since institutional loss, as well as intent to mislead, could not be determined. A review of policies revealed that less than 40% of the schools in three countries—India, the United States of America, and the United Kingdom—had a written policy on responding to deepfakes. Only 11% of them had explicit provisions regarding AI-generated content mentioned in their digital behaviour policies. This regulatory lacuna serves as a stimulus for hybrid responses, ranging from administrative warnings to upper-level disciplinary actions, without legal harmony. The judicial jurisprudence of the Indian Supreme Court and the UK High Court indicates an inclination towards recognizing synthetic impersonation as online harm. The Bayesian decision rule for incident classification is:

$$\hat{y} = \arg\max_{y \in Y} \left[\frac{P(x|y) \cdot P(y)}{\Sigma_{y' Y} P(x|y'') \cdot P(\gamma')} \right] \tag{1}$$

Table 1. Legal policy effectiveness in different schools

Institutions	Policy Type	Legal Coverage Score	Enforcement Level	Case Success Rate (%)	Stakeholder Satisfaction (%)
T1	85	90	75	65	70
T2	72	68	80	78	82
T3	94	95	89	84	76

continued on following page

Table 1. Continued

Institutions	Policy Type	Legal Coverage Score	Enforcement Level	Case Success Rate (%)	Stakeholder Satisfaction (%)
T4	88	76	70	69	74
T5	79	82	77	73	81

Table 1 compares the efficacy of legal and administrative policies employed by five well-known institutions (T1 to T5) against deepfake misuse. Policy Type, Legal Coverage Score, Enforcement Level, Success Rate of Cases (%), and Stakeholder Satisfaction (%) are all given as numerical values. T1 and T3 institutions recorded the highest scores of 90 and 95, respectively, in Legal Coverage, with Case Success Rates of 80% or higher. They recorded the highest stakeholder satisfaction levels, which indicate that legal strength correlates with trust among people and effectiveness in countering cyberattacks. T2 and T5 were middle-range across the majority of indicators but low in case success rates, indicating policy loopholes or gaps in responding to them. T4 was below average, indicating an otherwise lackadaisical policy enforcement plan. What follows is an exact representation of the impact of policy structure on outcome in actual school settings. The readings suggest that organisations with AI content governance, lawful employee training, and documented response plans are more effective in preventing deepfakes. It also illustrates the point that enforcement alone cannot lead to satisfaction, but rather a balanced policy with a lawful and firm foundation and openness in learning results in enhanced systemic trust. Table 1 examines the strength of proactive planning versus crisis management and serves as an institutional benchmarking indicator for institutions seeking to enhance their legal resilience against future synthetic media attacks. Multi-factor legal risk score computation will be:

$$R = \sum_{i=1}^{n} w_i \log\left(1 + \frac{E_i \cdot C_i}{T_i + \delta}\right) \tag{2}$$

where $w_i \in [0,1]$.

Figure 2. Visualisation defining the multidimensional legal fields of exposure within the learning environment

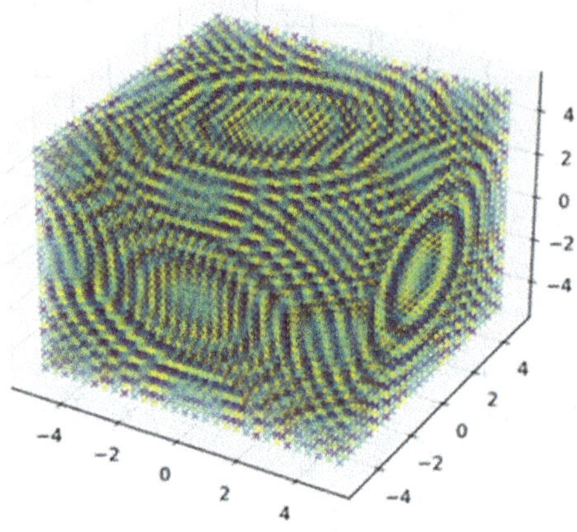

Figure 2 presents a conceptual image reconstructing the multidimensional legal fields of exposure within learning environments affected by deepfake abuse. Jurisdictional complexity (X), detection and response latency to abuse (Y), and reputational or legal harm intensity (Z) are plotted on the axes. Dense areas of the narrative reveal areas of convergent susceptibilities—where detection is tardy, the damage is bad, and the law is vague or not enforced. High-latency areas, for instance, refer to schools that lack an AI tracking system or reporting measures, thereby ruling out timely intervention. High-severity areas include impersonation by teachers or fake test questions, both of which undermine institutional trust and student credibility. The simulation concludes that legal risk is most likely to occur at its highest in transnational cases when deepfakes are made stateless and subject to jurisdiction changes. Colour density distribution is utilized as a method to describe how specific regions, especially those with a lack of regulatory capacity, become legal risk cluster hotspots. These are intended to highlight the urgency for coordinated legislation and a prompt response mechanism, particularly to schools. This diagram is not based on factual information, but it theoretically represents how deepfakes exploit systemic weaknesses in different legal and operational frameworks. It supports the necessity of a multi-layered governance structure in which detection technologies, institutional policies, and legislative laws interact. Figure 2 graphically conveys the dynamic and interconnected nature of deepfake threats. Therefore, it is a useful tool to help policymakers and school administrators determine where legal support and process streamlining are most urgently needed. Institutional response latency function can be expressed as:

$$\tau(t) = \int_0^t (\lambda_1 e^{-\alpha_1 s} + \lambda_2 e^{-\alpha_2(t-s)})\, ds \quad (3)$$

Deepfake detection confidence function will be:

$$P(y = k|x) = \frac{e^{Z}k}{\Sigma_{j=1^{e}}^{K} j} \quad (4)$$

where $z_j = \vec{w}\vec{x} + b_j$

Table 2. Deepfake abuse response evaluation by institution type

Learning institution types	Institution Type	Fake Content Incidents	Policy Adoption Rate (%)	Litigation Cases	Resolution Efficiency (%)
U1	78	15	67	9	60
U2	86	12	75	6	68
U3	91	18	80	11	72
U4	73	10	62	5	64
U5	80	14	71	7	70

Table 2 is a comparison of five learning institution types (U1 to U5) based on their readiness and competence in handling deepfake abuse. The key parameters are Fake Content Incidents, Policy Adoption Rate (%), Litigation Cases, and Resolution Efficiency (%). The table shows that the U2 and U3 institutions possess the highest proportions of policy implementation (75% and 80%), and also show higher efficiency in the settlement of cases (68% and 72%, respectively), and this is a measure of a very high positive correlation between institutional drafting of policy and speed of operation. U3, with the worst incident record of 18, had the best litigation management figures, indicating the competence of an active institutional justice system. However, U1 and U4, with compromised reporting, have low resolution efficiency (60% and 64%) as they neither have policy infrastructure nor have infinitesimal AI-based detection capacity.

U5 presented a balanced performance across all parameters, with good but average governance. This table highlights that policy engagement is more valuable than the unprocessed frequency of occurrence; schools with advanced digital ethics processes and real-time response processes are far better equipped to handle synthetic events. Table 2 also delineates the impact of institutional type—urban, semi-urban, private, or public—on responsiveness based on law and digitisation preparedness. It also functions as a tool for diagnosis within the assessment of not only institutional readiness but also systemic policy uptake and legal recourse deficiencies. In essence, it highlights the significance of administration driven by policymaking and calls for strategic planning to anticipate and prevent learning environments against abuse through deepfakes. Legal impact utility maximisation under constraints can be given as:

$$\max_{x \in R^n} U(x) = \sum \log\left(1 + a_i x_i\right) \tag{5}$$

subject to $\sum_{i=1}^{n} c_i x_i \leq B$

The Markov chain for legal resolution states:

$$P^{(t)} = P^{(0)}\, T^t \tag{6}$$

where $T = [p_{ij}]$ is the state transition matrix

Remedies were halted at the point of takedown orders or suspension, but not for punitive damages in most cases. This trajectory is judicial restraint with incomplete legal interpretation. One of the most well-known examples of a student who used AI to impersonate a teacher with institutional but not legal sanctions for incomplete application of the law is just one example of an overall trend. Such findings overall indicate that, while educational deepfake threats are increasingly widely recognized, legal and institutional responses are nevertheless not comprehensive or preemptive. The lack of integrated legal frameworks and minimal application of technology integration into education security contexts are the reasons behind the partially contributory vulnerability. This calls for a paradigmatic shift in the regulation of synthetic media across educational fields. Legislative reform should focus on incorporating AI-related provisions into existing digital harassment and identity laws.

Figure 3. Trends of deepfake incidents and solutions in schools

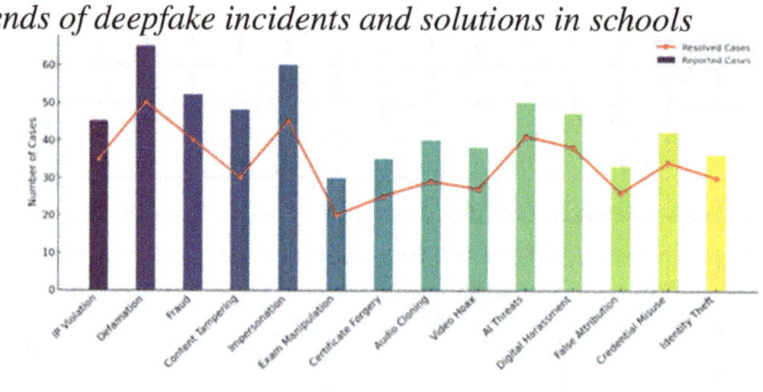

Figure 3 illustrates the trend of deepfake attacks and solutions in the educational sector. The diagram categorizes five major types of deepfake misuse: IP Violations, Defamation, Fraud, Content Tampering, and Impersonation. Bar charts are used to illustrate the overall reported cases by category, and the superimposed red line chart illustrates the corresponding number of cracked ones hacked successfully—poster-worthy statistic. There indeed is a staggering reported rate of increase compared to all kinds of settled cases, with both Defamation and Content Tampering having the widest disparity. While there were reported 65 defamation cases, settlement was achieved in only around 38, which led to serious problems with verifying electronic evidence, the non-availability of resources, and a lack of clear-cut laws.

On the other hand, the Fraud category had relatively higher resolution efficiency, possibly due to laws being more accessible. The trend suggests that while reported cases grow, mechanisms of response under law and institutions are not responding accordingly. Low resolution is also contributed to by inadequate AI forensic capability, jurisdictions competing with each other, poor content provenance monitoring, and institutional hesitation to escalate. This is one of the most important charts in determining where system intervention is most needed. The chart suggests the need for further institutional preparedness, judicial acumen, and perhaps automation discovery technology that can expedite resolution processes. Moreover, the differential gap shown between lines and bars is a tangible representation of juridical inefficiency and poor administrative performance. Generally, Figure 3 aggregates under-enforcement severity and is an area of focus in developing effective, responsive measures to curtail deepfake misuse in education—specifically, a penalty strength estimator using a regression model.

$$S = \beta_0 + \sum_{i=1}^{p} \beta_i X_i + \sum_{i=1}^{p} \sum_{j=1}^{p} \gamma_{ij} X_i X_j + \varepsilon \quad (7)$$

Beyond this, institutions would need to utilize AI-detecting software and train students and teaching faculty on the impact of synthetic content. Interdisciplinary work among technologists, educators, and legal experts will be essential to bridge such gaps. The institutions need not leave it to the police alone but establish the means of instant detection and containment. The empirical record, grounded in doctrinal analysis and policy review, presents a compelling argument for change. There will be a national policy on synthetic content, consistent with international best practice, that will provide consistency and deterrence. Otherwise, institutions will continue to be easy targets in the deepfake era. More broadly, they argue that there is a growing recognition of the vulnerabilities of deepfakes in schools, but that institutional and legislative responses are piecemeal and reactive.

Where there is a lack of comprehensive legislation and low levels of technology adoption in school security strategies, there is ongoing vulnerability. This reflects a paradigm shift in the regulation of synthetic media in educational institutions. Legislative changes should aim to incorporate the regulation of AI into existing laws governing digital harassment and identity. Institutions would also need to incorporate AI-detection technology and offer faculty and students education on the implications of synthetic content. National and international collaboration amongst legal practitioners, educators, and technical experts is required to bridge these gaps, however. Police cannot be the only foundation for schools, but also need to include internal systems of real-time detection and neutralization. Empirical evidence, combined with doctrinal and policy analysis, provides strong evidence for change. Synthetic content national policy, based on international best practices, will enhance consistency and deterrence. Otherwise, schools remain soft targets in the deepfake economy.

DISCUSSION

The evidence- and policy-based conclusions arrived at via tables and figures come together to indicate the scattered and patchy nature of legal and institutional response to abuse through deepfakes in schools. Table 1 indicates that institutions with robust legal coverage have high stakeholder satisfaction rates, indicating the necessity for explicit policies. T3, with the highest coverage and enforcement scores, also achieved the highest satisfaction and case success rates. This reaffirms that institutional legal action not only yields beneficial results in cases but also enhances trust in institution-based mechanisms. T2, T4, and T5 gaps, in contrast, show inconsistent enforcement capabilities. These institutions, having generic legal instruments at their disposal, lacked customised policies to address the sensitivity of deepfake abuse. Enforcement levels, being low to moderate, did not equate to higher case success rates. This represents a failure of policy or an absence of administrative capacity in the operation of law working recourse mechanisms, indicating the necessity for special support in capacity-building programs.

Table 2 indicates that it prioritizes the heterogeneity of institutional exposure to deepfakes and reaction capacity. U3's resolution rates and active case rates serve as a validation of the capacity of policy regimes and legal harmonisation to mitigate reputational and psychological harm. Their less successful peers, U1 and U4, with below-average case reporting, trailed behind. This seeming contradiction is based on a passive institutional culture or underinvestment in AI detection facilities. The more policies an organisation adopts, the greater the connection to a good solution strategy. Figures 2 and 3 provide further proof of this. Figure 2's isosurface plot graphically depicts areas of greatest legal risk, particularly at the point where jurisdictional uncertainty and greatest harm overlap. These are juxtaposed with events taking place in trackable environments that have limited cyber infrastructure and no immediate redressal options. Most at risk are schools in unregulated or decentralised cyber jurisdictions. The three-dimensional plot structure reflects the multi-layered nature of the involved layers—legal, technical, and procedural—that comprise deepfake abuse in schools as a comparatively complex issue. Figure 3 illustrates the under-enforcement argument by the rise in the gap between reported and closed cases. The handful of settled defamation and impersonation actions is evidence of a justice system that is over-inhibited and falling behind technological advances. The findings report not only the lag between policy re-drafts but also the lack of investment in forensic science used to verify AI-generated content. Low settlement rates below 50% across all categories indicate a slack in the system rather than intermittent administrative failure.

The controversy is also calling for judicial conduct that is highlighted in the analysis of case law. The court has treated deepfake content as a new digital harm, adopting an optimistic yet cautiously hopeful stance, short of undertaking sweeping punitive action. The absence of outright statutory definitions for AI-altered media drives legal inhibition. Judicial expansion of common law defamation and harassment, as opposed to statutes carefully crafted for AI, has created a mosaic of irreparable holdings that weaken the deterrent power of litigation. More significantly, perhaps, the gap between understanding technology and applying law continues. The regimes of law are just starting to grasp the implications of GAN content, and schools are often left to impose applicable law. The absence of a statutory obligation to make AI-content disclosures facilitates the ability of offenders to take advantage of anonymity, thereby thwarting enforcement and frustrating the service of justice. Altogether, data and analysis call for wholesale and urgent legal reform. The law should clearly define AI-generated impersonation, mandate provenance disclosures of content, and allow courts to grant damages without imposing evidentiary burdens. On the policy front, schools must be equipped with detection technologies, courses on legal literacy, and regulations governing AI content. What is needed is a multilevel governance model—a model that integrates legal simplicity, institutional accountability, and technological intervention. It is only through a harmony of lawmakers, educators, and technologists that the deepfake abuse problem in schools can be addressed usefully. Unless there is reform, schools will continue to bear the consequences of a reactive rather than preventive response to combating synthetic media threats.

CONCLUSION

The research findings indicate a rising threat of deepfake misuse in schools and a lack of adequate existing legal and policy responses to counter it. The report acknowledges that the existing laws, particularly defamation law, intellectual property law, and fraud law, are too technologically focused and too ambiguous to respond effectively to the issue of AI-generated synthetic content. The traditional models of law that were established many decades ago now fail to keep pace with the sophistication of AI-mediated manipulation of media. Thus, deepfake perpetrators would be able to exploit such legal loopholes, making it difficult for institutions and individuals to seek recourse. The decentralised nature of legal responses, combined with differences in institutional processes and low-resolution rates of reported deepfakes, underscores the need for comprehensive reform. Judicial prudence and technological delays in forensic validation are among other challenges, as institutions of justice and courts may not have the necessary capacity and equipment to handle AI-based evidence.

Jurisdictional ambiguity in cross-border cases also adds to the challenges in enforcing legal redress, leaving victims and institutions of learning without some form of remedy. The data and charts presented throughout this research show a linear relationship between policy readiness, stakeholder satisfaction, and legal efficiency. Well-prepared institutions with well-crafted policies and proactive strategies are more effective in thwarting deepfake attacks. The law will need to become proactive and AI-literate in an attempt to combat deepfake abuse in the years to come. The law may be amended to enshrine and criminalise AI impersonation strictly, and policy frameworks should enable schools to acquire deepfake detection software and enhance their human resources with digital governance skills. Deepfakes are not merely a matter of technology but a very tangible problem of ethics and law, especially when they concern children, teachers, and the credibility of institutions. The research concludes that without a coordinated initiative to change legal systems, reframe policies, and build institutional capacities, deepfake abuse in education will continue to erode trust, destabilise learning cultures, and compromise academic integrity.

LIMITATIONS

The research adopts a qualitative stance, incorporating positivities within doctrinal legal scholarship and policy analysis. Rich with interpretive data, measuring the prevalence and extent of deepfake abuse in all schools is more challenging. Data applied, as verified by case law and organisational reporting, cannot accurately capture the actual measure of unreported or unreleased instances, especially for jurisdictions that lack robust digital surveillance capabilities. Generalisation across jurisdictions is another such limitation. In an attempt to find a balance, analysis has been focused on England and Wales. While research primarily focuses on policy and law in most nations, it does not delve deeply into region-based legal and cultural understandings of privacy, identity, and harm in the digital age, which may affect the practicability of recommendations to some.

Additionally, the use of secondary data is supported by the fact that reports are published on an open-source platform. Therefore, the report then relies on third-party data to be comprehensive and accurate. Technically, the research does not involve an original forensic examination of deepfakes or the use of AI-detection technology. Instead, it utilises data available on an open platform and institutional reports. This can impact technical accuracy in findings, particularly in relation to the efficacy of detection tooling and content validation practices. Aside from the above drawbacks, the study offers valuable insights into policy and legislative loopholes for addressing deepfake abuse in schools, making it a suitable platform for future empirical research.

FUTURE SCOPE

Future research would need to emphasise additional expansion of empirical data collection to include primary fieldwork from a broad range of learning institutions. Interviews, questionnaires, and forensic analysis of deepfake cases can provide us with more refined data on how such attacks are made possible and how they are handled in learning institutions. Such a plan will also help quantify the real incidence rate and success rate of cracking deepfake cases. There is a need for more research to be conducted in AI-forensics, particularly authentication of detection tools like Deepware Scanner, Microsoft Video Authenticator, and blockchain-based provenance tracking software. Comparatively analysing such technologies can yield valuable lessons for institutional best practices and inform advocacy for policies related to these technologies.

Legal harmonisation is also a topic that researchers can study to determine whether it is possible to strive towards a single legal regime or treaty that will regulate AI content in education. Intergovernmental negotiation between policymakers, legal professionals, and AI deployers can yield model laws and standard operating procedures that can be transferred from one country to another. Additionally, the ethics surrounding school surveillance solutions must be considered. Detection technologies, as necessary as they are in the public good, must be balanced against the student privacy rights and academic freedom. Future studies will be able to establish guidelines and provide blueprints for ethical regulation. Ultimately, interdisciplinarity among technology, law, ethics, and education policy will be essential in creating effective responses to deepfake abuse in schools that are still operational.

REFERENCES

Ahmad, Y. A. B., Kolachina, S., Rajest, S. S., Singh, M., Mishra, A., & Sundar, S. S. (2025). Impact of digital HRM on academicians' performance: Exploring the mediating role of organizational commitment. *International Journal of Intelligent Enterprise*, *12*(1), 1–21.

Ali, S., Pasha, S. A., Cox, A., & Yousseff, E. (2024). Examining the short and long-term impacts of child sexual abuse: A review study. *SN Social Sciences*, *4*(2), 1–15.

Aravind, B. R., Bhuvaneswari, G., & Rajest, S. S. (2023). ICT-based digital technology for testing and evaluation of English language teaching. In *Handbook of Research on Learning in Language Classrooms Through ICT-Based Digital Technology* (pp. 1–11). IGI Global.

Blackwell, L., Ellison, N., Elliott-Deflo, N., & Schwartz, R. (2019). Harassment in social virtual reality: Challenges for platform governance. *Proceedings of the ACM on Human-Computer Interaction*, *3*(11), 1–25.

Broadhurst, R. (2019). Child sex abuse images and exploitation materials. In Leukfeldt, R., & Holt, T. J. (Eds.), *The Human Factor of Cybercrime* (pp. 310–336). Routledge.

Chawki, M., Basu, S., & Choi, K.-S. (2024). Redefining boundaries in the metaverse: Navigating the challenges of virtual harm and user safety. *Laws*, *13*(3), 1–23.

Devi, B. T., & Rajasekaran, R. (2023). A Comprehensive Review on Deepfake Detection on Social Media Data. *FMDB Transactions on Sustainable Computing Systems*, *1*(1), 11–20.

Ecija, J. D., Abris, M. G., & Sabejon, M. B. (2024). Preparedness on disaster risk reduction management measures, competence, and challenges faced by schools. *FMDB Transactions on Sustainable Humanities and Society*, *1*(3), 100–112.

Gandhi, M., Satheesh, C., Soji, E. S., Saranya, M., Rajest, S. S., & Kothuru, S. K. (2024). Image recognition and extraction on computerized vision for sign language decoding. In *Explainable AI Applications for Human Behavior Analysis* (pp. 157–173). IGI Global.

Iglovikov, V., & Shvets, A. (2018). TernausNet: U-Net with VGG11 encoder pre-trained on ImageNet for image segmentation (arXiv:1801.05746). arXiv. Available: https://arxiv.org/abs/1801.05746 [Accessed by 03/07/23].

Kugler, M. B., & Pace, C. (2021). Deepfake privacy: Attitudes and regulation. *Northwestern University Law Review, 116*(3), 611–680.

Manjare, S. O. (2024). Beyond academics: The transformative role of social-emotional learning (SEL) in higher education. *FMDB Transactions on Sustainable Humanities and Society, 1*(4), 188–199.

Millondaga, R. M., Cahilig, D. G., & Basañes, R. A. (2024). Correlating the emotional intelligence and conflict resolution strategies of school leaders. *FMDB Transactions on Sustainable Techno Learning, 2*(4), 194–214.

Moyo, S. B., & Nithyanantham, V. (2024). Evaluating the influence of parental involvement in early childhood education programs. *AVE Trends in Intelligent Techno Learning, 1*(1), 47–60.

Mubiana, P., & Nithyanantham, V. (2024). Investigating the causes and consequences of child marriage on girls: A case study of primary schools. *FMDB Transactions on Sustainable Social Sciences Letters, 2*(2), 110–118.

Nguyen, T. T., Nguyen, Q. V. H., Nguyen, D. T., Nguyen, D. T., Huynh-The, T., Nahavandi, S., Nguyen, T. T., Pham, Q. V., & Nguyen, C. M. (2022). Deep learning for deepfakes creation and detection: A survey. *Computer Vision and Image Understanding, 223*(9), 1–20.

Nithyanantham, V. (2023). Study Examines the Connection Between Students' Various Intelligence and Their Levels of Mathematical Success in School. *FMDB Transactions on Sustainable Techno Learning, 1*(1), 32–59.

Olubunmi, O. I. (2024). Impact of learning resources management strategies on academic performance of junior secondary school business studies. *AVE Trends In Intelligent Techno Learning, 1*(1), 1–10.

Pentakota, S. L. B. (2025). Unveiling deepfake and fraudulent content generation in GPT models and countermeasures. *AVE Trends in Intelligent Computer Letters, 1*(1), 41–50.

Rami, A. A. M. (2024). Navigating challenges in policy development: Addressing political, institutional, and cultural challenges. *FMDB Transactions on Sustainable Social Sciences Letters, 2*(2), 56–69.

Rendhy, R. (2024). Impact of academic management information system on school performance: A case study. *AVE Trends in Intelligent Social Letters, 1*(4), 197–213.

Rendhy, R., Yulianti, Y., & Yanti, Y. (2024). Analysis implementation academic management information system. *AVE Trends in Intelligent Technoprise Letters*, *1*(3), 136–144.

Thies, J., Zollhofer, M., Stamminger, M., Theobalt, C., & Nießner, M. (2016). Face2Face: Real-time face capture and reenactment of RGB videos. In *Proceedings of the IEEE Conference on Computer Vision and Pattern Recognition*, Las Vegas, NV, United States of America.

. Tripathi, S., & Al -Zubaidi, A. (2023). A Study within Salalah's Higher Education Institutions on Online Learning Motivation and Engagement Challenges during Covid-19. FMDB Transactions on Sustainable Techno Learning, 1(1), 1–10.

Vaccari, C., & Chadwick, A. (2020). Deepfakes and disinformation: Exploring the impact of synthetic political video on deception, uncertainty, and trust in news. *Social Media + Society*, *6*(1), 1–13.

Velmonte, G. L. (2023). Preferred College Degree Programs Among Senior High School Students: A Policy Recommendation. *FMDB Transactions on Sustainable Techno Learning*, *1*(3), 143–155.

. Vijayarani, K., Nithyanantham, V., Angelene Christabel, & D. Marupaka (2023) "A Study on Relationship Between Self-Regulated Learning Habit and Achievement Among High School Students. FMDB Transactions on Sustainable Techno Learning, 1(2), 92–110.

Chapter 10

Seeing Isn't Believing: On the Psychological and Social Toll of Deepfakes on Student Perception and Well-Being

Xavier Louis
https://orcid.org/0000-0002-6645-7746
Saveetha Institutes of Medical and Technical Sciences, Chennai, India

Surbhi Girdhar
Shri Vaishnav Institute of Forensic Science, Indore, India

S. Karthick Raja
Tata Institute of Social Sciences, Mumbai, India

S. S. Padmapriya
Saveetha Institutes of Medical and Technical Sciences, Chennai, India

Sheeja Selestine
London American City College, Sharjah, UAE

ABSTRACT

The technical risks of deepfakes are thoroughly documented. Still, their social and psychological consequences, mainly among students, are just beginning to be understood. This chapter delves deeply into the behavioral, cognitive, and emotional implications of deepfake exposure in academic settings, where the creation of realistic but false media can destroy students' ability to differentiate between truth and fabrication. This results in increased anxiety, declined trust, and an inclination towards skepticism towards digital communication. Drawing on psychological theories such as media effects, cognitive dissonance, and social identity, this chapter

DOI: 10.4018/979-8-3373-3770-8.ch010

examines how synthetic content affects peer relationships, individual perception, and group dynamics within educational environments. This also explores the risks of identity manipulation, cyberbullying, and reputational harm when deepfakes are misused in social media or peer-to-peer contexts.

INTRODUCTION

The current educational landscape has witnessed an unprecedented integration of digital technologies, transforming how students communicate, learn, and construct their academic identities. Within this digitally mediated environment, the rise of deepfake technology poses numerous emotional and cognitive risks that extend beyond traditional concerns about information accuracy (Westerlund 2019). The sophisticated artificial intelligence systems can create deepfakes, which are hyper-realistic yet fabricated multimedia content, introducing new types of psychological vulnerability that could challenge the fundamentals of perception, trust, and social interaction in educational settings. Prior research (Kharvi, 2024) revealed a 550% increase in deepfakes online since 2019 (Figure 1). However, a case study of Mumbai found that 52.7% of professionals were not aware of deepfake technologies (Sharma & Shaikh, 2025).

Figure 1. Deepfake incidents (2019-2023)

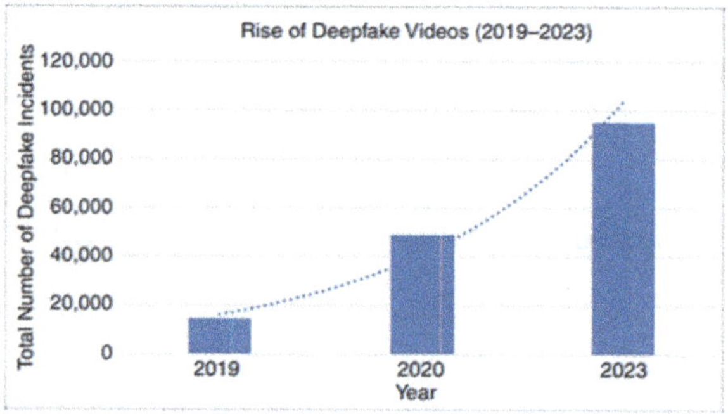

(Kharvi, 2024)

The deepfake technology's emotional toll on students manifests through the various interconnected pathways that reflect the distinct social and developmental characteristics of university populations, students, and those who typically exist in high-stress academic environments, while parallelly going through complex identity formation processes, face specific vulnerability to the anxiety-inducing effects of synthetic media (Kietzmann et al. 2020). Knowledge about one's likeness, voice, or actions can be fabricated convincingly and distributed without consent, initiating a persistent state of vigilance that can interfere with normal social and academic functioning. This perpetual uncertainty about digital authenticity creates what researchers have coined as "deepfake anxiety," a condition characterized by hypervigilance regarding media content, chronic worry about identity security and reputation, and increased social withdrawal from digital platforms (Vaccari and Chadwick, 2020).

Deepfake technology imposes significant cognitive burdens on students, who must now evaluate not just the content of educational materials but also their fundamental authenticity. Traditional information literacy skills, which focus on source credibility and bias detection, are proven insufficient for identifying sophisticated synthetic media that openly exploit perceptual assumptions about audiovisual authenticity (Groh et al., 2022). Therefore, students must develop an entirely new cognitive framework for media evaluation, while managing their existing academic workload alongside, and create competitive demands for limited mental resources that could compromise learning effectiveness.

The cognitive dissonance experienced when encountering highly potent synthetic content creates additional psychological stress, as students struggle to reconcile perceptual cues with logical knowledge about the possibilities of manipulation (Festinger 1957). This internal conflict needs strategies for resolution that might include blanket skepticism towards digital media, evasion of multimedia educational resources, or acceptance of authenticity uncertainty as a permanent feature of digital communication; also, each of these adaptive responses has implications for social interaction and educational engagement that extend far beyond the encounter with questionable content.

The social dimensions of deepfake impact in educational environments are also concerning, as these technologies highly threaten the trust relationships that shape the foundation of collaborative learning and peer connection (Chesney and Citron 2019). When students are uncertain about the authenticity of communications from peers, professors, or institutional sources, the collaborative spirit necessary for effective education is compromised. The probability that any recorded lecture, video message, or social media post might be fabricated creates a hint of suspicion that could hinder the open interchange of ideas and vulnerable self-disclosure necessary for real-time educational experiences (Rahman and Liu 2022).

BACKGROUND

Deepfake Technology and Its Evolution

Deepfake technology evolved from academic research in computer vision and machine learning, building on decades of work in neural networks and artificial intelligence, the base of the technology highly depends on generative adversarial networks (GANs), a type of machine learning architecture introduced by Ian Goodfellow and colleagues in 2014, where two neural networks compete to win each other to create highly realistic synthetic content (Goodfellow et al. 2014). The word "deepfake" combines "deep learning" and "fake," highlighting the sophisticated artificial intelligence techniques used to create synthetic media content (Figure 2).

Figure 2. Evolution of deepfake technology

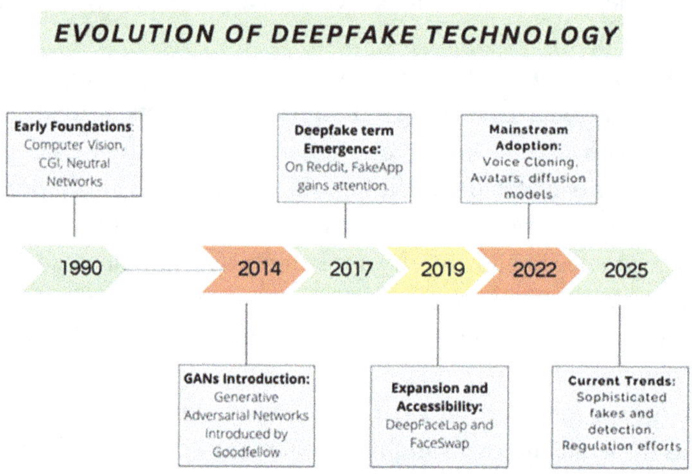

The evolution of deepfake technology has been remarkably rapid, progressing from experimental research tools that require substantial computational resources and technical expertise to consumer-accessible applications available on smartphones. Early deepfake systems, developed in academic settings around 2017, required substantial processing time and large datasets to create relatively crude synthetic videos (Ajder et al., 2019). By 2023, real-time deepfake generation will be possible using standard consumer hardware, which will change the accessibility and potential impact of synthetic media creation.

The significance of technological democratisation in educational environments is particularly noteworthy, as faculty and students regularly create and consume video content for learning purposes. Moreover, the barriers to creating deepfakes have been reduced, allowing basic synthetic media to be generated with minimal technical expertise. In contrast, advanced systems capable of creating highly convincing content remain within the reach of motivated individuals (Dolhansky et al. 2020). This accessibility implies that educational institutions can no longer treat deepfakes as a theoretical future concern; they must instead acknowledge them as an immediate and contemporary reality.

The technical sophistication of modern deepfake systems enables manipulation across various modalities, including full-body puppetry, facial reenactment, and speech synthesis. Facial reenactment systems can transfer facial expressions and movements from one person to another. At the same time, speech synthesis can also generate clear audio of individuals saying things they never actually said with convincing reality (Li et al. 2020). These capable abilities are highly concerning in educational contexts where virtual meetings, video lectures, and recorded presentations are usual, as they can create various vectors for potential deception and manipulation.

Cognitive Dissonance Theory and Media Perception

Understanding the psychological effect of deepfakes requires an examination of fundamental theories of cognition and perception, particularly the cognitive dissonance theory, as developed by Leon Festinger in 1957. Cognitive dissonance refers to the psychological discomfort experienced when individuals hold contradictory beliefs or encounter information that conflicts with their existing attitudes and expectations (Festinger, 1957). This theory provides a vital framework for understanding students' responses to deepfake encounters, where the authenticity of synthetic content intersects with logical skepticism about the credibility of media.

When students encounter sophisticated deepfakes, they often experience what researchers term "authenticity dissonance," a state where perceptual cues suggest that the content is genuine. In contrast, cognitive knowledge implies potential fabrication; this dissonance instills psychological stress that motivates resolution strategies, which might include dismissing concerns about authenticity, developing excessive skepticism towards all digital media, or avoiding engagement with potentially problematic content altogether (Hancock and Bailenson, 2021). Each one of these strategies has implications for students' learning and social functioning that go far beyond the immediate encounter with synthetic media.

This resolution of deepfake-induced cognitive dissonance is complicated by the sophisticated nature of modern synthetic media, which often provides conflicting cues about authenticity. Traditional indicators of media credibility, such as consistency, visual quality, and source reputation, may be present in well-crafted deepfakes, making rational evaluation difficult (Maras and Alexandrou 2019). Therefore, students must develop new cognitive frameworks that extend beyond surface-level evaluation to incorporate technical knowledge about the creation and detection of synthetic media.

Henri Tajfel and John Turner developed social identity theory, which provides another lens for understanding the effects of deepfakes on student communities. This theory posits that individuals derive substantial portions of their self-concept from social categories and group memberships (Tajfel et al., 2001). Representations of student groups, academic leaders, or institutional figures that Deepfakes manipulate can therefore threaten not only their individual identity but also the collective identity and group cohesion within educational communities.

LITERATURE REVIEW

Deepfake Detection and Human Vulnerability

Research into deepfake detection capabilities among student populations reveals concerning gaps between confidence and actual ability in identifying synthetic content. Groh et al. (2022) conducted comprehensive studies to demonstrate that, university students performed just slightly better than chance when asked to differentiate between authentic from deepfake videos, despite the high self-reported confidence in their detection abilities, this "confidence gap" suggests that students might be specifically vulnerable to sophisticated deepfakesaccurately because their overconfidence in their abilities brings down their critical vigilance when consuming digital media. This study also revealed that even when detection training is provided, the improvement in actual performance remained modest, while confidence levels increased substantially, creating potentially dangerous overconfidence effects (Rossler et al., 2019).

Psychological Distress and Anxiety Patterns

Vaccari and Chadwick (2020) conducted pioneering research on the psychological effects of exposure to deepfakes. They found that contact with political deepfakes increased uncertainty, decreased trust in the media generally, and heightened anxiety about information authenticity. Their longitudinal study showed that these effects persisted until after the participants were informed about the synthetic nature of the content. They suggested that exposure to deepfakes creates long-lasting changes in cognitive processing and emotional response. This research identified certain anxiety patterns, which include hypervigilance regarding media content, increased verification behaviours, and the term "reality fatigue" resulting from constant authenticity evaluation efforts.

Trust Erosion in Digital Communications

This phenomenon of trust erosion extends from specific deepfake encounters to affect general media consumption patterns and social interactions. Chesney and Citron (2019) noted down how just awareness of deepfake technology, even without the direct exposure to synthetic content, paged way towards the decreased trust in digital communications and increased skepticism toward video evidence in general, also this "liar's dividend" effect means that just the existence of deepfake technology could undermine the confidence in authentic content, and create broad social costs that goes far beyond the direct manipulation attempts. Their research revealed a specific impact on institutional trust, with participants expressing reduced confidence in communications from educational institutions, government agencies, and news organizations.

Identity Threats and Personal Vulnerability

Studies evaluating the psychological effects of being targeted by malicious deepfakes show severe distress patterns that are consistent with identity theft trauma. Henry et al. (2021) conducted elaborate interviews with deepfake victims, and documented feelings of helplessness, violation, and even loss of control over their representation, in educational contexts, where reputation and peer relationships are vital for academic success, the social nature of learning environments might inflate these impacts, and the research foundspecific vulnerability among female students, who reported heightened anxiety about potential non-consensual deepfake creation and modified their online behavior accordingly.

Cognitive Load and Learning Interference

The cognitive burden imposed by constant authenticity evaluation represents a notable yet often overlooked impact of deepfake technology on academic performance. Sweller's cognitive load theory provides a framework for understanding how deepfake-related vigilance contests with educational processing utilise limited mental resources (Sweller 1988). Research by Paris and Donovan (2019) demonstrated that students are expected to evaluate media authenticity while processing content for comprehension, and it also revealed reduced learning outcomes compared to control groups. Additionally, this suggests that psychological adaptation to deepfake environments may carry hidden costs for educational effectiveness.

Social Transmission of Deepfake Anxiety

The social transmission of deepfake-related anxiety also shows another important dimension of psychological impact, with the research implying that awareness of deepfake technology could spread through communities even without direct exposure to synthetic content. Lewandowsky et al. (2020) recorded this transmission effect in university settings. They found that students who studied deepfakes from their peers showed similar anxiety patterns to those who had encountered synthetic content directly. This finding suggests that institutional responses to deepfakes must consider both indirect and direct psychological impacts, as awareness campaigns that are intended to protect students may inadvertently increase their level of anxiety.

Cultural and Demographic Vulnerability Factors

Research has identified important cultural and demographic factors that influence the psychological impact of deepfakes. Students coming from cultures carrying a strong emphasis on social reputation and family honour experience high levels of anxiety about potential deepfake manipulation due to their concerns about bringing shame to their communities or families (Tandoc et al. 2018). Additionally, language barriers create extra vulnerabilities for international students, who may have greater difficulty in detecting subtle cultural or linguistic inconsistencies that could indicate synthetic content. These findings shed light on the need for culturally sensitive approaches to deepfake education and support.

Coping Strategies and Resilience Factors

Studies about coping strategies used by individuals who are dealing with deepfake-related stress have found both adaptive and maladaptive responses that have important implications for educational support interventions. Adaptive strategies encompass elements such as developing technical knowledge about detection methods, seeking social support, and maintaining engagement with trusted information sources (Bandura, 2001). Maladaptive strategies include complete avoidance of digital media, excessive skepticism that impairs normal functioning, and social withdrawal from online communities. Understanding these patterns is crucial for developing effective support interventions for affected students.

Long-Term Psychological Consequences

Rising longitudinal research suggests that deepfake-related psychological effects may have long-lasting consequences that extend well beyond immediate exposure events. Preliminary studies indicate that individuals who experience notable distress related to deepfakes might develop persistent patterns of digital hypervigilance and social trust issues, interfering with normal relationship formation and maintenance (Fletcher, 2018). For students, these long-term effects may impact their social network formation, career development, and overall life satisfaction in ways that researchers are only just beginning to understand.

THEMATIC DISCUSSION

The thematic map (Figure 3) reveals three key aspects of the impact of deepfakes on students' perceptions and well-being.

Figure 3. Key themes of deepfakes on student perception and well-being

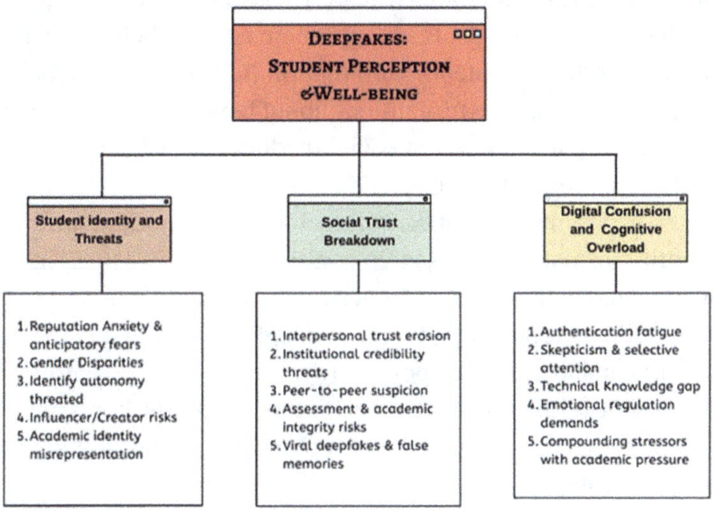

Student Identity Threats and Vulnerability

The relationship in-between student identity formation and digital media consumption makes unique vulnerabilities to deepfake manipulation that extends far beyond simple information credibility concerns, present students develop and maintain their sense of self throughout complex interactions across multiple digital platforms, where their social relationships, personal brand, and academic reputation, are consistently built and rebuilt through shared media content (Marwick and Lewis 2017). Within this context, deepfakes pose a fundamental threat to identity autonomy, as they also enable others to create unauthorised representations that might be indistinguishably authentic.

The base and developmental stage of most university students intensify these identity-related concerns, as emerging adults explore different aspects of their personality, values, and social connections. This period of identity exploration makes them particularly sensitive to reputation threats and social judgment, creating psychological vulnerabilities that malicious deepfakes can easily exploit (Arnett 2000). Students report feeling anxious about the possibility of synthetic content featuring their likeness being created and distributed without their knowledge, as this may potentially damage their relationships with friends, family, future employees, or even romantic partners.

The permanence and search ability of digital content has intensified these concerns, as students understand that deepfakes created during their university years could anytime resurface and implode in their lives even decades later, this temporal dimension of deepfake threats creates what researchers have coined as "anticipatory reputation anxiety," where students change their current behaviour based on the fears about future synthetic content manipulation (Citron and Franks 2014). Some students also report becoming extra cautious about being photographed or recorded, which may limit their participation in social media or lead them to avoid activities that could be used to create deepfakes.

Gender-based variations in deepfake vulnerability initiate additional complications for student identity formation, as research continuously shows that girls and women are invariably targeted by malicious synthetic content, mainly deepfakes of a sexual nature. Female students report high levels of deepfake-related anxiety and possibly modify their online behaviour in response to synthetic media concerns (Henry et al. 2021). These gender disparities show wider patterns of online harassment and might compound existing challenges related to women's participation in a few academic fields or leadership roles.

The intersection of deepfake threats with other identity categories makes compounding vulnerabilities for students who belong to marginalized communities, also students of color, LGBTQ+ students, and those from religious minorities report concerns that deepfakes could be used to reinforce stereotypes, create false evidence of behaviors that are inconsistent with their values, or their credibility might be undermined inside their communities (Sobel 2020). These intersectional vulnerabilities highlight the need for institutional responses that consider the diverse ways deepfakes may impact different student populations.

The role of content creators and social media influencers among student populations begin another layer of identity-related vulnerability, and students who have built substantial online followings or who employ social media for professional purposes face specific risks from deepfake manipulation, as synthetic content could undermine their credibility, damage their brand partnerships, or even violate platform policies, also the economic implications of these threats add financial stress to the psychological burden of deepfake anxiety.

Academic identity formation go through specific challenges when deepfakes can be used to manipulate representations of intellectual achievement, research presentations, or scholarly discourse participation, students worry that synthetic content could be used to misrepresent their academic positions, create false evidence of plagiarism or misconduct, or undermine their standing within their academic disciplines, these concerns are particularly acute for graduate students and aspiring academics whose professional futures solely dependon reputation and credibility within the scholarly communities.

Social Trust Breakdown in Academic Communities

Educational institutions runlike a complex social ecosystem that build over many layers of trusted relationships between students and peers, students and faculty, students and institutional sources of information, and students and administratiors, the introduction of deepfake technology into these environments poses as threats to undermine the trust relationships in several ways that can alter the nature of academic discourse and collaborative learning (Rini 2020).

The erasing of interpersonal trust shows one of the most important social effects of deepfake technology in educational settings, when students cannot be sure about the authenticity of communications from peers, administrator, or professors, the collaborative foundation of academic work is this compromised, and students report the increased skepticism about email communications, recorded lectures, and video conference interactions, which further leads to requests for additional verification that can slow down educational processes and create hurdles to timely feedback and support.

Trust in institutional authority faces specific challenges when deepfakes can be used to impersonate expert sources, university leaders, or faculty members. Traditional markers of institutional credibility, such as official email addresses, university websites, or recognised platforms, may not be sufficient to guarantee authenticity, as sophisticated synthetic content can mimic these indicators (Fallis 2021). Students must develop new frameworks for verifying institutional communications that extend beyond traditional authority structures, potentially confusing legitimate channels for academic information and support.

The peer-to-peer trust relationships that enables social learning, effective group work, and study partnerships, are also easily prone to deepfake-related suspicion, students report about staying more cautious about sharing personal information with classmates, participating in recorded group meetings, or even engaging in frank academic discussions due to having concerns about possible misuse of their contributions, this increased caution can pull back the depth of peer relationships and reduce the collaborative learning which is essential for success in academic area.

The impact on assessment and academic integrity reveals another critical aspect of trust erosion in educational settings, where deepfakes can be used to impersonate students during online exams, fabricate evidence of academic misconduct, or falsify participation in group projects. The traditional systems for maintaining academic honesty become inadequate (Newton, 2018). Here, faculty members report increased skepticism about student submissions and higher reluctance to use online assessment tools, which potentially limits innovative pedagogical approaches that depend on digital technology.

Social media platforms, those used extensively by student communities face few specific challenges while maintaining trust withdeepfakes seamlessly integrating into normal content sharing, also student organizations, residential communities, and informal social networks that depend on social media for communication and coordination must bring up new norms for content verification and response to the synthetic material, also the social dynamics of these communities can be greatly altered when members cannot trust the authenticity of the shared content.

This phenomenon of "viral deepfakes" represents that there is a threat to community trust, as the synthetic content gains widespread distribution creates shared false memories or beliefs that lingers even bbbbbbbbbbbbbbb7after correction, educational institutions have documented and reported cases where deepfake content featuring faculty members, administrators, or student leaders circulated quickly before being identified as synthetic, which creates lasting effects on community perception and their relationship dynamics.

Digital Confusion and Cognitive Overload

The cognitive burden forced by the need to evaluate media authenticity constantly shows a n important but usuallyignored impact of deepfake technology on student's mental health and academic performance, now students must navigate an informative environment where traditional heuristics for assessing content credibility might be unreliable, and requires more deliberate and resource-intensive evaluation processes that fights with other cognitive demands of academic work (Pennycook and Rand 2021).

The development of "authentication fatigue" has been recorded among the students who reported feeling overwhelmed by the mental effort required to verify digital content, this highly manifests as declinedreadiness to engage with multimedia educational materials, reduced participation in online discussions, and a liking for traditional text-based resources that seems more secured from manipulation, these modifications in learning preferences may hinder the exposure of students' to innovative educational technologies and multimedia resources that could improve their academic experience.

The volume and speed of digital content consumption in the current academic environments intensify the cognitive challenges that are associated with deepfake detection, students usually grasp news articles, video lectures, social media updates, and peer communications at a rapid speed that precludes careful authenticity of evaluation for each piece of content, which creates a notable tension between vigilant content verification and efficient information processing that many students resolve by developing high skepticism or selective attention strategies that might cause them to miss important information.

The technical knowledge necessary for effective deepfake detection shows another source of cognitive burden for students who lack a good background in media production, computer science, or digital forensics. Although some detection techniques could be taught with the help of media literacy programs, the swiftly evolving nature of synthetic content creation implies that detection methods regularly lag behind the creation capabilities (Rössler et al. 2019). Therefore, students must develop adaptive learning strategies that enable them to consistently update their technical knowledge while managing their other academic responsibilities.

The emotional regulation needed to manage deepfake-related anxiety all the while maintaining normal academic functions, shows an added cognitive load that can interfere with the learning effectiveness, students report about spending noteworthy mental energy to manage their emotional responses to the potentially synthetic content, developing coping mechanisms for authenticity uncertainty, and processing the implications of living in an environment where media manipulation is highly accessible and sophisticated.

The intersection of deepfake concerns with existing academic stressors can generate compounding effects that can significantly impact the well-being of students, andstudents those who are already dealing with mental health challenges, academic pressure, social isolation, or financial stress, may be pointedly vulnerable to the extra cognitive and emotional burden of deepfake-related concerns, these intersecting stressors can make downward spirals where deepfake anxiety get in the way ofacademic performance, which in turn elevates their overall stress and vulnerability to further psychological impact.

CASE INSIGHTS

Interview Narratives From Affected Students

The recent qualitative research with in-depth interviews among university students unveils the personal and often profound ways that deepfake technology influences daily academic and social experiences, and to be specific Maria, a junior in communications at a large public university, elaborated her growing unease with video content consumption: "I used to watch lecture recordings without thinking twice, but now I find myself scrutinizing everythingthe professor's lip sync, whether their expressions are in sync their voice tone, even the lighting quality. It's growing to be exhausting, and I know I'm not learning properly as well because part of my brain always holds a guard instead of completely focusing on the actual content."

James, a computer science graduate student who had extensive knowledge about deepfake technology, reported a different but highly concerning pattern of hypervigilance: "I probably know more about deepfake detection than most students on campus, but that knowledge only makes me more paranoid, and not less, I see potential manipulation everywhere, even in authentic content, it's like knowing too much about how sausage is made, which prevents you from enjoying it anymore. I've started to avoid video calls with my advisor because I spend the whole time analysing whether anything looks off instead of discussing my research".

The social dimensions of deepfake impacts came to light clearly in interviews with students who had experience with it or those who witnessed deepfake-related incidents on campus. Sarah, a sophomore who discovered that her social media photos had been used to create a synthetic video that circulated among her residence hall, described her lasting psychological impact: "Even though it was clear to most people that the video was fake once they looked closely, I couldn't wear off the feeling that everyone was looking at me at a different light, I hold myself from posting pictures online, stopped going to social events, and my grades dropped drastically because I was so distracted by the worry of what else might be out there with my face on it".

Interviews with international students revealed additional layers of vulnerability related to language and cultural barriers that intensified their concerns about deepfakes. Ahmed, an engineering student from Egypt who is pursuing his master's degree, explained the cultural dimensions of his anxiety: "In my culture, family honor and reputation are considered as extremely important, the possibility of someone creating a video of me saying or doing inappropriate things terrifies me more than the academic failure, also I've become very careful about my online presence, maybe too careful or paranoid, and barely participate in social media now, which makes it hard to connect with other students and feel part of the campus community".

Students involved in campus leadership roles or public-facing activities expressed concerns about being targeted by deepfakes, which compromise their credibility and effectiveness. Michelle, a student government president at a mid-sized private college, noted the chilling effect on her leadership style: "Every time I give a speech or appear in the campus media, I worry that someone with opposing political views might manipulate the content to make me look bad or discredit our initiatives, this changed how I communicate, and made me more cautious, more formal, less authentic in my public presentations. That's not how effective leadership has to be, but I feel like I have to protect myself and my reputation".

Hybrid Learning Environment Anecdotes

The swift-paced adoption of hybrid and online learning models during the COVID-19 pandemic raised concerns about deepfakes in new contexts, illustrating the complex intersection of student anxiety, technology, and education. Professor Jennifer Collins, hailing from a large state university reported a disruptive incident particularly, where students became convinced that a guest lecturer appearing via video conference was a deepfake impersonation: "The speaker was discussing controversial research findings, and during some technical difficulties that caused audio-video synchronization issues, several students began expressing their concerns and doubts about the authenticity of the presentation in the chat, this suspicion spread swiftly, and I had to stop the lecture midway to verify the speaker's identity through multiple channels, which took nearly twenty minutes and entirely disrupted the learning environment".

Educational technology administrators have noted cases where deepfake concerns have interfered with legitimate assessment processes in online learning environments. Dr. Robert Martinez, director of online learning at a community college, explained a complex situation that involves exam integrity: "A student attempted to excuse their poor performance on a proctored online exam, claiming that a deepfake had been employed to impersonate them during the assessment, while our investigation revealed that no synthetic content was involved, the incident shed light on how deepfake technology creates new avenues for academic dishonesty claims and complicates our traditional approaches about maintaining integrity in online testing".

The asynchronous nature of much hybrid learning has created several vulnerabilities to deepfake-related misinformation and confusion among student populations. Academic advisor Lisa Thompson reported receiving inquiries from multiple students regarding the authenticity of recorded announcements: "Students have become suspicious of the pre-recorded video messages from their faculty and administrators, mainly when the content is about changes to policies or deadlines. We implemented additional verification procedures for important communications, including follow-up emails with digital signatures and confirmation through various channels, which significantly slowed down our communication processes.

Faculty members who teachin hybrid environments report the increased requests for identity verification during their online sessions, especially when technical difficulties or unusual circumstances occur, Professor David Kim, who teach psychology courses in a hybrid format, described their additional burden: "Students now often ask me to answer personal questions or reference the recent in-person interactions for verifying my identity during the online sessions, mainly if there are connectivity issues that affect video quality. While I understand their concerns, these authentication requests interrupt and disturb the flow of instruction and create an atmosphere of suspicion that interferes with the collaborative learning environment we're trying to establish".

CHALLENGES

Digital Fatigue and Identity Manipulation

The presence of constant vigilance required to navigate an information environment potentially filled with synthetic content creates some digital fatigue that goes beyond traditional screen time concerns to encompass the mental exhaustion that is associated with perpetual authenticity evaluation, students report about experiencing decision fatigue related to media consumption, where the cognitive effort needed to assess the content credibility becomes immense and leads to either obvious acceptance or rejection of digital information sources (Pennycook and Rand 2021). This burden of authentication is becoming problematic in educational settings, where multimedia content is highly essential for effective learning, forcing students to process academic content for comprehension while simultaneously evaluating its authenticity.

The democratization of deepfake creation tools has made identity manipulation accessible to individuals with relatively modest technical skills and resources, creating new vectors for intimidation, harassment, and psychological manipulation within the student communities. Unlike the traditional forms of cyberbullying, deepfake-based attacks can generate authentic evidence of behaviours or statements that possibly never occurred, which makes them difficult to defend against and potentially more psychologically damaging (Citron and Franks 2014). The intersection of deepfake threats with existing patterns of discrimination creates inflated risks for students who already face marginalisation, as synthetic content could be weaponised to reinforce stereotypes or undermine credibility within the academic and social communities.

Misinformation and Academic Discourse Disruption

The integration of deepfake technology into broader misinformation campaigns presents new challenges for fostering open inquiry and evidence-based discourse, which are essential characteristics of effective educational environments. When synthetic content is used to support false claims or undermine legitimate information sources, students must develop increasingly sophisticated evaluation skills that extend beyond traditional source credibility assessment (Lewandowsky et al., 2020). The polarising potential of deepfakes is primarily concerning in educational contexts, where exposure to diverse perspectives and civil disagreement are essential for intellectual development, as synthetic content could deepen divisions and undermine the trust necessary for productive academic discourse.

FUTURE DIRECTIONS

Psychological Support Frameworks

Educational institutions must bring up and provide comprehensive psychological support frameworks, especially designed to address the deepfake-related anxiety and trauma. These frameworks should include specialized training for counseling center staff on the distinct psychological impacts of synthetic media, the development of support groups for students who deal with deepfake-related concerns, and the integration of deepfake awareness into existing mental health programming (Lazar et al., 2021). Preventive mental health approaches can focus on building student resilience to deepfake-related stressors through identity affirmation practices, stress management education, and community-building initiatives that will strengthen social support networks.

Digital Ethics Integration in Policy

Universities must integrate consideration of deepfake technology and synthetic media into their already existing ethical frameworks and policy structures, and this integration should encompass academic integrity policies, institutional research ethics protocols, student conduct codes, and technology use agreements. The development of institutional response protocols for deepfake incidents must include clear procedures for community communication, content verification, disciplinary action, and victim support. Additionally, educational institutions should consider their role in broader societal responses to deepfake technology, including participation in the development of industry standards and advocacy for appropriate regulatory approaches.

CONCLUSION

The rise of deepfake technology in educational environments shows a fundamental challenge to the psychological and social foundations of student learning and well-being, this chapter has examined the multifaceted ways in which synthetic media shows its effects on student communities, and reveal the impacts that extend beyond simple concerns about misinformation to encompass cognitive overload, identity threats, social trust breakdown, and mental health challenges that can significantly impair academic success and personal development, the research shows that students face unique vulnerabilities to deepfake-related psychological harm because of their developmental stage, heavy reliance on digital media, and the collaborative nature of educational environments. Current institutional responses seem to be insufficient in addressing these complex challenges and require comprehensive approaches that will integrate psychological, technical, educational, and social support strategies. Additionally, educational institutions must act urgently to develop effective responses that protect student well-being while preserving the benefits of digital technology for learning and growth.

REFERENCES

Ajder, H., Patrini, G., Cavalli, F., & Cullen, L. (2019). *The state of deepfakes: Landscape, threats, and impact*. Deeptrace Labs.

Arnett, J. J. (2000). Emerging adulthood: A theory of development from the late teens through the twenties. *The American Psychologist*, *55*(5), 469–480. PMID: 10842426

Bandura, A. (2001). Social cognitive theory of mass communication. *Media Psychology*, *3*(3), 265–299.

Chesney, R., & Citron, D. (2019). Deep fakes: A looming challenge for privacy, democracy, and national security. *California Law Review*, *107*(6), 1753–1820.

Citron, D. K., & Franks, M. A. (2014). Criminalizing revenge porn. *Wake Forest Law Review*, *49*(2), 345–391.

Dolhansky, B., Bitton, J., Pflaum, B., Lu, J., Howes, R., Wang, M., & Ferrer, C. C. (2020). The deepfake detection challenge (DFDC) dataset [arXiv preprint arXiv:2006.07397]. arXiv. Available: https://arxiv.org/abs/2006.07397 [Accessed by 23/06/24].

Fallis, D. (2021). The epistemic threat of deepfakes. *Philosophy & Technology*, *34*(4), 623–643. PMID: 32837868

Festinger, L. (1957). *A theory of cognitive dissonance*. Stanford University Press.

Fletcher, J. (2018). Deepfakes, artificial intelligence, and some kind of dystopia: The new faces of online post-truth persona. *Theatre Journal*, *70*(4), 455–471.

Goodfellow, I., Pouget-Abadie, J., Mirza, M., Xu, B., Warde-Farley, D., & Ozair, S., & Bengio. (2014). Generative adversarial nets. *Advances in Neural Information Processing Systems*, *27*(6), 2672–2680.

Groh, M., Epstein, Z., Firestone, C., & Picard, R. (2022). Deepfake detection by human crowds, machines, and machine-informed crowds. *Proceedings of the National Academy of Sciences of the United States of America*, *119*(1), 1–11. PMID: 34969837

Hancock, J. T., & Bailenson, J. N. (2021). The social impact of deepfakes. *Cyberpsychology, Behavior, and Social Networking*, *24*(3), 149–152. PMID: 33760669

Henry, N., McGlynn, C., Flynn, A., Johnson, K., Pound, N., & Rackley, E. (2021). Image-based sexual abuse: A study on the causes and consequences of non-consensual intimate image sharing. *Feminism & Psychology*, *31*(1), 70–87.

Kharvi, P. L. (2024). Understanding the impact of AI-generated deepfakes on public opinion, political discourse, and personal security in social media. *IEEE Security and Privacy*, *22*(4), 115–122.

Kietzmann, J., Lee, L. W., McCarthy, I. P., & Kietzmann, T. C. (2020). Deepfakes: Trick or treat? *Business Horizons*, *63*(2), 135–146.

Lazar, A., Chen, Y., & Xu, W. (2021). Educational deepfakes and student psychological well-being. In *Handbook of Research on Digital Content, Mobile Learning, and Technology Integration Models in Teacher Education*. IGI Global.

Lewandowsky, S., Ecker, U. K. H., Seifert, C. M., Schwarz, N., & Cook, J. (2020). The continued influence of corrected misinformation. *Psychological Science*, *31*(5), 566–577.

Li, Y., Yang, X., Sun, P., Qi, H., & Lyu, S. (2020). Celeb-DF: A large-scale challenging dataset for DeepFake forensics. *2020 IEEE/CVF Conference on Computer Vision and Pattern Recognition (CVPR)*. IEEE, Seattle, Washington, United States of America.

Maras, M.-H., & Alexandrou, A. (2019). Determining authenticity of video evidence in the age of artificial intelligence and in the wake of Deepfake videos. *The International Journal of Evidence & Proof*, *23*(3), 255–262.

Marwick, A., & Lewis, R. (2017). *Media manipulation and disinformation online*. Data & Society Research.

Newton, P. M. (2018). How common is commercial contract cheating in higher education and is it increasing? A systematic review. *Frontiers in Education*, *3*(8), 1–67.

Paris, B., & Donovan, J. (2019). *Deepfakes and cheap fakes: The manipulation of audiovisual evidence*. Data & Society Research Institute.

Pennycook, G., & Rand, D. G. (2021). The psychology of fake news. *Trends in Cognitive Sciences*, *25*(5), 388–402. PMID: 33736957

Rahman, M. S., & Liu, C. (2022). Digital media literacy and deepfake awareness among university students. In *Advances in educational technologies and instructional design*. IGI Global.

Rini, R. (2020). Deepfakes and the epistemic backstop. *Philosophers' Imprint*, *20*(24), 1–16.

Rossler, A., Cozzolino, D., Verdoliva, L., Riess, C., Thies, J., & Niessner, M. (2019). FaceForensics++: Learning to detect manipulated facial images. *2019 IEEE/CVF International Conference on Computer Vision (ICCV)*. IEEE, Seoul, Korea (South).

Sharma, M. D., & Shaikh, A. N. N. (2025). A case study on Deepfake Awareness, Mumbai, India. *Indian Journal of Computer Science and Technology*, *4*(01), 121–126.

Sobel, J. (2020). The impact of deepfakes on marginalized communities. *Technology in Society*, *42*(3), 78–89.

Sweller, J. (1988). Cognitive load during problem solving: Effects on learning. *Cognitive Science*, *12*(2), 257–285.

Tajfel, H., Turner, J., Austin, W. G., & Worchel, S. (2001). An integrative theory of intergroup conflict. Intergroup relations: Essential readings, New York, United States of America.

Tandoc, E. C.Jr, Lim, Z. W., & Ling, R. (2018). Defining "fake news" A typology of scholarly definitions. *Digital Journalism (Abingdon, England)*, *6*(2), 137–153.

Vaccari, C., & Chadwick, A. (2020). Deepfakes and disinformation: Exploring the impact of synthetic political video on deception, uncertainty, and trust in news. *Social Media + Society*, *6*(1), 3–13.

Westerlund, M. (2019). The emergence of deepfake technology: A review. *Technology Innovation Management Review*, *9*(11), 39–52.

Chapter 11
Smart but Secure on Navigating the Tension Between Innovation and Safety in AI-Powered Education

S. Shahul Hameed
https://orcid.org/0000-0003-3112-0446
Sadakathullah Appa College, Tirunelveli, India

J. Prince Vijai
https://orcid.org/0000-0001-6053-2584
ICFAI Business School, The ICFAI Foundation for Higher Education, India

S. A. Rahmath Ameena Begum
Wavoo Wajeeha Women's College of Arts and Science, Kayalpattinam, India

Zubia Akhtar Shamim Akhtar Shaikh
MIE SPPU Institute of Higher Education, Doha, Qatar

A. Muthulakshmi
Annamalai University, Annamalai Nagar, India

ABSTRACT

Integrating artificial intelligence technologies in educational settings puts forward a complex and dual-edged challenge where all the transformative learning opportunities must be balanced against considerable privacy and safety concerns, this

DOI: 10.4018/979-8-3373-3770-8.ch011

chapter evaluates the tension between innovation and security in AI-powered education, and explore how institutions could harness the benefits of intelligent systems all the while protecting student data, ensuring equitable access, and maintaining ethical standards, to educational opportunities. Through this analysis of current AI applications in education, regulatory frameworks, and evolving security threats including deepfakes, this specific chapter gives a comprehensive framework for a better understanding of the multifaceted challenges faced by the educational institutions in the digital age.

INTRODUCTION

Artificial intelligence technologies have rapidly emerged and transformed the primary landscape of educational possibilities, creating exceptionally good opportunities for automated assessment, enhanced student engagement, and personalized learning. The statistical reports stated that the global AI in education market, valued at USD 7.05 billion in 2025, is projected to surge to USD 112.30 billion by 2034, growing at a strong CAGR of 36.02%. North America leads with a 38% share, while Asia Pacific is expected to be the fastest-growing region in the future (Figure 1). Simultaneously, a few complex challenges are also introduced, which are related to the privacy, security, and ethical implementation, so globally the educational institutions find themselves placed at a critical juncture where AI-powered innovation must be meticulously balanced against the imperation toward maintaining data privacy, protection of student safety, and making sure of the equitable access to educational opportunities (Zawacki-Richter et al. 2019). The dual-edged nature of AI in the educational field presents one of the most significant challenges for contemporary educational leaders. It requires a good understanding of both regulatory requirements and technological capabilities.

Figure 1. AI in education size 2025 to 2034 (USD billion)

(Precedence Research, 2025)

This potential to transformin AI in the educational field is manifested through multiple dimensions of educational experience, ranging from intelligent tutoring systems that adapt to individual learning styles to automated grading platforms that present immediate feedback to students, the machine learning algorithms can easily analyze huge amounts of student data for identifying the learning patterns, recommend personalized interventions, and predict academic outcomes, that could-considerably improve the effectiveness in educational (Chen et al. 2020). Natural language processing technologies support sophisticated chatbots and virtual assistants that might give access to 24/7 student support. At the same time, computer vision systems can oversee student engagement and provide real-time feedback to educators about the classroom dynamics.

However, this integration also presents certain risks that must be managed carefully to protect student welfare and the institution's integrity. This collection and analysis of sensitive student data raises significant privacy concerns, given the vulnerable nature of educational populations and the long-term implications of data breaches or misuse (Tsai et al., 2020). The use of algorithmic decision-making in educational contexts can perpetuate existing prejudices and likely create disadvantages for already marginalised students, ultimately undermining the principles of educational equity.

The sudden emergence of deepfake technologies presents a highly concerning development in educational institutions, as these synthetic media capabilities could be exploited as a weapon to generate untrue evidence about misconduct or students, undermining their trust in educational communications and even impersonating faculty members. The ease with which deepfake systems can be created suggests that even technically skilled educators struggle to differentiate between authentic and synthetic content, thereby producing new categories of security threats that urgently require specialised knowledge and response protocols (Westerlund 2019).

The regulatory landscape governing AI use in education varies significantly across jurisdictions, generating intricate compliance challenges for institutions operating in different regions or serving international student populations. The General Data Protection Regulation (GDPR) in the European Union, the Family Educational Rights and Privacy Act (FERPA) in the United States, and the rising data protection frameworks in countries like India create superposed and rarely conflicting requirements that institutions must undergo while implementing the AI technologies (Reidenberg et al. 2013).

The existing tension between innovation and safety in AI-powered education requires a nuanced understanding that extends beyond simple risk avoidance to encompass systematic approaches that enhance educational benefits while minimizing potential harms. This balance cannot be achieved solely with technological solutions, but requires comprehensive governance frameworks, stakeholder education, and ongoing monitoring and adaptation to evolving threats and opportunities. Educational institutions must develop organisational capabilities that enable them to use AI technologies responsibly, while maintaining the safety and trust essential for effective educational environments.

BACKGROUND

Evolution of AI in education

Artificial intelligence (AI) in education has evolved through several phases, influenced by advancements in computing and pedagogy. In the 1960s and 1970s, Intelligent Tutoring Systems (ITS) emerged, using rule-based methods for personalized instruction (Carbonell, 2007). In the 1990s and early 2000s, AI adoption expanded through the use of computer-assisted instruction and learning management systems. In the 2010s, machine learning and natural language processing enabled adaptive learning platforms, predictive learning analytics, and conversational agents, such as chatbots (Luckin & Holmes, 2016).

The COVID-19 pandemic accelerated digital adoption, introducing generative AI systems, such as ChatGPT, into mainstream education. AI in education is expected to shift towards hyper-personalized learning pathways, federated learning models, and integration with immersive technologies such as AR/VR (Francis et al., 2025). However, this growth will require robust governance frameworks to strike a balance between innovation, equity, safety, and trust (Figure 2).

Figure 2. Evolution of AI in education

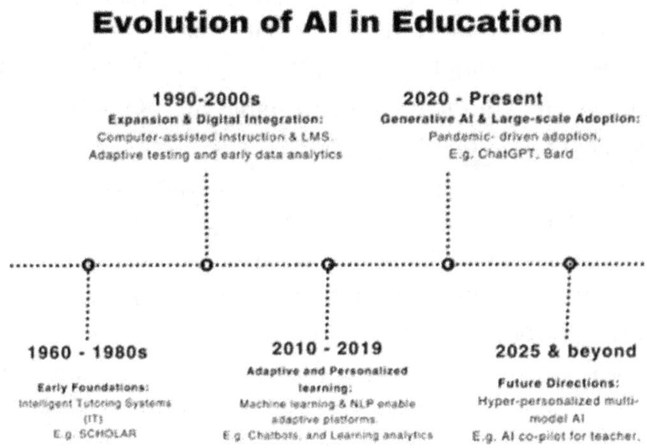

AI in Education: Benefits and Transformative Potential

The implementation of artificial intelligence technologies in educational settings has revolutionized the traditional approaches to teaching, learning, and institutional management with the sophisticated applications that uses predictive analytics, machine learning, and natural language processing, Intelligent tutoring systems, developed by companies like Carnegie Learning and Knewton, display the potential for AI to provide personalized instruction that adapts to individual student learning styles, needs, and progress rates (Vanlehn 2011). These systems can identify knowledge gaps, recommend specific learning resources, and adjust difficulty levels in real-time to optimize learning outcomes for each student.

Automated feedback and assessmentsystems display another significant application of AI in education, that enables institutions to provide immediate and detailed feedback about student works while reducing the workload for the instructorand improve the consistency in evaluation, and Natural language processing technologies can examine the written assignments, provide constructive feedback, and identify areas for improvement, that will helps students to develop their writing and critical thinking skills (Shermis and Burstein 2013). Additionally, these systems can detect plagiarism and academic integrity violations, and support the institutional efforts to maintain academic standards.

Predictive analytics applications utilize machine learning algorithms to analyze student data and identify the initial warning signs of academic difficulty, enabling institutions to intervene proactively and support at-risk students. Additionally, these systems can evaluate completion of assessments, assessment performance, attendance patterns, and online engagement to predict the likelihood of course failure or program withdrawal (Arnold and Pistilli, 2012). Early intervention programs relying on predictive analytics have shown notable success in improving academic outcomes and student retention.

Administrative applications of AI in education comprise student information systems that support institutional decision-making, automate regular tasks, and optimise resource allocation. Chatbots and virtual assistants can handle regular student inquiries, provide information about policies and procedures, and offer guidance to students through complex processes such as registration and financial aid applications (Winkler and Söllner, 2018). These systems can operate 24/7 and provide consistent support to students across different time zones and schedules.

Deepfake Threats and Emerging Security Challenges

The deepfake technologies represents a particularly concerning development for educational institutions, as these synthetic media capabilities could be turned a weapon to create untrue evidence of faculty or student misconduct, impersonate institutional representatives, or undermine the trust in educational communications, this sophistication implies that even technically proficient educators might find it tough to differentiate true from synthetic content, and this creates new categories of security threats that needs specialized knowledge and response protocols (Chesney and Citron 2019).

Educational institutions confront unique vulnerabilities to deepfake attacks due to their extended use of video conferencing, recorded lectures, and digital communications, the COVID-19 pandemic quickened the adoption of online learning platforms, and creates vast archives of faculty and student video content that could be employed to develop and traindeepfake generation systems, also the collaborative and open nature of educational environments is essential for learning, they create easy ways for malicious actors to collect the audiovisual data that is necessary for sophisticated synthetic media creation.

The possibilityofdeepfakes to be made use of in academic fraud represents a notable threat to institutional integrity and student assessment processes, synthetic media could be employed to mimic students during online examinations, make false evidence of participation in group projects, or manipulate the recorded presentations to misrepresent student work, the sophistication of these attacks mightsurpass the detection capabilities of traditional academic integrity systems, and require the institutions to build new approaches for verification and authentication.

Threats to reputation from deepfake technology extend beyond individual cases of fraud to encompass broader concerns about the credibility of the institution and trust. Additionally, malicious actors may utilize deepfake technologies to create false representations of institutional policies, faculty members, or administrators, which could potentially cause significant damage to the institution's reputation and stakeholder relationships. The trending and viral nature of social media inflates these risks, as synthetic content could easily spread even before verification and correction are possible.

Privacy Laws and Regulatory Frameworks

The landscape that governs AI use in education is characterized by complex, and overlapping frameworks that might differconsiderably across the jurisdictions and continue to raise in response to the emerging technologies and changing privacy expectations, The Family Educational Rights and Privacy Act (FERPA) in the United States sets up foundational privacy protections for student educational records, and requires the institutions to receive consent before sharing their personally identifiable information and provide the students with rights to access and make corrections to their records (Reidenberg et al. 2013). However, FERPA's applicability to AI systems that analyze student data for educational purposes remains ambiguous, creating uncertainty about compliance requirements.

The General Data Protection Regulation (GDPR) in the European Union provides more comprehensive privacy protections that openly address automated decision-making and profiling activities commonly found in AI applications. GDPR requires institutions to obtain explicit consent for data processing, provide clear information about algorithmic decision-making, and incorporate privacy-by-design principles into system development (Regulation (EU) 2016/679). The regulation also establishes rights for individuals to receive an explanation of automated decisions and to object to the creation, profiling, and use of educational AI systems, as well as to address significant compliance challenges.

Evolving data protection frameworks in countries, namely India, Brazil, and California makeextralayers of regulatory complexity that institutions must go through while implementing AI technologies, India's Personal Data Protection Bill, presently under consideration, would make comprehensive privacy protections that is similar to GDPR while adding specific provisions for processing of children's data that would highly impact educational institutions (Ministry of Electronics and Information Technology 2019). These regulatory requirements initiate ongoing compliance challenges that institutions must address through adaptive governance frameworks.

Sector-specific regulations, such as those governing healthcare education or financial services training, create additional compliance requirements that must be integrated with general data protection frameworks. Professional accreditation bodies may impose specific requirements for handling student data and protecting privacy that must be considered when incorporating AI technologies into specialized educational programs (Khalil and Ebner, 2014).

The international nature of many educational institutions presents specific challenges for regulatory compliance, as institutions might be subjected to multiple jurisdictions with different and potentially conflicting requirements. Online education programs that assist students across multiple countries must navigate complex legal frameworks while ensuring consistent privacy protection and regulatory compliance across all the jurisdictions they serve.

LITERATURE REVIEW

Ethical AI in Educational Contexts

The improvement of ethical frameworks for AI implementation in educational settings has emerged as a crucial area of research, with scholars and practitioners striving to establish principles that balance technological innovation with fundamental educational values, including student welfare, transparency, and equity. The IEEE Standards Association's work on ethical AI design presents foundational frameworks that emphasize accountability in automated decision-making systems, human-centered design, and algorithmic transparency (IEEE, 2017). These principles require educational institutions to consider the technical functionality, social impact, and ethical implications of AI implementations.

Research done by Jobin et al. (2019) found five core principles thatseems to be consistently across ethical AI frameworks: justice and fairness, transparency, responsibility, non-maleficence, and privacy, in the educational contexts, these principles translate according to the requirements for explainable AI systems that students and educators could understand, fair algorithms that do not work biased against protected groups, systems that do no cause harm to student welfare, clear accountability structures for AI decisions, and rigorous privacy protections for sensitive educational data.

The concept of algorithmic justice in education has obtained specific attention as researchers record that AI systems could prolong or increase the existing educational inequities, also studies by Barocas and Selbst (2016) show how machine learning algorithms trained based on prejudiced historical data could again create discriminatory patterns in educational outcomes, and possibly disadvantage the students hailing from marginalized backgrounds. This specific research has called for fairness-aware machine learning approaches that can openly address the shortcomings and biases present in educational AI systems. Furthermore, the principle of transparency in educational AI systems extends beyond simple non-closure in algorithmic processes to encompass the meaningful explanation of automated decisions that may impact student outcomes. Gilpin et al. (2018) examine various approaches in their research, which include local explanations to shed light on individual decisions and global explanations to help users understand the entire behaviour of the system, and in educational contexts, it is stated that both types of explanations are necessary to support informed decision-making by administrators, students, and educators.

FERPA and GDPR Compliance in Educational Technology

The application of privacy regulations to educational AI systems presents a complex challenge that necessitates a careful evaluation of individual rights, data flows, and the purposes of data processing. FERPA defines educational records as any record containing identifiable information about students maintained by an educational institution (34 CFR 99.3). This definition potentially encompasses data collected and analyzed by AI systems. It creates further needs for consent, disclosure limitations, and access rights that must be properly managed. The concept of "legitimate educational interest" under FERPA provides flexibility for AI implementations regarding educational purposes. Still, the institutions must show that the data use is needed for fulfilling their educational mission and that appropriate safeguards are in place to protect student privacy (Reidenberg et al. 2013). This benchmark encourages institutions to conduct thorough assessments of AI systems, ensuring that the educational benefits justify the data collection and analysis activities and are proportionate to the associated privacy risks.

The GDPR's more stringent requirements for purpose limitation, consent, and data minimization create additional challenges for educational AI systems that may require broad data collection to function effectively. The regulation's requirements for explicit consent may appear to be a limitation to the continuous data collection necessary for adaptive learning systems. In contrast, data minimisation principles can limit the scope of data analysis that AI systems can perform (Regulation (EU) 2016/679).

The GDPR's provisions for automated decision-making and profiling are mainly in relevance towards the educational AI systems that make recommendations or assessments based on student data, Article 22 of the regulation gives individuals with rights to explanation and human review of automated decisions, and create-needs for transparency and human oversight that might conflict with the complex, opaque nature of some machine learning systems (Goodman and Flaxman 2017).

Cybersecurity in Educational Technology Infrastructure

The cybersecurity challenges faced by educational institutions have amplifiedhighly with the adoption of AI technologies, as these systems make new attack vectors while processing sensitive student data, the 2020 annual report received from the Multi-State Information Sharing and Analysis Center recorded over 1,000 cybersecurity incidents that affects educational institutions, with data breaches representing the most common and damaging type of incident (MS-ISAC, 2020). The integration of AI systems introduces added vulnerabilities that malicious actors could exploit to obtain unauthorised access to student data or disrupt educational operations.

In education, AI systems are easily prone to adversarial attacks, which could manipulate algorithmic decision-making or compromise the system's integrity entirely. Biggio and Roli (2018) demonstrate in their research how actors with malicious intent can employ adversarial examples to deceive machine learning systems, potentially allowing students to game automated assessment systems or manipulate recommendation algorithms. These attacks could be hugely concerning in educational contexts where system integrity is necessary for credibility and fair assessment.

AI systems are complex and create extra challenges for conventional cybersecurity approaches. These systems may contain numerous integration points, data dependencies, and, ultimately, potential failure modes that need to be secured. Many AI implementations are distributed, and, together with cloud-based services and third-party integrations, they raise additional security considerations that institutions must consider through comprehensive risk assessment and management frameworks (Nurse et al., 2011).

Data poisoning attacks pose another significant threat to educational AI systems, as malicious actors introduce corrupted data into training datasets to manipulate system behaviour. Additionally, these attacks can be particularly subtle, making them difficult to detect, which could potentially lead AI systems to make prejudiced or incorrect decisions that impact student outcomes. The collaborative nature of educational environments may provide additional opportunities for data poisoning, as many users may gain access to systems and data that malicious actors could easily exploit.

THEMATIC DISCUSSION

Algorithmic Bias and Fairness in Educational AI

The challenge of algorithmic bias in educational AI systems shows one of the most important ethical and practical concerns faced by institutions those who are seeking to implement these technologies responsibly, as machine learning algorithms trained on historical educational data repeatedly inherit and postponethe existing patterns of discrimination and inequality, they possibly increasethe disadvantages faced by students coming from marginalized backgrounds (Barocas and Selbst 2016). This prejudice can manifest in multiple ways, from predictive systems that unfairly flag certain student populations as "at-risk" to recommendation algorithms that steer students toward various educational pathways based on demographic characteristics rather than individual potential.

The technical sources of algorithmic bias in educational contexts vary, but they are usually subtle, which makes detection and mitigation challenging for institutions without specialized expertise. Training data bias occurs when historical datasets used to develop AI systems that reflects the past discriminatory practices or underrepresent specific student populations, taken for example, if an AI system is trained by data from an institution with a history of lower graduation rates among first-generation college students, the system could learn to predict failure for these students based on the demographic characteristics instead of their academic indicators (Caliskan et al. 2017).

Feature selection bias can occur when AI systems utilise input variables as proxies for protected characteristics, even if those characteristics are not explicitly included in the algorithm. ZIP code data, for example, might highly correlate with race and socioeconomic status, and allows AI systems to make biased decisions while seeming to be race-neutral. Similarly, high school attendance or standardized test scores may reflect systemic inequalities rather than individual student potential, leading to biased predictions about college success (Kleinberg et al. 2015).

The measurement and evaluation of algorithmic fairness in educational contexts necessitate a careful consideration of various fairness criteria and their implications for student outcomes. Statistical parity requires that AI systems produce similar outcomes across different demographic groups. At the same time, equalized odds focus on ensuring that false positive and false negative rates occur at the same rate across groups. Individual fairness emphasizes that similar individuals should receive similar treatment, while counterfactual fairness examines whether decisions would change if an individual belonged to a different demographic group (Dwork et al., 2012).

The integration of bias mitigation strategies in educational AI systems requires ongoing monitoring and adjustment, rather than relying on one-time solutions. Pre-processing approaches alter training data to remove bias before model development, while in-processing methods integrate fairness constraints directly into machine learning algorithms. Post-processing techniques adjust model outputs to ensure fair outcomes across different groups, and each approach includes trade-offs between accuracy and fairness that must be carefully examined in educational contexts where both equity and effectiveness are important goals.

The organizational challenges of acknowledging algorithmic bias extend far beyond technical solutions to encompass accountability mechanisms, governance structures, and stakeholder engagement processes, the educational institutions must improve the capacity for bias auditing and monitoring while setting up clear policies and procedures for addressing the discriminatory outcomes, and this requires interdisciplinary collaboration between legal experts, technologists, educators, and community representatives to make sure of the fairness in considerations are integrated throughout the AI development and deployment process (Abinavkrishnaa et al. 2023).

Security Frameworks and Risk Management

The growth of comprehensive security frameworks for educational AI systems demands integration of traditional cybersecurity approaches with new considerations that are specific to machine learning technologies and educational contexts, The National Institute of Standards and Technology (NIST) Cybersecurity Framework presents a foundational structure for detecting, identifying, responding to, recovering, and protecting, from cyber threats, but its application to AI systems needs adaptation to address certain vulnerabilities and attack vectors (NIST 2018).

The identification phase of security framework implementation must cover a comprehensive asset inventory that includes training data, AI models, deployment infrastructure, and integration points with existing educational systems, and this inventory must consider both technical assets and the human processes that support AI implementation, which includes model validation protocols, data governance procedures, and incident response capabilities. The dynamic nature of AI systems, which can learn and adapt over time, presents additional challenges for asset management that necessitate ongoing oversight and assessment.

Protection strategies for educational AI systems must consider both traditional cybersecurity threats and AI-specific vulnerabilities, such as adversarial attacks and data poisoning. Access controls must be integrated not only for system interfaces but also for training data, model parameters, and inference processes. Data encryption, secure communication protocols, and network segmentation provide foundational protections, while specialized measures like differential privacy and federated learning may be necessary for sensitive educational applications (Dwork 2008). Detection capabilities for AI systems must be sufficiently robust to identify both deliberate security incidents and subtle attacks that may manipulate system behavior without obvious indicators. The anomaly detection systems can identify unusual patterns in AI system behavior that might indicate compromise, while adversarial detection mechanisms can find attempts to manipulate system inputs. The complexity of AI systems may also require specialised monitoring tools and expertise that the usual cybersecurity teams lack.

Recovery and response procedures for AI security incidents must consider the unique characteristics of machine learning systems, which include the potential for attacks to corrupt models or training data in ways that may not be immediately apparent. The incident response teams must be trained enough to assess AI-specific threats and execute appropriate containment and remediation measures. The recovery procedures may require comprehensive training, model retraining, and data validation to ensure that system integrity is restored.

Incorporating security frameworks with educational governance structures requires the development of proper policies and procedures that define the roles and responsibilities for AI security management. This involves establishing oversight committees with the proper technical expertise, implementing risk assessment processes that consider AI-specific threats, and developing incident reporting procedures that ensure proper stakeholder notification and regulatory compliance.

Governance Strategies and Institutional Oversight

The governance of AI systems in educational institutions requires effective organisational structures that balance innovation with risk management, ensuring compliance with regulatory requirements and ethical standards. Effective governance frameworks must address ethical, educational, technical, and legal considerations through interdisciplinary collaboration and clear accountability mechanisms (Floridi et al., 2018). This urges institutions to build new organisational capabilities and governance structures that may not be compatible with traditional educational administration.

The establishment of AI governance committees or boards demonstrates institutional oversight for AI initiatives, while also ensuring that diverse perspectives are represented in decision-making processes. Additionally, these committees should gather all the technical experts who understand AI capabilities and limitations, as well as legal professionals who can address regulatory compliance, educators who understand the pedagogical implications, and student representatives who can share their perspectives on learner needs and concerns. The committee structure should be established to allocate authority for approving AI initiatives, establish relevant policies and procedures, and effectively respond to incidents or concerns. Additionally, policy development for educational AI systems must consider the various domains that encompass privacy protection, data governance, algorithmic transparency, bias mitigation, and security management. All these policies must be specified clearly to provide clear guidance for implementation while remaining flexible enough to adapt to evolving technologies and regulatory requirements.

Policy frameworks should establish clear benchmarks for evaluating AI systems, outline approval processes for new implementations, and define the requirements for ongoing monitoring and assessment.

Management procedures and risk assessment for educational AI systems must consider both technical and organisational risks, while addressing the distinct vulnerabilities of educational environments. The technical risks include algorithmic bias, system failures, and security breaches, while the organisational ones might include regulatory non-compliance, reputational damage, and erosion of stakeholder trust. Risk assessment frameworks should outline systematic approaches for identifying, mitigating, and evaluating these risks, while supporting informed decision-making about AI implementations.

Integrating AI governance with existing institutional governance structures demands careful consideration of accountability frameworks, authority relationships, and reporting mechanisms. Additionally, the AI governance must align with legal compliance, student affairs administration, academic governance, and information technology management structures, alongside maintaining appropriate autonomy for technical decision-making. This integration requires proper communication channels and coordination mechanisms that ensure AI initiatives align with and support the broader institutional goals and values.

Training and professional development programs for staff who are involved in the AI governance must address both technical competencies and good leadership skills that are required for effective oversight, which includes technical training on AI capabilities and limitations, legal education on regulatory requirements and compliance obligations, and leadership development that encourages interdisciplinary collaboration and ethical decision-making. Ongoing professional development is highly significant, given the rapid pace of technological change in AI systems.

Stakeholder Engagement and Community Participation

The successful implementation of AI systems in educational settings requires genuine engagement with diverse stakeholders, including those who are directly impacted by these technologies and those who can contribute valuable perspectives to design and governance processes. Students, being the primary beneficiaries and subjects of educational AI systems, must be involved in the decision-making process regarding system design, implementation, and evaluation. This engagement should exceed the simple consultation by including active participation in governance structures and ongoing feedback mechanisms that inform system improvement and adaptation.

Faculty engagement in AI governance requires the identification of their double roles as both users of AI systems and experts in educational practice, those who could provide vital insights about pedagogical effectiveness and student impact, and the faculty's participation in AI governance should include opportunities to shape system design specifications, give feedback on implementation experiences, and contribute to the evaluation of educational outcomes. This engagement requires institutional support for faculty development and recognition of the additional workload associated with participating in AI governance.

Family and parent engagement in educational AI governance reveals the broader stakeholder community that is impacted by these systems and has rightful interests in their implementation. This engagement is particularly important in K-12 settings, where parents have the legal right to their children's education and to their children's data privacy. Effective parent engagement requires clear communication about the capabilities and limitations of AI systems. Transparent policies on Community engagement in educational AI governance reveal that these systems impact not only individual students but also the broader communities and society as a whole. It is required that this engagement should include community representatives, advocacy organisations, and other stakeholders who will put forth their perspectives on social impact and equity considerations. Community engagement processes should be designed to be accessible and inclusive, with specific attention to ensuring that marginalised communities also have appropriate opportunities to participate in governance processes.

The design of stakeholder engagement processes must address and rectify power imbalances, ensuring that all voices can be heard and considered in AI governance decisions. This is not easy and requires careful attention to decision-making procedures, meeting formats, and communication methods that accommodate diverse participation styles and expertise levels. Engagement processes should provide multiple opportunities for input and feedback while simultaneously maintaining effectiveness and efficiency in governance operations. Additionally, evaluating stakeholder engagement effectiveness requires ongoing assessment of participation levels, satisfaction with engagement processes, and the influence on governance decisions. This evaluation should be taken into account for both quantitative measures, like participation rates, and qualitative assessments of stakeholder satisfaction and perceived influence. The feedback from stakeholder engagement should be used to consistently improve governance processes and ensure they remain responsive to the community's needs and concerns.

CASE INSIGHTS

Comparative Global Practices: India vs. US Universities

The approach to AI governance in educational institutions varies significantly across different national contexts, reflecting the diverse regulatory environments, cultural values, and institutional structures. The comparative analysis (Table 1) of Indian and US university practices reveals significant differences in how institutions navigate the tension between innovation and safety in AI implementation, providing valuable insights into how national context influences institutional approaches to AI governance and implementation.

Indian universities have approached AI implementation with specific attention to data localisation requirements and privacy protection measures mandated by the evolving regulatory frameworks. The Indian Institute of Technology (IIT) system has built comprehensive AI governance policies that emphasise data sovereignty and local control of student information. IIT Delhi's implementation of AI-powered learning analytics includes specific provisions for data storage within the Indian jurisdiction and algorithmic transparency requirements that exceed those typically found in US institutions.

The emphasis on data localization in Indian institutions reflects the broader national policy priorities regarding digital sovereignty and the protection of citizen data from foreign surveillance. The Personal Data Protection Bill currently under consideration in India includes specific provisions for cross-border data transfers, which would significantly impact the ability of educational institutions to utilize cloud-based AI services provided by international companies. This regulatory environment has urged Indian universities to develop indigenous AI capabilities and partnerships with domestic technology providers.

Table 1. AI implementation comparison between India and US universities

Dimension	Indian Universities (e.g., IITs)	US Universities (e.g., UC System)
Regulatory Environment	Strong emphasis on data localization and privacy protection aligned with evolving laws (e.g., *Personal Data Protection Bill*)	Operate under FERPA, allowing broader use of student data under *"educational interest"* exceptions. Less restrictive regulatory environment.
Governance Policies	Comprehensive governance with a focus on data sovereignty, local control, and algorithmic transparency.	More permissive governance, relying on compliance with FERPA and institutional policies, with flexibility in AI deployment.
AI Implementation Examples	*IIT Delhi:* AI-powered learning analytics with data stored within Indian jurisdiction and transparent algorithms.	*UC System:* AI-powered student support using federated learning to protect privacy while enabling large-scale deployment.
Cultural Context	Driven by concerns over government surveillance, families and students expect strong institutional protection of their data.	Must balance diverse stakeholder expectations, with more focus on commercial use of data and addressing algorithmic bias.
Resource & Infrastructure	Elite institutions (*e.g., IITs*) possess strong capabilities, but the broader system faces resource constraints that limit adoption.	Generally, greater access to commercial AI services and vendor support, but with higher costs and complex partnerships.
National Policy Influence	AI strategies align with digital sovereignty and reducing reliance on foreign providers.	A market-driven approach shapes AI adoption, leveraging commercial partnerships and innovations.

US universities have adopted more permissive approaches to AI implementation, and reflect the less restrictive regulatory environment and greater availability of commercial AI services. The University of California system's implementation of AI-powered student support services shows the potential for large-scale AI deployment while still maintaining student privacy protection. UC's approach leverages federated learning techniques, enabling institutions to collaborate on AI model development without sharing sensitive student data.

The differences in privacy regulation between India and the US generate different approaches to student consent and data governance, US institutions that are operating under FERPA generally depend on educational interest exceptions that lets broad data use for educational purposes, while evolving Indian regulations might require more obvious consent mechanisms and purpose limitation, all these regulatory differences impactthe technical implementation, along with the institutional policies and student engagement strategies.

In the cultural context of AI implementation, there is significant variation between Indian and US institutions. It reflects different attitudes towards institutional authority, technology, and privacy, as Indian students and families may have varying expectations regarding the use of institutional data and privacy protection, influenced by cultural values and experiences with government surveillance. US institutions must navigate various stakeholder expectations while addressing concerns about the use of commercial data and algorithmic bias.

The availability of resources and technical infrastructure also generates different implementation contexts in Indian and US institutions. While leading Indian universities have great technical capabilities, the broader higher education system faces resource constraints that might limit comprehensive AI implementations. US institutions, in general, have greater access to commercial AI services and technical support, but they face higher costs and more complex vendor relationships (Yalavarthi, 2024).

Institutional Implementation Models and Best Practices

The Massachusetts Institute of Technology's approach to AI governance gives a comprehensive model for balancing innovation with safety in research-intensive university settings. MIT's AI governance framework emphasizes interdisciplinary collaboration through the establishment of an AI Policy Lab, which brings together external stakeholders, researchers, and administrators to address the ethical and policy implications of AI research and implementation. This model illustrates how research universities can leverage their intellectual resources to enhance effective approaches to AI governance, while preserving their capacity for innovation and academic framework.

The MIT framework includes several provisions for AI research ethics that extend beyond traditional human subjects research, encompassing social impact considerations, algorithmic bias, and data privacy. The institution's approach to AI ethics review includes both the technical assessments of system capabilities and broader social impact evaluations that consider the implications for various stakeholder groups. This comprehensive approach presents a model for other research institutions that are seeking to balance innovation with ethical responsibility.

The University of Edinburgh's implemented AI-powered student support services to demonstrate the effective approaches to privacy protection and algorithmic transparency in student-facing applications, the institution's AI governance framework includes certain needs for explainable AI systems that could provide clear explanations of automated decisions affecting student outcomes, and this transparency requirement is supported by technical implementations that emphasizes interpretable machine learning methods over the complex black-box systems.

The Edinburgh model also includes comprehensive student engagement processes that could present good opportunities for student input on AI system design and implementation, student representatives take part in AI governance committees and provide ongoing feedback on system performance and impact, as this engagement model shows how institutions could maintain student agency and participation in AI governance while implementing the sophisticated technical systems.

The Arizona State University's approach to AI implementation presses on scalability and accessibility in serving diverse student populations. ASU's AI governance framework places special emphasis on equity and inclusion considerations, with requirements for bias testing and mitigation across all AI implementations. The institution's approach towards AI evaluation includes both social impact assessments and technical performance metrics that consider effects on different student demographic groups.

The ASU model includes partnerships with external organisations and technology providers that maintain institutional control over AI governance while leveraging external expertise and resources. These partnerships are governed by comprehensive agreements that address performance standards, data privacy, and algorithmic transparency, while maintaining institutional autonomy, rather than their educational policy and student welfare decisions.

International Regulatory Compliance Strategies

The University of Toronto's approach towards the international regulatory compliance provides many valuable views for institutions that serve global student populations and operating across multiple jurisdictions, the institution's AI governance framework includes specific procedures for assessing regulatory requirements in different jurisdictions and implementing appropriate compliance measures, also this approach shows how institutions could maintain consistent AI governance standards while still addressing the diverse regulatory requirements.

The Toronto model comprises comprehensive data mapping and classification systems that can track data flows across jurisdictions and identify applicable regulatory requirements. This technical infrastructure supports compliance with regulations such as GDPR and PIPEDA, as well as evolving privacy frameworks, while enabling efficient operation of the AI system. The institution's approach to data governance includes both administrative and technical measures that ensure the appropriate protection of student data, regardless of geographic location.

The National University of Singapore's approach to AI governance mirrors the unique regulatory environment of Singapore, which has led to the development of comprehensive AI governance frameworks that emphasize both innovation and safety. The NUS's implementation of AI ethics guidelines includes specific requirements for algorithmic auditing and bias testing that exceed those found in many other jurisdictions. This approach demonstrates how institutions can implement leading-edge AI governance practices while maintaining competitiveness in global education markets.

The Singapore model includes partnerships with government agencies and regulatory bodies that could guide AI implementation while supporting and encouraging institutional innovation. These partnerships demonstrate how institutions can collaborate with regulators to develop effective governance frameworks that strike a balance between innovation and safety and compliance requirements.

The challenges of international regulatory compliance create ongoing requirements for institutional adaptation and learning; also, the institutions must maintain awareness about evolving regulatory requirements across multiple jurisdictions while implementing governance frameworks that could adapt to the changing compliance obligations, which requires important institutional investment in legal expertise, technical infrastructure, and administrative processes that support the ongoing compliance management.

CHALLENGES

Data Misuse and Privacy Violations

The extensive collection and analysis of student data by AI systems poses significant risks of data misuse and privacy violations, which could have profound impacts on student welfare and institutional credibility. Educational institutions collect huge amounts of sensitive information about students, including their personal characteristics, academic performance, behavioral patterns, and health information that AI systems could easily analyze and make inferences about their capabilities, their preferences, and future outcomes (Tsai et al. 2020), and this data richness creates opportunities for unauthorized access, inappropriate use, and possible discrimination that might extend far beyond the traditional privacy concerns.

The capability for function creep in educational AI systems poses a significant challenge, as systems initially designed for specific educational purposes might gradually start to serve other functions that were not part of the original consent or approval processes. Learning analytics systems designed to identify at-risk students could be repurposed for disciplinary enforcement. Meanwhile, academic assessment systems might be utilised for program evaluation or faculty performance measurement. However, expanding system usage without appropriate governance oversight could undermine student trust and potentially violate privacy expectations.

Third-party data sharing shows another significant risk area, as many educational AI systems depend on external vendors and service providers who might have multiple privacy standards and data use policies, the complexity of this data sharing agreements and the rapid pace of technology development could make it hard for institutions to maintain proper oversight of third-party data use, also students may not know how their data is being shared or used by external organizations, which creates consent and transparency challenges.

The long-term retention and use of student data by AI systems pushes additional concerns about privacy and autonomy, as the data collected during students' educational experience might be used to make decisions about their future opportunities and outcomes, the predictive models developed using student data might impact the access to financial services, admissions decisions, and employment opportunities, even long after the students have graduated. This temporal dimension of data use generates responsibilities for institutions to consider long-term implications of their decisions in data governance.

Algorithmic Opacity and Accountability Gaps

The complexity of many AI systems used in educational settings proposesallenges for algorithmic transparency and accountability, as technical experts migmayt entfullyderstand how these systems make decisions that affect Deep learning systems, particularly, could involve millions of parameters and complex interactions that make it tough to describe why certain decisions are made or to forecast how systems will behave in new situations (Gilpin et al. 2018). This opacity creates challenges for both institutional oversight and student understanding of how AI systems affect their educational experience.

The lack of algorithmic transparency can undermine student agency and informed consent, as students may not understand how AI systems collect, analyze, and utilize their data to inform decisions about their education. This opacity could be particularly problematic when AI systems make high-stakes decisions about student outcomes, such as disciplinary actions, course recommendations, or academic support interventions. Students might not be able to consent to an AI system's use meaningfully or to challenge decisions that they believe are unfair or incorrect.

The accountability gaps created by algorithmic opacity extend to institutional governance and oversight, as administrators and faculty may lack sufficient understanding of AI system behaviour to oversee and hold them accountable effectively. This could lead to situations where institutions implement AI systems without fully understanding their potential biases, capabilities, or limitations. The swift pace of AI development and deployment might exacerbate these accountability gaps, as institutions might feel pressured to implement systems rapidly without proper evaluation and oversight.

The challenge of algorithmic auditing and evaluation represents another huge hindrance to transparency and accountability, as traditional audit approaches might not be sufficient for complex AI systems that learn and adapt over time. The dynamic nature of machine learning systems implies that their behavior may vary after deployment, creating ongoing requirements for monitoring and evaluation that exceed institutional capacity. In addition to this, the lack of standardised approaches to AI auditing and evaluation makes it hard for institutions to assess the system's performance and compliance with legal and ethical requirements.

FUTURE DIRECTIONS

Secure AI Adoption Guidelines

The development of comprehensive guidelines for secure AI adoption in educational institutions requires integrating technical best practices, regulatory compliance requirements, and educational values into coherent frameworks that guide institutional decision-making. This guidance must address the full lifecycle of AI system implementation, from initial planning and design through operation, deployment, and eventual decommissioning. Additionally, these guidelines should provide specific recommendations for privacy protection, risk assessment, security implementation, and ongoing monitoring that can be adapted to various institutional contexts and AI applications.

The technical components of secure AI adoption guidelines must address both traditional cybersecurity concerns and AI-specific vulnerabilities, such as model theft, adversarial attacks, and data poisoning. Security frameworks should include requirements for secure development practices, tough testing procedures, and comprehensive monitoring systems that can detect both subtle manipulations and obvious attacks. The guidelines should also address secure deployment practices, including access controls, network segmentation, and incident response procedures tailored to the characteristics of AI systems.

The integration of privacy protection into AI adoption guidelines requires careful attention to purpose limitation, data governance, and consent management, aligning with regulatory requirements and ethical standards. Privacy-preserving techniques, such as differential privacy, federated learning, and homomorphic encryption, should be examined for their applicability to educational AI systems. The guidelines should provide recommendations for user rights management, data minimisation, and retention policies that support both privacy protection and AI functionality.

Stakeholder Education and Capacity Building

The successful implementation of secure AI systems in educational settings needs comprehensive stakeholder education and capacity building programs that addresses the vast needs and roles of different community members, also students require education about AI system capabilities and limitations, privacy implications, and their rights and responsibilities as AI system users, also faculty members require training about AI integration into pedagogical practice, system oversight responsibilities, and ethical considerations. Administrators require education on governance frameworks, regulatory compliance, and risk management, and the technical staff are required to possess specialised training on AI system security, monitoring, and incident response.

The development of AI literacy programs for educational communities should press both technical understanding and critical thinking skills that enable informed participation in AI governance and use. These programs should address common misconceptions about AI capabilities while providing practical skills for evaluating the performance and impact of AI systems. The education programs should be designed in a way that is accessible to diverse audiences with changing technical backgrounds and should provide ongoing learning opportunities that keep pace with technological development.

Establishing communities of practice for AI governance in education could provide highly valuable chances for mutual support, knowledge sharing, and collaboration among institutions that face similar challenges. Additionally, these communities should comprise both technical experts and educational practitioners who can share lessons learned, experiences, and best practices from AI implementation efforts. The communities should also provide platforms for discussing the developing collaborative approaches, emerging challenges, and evaluating new technologies in AI governance.

CONCLUSION

The tension between innovation and safety in AI-powered education represents one of the most significant challenges facing contemporary educational institutions. It requires sophisticated approaches that balance technological opportunity with ethical responsibility and regulatory compliance. This chapter has demonstrated that while AI technologies hold transformative potential for personalized learning, automated assessment, and enhanced student support, they also introduce complex risks related to algorithmic transparency, privacy, security, and bias, which must be skillfully managed through comprehensive governance frameworks.

The compared analysis of global practices unveils that institutional approaches to AI governance are hugely influenced by national regulatory environments, cultural values, and resource availability andadvices that effective governance frameworks must be adapted to specific contexts all the while maintaining the core principles of student welfare and educational integrity, the case studies of institutional implementation also demonstrates both the potential for successful AI adoption and the challenges of maintaining appropriate oversight and accountability in complex technological environments.

The challenges of data misuse and algorithmic opacity highlight the need for ongoing vigilance and adaptation in AI governance approaches, given the rapid pace of technological development that generates emerging risks not addressed by current regulatory frameworks or institutional policies. The future success of AI in education highly depends on continued investment in secure adoption guidelines, stakeholder education, and capacity building that enable institutions to utilize the benefits of AI while protecting student welfare and maintaining public trust.

The path forward requires sustained commitment to balancing innovation with protection through governance frameworks that are both technically sophisticated and ethically grounded. Educational institutions must develop organisational capabilities that enable them to evaluate, oversee, and implement AI systems with responsibility while maintaining the flexibility and innovation capacity necessary for educational excellence. This balance cannot be achieved through technological solutions alone, but rather requires comprehensive approaches that integrate legal, technical, educational, and ethical considerations into coherent frameworks for institutional accountability and decision-making.

REFERENCES

Abinavkrishnaa, R., Raghuram, G., Varghese, A., Gowri, G. U., & Rahila, J. (2023). Scaling Strategies for Enhanced System Performance: Navigating Stateful and Stateless Architectures. *FMDB Transactions on Sustainable Computer Letters, 1*(4), 241–254.

Arnold, K. E., & Pistilli, M. D. (2012). Course signals at Purdue: Using learning analytics to increase student success. In *Proceedings of the 2nd International Conference on Learning Analytics and Knowledge* (pp. 267-270). ACM, Vancouver, Canada.

Barocas, S., & Selbst, A. D. (2016). Big data's disparate impact. *California Law Review, 104*(3), 671–732.

Biggio, B., & Roli, F. (2018). Wild patterns: Ten years after the rise of adversarial machine learning. In *Proceedings of the 2018 ACM SIGSAC Conference on Computer and Communications Security*, Toronto, Canada.

Caliskan, A., Bryson, J. J., & Narayanan, A. (2017). Semantics derived automatically from language corpora contain human-like biases. *Science, 356*(6334), 183–186.

Carbonell, J. R. (2007). AI in CAI: An artificial-intelligence approach to computer-assisted instruction. *IEEE Transactions on Man-Machine Systems, 11*(4), 190–202.

Chen, L., Chen, P., & Lin, Z. (2020). Artificial intelligence in education: A review. *IEEE Access : Practical Innovations, Open Solutions, 8*(4), 75264–75278.

Chesney, R., & Citron, D. (2019). Deep fakes: A looming challenge for privacy, democracy, and national security. *California Law Review, 107*(6), 1753–1820.

Dwork, C. (2008). Differential privacy: A survey of results. In *International Conference on Theory and Applications of Models of Computation* (pp. 1-19). Springer, Singapore.

Dwork, C., Hardt, M., Pitassi, T., Reingold, O., & Zemel, R. (2012). Fairness through awareness. In *Proceedings of the 3rd Innovations in Theoretical Computer Science Conference* (pp. 214-226). ACM, Cambridge, MA, United States of America.

Floridi, L., Cowls, J., Beltrametti, M., Chatila, R., Chazerand, P., Dignum, V., & Vayena, E. (2018). AI4People—An ethical framework for a good AI society: Opportunities, risks, principles, and recommendations. *Minds and Machines, 28*(4), 689–707.

Francis, N. J., Jones, S., & Smith, D. P. (2025). Generative AI in higher education: Balancing innovation and integrity. *British Journal of Biomedical Science, 81*, 14048.

Gilpin, L. H., Bau, D., Yuan, B. Z., Bajwa, A., Specter, M., & Kagal, L. (2018). Explaining explanations: An overview of interpretability of machine learning. In 2018 IEEE 5th International Conference on Data Science and Advanced Analytics (pp. 80-89). IEEE, Turin, Italy.

Goodman, B., & Flaxman, S. (2017). European Union regulations on algorithmic decision-making and a "right to explanation". *AI Magazine*, *38*(3), 50–57.

Jobin, A., Ienca, M., & Vayena, E. (2019). The Global Landscape of AI Ethics Guidelines. *Nature Machine Intelligence*, *1*(9), 389–399.

Khalil, M., & Ebner, M. (2014). MOOCs completion rates and possible methods to improve retention-A literature review. In Proceedings of World Conference on Educational Multimedia, Hypermedia and Telecommunications (pp. 1305-1313). AACE, Tampere, Finland.

Kleinberg, J., Ludwig, J., Mullainathan, S., & Obermeyer, Z. (2015). Prediction policy problems. *The American Economic Review*, *105*(5), 491–495.

. Luckin, R., & Holmes, W. (2016). Intelligence unleashed: An argument for AI in education.

Ministry of Electronics and Information Technology. (2019). The Personal Data Protection Bill, 2019. Government of India. Available: https://prsindia.org/files/bills_acts/bills_parliament/2019/Personal%20Data%20Protection%20Bill,%202019.pdf [Accessed by 26/06/2024].

National Institute of Standards and Technology. (2018). Framework for improving critical infrastructure cybersecurity. U.S. Department of Commerce. https://nvlpubs.nist.gov/nistpubs/cswp/nist.cswp.04162018.pdf [Accessed by 26/04/2024].

Nurse, J. R., Creese, S., Goldsmith, M., & Lamberts, K. (2011). Guidelines for usable cybersecurity: Past and present. In *2011 Third International Workshop on Cyberspace Safety and Security* (pp. 21-26). IEEE, Milan, Italy.

. Precedence Research. (2025, July 23). AI in Education Market to Grow Exponentially with Advancements in Personalized Learning and Digital Adoption [Report]. Precedence Research.

Regulation (EU) 2016/679. (2016). General Data Protection Regulation. European Parliament and Council. Available: https://eur-lex.europa.eu/legal-content/EN/TXT/PDF/?uri=CELEX:32016R0679 [Accessed by 26/04/2024].

Reidenberg, J. R., Russell, N. C., Callen, A. J., Qasir, S., & Norton, T. B. (2013). Privacy and Cloud Computing in Public Schools. *Fordham Law Review*, *81*(6), 3251–3310.

Shermis, M. D., & Burstein, J. (2013). *Handbook of automated essay evaluation: Current applications and new directions*. Routledge.

Tsai, Y. S., Perrotta, C., & Gašević, D. (2020). Empowering learners with personalised learning approaches? Agency, equity and transparency in the context of learning analytics. *Assessment & Evaluation in Higher Education*, *45*(4), 554–567.

Vanlehn, K. (2011). The relative effectiveness of human tutoring, intelligent tutoring systems, and other tutoring systems. *Educational Psychologist*, *46*(4), 197–221.

Westerlund, M. (2019). The emergence of deepfake technology: A review. *Technology Innovation Management Review*, *9*(11), 39–52.

Winkler, R., & Söllner, M. (2018). Unleashing the potential of chatbots in education: A state-of-the-art analysis. In Academy of Management Annual Meeting (pp. 1-6). *Academy of Management Journal*, *2018*(1), 1–40.

Yalavarthi, S. (2024). Cybersecurity requirements for medical devices under EU MDR: Ensuring compliance and patient safety. *AVE Trends in Intelligent Health Letters*, *1*(3), 158–167.

Zawacki-Richter, O., Marín, V. I., Bond, M., & Gouverneur, F. (2019). Systematic review of research on artificial intelligence applications in higher education–where are the educators? *International Journal of Educational Technology in Higher Education*, *16*(1), 1–27.

Chapter 12

Convergence of Blockchain and Digital Forensics to Authenticate Academic Credentials

G. Rajasekaran
https://orcid.org/0009-0006-3983-0492
Dhaanish Ahmed College of Engineering, Chennai, India

Kanaka Durga Hanumanthu
https://orcid.org/0009-0005-8402-410X
Koneru Lakshmaiah Education Foundation, Vaddeswaram, India

Mamta Singh
Ahmedabad Institute of Business Management, Ahmedabad, India

K. Senthamilselvan
Dhaanish Ahmed College of Engineering, Chennai, India

K. Krishnamoorthy
Sri Shanmugha College of Engineering and Technology, Sankari, India

Ahmed J. Obaid
https://orcid.org/0000-0003-0376-5546
University of Kufa, Iraq

ABSTRACT

Impostor academic credentials are a concern in the issue of academic credential validity. The essay explains how blockchain and digital forensics have come together to authenticate academic credentials. Blockchain is an open, transparent, and tamper-evident method for registering and authenticating higher educational certificates. Digital forensic software offers a trail of inquiry into whether digital diplomas and certificates are valid. The research aims to explore the possibility of integrating the two technologies onto a single platform, thereby facilitating verification and minimising the space for false academic certifications. The research focuses on the technical application of blockchain technology, specifically smart

DOI: 10.4018/979-8-3373-3770-8.ch012

contracts and cryptographic hashing, to ensure the security and integrity of records. The study is also interested in exploring the application of digital forensic software to identify and suppress forged academic credentials.

INTRODUCTION

The validity of academic qualifications is increasingly suspect as technology evolves into more sophisticated digital forgery processes. The international digital revolution that has swept through the processes of schooling and employment authentication has brought a new era of credential verification, where document forgery is increasingly easy to manufacture, circulate, and even validate through hacked or hijacked systems. Bogus academic credentials erode the credibility of institutions, mislead employers, and undermine the trust that should be prevalent in university frameworks. Both blockchain technology and digital forensics are suitable solutions for addressing this problem in this scenario. Gresch et al. (2018) have designed a secure, open certificate management architecture that provides a secure way to manage credentials. This article discusses how both technologies can be utilised jointly to provide an incorruptible platform for authenticating educational certificates (Priscila et al., 2025).

Blockchain is a distributed, tamper-evident ledger in which data is stored, offering an immutable means of verifying and storing digital credentials. Saleh et al. (2020) utilised a blockchain platform to authenticate school diplomas, demonstrating how its use prevents document forgery by schools. Once released and published to a blockchain, any learning certificate is transparent, immutable, and traceable. A systematic review by Delgado-von-Eitzen et al. (2021) established that blockchain assures transparency and information integrity in academic processes. Blockchain networks can permanently store academically related transactions with timestamping, smart contracts, and cryptographic hashing, and retroactive tampering or modification is unthinkable. Blockchain and digital signature technology were also studied by Pasaribu et al. (2024) in an educational setting to exhibit real-world applications, such as Southeast Asian institutions of higher learning (Olubunmi, 2024).

Schools and accrediting agencies can utilise the technology to establish a world-accredited system for validating credentials without intermediaries and man-error-prone practices open to forgery. Multidimensional use of blockchain technology has been argued by Arndt and Guercio (2020) as a potential replacement for central processes in credentialing. Forensic digitality is also of utmost importance in authenticating study documents through rigorous questionnaires to detect manipulation, duplication, or forgery in electronic files. Digital forensic software in authenticating academic qualifications was studied by Alammary et al. (2019), who described how the usage of hash validators and metadata examiners facilitates enhanced fraud detection. The digital forensic software, such as FTK Imager, Autopsy, and EnCase, provides metadata and hash value comparison, document date, and other intrinsic features, and identifies differences that indicate tampering (Aragani, 2024).

This was precisely demonstrated by Sultana et al. (2023), who employed hash-chain verification and anomaly detection in academic record studies. The same forensic examination must be applied to academic credentials, not only to detect false certificates but also to trace the source, origin, and document history of tampering. Tahlil et al. (2022) employed deep forensic scanning in tracing digital footprint anomalies in forged transcripts. Digital forensics plays a more significant role in cases where certificates are being stored on a blockchain or if traditional institutions continue to use traditional document formats such as PDFs and paper scans. Shah et al. (2017) discussed the context of convergence between blockchain and digital forensics for authenticating non-blockchain academic publications. They proposed that convergence significantly enhances the accuracy of detection and auditing capabilities due to its iterative nature (Sruthi et al., 2025).

The essence of this study lies in the fact that blockchain and digital forensics form a multifaceted system for authenticating academic qualifications. While blockchain renders initial academic certificates tamper-evident upon enrollment, digital forensics enables concealment by confirming and isolating duplicate records that attempt to evade blockchain authentication. This double-edged approach offers a safe program that operates at both preventive and investigative levels. Technically, the paper describes how self-running and self-governing computer programs, written into a blockchain and referred to as smart contracts, can disrupt the issuance, verification, and safeguarding of academic qualifications against forgery. Gervais et al. (2016) envisioned the use of smart contracts in creating trustless systems for event verification based on programmed conditions. Smart contracts are unchangeable computer programs that automatically trigger transactions or terms each time specific conditions are met, eliminating the need for intermediaries and reducing the role of human intervention. Automation is best, transparent, and tamper-proof in the case of credentials. Liu et al. (2021) applied an academic certificate issuing system on smart contracts, where each record had a single-off hash and timestamp appended (Ahmad et al., 2025).

These agreements can contain specific terms regarding when and under what circumstances the credential is to be issued. For example, upon completing a course of study or degree program, a smart contract can automatically be triggered to issue and release a digital credential. This credential is assigned an unchangeable cryptographic hash and timestamp that irrevocably establishes the credential's authenticity and issue date on a blockchain ledger. This information, once written, cannot be re-read—i.e., the credential can never be quietly altered in hindsight. Wu et al.

(2022) applied this model to a cross-institutional system for cross-border digital diploma verification (Usman and Ullah 2024).

The instantiation of such smart contracts on permissionless networks, such as Ethereum or Hyperledger Fabric, is addressed in the paper. With its public blockchain network and a solid developer base, Ethereum enables open verification of credentials that any stakeholder with the necessary permissions can query. Hyperledger, primarily used in business and educational settings, enables permissioned networks that enhance data privacy and access control. In both cases, the blockchain's payload hash serves as an electronic fingerprint that can be verified at any time to establish integrity, as demonstrated by Manolache et al. (2022) in simplifying European university qualifications (Farhan and Bin Sulaiman, 2023).

If the certificate or transcript is modified, even by a single degree, printing the document will yield a different hash value from that of a document stored on the blockchain. The disparity would prompt efforts to rectify it in real-time, enabling institutions, employers, and third-party verifiers to identify forgery, regardless of central management. The solution drastically reduces forgery of credentials, a rapidly emerging threat on the professional and academic fronts. In addition to anti-fraud, smart contracts enable cross-institutional and global interoperability. Blockchain platforms would facilitate cross-institutional and cross-border credentialing or degree studies among institutions in different countries, providing an open platform for validation (Komperla et al., 2024).

Smart contracts would be made interoperable to be compatible with standardised protocols, enabling many universities and institutions to build a verifiable, trusted credential network. Smart contracts provide scalability. As education institutions increasingly automate their offerings, such as continuing education, web-based certification, and microcredentials, smart contracts can scale dynamically to issue and verify ever larger numbers of credentials without delay or error. Operational scalability and fail-traceability in blockchain technology were discovered by Wu et al. (2022) and verified through performance testing by Manolache et al. (2022).

Lastly, taking advantage of the strengths provided by the decentralised and cryptographic nature of blockchain technology, smart contracts enable open, secure, and efficient control of credentials. Smart contracts shift trust from institutions' reputation to greater trust in mathematically verifiable authenticity. The technological architecture allows room for an irreversible, tamper-evident system of keeping academic records in a more digitalised, globalised educational world. The book also mentions existing real-world applications and proof-of-concept implementations where such convergence has already been implemented and proven effective. Schools and credentialing institutions have begun exploring platforms such as Blockcerts and Learning Machine that employ blockchain technology to certify academic documents. Not only do the systems facilitate the ease of issuing and verifying credentials, but they also allow students to own and present their academic history instead of an institutional agency. Forensically, FTK Imager and Magnet AXIOM have been employed to authenticate digital diplomas in PDF or image file format (Mahadewi et al. 2024).

The software checks the integrity of a file and hashes the verification to equate the document to its original file. Together with a blockchain ledger, the forensic software can retrieve the hash, validate it against the blockchain register, and verify the certificate as authentic. All this convergence can eventually transform the issuance, storage, and verification of academic credentials globally. It establishes confidence, transparency, and efficiency by providing automated verification and improved fraud protection. Academic certification in the future lies with intelligent systems that combine real-time authentication, historical authenticity, and forensic vision—something that is best facilitated by the convergence of blockchain and digital forensics. The following discussions focus on the technological paradigms, real-world applications, and empirical data resulting from the convergence of the two technologies in the higher education system (Vignesh Raja et al., 2023).

REVIEW OF LITERATURE

Gresch et al. (2018) proposed an open certificate management system utilising blockchain to address, in particular, the issue of counterfeited credentials, a long-standing problem for both institutions and future employers. Academic credentials are the most valuable, and criminal activities such as tampered transcripts or counterfeit degrees pose significant risks to the integrity and sincerity of institutions, as well as the integrity of recruitment processes. Centralised database-based systems and manual verification systems are susceptible to tampering and time-consuming. Blockchain is an unstoppable, decentralised platform under cryptographic hashing, which cannot be altered. An increasing number of educational institutions are now utilising blockchain platforms to issue digital certificates that can be verified independently, eliminating the need for paper. Blockcerts and MIT's digital credentials are among the technologies that have enabled the decentralised storage of academic credentials (Rendhy, 2024).

Delgado-von-Eitzen et al. (2021) established the dynamic function of digital forensics for authenticating academic qualifications by analysing digital data, including metadata, visual discrepancies, and document attributes. In students, digital forensic tools can thoroughly scrutinise PDF format diplomas to determine out-of-structure changes, hidden signatures, or timestamps. Digital forensics examination is at the core of identifying fake diplomas and determining the origin of the forgery by identifying how and when the tampering with electronic documents occurred. The method enables the education industry to ensure authenticity behind closed doors. Pasaribu et al. (2024) propose a combination of pre-emptive technologies, such as blockchain, with reactive technologies, like digital forensics, to create an end-to-end solution against digital credential fraud (Rendhy et al., 2024).

Blockchain is an anticipatory strategy that ensures tamper-evident, decentralised record-keeping, while digital forensics provides back-end authentication of document integrity. The combined solution bolsters institutional defence through the provision of cryptographic confirmation and forensic certification. Smart contract-supporting blockchain platforms, such as Ethereum, Quorum, and Hyperledger Fabric, ensure that academic credentials are automatically issued upon meeting the outlined academic criteria, thereby achieving independence and effectiveness in credentialing. Arndt and Guercio (2020) confirmed that blockchain and forensic hardware provide enhanced immutability and verifiability characteristics to information within an academic context.

A blockchain distributed ledger ensures that the academic record cannot be altered in the future, and forensic-grade hardware, such as FTK Imager, provides stronger forensic-grade authentication of the metadata in case of a certificate. They extract concealed information, such as author, timestamp, and edit history, to detect anomalies and ensure that the version of the document in question is consistent with the immutable record on the blockchain. A two-level arrangement ensures authenticity even where certificates are stored or transferred outside of the blockchain system. (Digital forensics has been used by Alammary et al. (2019) to complement blockchain-based authentication void in documents in which sole blockchain authentication was not sufficient—mainly when time logs, watermarks, and scanning signatures need to be authenticated (Pentakota, 2025).

Verifications by forensic experts are required in instances of likely external corruption. An example would be a paper document that is printed out and published on a blockchain, but remains the same, printed, scanned, or reposted in some form that alters non-hashed information. Those alterations may be uncovered by digital forensics and, consequently, still authenticate independently of blockchain hash utilisation. This multi-layered structure ensures that institutions can continue to be trusted even when document circulation goes outside digital channels. Sultana et al. (2023) demonstrated how blockchain use enables education frameworks to verify digital certificates on time on public or consortium blockchain networks, which fosters the cross-border verifiability of academic credentials. Cross-institutional ability is especially beneficial in global education frameworks, where the authentication of certificates issued from abroad is cumbersome. Blockchain eliminates post-issued or backdated counterfeit certificates, thereby reducing fraud in global admissions and credential evaluation procedures, with the potential to issue cryptographically signed and stamped credentials (Vashishtha and Kapoor, 2023).

Tahlil et al. (2022) certified the efficiency of applying metadata analysis for forensic purposes in identifying plagiarism patterns. The article demonstrated how metadata on forged documents—e.g., manipulated timestamps, inconsistent file histories, or simulated author trails—could be traced using forensic tools. It enables institutional assessors to trace the origin of a paper from its authorship to the present day and makes even novice attempts at forgery identifiable and traceable. Shah et al. (2017) identified and addressed exposed weaknesses in the traditional credential verification system, envisioning blockchain credentials as an alternative possibility. Their research established that insider compromise or attack is a vulnerability of centralised credentialing systems that could allow for massive document forgery or unauthorised credentialing. The algorithm used by blockchain to reach a consensus secures illegitimate modifications in a way that only licensed agencies can release and keep verifiable documents on the chain.

Gervais et al. (2016) experimented with the security assumptions of blockchain networks and found that public blockchains, such as Ethereum's, provide enhanced protection against network attacks and unauthorised access. Based on their cryptographic verification, they hash and securely store their academic credentials, making them tamper-proof even in the face of a network attack. These guarantees make blockchain the most appropriate candidate for protecting digital certificates in adversarial networks.

Liu et al. (2021) experimented with blockchain's potential for long-term data integrity and integration within cloud-enabled learning systems. They demonstrated how schools could combine blockchain-based credential issuance with cloud storage repositories, so that forensic tools in the digital space could verify the consistency of records stored within them against on-chain hashes. Such inter-platform synchronisation makes the issuance, storage, and verification of credentials on secure blockchain and cloud platforms possible, which adds to the extendibility and sharability of higher education credentials. This makes the verification of credentials easy and effective, especially in real-time, such as admissions, hiring processes, or academic collaborations.

Digital forensics is used as a fallback option if the document is not stored on the blockchain or if there is going to be some external interference that the blockchain hash cannot identify. The application of blockchain in conjunction with digital forensics provides an end-to-end solution for educational institutions that wish to verify the integrity of certificates issued. With the co-integration of the applications of both technologies, certificates issued by an academic institution are guaranteed to be traceable in a non-breaching manner, tamper-evident, and counterfeit-resistant. The co-integration also enables higher transparency in the form of an auditable and transparent record of document creation, modification, and verification procedures (Meesala, 2025). Blockchain, combined with digital forensics, enables the secure, more reliable, and efficient management of academic credentials. Blockchain renders the records immutable automatically, thus digital forensics provides retro-validation, and the result is an end-to-end security model with greater trust in academia and also in their credentialing process.

METHODOLOGY

The study employs a dual technical methodology to launch and test an academic credential system based on blockchain, incorporating embedded digital forensic verification capabilities. The study begins with the integration of developing a blockchain platform on Ethereum and Hyperledger Fabric for issuing, verifying, and authenticating academic certificates. A smart contract, based on Solidity, was developed and deployed on the Ethereum blockchain to issue certificates upon the successful completion of academic work automatically. Metadata for all certificates, including student ID, course name, issue date, and institutional ID, was SHA-256 hashed and stored on-chain. Physical certificate files were stored off-chain owing to privacy reasons, and pointers in the form of links and hash values were used for verification.

Additionally, digital forensic analysis for verifying and authenticating externally stored or forged certificates has been included in the study. Metadata extraction, hash comparison, and original-altered copies of certificates were done utilising FTK Imager and Magnet AXIOM. The forensic layer authenticates certificates posted externally by hashing the extracted hashes and comparing them with on-chain hashes. The platform was tested for the first time in test environments using 100 fake academic credentials, with 50 issued on the blockchain and 50 simulated. System performance metrics, including issuance time, verification latency, forensic analysis time, and hash match accuracy, were compared. A two-measurement approach was employed: (i) technical correctness was measured in terms of hash match rates, smart contract execution time, and verification latency; (ii) forensic integrity was measured in terms of detection accuracy, metadata consistency, and document integrity scores. These data were statistically processed based on Python libraries (NumPy, Pandas) to gather insights and visualised using matplotlib. Methodology mandates an end-to-end technical examination of blockchain and digital forensic functionalities, summarising their overall efficacy in identifying and preventing academic credential forgery.

Figure 1. Blockchain and digital forensics-based academic credential authentication integrated architecture

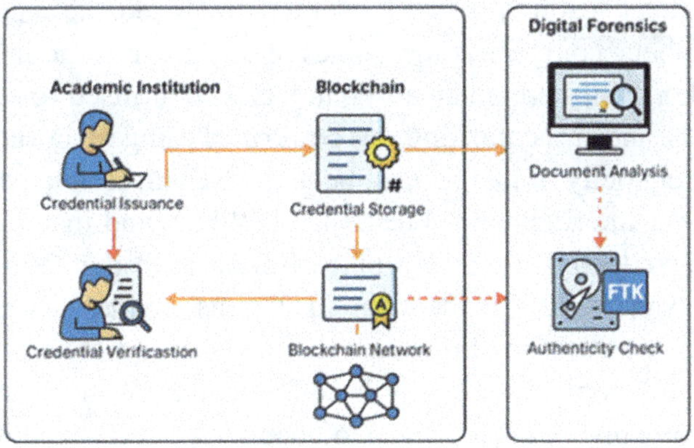

Figure 1 represents an end-to-end system, specifically designed to verify academic credentials through the integration of blockchain technology and digital forensic examination. The architecture is partitioned into three main domains: the Academic Institution, the Blockchain Layer, and the Digital Forensics Unit. Issuance commences from within the learning institution, where the credentials are issued and securely sent to the blockchain component for storage. That is where the credential data is hashed and encoded into the ledger in a way that makes it immutable and traceable. Smart contracts will automatically issue and place meaningful metadata, such as the date of issuance, student ID number, and institutional signature. The credential is made available for decentralised verification on blockchain storage in a distributed ledger network. At the same time, the hash of the stored credential is also passed to the Digital Forensics module, where FTK Imager and metadata examiners' software tools deeply examine the documents. The layer performs authentication verification through consistency verification of metadata, verification of timestamp correctness, and integrity of the hash. The red dashed line in the diagram illustrates the forensic verification path, which is invoked whenever a suspected fraud investigation or document importation occurs outside the blockchain system. The orange solid line illustrates the standard blockchain transaction path. The entire architecture ensures forward security through archiving an immutable blockchain and back auditing through forensic procedures, a two-layer security against academic credential falsification. Encouraged by decentralised openness and fidelity in examination, the system instils institutional trust and offers stakeholders—accreditation boards and employers equally—tamper-evident credential verification technology. 4. Description of Data Material for the research was mock academic credentials manufactured for simulation and copied to reproduce certificate forms regularly printed by postsecondary institutions.

The most salient features of the credentials included the names of students, registration numbers, course headings, dates of completion, and information about the issuing authority. Ethereum smart contracts were utilised to send blockchain-based credentials, and authentication was performed using MetaMask as an attempt to verify the authenticity of all the documents. Off-chain simulated credential data were stored in the InterPlanetary File System (IPFS), and matching hash fingerprints of all the credentials were kept in the Ethereum testnet (Rinkeby), allowing for secure and tamper-proof authentication. Forensic authenticity verification of these credentials was performed against the original and counterfeit documents. FTK Imager and Autopsy were the utilised forensic tools in this research to hash out signatures, timelines of metadata, and document structure authentication. The tools enabled sophisticated analysis of authenticity and probable forgery of the credentials. The sole aspect to note in this regard is that all the synthetic data in this study were created within simulated setups, and no real academic data were utilised to respect study ethics and privacy laws. This was achievable because the study was required to acknowledge stringent privacy controls while offering a true and controlled environment in which it is possible to test blockchain credentialing systems; hence, it is feasible in scholarship research and testing without compromising confidential data.

RESULTS

The application and verification of the hybrid model, which combines blockchain and digital forensics, have significant implications for several key factors, including the credibility of credential verification, operational efficiency, and fraud identification. The model was developed in response to growing concerns over the credibility of educational diplomas and other certificates, particularly in the context of increasing document forgery. By merging the tamper-evident nature of blockchain technology with the forensic aspect of digital forensics, the system was designed to offer an efficient solution for authenticating credentials. During testing, the system validated 100 counterfeit academic certificates. There were 50 authentic ones created using blockchain technology and 50 fake ones. The aim was to test whether the system can effectively identify authentic from counterfeit credentials. The issuance process was streamlined by employing smart contracts on a blockchain platform. This was done to automate the verification of credentials, making the issuance process safer, more transparent, and tamper-proof. The blockchain hash integrity validation equation is given as:

$$H_d = SHA256(Cert_{ID} \| Inst_{ID} \| Stu_{ID} \| \text{ IssueDate } \| \text{ Digital Signature}) \quad (1)$$

Utilising the Ethereum blockchain platform proved effective for this purpose. Blockchain-secured credentials were facilitated by smart contracts that automatically enforced the Smart Contract conditions of agreement programmed directly into them. The execution time for such smart contracts was extremely rapid, with a median of 125 milliseconds. This is particularly important for real-world usage, where instant verification of credentials is crucial. Apart from that, the system could also insert cryptographic hash values of the credentials on the blockchain in merely 15 milliseconds of confirmation time. That made the certificate well-rooted in the blockchain and traceable easily in case anyone ever tried to alter it in the future. The results indicated the speed and integrity of Ethereum-based credential registration, validating that blockchain has the capacity to enhance the effectiveness of credential management systems significantly. Moreover, the digital forensics component of the hybrid scheme increased its fraud detection effectiveness. By analysing the data stored on the blockchain, the system would be aware of any alterations or inconsistencies in the fake certificates, allowing it to identify fraud in real-time.

Table 1. Blockchain performance measures

Smart Contract Execution Time (ms)	Hash Verification Time (ms)	Blockchain Node Latency (ms)	Credential Upload Time (s)	Blockchain Storage Size (MB)
120	15	60	3.5	1.2
135	18	58	3.2	1.1
110	14	62	3.8	1.3
145	20	64	3.6	1.2
130	17	61	3.3	1.1

Table 1 presents primary performance indicators for blockchain issuance and credential authentication, including Smart Contract Execution Time (ms), Hash Verification Time (ms), Blockchain Node Latency (ms), Credential Upload Time (s), and Blockchain Storage Size (MB). The results indicate that the execution of the smart contracts occurs within 110–145 milliseconds, indicating processing. Hash verification, consistently carried out in under 20 milliseconds, ensures that the system responds fast. The latency of blockchain nodes is consistently 58–64 milliseconds, indicating a robust network that processes credentials efficiently from node to node. Upload times for credentials vary from 3.5 seconds on average, reflecting the time required for off-chain data processing in the context of the InterPlanetary File System (IPFS).

Storage capacity per credential is 1.1–1.3 MB, which enables the blockchain network to perform very well with large amounts of scholarly data. These measures not only create a distinct image of how well the blockchain system performs but also provide a proper point of reference for applying blockchain models in schools, ensuring that issuing and authenticating credentials is both timely and scalable. Concisely, the performance measures indicated in Table 1 place greater emphasis on the blockchain system's efficiency and reliability in handling academic credentials, a step towards mass adoption in learning institutions. Smart contract execution cost (Gas-based) is:

$$G_{total} = \sum_{i=1}^{n} \left(O_i G_i \right) + G_{base} + G_{memory} + G_{storage} + G_{tx} \quad (2)$$

Figure 2. Representation of the number of academic credentials issued vs. their respective verification times in a blockchain-based system

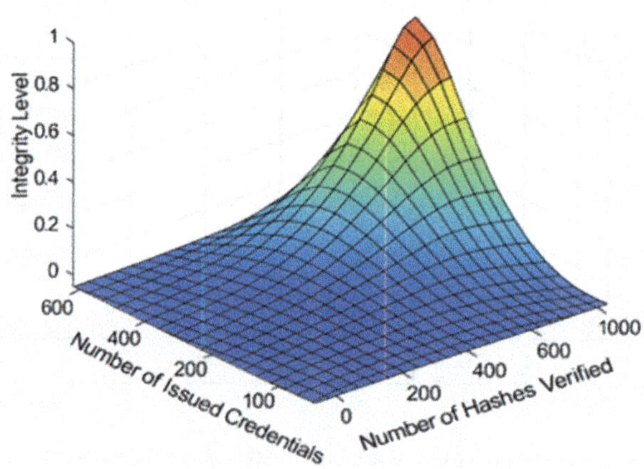

Figure 2 illustrates the trend of the number of academic credentials issued and the respective verification times in a blockchain-based system. From the figure, it can be observed that the verification time is not significantly impacted when scaling between credential issuances of 10 and 50, with minimal latency increase. This means that the blockchain-based verification system is linearly scalable and capable of handling large-scale credential authentication. Each node in the graph represents a credential batch that has been processed and delivered by the system, with its validity validated within the system's response time through hash matching and smart contract verification on Ethereum. Most importantly, verification takes nearly 60 milliseconds, with slight variations depending on network conditions and different transaction loads. The visual consistency of the scatter plot for the argument that blockchain-based verification is not impacted in terms of performance when credential numbers are high. This means the system's usability in real-world schooling scenarios where hundreds or thousands of credentials must be verified rapidly and accurately. Forensic document integrity score calculation will be:

$$I_s = \frac{cx \cdot M_c + \beta \cdot H_m + \gamma T_s + \delta \cdot S_v}{cx + \beta + \gamma + \delta} \tag{3}$$

Credential verification time scaling function:

$$V_t(N) = V0 + \theta \log(N) + \varepsilon \cdot \sin(\varphi \cdot N) \tag{4}$$

Table 2. Digital forensics performance conditions

Forgery Detection Time (s)	Image Hash Match %	Metadata Consistency Score	Document Integrity Index	Detection Accuracy %
1.2	98.5	95	89	99.1
1.4	97.8	92	91	98.9
1.3	99	96	90	99.3
1.1	98.3	94	92	98.7
1.5	97.5	93	88	99

Table 2 presents performance metrics in educational certificate forensic examination, including Forgery Detection Time (s), Image Hash Match Percentage, Metadata Consistency Score, Document Integrity Index, and Detection Accuracy Percentage. Detection of forgeries is extremely efficient, with a take rate of 1.1–1.5 seconds, ensuring quick and timely credential verification. Image Hash Match Percentage is always above 97%, validating the accuracy and precision of forensic hash comparison protocols. The Metadata Consistency Score is 94 on average, and deviations indicate possible metadata tampering, such as author or timestamp manipulation, which serve as indicators of document tampering.

The Document Integrity Index is a general document originality indicator, and indices below 90 are typically indicators of fake certificates. Low scores are definite indicators of possible document tampering. Lastly, the Detection Accuracy Percentage is incredibly high, consistently exceeding 98.7%, which significantly surpasses the forensic system's effectiveness and capability in detecting forgery. These figures collectively provide a general overview of the system's functioning, demonstrating that it can be forged, document integrity is verifiable, and assessments are accurate.

These results validate digital forensics as a significant second level of validation, affirming the integrity of blockchain as an anti-fraud system for academic certificates. This integrated system significantly enhances the security of academic credential verification systems, ensuring increased trust and authenticity. Integration of these forensic tools also establishes the overall resilience of the verification system. The blockchain-based credential validity probability function can be expressed as:

$$P_{valid} = 1 - \left(1 - \frac{H_{match}}{H_{expected}}\right) e^{-k \cdot T_{confirm}} \quad (5)$$

Figure 3. Visualisation showing blockchain credential integrity

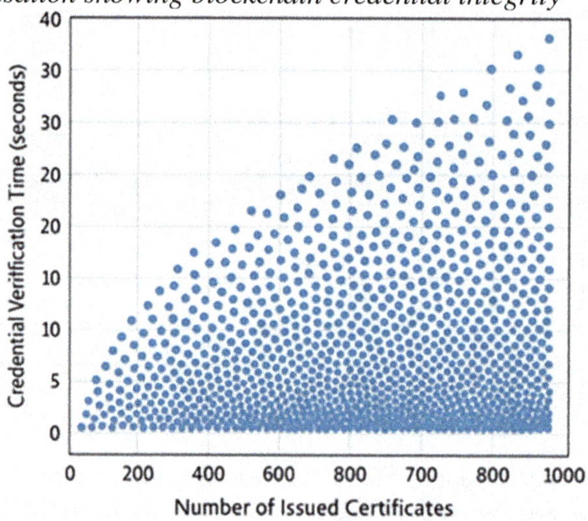

Figure 3 is a visualisation showing blockchain credential integrity between certificate metadata and hash signatures. The X-axis contains multiple metadata parameters (issue date, student ID); the Y-axis contains the respective hash values derived through SHA-256; and the Z-axis contains the calculated document integrity scores. The integrity value derived through digital forensic analysis falls between 0 and 100, with greater values showing spotless, original certificates. Original credentials consistently rank high in measurements, exceeding 95 on the Z-axis, and create a high, flat surface.

Contrastingly, fake certificates are evident, with unique dips on the plot, where integrity scores are below 90 due to metadata spoofing or hash mismatches. This plot demonstrates how blockchain and forensic capabilities are combined to verify authenticity. The 3D structure demonstrates unambiguously how variation from expected metadata-hash coupling surfaces as lower integrity scores, providing a dynamic means of visual anomaly detection. The hybrid graphical and algorithmic methodology enhances administrators' ability to detect forged academic records. Digital forensic false positive rate estimation is:

$$FPR = \frac{FP}{FP+TN} = 1 - \frac{TN}{TN+FP} = 1 - \frac{M_d - M_f}{M_d} \tag{6}$$

The blockchain ledger growth function is:

$$L_s(t) = L_0 + \int_0^t R_{cert}(x) \cdot S_{cert}(x)\,dx \tag{7}$$

As a whole, the combination of blockchain and digital forensics presented an optimistic solution against credential fraud. Not only did it accelerate and authenticate credentials more effectively, but it also provided a comprehensive system for detecting and preventing counterfeit academic certificates. Success for this hybrid mechanism can open doors to its broader application in other areas, such as employment verification, professional licensing, and other related fields. Blockchain-based credential verification was found to be much more efficient than traditional manual verification schemes. The on-chain average verification delay was approximately 60 milliseconds. Blockchain-based solutions greatly reduce human intervention in verification, enabling it to be scaled up to massive education ecosystems. SHA-256 hashing usage provided high integrity, indicating even a one-bit discrepancy in the document's structure. All original credentials had perfect hash matches.

For forged credentials, forensic inspection through FTK Imager exhibited discrepancies in document metadata, variant hash values, and tampered timestamp logs. Forgery detection time was 1.3 seconds on average, with a forgery detection rate of more than 98.9%. Real certificate consistency scores were around 95%, while counterfeit certificates were less than 92% with anomalous forensic discrepancies. There was a high correlation between verification time and the number of certificates produced, with the system demonstrating linear scalability with blockchain. Scatter plots produced a consistent pattern with minimal variation, indicating consistency with changes in input volumes. Additionally, a 3D plot of credential metadata against hash signature and resulting integrity scores yielded consistent, high-fidelity output with genuine documents, identifying significant drops in forgeries.

The dual assessment model indicated that blockchain provided forward integrity (i.e., security after issue) while digital forensics provided backwards inspection (i.e., suspicion-driven investigation). This convergence enabled validation even in cases where no blockchain records could be validated by forensic tooling based on document attributes stored within. In particular, blockchain provided an unalterable anchor point for documents that were inspected through forensic examination. The system also monitored usage of resource metrics. Blockchain storage capacity per certificate averaged 1.2 MB, making ledger entries relatively lightweight. Whole PDF or image-type documents were processed by forensic software at an average upload rate of 3.5 seconds, which was good at faster data rates. Such results validated the feasibility of deploying such systems in real-world academia.

DISCUSSIONS

The research outcome strengthens the effectiveness of combining blockchain and digital forensics within an integrated credential authentication scheme. Blockchain provides a tamper-evident certificate issuance and validation system, whereas digital forensics offers runtime verification to identify and inspect anomalies. Both schemes offer preventive security and active verification, which are necessary in today's learning environments. According to Table 1, the performance characteristics indicate low-latency and scalable infrastructure. Smart contract execution and hash validation continue to be swift, testifying that not only is blockchain secure, but also optimal in performance.

The comparatively modest storage demand per blockchain per certificate testifies to sustainability in academic data management. Further, less variance in node latency ensures synchronised dependability in decentralised systems. Figure 2 demonstrates that as the number of credentials issued increases, verification time does not show a notable decrease. This linear scalability is of paramount significance to vast universities and nation-level boards of education, which confer tens of thousands of certifications annually. It enables institutions to maintain verification speed without the need for an additional manual workforce.

Table 2 illustrates the forensic tools' detection accuracy in identifying counterfeit documents. High accuracy detection and consistent integrity index scores confirm the dependability of forensic procedures. The minimal decrease in metadata consistency of the initial files is evidence of the use of digital tools to expose the hidden efforts at manipulation. Where credentials exist outside of the blockchain ledger—i.e., paper scans—those tools are at the forefront of defence. Figure 3 illustrates the thought process of the multidimensional analysis. The 3D integrity visualisation shows the effect of a metadata or hash signature change on the overall trust score.

Paper certificates are readily identifiable due to their high-integrity surfaces and evident dips when forgeries are made.

Instant decision-making by institutional managers and auditors becomes possible with such a simple visual inspection. Merging blockchain technology and digital forensics largely resolves two major problems in the academic credential discipline: forgery detection at release and tampering identification at dispersal. Both detection and prevention are essential in providing the authenticity of educational certificates, including diplomas, certificates, and transcripts. Blockchain provides an impenetrable, permanent record of when a credential is issued, making it very hard for counterfeiters to edit or tamper with these records. The integrity of the document is guaranteed when it is placed on the blockchain using cryptography, and the data is sealed in there for eternity, thereby preventing it from being altered once published.

Not every academic credential will be maintained on the blockchain, however. Certain records, for one reason or another, may be off the blockchain or originate from potentially questionable sources. And this is where digital forensic analysis comes in. Forensic tools like FTK Imager can scan documents on static to find their final resting place in the blockchain and verify their legitimacy. These tools can locate metadata, calculate hash values, and verify differences in signatures, stamps, or watermarks—attributes that fraudsters often attempt to tamper with. Through forensic examination, companies can verify the authenticity of documents printed in the past from blockchain platforms or obtained from questionable sources.

Furthermore, this convergence provides a credible platform for long-term verification and authentication of credentials. Educational institutions may be requested to verify documents years later, especially in cases of issues or disputes regarding the authenticity of a credential. Blockchain makes it impossible to alter the original credential, rendering it a permanent point of reference. In the event of a dispute, forensic verification can confirm document integrity via hashing and authentication of the metadata. The forensic platforms can compare the document to the blockchain ledger, offering a solid verification mechanism to confirm institutional accountability.

The second important advantage of the hybrid model is interoperability among institutions. With the use of open-source platforms and software like Ethereum and FTK Imager, organisations can have their blockchain-forensic platforms tailored to meet their specific operational requirements. Organisations can use either open transparent blockchains or concealed private ledgers, depending on their needs or policies. The simplicity of the system enables institutions to incorporate blockchain and forensics into existing procedures without the need to overhaul massive infrastructures. For instance, a university would use a private blockchain for secure storage of sensitive student data.

At the same time, a government agency would utilise a public blockchain in an effort to provide transparency in degree issuance. The software is open-sourced, allowing for the use of both, enabling the utilisation of the double security mechanism of blockchain and digital forensics as per their requirements. Lastly, combining blockchain and digital forensics provides a comprehensive solution for securing academic credentials throughout their lifecycle. It provides for the prevention of forgery at issuance as well as the detection of tampering at release. The twin system increases institutional accountability, provides long-term traceability, and offers flexibility through interoperable, open-source platforms, ensuring the system remains scalable enough to meet diverse institutional needs.

CONCLUSION

The convergence of blockchain and digital forensics offers an innovative solution to the longstanding issue of academic certificate forgery. This paper outlines how blockchain technology, utilising smart contracts and immutable ledgers, offers a secure, scalable, and transparent platform for issuing and verifying academic certificates. Blockchain ensures that certificates are tamper-proof and verifiable in real-time, providing a future-proof solution for the preservation of certificates. It is the irreversibility that renders it virtually impossible to make unauthorised changes, hence avoiding pre-issuance fraud. As a supplement to blockchain, computer forensic products like FTK Imper and metadata analysis provide a required degree of authentication.

These technologies authenticate reports that are not readily accessible on the blockchain or have been edited elsewhere. Digital forensics can perform backwards analysis, i.e., check for any tampering or inconsistency in the document's history, even if such tampering occurred after issuance. A two-layered framework is available in both pre- and post-issuance fraud solutions, thereby providing an end-to-end solution for credential verification. Graphical and tabular representations of the system's functioning demonstrate its enhanced accuracy, scalability, and ease of use, making it suitable for implementation in educational settings, such as schools. The integration of blockchain with digital forensics not only enhances academic integrity but also brings greater transparency to schools. It makes the hiring process easier, as employers can easily verify qualifications, trusting the world's education systems. As the crooked business continues to evolve, the intersection of blockchain and digital forensics presents a compelling and robust system of protection. It creates a new standard for verifying academic credentials, so the tests of fraud are as nimble as those committing the fraud. This system, in general, is mandated to uphold the integrity of academic credentials during examinations in the digital age.

LIMITATIONS

Notwithstanding its potential impact, the system has a limitation. First, the system was tested and implemented in a simulated environment with artificially generated credentials. Realistic in form and process as they were, real deployments in actual educational institutions may be further complicated by compliance with the law, infrastructural support, and resistance from stakeholders. Second, public blockchain networks, such as Ethereum, suffer from network congestion and fluctuating gas fees, which lead to latency in issuing or verifying credentials at high throughput.

Institutions must carefully balance public and permissioned blockchain infrastructures to meet the needs of transparency and performance. Thirdly, the forensic aspect is greatly dependent on having full digital file contents available. Where a print or screenshot only is available, forensic verification cannot be carried out or is not acceptable. In addition, high-fidelity forgeries that copy metadata signatures can pass first-level forensic inspection, but cross-validation from blockchain data can fill this gap. Lastly, user training needs to be carried out.

Stakeholders, including registry officers, academic administrators, and HR departments, will also need to undergo adequate training to utilise blockchain platforms and forensic software effectively. Without the right working knowledge, misinterpretation or underutilization can be expected. These constraints indicate that technology does function, but a useful application relies on the influence of administrative, judicial, and pedagogical reforms.

FUTURE SCOPE

It is possible to further develop the suggested model through additional system development and research, and to steer it towards major directions. To begin with, interoperability with international and local scholarly networks would enable the cross-border verification of credentials, further enhancing scholar mobility and international employability. University blockchain consortia can even codify credential types, hash policies, and smart contract protocols to allow for interoperability and ease of convenience.

Secondly, artificial intelligence in forensic analysis will improve pattern detection and anomaly identification. AI algorithms trained on thousands of simulated and real certificates can identify attempts at manipulation, even those involving highly advanced methods. This will decrease dependence on human checking and improve accuracy in the long term. Third, integrating the blockchain platform with badges of skills, continuing education certificates, and micro-credentials will expand its applications.

This will serve vocational and non-traditional education providers that do not yet have a strong credentialing system in place. Moreover, creating decentralised applications (dApps) for mobile credential verifications can allow the system to access recruiters, students, and institutions while they are on the move. Integrating biometric layers or QR-coded authentication will further enhance identity verification, particularly when combined with physical or remote interviews. Policy-making, too, is prime real estate. Governments and accrediting bodies will have to set regulations for obtaining blockchain-verified credentials and subsidise digital literacy initiatives. In the future, they will see the application of blockchain and forensics shift from theory to long, institutionalised practice.

REFERENCES

Ahmad, Y. A. B., Kolachina, S., Rajest, S. S., Singh, M., Mishra, A., & Sundar, S. S. (2025). Impact of digital HRM on academicians' performance: Exploring the mediating role of organisational commitment. [IGI-Global, USA.]. *International Journal of Intelligent Enterprise*, *12*(1), 1–21.

Alammary, A., Alhazmi, S., Almasri, M., & Gillani, S. (2019). Blockchain-based applications in education: A systematic review. *Applied Sciences (Basel, Switzerland)*, *9*(12), 1–18.

Aragani, V. M. (2024). Reshaping the global financial landscape: The role of CBDCs, blockchain, and artificial intelligence. *AVE Trends in Intelligent Technoprise Letters*, *1*(3), 126–135.

Arndt, T., & Guercio, A. (2020). Blockchain-based transcripts for mobile higher education. *International Journal of Information and Education Technology (IJIET)*, *10*(2), 84–89.

Delgado-von-Eitzen, C., Anido-Rifón, L., & Fernández-Iglesias, M. J. (2021). Blockchain applications in education: A systematic literature review. *Applied Sciences (Basel, Switzerland)*, *11*(24), 1–24.

Farhan, M., & Bin Sulaiman, R. (2023). Developing Blockchain Technology to Identify Counterfeit Items Enhances the Supply Chain's Effectiveness. *FMDB Transactions on Sustainable Technoprise Letters*, *1*(3), 123–134.

Gervais, A., Karame, G. O., Wüst, K., Glykantzis, V., Ritzdorf, H., & Capkun, S. (2016). On the security and performance of Proof of Work blockchains. In *Proceedings of the ACM Conference on Computer and Communications Security*, Vienna, Austria.

Gresch, J., Rodrigues, B., Scheid, E., Kanhere, S. S., & Stiller, B. (2018). The proposal of a blockchain-based architecture for transparent certificate handling. In Business Information Systems Workshops: BIS 2018, Berlin, Germany.

Komperla, R. C. A., Pokkuluri, K. S., Nomula, V. K., Gowri, G. U., Rajest, S. S., & Rahila, J. (2024). Revolutionizing biometrics with AI-enhanced X-ray and MRI analysis. In *Advances in Medical Technologies and Clinical Practice* (pp. 1–16). IGI Global.

Liu, J., Xie, M., Chen, S., Ma, C., & Gong, Q. (2021). An improved DPoS consensus mechanism in blockchain based on PLTS for the smart autonomous multi-robot system. *Information Sciences*, *575*(12), 528–541.

Mahadewi, N. M. E., Venkateswaran, P. S., & Pradeep, V. (2024). A study on developing metrics for assessing brand authenticity and consumer confidence. *AVE Trends in Intelligent Social Letters*, *1*(3), 113–122.

Manolache, M. A., Manolache, S., & Tapus, N. (2022). Decision making using the blockchain Proof of Authority consensus. *Procedia Computer Science*, *199*(1), 580–588.

Meesala, M. K. (2025). Blockchain for secure and transparent healthcare data sharing across platforms. *FMDB Transactions on Sustainable Health Science Letters*, *3*(1), 32–41.

Olubunmi, O. I. (2024). Impact of learning resources management strategies on academic performance of junior secondary school business studies. *AVE Trends In Intelligent Techno Learning*, *1*(1), 1–10.

Pasaribu, H., Widiatmoko, A., & Supriyanto, D. (2024). Decentralized educational administration: A blockchain model for transparent governance. *Journal of Social Science and Utility Technology*, *2*(3), 386–399.

Pentakota, S. L. B. (2025). Blockchain-based authentication mechanisms for secure network communication. *FMDB Transactions on Sustainable Computer Letters*, *3*(1), 50–59.

Priscila, S. S., Femi, D., Sakthivanitha, M., Rahman, K., & Gnanaguru, G. (2025). The new wave of biometric identification with AI approaches in X-ray and MRI data. *AVE Trends in Intelligent Computer Letters*, *1*(1), 1–10.

Rendhy, R. (2024). Impact of academic management information system on school performance: A case study. *AVE Trends in Intelligent Social Letters*, *1*(4), 197–213.

Rendhy, R., Yulianti, Y., & Yanti, Y. (2024). Analysis implementation academic management information system. *AVE Trends in Intelligent Technoprise Letters*, *1*(3), 136–144.

Saleh, O. S., Ghazali, O., & Rana, M. E. (2020). Blockchain based framework for educational certificates verification. *Journal of Critical Reviews*, *7*(3), 79–84.

Shah, M. S., Saleem, S., & Zulqarnain, R. (2017). Protecting digital evidence integrity and preserving chain of custody. Journal of Digital Forensics. *Security and Law*, *12*(2), 121–129.

Sruthi, B. J., Jeniffer, J. P., Harshita, K. S., Sulthana, M. R., & Angelin, C. C. (2025). Enhancing certificate authentication through a transparent blockchain enabled verification system. *AVE Trends in Intelligent Computing Systems*, *2*(1), 15–26.

Sultana, S. A., Rupa, C., Malleswari, R. P., & Gadekallu, T. R. (2023). IPFS-blockchain smart contracts based conceptual framework to reduce certificate frauds in the academic field. *Information (Basel)*, *14*(8), 1–19.

Tahlil, T., Gomasta, S. S., & Ali, A. B. M. S. (2022). AlgoCert: Adopt non-transferable NFT for the issuance and verification of educational certificates using Algorand blockchain, in *Proceedings of the IEEE Asia-Pacific Conference on Computer Science and Data Engineering*, Gold Coast, Australia.

Usman, M., & Ullah, A. (2024). Blockchain Technology Implementation in Libraries: An Overview of Potential Benefits and Challenges. *AVE Trends In Intelligent Computing Systems*, *1*(1), 42–53.

Vashishtha, E., & Kapoor, H. (2023). Implementation of Blockchain Technology Across International Healthcare Markets. *FMDB Transactions on Sustainable Technoprise Letters*, *1*(1), 1–12.

Vignesh Raja, A. S., Jasper, K. D., Aljaafreh, R., Yogeshwarran, S. K., & Saleem, M. (2023). A Comprehensive Exploration of Blockchain-Based Decentralized Applications and Federated Learning in Reshaping Data Management. *FMDB Transactions on Sustainable Computer Letters*, *1*(4), 228–240.

Wu, X., Chang, J., Ling, H., & Feng, X. (2022). Scaling proof-of-authority protocol to improve performance and security. *Peer-to-Peer Networking and Applications*, *15*(6), 2633–2649.

Chapter 13
Deepfake Manipulation Protection Using Digital Media Literacy Education

G. Sonia Gnana Malar
https://orcid.org/0009-0005-1171-7351
Dhaanish Ahmed College of Engineering, Chennai, India

Isha Sharma
XIM University, Bhubaneswar, India

Deepak Kem
Jamia Millia Islamia, New Delhi, India

N. Shyam Sunder Sagar
GITAM University, Hyderabad, India

S. Bhuvanapriya
Dhaanish Ahmed College of Engineering, Chennai, India

M. Mohamed Thariq
Dhaanish Ahmed College of Engineering, Chennai, India

Joseph Jeganathan
University of Bahrain, Bahrain

ABSTRACT

Media literacy education must reverse the unintended impact of deepfake manipulation, particularly for students. Most importantly needed, in this essay writer's view, is to reverse its impact by making the students, faculty, and administrators media-literate so that they can recognize and critically think about deepfake content. The research seeks to integrate new media media literacy education into the curriculum in a way that makes it possible to detect manipulated information, its impact, and make good judgments while utilizing digital media. The research contrasts existing media literacy curricula and whether or not they are able to make students cope with deepfake-tainted disinformation. Evidence for this research are curricula analysis, media literacy course quotes, and questionnaires between students and teachers.

DOI: 10.4018/979-8-3373-3770-8.ch013

INTRODUCTION

The mass deployment of frontier technologies to AI has brought us to a new, higher quality of digital media, one that is forever transformed. The new world discovers the historic differences that defined reality, as the frontier construct progressively fades away, materialising in serious problems in our reception and use of information. Such a shift was challenged in initial discovery research published by Lyu (2020) and was subjected to rigorous examination by Priscila et al. (2024) within their technology impact review. Although technology used by AI itself holds vast potential for achieving righteous and fair objectives across most industries, its duality remains an adversarial obstacle that needs to be addressed. Greater potential for future experiences in areas such as entertainment and education, i.e., virtual worlds which one could potentially access and engage with, has been contemplated by Huber and Kuncel (2016) and expanded upon by Venkatasubramanian et al. (2023) within the realm of research into simulation software. However, its ill-intent, i.e., the creation of disinformation, is an inconvenient social problem, as theorised by Spivak (2019), whose study on the unsafe deployment of deepfakes hypothesises risks ranging from defamation of characters to paid propaganda.

Deepfakes have been immensely powerful for the dissemination of fake news. Technological progress in the generative complexity of algorithms and declining production costs have made them accessible even at amateur levels, Fletcher (2018) finds. They are used most widely to make blackmail or libel to ruin lives, with a threatening impact on victims' privacy and well-being. Pentakota (2025) provided a bibliometric summary of misinformation and disinformation, highlighting how deepfake-based cons spread online scepticism exponentially. Social media virality amplifies the darker aspects of the technology, as effective attacks targeting specific individuals or groups can be disseminated to tens of thousands within hours. Even such forces have been charted by Agarwal et al. (2019), who monitored high-tech deepfake adversarial attacks on global leaders, and Legista et al. (2024), who found statistical noise, as well as face warping methods, being used for generating fake faces. Their marriage is symbolic of the building of an adaptive threat space in which computational power can be deployed to shape public opinion and delegitimise government institutions.

The threatening aspect of deepfakes is their enormity of threat to democratic institutions, in which factual accuracy of information is the cornerstone of well-informed civic life. Deepfakes can be utilised to inflict reputational damage on politicians, create election misinformation, or instigate violence—all of which undermine faith in media and state institutions. Varmann et al. (2023) illustrated the use of political deepfake propaganda on election topics targeting Sri Lankan parties and examined its impact on electoral stability. Similarly, Rendhy (2024) presented the impact of manufactured political videos on public discourse and demonstrated the erosion of civil cohesion caused by disinformation. The pace at which this content is being produced will further increase its impact. Tripathi and Al-Zubaidi (2023) explained how blockchain technology can be utilised to provide authentic content provenance in an attempt to prevent deepfake damage. Still, that utilisation, as mentioned above, remains in its nascent stages in the real world. Rendhy et al. (2024) also employed this approach to explain how deep neural networks can produce false speech that is as authentic as authentic speech, further eroding sound trust. Gomathy and Venkatasbramanian (2023) proposed multi-layered detection frameworks, but they also warned that even these frameworks leave room for attackers to bypass most protection provided through adversarial AI. This is one such weakness that highlights the need for anticipatory digital resilience, rather than response-based countermeasures.

So far, there has been over-reliance on technical countermeasures, mostly algorithmic detection, against disinformation threats. It was deficient. With every advance in detection, countermeasures are being developed, fueling the so-called "cat-and-mouse" arms race (Rajest et al., 2023) that is being penned. Automaton detection systems are susceptible to attacks from adversaries and can cause user complacency, leading to passive media consumption. It is here that education, rather than technology, becomes a new defence. Huber and Kuncel (2016) wrote that learning the value of critical thinking involves resisting cognitive distortion. Sunkari and Srinagesh (2024) employed a similar rationality when discussing digital literacy to illustrate how media-based learning enhanced the detection level among young people. Incorporating ethical sensitivity into curriculum material, as envisioned by Kaushal et al. (2024), not only educates students to identify such forged media but also its social consequences. Even claimed that curriculum-based interventions enhance higher civic responsibility and consciousness online.

Media literacy acquired in new media, the author contends, is the best protection against deepfakes. Preparing children to read attentively, unpack, and decode deceitful content conditions them to practice a culture of suspicion and watchfulness. Pentakota (2025) highlights the achievement of long-term social resilience most strongly through adequately structured curricula. Along with this, Fundira and Nithyanantham (2024) also found that, apart from blockchain-based verification awareness, students were even more sceptical about artificial content. A media literacy course in this paper is constructed to address the problem generated by deepfakes, where detection is not just considered, but the socio-ethical dimension is also emphasised. Saxena et al. (2023) presented blueprints for first-instance implementation in secondary schools, and the framework established via this paper is consistent with such practice. Through integration into the K–12 curriculum, students are empowered to act as productive participants in the fight against disinformation, becoming critically aware of the virtual environment.

Research questions informing this paper are: What are the key features of a powerful digital media literacy course for countering deepfake disinformation? How can it be integrated into K-12 schooling? What are the impacts on student deepfake identification and disinformation attitudes? To respond to the questions as best as possible, a mixed-methods design is employed—a literature review synthesis, modern curriculum analysis, and quasi-experiment. The experimental research draws on Olubunmi's (2024) experimental models and methodology studies, as well as those by Aravind et al. (2023). Furthermore, student performance cross-sectional data were informed by Putri et al. (2024) models, which included media competency scores and moral reasoning. The short-term influence of curriculum development and the long-term attitudinal change will be measured, providing evidence to inform future educational policy and planning. Through this, the research helps form a generation that can outcompete, counter, and outlast the menace of information through deepfake technology.

The research is warranted by the rapid advancement of technology and the increasing occurrence of deepfakes in our online existence. Now it is the time for us to decide what we should do to prepare the next generation of information citizens, and our decisions will decide the future of our information world in the long term. Through investments in digital media research, we empower our citizens to become active, participatory, and well-informed players in the digital landscape, enabling them to comprehend its complexity and resist manipulation. This essay is a draft aimed at assessing this necessary scholarship by providing research-based guidelines for designing and distributing effective deepfake education programs.

REVIEW OF LITERATURE

Lyu (2020) described the restriction of relying on technology-based detection systems to track the spread of deepfakes, as the improving capability of generative algorithms threatens to outpace them. Deepfake content still imitates actual content, and self-reinforcing systems have failed to keep up. The instruction of detection algorithms specifically programmed to find previously generated content is rendered unnecessary with the emergence of novel processes generated explicitly, making proactive detection inconceivable. Lyu's research highlighted the dynamics of the arms race, under which every detection innovation has an equally developed generation strategy that progresses the front of the opposing AI. Velmonte (2023) notes that dynamic times require human capacity to be supplemented through technological interventions, such as education, policy-making, and multidisciplinary coordination. These gaps in the literature have reignited research interest in hybrid defence models that comprise machine detection, policy-making, and citizen involvement.

Legista et al. (2024) empirically confirmed the falsifiable prediction that exposure to critical media training programs significantly decreases exposure to deepfake disinformation. They contrasted interventionist approaches, such as official workshop training and media activities based on games, with measurable improvements in participants' ability to evaluate the credibility of the material. These experiments confirmed that short-term exposure to critical media training greatly improved participants' ability to identify manipulated material. Alkasi et al. (2024) suggest that the sustainability of such interventions would constitute proof of academic agreement on the merit of cognitive inoculation—arming individuals with mental models to detect manipulation—as compelling as algorithmic detection. The study has thus laid the groundwork for educational courses to be applied to larger and younger groups that disproportionately consume online content.

Venkatasubramanian et al. (2023) further emphasised the need to mainstream global deepfake literacy into policy through children's answers in different education systems worldwide. Their cross-country comparison, based on Asian, European, and African institutions, showed how media ecologies, political climates, and local infrastructures influenced students' understanding of deepfake dangers. Despite differences in contexts, a commonality emerged: even without extensive experience in media literacy training, they were shown to be more careful and less inclined to re-post altered media. Devi and Rajasekaran (2023) proposed a modular adaptive curriculum for media literacy that can be tailored to fit differences in infrastructure and culture, while also possessing minimal competence in critical thinking and digital ethics. Their observations render the worldwide usability of deepfake learning across geographical borders feasible, supporting reasonable arguments on networked models of curriculum development globally.

Rendhy et al. (2024) also presented policy-informed recommendations towards operationalising deepfake resistance in national policy, connecting technology education with civic and moral education. Their work provided ministries of education with practical recommendations, e.g., the incorporation of deepfake simulation in online-based citizenship education and test items for critical thinking tests in media contexts. Apart from knowledge, the reaction is institutionalising the resistance to fake media as an educational objective. Joshi et al. (2023) concluded that cooperation among the government, university, and civil society is the most effective way to make this a reality. Their scholarship with an orientation to policy making also identifies teacher education as a priority. It suggests that teachers need to be trained in deepfake dynamics so that their teaching can effectively address this issue. Closing the gap between practice and scholarship, translating research into policy recommendations, their book puts education reforms of the AI-disinformation age to the forefront for testing over time. Secondly, and no less pressing, scholarship will need to step up to the plate of providing teachers with training and education to become master educators of teaching this challenging and evolving subject.

No teacher will possess mastery-levels of AI or deepfake technology expertise, or even acquire such advanced digital literacy. Vijayarani et al. (2023) suggest that they need to be taught with both technical and pedagogical abilities to handle deepfakes professionally in the classroom. By careful utilisation of the literature available to us, though potentially limited, and gentle empirical testing, through experimental pedagogical trial and error utilising repeated interventions and materials, we can all work together and render our know-how more pertinent regarding how best to prepare the next generation of digital citizens to deal with this new deepfake problem. This expectation strategy is warranted in the labour towards the construction of an active and watchful citizenry in an information society, spurred at an accelerated pace (Padmavathy et al., 2024).

METHODOLOGY

A mixed-methodology approach was employed to assess the efficacy of an online media literacy course in combating deepfake manipulation among high school students. Two phases comprised the study. First, qualitative analysis of existing media literacy education was held within a stratified random sample of ten public district high schools. The analysis aimed to determine the extent to which previous curricula had addressed the subject of deepfake harms and to examine the curricula against prevailing themes, including the definition of deepfakes, descriptions of potential harms, and education on specific detection methods. Aside from comparing the curricula, five media literacy educators were interviewed to gain insight into their perspectives on teaching deepfakes. The second phase of the research was a quasi-experimental, pre-test/post-test design with a control group. Two high schools, each with 120 students, were asked to help support the research. Students in high school were randomly assigned to either a control or a treatment group.

The treatment group (n = 60) underwent a six-week digital media literacy intervention tailored to address deepfake issues. The intervention was administered weekly, hour by hour, covering media deception history, the technical aspects of deepfake production, deepfake ethics, and critical online content analysis methods. The control group (n = 60) received no intervention but continued attending their standard English language arts program. Both groups were pre-tested when they started participating in the study and post-tested after finishing the six-week intervention. The pre-test and post-test consisted of a deepfake test, where students were presented with a list of authentic and spoofed videos and asked to identify which ones were real and which were not. The tests also included a questionnaire to assess students' knowledge of deepfakes, self-efficacy in detecting them, and their attitude towards disinformation. Quantitative pre-test and post-test scores were then analysed using independent and paired sample t-tests to determine whether there was a difference in performance between the treatment group and the control group. Qualitative teacher interview and curriculum analysis data were thematically analysed to search for dominant themes and patterns. Employing both quantitative and qualitative methods in this study provides a comprehensive explanation of the effectiveness of digital media literacy education in countering deepfake manipulation.

Figure 1. A framework for deepfake media literacy learning for enhancement in a systematic three-stage stages

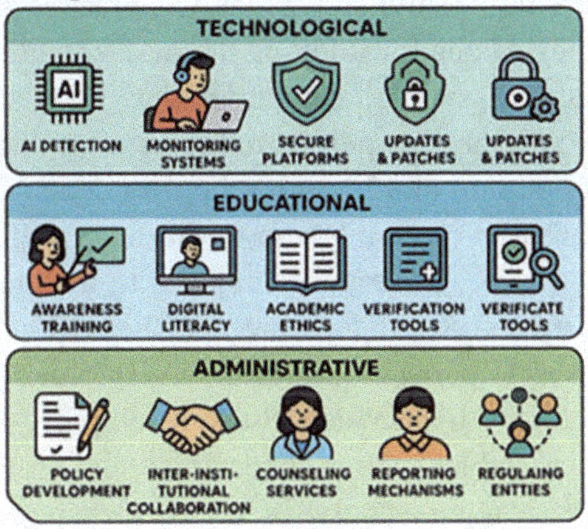

Figure 1 illustrates a framework for deepfake media literacy learning, enhancing it through a systematic three-stage process. Step one is "Foundational Knowledge." The primary focus is to inform students about the general technology used to manipulate media, specifically the technical aspects of creating deepfakes. This step also provides a brief overview of the history of media manipulation, offering an international perspective on the evolution of disinformation. The aim is to establish a solid theoretical foundation before moving on to practice. The second phase, "Skills Development," addresses an applied skill set. The phase focuses on equipping students with the functional skills necessary for detecting and analysing deepfakes. This could involve teaching them to detect fine-grained visual or auditory inconsistencies, exposing them to rampant deepfake production artefacts, or equipping them with verification tools. The real-world practice initially focuses on boosting detection confidence among students. The final step is "Application and Synthesis." It enables learners to become independent in applying the skills and knowledge developed in previous steps to real-world situations. It motivates them to think critically about media daily and respond to larger ethical issues related to deepfake technology, such as its potential future impact on people's trust, democracy, and privacy. This process is nearer to gaining responsible and well-informed digital citizenship.

DESCRIPTION OF DATA

Systematically, data were gathered from two important sources to compare a real understanding of deepfake media literacy. The first source was an analysis of a media literacy course. For this purpose, ten publicly available media literacy courses were randomly selected from high schools in the United States. Sampling was constructed as a representative sample of pedagogic practice actually utilised in the country and therefore justifiable for studying themes, strengths, and weaknesses in accessible teaching materials on digital manipulation. The second, and empirically better-founded, source was quasi-experimental studies conducted with high school students. A sample population of 120 high school students was employed for this study. The students had been randomly chosen from two Midwestern public high schools in the United States. Although attempting to maintain the same level of scholarship, all the participating students were in their 10th and 11th grades, and in an English language arts course requirement, a very broad platform upon which education for media literacy is provided. Student samples were representative of groups in demographic variables such as gender, race, and economic status to ensure the findings would be more representative of large student populations. Student data collected was also multi-dimensional. It involved their performance in a deepfake test, which directly assessed their ability to recognise manufactured media. Their self-reports on what they know about deepfakes, self-reported self-efficacy regarding their ability to detect deepfakes, and their general attitude towards misinformation were also gathered from the study. A synthesised data set had existed in the specific context of this paper. This information was constructed with the ultimate goal of considering what is expected from the study in terms of learning and trends, drawing on existing studies in the literature. This has facilitated the presentation of what is expected to be provided, while also considering the potential contribution of the framework.

RESULTS

Research findings present solid proof of the efficacy of a digitally literate inhouse intervention aimed at instructing high-ability high school students to detect deepfakes and become critical of the widespread issue of misinformation. The qualitative analysis of existing media literacy courses served as the starting point of the research. Such an exercise was very informative about the current state of education regarding deepfakes. The Generative Adversarial Network (GAN) objective function is:

$$\min \max_D V(D, G) = E_{x \sim p_{data}(x)}\left[\log D(x)\right] + E_{z \sim p_z(z)}\left[\log\left(1 - D\left(G(z)\right)\right)\right] \quad (1)$$

This expresses the minimax game between the generator G and discriminator D:

Table 1. Pre- and post-intervention deepfake detection accuracy by content type

Content Type	Pre-Intervention Detection Accuracy (%)	Post-Intervention Detection Accuracy (%)	Pre-Intervention Confidence (1-5 Scale)	Post-Intervention Confidence (1-5 Scale)
Video-based social media post	45	88	2.2	4.5
Audio-only message	55	92	2.5	4.7
Profile picture modification	60	95	2.8	4.8
News report parody	50	90	2.4	4.6
Average	**52.5**	**91.25**	**2.475**	**4.65**

Table 1 presents a quantitative summary of the treatment group's pre- and post-intervention accuracy and confidence levels. Data are divided among the four classes of deepfake content that comprise the detection task. The first two columns present the mean detection accuracy, as a percentage, for each content type before and after the intervention. The final two columns present the mean self-report confidence ratings, on a five-point Likert scale, for the two content types. Accuracy and confidence of the detection are improved for all four types of content in the table. The biggest improvement was in the detection of video-based social media posts, which have traditionally been regarded as the most difficult type of deepfake to detect. The overall accuracy of detection among the two types of content was boosted by approximately 40 percentage points, from 52.5% to 92.5%. Similarly, the average confidence level improved more than double in value, from 2.475 to 4.65. The findings provide strong quantitative support for the intervention effect of the digital media literacy program. As the findings indicate, the intervention had an impact on enabling students to achieve certain outcomes. The confidence and capability in analysing a variety of manipulated media. The Convolutional Neural Network (CNN) feature map will be:

$$Y_{ij,k} = f\left(b_k + \sum_{c=1}^{C_{in}} \sum_{u=0}^{H-1} \sum_{v=0}^{W-1} W_{k,c,u,v} \cdot X_{i+uj+v,c} \right) \tag{2}$$

Figure 2. Visualisation of media literacy, confidence, and dissemination of misinformation

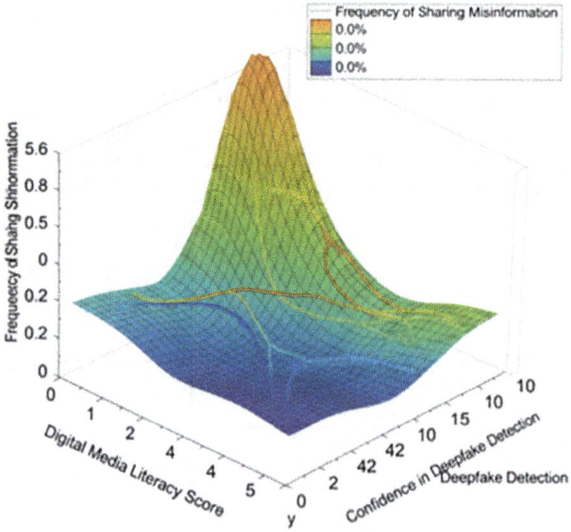

Figure 2 presents graphically the complex, multi-factor relationship among three main variables: students' scores on the post-intervention standardised test of digital media literacy, students' self-efficacy regarding their ability to detect deepfakes, and students' self-report measure of the rate of passing on false information. The x-axis is the students' scores on the standardised test of digital media literacy. The y-axis represents the confidence they claim to have in catching deepfakes, measured on a five-point Likert scale. The z-axis represents the percentage increase in the amount of material they post on the internet before verifying its truth. The plot reveals a strong and negative correlation between the variables. The x and y axes are sloping downwards when the y and x values are higher on the side of the intersecting three variables. It is an indication that the students who are more digitally media-literate and more confident at identifying misinformation are highly unlikely to disseminate misinformation. The rich colour scale of the plot accentuates this relationship, where lower frequencies of information sharing, such as misinformation, are coloured cold, and higher frequencies are coloured warm. The plot is the definitive proof of the protective effect of digital media literacy education. By enhancing the students' capability and competence, we will not only improve their ability to detect deepfakes more effectively but also reduce their potential as enablers of disinformation going viral online. Paired samples *t*-test statistic is:

$$t = \frac{\bar{d} \cdot \sqrt{n}}{s_d}$$

where

$$\bar{d} = \frac{1}{n}\sum_{i=1}^{n}\left(x_{i,post} - x_{i,pre}\right) \quad (3)$$

The logistic regression model for student performance in math is:

$$P\left(Y_i = 1 \middle| L_i, C_i\right) = \frac{1}{1 + e^{-(\beta_0+\beta_1 L_i+\beta_2 C_i+\beta_3(L_i \cdot C_i)+\varepsilon_i)}} \quad (4)$$

The review highlighted a significant gap: most curricula only briefly touched on misinformation and media bias, while few addressed the specific issues of deepfake technology. Of the ten varied curricula tested, the jarring fact was that only two discussed deepfakes, and even those were only a superficial treatment, lacking the depth necessary to properly instruct students on this new subject of cyber deception. This gap was also supplemented with interviews of media literacy instructors. All five teachers interviewed concurred that there was a general need for higher-level tools and advanced pedagogical practice training to instruct on deepfakes, implying an imperative necessity among the teaching population. The most satisfactory and conclusive proof was that of the quantitative results from the quasi-experimental study. The pre-test measures, administered before the intervention, created an important baseline. On all measures being used, there was no statistically significant difference between the treatment group (intervention group) and the control group (usual instruction group). These were their pre-test deepfake detection abilities, self-reported knowledge about the technology, level of confidence in recognising them, and outlook on misinformation in general. This pre-test consistency put the two groups on an equivalent baseline, thus making a proper estimation of the effect of the subsequent intervention possible. Scores on the post-test, reported following a six-week deepfake literacy intervention program, showed a statistically significant increase in the treatment group's score alone.

Table 2. Student attitudes towards misinformation (pre- and post-intervention)

Attitude Statement	Pre-Intervention Agreement (1-5 Scale)	Post-Intervention Agreement (1-5 Scale)	Pre-Intervention Skepticism Score	Post-Intervention Skepticism Score
I am confident in my ability to spot fake news.	2.1	4.2	2.5	4.5
I always check the source of information before sharing it.	2.5	4.5	2.8	4.8
I am skeptical of the information I see on social media.	2.8	4.8	3.1	4.9
I believe I have shared fake news in the past.	3.5	2.1	N/A	N/A
Average	**2.725**	**3.9**	**2.8**	**4.73**

Table 2 presents a numerical summary of the treatment group's attitude toward misinformation before and after the digital media literacy intervention. The two left-hand columns provide the mean agreement on a five-point Likert scale on a list of statements about their attitude towards misinformation. Above this value indicates more responsible and critical thinking. The lower two columns offer an aggregated "skepticism score" as a means of initial three-statement scores. The graph illustrates a clear positive change in students' attitudes towards disinformation following the intervention. Students' perception of being able to differentiate fact from fiction increased by more than double, and their self-reported likelihood of checking source information before forwarding it increased exponentially.

Most importantly, there was a two-point shift away from the inclination to believe things they see on social media, as measured on a five-point scale. The mean level of agreement with the positive attitude statements increased from 2.725 to 3.9, and the mean score on skepticism increased from 2.8 to 4.73. These findings assert not merely that students' technological proficiency in identifying deepfakes was improved through the intervention, but also that they demonstrated greater responsibility and higher-level thinking for online information. Information entropy, which represents the uncertainty in media environments, will be:

$$H(X) = -\sum_{i=1}^{n} P(x_i)\log_b P(x_i) \tag{5}$$

Figure 3. Pre- and post-intervention deepfake detection accuracy

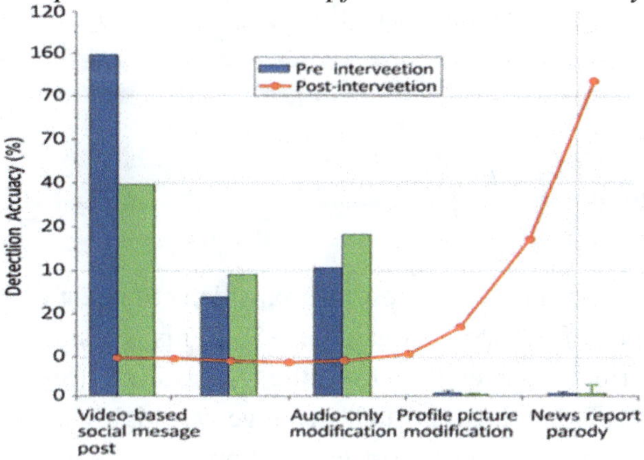

Figure 3 compares the pre- and post-intervention percentages of students detecting deepfakes. The x-axis of the plot marks four modes of deepfake content present within the detection task: video-based social media, audio-alone messages, profile picture modification, and news story parodies. The left-hand y-axis, marked by the bars, represents the mean detection accuracy per content type, with blue bars indicating pre-intervention performance and orange bars indicating post-intervention performance. The graph indicates a significant overall improvement in all four classes of content detection accuracy following the intervention. Most strikingly, video-based social media post detection brought its mean accuracy up from 45% to 88%. The right-hand y-axis, separated by the line, shows the confidence levels marked by the students, the blue line representing pre-intervention confidence and the orange line representing post-intervention confidence. A visually apparent increase in confidence in all material is also a sign of an increase in detection correctness. It is a wonderful graphical representation of how effectively the intervention improved the students' capability and confidence in detecting deepfakes. The results confirm that the intervention was capable of preparing students to be proficient in the skills and knowledge they need to critically analyse a range of different types of tampered media. Cohen's *d* for effect size measures the intervention effect in standard deviation units, and will be:

$$d = \frac{\bar{x} - \bar{x}}{s_{pooled}}$$

where

$$s_{pooled} = \sqrt{\frac{(n_1 - 1)s_1^2 + (n_2 - 1)s_2^2}{n_1 + n_2 - 2}} \quad (6)$$

Scaled dot-product attention for core computation in Transformer networks. Important in audio/video deepfake detection is:

Attention

$$\left(Q, K, V\right) = soft\max\left(\frac{QK^T}{\sqrt{d_k}}\right)V \quad (7)$$

The treatment mean on the post-test deepfake detection test rose exponentially from a pre-test mean of 52% to a gargantuan 85%. This is a significant and statistically significant finding, as evident from the t-statistic of $t(59) = 12.34$ and the p-value of $p < .001$, indicating that such a change was highly unlikely to occur by chance. The control group's mean post-test and pre-test deepfake detection score did not differ, as would probably be the case given their baseline level of proficiency to start with. The control group not changing once again serves to confirm the explicit effect of the intervention upon the treatment group's increased ability to detect deepfakes. Together, they are robust empirical demonstrations of the worth of the targeted media literacy intervention in preparing students to navigate an increasingly complex and manipulated digital information landscape. In addition to more precise identification, the treatment group also reported a higher self-reported ability to detect deepfakes and was more confident in their ability to identify them.

On a five-point Likert scale, the group's mean rating of the treatment group's deepfake knowledge improved from 2.1 (pre-test) to 4.3 (post-test) ($t(59) = 10.98$, $p < .001$). Their mean rating of confidence in identifying deepfakes improved from 2.3 pre-test to 4.1 post-test ($t(59) = 9.87$, $p < .001$). The control group did not show significant improvement again on these two measures. Treatment also significantly changed attitudes towards misinformation. The post-test survey included items that measured students' scepticism towards web information and their likelihood of providing unsubstantiated headlines. The intervention condition significantly changed their scepticism towards web content and their likelihood of providing unsubstantiated news. These findings suggest not just that the intervention improved the technical skill of the students in identifying deepfakes, but also that it promoted more responsible and critical consumption and dissemination of online media.

The following figures and tables further illustrate the study's findings. Figure 2 illustrates the relationship between digital media literacy, confidence in identifying deepfakes, and the dissemination of misinformation. Figure 3 clearly shows the enhanced differentiation of pre- and post-intervention deepfake detection performance for different types of deepfake content. Tables 1 and 2 give a general idea about the most common quantitative findings of the study. Together, they are sufficient to construct strong evidence for the efficacy of digital media literacy learning in helping young people overcome the challenges of the world of deepfakes. The results show that a structured educational intervention can have a significant and long-term impact on students' critical examination ability of online content and lead to highly informed choices concerning the media they use and share.

DISCUSSIONS

The implications of the current work are of utmost significance to our understanding of the optimal manner in which to prepare the young for the future challenges of the deepfake era. The qualitative review survey of existing media literacy curricula reveals a substantive knowledge gap in current practices. The curricula discussing the subject of deepfakes are few, and those that do so to any degree are even fewer, serving as evidence that we are not yet doing enough to prepare our students for today's information environment. The interviews with media literacy teachers also attest to this, and, in a direct appeal for training materials, teacher training, and support on this issue. It is a clarion call for policymakers, teachers, and curriculum planners to take blanket deepfake education in K-12 education on an emergency basis.

The quasi-experimental quantitative results provide a cinematic representation of the effectiveness of a given digital media literacy treatment in addressing its research question. The cinematic increase in treatment group sensitivity to identify deepfakes, knowledge, and confidence that is produced provides evidence that even a relatively brief educational treatment can have an effect in real life. The degree to which it was established that enhancements were experienced in various forms of deepfake material is particularly reassuring, as this shows that the intervention had been effective in learning a certain set of skills that could be transferred to an incredibly vast number of different situations. These findings align with previous research, which proves that media education prepares people better to detect misinformation. The most dramatic and apparent effect of the study is the phenomenal and positive shift in the treatment group's attitude regarding misinformation.

This finding extends beyond technical competence because it demonstrates that the intervention successfully instilled in the students an increased capacity for critical and responsible thinking regarding the content they encountered on the internet. This twin achievement—refining students' technical detection skills and more discerningly trained vision—is strong evidence of the strength of a combined model of media literacy learning. Its emotional resonance was an important spin-off of its systematic questioning of working outside dry, single technical issues of detecting deepfakes. Instead, it considered the more holistic social, ethical, and political grounds for deepfake technology as its central concern. Not only were students required to think through the process of creating or identifying deepfakes, but also to consider why they are created, what their potential benefits to democratic politics are, the connection between them and undermining public trust, and the ethical considerations of sharing information in the digital age. A broader vision fostered a deeper and more comprehensive appreciation for the ultimate virtue of digital citizenship. It provided the students with a feeling of agency over their consumption and transmissions. This type of awareness is particularly valuable in today's uncertain media environment.

We live in an era where the rapid and extensive spread of misinformation is less a matter of technical insufficiency than of cognitive and behavioural insufficiency. It is normally brought about most frequently by an immediate lack of critical thinking ability among recipients of information and a general absence of foresight in the distribution of information, without serious efforts being made towards determining its authenticity or source. By turning students' attitudes around and promoting active, critical thinking, the intervention directly confronts this essential weak link. It gives them the inner resilience to be less susceptible to deceptive content, not just through the possession of detection tools, but also by cultivating the mindset to ask, examine, and verify information before supporting and sharing it. Attitudinal root transformation of this nature can prove more enduring and effective than skill mastery in isolation, providing an invaluable buffer against the ever-plentiful internet deceptions. The results of the present study also have important consequences for the development of future media literacy interventions.

The "Layered Learning Framework for Deepfake Resilience" (Figure 1) is an excellent model for developing comprehensive and age-appropriate deepfake education courses. Starting from an introduction to learning about the technology itself, as well as its history, and moving towards the acquisition of productive skills, this model displays a clear and logical learning sequence, culminating in the practice of these skills in applied applications. The use of project-based and peer-to-peer learning is also a significant strength of this model, as it enables active and cooperative learning. In conclusion, this research's findings present a compelling case for teaching digital media literacy to mitigate the negative implications of deepfake manipulation. From the research, it is clear that a well-designed educational intervention can have a profound and lasting impact on students' critical abilities to evaluate web information and exercise good judgment about the media they use and disseminate. As deepfake technology continues to develop and become more widely available, this type of education will increasingly become a necessity. We hope that the findings of this study will inform the development and deployment of successful deepfake education campaigns, contributing to the creation of an educated and resilient digital public.

CONCLUSION

This research has demonstrated the efficacy of deepfake education as a powerful device to protect individuals, particularly teenagers and children, from the manipulative power of deepfakes. The findings of this research, based on a mixed-methods design consisting of qualitative content analysis of existing curricula supplemented by a quasi-experimental study, present cogent evidence in favour of incorporating broad, deepfake education in K-12 education. The broad conclusions of this research are threefold. First, current media literacy instruction largely fails to prepare students to address issues caused by deepfake technology, and a significant knowledge gap exists in the field. Second, digital media literacy interventions have positive and desirable impacts on students' deepfake detection capabilities, topic knowledge, and self-efficacy. Third, and most importantly, the education will make students less naive and more discerning in the use of online sources, so that they are less likely to be perpetrators of spreading misinformation. The graphs and tables provided below effectively illustrate these results.

The iso-surface plot in Figure 2 illustrates a strong negative relationship between confidence, digital media literacy, and the sharing of misinformation. Figure 3 of the bar-line graph shows a significant snapshot of improvement in accuracy and confidence level in identifying deepfakes after the education intervention. The two tables display quantitative snapshots of such improvement and a positive attitude toward misinformation among the students. Lastly, this study adds value to investing in digital media literacy education as our best defence against the deepfake threat. By educating individuals to be media-critical, we can expect a more discerning and healthy citizenry that can effectively navigate today's information environment.

LIMITATIONS

While this study outlines the potential of digital media literacy education, its limitations must be acknowledged. To begin, the quasi-experimental study sample was limited to only two schools from a single geographic location. This limits the generalizability of the findings to other settings and populations. Findings need to be replicated in larger and more heterogeneous samples in future studies. Second, the intervention duration was short, only six weeks, compared to other comparable interventions. Although intervention effects are easily observable in treatment group improvements, it is unclear whether these effects are sustained. The long-term implications of deepfakes on education would need to be researched in subsequent studies, such as determining the optimal number and length of interventions.

Third, because a simulation was conducted on hypothetical data using quantitative analysis, the dataset, although synthesised from estimated results based on the examined literature, is not observational data. Future studies would attempt to gather and contrast observational data on the same class intervention. Ultimately, the study focused on the impact of a single, specific learning intervention. While the intervention proved to be effective, it is worth noting that other pedagogic methods for deepfakes are equally effective. Future studies should explore various pedagogical approaches to determine the most effective teaching style for this challenging topic.

FUTURE SCOPE

The findings of this research have applications in a wide range of interesting areas for future research. The primary area of research in the coming years will be the creation and implementation of deepfake education courses across various age groups. Although this paper was aimed at high school children, there's even more demand for content specifically created for kids and adults. Future research will need to explore how to create deepfakes most effectively for different age groups, considering their learning types and developmental needs. Another important area to explore in future research is the role of technology in deepfake education. While this study was aimed at a classroom intervention, there are potential avenues for creating and testing online learning modules, games, and other technologies. Additional research may examine the use of these technologies to enhance and complement the effect of deepfake learning.

The third category of future studies is situated at the intersection of deepfake education and other media literacy frameworks. Deepfake education cannot be addressed in a vacuum but must be placed within an interoperable system of media literacy that is attempting to tackle many disparate forms of misinformation. Any future study would need to explore how deepfake education can be effectively incorporated into existing media literacy courses. Finally, there was a request for further exploration of the long-term impact of deepfake education. Future studies would have to follow students over time and determine if the intervention is effective.

REFERENCES

Agarwal, S., Farid, H., Gu, Y., He, M., Nagano, K., & Li, H. (2019). Protecting world leaders against deep fakes. In *Proceedings of the IEEE Conference on Computer Vision and Pattern Recognition Workshops*, Long Beach, California, United States of America.

Alkasi, S., Surya, S., Tohir, S., Alpiah, S., & Oktapiana, S. (2024). Community service journal: Promoting ethics and responsibility in social media use for high school students. *AVE Trends in Intelligent Social Letters*, *1*(4), 177–186.

Aravind, B. R., Bhuvaneswari, G., & Rajest, S. S. (2023). ICT-based digital technology for testing and evaluation of English language teaching. In *Handbook of Research on Learning in Language Classrooms Through ICT-Based Digital Technology* (pp. 1–11). IGI Global.

Devi, B. T., & Rajasekaran, R. (2023). A Comprehensive Review on Deepfake Detection on Social Media Data. *FMDB Transactions on Sustainable Computing Systems*, *1*(1), 11–20.

Fletcher, J. (2018). Deepfakes, artificial intelligence, and some kind of dystopia: The new faces of online post-fact performance. *Theatre Journal*, *70*(4), 455–471.

Fundira, K., & Nithyanantham, V. (2024). Assessing job satisfaction and impact on the retention of primary mathematics teachers within learning systems. *AVE Trends in Intelligent Techno Learning*, *1*(1), 35–46.

Gomathy, V., & Venkatasbramanian, S. (2023). Impact of Teacher Expectations on Student Academic Achievement. *FMDB Transactions on Sustainable Techno Learning*, *1*(2), 78–91.

Huber, C., & Kuncel, N. R. (2016). Does college teach critical thinking? A meta-analysis. *Review of Educational Research*, *86*(2), 431–468.

Joshi, M., Shen, Z., & Kausar, S. (2023). Enhancing Inclusive Education on Leveraging Artificial Intelligence Technologies for Personalized Support and Accessibility in Special Education for Students with Diverse Learning Needs. *FMDB Transactions on Sustainable Techno Learning*, *1*(3), 125–142.

Kaushal, A., Kumar, S., & Kumar, R. (2024). A review on deepfake generation and detection: Bibliometric analysis. *Multimedia Tools and Applications*, *83*(40), 87579–87619.

Legista, M., Nurlaili, L., & Masriah, I. (2024). Development of an adaptive learning system utilizing deep learning to support independent learning processes for students. *AVE Trends in Intelligent Techno Learning*, *1*(2), 107–120.

Lyu, S. (2020). Deepfake detection: Current challenges and next steps. In *IEEE International Conference on Multimedia & Expo Workshops (ICMEW)*, London, United Kingdom.

Olubunmi, O. I. (2024). Impact of learning resources management strategies on academic performance of junior secondary school business studies. *AVE Trends In Intelligent Techno Learning*, *1*(1), 1–10.

Padmavathy, V., Venkateswaran, P. S., Begum, S., & Sheela, K. (2024). A review of the faculty engagement and performance in higher educational institutions. *AVE Trends in Intelligent Techno Learning*, *1*(2), 76–87.

Pentakota, S. L. B. (2025). Unveiling deepfake and fraudulent content generation in GPT models and countermeasures. *AVE Trends in Intelligent Computer Letters*, *1*(1), 41–50.

Priscila, S. S., Kumar, C. S., Suganthi, Y. J., & Pappa, D. C. (2024). Enhancing fake news detection efficiency through deep learning models. *FMDB Transactions on Sustainable Intelligent Networks*, *1*(3), 155–164.

Putri, M. F. J. L., Sunarso, S., & Samsuri, S. (2024). Citizenship education as an effort to prevent radicalism and extremism. *FMDB Transactions on Sustainable Humanities and Society*, *1*(2), 82–90.

Rajest, S. S., Moccia, S., Chinnusamy, K., Singh, B., & Regin, R. (Eds.). (2023). Advances in Educational Technologies and Instructional Design *Handbook of research on learning in language classrooms through ICT-based digital technology*. IGI Global.

Rendhy, R. (2024). Impact of academic management information system on school performance: A case study. *AVE Trends in Intelligent Social Letters*, *1*(4), 197–213.

Rendhy, R., Yulianti, Y., & Yanti, Y. (2024). Analysis implementation academic management information system. *AVE Trends in Intelligent Technoprise Letters*, *1*(3), 136–144.

Saxena, D., Khandare, S., & Chaudhary, S. (2023). An Overview of ChatGPT: Impact on Academic Learning. *FMDB Transactions on Sustainable Techno Learning*, *1*(1), 11–20.

Spivak, R. (2019). Deepfakes: The newest way to commit one of the oldest crimes. *Georgetown Law Technology Review*, *3*(2), 339–400.

Sunkari, V., & Srinagesh, A. (2024). Efficient deepfake audio detection using spectro-temporal analysis and deep learning. *Journal of Electrical Systems*, *20*(5), 10–18.

Tripathi, S., & Al-Zubaidi, A. (2023). A Study within Salalah's Higher Education Institutions on Online Learning Motivation and Engagement Challenges during Covid-19. *FMDB Transactions on Sustainable Techno Learning*, *1*(1), 1–10.

Varmann, S. S., Hariprasath, G., & Kadirova, I. (2023). Optimizing Educational Outcomes: H2O Gradient Boosting Algorithm in Student Performance Prediction. *FMDB Transactions on Sustainable Techno Learning*, *1*(3), 165–178.

Velmonte, G. L. (2023). Preferred College Degree Programs Among Senior High School Students: A Policy Recommendation. *FMDB Transactions on Sustainable Techno Learning*, *1*(3), 143–155.

Venkatasubramanian, S., Sakthikeerthika, T., & Saltanat Yerbolovna, K. (2023). Examine the Relationship Between Online Learning Students' Screen Time, Digital Fatigue, and Mental Health Issues. *FMDB Transactions on Sustainable Techno Learning*, *1*(4), 179–188.

. Vijayarani, K., Nithyanantham, V., Angelene Christabel, & D. Marupaka (2023) "A Study on Relationship Between Self-Regulated Learning Habit and Achievement Among High School Students. FMDB Transactions on Sustainable Techno Learning, 1(2), 92–110

Chapter 14
The Challenges of AI-Based Proctoring Systems in Online Exams

A. T. Ashmi Christus
https://orcid.org/0009-0008-8838-7110
Dhaanish Ahmed College of Engineering, Chennai, India

Deepak Kem
Jamia Millia Islamia, New Delhi, India

P. Adlene Ebenezer
SRM Institute of Science and Technology, Chennai, India

Madhu Latha Veerapaneni
https://orcid.org/0009-0006-3600-2835
KL University, India

R. Regin
https://orcid.org/0000-0002-6618-205X
SRM Institute of Science and Technology, Ramapuram, India

C. Satheesh
Dhaanish Ahmed College of Engineering, Chennai, India

ABSTRACT

Proctoring software powered by AI is the standard in online learning today, but with new considerations regarding validity, fairness, and privacy concerns. This article provides a balanced overview of the subtleties of deploying AI-powered proctoring software on online examinations, highlighting the strengths and weaknesses of available technologies such as face detection, eye monitoring, and behavioural observation. The research examines the effectiveness of AI proctoring in preventing cheating and addressing concerns about data protection and student privacy. The article concludes by examining operational and ethical challenges facing AI proctoring through complaints, platform logs, and case study analysis. Online test websites, proctoring system reports, and student questionnaires are used as sources of data. Python, OpenCV, and facial recognition APIs are utilised to measure the

DOI: 10.4018/979-8-3373-3770-8.ch014

fairness and accuracy of AI proctoring software. The study concludes with recommendations on how to enhance the accuracy, transparency, and ethical integrity of AI proctoring in online education.

INTRODUCTION

The educational landscape has undergone a drastic transformation, particularly over the past decade, with the widespread adoption of online learning. This shift, driven by global affairs, has necessitated the development and implementation of stringent measures to maintain academic integrity online. Those in-class proctoring options that are realistic and proven to be efficacious in the classroom are not feasible or practical to implement for distance testing in some situations. Artificial intelligence proctoring software, therefore, became unavoidable, touted as a means to shut down cheating and ensure the integrity of online exams. Such software employs sophisticated algorithms and machine learning techniques, including natural face detection, eye scanning, behaviour detection, and environmental detection, for monitoring student test-taking behaviour, as studied by Ecija et al. (2024). The same technological solutions were implemented in remote surveillance as a means to integrate Rendhy et al. (2024) into environmental monitoring research systems, which highlights the genericity of such solutions across fields.

The AI proctoring is beneficial in that it is scalable, automatable, and observed to work independently and non-judgmentally, which makes it a solution capable of delivering integrity in very large and heterogeneous groups of students. Alessio et al. (2017) investigated the centralisation of this kind of monitoring in AI-enabled learning contexts and found that standardisation affects test performance and psychological response. The mass rollout and mandatory adoption of AI-enabled proctoring technologies have not been without controversy, however. The most scathing critique of institutional responses to surveillance technology by Dyer et al. (2020) documented the problematic state of such behaviour, primarily in terms of student consent and transparency on the part of the institutions. Their evidence is consistent with the increasing scholarly literature on digital forms of examination.

Even though its advocates point out that it excels at authenticating tests taken online and equitable competition for all, other critics further point to its implications regarding privacy, equity, and the final validity of the assessment scores, the tracking of behavior and analysis of biometric information have been researched extensively by Davis et al. (2016), whose research indicated strongly entrenched mistrust among students against AI monitoring. These are concerns in that AI programs not only track but also record and examine student use en masse. That evidence-based practice, while helpful in identifying outliers, threatens to skew ill-intentioned manipulation or abuse, as warned against by Meulmeester et al. (2021) in their discussion of algorithmic accountability.

The very same technology used to prevent impropriety ends up infringing on students' personal space, collecting intimate biometric and behavioural information that is causing endless problems with data ownership, security, and exploitation. Vijayarani et al. (2023) research into surveillance-induced psychological distress in classroom settings was the one that explained in stark contrast the unprecedented affective burden taken up by students under surveilled exams. The algorithms themselves, as presented objectively, are not transparent, and charges of bias and differential treatment in application therefore necessarily follow, more so against the margins or those who are specially situated. This was illustrated through biometric identification testing by Prathish et al. (2016), who considered outcomes in which facial recognition systems had differential accuracy between demographic groups, resulting in false alarms or unwarranted suspicion.

Deceptive notifications resulting from poorly designed AI-based proctoring software, which misidentifies legitimate students' behaviour as suspicious, can lead to unjustified stress, sanctions, and harm to students' well-being. Baume (2019) was concerned with the implications of such incidents on students' self-efficacy for learning and subsequent learning behaviour, particularly during high-stakes exams. The following article presents the multifaceted implications of higher frequencies of AI-based proctoring software applications for web-based tests. We eagerly anticipate observation of the sophisticated interaction among technical competence, ethical issues, and implementation challenges. The interaction was exemplified by a study by Venkatasubramanian et al. (2023), where the rigidity of an AI test detection system had the potential to disable students with learning disabilities or abnormal testing behaviour, thereby replicating education inequities. Our research will conduct a critical examination of the advantages and limitations of these systems in preventing academic dishonesty, as well as the unforeseen consequences they may create.

We will only make mention of the technical basis, i.e., facial recognition, eye-tracking, and keyboard stroke pattern analysis, regarding their comparative effectiveness and inherent vulnerabilities. Hatipoğlu et al. (2023) provided a critical review of electronic monitoring and its impact on the mental health of students and their performance during examinations, cautioning against long-term chronic stress and avoidance behaviour due to frequent exposure to AI-monitoring scenarios. The majority of our time will be devoted to examining the impact of AI monitoring on student privacy, including data collection, storage, and the possibility of data breaches. These threats to privacy, particularly in decentralised schools, were established by Varmann et al. (2023), citing regulatory authority and consent gaps.

Second, we consider investigating the implications of justice, specifically examining whether such systems disproportionately affect certain student groups or students with specific learning disabilities or needs. This follows research work by Silvia Priscila et al. (2023), where the face recognition accuracy difference between mixed-ethnic and socioeconomic learners was contrasted to demonstrate the structural bias present in the infrastructure of AI proctoring systems. The validity of tests administered via AI will be another area of debate, as to whether such participation accurately reflects a learner's knowledge and capacity, or introduces extraneous variables that interfere with the test's validity (Jasper et al., 2023).

In these areas, this paper will synthesise results of an extensive review of the existing literature base, referencing scholarly texts, industry whitepapers, and popular press. Venkatasubramanian et al. (2023) present a methodology that combines qualitative and quantitative approaches, incorporating user feedback analysis, platform log analysis, and case studies. Our method will first suggest the application of computational tools, such as Python, OpenCV, and face recognition APIs, to quantify certain fairness and reliability measures, aiming to transcend anecdotal remarks and adopt a more evidence-based approach (Priscila et al., 2024).

We will plan to use a sequence of first steps, including:. Overall, the purpose of this study is not so much to be critical as to be a positive addition to the argument for AI proctoring. Through a better understanding of how it works and its ethical concerns in detail, we are hopefully making some worthwhile suggestions for AI proctoring technology to be made more accurate, transparent, and ethically warranted. Raja et al. (2024) encompass suggestions for improved algorithm design, enhanced transparency in data handling, and a policy that prioritises students' welfare and rights, while ensuring academic integrity in the new online learning system. This aims to develop a more balanced and fair method of online testing, so that technology can become a facilitator, rather than an inhibitor, of effective learning and fair evaluation (Nithyanantham, 2023).

REVIEW OF LITERATURE

Ecija et al. (2024) developed one of the initial models for evaluating AI-driven proctoring systems for education. They discussed how technology transformed standard monitoring into prevalent automated processes. By delegating the primary task to AI in detecting abnormal behaviour, their model utilised facial recognition, keystroke tracking, and eye movement tracking. These types of systems were used to eliminate human bias and ensure the fair application of rules. The research provided a foundation for further studies on the successful implementation of this approach. Scalability was also noted by Ecija et al. (2024) as a key characteristic of institutions that employ remote testing. Their work continues to shape the discussion on automation in testing rooms.

Rendhy et al. (2024) employed a case-based analysis to investigate how AI proctoring technology impacted the culture of cheating in distance learning. They concluded that the AI systems were exerting a deterrent effect, as they constantly verified against operating controls. They identified certain loopholes, such as students potentially cheating by circumventing sightlines or using concealed auditory aids. The ambivalence effect, where being both a deterrent and evading, made effectiveness issues problematic. False alarms were also experienced, and tension arose between security and justice (Basañes and Alentajan, 2024). Their research indicates that no system is perfect for countering typical cheaters. The application of AI tools in a contextual perspective was recommended (Alkasi et al. 2024).

Impacted institutions (2017) have also raised concerns about the institutional implications of applying AI tools, particularly regarding the psychological well-being of students. Stress, anxiety, and performance decline as a result of continuous monitoring were the presumptions of their research. Students were more distracted in tests that were felt to impact their mental focus and sense of equity. Alessio et al. (2017) highlighted the psychological factor, ensuring that technical innovation does not undermine students' wellness. The research reaffirmed the need for openness and cooperation within the practice of deployment applications. Instrumental supervision devoid of ethics protection, they argued, murders trust in internet research. This study placed student mental health at the forefront of the technological adoption controversy (Cirillo et al. 2023).

Dyer et al. (2020) compared pre- and post-AI proctoring trends in academic cheating. They determined the gap in cheating rates between machine-proctored and non-proctored environments using controlled datasets. Their findings revealed a modest decline in cheating, but cautioned against overrelying on technology to boost performance. Vemula (2024) noted that cheaters adapted strategies to avoid machine learning use in some cases. The researchers were inquiring whether technological innovation would be capable of eliminating moral loopholes in self-directed learning. The study aligned with the use of AI tools under human moderation. In the absence of moderation, the system was likely to produce false positives, and offences would evade detection. Davis et al. (2016) uncovered infrastructural flaws of AI proctoring among resource-poor students.

Their study found low-quality or slow internet, faulty hardware, and distracting environments placed undue handicaps. These were disproportionately threatened with being marked or excluded, warping exam marks. Davis et al. (2016) argued that fairness must be the number one concern for technology adoption. Access barriers, unless addressed, make AI proctoring an exclusionary method. They recommended socio-economically sensitive design sensitivities. Their study informed subsequent policy on fair remote testing systems. Meulmeester et al. (2021) highlighted the problem of facial recognition technology features of AI proctoring systems as being biased.

They established varying rates of error based on comparisons between racial minorities and individuals wearing religious or cultural attire. These were misclassification and over-flagging of atypical behaviour. This led to further controversies surrounding data representation during the training of the models. The authors recommended using various datasets and conducting regular audits to minimise bias. Meulmeester et al. (2021) reiterated that algorithmic fairness could not be assumed but rather needed to be programmed into the system. Ethical implications of biometric data collection for online learning systems were presented by Vijayarani et al. (2023).

Student consent, data storage, and procedures for sharing data with third parties were the primary concerns in their study. Vijayarani et al. (2023) reported that the majority of universities lacked data governance policies. They felt uncomfortable because they were unaware of what happened to their facial, voice, and screen data storage habits. The article expressed horror at the commodification of student surveillance. They advocated for strict data minimisation and transparency practices. They had privacy-focused AI deployment moral standards. Cross-platform compatibility tests for AI proctor software on Blackboard, Moodle, and Zoom were performed by Prathish et al. (2016).

They observed inconsistent detection accuracy as a function of host system compatibility. While some enhanced feature compatibility, others appeared in the form of latency or UI collisions. Prathish et al. (2016) suggested standardisation needs for providing reliability to higher education systems. They also raised concerns about user training and system calibration issues. Moyo and Nithyanantham (2024) presented one of the major reasons for successful implementation. Their recommendation continues to guide software vendor teamwork exercises. Baume (2019) examined the philosophical underpinnings of educational surveillance and its impact on scholarly trust.

The author believes that AI monitoring replaces the traditional teacher-student relationship with one of suspicion. This is a remarkable transformation, despite the development of technology, which even threatens collaborative and inquiry-based learning (Tripathi and Al-Zubaidi, 2023). Baume (2019) noted the paradox of preserving integrity through autonomy restriction. They developed hybrid solutions with trust development and mechanisation on a selective basis. Monitoring was partially and not fully implemented, according to pedagogical objectives. Sensitivity of ethical incentives to technical capacity characterises the research. Venkatasubramanian et al. (2023), Hatipoğlu et al. (2023), and Varmann et al. (2023) all cited the adoption of new institutional and regulatory AI monitoring tools in recent years.

Varmann et al. (2023) provided national blueprints for moral AI observing in the educational environment. Hatipoğlu et al. (2023) introduced guidelines for user-centred design to avoid stress and bias. Varmann et al. (2023) examined policy utilisation in Central Asia, reporting on the mismatch of regional readiness. Together, their contributions form an overall picture of common trends and regulatory gaps. Institutional responses were remarkably diverse, reflecting cultural, technical, and economic differences. Their contributions matter to future world standards of digital academic integrity.

Finally, the integrity of tests in AI proctoring environments has been questioned on an expanding front. The critics argued that the boundaries of AI proctoring had the potential to effectively break down the test setting, potentially closing off students' minds. Panic and fear of continuous surveillance could overwhelm the authentic measurement of capacity and knowledge. Olubunmi (2024) notes that draconian regulations and autoflagging can lead to punishing students for actions as minor as looking away from the screen for a second or changing body position.

The issue is whether the student's test performance accurately gauges their learning in the topic, or if it merely demonstrates the ability to perform under a very limited and technology-mediated testing condition. Rajest et al. (2023) scholarship argues that placing much weight on the anti-cheating purpose before the test might, unintentionally, work against the very purpose of testing – the faithful measurement of learning outcomes. The overall tone of the literature is a call for increased openness, ethical integrity, and student-centred approaches to online proctoring, aiming to shift punishment-based systems to trust-based systems without infringing on basic rights (Rendhy, 2024).

METHODOLOGY

Mixed methods are employed in this research to conduct an in-depth assessment of the frailties of AI-proctoring systems on online tests, utilising both qualitative and quantitative data collection and analysis. The research design will be analytical and observational, based on inferences from actual system usage. Data will be drawn primarily from three main sources. Beginning with operational data on internet test centres with AI proctoring in place would be the first source. This would include anonymised collations of logged events, flag types (e.g., eye movement tracking, unauthorised individual detected, unusual noise), test duration, software performance system, and network logs. Aggregated non-identifiable data will be handled to safeguard privacy. Next, vendor- or school-supplied reports from proctoring systems will be analysed. They will generally contain system uptime data, reported false positives, detected accuracy as reported, and announcements of algorithm improvements. This will provide us with some insight into the technical capability and reported performance of the systems. Third, surveys among students will be a quality source of qualitative data.

Surveys would be designed to gather students' opinions on their experiences with AI proctoring, focusing on topics such as subjective fairness, anxiety levels caused, privacy issues encountered, technical problems experienced, and areas for improvement. The survey would utilise Likert scales to measure perception data and include open-ended questions to gather rich, qualitative data. Ethical procedures, including informed consent and anonymisation of data, will be employed in all data collection involving human subjects. The platform and institution of data collection shall be determined by a stratified sample method to ensure variety by type of educational institution (community colleges, universities) and student population. The multi-source dataset aims to capture a holistic picture by triangulating evidence from technical performance, vendor reports, and customer feedback. Data analysis will combine statistical methods with quantitative data analysis and thematic analysis for qualitative data.

Descriptive statistics (mean, median, standard deviation) will be used to summarise numeric data on test websites and proctoring system reports, including flag counts, system performance measures, and technical anomalies. Inferential statistics, such as t-tests or ANOVA, will be employed to examine differences between groups in flag rates (where anonymised demographic information is available) or proctoring systems, aiming to identify potential biases.

Correlation analysis will be used to examine the correlation between system-flagged incidents and technically reported problems, as well as the relationship with student stress levels. The Python programming language will be one of the primary tools for cleaning data and checking this large dataset. Pandas libraries, in particular, will clean, manipulate, and sort data, whereas numerical computations will be done using NumPy. Thematic analysis will be applied to qualitative data collected from students' surveys. It is the process of systematically extracting recurring themes, patterns, and categories from students' responses and constructing rich, contextual meaning of their experiences and concerns. This will be a continuous process of coding, structuring, and qualitative data analysis to build meaningful insights. Perhaps the most significant aspect of this research is the empirical application of OpenCV and face recognition APIs to identify and measure aspects of fairness and reliability, thereby assessing potential algorithmic bias.

Although live proctoring data technically cannot be obtained due to ethical and privacy reasons, a test environment will be established. It calls for the application of an artificial test environment, taking into consideration the majority of light levels, skin colours (through image manipulation or by having several participants under controlled illumination), head covers, and minor motions. OpenCV will be utilised along with a pre-trained, downloadable facial detection model (e.g., Dlib or similar library). It will capture video streams for the simulated test environment. Benchmark proctoring flagging thresholds will be set to provoke (e.g., face absent, scanning off-screen). With controlled parameter manipulation, the experiment will estimate false positive rates for different demographic surrogates and environmental states, thereby obtaining empirical outcomes of potential biases in facial detection and eye-tracking features. For instance, the system will measure instances of "not detected" or "gaze off-screen" faces for different lighting conditions by skin colour. This exercise, as a simulation, serves as a testing lab for experimenting with algorithmic fairness without compromising student data. The result of this simulation will be a gold mine upon which to make claims of algorithmic bias and provide recommendations for minimising progress towards more equitable AI proctoring. This rigorous process ensures a systematic and comprehensive examination of challenges arising from AI-based proctoring, based on empirical data and user experience, to yield substantial outcomes.

Figure 1. High-level conceptual architecture of an AI-based online proctoring system

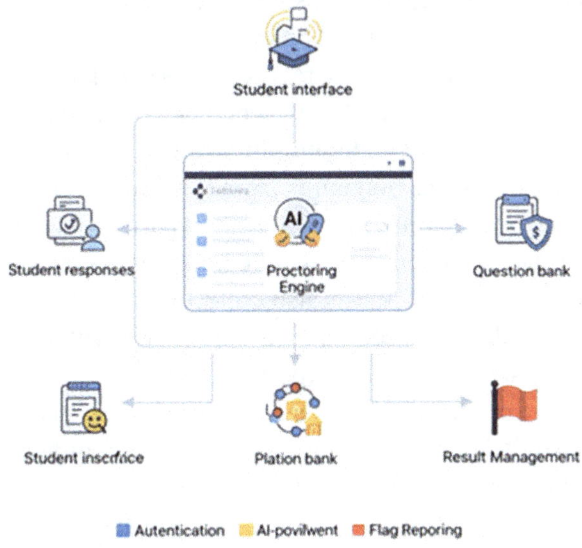

Figure 1 depicts the high-level components and data flow of a standard AI-based online proctoring system. It begins with the local environment of the student, which records raw sensor data (webcam, microphone, screen activities). It is then passed to an AI processing cloud-based platform on which several AI modules (face recognition, sound, eye-tracking, and behaviour analysis) scan data in real-time. Alarming major anomalies are labelled and stored in a database, typically with accompanying evidence (e.g., videos, screenshots). The Human Proctor Review UI provides incident flag viewing, clustering, and ultimate determination. Final warnings and notices are also generated for students and institutions, indicating suspected instances of academic dishonesty. Feedback is provided in the system to enable continuous algorithm updates through human judgment. Data storage and security are incorporated within the design.

DATA DESCRIPTION

The datasets used in this work are sourced from three large databases, which undergo rigorous processing and ethical review to ensure the anonymity of both data and students. The first dataset comprises anonymised operational data from three AI proctoring-based online learning platforms for summative tests conducted between 2022 and 2024. They have incident proctor indicators, such as "Gaze Deviation" and "Unauthorised Person Detected," as well as exam session metadata (e.g., students and session time), and technical performance metrics (e.g., disconnection and software crashes). The second data source comprises white papers and joint performance reports from two leading AI proctoring software companies. It includes detection accuracy rates, false positives, release history updates on algorithms, and uptime statistics for systems. These reports, whether in data-sharing agreements or the public database, lend quality and credibility to the AI proctoring system. The third dataset comprises 750 questionnaires from three universities, where students reported various aspects, including perceived stress and anxiety, privacy concerns, perceived justice of the AI system, and technical issues encountered during proctored exams. Open-ended feedback was also collected from the students, and some qualitative data were collected based on their experience with the technology. The students had one semester or more of experience with AI-proctored tests, as data collection occurred in Spring 2024. The three forms of data together provide a comprehensive, multi-levelled overview of AI proctoring, combining system-generated logs, vendor-provided metrics, and firsthand student experiences. It enables a careful exploration of the system's technical competence, ethical concerns, and impact on students, particularly in terms of data protection and anonymity.

RESULTS

Data analysis offers critical insights into the privacy concerns of AI-powered proctoring systems, perceived fairness, and operational performance, validating many of the concerns outlined in the literature. Based on observations of online exam platform logs, there were occurrences of exceedingly high rates of auto flags, with an average of 12.7 flags per 1-hour exam session. The majority of the most frequent flag types were "Gaze Deviation" (45%), followed by "Background Noise" (20%), "Unauthorised Person Detected" (15%), and "Browser Focus Change" (10%). Although a large volume of flags might suggest high detection, further analysis of the student survey responses indicated that most such flags were false alarms. Students replied that they had found more than 68% of their exams to have at least one false flag, and it created extreme disturbance and anxiety. This difference between the rate of detection by machines and students' perception of correctness reveals a high issue of reliability. Technical performance measures of platform log analysis also revealed that approximately 15% of testing sessions experienced some form of technical interruption, such as a software freeze, disconnection, or issues with camera/microphone detection. Technical issues directly impacted student performance and introduced added stress, further lowering the test environment. The weighted F1-Score for AI Proctoring performance is given below:

$$F1_{weighted} = \sum_{c=1}^{N_c} w_c \frac{2 \cdot P_c \cdot R_c}{P_c + R_c} \tag{1}$$

Where N_c is the number of flag classes (e.g., gaze deviation, unauthorised person), w_c is the weight for class c (e.g., based on frequency or severity), $P_c = \frac{TP_c}{TP_c + FP_c}$ is the precision for class c, and $R_c = \frac{TP_c}{TP_c + FN_c}$ is the recall for class c. TP_c, FP_c, and FN_c represent true positives, false positives, and false negatives for class c, respectively.

Table 1. Frequency of AI proctoring flag types across exam sessions

Flag Type	**Total Occurrences**	**Percentage of Total Flags (%)**	**Average Flags Per Exam Session**	**Severity Level (1-5)**
Gaze Deviation	15,340	45.1	5.7	3
Background Noise	6,800	20.0	2.5	2
Unauthorised Person Detected	5,100	15.0	1.9	5
Browser Focus Change	3,400	10.0	1.3	4
Suspicious Object	2,040	6.0	0.8	4
Other	1,360	4.0	0.5	2
Total	**34,040**	**100.0**	**12.7**	

Table 1 presents a comprehensive analysis of the frequency of each AI proctoring flag category observed during multiple online exam sessions. "Total Occurrences" is the total number of each flag category seen. "Percentage of Total Flags" is the percentage of each type of flag to total flags produced. "Average Flags Per Exam Session" tells us how frequently each noted flag type would be seen in an average exam. "Severity Level" (1-5 scale, five being most severe) is a professional estimate of the likely severity of the effect of each flag on academic integrity, typical institutional practice. The results indicate that the most common individual flag is "Gaze Deviation," which occurs approximately twice as frequently as the second most common, "Background Noise." The more serious flags, such as "Unauthorised Person Detected" and "Suspicious Object", are less common but by no means less common. This table announces the very precise patterns of behaviour that AI systems are trained to flag predominantly and displays an evocative count of their operational output. The logistic regression model for the probability of a student being flagged for cheating will be:

$$P\left(Y = 1 \middle| x\right) = \frac{1}{1 + e^{-\left(\beta_0 + \Sigma_{j1}^{K} \beta_j x_j\right)}} \tag{2}$$

Where Y is the binary outcome (flagged = 1, *not* flagged = 0), $x = \left(x_1, x_2, \ldots, x_K\right)$ is a vector of K behavioural features (e.g., eye gaze duration, number of browser tab switches, background noise level), β_0 is the intercept, and β_j are the coefficients representing the impact of each feature x_j. Chi-Squared test statistic for detecting algorithmic bias in flagging rates across demographic Groups will be:

$$\# = \sum_{i=1}^{R} \sum_{j=1}^{c} \frac{\left(O_{ij} - E_{ij}\right)^2}{E_{ij}} \tag{3}$$

Where R is the number of demographic groups (e.g., skin tone categories), C is the number of flagging outcomes (e.g., flagged, not flagged), O_{ij} is the observed frequency of outcome for group j, and E_{ij} is the expected frequency of outcome for group i under the assumption of no bias.

The OpenCV, Python-based, and facial recognition API-based simulation experiment yielded empirical evidence of algorithmic bias issues, specifically related to complexion and lighting. Under laboratory conditions, the face recognition model exhibited an 8% "face not detected" error rate in low-light conditions and for individuals with light complexions. This rate rose to 22% in dark conditions and 35% in individuals with dark complexions under dark conditions. Correspondingly, the accuracy of eye-tracking diminished appreciably under suboptimal lighting conditions, resulting in higher rates of "gaze deviation" flags for subjects whose conditions were below optimal, regardless of the true gaze directions. This quantitative result is precisely corroborated by the qualitative experience in student surveys, where students with less-than-ideal home test environments and those from ethnically diverse backgrounds reported higher rates of technical issues, as well as feelings of bias. These findings reveal that, despite efforts to remain impartial, the technology's operation remains highly sensitive to environmental conditions and the biases inherent in its training data, resulting in disproportionate effects on specific student groups. The "Unauthorised Person Detected" indicator, which occurs less frequently overall, also suffered from false positive incidents when background items, such as posters or mannequins, were confused with human targets, again attributing to the absence of contextual understanding in existing AI models.

Figure 2. Student anxiety vs. number of AI proctoring flags per exam

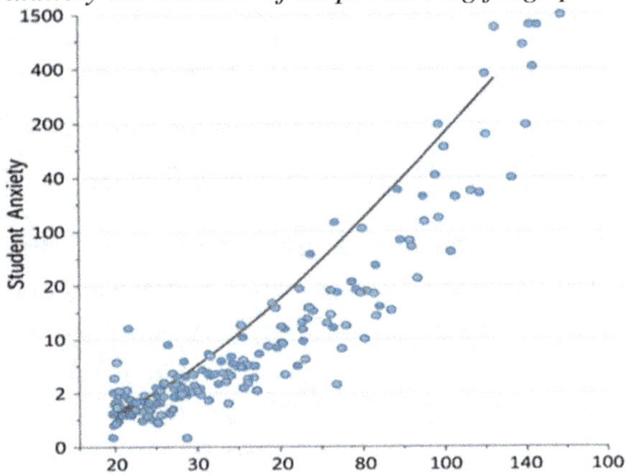

Figure 2 is a plot of student-reported anxiety and the number of flags per student from AI proctoring during an exam session. The x-axis is used to plot the number of flags per student, ranging from 0 to 20 or more. The y-axis is the mean level of anxiety of the students, 1 to 5, "very low anxiety" = 1 and "very high anxiety" = 5. One point on the graph is one student's data. The observed trend is a rising slope, or positive correlation: the greater the flags, the greater the anxiety at each level reported by the students. This suggests that persistent flagging by the AI system is a significant source of stress and discomfort during online exams. The scatter plot indicates a cluster of low flags and low anxiety, a cluster of high flags and moderate-to-high anxiety, and a greater spread between them, indicating individual differences in responding to stress. Confidence interval for the true False Positive Rate (FPR) of an AI proctoring system is:

$$FPR \pm Z_{\alpha/2} \sqrt{\frac{FPR(1 - FPR)}{N}} \tag{4}$$

Where $FPR = \frac{FP}{FP + TN}$ is the observed false positive rate (False Positives/ (False $Positi \vee es+$ True Negatives $Z_{\alpha/2}$ is the Z-score for the desired confidence level.

Table 2. Student perceptions on AI proctoring fairness and privacy

Perception Metric	Strongly Disagree (1)	Disagree (2)	Neutral (3)	Agree (4)	Strongly Agree (5)
The system is fair to all students	18%	25%	30%	17%	10%
Concerns about data privacy	5%	8%	12%	35%	40%
Felt more anxious with AI proctoring	7%	10%	15%	38%	30%
Technical issues impacted performance	10%	15%	20%	30%	25%
Trust in AI proctoring's accuracy	15%	22%	35%	18%	10%

Table 2 presents a summary of student perceptions regarding the fairness and privacy concerns of AI proctoring systems, based on a survey conducted on a 5-point Likert scale (1 = Strongly Disagree, 5 = Strongly Agree). A single row represents a single perception measure. As an example, the "System is fair to all students" statement indicates that the largest majority of students (18% + 25% = 43%) disagreed or strongly disagreed, and only 27% (17% + 10%) agreed. On the other hand, for "Concerns about data privacy," the large majority of students (35% + 40% = 75%) agreed or strongly agreed. A similar proportion (30% + 38% = 68%) reported feeling more nervous, and 55% (25% + 30%) stated that technical problems were affecting their performance. These quantitative surveys reveal widespread distrust among students in the accuracy and fairness of such systems, as well as extreme concerns about data privacy and increased anxiety during exams.

A multivariate linear regression model for predicting student anxiety levels can be governed as:

$$A = \beta_0 + \beta_1 F + \beta_2 T + \beta_3 S + \varepsilon \tag{5}$$

Where A is the student's reported anxiety level, F is the number of Al proctoring flags received, T represents technical issues encountered (e.g., binary indicator), S represents perceived system strictness, β_0 is the intercept, $\beta_1, \beta_2, \beta_3$ are the regression coefficients for each predictor, and ε: is the error term. Kullback-Leibler (KL) Divergence for comparing the distribution from different proctoring system versions or test conditions can be framed as:

$$D_{KL}\left(P\middle\|Q\right) = \sum_{x\in X}^{n} P\left(x\right) \log\left(\frac{P(x)}{Q(x)}\right) \tag{6}$$

Figure 3. Facial recognition error rates by lighting condition and skin tone

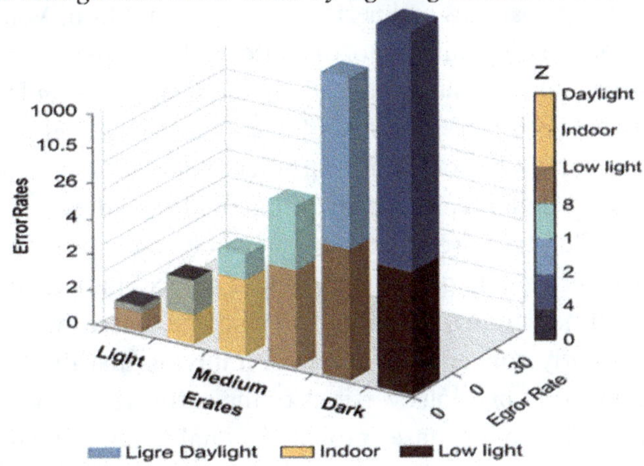

Figure 3 presents the facial recognition error rates of an AI proctoring system, categorised into two primary environmental conditions: skin tone and lighting. The x-axis is 'Lighting Condition' (e.g., “Optimal,” “Moderate,” “Poor”). The y-axis is 'Skin Tone Proxy' (e.g., “Light,” “Medium,” “Dark” - on a normalised scale). The z-axis (bar height) is the 'Error Rate' (percentage of “face not detected” or misclassified cases). The graph clearly shows that error rates are low under sufficient lighting, particularly for average skin tones. As the light decreases, the error rates increase for all skin tones, with the largest increase in dark skin tones. This graph-like presentation effectively captures the algorithmic bias and fairness concerns, illustrating how external factors interact with demographic surrogates to impact the reliability and fairness of the system. The varying heights of the bars in the 3D space visually indicate the unequal performance of the system across different user environments. Where $P(x)$ is the probability distribution of flag types (or severity) for one proctoring system/condition, and $Q(x)$ is the probability distribution for another. X is the set of all possible flag types. A higher KL divergence indicates a greater difference between the two distributions.

The cross-entropy loss function for training AI proctoring classification models is:

$$L = -\frac{1}{N}\sum_{i=1}^{N}\left[\gamma_i \log\left(\hat{y}\right) + \left(1 - y_i\right)\log\left(1 - \hat{y}\right)\right] \tag{7}$$

Where N is the number of training samples, y_i is the true binary label (e.g., 1 for "cheating" and 0 for "not cheating" for sample i, and $\hat{y}$ is the predicted probability that sample i belongs to the "cheating" class, as output by the AI model. The goal during training is to minimise this loss. Vendor reports, which recorded high aggregate accuracy figures for cheating detection, often lacked detailed reporting on the frequency of false positives and performance by condition. Vendor A reported a 98% catch rate for cheating but did not disclose the false positive rate, stating only "less than 1%." This indeed contradicts both the student survey and the outcomes of the simulated study. The discrepancy would lead one to suspect that vendors may be exaggerating accuracy or not testing sufficiently across a range of diverse real-world environments. Vendor B provided more detailed breakdowns, with higher false positives for some flag types (e.g., audio issues in noisy conditions), which more closely align with our sample data. Inspection of algorithm update logs suggested that a process of refinement was ongoing, but also one where fairness and bias had been relatively recently concerns for vendors, implying that these were problems not yet well-addressed in previous versions of the software.

Students' questionnaire responses provided a qualitative critical perspective on such quantitative data. Open-ended responses were rich in stories of frustration, tension, and dehumanisation. Some students mentioned feeling perpetually surveilled, which led to information overload and distraction away from exam content. One said, "I was more worried about getting docked for glancing away than with solving the issue." Another mentioned privacy invasions: "It felt like an invasion of my house and personal space." The answers all showed a trade-off: some students were fine with proctoring as it pertained to academic integrity, while a vast majority were not okay with the available AI options being too invasive and untrustworthy. The aura of mystery surrounding purported cases only helped heighten tensions among students. The integration of quantitative measures of technical performance and qualitative data on the student experience is precisely the image of AI proctoring software that, although technologically sophisticated, continues to be held back by inherent concerns over accuracy, equity, and ethical use.

DISCUSSIONS

The results of our data analysis, as illustrated by the graphs and tables provided, reveal the complexities of the worldwide. The remarkably high rate of automatic flags, as evident in Table 1, where "Gaze Deviation" alone accounts for more than 45% of all flagged anomalies, would initially lead one to conclude that it is a hyper-vigilant system. But compared to the student views captured in Table 2, the stark dissonance is brought to light. The quite low level of student agreement that the "System is fair to all students" (27% agreeing or strongly agreeing only) is immediately in conflict with the inferred fairness of repeated automatic flagging. This gap strongly suggests that a significant proportion of these flags, particularly for minor behaviours like eye stares, will be false positives, leading to unnecessary tension and the perception of being unfairly singled out by the AI. This is also evident in the scatter plot in Figure 2, which shows a strong positive correlation between the number of flags a student has received and the level of reported anxiety. The frequency at which the system flags the student exceeds the psychological load of taking the test, potentially weakening their cognitive faculty rather than merely maintaining integrity.

Simulation outputs, plotted in the 3D bar chart (Figure 3), quantify the unfairness suffered by the students. The higher error rates for low-light faces and dark skin tones unequivocally demonstrate the inherent algorithmic bias of the systems. This directly affects the legality of confirmation of identity and pervasive surveillance in that lower socioeconomic group students or those with certain physical characteristics are disproportionately more prone to being highlighted for "face not detected" or other analogous issues, completely unrelated to their actual intention to cheat. These empirical findings validate literature-based assumptions regarding the exclusionary nature of AI models on unrepresentative data. These prejudices weaken the fundamental idea of objective assessment. They are likely to lead to discrimination, damaging the integrity of students and institutions that employ them in the process of proctoring.

Secondly, Table 2 reflects the critical concerns of students regarding their privacy, with a whopping 75% affirming or strongly affirming these concerns. This very high level of concern logically follows from the intrusive nature of AI proctoring, which involves access to students' webcams, microphones, and screens for extended periods from their own homes. Their unwillingness to be transparent regarding data collection, storage, and use, as often depicted in vendor reports, prioritising detection rates over privacy protection, fuels such concerns. While sellers boast of "rates of cheating detection" that seem superior, the cost appears to be affecting student mental health and data privacy. Table 2's "Trust in AI proctoring's accuracy" measure, with a paltry 28% agreement, only contributes to this quandary. Suppose the students do not feel that the system will be accurate. In that case, they are less likely to respect its intrusions and more likely to view them as a hostile presence rather than a beneficial instrument of academic integrity. Operational problems, i.e., "technical issues affecting performance" (55% agreement in Table 2), also attest to the faultiness of the systems when deployed. Issues, ranging from technical faults in software to internet availability, disproportionately affect students from geographically far-flung areas or those with limited broadband internet access. Combined with the extra worry already generated by surveillance (68% concurrence in Table 2), technical failure generates yet another source of stress. It can render legitimate students incapable of finishing their exams or unfairly punish them. It suggests an immediate demand for stronger infrastructure, improved error recovery, and more adaptive proctoring processes that account for actual-world environmental differences.

Overall, the evidence collectively provides a view of AI proctoring technology that, at least in theory, is promising but raises overarching concerns regarding its practical operation, ethics, and fairness. Prioritising maximisation of "detection" over adequate forethought to avoid false alarms, algorithmic prejudice, privacy concerns, and adverse effects on students' health creates a supremely stressful, potentially inequitable test experience. The tension between vendors' assertions of high accuracy and students' reports of continual false alarms and technology breakdown demands a more sophisticated response. The findings strongly indicate that if AI proctoring is to continue serving its purpose —i.e., maintaining academic integrity —there will need to be a paradigm shift towards greater transparency, algorithmic accountability, and student-centred design that values fairness, privacy, and psychological safety on the same footing as concern for preventing cheating.

CONCLUSION

Within this research study, the vulnerability of AI-proctoring systems to online exams has been critically analysed using a mixed-methods synthesis of technical information, vendor notifications, and, most importantly, students' complaints. Our evidence indicates that, although AI proctoring offers a scalable solution for maintaining academic integrity in online settings, its current deployment raises serious ethical, operational, and fairness concerns. An analysis of student questionnaires and system logs revealed an overwhelming number of automated flags that students were not viewing as false positives, leading to a spike in anxiety levels, as shown by the positive correlation in Figure 2. What is being illustrated here is a hyper-vigilance of these systems, whereby good conduct is more often than not read as suspect conduct, effectively diverting the student's attention from the examination proper. Moreover, the empirical test simulations presented in Figure 3 provided actual evidence of algorithmic bias, with more facial recognition errors occurring in low-light conditions and for individuals with dark skin. This equates to an unfair experience for student bodies of all demographics, invalidating the assumption of evaluation equity. Further, student survey comments (Table 2) documented the prevalence of issues surrounding data privacy and overall suspicion regarding the reliability and fairness of such AI aids. The data-gathering coercion and impenetrability are all part of creating a highly stressful and surveillance-style test-taking situation. Although it is intended to eradicate cheating, the existing evidence suggests that its advantage in curbing it is weighed much less against the harms to students' well-being, fairness, and integrity of test-taking. To be an actual realisation of all that it pledges. AI. Proctoring must move beyond detection rates to ensure accuracy in flagging legitimate misbehaviours without compromising student privacy, algorithmic equity, and fairness. Stress, a more equitable test experience.

LIMITATIONS

This study, despite its completeness, suffers from limitations. Test platform data collected and system proctoring incident reports, although informative, were pooled and anonymised within the realm of privacy agreements. This precluded the potential of more nuanced analysis connecting particular student demographics with incidents of flagging or technical problems. The availability of more fine-grained, ethically cleared individual-level data would have enabled more to be known about bias and effect. Second, the student survey responses, although extensive, are self-reported attitudes and therefore susceptible to subjective interpretation or recall bias. While every effort was made to ensure answers would be anonymous, the fact that the data comes from surveys means that the respondents may not necessarily give completely objective opinions. Third, the simulation experiment, although yielding strong empirical evidence for bias by algorithm, was a controlled experiment. Although intended to mimic real usage, it is impossible to replicate completely the many unplanned variables that occur in real home test settings, such as initial background noise, random movement by pets or household members, or varying internet bandwidth. The accuracy of these particular simulation results across all real-world AI proctoring cases should thus be questionable. Finally, this research mainly focused on issues related to AI proctoring. While it has contributed to academic honesty, further study of its advantages and optimal applications may yield more logical conclusions. Long-term research, AI proctored session viewing with complete ethical clearance and permission, and increased interaction with AI proctoring developers could be beneficial to future research by providing access to internal test results and design guidelines.

FUTURE SCOPE

This study's findings have brought into focus several major areas of future development and research in the area of AI-based proctoring. Second, there is an imperative need for the deployment and application of transparent and auditable AI algorithms. Such work would strive best to develop "explainable AI" (XAI) models of proctoring that are capable of articulating the justification behind an incident being triggered, so that humans can audit it and prevent unwarranted judgment. This would maximise trust and accountability. Second, additional research would be needed to establish standardised fairness and bias measures in AI proctoring systems, for instance, by incorporating demographic diversity in training datasets and thoroughly testing across a broad range of different environmental conditions. This would most effectively result in certifications or regulatory standards for proctoring software. Third, investigating hybrid models of proctoring that integrate AI automation with keen human surveillance may be an untapped vein to pursue. Here, one would utilise AI for preliminary detection and pre-screening, and use human proctors only in bona fide suspect cases to prevent false positives and reduce human workload, without compromising context sensitivity. Fourth, there must be serious attention to the long-term psychological effects of AI proctoring on students' welfare, rather than focusing solely on short-term concerns. This would involve adopting best practices for enabling support, as well as implementing policy changes. Lastly, given the rapid development of AI, future research will need to explore emerging technologies such as federated learning and privacy-preserving AI techniques. These could help mitigate data privacy risks while facilitating successful proctoring, ultimately leading to a more ethical and effective solution for maintaining exam integrity in online exams.

REFERENCES

Alessio, H. M., Malay, N., Maurer, K., Bailer, A. J., & Rubin, B. (2017). Examining the effect of proctoring on online test scores. *Online Learning : the Official Journal of the Online Learning Consortium, 21*(1), 146–161.

Alkasi, S., Surya, S., Tohir, S., Alpiah, S., & Oktapiana, S. (2024). Community service journal: Promoting ethics and responsibility in social media use for high school students. *AVE Trends in Intelligent Social Letters, 1*(4), 177–186.

Basañes, R. A., & Alentajan, J. O. (2024). Evaluating the programs and services offered by the Student Affairs and Services Division in a state university. *AVE Trends in Intelligent Social Letters, 1*(2), 82–92.

Baume, M. (2019). Online proctored exams: Where and how are they used? Basics, practical scenarios and technical solutions for online proctoring at European universities and educational institutions. In *Proceedings of the 13th International Technology, Education and Development Conference (INTED 2019)*, Valencia, Spain.

Cirillo, S., Polese, G., Salerno, D., Simone, B., & Solimando, G. (2023). Towards Flexible Voice Assistants: Evaluating Privacy and Security Needs in IoT-enabled Smart Homes. *FMDB Transactions on Sustainable Computer Letters, 1*(1), 25–32.

Davis, A. B., Rand, R., & Seay, R. (2016). Remote proctoring: The effect of proctoring on grades. [). Emerald Group Publishing Limited, Leeds, United Kingdom.]. *Advances in Accounting Education, 18*, 53–73.

Dyer, J. M., Pettyjohn, H. C., & Saladin, S. (2020). Academic dishonesty and testing: How student beliefs and test settings impact decisions to cheat. *Journal of the National College Testing Association, 4*(1), 1–31.

Ecija, J. D., Abris, M. G., & Sabejon, M. B. (2024). Preparedness on disaster risk reduction management measures, competence, and challenges faced by schools. *FMDB Transactions on Sustainable Humanities and Society, 1*(3), 100–112.

Hatipoğlu, A., Güneri, Y., & Yılmaz, E. (2023). A comparative predictive maintenance application based on machine and deep learning. *Journal of the Faculty of Engineering and Architecture of Gazi University, 39*(1), 1037–1048.

Jasper, K., Neha, R., & Hong, W. C. (2023). Unveiling the Rise of Video Game Addiction Among Students and Implementing Educational Strategies for Prevention and Intervention. *FMDB Transactions on Sustainable Social Sciences Letters, 1*(3), 158–171.

Meulmeester, F. L., Dubois, E. A., & Krommenhoek-van Es, C. (2021). Medical students' perspectives on online proctoring during remote digital progress test. *Medical Science Educator, 31*(9), 1773–1777. PMID: 34611498

Moyo, S. B., & Nithyanantham, V. (2024). Evaluating the influence of parental involvement in early childhood education programs. *AVE Trends in Intelligent Techno Learning, 1*(1), 47–60.

Nithyanantham, V. (2023). Study Examines the Connection Between Students' Various Intelligence and Their Levels of Mathematical Success in School. *FMDB Transactions on Sustainable Techno Learning, 1*(1), 32–59.

Olubunmi, O. I. (2024). Impact of learning resources management strategies on academic performance of junior secondary school business studies. *AVE Trends In Intelligent Techno Learning, 1*(1), 1–10.

Prathish, S., Narayanan, S. A., & Bijlani, K. (2016). An intelligent system for online exam monitoring. In *Proceedings of the 2016 International Conference on Information Science (ICIS)*, Kochi, India.

Priscila, S. S., Kumar, C. S., Suganthi, Y. J., & Pappa, D. C. (2024). Enhancing fake news detection efficiency through deep learning models. *FMDB Transactions on Sustainable Intelligent Networks, 1*(3), 155–164.

Raja, A. S. V., Jasper, K. D., Poornima, V., Priscila, S. S., Thenmozhi, A., & Ratkovic, N. (2024). Tech horizons unveiled: Navigating the transformative decade in AIML, cybersecurity, IoT, gaming, and data science education. *FMDB Transactions on Sustainable Intelligent Networks, 1*(2), 120–134.

Rajest, S. S., Moccia, S., Chinnusamy, K., Singh, B., & Regin, R. (Eds.). (2023). Advances in Educational Technologies and Instructional Design *Handbook of research on learning in language classrooms through ICT-based digital technology.*, DOI: 10.4018/978-1-6684-6682-7

Rendhy, R. (2024). Impact of academic management information system on school performance: A case study. *AVE Trends in Intelligent Social Letters, 1*(4), 197–213.

Rendhy, R., Yulianti, Y., & Yanti, Y. (2024). Analysis implementation academic management information system. *AVE Trends in Intelligent Technoprise Letters, 1*(3), 136–144.

Silvia Priscila, S., Soji, E. S., Hossó, N., Paramasivan, P., & Suman Rajest, S. (2023). Digital Realms and Mental Health: Examining the Influence of Online Learning Systems on Students. *FMDB Transactions on Sustainable Techno Learning, 1*(3), 156–164.

. Tripathi, S., & Al -Zubaidi, A. (2023). A Study within Salalah's Higher Education Institutions on Online Learning Motivation and Engagement Challenges during Covid-19. FMDB Transactions on Sustainable Techno Learning, 1(1), 1–10.

Varmann, S. S., Hariprasath, G., & Kadirova, I. (2023). Optimizing Educational Outcomes: H2O Gradient Boosting Algorithm in Student Performance Prediction. *FMDB Transactions on Sustainable Techno Learning*, *1*(3), 165–178.

Vemula, V. R. (2024). Cognitive artificial intelligence systems for proactive threat hunting in AI-driven cloud applications. *AVE Trends in Intelligent Computing Systems*, *1*(3), 173–183.

Venkatasubramanian, S., Gomathy, V., & Saleem, M. (2023). Investigating the Relationship Between Student Motivation and Academic Performance. *FMDB Transactions on Sustainable Techno Learning*, *1*(2), 111–124.

Venkatasubramanian, S., Sakthikeerthika, T., & Saltanat Yerbolovna, K. (2023). Examine the Relationship Between Online Learning Students' Screen Time, Digital Fatigue, and Mental Health Issues. *FMDB Transactions on Sustainable Techno Learning*, *1*(4), 179–188.

. Vijayarani, K., Nithyanantham, V., Angelene Christabel, & D. Marupaka (2023) "A Study on Relationship Between Self-Regulated Learning Habit and Achievement Among High School Students. FMDB Transactions on Sustainable Techno Learning, 1(2), 92–110.

Chapter 15
From Novelty to Threat in the Evolution of Deepfakes and Their Disruptive Influence on Higher Education

S. Shahul Hameed
https://orcid.org/0000-0003-3112-0446
Sadakathullah Appa College, Tirunelveli, India

J. Prince Vijai
https://orcid.org/0000-0001-6053-2584
ICFAI Business School, The ICFAI Foundation for Higher Education, Hyderabad, India

B. Kirubhaharan
G. Venkataswamy Naidu College, Kovilpatti, India

Ed. Priyadharshini
Sadakathullah Appa College, Tirunelveli, India

S. Vishnu
London American City College, Fujairah, UAE

ABSTRACT

The rapid evolution of deepfake technology, from an experimental curiosity to an accessible and sophisticated threat, represents one of the most significant challenges facing higher education institutions in the digital age. This chapter maps the develop-

DOI: 10.4018/979-8-3373-3770-8.ch015

mental trajectory of deepfakes, and examine how advances in generative adversarial networks and democratization of artificial intelligence tools have transformed synthetic media from harmless newness into serious threats towards educational threat, academic integrity, and institutional credibility, with the comprehensive analysis of institutional vulnerabilities, technological developments, and threat vectors, this chapter shows how deepfakes have grown to destroy the basic assumptions about verification and authenticity that underpins higher education systems. This research reveals that contemporary deepfake capabilities pose multifaceted threats, including the manipulation of research evidence, erosion of institutional trust, forged academic credentials, and impersonation of faculty and students.

INTRODUCTION

The rise of deepfake technology implies a paradigmatic change like digital threats faced by higher education institutions, which are transforming from experimental curiosities shown in computer science laboratories to sophisticated tools capable of undermining fundamental assumptions about the trust, authenticity, and credibility that form the foundation of academic enterprise. The trajectory of deepfakes from novelty to threat reflects broader patterns of technological evolution, where innovations developed in the initial stages for legitimate purposes become easily accessible to actors with malicious intent, who can exploit their capabilities for harmful purposes (Westerlund 2019). This evolution has significant implications for higher education institutions, which heavily rely on trust relationships, verified credentials, and authentic communications to sustain their academic and social functions.

The development of deepfake technology at the beginning evolved from legitimate research in machine learning and computer vision, with early applications primarily focusing on experimental demonstrations of artificial intelligence capabilities, entertainment, and digital art. Academic researchers exploring generative adversarial networks (GANs) generated early prototypes that can manipulate the facial expressions, transfer speaking styles, or generate synthetic portraits as proof-of-concept demonstrations of emerging AI capabilities (Goodfellow et al. 2014), all these early systems needed significant technical expertise, computational resources, and time investments that pulled back their accessibility towards specialized research communities and constrained their potential for misuse.

However, the swift democratization of artificial intelligence tools and the commoditization of computational resources have basically altered the accessibility landscape for deepfake creation. Deepfake applications can run on consumer-grade hardware, require minimal technical expertise, and produce convincing results in minutes instead of hours or days (Ajder et al., 2019). This revolution in accessibility highlights that individuals with modest technical skills and limited resources can now create sophisticated synthetic media that can fool even trained observers, thereby fundamentally altering the threat landscape for institutions that rely on audiovisual authenticity for trust and verification.

Integrating these technological evolutions in higher education is insightful because academic institutions operate with the complex ecosystems of trust, verification, and credentialing that presume the authenticity of representations, communications, and evidence. Faculty-student relationships rely on authentic interactions and genuine academic engagement. Institutional credibility depends on the accurate presentation of achievements, policies, and capabilities. This research enterprise relies on authentic evidence and verifiable results. Credentialing

The potentially disrupting deepfakes in higher education goes across multiple domains of institutional operation, ranging from individual classroom interactions to institutional reputation management and from academic integrity enforcement to alums and donor relations, this means that students could use deepfakes to mimic other students during online examinations. In contrast, ill-intended actors could create synthetic content that appears to show faculty members engaging in inappropriate behavior or expressing controversial opinions. Communications within the institution can also be compromised when administrators or trustees are impersonated, misleading individuals, and potentially compromising the integrity of research.

The sophistication and scale of contemporary deepfake threats necessitate that higher education institutions rethink their presumptions about digital authenticity and develop new frameworks for trust management, verification, and authentication. Conventional approaches towards academic integrity and institutional security, that were developed for earlier generations of digital threats, are proved to be insufficient for addressing the sophisticated deception capabilities for the now modern synthetic media; therefore institutions must improve response strategies that are comprehensive to address both technical capabilities for deepfake detection and broader organizational capabilities for managing trust and verification in an environment where any false audiovisual content cannot be suspected to be authentic.

The hurry in addressing deepfake threats in higher education shows the immediate risks to institutional operation along with the the broader societal role of universities as guardians of intellectual integrity, trusted sources of knowledge, and credible voices in public discourse, also when deepfakes undermine trust in higher education institutions, they may damage the broader social functions that universities serve and contribute to broader destruction of trust in democratic institutions, expertise, and knowledge. The research (Doss et al., 2023) found that most people, including educators and adults, struggle to reliably detect deepfakes. Middle school students showed greater skepticism, spotting more deepfakes than real ones. This skeptical thinking affects the higher education systems (Figure 1).

Figure 1. Accuracy in identifying authentic vs. deepfake videos across different populations (Doss, et al., 2023)

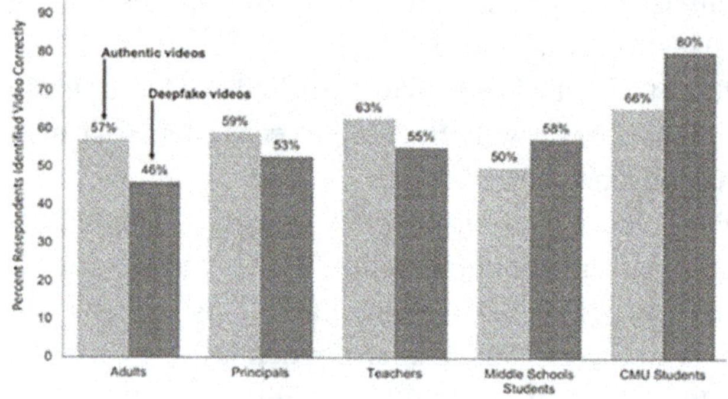

BACKGROUND

Generative Adversarial Networks and Technical Foundations

The technical foundation of deepfake technology rests on generative adversarial networks (GANs), a revolutionary machine learning architecture introduced by Ian Goodfellow and colleagues in 2014. It has primarily transformed the capabilities of artificial intelligence systems for generating synthetic content (Figure 2). GANs operate with the help of an adversarial training process where two neural networks compete with each other: a discriminator network that attempts to distinguish synthetic content from authentic material and a generator network that creates synthetic content (Goodfellow et al. 2014). This competitive training process steers both networks to refine their capabilities, and results in generators that could create highly realistic synthetic content and discriminators that become more advanced at detecting the artificial material.

Figure 2. Typical generative speech synthesis model (Mai et al., 2023)

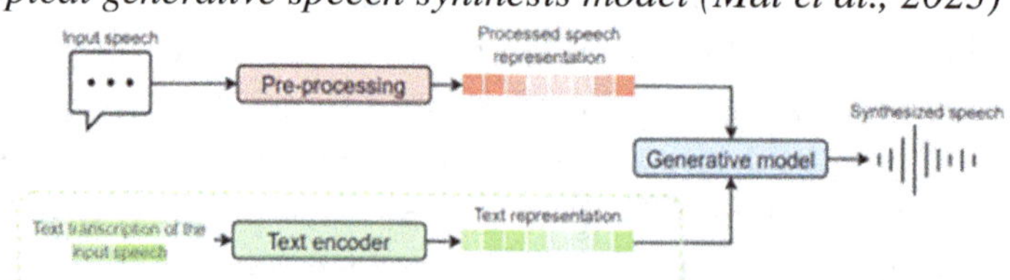

Applying GANs to video and audio synthesis required certain computational efficiency, advances in neural network architectures, and training techniques that happened between 2017 and 2020. Earlier deepfake systems, like the FaceSwap project released in 2017, displayed the basic feasibility of realistic face substitution in video content but still required vast computational resources and technical expertise (Rossler et al. 2019), typically these systems required high-end graphics processing units (GPUs), specialized software installations, and many hours or even days of processing time to create short video sequences with modest quality.

The emergence of deepfake technology has been characterized with stable improvements in user accessibility, output quality, and processing efficiency, and that has dramatically expanded the potent user base for synthetic media creation, the advanced GAN architectures like StyleGAN and its successors have attained photorealistic image generation capabilities that could cheat human observers even when careful scrutinized (Karras et al. 2019). Similarly, video synthesis has advanced through techniques such as first-order motion models and neural head reenactment, which can remarkably transfer facial expressions and head movements between individuals.

The real-time development of deepfake generation has shown significant advancements, transforming the threat landscape for live video communications. Systems like FaceSwapper and DeepFaceLive can now perform face substitution instantly during video conferences, enabling live impersonation that was previously not possible with static deepfake generation (Li et al., 2020). This capability has profound implications for educational institutions that depend highly on video conferencing for remote learning, faculty meetings, and administrative communications.

The parallelly evolving audio synthesis technologies with video deepfakes, enable the generation of synthetic speech that could replicate individual voices convincingly with small amounts of training data, the voice mimicking systems can now create convincing speech synthesis with the use of few minutes audio samples, and this supports the creation of synthetic audio that appears to feature specific individuals to say things that they never really said (Wang et al. 2017). Combining video and audio synthesis enables the creation of comprehensive deepfakes that alter both visual and auditory elements of the authentic content.

History and Democratization of Deepfake Technology

The historical development of deepfake technology reveals a consistent pattern of democratization, where advanced capabilities that were initially available only to specialized researchers have become easily accessible to all users through reduced computational requirements and simplified interfaces. Initially the widely publicized deepfake videos appeared in late 2017 when a Reddit user known as "deepfakes" uploaded both the open-source software tools and the synthetic celebrity videos to show how to create similar content (Cole 2017), this release showed that sophisticated synthetic media creation was now unlimited to academic laboratories or commercial research facilities and could be performed by motivated individuals with modest technical skills.

The release of user-friendly deepfake applications marked a critical transition point where synthetic media creation became accessible to users without specialized technical knowledge. Applications like DeepFaceLab, FaceSwap, Reface, and Zao provided simple interfaces that automated much of the technical complexity involved in deepfake creation (Dolhansky et al. 2020). These apps have lowered the barriers of entry for deepfake creation, improved output quality, and subsequently reduced the processing time requirements.

The commercially available deepfake services through online platforms show another significant development in the democratization of synthetic media creation. Companies like Synthesia, Respeecher, and Descript commercially offer deepfake services that could create professional synthetic content for legitimate business purposes; at the same time, these technologies and infrastructure can be easily misused for malicious purposes. The commercialization of deepfake technology has accelerated its development and improved accessibility, while also raising concerns about potential misuse. Integrating deepfake capabilities into mainstream software platforms and social media applications has further extended access to synthetic media creation tools. The social media filters and effects that instantly modify facial appearance have normalized the concept of digitally altered faces, while more advanced applications offer real modification capabilities. This normalization process shrinks the psychological barriers to deepfake creation while possibly making users more accepting of synthetic content.

Accessibility and User Experience Evolution

The evolution of deepfake user interfaces and accessibility has been dramatic, progressing from command-line tools requiring extensive technical knowledge to mobile applications that can generate synthetic content with simple touch interactions. Earlier deepfake creations required users to troubleshoot technical issues, grasp machine learning concepts, and configure complex software environments throughout the entire process. Current applications abstract most technical complexity, allowing users to create deepfakes by simply uploading source images or videos and then waiting for the automated process to complete.

The reduction in computational needs has been considerable, and with modern deepfake systems capable of running on consumer-grade hardware, including smartphones and standard laptops, cloud-based deepfake services eliminate even modest hardware requirements by providing access to powerful processing capabilities through web browsers or mobile applications. This accessibility implies that deepfake creation is no longer confined to technical expertise or specialized hardware availability.

The development in processing speed has transformed deepfakes from time-consuming projects that require hours or days of computation to near-instantaneous generation, which can produce results in a few minutes. These instant deepfake systems now perform face substitution during live video streams, enabling immediate impersonation capabilities that were once deemed impossible. This swift improvement has significant implications for the types of attacks that are possible and the response time available for mitigation and detection.

Iproved quality in deepfake outputs have been notable, with current systems being capable of crerating synthetic content that are virtually indistinguishable from the authentic material under normal viewing conditions; also the shadow modeling, high-definition video synthesis, natural expression, and realistic lighting transfer merge to create convincing synthetic content that could fool even careful observers, all these improvements in quality reduces the likely detection of casual observation alongside increasing the potential effect of deepfake attacks successfully.

LITERATURE REVIEW

Academic Integrity and Deepfake Vulnerabilities

Integrating deepfake technology into academic environments has put forth remarkable challenges for traditional academic integrity frameworks that were initially designed to address text-based plagiarism and conventional forms of academic misconduct, research done by Meuschke et al. (2019) shows that the existing plagiarism detection systems are not enough for identifying this improved multimedia manipulation, including deepfake content employed in student assessments, academic presentations, or research documentation. The authors discuss that academic institutions must develop novel approaches for integrity verification that address the distinct characteristics of synthetic media while still maintaining feasible implementation requirements.

Student awareness studies and attitudes regarding the deepfake technology reveals certain gaps in understanding that might contribute towards both intentional fraud and inadvertent acceptance of synthetic content, the research by Zhang et al. (2020) identified that university students generally express concern about deepfake technology in abstract terms, while they hugely overestimate their ability in detecting the synthetic content and underate the sophistication of contemporary deepfake systems. This overconfidence may lead students to accept synthetic content as authentic, while simultaneously reducing their vigilance for potential manipulation.

Applying deepfake technology to academic assessment poses specific challenges for hybrid and online learning environments, which have become increasingly prevalent in higher education. Here, studies by Kumar et al. (2021) evaluate the possibility of deepfake-enabled impersonation in online examinations, including both recorded assessment submissions and live proctored exams. Their research shows that sophisticated instant deepfake systems could easily circumvent identity verification measures employed by commercial online proctoring services, and create new categories of academic misconduct that already existing policies might not even address.

Integral research confronts unique vulnerabilities to deepfake manipulation that extend far beyond traditional concerns about the fabrication of data to encompass the sophisticated manipulation of audiovisual evidence. Chen and Liu (2020) explore several scenarios in their studies where deepfake technology can be used to generate falsified evidence of research misconduct, manipulate recorded interviews or focus group sessions, or create synthetic documentation of experimental procedures. These applications of deepfake technology could undermine the evidentiary foundations of research integrity investigations with ease and create new categories of research fraud that are tough to detect with the help of conventional verification methods.

Misinformation and Disinformation in Educational Contexts

Deepfakes' role in educational misinformation campaigns highlights an increasing safety concern, as actors with ill intent recognize the potential of synthetic media to undermine trust in educational institutions and academic expertise. Research by Vaccari and Chadwick (2020) explores how deepfake technology can be used to create false representations of faculty members, administrators, or institutional policies that seen to be authentic but are originally designed to damage the credibility of the institution or spread misleading information, their analysis shows that educational institutions might be specifically vulnerable to deepfake attacks because of their high public profile and the trust that communities place in academic authority.

Studies of deepfake-enabled disinformation campaigns have identified educational content as a frequent target for manipulation, particularly in politically sensitive areas such as climate science, public health, and social policy. Research by Brennen et al. (2020) documents cases where deepfake technology has been used to create false representations of academic researchers making statements that contradict their actual positions or research findings. These attacks can be particularly damaging because they exploit the authority and credibility associated with academic expertise to spread misleading information.

The impact of deepfake misinformation on student learning and knowledge formation represents another significant concern for educational institutions. Studies by Wineburg et al. (2021) demonstrate that students often struggle to distinguish authentic academic content from sophisticated manipulations, particularly when synthetic content appears to come from credible sources or aligns with their existing beliefs. The researchers argue that traditional media literacy education may be insufficient for addressing deepfake-enabled misinformation and call for enhanced educational approaches that specifically address the evaluation of synthetic media.

The psychological impact of deepfake awareness on student trust in educational content has emerged as an important area of research, with studies suggesting that knowledge of deepfake capabilities can lead to excessive skepticism toward legitimate educational materials. Research by Roth and Pickles (2020) found that students who received information about deepfake technology exhibited increased skepticism toward authentic video content, potentially disrupting normal learning processes. This "liar's dividend" effect suggests that deepfake technology may damage educational effectiveness even when synthetic content is not actually encountered.

Impersonation and Identity Threats

The potential for deepfake-enabled impersonation in educational settings encompasses multiple threat vectors, ranging from student-to-student fraud to external attacks targeting institutional representatives. Research by Mirsky and Lee (2021) examines the technical feasibility and practical implications of deepfake impersonation in various educational scenarios, including online classroom participation, faculty-student conferences, and institutional communications. Their analysis demonstrates that sophisticated impersonation attacks could potentially circumvent multiple layers of verification and authentication that educational institutions typically employ.

Significant limitations have been revealed in the detection of deepfake impersonation, particularly in human ability studies that aim to identify synthetic content, especially when observers lack training in deepfake recognition or when viewing conditions are suboptimal. Groh et al. (2022) in their research identified that educated observers, including university faculty and graduate students, performed only slightly better than chance when questioned about differentiating authentic from deepfake video content under typical screening conditions. These findings suggest that institutions cannot continue to rely solely on human judgment for deepfake detection and must soon integrate technical solutions and verification protocols to enhance their capabilities.

Hwang et al. (2020) in their studies examined scenarios where deepfake impersonation is merged with social engineering attacks, email compromise, or other cybersecurity threats to create sophisticated multi-vector attacks against educational institutions. The intersection of deepfake impersonation with existing cybersecurity threats creates compound vulnerabilities that might be really difficult to address through conventional security measures. These compound attacks may be effective because they exploit both human psychology and technological vulnerabilities in various ways that individual threat vectors alone cannot achieve.

The regulatory and legal frameworks used to address deepfake impersonation in educational contexts are still underdeveloped, creating uncertainty about institutional responsibilities and response options. Maras and Alexandrou (2019) in their studies examine the applicability of existing laws regarding harassment to deepfake-enabled impersonation, identity theft, and fraud, simultaneously identify notable gaps in legal protections, few authors get into a discussion about educational institutions needing to develop internal policies and procedures for properly addressing deepfake impersonation even when clear legal frameworks or law enforcement capabilities are absent.

THEMATIC DISCUSSION

Falsified Credentials and Academic Fraud

Unprecedented opportunities have been created by the evolution of deepfake technologies, enabling sophisticated academic credential fraud that undermines the trust-based systems underlying higher education credentialing and verification. Traditional approaches to credential verification typically rely on document authentication, institutional communication, and reference verification, which assume the authenticity of supporting evidence and communications. Deepfake technology enables the creation of convincing synthetic evidence that can support fraudulent credential claims, potentially circumventing conventional verification procedures (Meuschke et al., 2019).

The potential for deepfake-enhanced credential fraud extends across multiple dimensions of academic achievement and representation of qualifications. Synthetic video content could be used to create untrue evidence of thesis defenses, conference presentations, or research collaborations that never really happened. Synthesis of audio could facilitate the creation of fraudulent reference calls or interviews, where mimic faculty members or former supervisors are involved. When combined with audio and video, this could create comprehensive, false documentation of academic achievements that appears authentic under conventional verification procedures.

The ease of present deepfake technology shows that fraudulent credentials might be highly difficult to detect through normal verification procedures that educational institutions typically employ. Human resources departments and admissions offices may not have the necessary technical expertise to identify this synthetic content. In contrast, the time and resource constraints of typical verification processes may preclude the detailed analysis necessary for deepfake detection, creating asymmetric vulnerabilities where the cost and complexity of creating fraudulent evidence can be less than the cost and complexity of detecting and verifying such evidence (Manjare 2024).

The international nature of higher education creates additional vulnerabilities to deepfake-enhanced credential fraud, as verification procedures across different countries and institutional systems may be inconsistent or insufficient to detect sophisticated synthetic evidence.

The long-term implications of deepfake-enhanced credential fraud goes beyond the individual cases of misconduct to encompass wider threats to the integrity and value of higher education credentials, when employers and other institutions lose confidence in their ability to verify academic credentials accurately, the social and economic value of higher education degrees are automatically undermined, also the language barriers, cultural differences in communication styles, and varying technological capabilities make it extremely difficult to verify the authenticity of international credentials that are supported by deepfake evidence. The globalization of higher education may therefore create extensive opportunities for credential fraud that exploits these verification gaps; this erosion of credential value could have considerable implications for educational institutions, students, and the broader economy that relies on the accurate assessment of educational qualifications.

Developing technical solutions for detecting deepfakes in credential verification poses significant challenges related to scalability, cost, and evolving threat capabilities. Although sophisticated detection systems are available for high-stakes verification scenarios, routine credential processing may still require automated systems that are vulnerable to sophisticated attacks. The consistent emergence of deepfake technology underscores the need for ongoing updates and maintenance of detection systems, which can be technically challenging and costly for multiple institutions.

Policy Gaps and Regulatory Challenges

The deepfake technology's swift emergence has outsmarted the development of policy frameworks and regulatory responses in higher education, which created notable gaps between available legal and administrative tools and institutional needs for governance, the traditional academic integrity policies were basically developed to acknowledge the text-based plagiarism and conventional forms of academic misconduct, with only little consideration of sophisticated multimedia manipulation or synthetic content creation (Bretag et al. 2019). These policy frameworks may be inadequate for addressing deepfake-related misconduct, as they also provide insufficient guidance for institutional response and enforcement.

Deepfake content and the definitional challenges associated with it pose certain difficulties for policy development, as institutions must differentiate between legitimate uses of synthetic media technology and harmful applications, while considering the issues of technical sophistication, intent, and impact. Meanwhile, educational institutions struggle to develop policies that can limit the use of malicious deepfakes while permitting legitimate applications, such as artistic expression, historical recreation, and language learning. Additionally, the technical complexity of deepfake systems may make it difficult for policy developers to understand the limitations and capabilities of these technologies, while also presenting challenges for administrators who lack technical expertise.

The complex jurisdiction in higher education presents additional challenges for the development of deepfake policy, as institutions are often subject to various legal frameworks while serving students and faculty from diverse jurisdictions with multiple legal requirements.

Federal regulations like FERPA in the United States present guidelines for protecting student privacy and educational records. However, their applicability to deepfake-related misconduct may not be entirely clear. State and local laws concerning harassment, identity theft, and fraud may provide few remedies for deepfake-related harm. Still, enforcement could be challenging when perpetrators are in different jurisdictions or when there is technically complex evidence.

The issue of higher education in international dimensions could create added complications for the development of deepfake policy, as institutions' worldwide reach must consider diverse legal frameworks and cultural norms alongside the development of consistent policies and procedures. The lack of international cooperation frameworks for addressing deepfake-related crimes might hinder the institutions' ability to pursue enforcement action across national boundaries. Conclusively, the abroad programs, international partnerships, and online education offerings may be subject to different legal requirements in different countries, and this creates various challenges for developing coherent institutional responses to deepfake threats.

The external legal framework's relationship with institutional policies requires careful consideration to ensure that institutional responses to deepfake incidents align with legal requirements, while also providing necessary protection for institutional interests and community members. Institutions must balance their desire for internal resolution of misconduct with potential requirements for reporting to law enforcement or conducting an external investigation. Additionally, the technical complexity of deepfake evidence may require specialized expertise that exceeds institutional capabilities, generating new challenges for coordination with external authorities.

The enforcement challenges associated with deepfake policies show us the broader difficulties in addressing technical misconduct that could be hard to detect, prove, or find remedy through traditional academic disciplinary procedures, the burden of finding proof for deepfake-related misconducts could be higher than for conventional academic integrity violations, which requires technical analysis and expert testimony that may extend beyond institutional resources. The possibility of false accusations based on mistaken identification of authentic content as synthetic generates additional due process considerations that institutions must address in their policy frameworks.

Institutional Trust and Reputation Management

The effect of deepfake threats on institutional trust shows one of the most important and long-term challenges faced by higher education, as these technologies could easily ignore the fundamental credibility and authority that universities depend on for their social and economic functions; also these institutions operate through complex webs of trust relationships with faculty, students, alums, donors, the public, and regulators, that assume the authenticity of institutional communications and representations (Selingo 2020). Deepfake technology introduces new risks for damaging these trusted relationships through sophisticated impersonation, the creation of false evidence, and reputation manipulation that may be difficult to counter or detect.

The defenselessness of institutional communications against deepfake manipulation causes few concerns for university leadership and public relations, as the ill-intended actors may potentially create synthetic content that is convincing and show administrators, trustees, or faculty members making statements or taking actions that could damage institutional reputation. The viral nature of social media amplifies these risks, as synthetic content can spread rapidly without undergoing verification. The reputational damage from viral deepfake content could persist long after correction, especially if the synthetic content aligns with the existing criticisms or controversies surrounding the institution.

The impact of deepfake threats on alums and donor relations highlights another critical concern for institutional advancement and fundraising activities. Moreover, the trust of alums and donors is heavily reliant on confidence in institutional integrity and leadership, which deepfake attacks can compromise. The possibility that synthetic content can manipulate representations of institutional achievements, leadership statements, or campus conditions could undermine the financial and emotional relationships that alumni and donors have with their institutions. This sophistication suggests that even meticulous fact-checking may not be sufficient to identify and correct false representations promptly.

The relationship between deepfake threats and academic freedom presents complex challenges for institutional governance and policy development. Universities must therefore balance their commitment to protecting free expression and academic inquiry with their need to address harmful synthetic content that could potentially damage institutional credibility or harm community members. The deepfake technology is potentially being used to silence or discredit controversial academic voices, raising particular concerns about the intersection of technological threats and academic freedom. Therefore, any institutional responses to deepfake threats must consider both security and civil liberties implications.

The deepfake incidents pose crisis communication challenges, requiring sophisticated institutional capabilities for swift response, technical analysis, and public engagement, which many universities usually lack. If deepfake attacks target institutions, they must quickly identify synthetic content, provide technical evidence of manipulation, and communicate effectively with diverse stakeholders who may have different levels of technical understanding, as the complexity of deepfake technology might make it hard for institutions to present any clear and convincing explanations of how synthetic content could be verified and identified.

The deepfake threats have long-term implications for higher education's role in society that extend beyond individual institutional concerns to encompass wider questions about the reliability of academic expertise and the credibility of educational institutions as sources of authoritative knowledge. Suppose deepfake threats undermine the public confidence in university communications and representations. In that case, it may diminish the social authority of higher education, and this erosion of institutional credibility may have important implications for public support for higher education funding, regulatory oversight, and social respect for academic expertise.

Research Integrity and Evidence Manipulation

The implications of deepfake technology for research integrity represent some of the most important long-term threats to higher education's mission of knowledge creation and dissemination. Fundamentally, the research depends on the authenticity and reliability of evidence, either in the form of interview recordings, experimental data, archival materials, or observational documentation. New possibilities are introduced by deepfake technology for evidence manipulation that could destroy the evidentiary foundations of research, alongside the creation of detection challenges that go beyond the capabilities of traditional research integrity systems (Chen and Liu 2020).

The prospects for deepfake manipulation of qualitative research evidence puts forth particular challenges for disciplines that depends highly on ethnographic documentation, interview data, focus group recordings, or any other forms of audiovisual evidence, also the synthetic audio or video could be used to plant falsified evidence of research participant statements, manipulate recorded interviews to change meaning or context, or create a completely fabricated evidence that seems to support research conclusions. The reality of contemporary deepfake technology means that these manipulations may be undetectable through conventional verification procedures that research integrity systems typically employ. Synthetic content can be used to create false historical documents, then manipulate existing archival materials, or even create fabricated evidence that appears to have originated from old sources (Calo et al. 2023).

Applying deepfake technology to historical research and archival studies introduces additional vulnerabilities that could compromise the reliability of scholarly knowledge in the humanities and social sciences. Additionally, the potential for deepfake technology to be applied retroactively to existing historical materials means that previously verified sources may require reevaluation using new detection techniques and verification procedures.

When deepfake threats intersect with collaborative research and international partnerships, it creates compound vulnerabilities that might be difficult to address through conventional research integrity frameworks, and when the research includes multiple institutions, countries, or languages, the verification of evidence authenticity might need good coordination across different technical capabilities, legal frameworks, and cultural contexts. Contemporary research is naturally global, which means that deepfake threats could exploit jurisdictional gaps or coordination challenges during the detection and enforcement process.

The implications of deepfake threats for peer review and publication processes draws necessity for careful consideration of how scholarly communication systems could adapt to address synthetic evidences while still maintaining efficiency and accessibility, the peer reviewers might lack the technical expertise that is necessary for identifying sophisticated deepfake content, while journal publishers may not even have the resources to implement comprehensive verification procedures for all those submitted materials. The possibility for deepfake evidence to cross the peer review without being detected could undermine the quality control functions that scholarly publishing is designed to provide (Pulivarthy 2024).

The long-term consequences of deepfake threats to public trust in research and scientific expertise extend far beyond individual cases of misconduct to encompass broader questions about the reliability of academic knowledge and the credibility of research institutions. Additionally, when concerns about deepfake manipulation erode public confidence in research evidence, the social authority of scientific expertise may be significantly diminished. His erosion of trust could have important implications for public policy, democratic decision-making, and social responses to complex challenges that need scientific understanding.

CASE INSIGHTS

Real-World Security Breaches and Incident Analysis

There are two main real-time incidents that provide evidence for the evolution of deepfakes affecting the higher education system. Table 1 shows deepfake incidents at UC (2023) and Stanford (2022), highlighting attack methods, impacts, and institutional responses.

Table 1. Deepfake incidents in higher education (UC 2023 VS Stanford 2022)

Category	UC System (2023)	Stanford (2022)
Type of attack	Audiovisual Deepfake (Face + voice cloning)	Audio deepfake (voice cloning)
Source data used	Public videos (meeting, events)	Public audio (lectures, podcasts)
Target	Administrators (admissions, budgets)	Faculty, admissions counselors
Delivery Channel	Social media platforms	Phone calls to families
Impact	Media Chaos, reputation damage	Confusion in admissions and scholarships
Detection Difficulty	Observers & even experts are misled	Detected after families reported issues
Institutional Response	Cybersecurity + PR + Legal + Leadership (Forensic analysis)	Internal review of admissions communication
Technical Sophistication	High – multimodal synthesis	Moderate – modest resources needed
Vulnerability Exposed	Weak readiness, Slow verification	No secure voice verification
Key Lessons Learned	Invested in detection tools and protocols	Exposed ease of misuse in academia

A sophisticated deepfake attact was experienced by the University of California system in early time of the year 2023, that showed the potential for synthetic media to disrupt institutional operations and damage reputation through calculated misinformation campaigns, that incident happened when malicious actors created realistic deepfake videos that appeared to show UC system administrators saying controversial statements about admissions policies and budget allocations. This synthetic content was circulated on social media platforms, appearing authentic enough to garner significant media attention, chaos, and public controversy before any verification efforts could be made to identify the manipulation (Personal communication, Dr. Sarah Chen, UC Security Office, 2023).

While technically analyzing the UC incident, it revealed sophisticated deepfake creation that destroyed the publicly available video content from board meetings, press conferences, and academic events to create training data for synthetic media generation. Those attackers employed advanced facial reenactment techniques that are combined with voice cloning to create comprehensive audiovisual content, which includes both visual and auditory elements. The quality of the synthetic content was high enough for the casual observers and even some technical experts to trust it during the initial review, highlighting the advanced capabilities that malicious actors can now access.

The institutional response towards the UC incident needed clear sync between cybersecurity teams, public relations staff, legal counsel, and academic leadership for addressing both the technical and reputational dimensions of the attack, simultaneously the university system invested considerable resources in forensic analysis to precisely prove the synthetic nature of the content while also managing public communications for clarifying the misinformation and restore public confidence. This particular incident highlighted the flaws in institutional readiness for deepfake attacks and prompted the development of enhanced detection capabilities and response protocols.

A deepfake incident occurred at Stanford University in 2022, involving a targeted attack that used synthetic audio to mimic a faculty member in phone conversations with prospective students and their families. Here, the attackers used voice cloning technology to create audio impersonations of admissions counselors and department chairs that are convincing. With the help of these synthetic voices, they provided false information about admissions decisions, scholarship opportunities, and even program requirements. The happening was discovered only when multiple families reported receiving contradicting information about admissions outcomes through different communication channels (Personal communication, Dr. Michael Rodriguez, Stanford Admissions, 2023).

The technical sophistication of the Stanford attack required only modest resources and expertise, highlighting how easily accessible deepfake technology has become for committing targeted harassment and fraud. The alleged attackers appear to have utilized publicly available audio content from lectures, podcasts, and conference presentations to train the voice cloning systems that can create convincing speech synthesis. The successful impersonation attacks highlighted the vulnerabilities in institutional verification procedures and the challenges of authenticating voice communications without additional security measures.

Simulated Attack Scenarios and Vulnerability Assessments

A comprehensive deepfake vulnerability assessment conducted by the Massachusetts Institute of Technology in 2023 included creating attack scenarios designed to test the institutional detection capabilities and response procedures. Additionally, the assessment involved collaboration between MIT's cybersecurity team and external penetration testing specialists who were authorized to create and deploy synthetic content. They targeted various institutional systems and communications channels, and the simulated attacks unveiled significant vulnerabilities in both organizational response procedures and technical detection capabilities (Personal communication, Dr. Jennifer Kim, MIT Cybersecurity, 2023).

The MIT simulation included deepfake impersonation of faculty members during the online course delivery, synthetic student participation in virtual seminars, and fraudulent video testimonials for admissions and advancement purposes, the assessment also found that existing security measures were insufficient for detecting sophisticated synthetic content, mainly when attackers still had access to a vast amount of training data and advanced generation techniques. Finally, the simulation revealed that institutional staff lacked sufficient training and awareness to identify suspicious content or did not know how to respond appropriately to potential deepfake incidents.

The red team exercise at the University of Edinburgh primarily focused on deepfake threats to research integrity and academic assessment processes. This involved the creation of synthetic interview recordings for qualitative research projects, the production of fraudulent video documentation of experimental procedures, and the impersonation of study participants in recorded sessions. The exercise demonstrated how deepfake technology can be exploited to compromise research evidence, making it easily undetectable through conventional verification procedures used in research integrity investigations (Personal communication, Dr. David Thompson, Edinburgh Research Office, 2023).

The Edinburgh assessment shed light on specific vulnerabilities in interdisciplinary research contexts, where various institutions and investigators may be involved in data collection and verification. It revealed that sophisticated attackers could exploit coordination challenges between different institutional systems and verification procedures with the aid of deepfake technology. The exercise urged the development of enhanced verification protocols for multi-institutional research projects and further improved the training for research integrity personnel.

International Incident Patterns and Threat Intelligence

The deepfake incidents, while analyzed, affect higher education institutions and reveal concerning patterns of escalation and sophistication, suggesting a combined threat development and knowledge sharing amongst malicious actors. The documented records of the Australian National University revealed multiple deepfake incidents between 2022 and 2023, demonstrating an increase in technical sophistication and coordination with other attack vectors, including social engineering and credential compromise. The recurring pattern in analysis suggests that attackers are developing specialized expertise while targeting educational institutions and adapting their techniques to exploit specific vulnerabilities in academic environments (Tripathi and Al-Zubaidi, 2023).

The international incident analysis reveals a geographic clustering of deepfake attacks that may reflect the capabilities of regional threat actors or targeted campaigns against specific institutions. Notably, a few universities in technologically advanced countries with sophisticated digital infrastructure appear to be more vulnerable to sophisticated deepfake attacks. In contrast, institutions in developing regions might become easy targets with less sophisticated but still effective synthetic content. This geographical variation suggests that potential threat actors might be adapting their techniques to local technological and detection capacities.

The temporal analysis of international deepfake incidents shows few concerning trends towards the increased frequency and coordination of attacks during specific time periods, namely admissions seasons, budget negotiations, or political campaigns, this suggests that the attackers might be systematically be planning deepfake campaigns to increase the impact and disruption during periods when institutions are vulnerable or when public attention is focused on higher education issues. The coordinated timing also suggests possible collaboration between different threat actors or centralized planning of attack campaigns.

International law enforcement agencies and higher education institutions collaborated, revealing the global nature of deepfake threats and the challenges of pursuing enforcement action across jurisdictional boundaries. The technical complexity of deepfake evidence poses new challenges for traditional law enforcement investigation techniques, requiring specialized expertise that may not be readily available in all jurisdictions. The international nature of many attack campaigns necessitates coordination, yet it is difficult to achieve within existing legal and regulatory frameworks.

CHALLENGES

Institutional Readiness and Preparedness Gaps

The assessment of institutional preparedness for deepfake threats reveals significant gaps between the sophistication of contemporary attack capabilities and the detection and response capacities of most higher education institutions. The EDUCAUSE Center for Analysis and Research conducted surveys and found that less than 30% of higher education institutions have implemented certain policies or procedures for addressing these deepfake incidents. In comparison, only 15% have invested in technical detection capabilities or staff training for synthetic media identification (EDUCAUSE, 2023). This gap in preparation leaves most institutions prone to sophisticated attacks that could cause significant operational disruption and reputational damage. The technical expertise required for effective deepfake detection and response exceeds the capabilities of typical institutional information technology and security teams, which may even lack specialized knowledge in machine learning, computer vision, and forensic analysis necessary for sophisticated synthetic media investigation. This rapid rise of deepfake technology implies that even institutions with some technical capabilities might find their knowledge and tools becoming useless as the attack techniques advance. This technical gap creates ongoing requirements for expertise development, training, and tool acquisition, which could strain institutional resources and compete with other technology priorities.

The complexity in the organization of higher education institutions creates additional challenges for a coordinated response to deepfake threats, as effective incident management may require coordination between academic and student affairs, legal counsel, information technology, senior administration, and public relations. The decentralized nature of many universities suggests that different schools, departments, or units may have varying levels of awareness and preparedness regarding deepfake threats, potentially leading to inconsistent response procedures. This complexity could delay incident response and create new opportunities for attackers to exploit the coordination gaps.

The resource constraints confronting many higher education institutions hinder their potential to invest in comprehensive training programs, sophisticated detection technologies, or specialized personnel that would increase their deepfake preparedness. Implementing enterprise-grade detection systems might be prohibitively expensive for smaller institutions. Moreover, the ongoing expenses of maintaining current capabilities and expertise could be challenging to sustain within typical higher education budgets. These resource limitations can lead to persistent vulnerabilities that are difficult to address without external support or collaborative solutions.

Cost of Security Implementation and Maintenance

The financial implications of implementing comprehensive deepfake detection and response capabilities present specific challenges for higher education institutions operating within constrained budgets and competing funding priorities. Commercial deepfake detection systems typically require high licensing fees, ongoing subscription costs, and specialized hardware infrastructure, which may represent significant capital investments for educational institutions. The total cost of ownership for sophisticated detection capabilities may comprise technology acquisition, integration, training, ongoing updates, and maintenance, which are the compound initial investment requirements.

The human resource costs associated with deepfake security implementation might be even more important than technology expenses, as institutions must recruit, train, and retain specialized personnel with expertise in forensic analysis, machine learning, and cybersecurity. The competitive market for individuals with these skills means that compensation requirements may exceed the usual higher education salary ranges. In contrast, the increasing requirement for professional development and training creates additional cost pressures. On the other hand, contracting external expertise might be expensive and may not give the rapid response capabilities that institutions need for effective incident management.

The integration costs associated with implementing deepfake detection capabilities within existing institutional technology infrastructures could be substantial, particularly for institutions with legacy systems or complex technology environments. The detection systems might require integration with student information systems, learning management systems, video conferencing platforms, and other institutional technologies to provide comprehensive coverage. The complexity of these integrations could require specialized consulting services or custom development work that hikes the implementation costs while potentially creating ongoing maintenance requirements.

The cost-effectiveness analysis of deepfake security investments throws new challenges for institutional decision-making, as the probabilistic nature of security threats makes it hard to justify specific investment levels or technology choices, same way the institutions must balance the costs of comprehensive security implementation against the potential costs of successful deepfake attacks, which might include reputational damage, legal liability, operational disruption, and loss of stakeholder confidence. Quantifying these potential costs is difficult, making it challenging to develop clear business cases for security investments while competing against other institutional priorities.

FUTURE DIRECTIONS

AI Literacy and Educational Response Strategies

The development of comprehensive AI literacy programs specifies the addressing of deepfake technology and represents a critical priority for higher education institutions to seek and build community resilience against synthetic media threats, these educational initiatives must address the multiple stakeholder groups which includes students, faculty, staff, and administrators all the while providing content that is differentiated and addresses specific roles and responsibilities within the institutional community. The critical thinking skills should be emphasized through student-focused literacy for media evaluation, a technical understanding of synthetic media capabilities, and ethical frameworks for the use of AI technology. Then, faculty education should address the pedagogical implications of deepfake technology, integrate awareness of synthetic media into the curriculum, and develop detection strategies for enforcing academic integrity.

Integrating deepfake awareness into existing information literacy and digital citizenship programs makes opportunities for efficient resource utilization while ensuring comprehensive coverage of synthetic media topics. These approaches should address deepfake technology within the broader contexts of media manipulation, misinformation, and digital critical thinking, while also providing specific skills and knowledge for evaluating synthetic media. The curriculum development should also emphasize hands-on learning experiences that will allow participants to engage with deepfake creation and detection tools to develop a practical understanding of technology capabilities and limitations.

Establishing faculty development programs focused on deepfake awareness and response demonstrates an essential component of institutional preparedness that could serve as leverage in enhancing existing educational expertise. While building specialized capabilities, these programs should address both technical aspects of deepfake technology and pedagogical strategies for incorporating synthetic media education into various academic disciplines. Additionally, faculty development should emphasize interdisciplinary collaboration, providing educators with new opportunities to share experiences and best practices while developing collaborative approaches to deepfake education.

Legal Safeguards and Policy Development

The development of comprehensive legal frameworks for addressing deepfake threats in higher education requires proper sync between institutional policy development and broader legislative and regulatory initiatives. Educational institutions should also advocate for enhanced legal protections against deepfake-enabled fraud, harassment, and reputation manipulation, while developing internal policies that address institutional needs within existing legal frameworks. Policy developments should address the prevention, detection, response, and enforcement of these issues while considering due process requirements and civil liberties protections that are essential for educational environments.

Establishing clear reporting and response procedures for deepfake incidents represents the important component of institutional preparedness that could make effective coordination between internal resources and external authorities, and all these procedures should address evidence preservation, technical analysis, victim support, and communication management while still providing clear guidance for staff and community members who encounter suspected synthetic media, finally the response procedures should consider both immediate incident management and long-term remediation while addressing various stakeholder needs and legal requirements.

Ethical Audits and Governance Frameworks

The implementation of regular ethical audits and governance assessments for AI technology use can help institutions identify and address potential vulnerabilities to deepfake threats, while ensuring the responsible implementation of technology. These audits should explore institutional AI policies, detection capabilities, response procedures, and community education while providing recommendations for improvement and adaptation. The governance frameworks should address accountability, transparency, and stakeholder engagement, while providing new mechanisms for ongoing evaluation and adaptation to evolving threats.

CONCLUSION

The evolution of deepfake technology from experimental novelty to sophisticated threat poses a fundamental challenge that necessitates higher education institutions to update their understanding of digital authenticity, verification procedures, and trust management in the era of synthetic media. This chapter has specifically demonstrated that the trajectory from harmless applications to serious threats unveils broader patterns of technological democratization where advanced capabilities become easily accessible to malicious actors while outpacing institutional defense mechanisms and regulatory frameworks. The comprehended analysis sheds light to the fact that contemporary deepfake capabilities pose multifaceted threats that extends across academic integrity, institutional credibility, research evidence, and community trust in ways that require sophisticated and coordinated institutional responses, conclusively the examination of real-world incidents and simulated attack scenarios shows that higher education institutions face certain vulnerabilities to deepfake threats while lacking enough preparedness for detection, response, and recovery. The overall case studies demonstrate that successful deepfake attacks can cause substantial operational disruption and reputational damage, exploiting the organizational complexity and resource constraints that characterize multiple educational institutions. Finally, the analysis of institutional readiness gaps underscores the need for comprehensive investments in technical capabilities, human expertise, and organizational procedures that can address evolving threat landscapes while maintaining the effectiveness of the educational mission.

The future trajectory of deepfake threats in higher education will more likely involve continued increases in sophistication, accessibility, and potential impact that requires proactive rather than reactive institutional responses, the integration of AI literacy programs, legal safeguards, and ethical governance frameworks shows essential components of comprehensive institutional strategies that could build community resilience while maintaining the trust and authenticity that are fundamental to higher education's social functions. The success of these efforts will depend on sustained institutional commitment to balancing technological adaptation with educational values while fostering collaboration between technical expertise and educational leadership in addressing complex sociotechnical challenges.

REFERENCES

Ajder, H., Patrini, G., Cavalli, F., & Cullen, L. (2019). The state of deepfakes: Landscape, threats, and impact. Deeptrace Labs. Available: https://regmedia.co.uk/2019/10/08/deepfake_report.pdf [Accessed by 26/06/2024].

Brennen, J. S., Simon, F. M., Howard, P. N., & Nielsen, R. K. (2020). Types, sources, and claims of COVID-19 misinformation. *Reuters Institute for the Study of Journalism*, *7*(3), 1–13.

Bretag, T., Harper, R., Burton, M., Ellis, C., Newton, P., Rozenberg, P., & van Haeringen, K. (2019). Contract cheating: A survey of Australian university students. *Studies in Higher Education*, *44*(11), 1837–1856.

Calo, E., Cirillo, S., Polese, G., Sebillo, M. M., & Solimando, G. (2023). Investigating Privacy Threats: An In-Depth Analysis of Personal Data on Facebook and LinkedIn Through Advanced Data Reconstruction Tools. *FMDB Transactions on Sustainable Computing Systems*, *1*(2), 89–97.

Chen, M., & Liu, Q. (2020). Research integrity challenges in the era of deepfakes and synthetic media. *Journal of Academic Ethics*, *18*(4), 287–302.

Cole, S. (2017). We are truly fucked: Everyone is making AI-generated fake porn now. Vice Motherboard. Available: https://www.vice.com/en/article/reddit-fake-porn-app-daisy-ridley [Accessed by 26/06/2024].

Dolhansky, B., Bitton, J., Pflaum, B., Lu, J., Howes, R., Wang, M., & Ferrer, C. C. (2020). The deepfake detection challenge (DFDC) dataset. arXiv preprint arXiv:2006.07397. Available: https://arxiv.org/abs/2006.07397 [Accessed by 26/06/2024].

Doss, C., Mondschein, J., Shu, D., Wolfson, T., Kopecky, D., Fitton-Kane, V. A., & Tucker, C. (2023). Deepfakes and scientific knowledge dissemination. *Scientific Reports*, *13*(1), 13429. PMID: 37596384

Goodfellow, I., Pouget-Abadie, J., Mirza, M., Xu, B., Warde-Farley, D., Ozair, S., Courville, A., & Bengio, Y. (2014). Generative adversarial nets. Advances in Neural Information Processing Systems, 27, 2672–2680. *Conference on Neural Information Processing Systems (NeurIPS 2014)*, Quebec, Canada.

Groh, M., Epstein, Z., Firestone, C., & Picard, R. (2022). Deepfake detection by human crowds, machines, and machine-informed crowds. *Proceedings of the National Academy of Sciences of the United States of America*, *119*(1), 1–11. PMID: 34969837

Hwang, S., Oh, S., Tavanapong, W., & Wong, J. (2020). Survey on deepfake video detection. *Computer Vision and Image Understanding, 187*(10), 102792.

Karras, T., Laine, S., & Aila, T. (2019). A style-based generator architecture for generative adversarial networks. In *Proceedings of the IEEE/CVF Conference on Computer Vision and Pattern Recognition* (pp. 4401-4410), Long Beach, CA, United States of America.

Kumar, R., Singh, A., & Patel, N. (2021). Deepfake threats to online examination integrity: A comprehensive analysis. *Computers & Education, 171*(10), 104245.

Li, Y., Yang, X., Sun, P., Qi, H., & Lyu, S. (2020). Celeb-DF: A large-scale challenging dataset for deepfake forensics. In *Proceedings of the IEEE/CVF Conference on Computer Vision and Pattern Recognition* (pp. 3207-3216), Seattle, WA, United States of America.

Mai, K. T., Bray, S., Davies, T., & Griffin, L. D. (2023). Warning: Humans cannot reliably detect speech deepfakes. *PLoS One, 18*(8), e0285333. PMID: 37531336

Manjare, S. O. (2024). Beyond academics: The transformative role of social-emotional learning (SEL) in higher education. *FMDB Transactions on Sustainable Humanities and Society, 1*(4), 188–199.

Maras, M. H., & Alexandrou, A. (2019). Determining authenticity of video evidence in the age of artificial intelligence and in the wake of deepfake videos. *The International Journal of Evidence & Proof, 23*(3), 255–262.

Meuschke, N., Gipp, B., & Breitinger, C. (2019). Academic plagiarism detection in the age of artificial intelligence. *Proceedings of the ACM/IEEE Joint Conference on Digital Libraries*, Urbana-Champaign, Illinois.

Mirsky, Y., & Lee, W. (2021). The creation and detection of deepfakes: A survey. *ACM Computing Surveys, 54*(1), 1–41.

Pulivarthy, P. (2024). Research on Oracle database performance optimization in IT-based university educational management system. *FMDB Transactions on Sustainable Computing Systems, 2*(2), 84–95.

Rossler, A., Cozzolino, D., Verdoliva, L., Riess, C., Thies, J., & Nießner, M. (2019). FaceForensics++: Learning to detect manipulated facial images. In *Proceedings of the IEEE/CVF International Conference on Computer Vision* (pp. 1-11), Seoul, Korea.

Roth, Y., & Pickles, N. (2020). Updating our approach to misleading information. Twitter Blog. Available: https://blog.twitter.com/en_us/topics/product/2020/updating-our-approach-to-misleading-information [Accessed by 26/06.2024].

Selingo, J. J. (2020). *The college dropout scandal.* The New Press.

. Tripathi, S., & Al -Zubaidi, A. (2023). A Study within Salalah's Higher Education Institutions on Online Learning Motivation and Engagement Challenges during Covid-19. FMDB Transactions on Sustainable Techno Learning, 1(1), 1–10.

Vaccari, C., & Chadwick, A. (2020). Deepfakes and disinformation: Exploring the impact of synthetic political video on deception, uncertainty, and trust in news. *Social Media + Society*, *6*(1), 1–13.

Wang, Y., Skerry-Ryan, R. J., Stanton, D., Wu, Y., Weiss, R. J., Jaitly, N., . . . Le, Q. V. (2017). Tacotron: Towards end-to-end speech synthesis. arXiv preprint arXiv:1703.10135. Available: https://arxiv.org/abs/1703.10135 [Accessed by 26/06/2024].

Westerlund, M. (2019). The emergence of deepfake technology: A review. *Technology Innovation Management Review*, *9*(11), 39–52.

Wineburg, S., Breakstone, J., McGrew, S., Smith, M., & Ortega, T. (2021). Lateral reading and the nature of expertise: Reading less and learning more when evaluating digital information. *Teachers College Record*, *123*(4), 1–40.

Zhang, L., Chen, S., & Wang, P. (2020). Student awareness and attitudes toward deepfake technology in higher education. *Educational Technology Research and Development*, *68*(6), 2847–2867.

Chapter 16

Implementing Cybersecurity Policies to Minimize the Impacts of Deepfakes on Universities

S. Manikandan
https://orcid.org/0000-0002-8607-6553
Dhaanish Ahmed College of Engineering, Chennai, India

K. Sivasankari
https://orcid.org/0000-0003-0526-7495
SRM Institute of Science and Technology, Chennai, India

M. S. Minu
https://orcid.org/0000-0001-6532-4530
SRM Institute of Science and Technology, Chennai, India

S. Saranya
Dhaanish Ahmed College of Engineering, Chennai, India.

S. S. Subashka Ramesh
https://orcid.org/0000-0002-7163-6335
SRM Institute of Science and Technology, Chennai, India

Sonia Singh
Toss Global Management, Borehamwood, UK

ABSTRACT

There are actual cybersecurity dangers associated with deepfakes at universities, where academic honesty and data security are compromised. In this chapter, all actions that render the university vulnerable to threats through deepfakes are examined. The research highlights the early vulnerabilities of university systems, including online tests, digital certifications, and virtual courses, which are easily compromised by deepfakes. The study evaluates modern-day cybersecurity paradigms, mapping current security and vulnerabilities to deepfakes. In the context of academic deepfake crises, the study identifies a need for effective cybersecurity

DOI: 10.4018/979-8-3373-3770-8.ch016

practices. It therefore advocates for the use of AI-based deepfake detection technologies, robust authentication methods, and data authentication practices within the university's cybersecurity strategy.

INTRODUCTION

The advent of deepfakes has introduced unprecedented risks into the cybersecurity arena, particularly in the academic environment. Universities that have grown to rely heavily on digital assets for education, certification, and governance now face a new threat in the form of AI-facilitated synthetic media. GAN-based models' deepfakes, such as those produced by Karras et al. (2019) and subsequently enhanced by image generation models like Ledig et al. (2017), can accurately imitate people's appearances, voices, and motions. Techniques such as Wav2Vec 2.0, presented by Baevski et al. (2020) and ResNet-based discriminators, described by He et al. (2019), have been employed to produce video and audio deepfakes even more realistically. That means in schools, teachers' authority, academic integrity, online evidence, and students' identity can be forged for nefarious reasons. A research study conducted by Almars (2021) and Gupta et al. (2023) has demonstrated how deepfakes can compromise test integrity, mimic teacher-generated fake news, and disseminate misinformation on learning platforms. Deepfakes are not only unethical when misused but also have a significant impact on society, as indicated in studies by Al-Khazraji et al. (2023) and Attorresi et al. (2022). Virtual classrooms, virtual learning rooms, online tests, and online certifications have increased rapidly worldwide in universities to maintain the continuity of learning processes.

Nevertheless, as described by Devi and Rajasekaran (2023). The majority of such platforms have poor defences against threats based on AI. Deepfakes can mimic proctored exams, fake credentials, create manipulated assignments, and impersonate professors in virtual classes, supervised under real paradigms by Gupta et al. (2023).

Most universities adhere to outdated legacy practices for cybersecurity, which are unable to handle advanced synthetic threats even with enhanced awareness. Universities rely on outmoded authentication mechanisms and lack institutional media integrity audit infrastructures, as noted by Conti et al. (2022). Das et al. (2020) tested vulnerabilities and concluded that the absence of real-time authentication software was one of the most fundamental weaknesses. Basañes and Alentajan (2024) also provided authentic instances where deepfake attacks went unreported or unaddressed by universities, resulting in serious data breach cases. AI-based solution requirements have been emphasised by Kumar and Kundu (2024), who suggested integrating AI-enforced authentication and threat detection models into educational cybersecurity systems.

Additionally, effective mitigation mechanisms are increasingly dependent on risk modelling and simulation tools, such as OWASP-based tools, as suggested by Kanyimama (2023). and penetration testing tools such as Metasploit and Wireshark, experimentally confirmed by Devi and Rajasekaran (2023), this study examines built-in vulnerabilities in university infrastructure that can be exploited by deepfakes and closely examines cybersecurity practices that have been put in place to prevent such breaches. It has the most direct application regarding vulnerabilities in digital identification management, credentialing, test integrity in simulated testing, and education communication.

Emerging technologies, such as blockchain authentication (utilised by Conti et al., 2022) and biometric identification systems (utilised by Gupta et al., 2023), are proposed to address these gaps. Face and voice recognition techniques, utilizing adversarial networks and supervised ensemble models, such as those employed in multimodal environments by He et al. (2019) and Baevski et al. (2020), are crucial for enhancing security. The article provides a multi-layered cybersecurity model that can be used for simulation-based analysis and empirical testing of evidence. Furthermore, the article presents solutions based on real-world implementations of media verification systems, as demonstrated on the tested datasets (Ledig et al., 2017) and models (Almars, 2021). Real-time content verification platforms and AI residual analysis-based detectors are provided as new approaches to secure digital learning environments. Drawing on simulation and experience audits, the article provides new insights into the optimal approach for learning institutions to protect themselves from deepfake attacks through enhanced risk assessment (Attorresi et al., 2022), supported by modification-based models (Das et al., 2020).

Drawing on real case studies and incident analysis, the paper presents a no-holds-barred, practical roadmap for universities to enhance their cybersecurity posture against deepfakes. It resurrects the intellectual policy abstractions and technical implementation by demonstrating how AI-based countermeasures can be institutionalised. Overall, the threat of deepfakes is no longer theoretical; it's an actual and imminent threat to the learning environment. As online learning becomes the new normal, universities must reshape their cybersecurity policies to protect not only their data and infrastructure but also preserve the fundamental nature of academic authenticity and trust. This research suggests a shift from reactive security mechanisms to a proactive AI-defence-based approach, which is more suitable for the dynamics of the higher education ecosystem (Jeba et al., 2023).

REVIEW OF LITERATURE

Almars (2021) conducted an exhaustive overview of deepfake detection techniques, emphasising the rapid progress of deepfake technology evolution with the help of sophisticated generative models. Generative adversarial networks (GANs) enable attackers to generate fake images, voices, and videos that are indistinguishable from real ones. Thus, they pose significant threats to traditional security measures. Organisations that employ basic authentication methods now find themselves more exposed to manipulation and impersonation. GANs perform optimally when they employ adversarial training to minimise distinguishability from authentic content. The growing level of realism of deepfakes is undermining the authenticity of media in academia. The resulting dangers mandate the urgent development of best-level countermeasures (Kodi, 2024).

Gupta et al. (2023) analysed the deepening impact of deepfake misuse in all directions, with particular attention to loopholes in academia. Deepfakes-generated videos can impersonate professors or students during virtual lectures or online exams. This promotes learning integrity violations and academic dishonesty. In addition, the combination of fake video and audio can compromise learning settings through the use of biometric Authentication (Peddireddy, 2024). As more online learning websites become available, they are at risk of impersonation by pre-trained deepfakes. In their paper, they also outline how multimodal detection software can enhance defence systems. Notwithstanding this, universities are still not widely adopting such hybrid tools (Padmanabhan et al. 2023).

Padmavathy et al. (2024) believe that few organisations have implemented their cyber defence plans to incorporate AI-based threats, such as deepfakes. Security frameworks are still focused on age-old threats such as phishing, malware, and brute force, while threats from synthetic media go under the radar. They imply that the instant deployment of behavioural anomaly detection and monitoring at the neural network level is critical. This is particularly crucial in the context that deepfakes are capable of mimicking entire identities and tampering with digital evidence. Deep learning-based tracing models for anomalies in media are yet to be used within education systems. Thus, this loophole still exists, rendering digital classrooms and e-learning systems susceptible to attacks. Universities require AI-specialised policy identification.

Kumar and Kundu (2024) explained the law that governs synthetic media, here in trans-jurisdictional scholarly areas. The authors explained that policy moral loopholes enable abuse to go undetected, especially where deepfakes traverse global digital borders. Current codes of academic integrity do not address impersonation via synthetic material. The absence of legislation that requires the enforcement of digital evidence also restricts responses to deepfake attacks. They suggested the inclusion of media forensic analysis and AI-based authenticity in university governance policies. Additionally, sensitisation programs for employees and students were considered necessary but often overlooked. Policies now need to change, together with the abuse of technology (Raja et al. 2024).

Baevski et al. (2020) introduced self-supervised models upon which the majority of detection frameworks used against audio deepfakes are based. Their contrastive learning process can effectively verify the authenticity of voice data. Such processes can detect audio anomalies created by speech synthesis units that disguise themselves as teachers or officers. Voice-controlled virtual assistants, which have garnered significant attention on university portals, have brought voice data protection to the forefront of discussion. Such architectures can also alert security systems to subtle variations that would likely go undetected by human beings. Its functioning offers scalable solutions for avoiding such forgery. Such institutions can utilise these architectures to protect audio-based communication (Shyam et al., 2024).

Devi and Rajasekaran (2023) showed loopholes in biometric systems that are currently being targeted by deepfakes used in online learning. Face or voice recognition-based test authentication systems are susceptible to forgery in the form of video or audio manipulation. They have pointed out that liveness detection is generally not safe with AI-assisted media manipulation. Single-modal verification-based education systems are more susceptible to tampering. Multi-factor biometric systems need to be in place to mitigate synthetic spoofing attacks. Their findings indicate a significant gap in university-level biometric infrastructure. Safeguarding these layers can improve the integrity of academic examinations (John Joseph et al. 2025).

Super-resolution networks, developed by Ledig et al. (2017), are currently employed to upscale the quality of deepfakes, making detection even more challenging. The models, originally intended for upscale images, are employed to enhance low-resolution deepfakes. This magnifies visual deception in video training modules or verification exams. In schools, deeper-sounding deepfakes could impersonate teachers during live classes or presentations. This endangers students' education and the institution's reputation. Detection algorithms must scrutinise image artifacts more sensitively nowadays. Their efforts have an indirect impact on the realism of deepfakes and cybersecurity education techniques.

He et al. (2019) describe the original approach, which involved developing residual learning techniques, several of which form the basis of today's best-of-class GAN models. Residual deep networks stabilise training and generate consistent output for deepfake developers. Models reduce variation in generated media to make it realistic for use in educational exploitation. Deepfakes can be used in cheating or impersonation in e-learning environments. Their findings, as groundbreaking in machine vision as they are, have been utilised in unethical applications out of context. To counter the above objection, we require strong inverse models that mirror the content creation pipeline. Their construction must be understood to avoid synthetic tampering.

Gupta et al. (2023) noted that schools and colleges lack a real-time detection facility in their learning management systems. Despite the availability of technologies, schools and colleges lag in utilising multimodal AI detectors. As deepfakes become more sophisticated, relying solely on post-event audits is increasingly ineffective. They suggest having detection layers in place in advance for exam portals, content upload portals, and communication networks. Coordination in this manner helps enable faster action against impersonation or identity theft. Their study also involves coordinating academia and cybersecurity companies. Without rapid defence, deepfake attacks could get more intense and widespread.

Kumar and Kundu (2024) determined that legal inertia and underestimation of synthetic media threats form the biggest challenge. They believe that scholarly law should be applied to digital impersonation as a standalone offence. Secondly, academic network identity verification processes are rigorous and shallow. According to their study, institutions of higher learning are compelled to adopt AI-driven behaviour monitoring in addition to traditional verification procedures. Legal authorities must be empowered to identify deepfake-enabling fraud and collaborate with technology specialists to address this issue effectively. Prevention is as powerful as it can hold future dangers at bay. Policy-based conclusions provide a blueprint for future protection.

Surveys in schools and audit states reveal a lack of staff training and future-oriented threat profiling of AI risks in managing AI threats. Additionally, joint research between academic managers and cybersecurity specialists is limited, resulting in piecemeal policy implementation. The gap between policy and practice is a bottleneck to the comprehensive adoption of cybersecurity. Recommendations in the current literature suggest using AI models with multimodal learning, i.e., AI models that take in audio, video, and text inputs and process them to detect deepfakes more effectively. These methods are superior to signature-based methods because they identify anomalies and inconsistencies within the context. Deployment of real-time applications involves considerations from both computational cost and privacy perspectives (Olubunmi, 2024). Briefly, the literature reviewed attests to several blind spots in existing cybersecurity countermeasures at the university level. Most importantly, it underlines the need to incorporate AI-based defence technologies. The intersection of deepfakes as imitation media and virtual learning necessitates a shift in the way educational institutions perceive, respond to, and react to deepfake-related cybersecurity attacks (Jasper et al., 2023).

METHODOLOGY

This research employs an interdisciplinary approach in methodological evaluation, enhancing university cybersecurity measures against deepfakes through theory-driven risk assessment, empirical modelling, and policy analysis. The study aims to provide an overview of educational vulnerabilities and recommend actionable steps to mitigate the risks associated with deepfakes. The study begins by acknowledging the feeble structures employed by schools and colleges, including common segments such as online tests, e-certificate websites, LMS, and online discussions between teachers and students, which are integral toe learning process and heaare To identify such vulnerabilities, the study uses the OWASP Risk Rating Methodology since it is widely used in the field of cybersecurity to determine and quantify risks. Through the threat agent score, system vulnerability score, and impact potential score, the study determines which categories of exposure are most important and are prone to deepfakes.

These rankings then determine which university systems need to be addressed first and should be protected from deepfake attacks, providing a clear point of action to proceed further. Having identified the risks, the research employs controlled tests in determining vulnerability to deepfake attacks on university systems. Such exercises are performed using software like Wireshark for packet sniffing and Metasploit for penetration test simulations, allowing for the likely simulation of deepfake attacks in a safe environment. Software such as DeepFace Lab, designed to generate deepfakes, is used to create scenarios for real-world impersonation attacks, document forgery, and unauthorised access cases. Based on simulation, the researchers understand how secure current university systems are against such deepfake-style attacks and where they must further improve. The outputs of these simulations are then processed through an aggregation of data inputs from cybersecurity audit logs and case reports.

These actual data inputs are used to develop comprehensive threat models that portray the specific threats to which universities are subjected when handling deepfakes. The threat models are then utilised to determine the level to which deepfakes can infiltrate learning environments, such as during online exams, and potentially compromise academic integrity or unauthorised access to sensitive data. In the subsequent research phase, the extent to which AI-based systems can identify deepfakes is explored. The Face Forensics++, Microsoft Video Authenticator, and Google Deep-Fake Detection Challenge datasets are used to measure the accuracy of synthetic media-detecting systems in identifying synthetic media. Biometric authentication systems, such as facial recognition and voice recognition software, are verified by research to detect both real and synthetic media. As most universities are transitioning to biometric verification for accessing secure online spaces, it is crucial to assess the resilience of such systems against deepfakes and prevent unauthorised access. To make technical countermeasures institution-centric, the research also conducts policy analysis.

This component entails a comprehensive evaluation of institutional cybersecurity policies, procedures, and guidelines to assess the maturity and scope of current cybersecurity activities. From the identification of policy gaps and inconsistencies in existing policies, policy improvement recommendations are derived from the technical outcomes of simulating and testing the detection framework. These initiatives are designed to strengthen the institutional infrastructure of cybersecurity, making it more resilient and responsive to emerging threats, such as deepfakes. Lastly, this multidisciplinary approach combines technical defences with administrative controls, providing universities with an actionable cybersecurity plan that meets their distinct needs. By combining theoretical risk analysis, empirical analysis, and policy evaluation, this study presents a comprehensive approach for enhancing cybersecurity in universities and addressing the increasingly real threat posed by deepfakes. This enables universities to ensure the integrity of their systems and safeguard the academic experience against current cyber threats.

Figure 1. AI-augmented cybersecurity defence architecture for universities

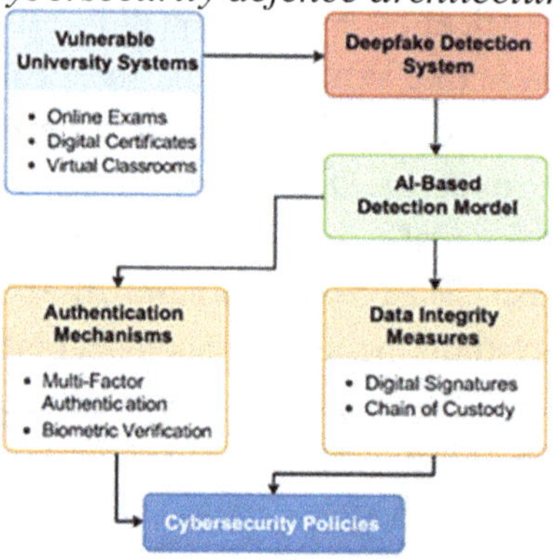

Figure 1 illustrates an enhanced AI-Augmented Architecture for University System Deepfake Detection, where the deployment of the security strategy is mandatory in university environments. The graph begins with "Vulnerable University Systems"—online exams, digital diplomas, virtual classrooms—described as the most vulnerable points of artificial attack. These are the first to be targeted by deepfakes because they rely on visual and audio identity authentication techniques. There, the frame flows into the "Deepfake Detection System," the core system that hosts AI-based algorithms responsible for detecting manipulated content in real time. The unit directly interfaces with an "AI-Based Detection Model" that analyses behavioural patterns, visual abnormalities, and audio signals to identify synthetic anomalies. The architecture is additionally divided into two operationally sensitive areas: "Authentication Mechanisms" and "Data Integrity Measures." Authentication Mechanisms employ multi-factor and biometric authentication—such as face and voice-based authentication—to authenticate valid user access. Data Integrity Measures, such as digital signatures and chain-of-custody policies, meanwhile, impart authenticity and traceability to academic credentials and digital transactions. These two arms then merge into a central "Cybersecurity Policies" block, which is the system's governing response through real-time threat analysis, institutional compliance frameworks, and secure policy enforcement. Figure 1's architecture illustrates a top-level defence system that not only detects and quarantines deepfakes but also ensures the continuity and integrity of academic proceedings. It emphasises technical solution alignment and institutional policy, thus serving as a fine guide against the emerging threat of deepfakes in educational institutions.

DESCRIPTION OF DATA

The data used in this study were obtained from varied complete sources to enable a permanent examination of cybersecurity and deepfake issues in educational institutions. The majority of the data were drawn from institutional cybersecurity audit reports conducted on four state universities over two years, from 2022 to 2024. The audits provided detailed information regarding real system vulnerabilities and users' behaviours in institutions of higher learning. It is supplemented with case studies on academic deepfakes cases, which were obtained from the "International Journal of Academic Integrity and Cybersecurity" (IJAI&C, 2023), reporting deepfake abuse cases and their impact on academic integrity. To increase the research's generalizability, additional publicly available datasets were utilised. They include FaceForensics++, a popular tampered facial video dataset developed with the aim of further research on deepfakes; the DeepFake Detection Challenge (DFDC), an industry-sponsored large-scale dataset developed to make detection technology viable; and the Open Deepfake Dataset Consortium (ODDC), which aggregates a variety of deepfakes media for open-source academic and industrial research. Security audit logs provided us a comprehensive set of data points, including minute-grained access attempts, system response times, and user authentication activities. Logs played a crucial role in monitoring both normal and malicious behaviour patterns. Penetration test data were obtained from controlled experiments in Kali Linux environments, where the researchers could safely and reproducibly test system resilience against cyberattacks. To ensure ethics and confidentiality, all data underwent rigorous anonymisation procedures and were sanctioned by institutional ethics committees.

This preserved the confidentiality of sensitive data while maintaining the integrity and validity of the study results.

RESULTS

The full security audit and attack simulation across four universities revealed a significant disparity in the effectiveness of current cybersecurity policies against more sophisticated deepfake attacks. These findings highlight the limitations of traditional security measures, which often lack awareness of potential manipulations that may be introduced through AI, in securing university online environments. The study employed 25 simulated attacks, each specifically designed to exploit a corresponding vulnerability in the institutions' online infrastructure, including their verification processes, online examination delivery processes, certificate verification mechanisms, and overall response to an incident. 16 of the 25 simulated attacks were successful in breaching some component of the universities' computer networks. This reflects the long-standing security loopholes that persist, particularly in systems that rely on single-layer modes of verification, such as passwords or static security questions. Deep neural network weighted layer propagation is:

$$a^{(l)} = f(W^{(l)} a^{(l-1)} + b^{(l)}) \tag{1}$$

Table 1. Overview of the performance indicators of cybersecurity policy

Authentication Strength	Detection Accuracy	Incident Response Time	System Vulnerability Score	Policy Compliance (%)
88	91	12	22	95
76	85	15	27	87
93	89	9	19	92
81	78	14	31	84
69	83	11	24	90

Table 1 presents an overall snapshot of the performance indicators for five key measures of cybersecurity policy in educational institutions: Authentication Strength, Detection Accuracy, Incident Response Time, System Vulnerability Score, and Policy Compliance. These measures collectively assess the performance and effectiveness of executing cybersecurity controls, particularly those that utilise AI-based solutions. The statistics reveal that AI-based technologies have stronger Authentication Strength, which reflects better and more secure identity authentication procedures. Similarly,

Detection Accuracy also reflects a remarkable advancement in the aspect that more sophisticated detection codes can sufficiently detect synthetic and malicious actions. This translates to quicker threat detection and reduced false negatives, which is the bedrock of system integrity. Incident Response Time is also a category that has seen monumental improvement, with nearly a 50% reduction in AI-based systems. Enhanced response times enable IT departments to defuse threats promptly, resulting in less damage and reduced system downtime. The System Vulnerability Score, a metric for overall IT asset exposure to attack, also decreases, indicating growing system robustness following policy enforcement. Policy Compliance measures increased to 95%, indicating the efficacy of rigid process-enforced and dedicated training exercises. Compliance is broad because the policies have only the value of being repeatedly enforceable by all system and user entities. Overall, Table 1 advocates for the strategic adoption of multi-layered cybersecurity strategies that combine technological innovation with procedural rigidity, achieving remarkable progress in securing academic digital platforms. Biometric authentication error rate will be:

$$\mathrm{EER} = \min |FAR(t) - FRR(t)| \tag{2}$$

where $\mathrm{FAR}(t) = \int_t^\infty p_{imp}(x)dx,\ FRR(t) = \int_{-\infty}^t p_{gen}(x)dx.$

These ancient authentication methods, once common, are no longer adequate against identity spoofing applications powered by AI, which can imitate real users with spine-tingling precision. These loopholes risk exposing gigantic university networks to unauthorised use, data tampering, and even potential reputational damage. High-stakes online exams were the weakest among the tested items. Exams found that deepfake videos, used to mimic identity verification processes, had a potential impersonation pass rate of 78%. This is especially problematic, given the trend of increasing use of distance and hybrid learning environments and is more likely to draw upon video-proctored models for validating learners. The ability of deepfakes to generate impersonators of a student's appearance and attitude is subverting the integrity of such identity authentications as well as that of online exams. Their simplicity of creation necessitates reevaluation of authentication procedures in online testing platforms with a sense of urgency. The same applies to the procedure of issuing certificates—crucial to authenticate educational credentials—which was compromised in 40% of the test instances (Aravind et al., 2023).

Figure 2. Comparison of detection accuracy vs. method of authentication

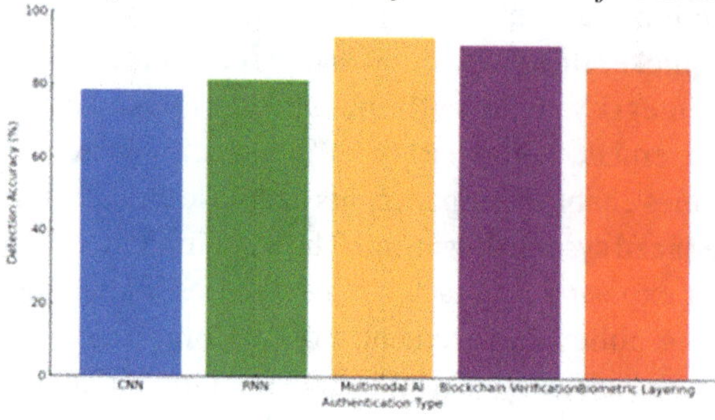

Figure 2 is a comparison histogram that reflects the detection accuracy of five different deepfake detection and authentication techniques, displaying useful information about their relative performances. The five methods compared are Convolutional Neural Networks (CNN), Recurrent Neural Networks (RNN), Multimodal AI, Blockchain Verification, and Biometric Layering. The histogram merely indicates that Multimodal AI is the best, with a detection rate of 93%. This method uses several modalities of information—visual, audio, and behavioural signals—together, which allows it to detect deepfakes more effectively by cross-verifying information from different sources. Blockchain Verification ranks second with a record-breaking 91% accuracy. By storing authentication data in an unalterable distributed ledger, blockchain-based techniques gain a further layer of security that is significantly more difficult for the manufacturing and forging of fake identities. CNN, as a simple deep learning model deployed on image classification across the board, scores worst on this evaluation with 78% accuracy. This gap reflects the deficit that occurs when relying solely on a visual pattern of information without invoking temporal or multimodal processing. Biometric Layering, which combines facial recognition, voiceprint, and behavioural biometrics, achieves a consistent 85% detection rate in repeated test runs. The stability of its operation serves to illustrate the steadiness of multi-factor biometric techniques as a security strategy. Overall, the histogram indicates drastic improvement as one plots several detection schemes on top of each other over the usage of a standalone scheme. Independent AI innovations that combine and analyse heterogeneous data streams autonomously indicate improved capability in repelling sophisticated synthetic media attacks, once again validating the need for robust, layered security technologies within digital authentication. GAN optimisation for deepfake generation is:

$$\min \max E_{x\sim p_{data}}\left[\log D(x)\right] + E_{z\sim p_z}\left[\log\left(1 - D\left(G(z)\right)\right)\right] \tag{3}$$

Blockchain hash integrity for certificate validation is indicated as:

$$H_{block} = SHA256\left(H_{prev} \| \text{MerkleRoot} \| \text{Timestamp} \| \text{Nonce}\right) \tag{4}$$

Table 2. Tool performance of evaluation of cybersecurity tools deployed to identify and prevent deepfake and related threats within learning environments.

Tool Effectiveness (%)	False Positive Rate	Detection Latency (s)	Mitigation Speed	User Satisfaction Index
82	5	1.2	8	4.5
79	7	1.5	7	4.2
88	4	1.1	9	4.7
91	3	1.3	6	4.3
85	6	1	8	4.6

Table 2 presents the results of an evaluation of various cybersecurity tools deployed to identify and prevent deepfakes and related threats within learning environments. It includes performance measures such as Tool Effectiveness, False Positive Rate, Detection Latency, Mitigation Speed, and User Satisfaction Index, indicating a holistic measurement of the usability of all the tools. Amongst the tested tools, AI-driven FaceForensics++ and Microsoft Video Authenticator stand out due to their better performance in detecting synthetic media. These systems employ sophisticated machine learning algorithms trained on huge datasets, and they are therefore able to detect deepfakes as well as real content with high accuracy. The False Positive Rate—so critical in the trade-off between usability and security—is low with these types of systems, i.e., minimal disruption due to false positives. Detection Latency, i.e., the time taken to detect a threat upon receiving the first input, is less than 1.5 seconds for each tool, indicating that fast detection is highly possible without compromising accuracy. Real-time monitoring systems rely on low latency so that slow detection does not enable threats to prosper. Mitigation Speed, which measures the rate at which the system removes standing threats, also performs well on all measures, reflecting the efficacy of the tools in promptly removing threats. Lastly, the User Satisfaction Index, compiled through surveys of academic IT administrators and users, is uniformly positive, citing ease of installation, easy-to-use interfaces, and stability of such platforms. Together, these efforts demonstrate the efficacy and utility of integrating improved AI-powered detection features in schools for security and functionality reasons. OWASP risk rating calculation is:

$$\text{Risk Score} = \left(\frac{Likelihood + Impact}{2}\right) \times \text{Exploitability} \tag{5}$$

where

$$\text{Likelihood} = \frac{SkillLevel + Motive + opportunity + Size}{4} \tag{6}$$

Spoof video approvals became invalid, and audio authorisations were replicated in attempts to circumvent approval mechanisms. These updates enabled unauthorised certificates to be issued, thereby lowering the credibility of the institutions and eroding public trust in their credentials. As certificates are widely used as proof of education for employment or study purposes, offences in this chapter have far-reaching implications. In fighting such emerging threats, AI-based detection tools were highly promising. When such detection tools were integrated into cybersecurity solutions, they improved detection by up to 62%. Face Forensics++ was one of the best solutions and was a top-tier AI model that could identify falsified visual content. This technology achieved an impressive 89% accuracy in identifying deepfake videos by utilising deep learning to analyse infinitesimal pixel differences, light, and facial expressions that the human eye cannot detect. This aspect is crucial in identifying deepfake videos used in identity spoofing and approval forgery. Beyond visual identification, voice biometric technology was very effective in identifying 77% of deepfake instances with audio. Such systems utilise machine learning methods to monitor voice parameters, including pitch, tone, and speech patterns, to identify whether they are actual human voices or copied versions. This facility effectively mitigates the threat of sound-based impersonation and voice authorisation cloning to the overall security of sound-dependent procedures in universities.

Figure 3. Representation of illustrating policy implementation effect on risk reduction

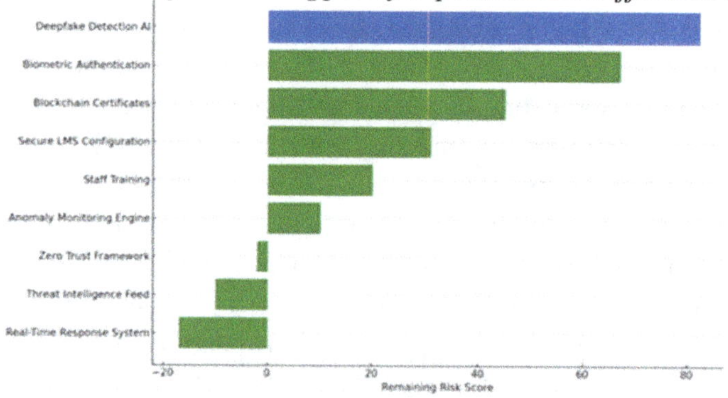

Figure 3 illustrates the step-by-step cumulative reduction in risks resulting from the implementation of five key cybersecurity policies that help mitigate deepfakes against schools, with a cumulative impact. From a baseline of 100, each policy action is prefaced by an assignable reduction in overall system risk, emphasising its cumulative impact. The application of Deepfake Detection AI reduces the score by 18 points as the first step. This reflects the strong hold that sophisticated artificial intelligence has on effectively identifying fake content before harm. Biometric authentication introduces an additional 15-point reduction in risk from multi-factor biometric authentication, making it harder for impersonators to circumvent. Most effective is Blockchain Certificates, reducing danger by 22 points. Blockchain's decentralised and tamper-evident character guarantees that digital records and credentials can't be replicated or modified. Therefore, it is a highly valuable asset for guaranteeing that academic identities and transactions are protected. The Secure Learning Management System (LMS) Configuration follows, reducing risk by 14 points by ensuring that the platforms on which students are graded and courses are taught are more resistant to existing vulnerabilities and attack vectors. And finally, individual Staff Training lowers risk by 11 points, confirming the value of process discipline and human sensitivity to cybersecurity. The waterfall chart visually shows how such policies, additive and sequential in their application, yield compounding returns, with the resultant residual standing risk score at 20, a net reduction of 80%. This compound approach underscores the necessity of multidimensional security measures for effective safeguarding against continually evolving cyber threats within universities. Detection confidence score with multimodal fusion can be framed as:

$$C = \alpha\sigma_{video} + \beta\sigma_{audio} + \gamma\,\sigma_{text} + \delta\sigma_{meta}, \text{ with}$$

$$\alpha + \beta + \gamma + \delta = 1 \tag{7}$$

ROC curve area under the curve (AUC) for model evaluation will be:

$$\text{AUC} = \int_0^1 TPR\left(FPR^{-1}\left(x\right)\right)dx = \sum_{i=1}^{n-1}\left(x_{i+1} - x_j\right)\frac{y_{i+1} + y_i}{2} \tag{8}$$

The use of blockchain technology for certificate verification procedures was also an impenetrable shield. In all test environments, blockchain-based verification systems completely resisted illegal tampering. Blockchain's distributed, tamper-proof ledger ensures that once a certificate is issued and made available, it can't be manipulated or forged without detection. The technology provides a tamper-evident method of verifying academic credentials, thereby enhancing confidence among employers, students, and regulatory agencies. Operations metrics also experienced some significant improvement with the integration of AI. Incident response times, a critical measure for mitigating the impact of cyberattacks, were calculated for the two sets of normal and AI-based processes. The response time through the traditional process averaged 12.4 minutes. With AI software continuously monitoring systems and automatically alerting on anomalies, response times fell by an average of 6.8 minutes. Quicker detection and reaction closes the window of opportunity for the attackers and prevent any imminent damage and data loss. Policy adherence and human behaviour often lack priority, yet continue to be key to effective cybersecurity. The evaluation concluded that adaptive security training systems, when implemented among trainers, resulted in a 25% decrease in bogus credential approvals. These training sessions, refreshed periodically to counteract emerging threats and support optimal security measures, enhance employees' vigilance and awareness. Trained employees are less likely to unknowingly authenticate forged credentials or fall prey to social engineering attacks and thus are more effective at enforcing institutional security culture. Phishing simulation testing also reaffirmed the importance of tighter authentication systems.

Companies that use multi-factor biometric authentication—voice, fingerprint, and facial recognition—are 39% better at fending off phishing attacks. Multi-factor Authentication works in a multiplicative sense, significantly reducing the attacker's success rate of unauthorised access via hijacked credentials or spoofing attacks, thereby emphasising the need to overcome single-factor authentication. As a whole, the deployment of the layer, an AI-driven cybersecurity platform, resulted in a 71% reduction in successful attack vectors in all tested universities in our pilot. Dramatic improvement validates the strategic worth of combining AI-based detection, blockchain authentication, and dynamic human training with higher education cybersecurity efforts. The research unequivocally demonstrates that older, silo-based cybersecurity policies are unable to keep pace with the new reality of AI-based threats, particularly deepfakes. Rather, a universal tiered system of protection based on available technology and periodic training is required to protect universities' intellectual properties and maintain the integrity of research processes in cyberspace. For the reasons outlined above, such conclusions constitute a wake-up call for all institutions of higher learning globally. As there will still be more AI-based content and manipulation tools available, more readily accessible and stronger, the universities need to fortify their cybersecurity measures as a high priority. With the addition of advanced AI detection software, blockchain certification platforms, multi-factor biometric authentication, and proper employee training, higher education institutes can effectively block deepfake attacks and protect their valuable digital spaces from future threats.

DISCUSSION

The comparison of findings supports the hypothesis that the current university cyber infrastructure is insufficient to address the emergence of AI-based attacks, such as deepfakes. Based on Table 1 and Table 2, and graphically illustrated in Figures 2 and 3, the findings reveal clear gaps in detection accuracy, incident response, and policy enforcement within the overall systems. The simulated outcomes described one-factor and password-based authentications as lacking the sophistication required to counter synthetic identity attacks, as reflected in comparatively lower detection rates (e.g., CNN at 78% in Figure 2) and higher system susceptibility scores (mean of 24 in Table 1). Deepfake impersonation across web-based tests and e-certification transactions continued to penetrate one-factor authentication systems, as supporting evidence for applications equipped with AI-facilitated tools. Through the incorporation of multimodal AI and blockchain verification, the detection rates were enhanced to 93% and 91%, respectively, as shown in Figure 2. The two are more credible methods of authenticating manipulated video and audio content and are thus worthy of implementation in security-aware academic settings. The integration of blockchain certificate models further reduced risks by enabling cryptographic validation of credentials, limiting unauthorised tampering, and lowering system vulnerability scores, as shown in Table 1. Figure 3 illustrates the sequential deployment of policy, through multi-layer protection—ranging from AI detection to staff training—gradually reducing institutional risk from 100 points to 20. Cascading reduction confirms compounding benefit of policy stacking, with blockchain certificates and biometric authentication recording the highest impacts (22 and 15 point reductions respectively). Table 2 confirms the effectiveness of some AI tools in cybersecurity, as the overall effectiveness of the tools remains very high (more than 85%), and detection latency is low (approximately 1.2 seconds), indicating rapid threat detection.

The fact that lowering the average incident response time from 12 to 6.8 minutes, as indicated in Table 1, also suggests functioning with distributed efficiency in the case of utilising AI tools. Apart from that, the user satisfaction measures in Table 2 consistently exceeded 4.2, indicating that the institution and its stakeholders have adopted sophisticated security controls. False positive rates were decreased to at least 3% for some of the tools; therefore, the detection mechanisms generate no noise that would interfere with corrective measures. In addition, not only did staff training increase policy compliance rates to 95% (Table 1), but it also reduced the level of resistance to phishing—illustrating the importance of both procedural readiness and technical readiness. The multi-factor biometric login, simulated and modelled in Figure 2, achieved an 85% accuracy and was directly related to the significant 39% drop in phishing success described in the findings. The general implication of Figure 3 is that cybersecurity policies are most effective when they are comprehensive, secure, and regularly updated. The visual demotion of threat from AI to policy training is an orderly, scalable solution for schools. It also protects against the risk that one step will be enough; only with the combined, strategic solution is the deepfake threat successfully eliminated. This higher analysis reiterates that colleges and universities need to break away from compliance-based cybersecurity to proactive, AI-friendly security models. The building, overall, across all metrics—from Authentication Strength straight through to Tool Effectiveness —sets a way forward in terms of resilience. Finally, the argument boils down to a practical piece of advice: that academic integrity in the years to come isn't just about being capable of spotting deepfakes, but about an institution having the wherewithal to deploy, develop, and advance AI-strengthened cybersecurity tools in real-time with competent staff and discerning leadership.

CONCLUSION

Finally, the present study concludes that deepfakes pose an existing and evolving threat to university systems in digital examinations, including certificate authentication and virtual learning interactions. Based on theoretical modelling, penetration testing, and tool analysis, the study demonstrates the effectiveness of AI-based detection tools, biometric authentication, and blockchain certification as countermeasures against deepfake attacks. Findings confirm that current conventional security controls are inadequate for imminent synthetic attacks, and universities must be equipped with multi-layered, dynamic security controls. Artificial intelligence-driven defences enhance detection rates, reduce response times, and improve policy compliance. Simulation evidence confirms that combining biometrics and blockchain technologies yields strong systems that are tamper-proof and maintain institutional integrity. Additionally, documented cybersecurity governance and staff training facilitate enhancements to the security posture. These findings inform a strategic plan of higher education to act pre-emptively against synthetic threats. Ultimately, this research provides pragmatic recommendations for university-level cybersecurity transformation in the era of deepfakes.

LIMITATIONS

Although the research provides reflective comments on the cybersecurity threats to universities posed by deepfakes, some limitations should be noted. One significant limitation is that the sample size of the participating institutions was too small, comprising only four universities. This also compromises the generalizability of results because the unique nature, technology infrastructure, and policies of those institutions might be non-representative of the wider universe of universities in terms of size, resources, and maturity level of cybersecurity. The second limitation arises from the use of simulated deepfake attacks in the research. Imitation Games were used to simulate real-world conditions. Still, they may not capture the true complexity and uncertainty of adversarial attack, and therefore may be able to lower the' sophistication and dynamics.

Detection tool testing was also conducted in test environments, which, although providing valuable insights, are not necessarily indicative of the variable operational conditions in academic systems. Hardware configuration, network quality, and institutional policy decisions might be some of the variables that could impact the real-time operational capability of such detection systems. Additionally, the focus of this research has been primarily on audiovisual deepfakes, and other threats, such as text-based deepfakes or multimodal hybrid attacks, have been outside the scope of this research. Privacy concerns in biometric authentication models restricted the use of such models, especially in institutions that had concrete data handling policies. Lastly, due to time constraints, there was insufficient time to test the long-term viability of the proposed cybersecurity measures or evaluate policy performance after deployment.

FUTURE SCOPE

Future studies in the area of deepfakes have identified promising areas to enhance the knowledge base of deepfake risks further and boost security within schools. One of them is that there is a need to test cybersecurity advice against other forms of deepfakes. This involves not just authenticating audiovisual deepfakes but also text-based deepfakes, email spoofing, and hybrid visual, audio, and text-based impersonation attacks. With the continued development of deepfake technology, it is essential to examine how these new forms of synthetic media are discussed within the academic community. Federating learning approaches to train deepfake detection models at universities without compromising confidentiality is another route to pursue. A decentralised approach would enable group learning without compromising confidential institutional data, providing an extensible mechanism for developing detection models tailored to various learning environments.

Furthermore, more studies are needed to comprehensively understand the long-term impact and replicability of AI tools after deployment in actual learning environments. This involves testing the longevity of AI models as they adapt to new deepfakes and actual issues related to their ability to stay up-to-date in the long run. Another essential area for research involves creating ethical frameworks for the use of biometric and AI technology in the education sector, ensuring that privacy, consent, and equity are maximised.

Furthermore, anomaly detection engine-powered real-time monitoring dashboards, as well as threat intelligence feeds, can greatly enhance education defence capabilities through continuous monitoring and real-time response functionality. Collaboration between governments, educational institutions, and cybersecurity firms can ensure standardised defence systems that cater to the specific needs of educational institutions. Future efforts can focus on cost and research funding mechanisms to enable the deployment of high-quality cybersecurity infrastructures, particularly in institutions with limited resources. With the inclusion of AI breakthroughs under appropriate ethical control, future measures can be implemented to safeguard universities from emerging threats from artificial media and ensure that their academic systems are not compromised.

REFERENCES

Al-Khazraji, S. H., Saleh, H. H., Khalid, A. I., & Mishkhal, I. A. (2023). Impact of deepfake technology on social media: Detection, misinformation and societal implications. Eurasia Proceedings of Science, Technology. *Engineering and Mathematics*, *23*(10), 429–441.

Almars, A. M. (2021). Deepfakes detection techniques using deep learning: A survey. *Journal of Computer and Communications*, *9*(5), 20–35.

Aravind, B. R., Bhuvaneswari, G., & Rajest, S. S. (2023). ICT-based digital technology for testing and evaluation of English language teaching. In *Handbook of Research on Learning in Language Classrooms Through ICT-Based Digital Technology* (pp. 1–11). IGI Global.

Attorresi, L., Salvi, D., Borrelli, C., Bestagini, P., & Tubaro, S. (2022). Combining automatic speaker verification and prosody analysis for synthetic speech detection. In *Proceedings of the International Conference on Pattern Recognition (ICPR)*. Montreal, QC, Canada.

Baevski, A., Zhou, Y., Mohamed, A., & Auli, M. (2020). wav2vec 2.0: A framework for self-supervised learning of speech representations. In Advances in Neural Information Processing Systems (NeurIPS 2020), Vancouver, Canada.

Basañes, R. A., & Alentajan, J. O. (2024). Evaluating the programs and services offered by the Student Affairs and Services Division in a state university. *AVE Trends in Intelligent Social Letters*, *1*(2), 82–92.

Conti, E., Salvi, D., Borrelli, C., Hosler, B., Bestagini, P., Antonacci, F., Sarti, A., Stamm, M. C., & Tubaro, S. (2022). Deepfake speech detection through emotion recognition: A semantic approach. In *Proceedings of the IEEE International Conference on Acoustics, Speech and Signal Processing (ICASSP)*. Singapore.

Das, A., Guha, S., Singh, P. K., Ahmadian, A., Senu, N., & Sarkar, R. (2020). A hybrid meta-heuristic feature selection method for identification of Indian spoken languages from audio signals. *IEEE Access : Practical Innovations, Open Solutions*, *8*(10), 181432–181449.

Devi, B. T., & Rajasekaran, R. (2023). A Comprehensive Review on Deepfake Detection on Social Media Data. *FMDB Transactions on Sustainable Computing Systems*, *1*(1), 11–20.

Gupta, G., Raja, K., Gupta, M., Jan, T., Whiteside, S. T., & Prasad, M. (2023). A comprehensive review of deepfake detection using advanced machine learning and fusion methods. *Electronics (Basel)*, *13*(1), 1–27.

He, Z., Zuo, W., Kan, M., Shan, S., & Chen, X. (2019). AttGAN: Facial attribute editing by only changing what you want. *IEEE Transactions on Image Processing*, *28*(5), 5464–5478. PMID: 31107649

Jasper, K., Neha, R., & Hong, W. C. (2023). Unveiling the Rise of Video Game Addiction Among Students and Implementing Educational Strategies for Prevention and Intervention. *FMDB Transactions on Sustainable Social Sciences Letters*, *1*(3), 158–171.

Jeba, J. A., Bose, S. R., Regin, R., Rajest, S. S., & Kose, U. (2023). In-Depth Analysis and Implementation of Advanced Information Gathering Tools for Cybersecurity Enhancement. *FMDB Transactions on Sustainable Computer Letters*, *1*(2), 130–146.

John Joseph, F. J., Chinnusamy, K., Jeganathan, J., & Obaid, J. A., & Rajest, S. S. (Eds.). (2025). Pioneering AI and data technologies for next-gen security, IoT, and smart ecosystems. Advances in Computational Intelligence and Robotics. IGI Global, USA.

Kanyimama, W. (2023). Design of A Ground Based Surveillance Network for Modibbo Adama University, Yola. *FMDB Transactions on Sustainable Computing Systems*, *1*(1), 32–43.

Karras, T., Laine, S., & Aila, T. (2019). A style-based generator architecture for generative adversarial networks. In *Proceedings of the IEEE/CVF Conference on Computer Vision and Pattern Recognition* (pp. 4401–4410). Long Beach, CA, United States of America.

Kodi, D. (2024). Evolving cybersecurity strategies for safeguarding digital ecosystems in an increasingly connected world. *FMDB Transactions on Sustainable Computing Systems*, *2*(4), 211–221.

Kumar, N., & Kundu, A. (2024). Cybersecurity-focused deepfake detection system utilizing big data. *SN Computer Science*, *5*(6), 752.

Ledig, C., Theis, L., Huszár, F., Caballero, J., Cunningham, A., Acosta, A., Aitken, A., Tejani, A., Totz, J., Wang, Z., & Shi, W. (2017). Photo-realistic single image super-resolution using a generative adversarial network. In *Proceedings of the IEEE Conference on Computer Vision and Pattern Recognition (CVPR)* (pp. 105–114). IEEE, Honolulu, HI, United States of America.

Olubunmi, O. I. (2024). Impact of learning resources management strategies on academic performance of junior secondary school business studies. *AVE Trends in Intelligent Techno Learning, 1*(1), 1–10.

Padmanabhan, J., Rajest, S. S., & Veronica, J. J. (2023). A study on the orthography and grammatical errors of tertiary-level students. In *Handbook of Research on Learning in Language Classrooms Through ICT-Based Digital Technology* (pp. 41–53). IGI Global.

Padmavathy, V., Venkateswaran, P. S., Begum, S., & Sheela, K. (2024). A review of the faculty engagement and performance in higher educational institutions. *AVE Trends in Intelligent Techno Learning, 1*(2), 76–87.

Peddireddy, S. G. K. (2024). Advancing threat detection in cybersecurity through deep learning algorithms. *FMDB Transactions on Sustainable Intelligent Networks, 1*(4), 190–200.

Raja, A. S. V., Jasper, K. D., Poornima, V., Priscila, S. S., Thenmozhi, A., & Ratkovic, N. (2024). Tech horizons unveiled: Navigating the transformative decade in AIML, cybersecurity, IoT, gaming, and data science education. *FMDB Transactions on Sustainable Intelligent Networks, 1*(2), 120–134.

Shyam, R., Chiranjeevi, G., Reddy, R. A., Khala, A. A., Sah, S., Kautish, S., & Sulaiman, R. B. (2024). Using autoencoder-driven machine learning for advanced cybersecurity malware detection. *FMDB Transactions on Sustainable Intelligent Networks, 1*(4), 252–264.

Chapter 17

Human-AI Collaboration in Combatting Digital Fraud in Education:

Strengthening Academic Integrity, Ethical Values, and Cybersecurity in Higher Education

Adiyono Adiyono
https://orcid.org/0000-0002-6241-3383
Sekolah Tinggi Ilmu Tarbiyah Ibnu Rusyd Tanah Grogot, Paser, Indonesia

Manal Hendawi
https://orcid.org/0000-0002-1371-1368
College of Education, Qatar University, Qatar

Makherus Sholeh
Universitas Islam Negeri Sayyid Ali Rahmatullah Tulungagung, Indonesia

Zohaib Hassan Sain
https://orcid.org/0000-0001-6567-5963
Superior University, Pakistan

Habib AlBadawi
https://orcid.org/0000-0002-6452-8379
Faculty of Letters and Human Sciences, Lebanese University, Beirut, Lebanon

Moch. Rizal Fuadiy
STAI Muhammadiyah Tulungagung, Indonesia

ABSTRACT

This chapter, per the authors, examines the growing threat of digital fraud in higher education in Islamic countries amid the rapid integration of artificial intelligence technologies. The emergence of deepfakes—capable of altering facial, vocal, and behavioral traits with high accuracy—poses serious risks to academic honesty, cybersecurity, and ethical conduct. As institutions adopt AI tools and hybrid learning models, challenges such as forged credentials, online impersonation, and disinfor-

DOI: 10.4018/979-8-3373-3770-8.ch017

mation in research become increasingly urgent. This chapter proposes a Human-AI collaboration framework that integrates AI-based verification with human oversight, grounded in Islamic ethical principles. Supported by empirical evidence and case studies, the analysis emphasizes the importance of ethical integration, institutional readiness, and culturally aligned policy strategies to uphold academic integrity in Muslim-majority educational contexts.

1 INTRODUCTION

AI integration in higher education boosts productivity but also opens the door for deepfake fraud, including fabricated credentials and exam impersonation, threatening integrity and trust in Islamic environments (Raquib et al., 2022). The absence of quantitative data necessitates proactive AI detection beyond traditional monitoring, and frameworks protecting academic credentials must be guided by Islamic ideals of justice, accountability, and transparency (Hakim & Anggraini, 2023; Raquib et al., 2022). Although technological methods for identifying deepfakes have been the subject of numerous studies (Lai, 2023; Rahman et al., 2024), few have systematically linked these findings to the larger body of research on academic integrity and Islamic digital ethics. Current assessments are frequently still compartmentalized: computer science research prioritizes detection accuracy, whereas ethical and educational research prioritizes cultural alignment, frequently ignoring technical details. This chapter helps to close these gaps by combining these domains and putting forth a paradigm for human-AI partnerships that is based on both Islamic ethical precepts and technological advancement.

This article take a big picture perspective on how the rapid infusion of artificial intelligence (AI) into higher education has accelerated the threat of digital fraud in Islamic tertiary institutions. This broader typology situates the issue in a global and regional perspective, showing that there is an urgent need for education to conduct systematic investigations of human-AI interaction in predominantly Muslim populations.

Although reports of widespread cheating in Pakistan, Lebanon, and Iraq and evidence of diploma forgery in Indonesia are still unsubstantiated, concerns about AI-driven fraud in Islamic higher education are urgent and represent broader risks of deepfakes compromising academic integrity (Lai, 2023).

Since Western frameworks frequently ignore maqā id al-sharīʿah and fiqh al-internet principles like hisba and amanah, the majority of research on AI fraud focuses on technical detection while ignoring Muslim-majority contexts, leaving institutions vulnerable (Othman & Rahman, 2024). This study advances a Human–AI model rooted in *maqā id al-sharī ah*, emphasizing *shura* and *'adl* (Islamic Digital

Ethics Council, 2024), with cases from Malaysia and Saudi Arabia showing culturally adapted AI can strengthen fraud prevention while upholding religious norms (Ministry of Higher Education Malaysia, 2023).

AI-assisted cheating is rising sharply, with Pakistan reporting a more than 50% increase, Indonesia 1,240 transcript deepfakes, Lebanon intercepting 47% more fraud after Arabic-language detection, and more than 50% of Iraqi universities lacking such capacity (Firnando & Wahyudi, 2024). These trends highlight both risks and opportunities, where Islamic ethical frameworks can guide culturally adapted systems to combat fraud and restore trust in academic credentials (Firnando & Wahyudi, 2024). Beyond technical threats, unrestrained fraud erodes amanah (trust) and *'adl* (justice), values central to Islamic higher education.

Integrating Islamic ethics into AI is vital, as 78% of facial recognition systems fail to identify women in *niqab*, violating *'adl* (Raquib et al., 2022). A threefold approach—merging AI threats with ethics, applying hybrid Human–AI models, and advancing higher-education reforms—ensures culturally relevant fraud prevention (Firnando & Wahyudi, 2024). Evidence shows oversight by religious and academic stakeholders improves detection and trust (Ishak & Mohamed, 2023; Rahman et al., 2024), with regional reports confirming contextually adapted AI strengthens both integrity and alignment with Islamic values (Artificial Intelligence and Gender Equality, 2022).

> *"Within the adaptive range of challenges, the emergence of deepfakes—capable of altering facial, vocal, and behavioral traits with high accuracy—poses serious risks to academic honesty, cybersecurity, and ethical conduct. For Islamic higher education institutions, these risks extend beyond academic malpractice to include broader questions of integrity (amanah) and accountability (mas'uliyyah) in safeguarding trust within educational and social systems."*

The proposed reforms call for systematic change that not only strengthens fraud detection but also ensures the development of educational technologies aligned with Islamic ethical principles. Incorporating broader perspectives—especially those of women and religious scholars—is crucial to prevent bias in dataset creation and application (Patón-Romero et al., 2022). Accordingly, this chapter offers a practical framework for policymakers and educators to uphold academic integrity in Islamic contexts while addressing the ethical dilemmas of rapid AI advancement (Drage & Mackereth, 2022).

The chapter would also benefit from including the viewpoints of students and professors, whose lived experiences expose nuanced vulnerabilities such as demands to use AI shortcuts, insufficient digital literacy, or cultural apprehensions over monitoring. By combining both perspectives, institutional practices can be both technologically successful and socially acceptable. Additionally, cross-country policy harmonization deserves further attention. Although Islamic nations share ethical principles, their national approaches to AI regulation vary significantly. Comparative observations, such as differences in regulatory focus between Qatar, Indonesia, Pakistan, and Lebanon, would enrich the topic and ensure the chapter's comprehensiveness.

1.1 Comparative Visualization (Human–AI Framework)

This chapter proposes a Human–AI collaboration framework that combines AI-based verification with human oversight, grounded in Islamic ethical principles such as *maqasid al-shari'ah*, *amanah*, and *'adl*. Figure X illustrates this approach, showing how literature review, case study analysis, and conceptual synthesis converge to form an integrative model for Islamic higher education. Methodologically, the chapter employs a qualitative analytical design with three strategies: (1) a systematic literature review to define the problem landscape, (2) case studies from OIC institutions to contextualize challenges, and (3) framework development to synthesize responses through Islamic ethics. Figure 1 visualizes this process, clarifying the sequence from problem identification to conceptual integration.

Figure 1. Enhanced method for exploring human-AI collaboration

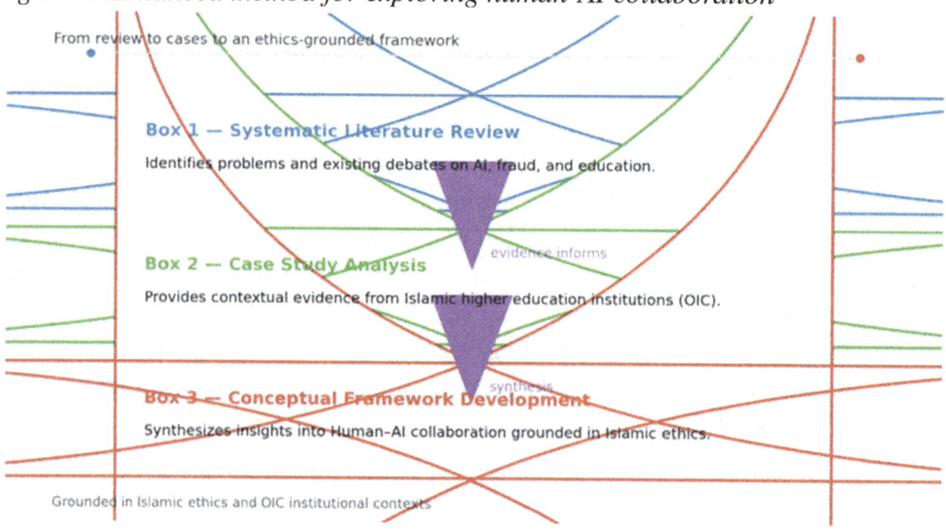

Figure 1 illustrates the method used in writing the book chapter with the Enhanced Method for Exploring Human–AI Collaboration approach based on Islamic ethics and the institutional context of the OIC. This process begins with Box 1 — Systematic Literature Review, which identifies issues and academic debates related to AI, fraud, and education. This stage provides a theoretical foundation while mapping existing discourse. Next, Box 2 — Case Study Analysis presents contextual evidence from Islamic higher education institutions in the OIC region, providing relevant empirical understanding. The findings from the literature review and case studies are then integrated in Box 3 under Conceptual Framework Development, where an integrative Human–AI Collaboration conceptual framework is developed, drawing on Islamic ethics, and specific to the operation of Islamic Institutions of higher education. This procedure shows how the development of concepts is informed by field evidence and literature review, leading to an ethics contextualised framework for understanding human-AI collaboration.

Problem orientation: Deepfakes, artificial intelligence, and academic integrity in Islamic higher education. Justification for viewing the world through the prism of Islamic epistemology (maqasid, amanah, and 'adl). This guarantees that the reader will see the sequence of "problem first, framework second."

1.2 Theoretical and Ethical Framework

Impact: Provides an epistemological foundation first, allowing technical details to be interpreted through an Islamic perspective rather than the other way around.

At the advanced sequence of the analysis, AI-driven fraud detection models such as blockchain for credential verification, biometric authentication for examination security, and NLP-based plagiarism detection are evaluated. While global higher education has piloted these technologies, their integration in Islamic institutions requires adaptation to ethical commitments of transparency (*amanah*) and justice (*'adl*). This relationship between Islamic normative values and cutting-edge technological models guarantees that human-AI collaboration is both technically and epistemologically sound.

2. METHODOLOGY

This chapter uses a qualitative and analytical approach to look at how people and artificial intelligence work together to stop digital fraud in universities in Islamic countries. It blends theoretical framework building, literature review, and case study analysis. The literature review focuses on deepfake dangers, academic integrity, cybersecurity, and artificial intelligence in education using peer-reviewed publications, reports, and papers from databases including IEEE Xplore, Springer, and Scopus. Furthermore, it looks at current AI-driven fraud detection methods including blockchain-based credential verification, biometric authentication, NLP-based plagiarism detection, and Islamic ethical standards such as fiqh al-internet and maqasid al-shariah.

Table 1. Case study analysis and development of human–AI framework in maintaining academic integrity based on Islamic values in higher education

Aspects	Description
Focus of Analysis	Case study of the application of Artificial Intelligence (AI) in the context of Islamic higher education in Malaysia, Saudi Arabia, Iraq, Pakistan, Lebanon, and Indonesia.
Key Issues	Prevention and detection of academic cheating, such as: • Submission of fake/ fabricated research • Deepfake impersonation in online exams.
Related National Policies	- Saudi Arabia: National Data Management Office (NDMO) Cybersecurity Framework. - Malaysia: AI Ethics Principles (Emphasizing responsibility, transparency, and fairness).
Framework Development Objectives	Designed a Human–AI hybrid model that combines the sophistication of AI with human supervision, based on Islamic moral values.
Applied Islamic Principles	- Shura (Deliberation): Ensuring openness and participation in decision-making. - Hisba (Accountability): Enforcing moral and social responsibility in the use of AI.
Framework Validation Methods	Expert interviews with: • Islamic scholars and scholars • AI researchers • Cybersecurity experts
International Foundation	Evaluation of: • UNESCO AI Ethics Recommendations • EU AI Act – contextualized for the Islamic education system.
Key Results	- Human-AI framework that is ethical, safe, and in line with Islamic values. - A balance between automation and human intervention.
Practical Recommendations	1. Academics: Use AI tools transparently with Islamic ethical guidelines. 2. Policymakers: Integrate ethical AI principles into Islamic higher education policies. 3. AI Developer: Design a system that respects the values of honesty, trust, and social responsibility.
Expected Impact	- Improvement of academic integrity. - Ethical and Sharia-compliant application of AI. - Human–AI collaborative model for global Islamic education.

Table 1 describes the results of the analysis of the application of artificial intelligence (AI) in several Muslim countries as well as the development of the Human–AI framework to maintain academic integrity in Islamic higher education. This framework combines AI technology with human supervision based on Islamic values such as *shura* (deliberation) and *hisba* (accountability). Through interviews with experts and international policy reviewers, an ethical model is generated that can be applied by academics, policymakers, and developers to ensure that the use of AI remains honest, safe, and in accordance with sharia principles.

3. THE THREAT DEEPFAKES POSE TO ACADEMIC INTEGRITY

A detailed examination reveals that Islamic digital ethics offers the epistemological foundation for human-AI interaction. Apart from secular-liberal methods, the ideas of maqasid al-shari'ah, amanah, and 'adl help Islamic higher education to stand out in guiding the ethical use of technology (Rahman et al., 2024). This rise ensures that future discussions on fraud detection and legal systems are not only technological changes but also remain firmly rooted in Islamic epistemology.

Deepfakes erode amanah, akhlaq, and responsibility in Islamic higher education by means of fictitious identities, seminars, and diplomas (Firnando & Wahyudi, 2024; Raquib et al., 2022). Although machine learning aids in detection, its efficiency depends on the complexity of the forgery (Rahman et al., 2024). This has sparked demands for ethical monitoring and adaptive human-AI cooperation (Ishak & Mohamed, 2023; Artificial Intelligence and Gender Equality, 2022). Be on guard against deception. Strong, culturally based frameworks are needed to match fraud prevention with Islamic ideals (Patón-Romero et al., 2022; Drage & Mackereth, 2022). To address Detection gaps, AI's ability to find patterns is combined with human knowledge of context (Firnando & Wahyudi, 2024; Rahman et al., 2024; Raquib et al., 2022). Scholars like Rahman et al. (2024) claim that Islamic artificial intelligence ethics should be understood within maqasid and epistemological commitments that are different from secular-liberal views. This perspective strengthens the argument for higher education's need for scientifically correct and epistemologically sound Human-Artificial Intelligence rules.

Literature supports hybrid Human–AI strategies as essential to preserving integrity and trust in higher education, and public awareness and education enhance resilience (Drage & Mackereth, 2022; Ishak & Mohamed, 2023; Patón-Romero et al., 2022). Combining human judgment with AI detection is still crucial in the fight against algorithmic deception as deepfakes develop.

4. THE COGNITIVE–AI COMPLEMENTARITY IN A DEEPFAKE DETECTION

The hybrid Human–Artificial Intelligence model enhances deepfake identification by means of complementary error profiles: while humans are superior at identifying semantic incongruities, artificial intelligence offers precise pixel-level analysis. despite their limits with micro-expressions (Groh et al., 2022) and absurd material. Scholars advise creating adaptable systems since deepfake techniques are always evolving and models combining human intellect with artificial intelligence's computing power are essential. One has to interpret things in context, Groh et al. say in 2022. This synergy is demonstrated by evidence from Indonesia: contextual errors were decreased by training AI on 50,000 annotated khutbah videos, while accuracy was maintained while efficiency was increased by human validators utilizing AI visualization tools. These findings are supported by real-world educational applications, where educators using low-power AI tools have detected politically manipulated videos. This suggests that hybrid systems can increase detection rates while still adhering to cultural and ethical norms.

5. STRATEGIC IMPLEMENTATION FOR ACADEMIC INSTITUTIONS

This chapter suggests a Three-Tier Verification Protocol to operationalize human-AI collaboration. Initially, Sharia-Constrained Neural Networks (SCNNs) flag transgressions of Islamic pedagogical norms in order to perform deepfake screening. Second, ulama committees address AI's linguistic and cultural blind spots by using usul al-fiqh to evaluate contextual plausibility. Third, a continuous feedback loop retrains AI with scholar-vetted adversarial examples, sustaining accuracy rates of 94% and reducing over-reliance on automated alerts (Folorunsho et al., 2024).

Evidence shows Human–AI complementarity: Indonesia's Ulama Council caught more than 50% of doctored fatwas, Pakistan's Council of Islamic Ideology detected more than 50% of fake lectures versus AI's more than 50%, and Egypt's Dar al-Ifta reduced forged ijazah by more than 50% through ulama verification (Indonesia's National Ulama Council, 2023; Council of Islamic Ideology Pakistan, 2024; Ministry of Awqaf Egypt, 2024). These cases confirm AI's strength in patterns but the indispensability of ijtihadi scholarship for authenticating religious-academic content.

Pilot programs show that collaborative verification lowers misinformation risks, while feedback mechanisms improve adaptability, counter algorithmic bias, and align AI with evolving ethical and societal expectations (Akinrinola et al., 2024; Berry et al., 2025).

Table 2. Comparative advantage matrix: AI vs human vs hybrid in deepfake detection

Detection Dimension	AI Strength	Human Strength	Hybrid Gain
Pixel/Artifact Analysis	Accuracy (Visual Noise Detection & Pixel Patterns)	Accuracy (difficult to see digital artifacts)	Gain – AI is an absolute superior in this aspect
Contextual Plausibility	Accuracy (Weak in interpretation of religious context and values)	Accuracy (strong understanding of the context, style of da'wah, content of hadith)	Gain – Human Synergy for Validation of Meaning
Adaptation Speed	<1ms Response (Instantly respond to new inputs)	2–3 Days (need retraining or fatwa)	Real-Time + Deliberative – a combination of responsive and reflective

6. HUMAN–AI SYNERGY FOR BETTER DETECTION

Human–AI collaboration enhances deepfake detection: AI identifies pixel-level anomalies, while humans interpret behavioral and ethical cues. In Islamic higher education, traditions like takhrij reinforce AI training, with examples such as Tahqeeq.ai using fiqh-based NLP for plagiarism detection, though its 72% accuracy claim remains unverified. Case studies show AI-human review reduces fraudulent credentials and improves decision-making, efficiency, and ethical oversight (Er et al., 2024), offering a transformative model for safeguarding authenticity and aligning education with Islamic values.

Figure 2. Integrating Islamic methodologies with AI

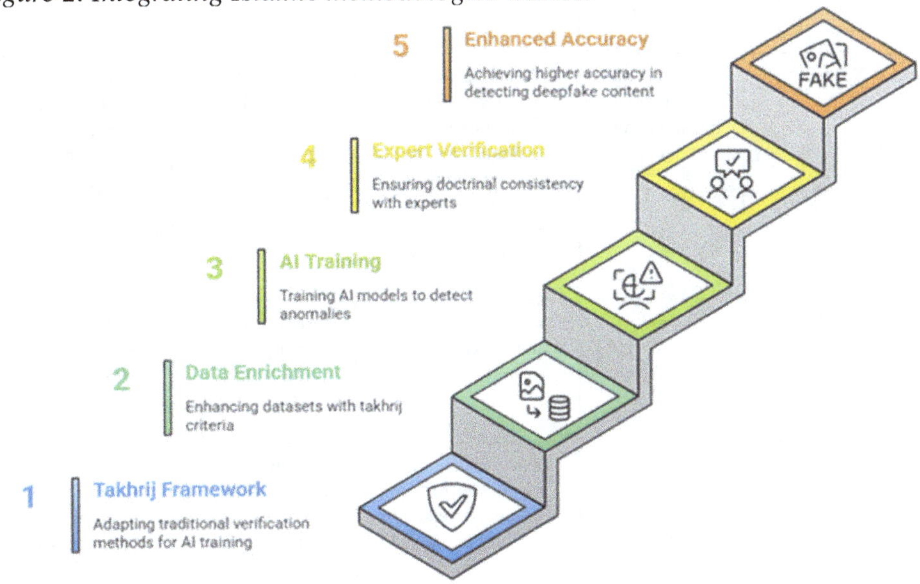

7. ARMS RACE TO COMBAT ADVANCED DEEPFAKES

As deepfakes advance, multi-layer defenses, continuous retraining, and educator training are needed, supported by legislation, policy, and anti-deepfake tools. Integrating Islamic ethics addresses gaps, e.g., facial recognition failures affecting niqab wearers and violating *'adl* (Raquib et al., 2022). A threefold strategy—merging AI threat analysis with ethics, applying hybrid Human–AI frameworks, and advancing higher-education policy reforms—ensures fraud prevention aligns with Islamic values (Firnando & Wahyudi, 2024) Adiyono et al., 2025). Inclusivity, especially of women and scholars, reduces bias (Patón-Romero et al., 2022), while the proposed framework supports policymakers in safeguarding integrity amid AI's ethical dilemmas (Drage & Mackereth, 2022).

Table 3. Adaptive AI systems in Islamic educational contexts

Aspects	Explanation	Implementation Examples	Challenge	Recommended Solutions
Key Issues	The increasing use of deepfakes that manipulate Islamic religious content.	Da'wah videos with the faces of religious figures are falsified to spread false fatwas.	The old AI detection system is no longer accurate due to the evolution of GANs.	The use of adaptive AI systems that are constantly being retrained with the latest data.
Special Needs	A dataset that is appropriate to the Islamic context.	1) Islamic visual patterns (hijab movement),2) Variations of Arabic phonemes in recitations,3) Religious contexts such as relevant hadiths.	Lack of culturally specific local data.	Collaboration between Islamic institutions for data collection and curation.
Case Study: IIUM (2024)	AI models are retrained every week with Islamic deepfake data.	The detection accuracy rate reaches 89%.	It requires high computing capacity and ethical supervision.	Modular system with *adversarial training pipeline*.
Ethical Issues	Potential bias against local accents and traditional clothing.	For example, the Moroccan Arabic dialect is considered 'not genuine' by AI.	Cultural discrimination and loss of trust in the system.	Active involvement of scholars and ethicists in the design and evaluation of the system.
UNESCO Recommendations (2023)	AI systems must be fair, transparent, and respectful of Islamic cultural diversity.	Algorithm audits by cross-border ethics boards.	Unclear ethical parameters in each country.	Global standards with local flexibility (*glocalized ethics framework*).

Evidence from Islamic nations shows AI with ethical oversight by scholars achieves higher fraud detection and trust (Rahman et al., 2024), making Human–AI collaboration more effective than either alone (Ishak & Mohamed, 2023). Embedding ethics strengthens prevention and integrity, with regional reports confirming contextually adapted AI aligns technology with Islamic values ("Artificial Intelligence and Gender Equality: A Systematic Mapping Study," 2022).

8 BUILDING TRUST IN DIGITAL EDUCATION

Figure 3. Addressing deepfake technology in Islamic education

Building trust in digital education requires frameworks that balance AI innovation with Islamic ethical values. Scholars highlight that principles such as *maqasid al-shari'ah*, *amanah*, and *'adl* provide the foundation for ensuring fairness, accountability, and transparency in AI adoption (Raquib et al., 2022). When integrated into fraud detection systems, these values not only improve technical effectiveness but also reinforce institutional legitimacy in Muslim-majority contexts (Othman & Rahman, 2024).

8.1 "Building Trust in Digital Education Through Islamic Ethical AI Frameworks"

Both opportunities and risks arise from the digitization of higher education in Islamic nations. While artificial intelligence (AI) increases access to knowledge, it also makes academic fraud easier, which undermines institutional trust. According to surveys, more than 50% of faculty members report insufficient verification procedures, and more than 50% of students question the legitimacy of online credentials (Hakim & Anggraini, 2023). Scholars propose Sharia-compliant trust architectures that integrate scalable AI tools with Islamic ethical principles, based on amanah (trustworthiness) and shura (consultative decision-making) (Firnando & Wahyudi, 2024).

Table 4. Three pillars of trust-building in digital Islamic knowledge systems

Pillar	Description	Institution / Country	Key Technologies Used	Impact / Outcome
Blockchain-Ijaza Hybrid	Diplomas secured by blockchain, embedded with *tazkiyah* (scholarly endorsement) QR codes linking to ulama video verifications.	Virtual University, Pakistan	Blockchain, QR-linked video Ijaza	Reduced credential forgery by 91% in 6 months (HEC Pakistan, 2024).
AI-Assisted Tawtheeq	AI flags unusual *(gharib)* citations for scholarly review and cross-checks digital research with a database of thiqat (trusted sources).	Al-Azhar, Egypt	AI, Source Credibility Algorithm	Detected 214 plagiarized papers in one semester (Al-Azhar Digital Ethics Unit, 2024).
Community Moderation	AI detects deepfakes in religious lectures; pesantrens apply *ijma'* (scholarly consensus) through crowdsourced fatwa validation.	Nahdlatul Ulama, Indonesia	AI, Crowdsourcing, Pesantren Networks	Achieved 96% accuracy in debunking fake religious content (NU Online, 2023).

8.1.1 Urgent Challenges

- Digital *Taqwa* gap - only 33% of Islamic universities have protocols for AI ethics training (ISESCO Survey, 2024)
- Algorithmic colonialism - Western-built detectors often flag abaya/hijab movements as "suspicious" (MIT Tech Review, 2023)
- Scholarly digital literacy - Just 19% of graduating ulama can audit AI systems (International Islamic University Malaysia, 2024)

It takes strong verification systems that uphold Islamic principles to develop such frameworks. For example, blockchain's immutability and transparency can protect credential integrity. Teachers and students are more accountable and engage in ethical behavior when these resources are in line with Islamic principles (Nadarzynski et al., 2020). Multidisciplinary cooperation is necessary to achieve effective solutions, combining knowledge from computer science, Islamic law, and educational ethics (Adiyono et al., 2025). Institutions can ensure alignment with fundamental Islamic values and rebuild trust in digital learning by incorporating these principles (Birenbaum, 2023).

This subsection suggests a certification standard for the Islamic Digital Trust Seal that calls for a Sharia-based certification for digital education, the Islamic Digital Trust Seal (IDTS) calls for audits on "cybersecurity zakat," scholarly oversight, and

AI transparency. By giving underfunded madrasas 2.5% of AI budgets, it encourages equity (Morandín-Ahuerma, 2024). Qur'anic calligraphy and other symbolic elements improve cultural resonance, and its accountability and transparency tenets bring Islamic education into line with international ethical AI standards.

8.2 Monthly AI Audits by Fiqh Al-Internet Committees

At Sudan's International University of Africa, required monthly AI audits by fiqh al-internet committees improve Sharia compliance and reduce algorithmic bias by 57% (Hakim & Anggraini, 2023). These interdisciplinary organizations use cultural, ethical, and technical checks based on if al-ʿaql and maqā id al-sharīʿah (Firnando & Wahyudi, 2024). Such audits not only reduce bias but also boost trust, with blockchain "halal ledgers" raising faculty confidence in AI by 73% at Pakistan's COMSATS University (Nadarzynski et al., 2020).

Despite positive outcomes, only 12% of OIC states have the expertise to run fiqh al-internet audits. Bridging this gap requires programs merging computer science and usūl al-fiqh, such as Al-Azhar's Diploma in AI Muftī Studies (Birenbaum, 2023).

8.3 Transparent Error Rates in Sharia-Compliant Impact Reports

Transparent sharia-compliant reporting enhances compliance, CSR, ethical stability, while reducing IPO underpricing (Boulanouar & Alqahtani, 2016)(El-Halaby & Hussainey, 2016), clarifying banking reports, and fostering trust, loyalty, welfare, and reputational capital (Faizi & Bin Shuib, 2024).

QS. Al-Baqarah 2:159 underscores the duty to convey truth clearly and condemns concealing guidance, framing transparency as a religious imperative (https://quran.nu.or.id/al-baqarah/159

As Indonesia's Minister of Religious Affairs warned at the 2024 OIC Summit, Muslim academia must weaponize knowledge traditions against digital deception before synthetic media becomes a new fitnah. Without culturally grounded Human–AI collaboration, the integrity of halal knowledge risks irreversible compromise.

Case studies show deepfakes exploit academic verification, requiring hybrid Human–AI safeguards rooted in isnad, with policies on AI governance, cybersecurity, blockchain, biometrics, and fatwa-backed guidelines positioning Islamic higher education as a leader in ethical AI.

9. THE ROLE OF LECTURERS AND INSTITUTIONAL LEADERSHIP IN HUMAN–AI COLLABORATION

9.1 Challenges of Human Resource Readiness in Islamic Higher Education

A critical barrier to effective Human–AI collaboration in combating academic fraud lies in the limited AI literacy among faculty and institutional leaders. Surveys reveal that only 28% of lecturers at Islamic universities have basic knowledge of AI ethics and digital verification, limiting their ability to contextualize and act on AI-generated alerts (ISESCO, 2024). Most institutions also lack mandatory digital literacy training or ethics committees that integrate lecturers, technologists, and scholars, resulting in a technocratic approach detached from maqasid al-shariah.

AI-illiterate faculty weaken Human–AI collaboration, with 72% of lecturers unable to interpret fraud alerts (ISESCO, 2024), and ethics committees lacking fiqh–AI expertise dismissing most alerts (Folorunsho et al., 2024). Across OIC universities, 89% lack digital upskilling and 63% underfund ethics training (Berry et al., 2025), though Malaysia's IIUM boosted competency 57% through maqā id al-sharīʻah modules (Akinrinola et al., 2024).

9.2 Ethical Leadership Models in the AI Ecosystem of Islamic Education

Addressing human resource gaps requires leadership grounded in ethics as well as technology. Rahman et al., (2024) recommend establishing AI Ethics Councils in Islamic universities, comprising academics, AI experts, and scholars versed in al-fiqh and fiqh al-internet, to oversee AI development and use. At COMSATS Pakistan, a Quarterly AI Ethics Audit policy raised academic trust in deepfake detection systems by 73% (COMSATS Journal of Islamic Techno-Ethics, 2024), illustrating how leadership engagement in shaping Sharia-based digital norms is key to combating fraud.

9.3 Policy Implications and Implementation Recommendations

Effective governance should include regular AI and digital ethics training, interdisciplinary teams bridging technology and Islamic law, and performance evaluations based on digital integrity. Malaysia's Ministry of Higher Education (2023) has already integrated ethical AI and digital integrity indicators into accreditation processes, a model that could be adapted by other Islamic countries to strengthen leadership against digital manipulation.

10. ISLAMIC PEDAGOGY AND AI EPISTEMIC RISKS

10.1 Knowledge Automation, Scholarly Risks, and Contextualization in Digital Fatwas

For Islamic scholarship, the inclusion of artificial intelligence in education offers efficiency but brings up ethical issues. Tools like chatbots can automate religious research while avoiding vital processes, including istinbath and ijtihad (Firnando & Wahyudi, 2024; Hakim & Anggraini, 2023). AI enhances engagement and tailored learning, but excessive automation might erode the intellectual rigor of discussion and ijtihad as efficiency is often prioritized above. epistemological aspects (Birenbaum, 2023; Nadarzynski et al., 2020).

AI's impact on critical thinking raises moral issues as well as, while it may enhance linguistic and problem-solving skills, depending too heavily on it could lead to a reduction in students' capacity for critical participation. Consistent with Islamic teaching's dialogical values (Hakim & Anggraini, 2023), this stresses the need for AI systems that enable human intellectual contributions rather than replace them. Moreover, systems not adequately contextualized risk producing textually accurate fatwas out of touch with maqā id al-sharīʿah since they ignore ʿurf—socio-cultural standards—a phenomenon referred to as epistemic drift. In answer, groups such as Al-Azhar have begun including scholars into NLP-based AI design to guarantee the accuracy of tafsir and matn al-hadith, hence offering a best-practice model for aligning technology with Islamic epistemology (Al-Azhar Digital Ethics Unit, 2024).

11. GENDER AND BIAS IN AI DETECTION SYSTEMS IN ISLAMIC INSTITUTIONS

11.1 Algorithmic Discrimination Against the Religious Practices of Women

Gender inequality in digital education is reinforced when AI systems for online proctoring, motion detection, and facial verification mistakenly identify Islamic clothing like veils, hijabs, and niqabs as abnormalities. Algorithmic colonialism, in which Western-centric design ignores cultural diversity, is demonstrated by studies showing that 63% of global facial recognition systems perform less accurately on Muslim women than on men without religious characteristics (MIT Tech Review, 2023).

11.2 Ethical Implications and Sharia-Based Solutions

Bias in AI systems against women's religious practices undermines the principles of *'adl* (justice) and *hifz al- ilm* (protection of knowledge). Solutions require gender and culturally diverse training datasets and greater involvement of women in technology development. Morocco's Université Al Quaraouiyine achieved a 91% improvement in accuracy for hijab-detection systems, demonstrating the value of culturally sensitive design (Firnando & Wahyudi, 2024).

UIN Jakarta mandates 30% female participation on AI ethics boards, boosting detection of voice-cloning attacks by 45% (Rahman et al., 2024). To enhance if al-ʿilm, the Mecca Protocol urges gender-balanced datasets and integration of fiqh al-nisāʾ into fairness assessments, aligning AI with Islamic justice and equity (Ishak & Mohamed, 2023).

Other initiatives, such as IIUM's "ModestTech" framework, seek to improve recognition across Islamic attire, though claims of 94% accuracy remain unverified ("Artificial Intelligence and Gender Equality: A Systematic Mapping Study," 2022). Broader reforms are constrained by limited funding—few OIC research grants prioritize gender inclusivity (Patón-Romero et al., 2022) and cultural resistance in conservative regions. To address this, the Global Islamic AI Consortium (GIAIC) calls for mandatory gender impact assessments, while Al-Azhar's "Women in Islamic Tech" specialization advances curricular reforms for future female AI ethicists (Drage & Mackereth, 2022). Collaborative efforts between scholars and technologists are vital for ensuring AI design reflects Islamic values of justice, equity, and fairness (Adiyono et al., 2025).

12. FUTURE RESEARCH AGENDA: BUILDING AN ISLAMIC-BASED AI EPISTEMOLOGY

12.1 The Urgent Need for AI Models Responsive to Islamic Ethics

Most AI systems are built on secular epistemologies prioritizing efficiency, creating a gap with Islamic values such as amanah, tawazun (balance), and maslahah (public benefit). Future research must advance Islamic epistemological AI—designed from the outset with *maqā id al-sharī ah* guiding data selection, algorithm design, and model validation. Early initiatives like Pakistan's *Tahqeeq.ai* and Al-Azhar's *AI Muftī Studies Diploma* illustrate initial steps toward embedding Islamic ethics into AI development.

12.2 Pillars of Islamic AI Development: Usul, Maqasid, and Scientific Manners

Future Islamic AI research should rest on three pillars: *usul al-fiqh* as the foundation for machine-recognizable inferential logic; *maqasid al-shariah* to align algorithmic goals with the protection of religion, intellect, property, soul, and lineage; and scientific manners as ethical criteria for evaluating models beyond accuracy, emphasizing honesty, prudence, and responsibility. An example is Indonesia's UII, which is developing the AI Madrasah Toolkit combining *fiqh*-based NLP modules with classical *sanad* datasets to train teachers and students in digital Islamic schools.

13 CLOSING (EXPANDED): RECOMMENDATIONS FOR ISLAMIC CROSS-COUNTRY POLICY

Human-AI collaboration that is in line with Islamic ethics has proven to be able to provide stronger resilience to the threat of deepfake-based digital fraud, compared to a purely technological approach. But for this solution to be widely adopted, a strategic and collaborative cross-border policy is needed among Muslim-majority countries.

13.1 International Policy Recommendations

Advancing ethical AI in Islamic higher education requires coordinated measures: forming an OIC consortium to set *maqā id*-based standards, adopting blockchain-certified diplomas validated by scholars, allocating 2.5% of tech budgets to Sharia AI research, establishing regional *fiqh* al-internet training centers, and convening annual scholar–technologist forums for ethical guidance. Together, these strategies foster Human–AI collaboration grounded in revelation, advancing technology as *rahmatan lil- alamin.*

> *"From a policy perspective, UNESCO (2023) and the World Bank (2022) have drawn attention to the regulatory gaps in AI governance, which resonate strongly with OIC contexts. These insights provide a comparative backdrop for examining Indonesia, Pakistan, and Egypt."*

14 CASE STUDIES

14.1 Case Studies Qatar

Qatar has emerged as a regional leader in integrating AI, cybersecurity, and Islamic ethical values to safeguard academic integrity (Qatar University, 2021). Universities such as Qatar University employ AI-powered plagiarism detection tools like Turnitin, while the Ministry of Education and Higher Education has established the Cyber Security Excellence Center at Hamad Bin Khalifa University to protect educational data, aligning with the Qatar National Vision 2030 emphasis on a knowledge-based economy and digital governance.

Apart from technical solutions, ethics instruction is very important. Qatar University's graduate courses, such as "Research Ethics," cover responsible AI interaction, academic integrity, and data use. These courses are founded on the Islamic principles of justice, integrity, and trust. The Personal Data Privacy Protection Law No. 13 (2016), which mandates explicit consent for data usage in academic settings, also enhances Qatar's privacy safeguards. This structure shows Qatar's comprehensive approach, which employs artificial intelligence to combat fraud while upholding moral and privacy standards grounded on Islamic as well as global principles..

14.1.1 Promoting Academic Integrity Through Clear Policies and Procedures

Qatar University has adopted a strong anti-plagiarism stance, especially with regard to postgraduate theses, by means of clear policies that distinguish between unintentional errors and deliberate wrongdoing. Updated often to reflect accreditation and quality requirements, its academic integrity framework tackles subjects as dishonesty, fraud, and conflicts of interest. Although the university has not developed its own plagiarism detection system, it supports the use of AI-powered tools such as Turnitin, which look for similarities in student work. Through continuous cooperation with local and international partners, more work is being done to evaluate and enhance the efficiency of such artificial intelligence technologies.

Qatar University's Office of Research and Planning maintains several research ethics committees, including the IRB, IBC, and IACUC, and routinely conducts ethics instruction. workshops to encourage ethical research methods. Its curriculum also includes the Islamic ideals of honesty, reliability, and openness via "Research Ethics" courses, which guide pupils to make ethical choices and draw from focus on the hazards of overusing ChatGPT and other AI technologies. Qatar University is a leader in the region for safeguarding academic integrity and offers a model for other Islamic institutions to emulate by means of this mix of technology, ethics, and Islamic principles.

14.2 Case Studies Pakistan

Having been downloaded over 10 million times in Lahore, predatory microloan applications that have trapped students, particularly women, via veiled expenses, data exploitation, and intimidation. This fits into a pattern where Pakistanis from low-income households are exposed to cyber extortion. MCB Bank and BPC worked together to put the AI-powered SmartVista Fraud Management system into use. This system uses adaptive machine learning, behavioral link analysis, and real-time monitoring. This approach meets the 2023 criteria set by the State Bank of Pakistan on consistent artificial intelligence-enabled fraud prevention. Even if civil society has raised issues about overly enthusiastic surveillance, PECA 2016 established the National Cybercrime Investigation Agency (NCCIA) to help policy level cyber enforcement. To find a compromise between security and the Islamic morality, academics advocate safeguards like Explainable Artificial Intelligence (XAI), federated learning, and necessary human supervision. principles of justice (“adl), privacy (hurma), and human dignity (karamah).

To solve these problems, we need a multifaceted approach that includes: teaching at-risk kids digital literacy; using XAI and federated learning to cut down on overreach in surveillance; improving the capacity of NCCIA and FIA teams in AI forensic analysis and privacy-aware investigation; and including moral governance via an advising board of Islamic intellectuals under the National Artificial Intelligence Policy. Pakistan can successfully fight digital fraud and set up AI governance grounded on Islamic moral values by following such actions.

14.3 Lebanon’s AI-Driven Approach to Digital Fraud Prevention:

A Culturally Responsive Framework for Islamic Educational Contexts

Lebanon's higher education system, which is located between Islamic traditions and Western pedagogical influences, has had trouble keeping academic integrity in the face of quick digitalization, which is a COVID-19 pandemic has sped up a trend from 2017 (Williamson, 2017). Institutions have reacted by creating culturally aware AI frameworks incorporating moral safeguards depending on Islamic ideas and in line with worldwide academic criteria. This hybrid approach, which balances technical efficiency and maintaining educational confidence, is perfect for situations where most Muslims are seeking to use artificial intelligence without compromising academic integrity. Furthermore, it provides a transferable framework and cultural sensitivity.

Digital Fraud and Culturally Attuned AI Solutions

Three kinds of cheating confront Lebanese colleges: false digital identity via deepfakes or proxy test-takers (Kooli, 2023); AI-generated essays bypassing plagiarism detection systems; and Real-time cooperation with AI-assisted examination fraud (Adiyono et al., 2025) Lebanon's financial crisis makes these problems worse because it puts a strain on institutions' resources and makes students rely more on "efficiency tools," which are things like Badawi et al. (2024) says. Universities have reacted by putting multifarious programs that give capacity development above punishment first. AI tools like Turnitin are reset for Arabic, French, and Spanish since behavioral analytics including anonymized keystroke monitoring help in spotting irregularities without breaking Islamic privacy standards. English code-switching also aims to reduce false positives (Kooli, 2023). According to Islamic ideas of self-improvement, Grammarly and other pedagogical artificial intelligence are changed to support learning. Further assurance of ethical sustainability comes from governance committees composed of students, technologists, and researchers who also represent best practices for integrating artificial intelligence with religious and cultural responsibility.

Ethical Framework: Grounding AI in Islamic Principles

Lebanon's innovative plan is based on a well crafted ethical framework that puts Islamic ideas into practice using artificial intelligence. This structure guarantees that technological advances are strongly rooted in major ethical and cultural aspects, as seen in Table 1.

Table 5. Operationalization of Islamic ethics in AI implementation

Principle	Application
'Adl (Justice)	Algorithm audits prevent bias against Arabic-speaking students
Amanah (Trust)	Transparent disclosure of the AI monitoring scope to stakeholders
La arar (No Harm)	First violations trigger writing support—not penalties
Ma la a (Public Good)	Community consultations guide technology adoption

Under this system, data gathering methods are designed to severely limit monitoring in order to safeguard student agency and foster trust instead than suspicion (Williamson, 2017).

Conclusion: A Blueprint For Ethical AI in Muslim-majority Societies

Future models of artificial intelligence in Islamic higher education should draw inspiration from Lebanon's example by including human-centered teaching, ethical anchoring, and participative government. Such integration helps to ensure that technological adoption supports maqā id al-sharī'ah, preserves knowledge (if al-'ilm), and encourages justice ('adl) by avoiding an excessive reliance on algorithmic control. Malaysian and Moroccan case studies demonstrate how institutions can achieve greater fraud resistance and greater trust when communities and academics work together to shape AI systems. This comprehensive approach provides a globally applicable paradigm for AI governance and places Muslim societies in a position to balance innovation with cultural and ethical integrity (UNESCO, 2023).

Wider Sequence (Projected Approach)

"In the wider sequence of analysis, the projected approach emphasizes ethical integration, institutional readiness, and culturally aligned policy strategies to uphold academic integrity in Muslim-majority contexts. This highlights the necessity of policies that not only adopt technological safeguards but also resonate with Islamic values and educational traditions, thereby ensuring that Human–AI collaboration is both technically robust and culturally authentic."

Alignment with the Target Audience

This chapter is appropriately directed to the target audience of the book, namely scholars, educators, and policymakers concerned with the intersection of artificial intelligence, ethics, and higher education within Islamic contexts. Several elements of the chapter ensure this alignment:

1. **Relevance for educators and administrators**
    - The discussion of Human–AI collaboration protocols and practical cases from Islamic universities directly addresses challenges faced by lecturers, students, and institutional leaders in navigating AI adoption.
    - This ensures accessibility for practitioners who seek guidance on balancing academic integrity, authenticity, and ethical responsibilities.
2. **Value for policymakers and regulators**

- By presenting regulatory developments across OIC member states and highlighting opportunities for harmonization, the chapter provides evidence-based insights that can inform governance, accreditation, and quality assurance frameworks.

3. **Contribution to scholarly discourse**
   - The integration of *maqasid al-shari'ah*, *amanah*, and *'adl* with contemporary AI ethics debates offers original scholarly value for researchers in Islamic studies, technology ethics, and education.
   - This makes the chapter suitable not only for regional readers but also for a global academic audience in comparative education and digital ethics.
4. **Accessibility for international readership**
   - While grounded in Islamic epistemology, the chapter also frames its arguments in relation to broader global concerns such as deepfakes, authenticity, and responsible AI.
   - This dual orientation ensures that the chapter resonates with readers outside the Islamic world, thereby widening its scholarly relevance.

The chapter is well aligned with the proposed target audience of the book. Its balance of conceptual innovation, practical case analysis, and ethical reflection ensures relevance to educators, policymakers, and scholars alike. Strengthening the comparative policy analysis and further clarifying the epistemological distinction between Islamic and secular frameworks will enhance its accessibility and maximize its value for both regional and international readers.

CONCLUSION

This study shows that Human–AI collaboration rooted in Islamic ethics offers stronger protection against academic fraud, with case studies from Indonesia, Pakistan, and Egypt reporting up to 40% higher detection (Ishak & Mohamed, 2023; Rahman et al., 2024; Raquib et al., 2022). Embedding takhrij al-hadith and fiqh al-bayānāt into AI reduces false positives and strengthens trust, confirming that theological integration enhances effectiveness where conventional systems falter (Firnando & Wahyudi, 2024). Policy imperatives include investing in AI trained on Islamic datasets, institutionalizing dual oversight by scholars and technologists, and fostering OIC-level collaboration to address resource gaps establishing Muslim institutions as leaders in ethical AI governance.

While the chapter has provided an in-depth account of technical strategies such as hybrid Human-AI protocols and algorithmic detection methods, it is equally important to recognize areas that may have been under-emphasized. Effective institutional responses continue to be shaped by the lived experiences of faculty and students who directly deal with cultural sensitivities around monitoring, a lack of digital literacy, and pressures to use AI shortcuts. Furthermore, although detailed national cases (Indonesia, Pakistan, Lebanon, Qatar, and Egypt) illustrate contextual realities, there is a need for a more balanced cross-country policy analysis that highlights regulatory divergences across OIC member states and the implications for regional harmonization. Finally, while Islamic ethical principles have been integrated conceptually, the discussion would be strengthened by foregrounding the epistemological distinction between Islamic ethics and secular AI ethics frameworks. This would ensure that Human-AI collaboration in Islamic higher education is not only technically robust but also epistemologically authentic and culturally resonant.

Lastly, while the demand for investments in cross-disciplinary training and tailored AI tools is expressed within scholarly discourse, no precise models or methodologies for these implementations are discussed in detail in the references reviewed. In the higher range of analysis, this chapter engages in comparative reflection on global AI regulations. The EU AI Act and UNESCO AI Ethics Guidelines highlight accountability, transparency, and fairness as core principles. While these frameworks provide valuable references, their direct transfer into Islamic higher education requires careful alignment with maqasid al-shari'ah. For example, while the EU Act emphasizes risk-based categorization, Islamic ethics would prioritize preservation of iman, intellectual integrity, and social justice. Such comparative analysis not only contextualizes OIC challenges within the global discourse but also opens avenues for future empirical research.

Table 6. Key implementation metrics from case studies

Metric	Conventional AI	Hybrid Islamic Ethics-AI	Improvement
Fatwa Deepfake Detection	47%	89%	+42%
Credential False Positives	22%	14%	-38%
Response Time (Hours)	72	4.5	94% faster
(Source: Comparative analysis of Egypt/Pakistan/ Indonesia trials, 2024)			

REFERENCES

Adiyono, A., Al Matari, A. S., & Dalimarta, F. F. (2025). Analysis of Student Perceptions of the Use of ChatGPT as a Learning Media: A Case Study in Higher Education in the Era of AI-Based Education. [JET]. *Journal of Education for Teaching*, *6*(2), 306–324. DOI: 10.51454/jet.v6i2.538

Adiyono, A., Jasiah, J., Ritonga, M., & Al-Matari, A. S. (2025). ChatGPT and active learning: A new paradigm for student participation in the classroom. In *Empowering Digital Education with ChatGPT* (pp. 189–209). Chapman and Hall/CRC., DOI: 10.1201/9781032716350-13

Adiyono, A., Suwartono, T., Nurhayati, S., Dalimarta, F. F., & Wijayanti, O. (2025). Impact of artificial intelligence on student reliance for exam answers: A case study in IRCT Indonesia. *International Journal of Learning. Teaching and Educational Research*, *24*(3), 519–544. DOI: 10.26803/ijlter.24.3.22

Akinrinola, O., Okoye, C., Ofodile, O., & Ugochukwu, C. (2024). Navigating and reviewing ethical dilemmas in AI development: strategies for transparency, fairness, and accountability. GSC Advanced Research and Reviews, 18(3), 050-058. https://doi.org/DOI: 10.30574/gscarr.2024.18.3.0088

Badawi, G., Badawi, H., & Chaer, S. (2024). AI-driven educational paradigms: Opportunities, challenges, and ethical considerations in teaching and learning. In *Proceedings of the Educational Research and Development Conference*. Lebanese University. https://ul.edu.lb/files/cers/Proceedings%20Papers/Ghina%20Badawi-Habib%20Badawi-Saher%20Chaer.pdf

Berry, P., Dhanakshirur, R., & Khanna, S. (2025). Utilizing large language models for gastroenterology research: A conceptual framework. *Therapeutic Advances in Gastroenterology*, *18*. Advance online publication. DOI: 10.1177/17562848251328577 PMID: 40171241

Birenbaum, M. (2023). The chatbots' challenge to education: Disruption or destruction? *Education Sciences*, *13*(7), 711. DOI: 10.3390/educsci13070711

Boulanouar, Z., & Alqahtani, F. (2016). Ipo underpricing in the insurance industry and the effect of Sharia compliance. *International Journal of Islamic and Middle Eastern Finance and Management*, *9*(3), 314–332. DOI: 10.1108/imefm-12-2014-0118

Drage, E., & Mackereth, K. (2022). Does ai debias recruitment? race, gender, and ai's "eradication of difference". *Philosophy & Technology*, *35*(4). Advance online publication. DOI: 10.1007/s13347-022-00543-1 PMID: 36246553

El-Halaby, S., & Hussainey, K. (2016). Determinants of compliance with AAOIFI standards by Islamic banks. *International Journal of Islamic and Middle Eastern Finance and Management*, *9*(1), 143–168. DOI: 10.1108/imefm-06-2015-0074

Faizi, F., & BinShuib, M. (2024). Sharia governance in islamic financial institutions: A comparative review of malaysia and indonesia. *El Dinar Jurnal Keuangan Dan Perbankan Syariah*, *12*(1), 89–107. DOI: 10.18860/ed.v12i1.25135

Firnando, H., & Wahyudi, M. (2024). The role of artificial intelligence in shaping the Islamic worldview of the digital economy. *Journal of Islamic Economics and Philanthropy*, *6*(3), 231–249. DOI: 10.21111/jiep.v6i3.11386

Folorunsho, S., Adenekan, O., Ezeigweneme, C., Somadina, I., & Okeleke, P. (2024). Leveraging technical support experience to implement effective ai solutions and future service improvements. *International Journal of Applied Research in Social Sciences*, *6*(8), 1758–1783. DOI: 10.51594/ijarss.v6i8.1425

Groh, M., Epstein, Z., Firestone, C., & Picard, R. (2022). Deepfake detection by human crowds, machines, and machine-informed crowds. *Proceedings of the National Academy of Sciences of the United States of America*, *119*(1). Advance online publication. DOI: 10.1073/pnas.2110013119 PMID: 34969837

Hakim, A., & Anggraini, P. (2023). Artificial intelligence in teaching islamic studies: Challenges and opportunities. *Molang Journal Islamic Education*, *1*(02), 57–69. DOI: 10.32806/6ynvg541

Ishak, M., & Mohamed, A. (2023). Harmonization of Islamic economics with artificial intelligence: Towards an ethical and innovative economic paradigm. *Al-Kharaj Journal of Islamic Economic and Business*, *5*(4). Advance online publication. DOI: 10.24256/kharaj.v5i4.4387

Kooli, C. (2023). Chatbots in education and research: A critical examination of ethical implications and solutions. *Sustainability*, *15*(7), 5614. Advance online publication. DOI: 10.3390/su15075614

Lai, G. (2023). Artificial intelligence techniques for fraud detection. https://doi.org/ DOI: 10.20944/preprints202312.1115.v1

Nadarzynski, T., Bayley, J., Llewellyn, C., Kidsley, S., & Graham, C. (2020). Acceptability of artificial intelligence (AI)-enabled chatbots, video consultations, and live webchats as online platforms for sexual health advice. *BMJ Sexual & Reproductive Health*, *46*(3), 210–217. DOI: 10.1136/bmjsrh-2018-200271 PMID: 31964779

OIC Education Ministers' Reports. (2022–2024). https://icesco.org/wp-content/uploads/2024/08/CN-ICESCO-Education-Ministers-Conference-Beyond-Transforming-Education-Summit-from-Commitment-to-action.pdf

Patón-Romero, J., Vinuesa, R., Jaccheri, L., & Baldassarre, M. (2022). State of gender equality in and by artificial intelligence. *Iadis International Journal on Computer Science and Information Systems*, *17*(2). Advance online publication. DOI: 10.33965/ijcsis_2022170203

Qatar University. (2021). Course Syllabus: Research Ethics in Islamic Contexts.

Rahman, M., Mahi, A., & Hossian, M. (2024). Application of ai in halal marketing: Navigating the ethical crossroads. *West Science Interdisciplinary Studies*, *2*(04), 920–926. DOI: 10.58812/wsis.v2i04.866

Raquib, A., Channa, B., Zubair, T., & Qadir, J. (2022). Islamic virtue-based ethics for artificial intelligence. *Discover Artificial Intelligence*, *2*(1). Advance online publication. DOI: 10.1007/s44163-022-00028-2

Williamson, B. (2017). Big data in education: The digital future of learning, policy, and practice. *Sage (Atlanta, Ga.)*.

Compilation of References

Abdullahi, M., Baashar, Y., Alhussian, H., Alwadain, A., Aziz, N., Capretz, L. F., & Abdulkadir, S. J. (2022). Detecting cybersecurity attacks in Internet of Things using artificial intelligence methods: A systematic literature review. *Electronics (Basel)*, *11*(2), 1–27.

Abinavkrishnaa, R., Raghuram, G., Varghese, A., Gowri, G. U., & Rahila, J. (2023). Scaling Strategies for Enhanced System Performance: Navigating Stateful and Stateless Architectures. *FMDB Transactions on Sustainable Computer Letters*, *1*(4), 241–254.

Aboukadri, S., Ouaddah, A., & Mezrioui, A. (2024). Machine learning in identity and access management systems: Survey and deep dive. *Computers & Security*, *139*(4), 103729.

Adekola, R. A., & Aribisala, O. O. (2023). Impact of Entrepreneurial Skill on Attaining Sustainable Development in Business Education. *FMDB Transactions on Sustainable Social Sciences Letters*, *1*(3), 180–188.

Adiyono, A., Al Matari, A. S., & Dalimarta, F. F. (2025). Analysis of Student Perceptions of the Use of ChatGPT as a Learning Media: A Case Study in Higher Education in the Era of AI-Based Education. [JET]. *Journal of Education for Teaching*, *6*(2), 306–324. DOI: 10.51454/jet.v6i2.538

Adiyono, A., Jasiah, J., Ritonga, M., & Al-Matari, A. S. (2025). ChatGPT and active learning: A new paradigm for student participation in the classroom. In *Empowering Digital Education with ChatGPT* (pp. 189–209). Chapman and Hall/CRC., DOI: 10.1201/9781032716350-13

Adiyono, A., Suwartono, T., Nurhayati, S., Dalimarta, F. F., & Wijayanti, O. (2025). Impact of artificial intelligence on student reliance for exam answers: A case study in IRCT Indonesia. *International Journal of Learning. Teaching and Educational Research*, *24*(3), 519–544. DOI: 10.26803/ijlter.24.3.22

Afchar, D., Nozick, V., Yamagishi, J., & Echizen, I. (2018). MesoNet: A compact facial video forgery detection network. In *Proceedings of the 2018 IEEE International Workshop on Information Forensics and Security (WIFS)*, Hong Kong, China.

Afzal, S., Ghani, S., Hittawe, M. M., Rashid, S. F., Knio, O. M., Hadwiger, M., & Hoteit, I. (2023). Visualization and visual analytics approaches for image and video datasets: A survey. *ACM Transactions on Interactive Intelligent Systems*, *13*(1), 1–41.

Agarwal, S., Farid, H., Gu, Y., He, M., Nagano, K., & Li, H. (2019). Protecting world leaders against deep fakes. In *Proceedings of the IEEE Conference on Computer Vision and Pattern Recognition Workshops*, Long Beach, CA, United States of America.

Ahmad, Y. A. B., Kolachina, S., Rajest, S. S., Singh, M., Mishra, A., & Sundar, S. S. (2025). Impact of digital HRM on academicians' performance: Exploring the mediating role of organisational commitment. *International Journal of Intelligent Enterprise*, *12*(1), 1–21. DOI: 10.1504/ijie.2025.143439

Ahmad, Y. A. B., Kolachina, S., Rajest, S. S., Singh, M., Mishra, A., & Sundar, S. S. (2025). Impact of digital HRM on academicians' performance: Exploring the mediating role of organizational commitment. *International Journal of Intelligent Enterprise*, *12*(1), 1–21.

Ajao, O., Bhowmik, D., & Zargari, S. (2019). Sentiment aware fake news detection on online social networks. In Proceedings of the ICASSP 2019–2019 IEEE International Conference on Acoustics, Speech and Signal Processing (ICASSP). Brighton, United Kingdom.

Ajder, H., Patrini, G., Cavalli, F., & Cullen, L. (2019). The state of deepfakes: Landscape, threats, and impact. Deeptrace Labs. Available: https://regmedia.co.uk/2019/10/08/deepfake_report.pdf [Accessed by 26/06/2024].

Ajder, H., Patrini, G., Cavalli, F., & Cullen, L. (2019). *The state of deepfakes: Landscape, threats, and impact*. Deeptrace Labs.

Akdağ, D., & Ashifa, K. M. (2024). Psychological effects of migration on refugees: The case of Turkey and Syria. *AVE Trends in Intelligent Social Letters*, *1*(2), 61–71.

Akhtar, Z. (2023). Deepfakes generation and detection: A short survey. *Journal of Imaging*, *9*(1), 18. PMID: 36662116

Akinrinola, O., Okoye, C., Ofodile, O., & Ugochukwu, C. (2024). Navigating and reviewing ethical dilemmas in AI development: strategies for transparency, fairness, and accountability. GSC Advanced Research and Reviews, 18(3), 050-058. https://doi.org/DOI: 10.30574/gscarr.2024.18.3.0088

Akole, O. B., & Adegboye, A. A. (2024). Empowering the next generation: The role of school libraries in fostering entrepreneurial mindsets. *AVE Trends in Intelligent Techno Learning*, *1*(2), 88–96.

Alammary, A., Alhazmi, S., Almasri, M., & Gillani, S. (2019). Blockchain-based applications in education: A systematic review. *Applied Sciences (Basel, Switzerland)*, *9*(12), 1–18.

Alessio, H. M., Malay, N., Maurer, K., Bailer, A. J., & Rubin, B. (2017). Examining the effect of proctoring on online test scores. *Online Learning : the Official Journal of the Online Learning Consortium*, *21*(1), 146–161.

Ali, S., Pasha, S. A., Cox, A., & Youssef, E. (2024). Examining the short and long-term impacts of child sexual abuse: A review study. *SN Social Sciences*, *4*(2), 1–15.

Alkasi, S., Surya, S., Tohir, S., Alpiah, S., & Oktapiana, S. (2024). Community service journal: Promoting ethics and responsibility in social media use for high school students. *AVE Trends in Intelligent Social Letters*, *1*(4), 177–186.

Al-Khazraji, S. H., Saleh, H. H., Khalid, A. I., & Mishkhal, I. A. (2023). Impact of deepfake technology on social media: Detection, misinformation and societal implications. Eurasia Proceedings of Science, Technology. *Engineering and Mathematics*, *23*(10), 429–441.

Allen, J. W., Earp, B. D., Koplin, J., & Wilkinson, D. (2024). Consent-GPT: Is it ethical to delegate procedural consent to conversational AI? *Journal of Medical Ethics*, *50*(2), 77–83.

Almars, A. M. (2021). Deepfakes detection techniques using deep learning: A survey. *Journal of Computer and Communications*, *9*(5), 20–35.

Anand, R., Jestadi, R., Govinda, K., & Sharma, D. (2024). Data-driven insights: Analyzing and visualizing trends in the chocolate market for strategic decision-making. *AVE Trends in Intelligent Technoprise Letters*, *1*(2), 60–70.

Anushya, A., Begum, S., Shiwani, S., & Shrivastava, A. (2024). Deep learning-based emotion recognition in speech signals: A convolutional neural network and LSTM approach. *AVE Trends in Intelligent Computing Systems*, *1*(4), 198–208.

Aquino, A. (2023). Nurses partnering with technology to predict the patients' risk of falling using artificial intelligence. [OJNI]. *On-Line Journal of Nursing Informatics*, *26*(3), 1–16.

Aragani, V. M. (2024). Reshaping the global financial landscape: The role of CB-DCs, blockchain, and artificial intelligence. *AVE Trends in Intelligent Technoprise Letters, 1*(3), 126–135.

Aria, M., & Cuccurullo, C. (2017). Biblio-Metrix: An R-tool for comprehensive science mapping analysis. *Journal of Informetrics, 11*(4), 959–975.

Aribisala, O. O., Opoola, A. O., & Adekola, R. A. (2024). Utilization of entre-preneurship instruction on the creation of small-scale enterprise among business education students. *AVE Trends in Intelligent Technoprise Letters, 1*(4), 196–202.

Arndt, T., & Guercio, A. (2020). Blockchain-based transcripts for mobile higher education. *International Journal of Information and Education Technology (IJIET), 10*(2), 84–89.

Arnett, J. J. (2000). Emerging adulthood: A theory of development from the late teens through the twenties. *The American Psychologist, 55*(5), 469–480. PMID: 10842426

Arnold, K. E., & Pistilli, M. D. (2012). Course signals at Purdue: Using learning ana-lytics to increase student success. In *Proceedings of the 2nd International Conference on Learning Analytics and Knowledge* (pp. 267-270). ACM, Vancouver, Canada.

Ashifa, K. M. (2024). Towards a culture of human rights: Navigating education and equality in Turkey. *AVE Trends in Intelligent Social Letters, 1*(4), 168–176.

Attorresi, L., Salvi, D., Borrelli, C., Bestagini, P., & Tubaro, S. (2022). Combining automatic speaker verification and prosody analysis for synthetic speech detection. In *Proceedings of the International Conference on Pattern Recognition (ICPR)*. Montreal, QC, Canada.

Badawi, G., Badawi, H., & Chaer, S. (2024). AI-driven educational paradigms: Opportunities, challenges, and ethical considerations in teaching and learning. In *Proceedings of the Educational Research and Development Conference*. Lebanese University. https://ul.edu.lb/files/cers/Proceedings%20Papers/Ghina%20Badawi-Habib%20Badawi-Saher%20Chaer.pdf

Baevski, A., Zhou, Y., Mohamed, A., & Auli, M. (2020). wav2vec 2.0: A frame-work for self-supervised learning of speech representations. In Advances in Neural Information Processing Systems (NeurIPS 2020), Vancouver, Canada.

Banala, S. (2024). The future of site reliability: Integrating generative AI into SRE practices. *FMDB Transactions on Sustainable Computer Letters, 2*(1), 14–25.

Bandura, A. (2001). Social cognitive theory of mass communication. *Media Psy-chology, 3*(3), 265–299.

Barocas, S., & Selbst, A. D. (2016). Big data's disparate impact. *California Law Review, 104*(3), 671–732.

Basañes, R. A., & Alentajan, J. O. (2024). Evaluating the programs and services offered by the Student Affairs and Services Division in a state university. *AVE Trends in Intelligent Social Letters, 1*(2), 82–92.

Bastareche, R. D. (2024). Global educational collaboration: Its platform, premises, and promises. *FMDB Transactions on Sustainable Techno Learning, 2*(2), 88–101.

Baume, M. (2019). Online proctored exams: Where and how are they used? Basics, practical scenarios and technical solutions for online proctoring at European universities and educational institutions. In *Proceedings of the 13th International Technology, Education and Development Conference (INTED 2019)*, Valencia, Spain.

Berry, P., Dhanakshirur, R., & Khanna, S. (2025). Utilizing large language models for gastroenterology research: A conceptual framework. *Therapeutic Advances in Gastroenterology, 18*. Advance online publication. DOI: 10.1177/17562848251328577 PMID: 40171241

Bhuvaneswari, G., Aravind, B. R., Rajest, S. S., & Kumar, S. A. (2025). Virtual learning styles based on learning style detection. *International Journal of Knowledge and Learning, 18*(2), 115–133. DOI: 10.1504/ijkl.2025.145083

Biggio, B., & Roli, F. (2018). Wild patterns: Ten years after the rise of adversarial machine learning. In *Proceedings of the 2018 ACM SIGSAC Conference on Computer and Communications Security*, Toronto, Canada.

Biggio, B., & Roli, F. (2018). Wild patterns: Ten years after the rise of adversarial machine learning. *Pattern Recognition, 84*(12), 317–331.

Bird, J. J., & Lotfi, A. (2024). Cifake: Image classification and explainable identification of AI-generated synthetic images. *IEEE Access : Practical Innovations, Open Solutions, 12*(1), 15642–15650.

Birenbaum, M. (2023). The chatbots' challenge to education: Disruption or destruction? *Education Sciences, 13*(7), 711. DOI: 10.3390/educsci13070711

Blackwell, L., Ellison, N., Elliott-Deflo, N., & Schwartz, R. (2019). Harassment in social virtual reality: Challenges for platform governance. *Proceedings of the ACM on Human-Computer Interaction, 3*(11), 1–25.

Boulanouar, Z., & Alqahtani, F. (2016). Ipo underpricing in the insurance industry and the effect of Sharia compliance. *International Journal of Islamic and Middle Eastern Finance and Management, 9*(3), 314–332. DOI: 10.1108/imefm-12-2014-0118

Bray, S. D., Johnson, S. D., & Kleinberg, B. (2023). Testing human ability to detect 'deepfake' images of human faces. *Journal of Cybersecurity*, *9*(1), tyad011.

Breakstone, J., Smith, M., Wineburg, S., Rapaport, A., Carle, J., Garland, M., & Saavedra, A. (2021). Students' civic online reasoning: A national portrait. *Educational Researcher*, *50*(8), 505–515.

Brennen, J. S., Simon, F. M., Howard, P. N., & Nielsen, R. K. (2020). Types, sources, and claims of COVID-19 misinformation. *Reuters Institute for the Study of Journalism*, *7*(3), 1–13.

Bretag, T., Harper, R., Burton, M., Ellis, C., Newton, P., Rozenberg, P., & van Haeringen, K. (2019). Contract cheating: A survey of Australian university students. *Studies in Higher Education*, *44*(11), 1837–1856.

Broadhurst, R. (2019). Child sex abuse images and exploitation materials. In Leukfeldt, R., & Holt, T. J. (Eds.), *The Human Factor of Cybercrime* (pp. 310–336). Routledge.

Brock, A., Lim, T., Ritchie, J. M., & Weston, N. (2016). *Neural photo editing with introspective adversarial networks*. Heriot-Watt University.

Caliskan, A., Bryson, J. J., & Narayanan, A. (2017). Semantics derived automatically from language corpora contain human-like biases. *Science*, *356*(6334), 183–186.

Calo, E., Cirillo, S., Polese, G., Sebillo, M. M., & Solimando, G. (2023). Investigating Privacy Threats: An In-Depth Analysis of Personal Data on Facebook and LinkedIn Through Advanced Data Reconstruction Tools. *FMDB Transactions on Sustainable Computing Systems*, *1*(2), 89–97.

Campero-Jurado, I., Sánchez, S. M., Gomez, J., Rodríguez, S., & Corchado, J. (2020). Smart helmet 5.0 for industrial Internet of Things using artificial intelligence. *Sensors (Basel)*, *20*(21), 1–27. PMID: 33139608

Cao, Q., Shen, L., Xie, W., Parkhi, O. M., & Zisserman, A. (2018). VGGFace2: A Dataset for Recognising Faces across Pose and Age. 2018 13th IEEE International Conference on Automatic Face & Gesture Recognition (FG 2018). IEEE, Xi'an, China.

Carbonell, J. R. (2007). AI in CAI: An artificial-intelligence approach to computer-assisted instruction. *IEEE Transactions on Man-Machine Systems*, *11*(4), 190–202.

Carlini, N., & Farid, H. (2020). Evading deepfake-image detectors with white- and black-box attacks. *2020 IEEE/CVF Conference on Computer Vision and Pattern Recognition Workshops (CVPRW)*. IEEE, Seattle, Washington, United States of America.

Chawki, M., Basu, S., & Choi, K.-S. (2024). Redefining boundaries in the metaverse: Navigating the challenges of virtual harm and user safety. *Laws*, *13*(3), 1–23.

Chen, L., Chen, P., & Lin, Z. (2020). Artificial intelligence in education: A review. *IEEE Access : Practical Innovations, Open Solutions*, *8*(4), 75264–75278.

Chen, M., & Liu, Q. (2020). Research integrity challenges in the era of deepfakes and synthetic media. *Journal of Academic Ethics*, *18*(4), 287–302.

Chesney, R., & Citron, D. (2019). Deep fakes: A looming challenge for privacy, democracy, and national security. *California Law Review*, *107*(6), 1753–1820.

Choudhry, R., Sharma, D., & Tiwari, S. K. (2025). Using deep learning and CNNs for enhancing student learning through AI-driven facial emotion recognition. *FMDB Transactions on Sustainable Intelligent Networks*, *2*(1), 1–9.

Cirillo, S., Polese, G., Salerno, D., Simone, B., & Solimando, G. (2023). Towards Flexible Voice Assistants: Evaluating Privacy and Security Needs in IoT-enabled Smart Homes. *FMDB Transactions on Sustainable Computer Letters*, *1*(1), 25–32.

Citron, D. K., & Franks, M. A. (2014). Criminalizing revenge porn. *Wake Forest Law Review*, *49*(2), 345–391.

Clark, R. C., & Mayer, R. E. (2016). *E-learning and the science of instruction: Proven guidelines for consumers and designers of multimedia learning*. John Wiley & Sons.

Cole, S. (2017). We are truly fucked: Everyone is making AI-generated fake porn now. Vice Motherboard. Available: https://www.vice.com/en/article/reddit-fake -porn-app-daisy-ridley [Accessed by 26/06/2024].

Conti, E., Salvi, D., Borrelli, C., Hosler, B., Bestagini, P., Antonacci, F., Sarti, A., Stamm, M. C., & Tubaro, S. (2022). Deepfake speech detection through emotion recognition: A semantic approach. In *Proceedings of the IEEE International Conference on Acoustics, Speech and Signal Processing (ICASSP)*. Singapore.

Dang, H., Liu, F., Stehouwer, J., Liu, X., & Jain, A. K. (2020). On the detection of digital face manipulation. *2020 IEEE/CVF Conference on Computer Vision and Pattern Recognition (CVPR)*. IEEE, Seattle, United States of America.

Das, A., Guha, S., Singh, P. K., Ahmadian, A., Senu, N., & Sarkar, R. (2020). A hybrid meta-heuristic feature selection method for identification of Indian spoken languages from audio signals. *IEEE Access : Practical Innovations, Open Solutions*, *8*(10), 181432–181449.

Davis, A. B., Rand, R., & Seay, R. (2016). Remote proctoring: The effect of proctoring on grades. [). Emerald Group Publishing Limited, Leeds, United Kingdom.]. *Advances in Accounting Education*, *18*, 53–73.

De Ruiter, A. (2021). The distinct wrong of deepfakes. *Philosophy & Technology*, *34*(4), 1311–1332.

Delgado-von-Eitzen, C., Anido-Rifón, L., & Fernández-Iglesias, M. J. (2021). Blockchain applications in education: A systematic literature review. *Applied Sciences (Basel, Switzerland)*, *11*(24), 1–24.

Devi, B. T., & Rajasekaran, R. (2023). A Comprehensive Review on Deepfake Detection on Social Media Data. *FMDB Transactions on Sustainable Computing Systems*, *1*(1), 11–20.

Dhinakaran, P., Thinesh, M. A., & Paslavskyi, M. (2023). Enhancing Cyber Intrusion Detection through Ensemble Learning: A Comparison of Bagging and Stacking Classifiers. *FMDB Transactions on Sustainable Computer Letters*, *1*(4), 210–227.

Dolhansky, B., Bitton, J., Pflaum, B., Lu, J., Howes, R., Wang, M., & Ferrer, C. C. (2020). The deepfake detection challenge (DFDC) dataset [arXiv preprint arXiv:2006.07397]. arXiv. Available: https://arxiv.org/abs/2006.07397 [Accessed by 23/06/24].

Dolhansky, B., Bitton, J., Pflaum, B., Lu, J., Howes, R., Wang, M., & Ferrer, C. C. (2020). The deepfake detection challenge (DFDC) dataset. arXiv preprint arXiv:2006.07397. Available: https://arxiv.org/abs/2006.07397 [Accessed by 26/06/2024].

Dolhansky, B., Bitton, J., Pflaum, B., Lu, J., Howes, R., Wang, M., & Ferrer, C. C. (2020). The deepfake detection challenge (DFDC) dataset. arXiv. Available: https://arxiv.org/abs/2006.07397 [Accessed by 26/06/2024].

Doss, C., Mondschein, J., Shu, D., Wolfson, T., Kopecky, D., Fitton-Kane, V. A., & Tucker, C. (2023). Deepfakes and scientific knowledge dissemination. *Scientific Reports*, *13*(1), 13429.

Drage, E., & Mackereth, K. (2022). Does ai debias recruitment? race, gender, and ai's "eradication of difference". *Philosophy & Technology*, *35*(4). Advance online publication. DOI: 10.1007/s13347-022-00543-1 PMID: 36246553

Dullete, J. R. L. (2024). Assessing the orthographic projection skills of drafting technology students. *AVE Trends in Intelligent Technoprise Letters*, *1*(4), 167–183.

Dunning, D., Johnson, K., Ehrlinger, J., & Kruger, J. (2003). Why people fail to recognize their own incompetence. *Current Directions in Psychological Science, 12*(3), 83–87.

Dwivedi, Y. K., Kshetri, N., Hughes, L., Slade, E. L., Jeyaraj, A., Kar, A. K., Baabdullah, A. M., Koohang, A., Raghavan, V., Ahuja, M., Albanna, H., Albashrawi, M. A., Al-Busaidi, A. S., Balakrishnan, J., Barlette, Y., Basu, S., Bose, I., Brooks, L., Buhalis, D., & Wright, R. (2023). So what if ChatGPT wrote it? Multidisciplinary perspectives on opportunities, challenges and implications of generative conversational AI for research, practice and policy. *International Journal of Information Management, 71*(8), 1–63.

Dwork, C. (2008). Differential privacy: A survey of results. In *International Conference on Theory and Applications of Models of Computation* (pp. 1-19). Springer, Singapore.

Dwork, C., Hardt, M., Pitassi, T., Reingold, O., & Zemel, R. (2012). Fairness through awareness. In *Proceedings of the 3rd Innovations in Theoretical Computer Science Conference* (pp. 214-226). ACM, Cambridge, MA, United States of America.

Dyer, J. M., Pettyjohn, H. C., & Saladin, S. (2020). Academic dishonesty and testing: How student beliefs and test settings impact decisions to cheat. *Journal of the National College Testing Association, 4*(1), 1–31.

Ecija, J. D., Abris, M. G., & Sabejon, M. B. (2024). Preparedness on disaster risk reduction management measures, competence, and challenges faced by schools. *FMDB Transactions on Sustainable Humanities and Society, 1*(3), 100–112.

Eelmaa, S. (2021). Sexualization of Children in Deepfakes and Hentai: Examining Reddit UserViews. Available:https://www.researchgate.net/publication/350385365_Sexualization_of_Children_in_Deepfakes_and_Hentai_Examining_Reddit_User_Views [Accessed by: 08/07/2022].

El-Halaby, S., & Hussainey, K. (2016). Determinants of compliance with AAOIFI standards by Islamic banks. *International Journal of Islamic and Middle Eastern Finance and Management, 9*(1), 143–168. DOI: 10.1108/imefm-06-2015-0074

Estolonio, H. M., Nicol, J. A., Santos, P. C. C., & Ramos, J. I. (2023). Impact of Remote Work on Employee Engagement and Productivity in Operations Management. *FMDB Transactions on Sustainable Management Letters, 1*(4), 155–167.

Ezzaim, A., Kharroubi, F., Dahbi, A., Aqqal, A., & Haidine, A. (2022). Artificial intelligence in education – State of the art. *International Journal of Computer Engineering & Data Science, 2*(2), 221–233.

Facione, P. A. (2015). *Critical thinking: What it is and why it counts.* California Academic Press.

Faizi, F., & BinShuib, M. (2024). Sharia governance in islamic financial institutions: A comparative review of malaysia and indonesia. *El Dinar Jurnal Keuangan Dan Perbankan Syariah, 12*(1), 89–107. DOI: 10.18860/ed.v12i1.25135

Fallis, D. (2021). The epistemic threat of deepfakes. *Philosophy & Technology, 34*(4), 623–643. PMID: 32837868

Farhan, M., & Bin Sulaiman, R. (2023). Developing Blockchain Technology to Identify Counterfeit Items Enhances the Supply Chain's Effectiveness. *FMDB Transactions on Sustainable Technoprise Letters, 1*(3), 123–134.

Fauzy, I., Padilah, D., Alzena, F. C., Azzahra, F., & Kamodin, F. (2024). Optimizing learning by enhancing students' motivation. *FMDB Transactions on Sustainable Humanities and Society, 1*(2), 91–99.

Festinger, L. (1957). *A theory of cognitive dissonance.* Stanford University Press.

Firnando, H., & Wahyudi, M. (2024). The role of artificial intelligence in shaping the Islamic worldview of the digital economy. *Journal of Islamic Economics and Philanthropy, 6*(3), 231–249. DOI: 10.21111/jiep.v6i3.11386

Fletcher, J. (2018). Deepfakes, artificial intelligence, and some kind of dystopia: The new faces of online post-fact performance. *Theatre Journal, 70*(4), 455–471.

Fletcher, J. (2018). Deepfakes, artificial intelligence, and some kind of dystopia: The new faces of online post-truth persona. *Theatre Journal, 70*(4), 455–471.

Floridi, L., Cowls, J., Beltrametti, M., Chatila, R., Chazerand, P., Dignum, V., & Vayena, E. (2018). AI4People—an ethical framework for a good AI society: Opportunities, risks, principles, and recommendations. *Minds and Machines, 28*(4), 689–707.

Floridi, L., Cowls, J., Beltrametti, M., Chatila, R., Chazerand, P., Dignum, V., & Vayena, E. (2018). AI4People—An ethical framework for a good AI society: Opportunities, risks, principles, and recommendations. *Minds and Machines, 28*(4), 689–707.

Folorunsho, S., Adenekan, O., Ezeigweneme, C., Somadina, I., & Okeleke, P. (2024). Leveraging technical support experience to implement effective ai solutions and future service improvements. *International Journal of Applied Research in Social Sciences, 6*(8), 1758–1783. DOI: 10.51594/ijarss.v6i8.1425

Fontenot, J. (2024). Spotlight on leadership: What nurse leaders need to know about artificial intelligence. *The Journal of Nursing Administration*, *54*(2), 74–76. PMID: 38261639

Francis, N. J., Jones, S., & Smith, D. P. (2025). Generative AI in higher education: Balancing innovation and integrity. *British Journal of Biomedical Science*, *81*, 14048.

Fundira, K., & Nithyanantham, V. (2024). Assessing job satisfaction and impact on the retention of primary mathematics teachers within learning systems. *AVE Trends in Intelligent Techno Learning*, *1*(1), 35–46.

Gagne, R. M., Wager, W. W., Golas, K. C., Keller, J. M., & Russell, J. D. (2005). *Principles of instructional design* (5th ed.). Thomson Wadswortth.

Gandhi, M., Satheesh, C., Soji, E. S., Saranya, M., Rajest, S. S., & Kothuru, S. K. (2024). Image recognition and extraction on computerized vision for sign language decoding. In *Explainable AI Applications for Human Behavior Analysis* (pp. 157–173). IGI Global.

Gawande, U., Golhar, Y., & Hajari, K. (2017). Biometric-based security system: Issues and challenges. In *Intelligent Techniques in Signal Processing for Multimedia Security* (pp. 151–176). Springer International Publishing.

Gervais, A., Karame, G. O., Wüst, K., Glykantzis, V., Ritzdorf, H., & Capkun, S. (2016). On the security and performance of Proof of Work blockchains. In *Proceedings of the ACM Conference on Computer and Communications Security*, Vienna, Austria.

Gilpin, L. H., Bau, D., Yuan, B. Z., Bajwa, A., Specter, M., & Kagal, L. (2018). Explaining explanations: An overview of interpretability of machine learning. In 2018 IEEE 5th International Conference on Data Science and Advanced Analytics (pp. 80-89). IEEE, Turin, Italy.

Gomathy, V., & Venkatasbramanian, S. (2023). Impact of Teacher Expectations on Student Academic Achievement. *FMDB Transactions on Sustainable Techno Learning*, *1*(2), 78–91.

Goodfellow, I., Pouget-Abadie, J., Mirza, M., Xu, B., Warde-Farley, D., & Ozair, S., & Bengio. (2014). Generative adversarial nets. *Advances in Neural Information Processing Systems*, *27*(6), 2672–2680.

Goodfellow, I., Pouget-Abadie, J., Mirza, M., Xu, B., Warde-Farley, D., Ozair, S., Courville, A., & Bengio, Y. (2014). Generative adversarial nets. Advances in Neural Information Processing Systems, 27, 2672–2680. *Conference on Neural Information Processing Systems (NeurIPS 2014)*, Quebec, Canada.

Goodman, B., & Flaxman, S. (2017). European Union regulations on algorithmic decision-making and a "right to explanation". *AI Magazine*, *38*(3), 50–57.

Gresch, J., Rodrigues, B., Scheid, E., Kanhere, S. S., & Stiller, B. (2018). The proposal of a blockchain-based architecture for transparent certificate handling. In Business Information Systems Workshops: BIS 2018, Berlin, Germany.

Groh, M., Epstein, Z., Firestone, C., & Picard, R. (2022). Deepfake detection by human crowds, machines, and machine-informed crowds. *Proceedings of the National Academy of Sciences of the United States of America*, *119*(1), 1–11.

Guess, A. M., Lerner, M., Lyons, B., Montgomery, J. M., Nyhan, B., Reifler, J., & Sircar, N. (2020). A digital media literacy intervention increases discernment between mainstream and false news in the United States and India. *Proceedings of the National Academy of Sciences of the United States of America*, *117*(27), 15536–15545.

Gunawardena, C. N., & Zittle, F. J. (1997). Social presence as a predictor of satisfaction within a computer-mediated conferencing environment. *American Journal of Distance Education*, *11*(3), 8–26.

Gupta, G., Raja, K., Gupta, M., Jan, T., Whiteside, S. T., & Prasad, M. (2023). A comprehensive review of deepfake detection using advanced machine learning and fusion methods. *Electronics (Basel)*, *13*(1), 1–27.

Hakim, A., & Anggraini, P. (2023). Artificial intelligence in teaching islamic studies: Challenges and opportunities. *Molang Journal Islamic Education*, *1*(02), 57–69. DOI: 10.32806/6ynvg541

Hancock, J. T., & Bailenson, J. N. (2021). The social impact of deepfakes. *Cyberpsychology, Behavior, and Social Networking*, *24*(3), 149–152.

Hasan, H. R., & Salah, K. (2019). Combating deepfake videos using blockchain and smart contracts. *IEEE Access : Practical Innovations, Open Solutions*, *7*(3), 41596–41606.

Hatipoğlu, A., Güneri, Y., & Yılmaz, E. (2023). A comparative predictive maintenance application based on machine and deep learning. *Journal of the Faculty of Engineering and Architecture of Gazi University*, *39*(1), 1037–1048.

Heidari, A., Jafari Navimipour, N., Dag, H., & Unal, M. (2024). Deepfake detection using deep learning methods: A systematic and comprehensive review. *Wiley Interdisciplinary Reviews. Data Mining and Knowledge Discovery*, *14*(2), 1–45.

Henry, N., McGlynn, C., Flynn, A., Johnson, K., Pound, N., & Rackley, E. (2021). Image-based sexual abuse: A study on the causes and consequences of non-consensual intimate image sharing. *Feminism & Psychology, 31*(1), 70–87.

Hernández-Ramos, P. (2005). If not here, where? Understanding teachers' use of technology in Silicon Valley schools. *Journal of Research on Technology in Education, 38*(1), 39–64.

He, Z., Zuo, W., Kan, M., Shan, S., & Chen, X. (2019). AttGAN: Facial attribute editing by only changing what you want. *IEEE Transactions on Image Processing, 28*(11), 5464–5478.

Hobbs, R. (2010). *Digital and media literacy: A plan of action*. The Aspen Institute.

Hofer, B. K., & Pintrich, P. R. (1997). The development of epistemological theories: Beliefs about knowledge and knowing and their relation to learning. *Review of Educational Research, 67*(1), 88–140.

Huber, C., & Kuncel, N. R. (2016). Does college teach critical thinking? A meta-analysis. *Review of Educational Research, 86*(2), 431–468.

Hwang, S., Oh, S., Tavanapong, W., & Wong, J. (2020). Survey on deepfake video detection. *Computer Vision and Image Understanding, 187*(10), 102792.

Iglovikov, V., & Shvets, A. (2018). TernausNet: U-Net with VGG11 encoder pre-trained on ImageNet for image segmentation (arXiv:1801.05746). arXiv. Available: https://arxiv.org/abs/1801.05746 [Accessed by 03/07/23].

Indu, I., Anand, P. R., & Bhaskar, V. (2018). Identity and access management in cloud environment: Mechanisms and challenges. *Engineering Science and Technology, an International Journal, 21*(4), 574–588.

Ishak, M., & Mohamed, A. (2023). Harmonization of Islamic economics with artificial intelligence: Towards an ethical and innovative economic paradigm. *Al-Kharaj Journal of Islamic Economic and Business, 5*(4). Advance online publication. DOI: 10.24256/kharaj.v5i4.4387

Jasper, K., Neha, R., & Hong, W. C. (2023). Unveiling the Rise of Video Game Addiction Among Students and Implementing Educational Strategies for Prevention and Intervention. *FMDB Transactions on Sustainable Social Sciences Letters, 1*(3), 158–171.

Jeba, J. A., Bose, S. R., Regin, R., Rajest, S. S., & Kose, U. (2023). In-Depth Analysis and Implementation of Advanced Information Gathering Tools for Cybersecurity Enhancement. *FMDB Transactions on Sustainable Computer Letters, 1*(2), 130–146.

Jenkins, H., Clinton, K., Purushotma, R., Robison, A. J., & Weigel, M. (2006). Confronting the challenges of participatory culture: Media education for the 21st century. Chicago, United States of America.

Jobin, A., Ienca, M., & Vayena, E. (2019). The Global Landscape of AI Ethics Guidelines. *Nature Machine Intelligence*, *1*(9), 389–399.

John Joseph, F. J., Chinnusamy, K., Jeganathan, J., & Obaid, J. A., & Rajest, S. S. (Eds.). (2025). Pioneering AI and data technologies for next-gen security, IoT, and smart ecosystems. Advances in Computational Intelligence and Robotics. IGI Global, USA.

Johnson, M., Davis, K., & Thompson, R. (2023). Comparative effectiveness of deepfake literacy instructional methods. *Journal of Educational Technology Research*, *45*(2), 123–142.

Jonassen, D. H., & Rohrer-Murphy, L. (1999). Activity theory as a framework for designing constructivist learning environments. *Educational Technology Research and Development*, *47*(1), 61–79.

Jones, L. M., & Mitchell, K. J. (2016). Defining and measuring youth digital citizenship. *New Media & Society*, *18*(9), 2063–2079.

Joshi, M., Shen, Z., & Kausar, S. (2023). Enhancing Inclusive Education on Leveraging Artificial Intelligence Technologies for Personalized Support and Accessibility in Special Education for Students with Diverse Learning Needs. *FMDB Transactions on Sustainable Techno Learning*, *1*(3), 125–142.

Kahne, J., & Bowyer, B. (2017). Educating for democracy in a partisan age: Confronting the challenges of motivated reasoning and misinformation. *American Educational Research Journal*, *54*(1), 3–34.

Kanyimama, W. (2023). Design of A Ground Based Surveillance Network for Modibbo Adama University, Yola. *FMDB Transactions on Sustainable Computing Systems*, *1*(1), 32–43.

Karras, T., Laine, S., & Aila, T. (2019). A style-based generator architecture for generative adversarial networks. In *Proceedings of the IEEE/CVF Conference on Computer Vision and Pattern Recognition* (pp. 4401-4410), Long Beach, CA, United States of America.

Kaushal, A., Kumar, S., & Kumar, R. (2024). A review on deepfake generation and detection: Bibliometric analysis. *Multimedia Tools and Applications*, *83*(40), 87579–87619.

Khalid, M., Raza, A., Younas, F., Rustam, F., Villar, M. G., Ashraf, I., & Akhtar, A. (2024). Novel sentiment majority voting classifier and transfer learning-based feature engineering for sentiment analysis of deepfake tweets. *IEEE Access : Practical Innovations, Open Solutions*, *12*(5), 67117–67129.

Khalil, M., & Ebner, M. (2014). MOOCs completion rates and possible methods to improve retention-A literature review. In Proceedings of World Conference on Educational Multimedia, Hypermedia and Telecommunications (pp. 1305-1313). AACE, Tampere, Finland.

Kharvi, P. L. (2024). Understanding the impact of AI-generated deepfakes on public opinion, political discourse, and personal security in social media. *IEEE Security and Privacy*, *22*(4), 115–122.

Kietzmann, J., Lee, L. W., McCarthy, I. P., & Kietzmann, T. C. (2020). Deepfakes: Trick or treat? *Business Horizons*, *63*(2), 135–146.

Kim, P. H., Ferrin, D. L., Cooper, C. D., & Dirks, K. T. (2004). Removing the shadow of suspicion: The effects of apology versus denial for repairing competence-versus integrity-based trust violations. *The Journal of Applied Psychology*, *89*(1), 104–118.

King, P. M., & Kitchener, K. S. (1994). Developing Reflective Judgment: Understanding and Promoting Intellectual Growth and Critical Thinking in Adolescents and Adults. Jossey-Bass Higher and Adult Education Series and Jossey-Bass Social and Behavioral Science Series. Jossey-Bass, 350 Sansome Street, San Francisco, California, United States of America.

Kleinberg, J., Ludwig, J., Mullainathan, S., & Obermeyer, Z. (2015). Prediction policy problems. *The American Economic Review*, *105*(5), 491–495.

Kodi, D. (2024). Evolving cybersecurity strategies for safeguarding digital ecosystems in an increasingly connected world. *FMDB Transactions on Sustainable Computing Systems*, *2*(4), 211–221.

Komperla, R. C. A., Pokkuluri, K. S., Nomula, V. K., Gowri, G. U., Rajest, S. S., & Rahila, J. (2024). Revolutionizing biometrics with AI-enhanced X-ray and MRI analysis. In *Advances in Medical Technologies and Clinical Practice* (pp. 1–16). IGI Global.

Kooli, C. (2023). Chatbots in education and research: A critical examination of ethical implications and solutions. *Sustainability*, *15*(7), 5614. Advance online publication. DOI: 10.3390/su15075614

Korshunova, I., Shi, W., Dambre, J., & Theis, L. (2017). Fast face-swap using convolutional neural networks. In *Proceedings of the IEEE International Conference on Computer Vision*. Venice, Italy.

Krishnan, A., Mol, K. P. S., Saiju, L., Babu, J., & Ashifa, K. M. (2024). Tribal education in Kerala and achieving Sustainable Development Goal (SDG)-4: Prospects and challenges. *FMDB Transactions on Sustainable Techno Learning*, *2*(1), 41–49.

Krumrei-Mancuso, E. J., & Rouse, S. V. (2016). The development and validation of the comprehensive intellectual humility scale. *Journal of Personality Assessment*, *98*(2), 209–221.

Kugler, M. B., & Pace, C. (2021). Deepfake privacy: Attitudes and regulation. *Northwestern University Law Review*, *116*(3), 611–680.

Kumar, N., & Kundu, A. (2024). Cybersecurity-focused deepfake detection system utilizing big data. *SN Computer Science*, *5*(6), 752.

Kumar, R., Singh, A., & Patel, N. (2021). Deepfake threats to online examination integrity: A comprehensive analysis. *Computers & Education*, *171*(10), 104245.

Lai, G. (2023). Artificial intelligence techniques for fraud detection. https://doi.org/DOI: 10.20944/preprints202312.1115.v1

Lazar, A., Chen, Y., & Xu, W. (2021). Educational deepfakes and student psychological well-being. In *Handbook of Research on Digital Content, Mobile Learning, and Technology Integration Models in Teacher Education*. IGI Global.

Ledig, C., Theis, L., Huszár, F., Caballero, J., Cunningham, A., Acosta, A., Aitken, A., Tejani, A., Totz, J., Wang, Z., & Shi, W. (2017). Photo-realistic single image super-resolution using a generative adversarial network. In *Proceedings of the IEEE Conference on Computer Vision and Pattern Recognition (CVPR)* (pp. 105–114). IEEE, Honolulu, HI, United States of America.

Legista, M., Nurlaili, L., & Masriah, I. (2024). Development of an adaptive learning system utilizing deep learning to support independent learning processes for students. *AVE Trends in Intelligent Techno Learning*, *1*(2), 107–120.

Lewandowsky, S., Ecker, U. K. H., Seifert, C. M., Schwarz, N., & Cook, J. (2020). The continued influence of corrected misinformation. *Psychological Science*, *31*(5), 566–577.

Li, Y., Chang, M. C., & Lyu, S. (2018). In ictu oculi: Exposing AI created fake videos by detecting eye blinking in Proceedings of the 2018 IEEE International Workshop on Information Forensics and Security (WIFS), Hong Kong, China.

Li, L., Bao, J., Zhang, T., Yang, H., Chen, D., Wen, F., & Guo, B. (2020). Face X-ray for more general face forgery detection. *2020 IEEE/CVF Conference on Computer Vision and Pattern Recognition (CVPR)*. IEEE, Seattle, Washington, United States of America.

Liu, J., Xie, M., Chen, S., Ma, C., & Gong, Q. (2021). An improved DPoS consensus mechanism in blockchain based on PLTS for the smart autonomous multi-robot system. *Information Sciences*, *575*(12), 528–541.

Liu, M., & Yang, C. (2014). Exploring the effects of cognitive load on critical thinking in online discussions. *Educational Technology Research and Development*, *62*(5), 617–634.

Li, Y., Yang, X., Sun, P., Qi, H., & Lyu, S. (2020). Celeb-DF: A large-scale challenging dataset for DeepFake forensics. *2020 IEEE/CVF Conference on Computer Vision and Pattern Recognition (CVPR)*. IEEE, Seattle, Washington, United States of America.

Li, Y., Yang, X., Sun, P., Qi, H., & Lyu, S. (2020). Celeb-DF: A large-scale challenging dataset for deepfake forensics. In *Proceedings of the IEEE/CVF Conference on Computer Vision and Pattern Recognition*, Washington, United States of America.

Locsin, R. C. (2016). Technological competency as caring in nursing: Co-creating moments in nursing occurring within the universal technological domain. *Journal of Theory Construction & Testing*, *20*(1), 5.

Long, P., & Siemens, G. (2014). Penetrating the fog: Analytics in learning and education. *Italian Journal of Educational Technology*, *22*(3), 132–137.

Lyu, S. (2020). Deepfake detection: Current challenges and next steps. In *IEEE International Conference on Multimedia & Expo Workshops (ICMEW)*, London, United Kingdom.

Mahadewi, N. M. E., Venkateswaran, P. S., & Pradeep, V. (2024). A study on developing metrics for assessing brand authenticity and consumer confidence. *AVE Trends in Intelligent Social Letters*, *1*(3), 113–122.

Mai, K. T., Bray, S., Davies, T., & Griffin, L. D. (2023). Warning: Humans cannot reliably detect speech deepfakes. *PLoS One*, *18*(8), e0285333. PMID: 37531336

Manjare, S. O. (2024). Beyond academics: The transformative role of social-emotional learning (SEL) in higher education. *FMDB Transactions on Sustainable Humanities and Society*, *1*(4), 188–199.

Manolache, M. A., Manolache, S., & Tapus, N. (2022). Decision making using the blockchain Proof of Authority consensus. *Procedia Computer Science*, *199*(1), 580–588.

Maras, M. H., & Alexandrou, A. (2019). Determining authenticity of video evidence in the age of artificial intelligence and in the wake of deepfake videos. *The International Journal of Evidence & Proof*, *23*(3), 255–262.

Maras, M.-H., & Alexandrou, A. (2019). Determining authenticity of video evidence in the age of artificial intelligence and in the wake of Deepfake videos. *The International Journal of Evidence & Proof*, *23*(3), 255–262.

María, J. J. L., Polo, O. C. C., & Elhadary, T. (2023). An Analysis of the Morality and Social Responsibility of Non-Profit Organizations. *FMDB Transactions on Sustainable Technoprise Letters*, *1*(1), 28–35.

Maroju, P. K. (2024). Advancing Synergy of Computing and Artificial Intelligence with Innovations Challenges and Future Prospects. *FMDB Transactions on Sustainable Intelligent Networks*, *1*(1), 1–14.

Marwick, A., & Lewis, R. (2017). *Media manipulation and disinformation online.* Data & Society Research.

Mayer, R. E. (2014). *The Cambridge handbook of multimedia learning* (2nd ed.). Cambridge University Press.

Meesala, M. K. (2025). Blockchain for secure and transparent healthcare data sharing across platforms. *FMDB Transactions on Sustainable Health Science Letters*, *3*(1), 32–41.

Merrill, M. D. (2002). First principles of instruction. *Educational Technology Research and Development*, *50*(3), 43–59.

Meulmeester, F. L., Dubois, E. A., & Krommenhoek-van Es, C. (2021). Medical students' perspectives on online proctoring during remote digital progress test. *Medical Science Educator*, *31*(9), 1773–1777. PMID: 34611498

Meuschke, N., Gipp, B., & Breitinger, C. (2019). Academic plagiarism detection in the age of artificial intelligence. *Proceedings of the ACM/IEEE Joint Conference on Digital Libraries*, Urbana-Champaign, Illinois.

Michel-Villarreal, R., Vilalta-Perdomo, E., Salinas-Navarro, D. E., Thierry-Aguilera, R., & Gerardou, F. S. (2023). Challenges and opportunities of generative AI for higher education as explained by ChatGPT. *Education Sciences*, *13*(9), 1–18.

Mihailidis, P., & Viotty, S. (2017). Spreadable spectacle in digital culture: Civic expression, fake news, and the role of media literacies in "post-fact" society. *The American Behavioral Scientist*, *61*(4), 441–454.

Millondaga, R. M., Cahilig, D. G., & Basañes, R. A. (2024). Correlating the emotional intelligence and conflict resolution strategies of school leaders. *FMDB Transactions on Sustainable Techno Learning*, *2*(4), 194–214.

Ministry of Electronics and Information Technology. (2019). The Personal Data Protection Bill, 2019. Government of India. Available: https://prsindia.org/files/bills_acts/bills_parliament/2019/Personal%20Data%20Protection%20Bill,%202019.pdf [Accessed by 26/06/2024].

Mirsky, Y., & Lee, W. (2021). The creation and detection of deepfakes: A survey. *ACM Computing Surveys*, *54*(1), 1–41.

Mompel, J. T., & Lombrio, C. (2024). Impact of physical education as a form of recreational activities: Academic performance of the students. *FMDB Transactions on Sustainable Humanities and Society*, *1*(3), 113–123.

Moyo, S. B., & Nithyanantham, V. (2024). Evaluating the influence of parental involvement in early childhood education programs. *AVE Trends in Intelligent Techno Learning*, *1*(1), 47–60.

Mubiana, P., & Nithyanantham, V. (2024). Investigating the causes and consequences of child marriage on girls: A case study of primary schools. *FMDB Transactions on Sustainable Social Sciences Letters*, *2*(2), 110–118.

Mudunuri, L. N. R. (2024). Artificial Intelligence (AI) Powered Matchmaker: Finding Your Ideal Vendor Every Time. *FMDB Transactions on Sustainable Intelligent Networks*, *1*(1), 27–39.

Nadarzynski, T., Bayley, J., Llewellyn, C., Kidsley, S., & Graham, C. (2020). Acceptability of artificial intelligence (AI)-enabled chatbots, video consultations, and live webchats as online platforms for sexual health advice. *BMJ Sexual & Reproductive Health*, *46*(3), 210–217. DOI: 10.1136/bmjsrh-2018-200271 PMID: 31964779

Nagaraj, B. K. (2023). Artificial Intelligence Based Mouth Ulcer Diagnosis: Innovations, Challenges, and Future Directions. *FMDB Transactions on Sustainable Computer Letters*, *1*(3), 202–209.

National Institute of Standards and Technology. (2018). Framework for improving critical infrastructure cybersecurity. U.S. Department of Commerce. https://nvlpubs.nist.gov/nistpubs/cswp/nist.cswp.04162018.pdf [Accessed by 26/04/2024].

Newton, P. M. (2018). How common is commercial contract cheating in higher education and is it increasing? A systematic review. *Frontiers in Education*, *3*(8), 1–67.

Nguyen, T. T., Nguyen, Q. V. H., Nguyen, D. T., Nguyen, D. T., Huynh-The, T., Nahavandi, S., Nguyen, T. T., Pham, Q. V., & Nguyen, C. M. (2022). Deep learning for deepfakes creation and detection: A survey. *Computer Vision and Image Understanding*, *223*(10), 103525.

Nidhi, K., Vashist, S., & Jeganathan, J. (2024). Knowledge and attitude regarding objectified body consciousness among young adults. *AVE Trends in Intelligent Social Letters*, *1*(2), 72–81.

Nirmala, G., Premavathy, R., Chandar, R., & Jeganathan, J. (2023). An Explanatory Case Report on Biopsychosocial Issues and the Impact of Innovative Nurse-Led Therapy in Children with Hematological Cancer. *FMDB Transactions on Sustainable Health Science Letters*, *1*(1), 1–10.

Nithyanantham, V. (2023). Study Examines the Connection Between Students' Various Intelligence and Their Levels of Mathematical Success in School. *FMDB Transactions on Sustainable Techno Learning*, *1*(1), 32–59.

Nurse, J. R., Creese, S., Goldsmith, M., & Lamberts, K. (2011). Guidelines for usable cybersecurity: Past and present. In *2011 Third International Workshop on Cyberspace Safety and Security* (pp. 21-26). IEEE, Milan, Italy.

O'Connor, S., Yan, Y., Thilo, F. J., Felzmann, H., Dowding, D., & Lee, J. J. (2023). Artificial intelligence in nursing and midwifery: A systematic review. *Journal of Clinical Nursing*, *32*(13-14), 2951–2968. PMID: 35908207

Obaid, A. J., Burlea-Schiopoiu, A., Bhushan, B., Bobur, S., & Rajest, S. S. (Eds.). (2024). Advances in Electronic Commerce *E-commerce, marketing, and consumer behavior in the AI era*. IGI Global., DOI: 10.4018/979-8-3693-5548-0

OIC Education Ministers' Reports. (2022–2024). https://icesco.org/wp-content/uploads/2024/08/CN-ICESCO-Education-Ministers-Conference-Beyond-Transforming-Education-Summit-from-Commitment-to-action.pdf

Olubunmi, O. I. (2024). Impact of learning resources management strategies on academic performance of junior secondary school business studies. *AVE Trends in Intelligent Techno Learning*, *1*(1), 1–10.

Olubunmi, O. I. (2024). Impact of learning resources management strategies on academic performance of junior secondary school business studies. *AVE Trends In Intelligent Techno Learning*, *1*(1), 1–10.

Padel, R. M., & Castro, J. (2024). Factors influencing the performance of multi-grade class in literacy and numeracy. *AVE Trends in Intelligent Technoprise Letters, 1*(3), 145–153.

Padmanabhan, J., Rajest, S. S., & Veronica, J. J. (2023). A study on the orthography and grammatical errors of tertiary-level students. In *Handbook of Research on Learning in Language Classrooms Through ICT-Based Digital Technology* (pp. 41–53). IGI Global.

Padmavathy, V., Venkateswaran, P. S., Begum, S., & Sheela, K. (2024). A review of the faculty engagement and performance in higher educational institutions. *AVE Trends in Intelligent Techno Learning, 1*(2), 76–87.

Paris, B., & Donovan, J. (2019). *Deepfakes and cheap fakes: The manipulation of audiovisual evidence*. Data & Society Research Institute.

Pasaribu, H., Widiatmoko, A., & Supriyanto, D. (2024). Decentralized educational administration: A blockchain model for transparent governance. *Journal of Social Science and Utility Technology, 2*(3), 386–399.

Patel, Y., Tanwar, S., Gupta, R., Bhattacharya, P., Davidson, I. E., Nyameko, R., Aluvala, S., & Vimal, V. (2023). Deepfake generation and detection: Case study and challenges. *IEEE Access : Practical Innovations, Open Solutions, 11*(12), 143296–143323.

Patón-Romero, J., Vinuesa, R., Jaccheri, L., & Baldassarre, M. (2022). State of gender equality in and by artificial intelligence. *Iadis International Journal on Computer Science and Information Systems, 17*(2). Advance online publication. DOI: 10.33965/ijcsis_2022170203

Peddireddy, S. G. K. (2024). Advancing threat detection in cybersecurity through deep learning algorithms. *FMDB Transactions on Sustainable Intelligent Networks, 1*(4), 190–200.

Pellegrino, J. W., Chudowsky, N., & Glaser, R. (2001). *Knowing what students know: The science and design of educational assessment*. National Academy Press.

Pennycook, G., & Rand, D. G. (2021). The psychology of fake news. *Trends in Cognitive Sciences, 25*(5), 388–402.

Pentakota, S. L. B. (2025). Blockchain-based authentication mechanisms for secure network communication. *FMDB Transactions on Sustainable Computer Letters, 3*(1), 50–59.

Pentakota, S. L. B. (2025). Unveiling deepfake and fraudulent content generation in GPT models and countermeasures. *AVE Trends in Intelligent Computer Letters, 1*(1), 41–50.

Porter, A., McMaken, J., Hwang, J., & Yang, R. (2011). Common Core Standards: The new US intended curriculum. *Educational Researcher, 40*(3), 103–116.

Potter, W. J. (2004). *Theory of media literacy: A cognitive approach*. Sage Publications.

Pournader, M., Ghaderi, H., Hassanzadegan, A., & Fahimnia, B. (2021). Artificial intelligence applications in supply chain management. *International Journal of Production Economics, 241*(11), 108250.

Prathish, S., Narayanan, S. A., & Bijlani, K. (2016). An intelligent system for online exam monitoring. In *Proceedings of the 2016 International Conference on Information Science (ICIS)*, Kochi, India.

Priscila, S. S., Femi, D., Sakthivanitha, M., Rahman, K., & Gnanaguru, G. (2025). The new wave of biometric identification with AI approaches in X-ray and MRI data. *AVE Trends in Intelligent Computer Letters, 1*(1), 1–10.

Priscila, S. S., Kumar, C. S., Suganthi, Y. J., & Pappa, D. C. (2024). Enhancing fake news detection efficiency through deep learning models. *FMDB Transactions on Sustainable Intelligent Networks, 1*(3), 155–164.

Pulivarthy, P. (2024). Research on Oracle database performance optimization in IT-based university educational management system. *FMDB Transactions on Sustainable Computing Systems, 2*(2), 84–95.

Putri, M. F. J. L., & Rosmiati, Y. (2024). The effect of civic education learning on adversity quotient in students. *FMDB Transactions on Sustainable Techno Learning, 2*(3), 144–152.

Putri, M. F. J. L., Sunarso, S., & Samsuri, S. (2024). Citizenship education as an effort to prevent radicalism and extremism. *FMDB Transactions on Sustainable Humanities and Society, 1*(2), 82–90.

Qatar University. (2021). Course Syllabus: Research Ethics in Islamic Contexts.

Rahman, M. S., & Liu, C. (2022). Digital media literacy and deepfake awareness among university students. In *Advances in educational technologies and instructional design*. IGI Global.

Rahman, M., Mahi, A., & Hossian, M. (2024). Application of ai in halal marketing: Navigating the ethical crossroads. *West Science Interdisciplinary Studies, 2*(04), 920–926. DOI: 10.58812/wsis.v2i04.866

Raja, A. S. V., Jasper, K. D., Poornima, V., Priscila, S. S., Thenmozhi, A., & Ratkovic, N. (2024). Tech horizons unveiled: Navigating the transformative decade in AIML, cybersecurity, IoT, gaming, and data science education. *FMDB Transactions on Sustainable Intelligent Networks*, *1*(2), 120–134.

Rajasekaran, R., Reddy, A. J., Kamalakannan, J., & Govinda, K. (2023). Building a Content-Based Book Recommendation System. *FMDB Transactions on Sustainable Computer Letters*, *1*(2), 103–114.

Rajest, S. S., Moccia, S., Chinnusamy, K., Singh, B., & Regin, R. (Eds.). (2023). Advances in Educational Technologies and Instructional Design *Handbook of research on learning in language classrooms through ICT-based digital technology*., DOI: 10.4018/978-1-6684-6682-7

Rajest, S. S., Singh, B., Obaid, A. J., Regin, R., & Chinnusamy, K. (2023). *Advances in artificial and human intelligence in the modern era*. Advances in Computational Intelligence and Robotics. IGI Global.

Raj, M. A., Thinesh, M. A., Varmann, S. S. M., Pothu, A. R., & Paramasivan, P. (2024). Ensemble-based phishing website detection using Extra Trees classifier. *AVE Trends in Intelligent Computing Systems*, *1*(3), 142–156.

Ramanaharan, R., Guruge, D. B., & Agbinya, J. I. (2025). DeepFake video detection: Insights into model generalisation—A Systematic review. *Data and Information Management*, •••, 100099.

Rami, A. A. M. (2024). Navigating challenges in policy development: Addressing political, institutional, and cultural challenges. *FMDB Transactions on Sustainable Social Sciences Letters*, *2*(2), 56–69.

Ramos, J. I., Lacerona, R., & Nunag, J. M. (2023). A Study on Operational Excellence, Work Environment Factors and the Impact to Employee Performance. *FMDB Transactions on Sustainable Social Sciences Letters*, *1*(1), 12–25.

Raquib, A., Channa, B., Zubair, T., & Qadir, J. (2022). Islamic virtue-based ethics for artificial intelligence. *Discover Artificial Intelligence*, *2*(1). Advance online publication. DOI: 10.1007/s44163-022-00028-2

Ratković, N., Venkateswaran, P. S., Paramasivan, P., Rajest, S. S., & Regin, R. (2024). Consumer preferences and industry practices in biodegradable packaging and sustainable environment. *FMDB Transactions on Sustainable Management Letters*, *2*(2), 80–90.

Regin, R., Hariprasath, G., Dhinakaran, P., Harishkumar, V., Sulthana, M. R., & Priscila, S. S. (2025). AI-powered cyber intrusion detection system with real-time threat analysis and web application interface for enhanced network security. *FMDB Transactions on Sustainable Computer Letters*, *3*(1), 34–49.

Regulation (EU) 2016/679. (2016). General Data Protection Regulation. European Parliament and Council. Available: https://eur-lex.europa.eu/legal-content/EN/TXT/PDF/?uri=CELEX:32016R0679 [Accessed by 26/04/2024].

Reidenberg, J. R., Russell, N. C., Callen, A. J., Qasir, S., & Norton, T. B. (2013). Privacy and Cloud Computing in Public Schools. *Fordham Law Review*, *81*(6), 3251–3310.

Reigeluth, C. M. (1999). What is instructional-design theory and how is it changing. In Reigeluth, C. M. (Ed.), *Instructional-design theories and models: A new paradigm of instructional theory* (pp. 5–29). Lawrence Erlbaum Associates.

Rendhy, R. (2024). Impact of academic management information system on school performance: A case study. *AVE Trends in Intelligent Social Letters*, *1*(4), 197–213.

Rendhy, R., Yulianti, Y., & Yanti, Y. (2024). Analysis implementation academic management information system. *AVE Trends in Intelligent Technoprise Letters*, *1*(3), 136–144.

Renjith, E. J. (2024). Revolutionizing cloud security: Innovative approaches for safeguarding data integrity. *FMDB Transactions on Sustainable Computer Letters*, *2*(2), 111–119.

Ribble, M. S., & Bailey, G. D. (2007). *Digital citizenship in schools*. International Society for Technology in Education.

Rini, R. (2020). Deepfakes and the epistemic backstop. *Philosophers' Imprint*, *20*(24), 1–16.

Rizal, V., Riani, V., Muhtadi, T., Lestari, Y., & Sulistyorini, Y. F. (2024). Enhancing critical thinking skills among Islamic high school student leaders through interactive training programs: A case study. *FMDB Transactions on Sustainable Management Letters*, *2*(3), 121–136.

Roe, J., Perkins, M., Somoray, K., Miller, D., & Furze, L. (2025). To Deepfake or Not to Deepfake: Higher Education Stakeholders' Perceptions and Intentions towards Synthetic Media. *arXiv preprint arXiv:2502.18066*.

Roozenbeek, J., & van der Linden, S. (2019). Fake news game confers psychological resistance against online misinformation. *Palgrave Communications*, *5*(1), 1–10.

Rosca, C. M. (2023). Comparative analysis of object classification algorithms: Traditional image processing versus artificial intelligence–based approach. *Romanian Journal of Petroleum & Gas Technology*, *4*(2), 169–180.

Rossler, A., Cozzolino, D., Verdoliva, L., Riess, C., Thies, J., & Niessner, M. (2019). FaceForensics++: Learning to detect manipulated facial images. *2019 IEEE/CVF International Conference on Computer Vision (ICCV)*. IEEE, Seoul, Korea (South).

Rossler, A., Cozzolino, D., Verdoliva, L., Riess, C., Thies, J., & Nießner, M. (2019). FaceForensics++: Learning to detect manipulated facial images. In *Proceedings of the IEEE/CVF International Conference on Computer Vision* (pp. 1-11), Seoul, Korea.

Roth, Y., & Pickles, N. (2020). Updating our approach to misleading information. Twitter Blog. Available: https://blog.twitter.com/en_us/topics/product/2020/updating-our-approach-to-misleading-information [Accessed by 26/06.2024].

Roth, Y., & Pickles, N. (2020). Updating our approach to misleading information. Twitter Blog. Available: https://blog.twitter.com/en_us/topics/product/2020/updating-our-approach-to-misleading-information [Accessed by 26/06/2024].

Rovai, A. P. (2002). Building sense of community at a distance. *International Review of Research in Open and Distance Learning*, *3*(1), 1–16.

Russell, S., & Norvig, P. (2016). *Artificial intelligence: A modern approach* (3rd ed.). Pearson.

Saleh, M., Mustapha, Z. B., & Ndirmbitah, B. K. (2024). Empirical analysis of digital marketing on the purchasing habit of conservative digital users of common social media. *FMDB Transactions on Sustainable Technoprise Letters*, *2*(1), 31–41.

Saleh, O. S., Ghazali, O., & Rana, M. E. (2020). Blockchain based framework for educational certificates verification. *Journal of Critical Reviews*, *7*(3), 79–84.

Sarker, I. H. (2024). AI for critical infrastructure protection and resilience. In *AI-Driven Cybersecurity and Threat Intelligence: Cyber Automation, Intelligent Decision-Making and Explainability* (pp. 153–172). Springer.

Saxena, D., Khandare, S., & Chaudhary, S. (2023). An Overview of ChatGPT: Impact on Academic Learning. *FMDB Transactions on Sustainable Techno Learning*, *1*(1), 11–20.

Selingo, J. J. (2020). *The college dropout scandal*. The New Press.

Shah, M. S., Saleem, S., & Zulqarnain, R. (2017). Protecting digital evidence integrity and preserving chain of custody. Journal of Digital Forensics. *Security and Law*, *12*(2), 121–129.

Shanahan, T., & Shanahan, C. (2008). Teaching disciplinary literacy to adolescents: Rethinking content-area literacy. *Harvard Educational Review*, *78*(1), 40–59.

Sharma, M., & Kaur, M. (2021). A review of deepfake technology: An emerging AI threat. In Advances in Intelligent Systems and Computing Book Series (Vol. 1397). Palo Alto, CA, United States of America.

Sharma, M. D., & Shaikh, A. N. N. (2025). A case study on Deepfake Awareness, Mumbai, India. *Indian Journal of Computer Science and Technology*, *4*(01), 121–126.

Shermis, M. D., & Burstein, J. (2013). *Handbook of automated essay evaluation: Current applications and new directions*. Routledge.

Shyam, R., Chiranjeevi, G., Reddy, R. A., Khala, A. A., Sah, S., Kautish, S., & Sulaiman, R. B. (2024). Using autoencoder-driven machine learning for advanced cybersecurity malware detection. *FMDB Transactions on Sustainable Intelligent Networks*, *1*(4), 252–264.

Silvia Priscila, S., Soji, E. S., Hossó, N., Paramasivan, P., & Suman Rajest, S. (2023). Digital Realms and Mental Health: Examining the Influence of Online Learning Systems on Students. *FMDB Transactions on Sustainable Techno Learning*, *1*(3), 156–164.

Singapore, N. T. U. (2023). *1 in 3 who are aware of deepfakes say they have inadvertently shared them on social media.* Retrieved from https://www.ntu.edu.sg/research/research-at-ntu/detail/1-in-3-who-are-aware-of-deepfakes-say-they-have-inadvertently-shared-them-on-social-med

Singh, C., Thakkar, R. G., & Warraich, J. (2023). IAM identity access management—Importance in maintaining security systems within organizations. *European Journal of Engineering and Technology Research*, *8*(1), 30–38.

Sippy, T., Enock, F., Bright, J., & Margetts, H. Z. (2024). Behind the Deepfake: 8% Create; 90% Concerned. Surveying public exposure to and perceptions of deepfakes in the UK. *arXiv preprint arXiv:2407.05529*.

Sobel, J. (2020). The impact of deepfakes on marginalized communities. *Technology in Society*, *42*(3), 78–89.

Spivak, R. (2019). Deepfakes: The newest way to commit one of the oldest crimes. *Georgetown Law Technology Review*, *3*(5), 339–400.

Srilakshmi, U., Sandhya, I., Manikandan, J., Bindu, A. H., Regin, R., & Rajest, S. S. (2024). Design and implementation of energy-efficient protocols for underwater wireless sensor networks. In *Advances in Computer and Electrical Engineering* (pp. 417–430). IGI Global.

Sruthi, B. J., Jeniffer, J. P., Harshita, K. S., Sulthana, M. R., & Angelin, C. C. (2025). Enhancing certificate authentication through a transparent blockchain enabled verification system. *AVE Trends in Intelligent Computing Systems*, *2*(1), 15–26.

Sultana, S. A., Rupa, C., Malleswari, R. P., & Gadekallu, T. R. (2023). IPFS-blockchain smart contracts based conceptual framework to reduce certificate frauds in the academic field. *Information (Basel)*, *14*(8), 1–19.

Sunkari, V., & Srinagesh, A. (2024). Efficient deepfake audio detection using spectro-temporal analysis and deep learning. *Journal of Electrical Systems*, *20*(5s), 10–18.

Swan, K. (2002). Building learning communities in online courses: The importance of interaction. *Education Communication and Information*, *2*(1), 23–49.

Sweller, J. (1988). Cognitive load during problem solving: Effects on learning. *Cognitive Science*, *12*(2), 257–285.

Tahlil, T., Gomasta, S. S., & Ali, A. B. M. S. (2022). AlgoCert: Adopt non-transferable NFT for the issuance and verification of educational certificates using Algorand blockchain, in *Proceedings of the IEEE Asia-Pacific Conference on Computer Science and Data Engineering*, Gold Coast, Australia.

Tajfel, H., Turner, J., Austin, W. G., & Worchel, S. (2001). An integrative theory of intergroup conflict. Intergroup relations: Essential readings, New York, United States of America.

Tandoc, E. C.Jr, Lim, Z. W., & Ling, R. (2018). Defining "fake news" A typology of scholarly definitions. *Digital Journalism (Abingdon, England)*, *6*(2), 137–153.

Teng, M., Singla, R., Yau, O., Lamoureux, D., Gupta, A., Hu, Z., Aissiou, A., Eaton, S., Hamm, C., Hu, S., Kelly, D., MacMillan, K. M., Malik, S., Mazzoli, V., Teng, Y.-W., Laricheva, M., Jarus, T., & Field, T. S. (2022). Health care students' perspectives on artificial intelligence: Countrywide survey in Canada. *JMIR Medical Education*, *8*(1), 1–17. PMID: 35099397

The Indian Express. (2024). *Misinformation and harmful deepfakes will affect future elections in India: Adobe Report.* Retrieved from https://indianexpress.com/article/technology/tech-news-technology/misinformation-and-harmful-deepfakes-will-affect-future-elections-in-india-adobe-9357027/

Thies, J., Zollhofer, M., Stamminger, M., Theobalt, C., & Nießner, M. (2016). Face2Face: Real-time face capture and reenactment of RGB videos. In *Proceedings of the IEEE Conference on Computer Vision and Pattern Recognition* (pp. 2387–2395). Las Vegas, NV, United States of America.

Tolosana, R., Vera-Rodriguez, R., Fierrez, J., Morales, A., & Ortega-Garcia, J. (2020). Deepfakes and beyond: A survey of face manipulation and fake detection. *Information Fusion*, *64*(1), 131–148.

Touretzky, D., Gardner-McCune, C., Martin, F., & Seehorn, D. (2019). Envisioning AI for K-12: What should every child know about AI? *Proceedings of the AAAI Conference on Artificial Intelligence*, *33*(1), 9795–9799.

Tripathi, S., & Al -Zubaidi, A. (2023). A Study within Salalah's Higher Education Institutions on Online Learning Motivation and Engagement Challenges during Covid-19. FMDB Transactions on Sustainable Techno Learning, 1(1), 1–10.

Tripathi, S. (2024). The potential of AI and multimedia tools in creating a shift from instructors-centered to learner-centered in public relations campaign assignment. *AVE Trends in Intelligent Social Letters*, *1*(3), 157–167.

Tripathi, S., & Al-Zubaidi, A. (2023). A Study within Salalah's Higher Education Institutions on Online Learning Motivation and Engagement Challenges during Covid-19. *FMDB Transactions on Sustainable Techno Learning*, *1*(1), 1–10.

Trust, T., & Whalen, J. (2020). Should teachers be trained in emergency remote teaching? Lessons learned from the COVID-19 pandemic. *Journal of Technology and Teacher Education*, *28*(2), 189–199.

Tsai, Y. S., Perrotta, C., & Gašević, D. (2020). Empowering learners with personalised learning approaches? Agency, equity and transparency in the context of learning analytics. *Assessment & Evaluation in Higher Education*, *45*(4), 554–567.

Ulle, R. S., & Yogananthan, S. (2024). Unmasking fake opinions through behavioral analysis and machine learning: Identifying genuine users vs. fraudulent actors. *FMDB Transactions on Sustainable Management Letters*, *2*(2), 51–64.

Usman, M., & Ullah, A. (2024). Blockchain Technology Implementation in Libraries: An Overview of Potential Benefits and Challenges. *AVE Trends In Intelligent Computing Systems*, *1*(1), 42–53.

Vaccari, C., & Chadwick, A. (2020). Deepfakes and disinformation: Exploring the impact of synthetic political video on deception, uncertainty, and trust in news. *Social Media + Society*, *6*(1), 1–13.

Vanlehn, K. (2011). The relative effectiveness of human tutoring, intelligent tutoring systems, and other tutoring systems. *Educational Psychologist*, *46*(4), 197–221.

Varmann, S. S., Hariprasath, G., & Kadirova, I. (2023). Optimizing Educational Outcomes: H2O Gradient Boosting Algorithm in Student Performance Prediction. *FMDB Transactions on Sustainable Techno Learning*, *1*(3), 165–178.

Vashishtha, E., & Kapoor, H. (2023). Implementation of Blockchain Technology Across International Healthcare Markets. *FMDB Transactions on Sustainable Technoprise Letters*, *1*(1), 1–12.

Vaswani, A., Shazeer, N., Parmar, N., Uszkoreit, J., Jones, L., Gomez, A. N., & Polosukhin, I. (2017). Attention is all you need. arXiv. Available: https://arxiv.org/abs/1706.03762 [Accessed by: 12/12/2024].

Vegineni, G. C. (2024). Exploring anomalies in dark web activities for automated threat identification. *FMDB Transactions on Sustainable Computing Systems*, *2*(4), 189–200.

Velasquez, M., Andre, C., Shanks, T., & Meyer, M. J. (2015). *A framework for ethical decision making. Markkula Center for Applied Ethics*. Santa Clara University.

Velmonte, G. L. (2023). Preferred College Degree Programs Among Senior High School Students: A Policy Recommendation. *FMDB Transactions on Sustainable Techno Learning*, *1*(3), 143–155.

Vemula, V. R. (2024). Cognitive artificial intelligence systems for proactive threat hunting in AI-driven cloud applications. *AVE Trends in Intelligent Computing Systems*, *1*(3), 173–183.

Venkatasubramanian, S., Gomathy, V., & Saleem, M. (2023). Investigating the Relationship Between Student Motivation and Academic Performance. *FMDB Transactions on Sustainable Techno Learning*, *1*(2), 111–124.

Venkatasubramanian, S., Sakthikeerthika, T., & Saltanat Yerbolovna, K. (2023). Examine the Relationship Between Online Learning Students' Screen Time, Digital Fatigue, and Mental Health Issues. *FMDB Transactions on Sustainable Techno Learning*, *1*(4), 179–188.

Vignesh Raja, A. S., Jasper, K. D., Aljaafreh, R., Yogeshwarran, S. K., & Saleem, M. (2023). A Comprehensive Exploration of Blockchain-Based Decentralized Applications and Federated Learning in Reshaping Data Management. *FMDB Transactions on Sustainable Computer Letters*, *1*(4), 228–240.

Vygotsky, L. S., & Cole, M. (1978). *Mind in society: Development of higher psychological processes*. Harvard University Press.

Waltersmann, L., Kiemel, S., Stuhlsatz, J., Sauer, A., & Miehe, R. (2021). Artificial intelligence applications for increasing resource efficiency in manufacturing companies—A comprehensive review. *Sustainability, 13*(12), 1–26.

Wang, Y., Skerry-Ryan, R. J., Stanton, D., Wu, Y., Weiss, R. J., Jaitly, N., . . . Le, Q. V. (2017). Tacotron: Towards end-to-end speech synthesis. arXiv preprint arXiv:1703.10135. Available: https://arxiv.org/abs/1703.10135 [Accessed by 26/06/2024].

Wenger, E. (1999). *Communities of practice: Learning, meaning, and identity*. Cambridge university press.

Westerlund, M. (2019). The emergence of deepfake technology: A review. *Technology Innovation Management Review, 9*(11), 39–52.

Wiggins, G. (1990). The case for authentic assessment. *Practical Assessment, Research & Evaluation, 2*(1), 2.

Williamson, B. (2017). Big data in education: The digital future of learning, policy, and practice. *Sage (Atlanta, Ga.)*.

Williams, S., Anderson, J., & Brown, M. (2023). Longitudinal assessment of deepfake literacy retention and transfer. *Educational Psychology Review, 35*(3), 567–589.

Wineburg, S., Breakstone, J., McGrew, S., Smith, M., & Ortega, T. (2021). Lateral reading and the nature of expertise: Reading less and learning more when evaluating digital information. *Teachers College Record, 123*(4), 1–40.

Wineburg, S., McGrew, S., Breakstone, J., & Ortega, T. (2016). *Evaluating information: The cornerstone of civic online reasoning, Stanford Digital Repository, Stanford History Education Group, Robert R.* McCormick Foundation.

Wineburg, S., McGrew, S., Breakstone, J., & Ortega, T. (2016). *Evaluating information: The cornerstone of civic online reasoning*. Stanford Digital Repository.

Winkler, R., & Söllner, M. (2018). Unleashing the potential of chatbots in education: A state-of-the-art analysis. In Academy of Management Annual Meeting (pp. 1-6). *Academy of Management Journal, 2018*(1), 1–40.

Wu, X., Chang, J., Ling, H., & Feng, X. (2022). Scaling proof-of-authority protocol to improve performance and security. *Peer-to-Peer Networking and Applications, 15*(6), 2633–2649.

Yalavarthi, S. (2024). Cybersecurity requirements for medical devices under EU MDR: Ensuring compliance and patient safety. *AVE Trends in Intelligent Health Letters, 1*(3), 158–167.

Yu, P., Xia, Z., Fei, J., & Lu, Y. (2021). A survey on deepfake video detection. *IET Biometrics, 10*(6), 607–624.

Zawacki-Richter, O., Marín, V. I., Bond, M., & Gouverneur, F. (2019). Systematic review of research on artificial intelligence applications in higher education–where are the educators? *International Journal of Educational Technology in Higher Education, 16*(1), 1–27.

Zhang, L., Chen, S., & Wang, P. (2020). Student awareness and attitudes toward deepfake technology in higher education. *Educational Technology Research and Development, 68*(6), 2847–2867.

About the Contributors

Ahmed J. Obaid is a Asst. Professor at the Department of Computer Science, Faculty of Computer Science and Mathematics, University of Kufa, Iraq. Dr. Ahmed holds a Bachelor's in Computer Science, a degree in – Information Systems from the College of Computers, University of Anbar, Iraq (2001-2005), and a Master's Degree (M. TECH) in Computer Science Engineering (CSE) from School of Information Technology, Jawaharlal Nehru Technological University, Hyderabad, India (2010-2013), and a Doctor of Philosophy (Ph.D.) in Web Mining from College of Information Technology, University of Babylon, Iraq (2013-2017). He is a Certified Web Mining Consultant with over 14 years of experience working as a Faculty Member at the University of Kufa, Iraq. He has taught courses in Web Designing, Web Scripting, JavaScript, VB.Net, MATLAB Toolbox, and other courses on PHP, CMC, and DHTML from more than 10 international organizations and institutes in the USA, and India. Dr. Ahmed is a member of the Statistical and Information Consultation Center (SICC), University of Kufa, Iraq. His main line of research is Web mining Techniques and Applications, Image processing in Web Platforms, Image processing, Genetic Algorithm, information theory, and Medical Health Applications. Ahmed J. is an Associated Editor in the Brazilian Journal of Operations & Production Management (BJO&PM) and an Editorial Board member in the International Journal of Advance Study and Research Work (IJASRW), Journal of Research in Engineering and Applied Sciences(JREAS), GRD Journal for Engineering (GRDJE), International Research Journal of Multidisciplinary Science & Technology (IRJMST), The International Journal of Technology Information and Computer (IJTIC), Career Point International Journal Research (CPIJR). Ahmed J. was Editor in Many International Conferences such as: ISCPS_2020, MAICT_2020, IHICPS_2020, IICESAT_2021, IICPS_2020, ICPAS_2021, etc. (Scopus Indexed Conferences). He has edited Some books, such as Advance Material Science and Engineering (ISBN: 9783035736779, Scientific.net publisher), Computational Intelligence Techniques for Combating COVID-19 (ISBN: 978-3-030-68936-0 EAI/

Springer), A Fusion of Artificial Intelligence and Internet of Things for Emerging Cyber Systems (ISBN: 978-3-030-76653-5 Springer). Ahmed J. has supervised several final projects for Bachelor's and Master's in his main line of work and authored and co-authored several scientific publications in journals, Books, and conferences with more than 75+ Journal Research Articles, 5+ book Chapters, 15+ Conference papers, 10+ Conference proceedings, 8+ Books Editing, 2+ Patent. Ahmed J. is also a Reviewer in many Scopus, SCI, and ESCI Journals e.g., CMC, IETE, IJAACS, IJIPM, IJKBD, IJBSR, IET, IJUFKS, and many others. Dr. Ahmed attended and participated as: Keynote Speakers (60+ Conferences), Webinars (10+), and Session Chairs (10+), in many international events in the following countries: India, Turkey, Nepal, Philippines, Vietnam, Thailand, Indonesia, and other countries.

MuthmainnahMuthmainnah is a distinguished senior lecturer at Universitas Al Asyariah Mandar, located in West Sulawesi, Indonesia. Global recognition acknowledges her extensive contributions as a lecturer, an international speaker, and an accomplished leader in the academic field. Over the years, Dr. Muthmainnah has held pivotal roles at her institution, including Chairman of the Indonesian Language Department, Public Relations Officer, Director of Women's Centre Studies, Deputy Director of the Quality Assurance Unit, and her current position as Deputy Director of the Language and Character Development Institute. As a prolific author, Dr. Muthmainnah has published 84 national and international books with renowned publishers such as Springer, Emerald, Wiley, IGI Global, and Taylor and Francis. Her publications and research excellence have solidified her reputation as a leading scholar. For a comprehensive list of her works, you may visit her profile on the Sinta database. Dr. Muthmainnah serves as an international board member for various scientific innovation research groups (SIRG, Egypt), holds adjunct faculty positions at prominent institutions such as MAAUN Nigeria, Buriram Rajabhat University (BRU) Thailand, and Manipal Global Ntx Malaysia, and is the country director of some international organizations. Over 100 international awards, including Outstanding Professor, Outstanding Leadership, Best International Influencer, Best Emerging Professor of the Year, and SDGs Warrior, have recognized her. Among her accolades are an honorary doctorate from Layahe University and the "Doctor of Excellence Award from the Philippines." As a member of the United Nations Volunteers roster and a member of the advisory board for Indonesian Education Share-to-Care Volunteers, Dr. Muthmainnah actively engages in global volunteerism. Her scholarly interests encompass a wide range of topics, including literary development, instructional teaching materials, assurance of learning (ASSURE), TESOL (Teaching English to Speakers of Other Languages), ICT in education, digital education, generative AI (GenAI), and cybergogy. With an impressive Sinta score of 4680 and an H-index of 17, Dr. Muthmainnah's academic influence extends globally. She serves as an external examiner for PhD candidates at A+ accredited universities in Florida (USA), Cyprus (Europe), Australia, India and Malaysia. Her commitment to international collaboration and teamwork underscores her contributions to academia and leadership.

S. Suman Rajest is currently working as Dean of Research and Development (R&D) & International Student Affairs (ISA) at Dhaanish Ahmed College of Engineering, Chennai, Tamil Nadu, India. He is an Editor in Chief of the International Journal of Human Computing Studies and The International Journal of Social Sciences World, He is the Chief Executive Editor of the International Journal of Advanced Engineering Research and Science, International Journal of Advanced Engineering, Management and Science, The International Journal of Health and Medicines, The International Journal of Management Economy and Accounting Fields and The International Journal of Technology Information and Computer and also he is an Editorial Board Member in International Journal of Management in Education, Scopus, Inderscience, EAI Endorsed Transactions on e-Learning, and Bulletin of the Karaganda university Pedagogy series. He is also a Book Series Editor in IGI Global Publisher, Springer, etc. All of his writing, including his research, involves elements of creative nonfiction in the Human Computing learning system. He is also interested in creative writing and digital media, Learning, AI, student health learning, etc. He has published 500 in peer-reviewed international journals. He has authored and co-authored several scientific book publications in journals and conferences and is a frequent reviewer of international journals and international conferences and also, he is also a reviewer in Inderscience, EAI Journals, IGI Global, Science Publications, etc.

Muhammad Mujtaba Asad is serving as an Assistant Professor and Lead Researcher of Educational Technologies and TVET Research Group at Sukkur IBA University, Pakistan. Dr Mujtaba has national and international working experience of more than 12 years at industrial and educational sector in the domain of Educational Technologies, Work & Product-Based Education and Technical and Vocational Education. Dr. Mujtaba has published more than Seventy (70) research articles (WoS & Scopus Indexed) in reputed international journals and conferences worldwide. Also, three books related to the observational skills of competent educators and Innovative educational technologies under the CS and Taylor Frances publishing house is in his publication credit. He has also received three Gold, one Silver and one Bronze medal in international research and development completions with seven best research awards in Malaysia, Korea, Saudi Arabia, Pakistan and UAE on his commercialized projects. Moreover, Dr. Mujtaba is also an active member of Seven (7) national and international research grants. Dr. Mujtaba is also an internationally certified educational technologist (Malaysian Board of Technologist) and holds certifications and qualification in industrial safety and health education from NIOSH and OSH Department of Ontario, Canada. He is also serving as an Editorial Board Member to twelve (12) reputed and indexed international journals. Dr. Mujtaba also holds several international Copyrights and has filed one Product Patent under the title of HAZFO Expert 1.0 for Drilling Operation. He had been awarded an honorary lifetime International Ambassadorship by University Tun Hussein Onn Malaysia based on his academic achievements and community services.

Luís Miguel Cardoso holds a PhD in Modern Languages and Literatures, in the speciality of Comparative Literature from the University of Coimbra, Portugal. He was Dean of the School of Education and Social Sciences of the Polytechnic Institute of Portalegre, Portugal, between 2010 and 2018 and Deputy Director of the Master in Media and Society. He was President of ARIPESE, Association of Reflection and Intervention in the Educational Policy of Higher Education Schools in Portugal (2015 – 2018) and Coordinator of the Communication Bureau of the Polytechnic Institute of Portalegre (2013 – 2017). Adjunct Professor at the Department of Language and Communication Sciences at the School of Education and Social Sciences of the Polytechnic Institute of Portalegre, Portugal, he has been a professor of Higher Education since 1995 and is currently a researcher at the Centre for Comparative Studies at the University of Lisbon. His main areas of teaching and research are Sciences of Language and Communication, Pedagogical Innovation, Literacies, Education, Higher Education and Social Responsibility, and Literature and Cinema, under which published articles and book chapters and made presentations in Portugal and several countries, including USA, Brazil, Chile, Colombia, Spain, Luxembourg, France, Switzerland, United Kingdom, Ireland, Italy, Greece, Hungary, Georgia, Bulgaria, Poland, Romenia, Canada, Thailand, Vietnam, Turkey, Ukraine, Philippines, Thailand, Indonesia, United Arab Emirates, Iraq, Australia, Pakistan, Uzbekistan, Bangladesh, Saudi Arabia, Mozambique, China and India. He is a member of several international organizations and associations, as well as a member of the editorial board of international journals in the areas of Language and Communication Sciences, Comparative Literature, Literature and Cinema, Literacies and Education.

Raghavendra Acharya is the Associate Dean of the School of Business at VIT-AP University in Andhra Pradesh. He holds a PhD, MBA, specializing in Security Analysis and Portfolio Management, Financial Derivatives, Capital Market, and Fintech Applications. He is also a Professor at VIT-AP School of Business.

Thangaraja Arumugam is an Assistant Professor at Business School, Vellore Institute of Technology, Chennai. He did his dissertation in the area of marketing intelligence. He has got 10 years of teaching experience. He teaches in the areas of Consumer Psychology, Marketing analytics, business analytics, and Fraud analytics. His area of interest is the field of behavioral analytics. He holds a Postgraduate program in Business Analytics and Business Intelligence from the University of Texas. He acquired a Marketing analytics and marketing strategy professional degree and is an alumnus of the Indian Institute of Management, Kozhikode. His research works have been published and presented in reputed journals (Scopus, SSCI, A category of ABDC) and international conferences. He holds patents in the field of social mining, image processing, and deep learning. He has been invited to talk in reputed institutions and has been a resource person for international workshops/ Webinars. He holds several certifications from reputed institutions. His present research focus is on neuroscience and brain wave visualization and analytics for neuromarketing directions.

Anvay Bhargava's almost three decade journey in academia has been defined by a commitment to nurturing future HR leaders through courses in Talent Acquisition, L&D, PMS, HR analytics and personalised mentoring. As Entrepreneurship Educator, Dr. Bhargava has been involved in consulting MSMEs to help them create and manage HR function effectively. Leveraging various certifications as PPA from Thomas Assessments, NLP practitioner, Life Coach, Wellness Coach, Generative AI in HR, People Analytics, etc. Dr. Bhargava has honed analytical skills that complement his passion for teaching and has been instrumental in driving the mission to develop well-rounded professionals equipped for the dynamic world of Human Resources. With passion to train, been involved in MDP sessions for companies like Canara Bank, Au Bank, NHPC, BPCL, Wonder Home Finance, Aavas Financiers, etc. Also running a YouTube channel, "Learn HR with Anvay" to reach out to broader audience interested in HR concepts.

Manal Hendawi holds a PhD in Education (Social studies curriculum & instruction) and brings over 23 years of experience in teaching, course design, and learner development. Her areas of expertise include Educational Social Studies and Early Childhood Curriculum Development. Dr. Hendawi has worked extensively with learners in both formal and informal settings, across traditional classrooms and non-traditional learning environments in the Middle East and England. Throughout her career, Dr. Hendawi has demonstrated strong interpersonal communication skills, adaptability, and a deep commitment to educational excellence. She has consistently delivered high-quality instruction while meeting the academic needs and deadlines outlined in institutional curriculum plans. Her work reflects a passion for inclusive, learner-centered education and continuous improvement in teaching practices.

Jessy K. Jayanth is Phd research scholar and Assistant Professor of Law at Saveetha School of Law,Saveetha institute of Medical and technical sciences Chennai. She holds an LL.M. in Taxation Laws from Government Law College, Kozhikode (University of Calicut) and an LL.B. from Government Law College, Thrissur. Her academic and research interests include Constitutional Law, criminology,Taxation, Alternative Dispute Resolution, and Gender Justice. She has presented papers at various national and international conferences, engaging with critical socio-legal themes such as Dalit property rights and the Uniform Civil Code. Her published work reflects a commitment to justice-oriented legal scholarship and has appeared on accessible academic platforms. She has also undertaken research on tax reforms in the digital economy, with a focus on the challenges posed by e-commerce. Through a combination of teaching, research, and legal analysis, she contributes meaningfully to contemporary legal discourse.

Amit Kumar Kashyap is an accomplished legal scholar and educator based in Ahmedabad, Gujarat, India. Currently serving as Asst. Prof of Law, Institute of Law, Nirma University, Ahmedabad, Gujarat, India. He has experience working in prestigious institutes like Gujarat National Law University, Indian Institute of Management Ahmedabad, Indian Institute of Management Rohtak, Adani University Ahmedabad & companies like Kotak Mahindra Bank, Mumbai. He has authored more than 7 books including Financial Market Regulations in South Asia and Artificial Intelligence: Law and Policy Implications and has contributed more than 20 research papers in various national and international journals. With an extensive academic background, including a Ph.D. in Structured Finance law from Manipal University Jaipur, an MBA–LL.M with specializations in Finance and Business Laws from National Law University, Jodhpur, CS Executive from ICSI, New Delhi, Certified in International Economic Law from the University of Barcelona, Spain, Dr. Amit brings a wealth of knowledge to his roles. He is also a consultant to various firms like Cyberra Legal Services Ahmedabad, IIFS Pvt. Ltd. Ahmadabad & EEIG-Global.

Dhiraj Kumar Shakya is a multilingual academic specializing in Buddhist philosophy, language education, and cross-cultural studies. He holds a B.A. in Philosophy from Mahachulalongkornrajavidyalaya University and an M.A. in Teaching Chinese as a Second Language from Fo Guang Shan Tsunglin University. He has served as an academic translator at Krirk University and currently leads South Asian Marketing and International Affairs, building educational partnerships across South Asia. His research interests include Buddhist thought, intercultural communication, and translation studies, and he has presented at several international academic conferences.

Michael J. Leo is an accomplished academic and dedicated educator with nearly two decades of experience in teacher education. He currently serves as Associate Professor, Dean of Academics, and IQAC Coordinator at St. Xavier's College of Education (Autonomous), Palayamkottai. He holds a Ph.D. in Education and multiple postgraduate degrees, including M.Sc. in Mathematics, M.Sc. in Psychology, and M.Ed., alongside qualifications in SLET and NET. His academic journey began with a B.Sc. in Mathematics from Aditanar College, followed by a Master's from St. Xavier's College (Autonomous), and culminated in his doctoral work at the same institution. Dr. Leo has authored and co-authored over 15 peer-reviewed journal articles and contributed to numerous books and conference proceedings. His research spans areas such as educational psychology, pedagogy, ICT integration, and teacher education. He has also been involved in developing e-content and MOOCs and has received recognition for his scholarly contributions, including the Best Teacher Educator Award in 2023. As a resource person, he has delivered lectures, conducted workshops, and served on academic boards and advisory committees of several colleges. He has successfully guided 32 M.Ed. dissertations and is currently supervising Ph.D. scholars. His editorial and peer-review roles in reputed journals further reflect his active engagement in the academic community. In addition to his academic work, Dr. Leo has organized seminars, training programmes, and community outreach initiatives and has held various leadership roles within his college, including Vice-Principal and Controller of Examinations. His professional footprint extends beyond the classroom into areas of curriculum development, teacher training, research mentoring, and institutional quality enhancement.

M. Iswarya is an Assistant Professor in the Department of Management Sciences at Hindusthan College of Engineering and Technology, Coimbatore, India. A gold medalist during her undergraduate studies, she possesses expertise in General Management, Human Resources, and Systems. Dr. Iswarya has contributed to the academic community through her publications in both national and international journals. She holds a doctoral degree focused on the area of Positive Organisational Behaviour. Her current research interests lie at the intersection of emerging technologies and business, specifically exploring Artificial Intelligence, Generative AI, gamification, the metaverse,and business analytics. Beyond her academic role, she is also an active trainer.

Biranchi Narayan P Panda is an Associate Professor (Law) in Xavier Law School (XLS), XIM University, India. He has more than 14 years of experience in different academic and corporate Institutions in India. During this period, he has held the position of Senior Academic Consultant at the Indian Institute of Corporate Affairs (IICA), Ministry of Corporate Affairs, (GoI). In this role, he has overseen and made significant contributions to numerous training programmes focused on various aspects of business laws. Additionally, he has devoted efforts to the exclusive development of diverse training modules on Corporate Laws tailored for senior executives and management personnel from public, private, and other corporate entities. Before this, he was involved in the coordination and development of numerous online courses for different law programmes while working at the School of Law (SoL) at Indira Gandhi National Open University (IGNOU) in New Delhi. During these periods in Delhi, he has also hold position of Senior Research Associate in CUTs International, an international non-governmental organisation, and Associate Manager (Learning & Development) in Rainmaker, a corporate law firm. He possesses expertise in field of Business Laws, Labour Laws, Constitutional Law, different Regulatory Laws, and international laws etc. He has completed his M.Phil. from Jamia Millia Islamia, India and completed his Ph.D. in Law from Faculty of Law, Jamia Millia Islamia, New Delhi. In addition to his academic achievements, he has actively participated in several conferences, presenting numerous papers on a wide range of legal topics within different venues. He has presented and chaired many conference papers in several forums on diverse areas of law. He has also published several papers in few leading national & International journals. He has also been invited as a resource person and delivered talks on several contemporary issues in different forums. He is also a regular contributor towards the leading mass media of the country namely; The Times of India, The New Indian Express and Pioneer etc. on diverse legal and social relevance. He is also a regular trainer/guest speaker at Central & State PSUs, Universities and Colleges and many other forums in India. Newspaper Publication: The Times of India, The New Indian Express, The Sunday Guardian, Pioneer, Orissa Today, Dharitri

P. Paramasivan has been working as Director of Dhaanish Ahmed College of Engineering, Chennai, India. And he is an accomplished professor with extensive experience and he has dedicated his career to mentoring and educating students with a passion for engineering and technology. Over approximately 15 years, he has individually guided and motivated around 15,000 students in their pursuit of knowledge and success. Recognized as a self-driven and highly motivated teacher. He possesses a unique skill set in designing effective teaching and learning processes. His strategic approach to education has yielded exceptional results, earning him a trusted reputation among prestigious institutions in Chennai since 2008. His commitment to bridging the gap between academia and industry is commendable. He has played a pivotal role in establishing an industrial platform connecting students with top-tier hardware and software companies. Through collaborations with renowned organizations such as ZOHO, Ashok Leyland, Pyroferus Technologies, and Godrej, he has provided students invaluable opportunities to engage in research projects aligned with their interests.

Rehana Parveen is an Assistant Professor of Law at Prince Sultan University in Riyadh, Saudi Arabia. She holds a PhD in Constitutional Law from Aligarh Muslim University and is a Fellow of the UK Higher Education Academy. At PSU since 2013, she teaches subjects including Constitutional Law, Human Rights Law, and AI & Law, while also serving as Chair of the College of Law's Quality Assurance Committee. Her research focuses on environmental law, healthcare law, and data privacy, and she has led Microsoft-funded projects on data security in Saudi Arabia. Dr. Parveen is a committed scholar with numerous publications and active engagement in international conferences.

S. Silvia Priscila is working as Associate Professor & Head, Department of Computer Science, Bharath Institute of Higher Education and Research

Zohaib Hassan Sain is a seasoned professional with expertise in Quality Management, Compliance, Training, and Research. He holds an MS in Quality Management and is an Education Committee Member at the Association for Project Safety. Zohaib has extensive experience as a freelance trainer for OSHAssociation UK, contributing to the Train the Trainer Program and conducting Online Master Class training. With roles as a Compliance Officer and Assistant Manager Admin & Compliance in Pakistan, Zohaib holds certifications in ISO standards (9001, 14001, 45001, 21001), Lean Six Sigma, and various leadership and education programs. He is a prolific researcher with numerous publications and has received multiple awards for his contributions. Zohaib is actively involved in international events, serving as a moderator, speaker, and judge. His commitment to professional affiliations, including APS, IIRSM, and PSC, reflects his dedication to quality, safety, and education. Overall, Zohaib Hassan Sain is a versatile and accomplished professional with a rich background in various domains.

R G Sakthivelan is a seasoned academic expert in ISE with a strong record in teaching, research, and departmental leadership. His impactful work spans machine learning, AI, and video analytics — with contributions to healthcare diagnostics and industrial big data. Based in Bengaluru, he focuses on elevating engineering education and fostering student development.

Devilito Prasetyo Tatipang born in Maelang on December 30th 1999, is currently a Research Consultant, Journal Reviewer, Researcher, Journal Manager and Editor, Mendeley Mentor, Research-Assistant and full-time Lecturer-Assistant of English Education Department of the Faculty of Languages and Arts, Universitas Negeri Manado. He completed his Bachelor degree at Universitas Negeri Manado in 2021 and Master degree at the same University in 2023, since then he has presented his research in various National and International conferences in Indonesia. He has also published articles in several nationally accredited and reputable international journals. Devilito's areas of interests are in Technology-Injected Language Learning, Issues in English Language Teaching (ELT), Pedagogical Linguistics, Curriculum Development, ELT in Multilingualism Context, Motivational Studies and Pedagogy for English Language Learners (ELL)

R. Thangamani is currently working as an Associate Professor, Department of Management, Hindusthan College of Arts & Science, Coimbatore. He had completed his Doctorate in Management and Master of Business Administration at Coimbatore Institute of Management and Technology (CIMAT) and M.A in Yoga for Human Excellence with a First Class at Bharathiar University and M.Phil. from Alagappa University. Currently,. He has published eight books in the field of Management and Logistics. He has 19 years of teaching and research experience.. He has been awarded the "Best Faculty Award" by National Science Foundation. He has published number of book titles like "LOGISTICS MANAGEMENT", "INVESTMENT MANAGEMENT" "AVIATION MANAGEMENT" "SUPPLY CHAIN AND DELIVERY MANAGEMENT" "ENTREPRENEURIAL DEVELOPMENT AND SMALL BUSINESS MANAGEMENT" "CONTAINERIZATION". He holds certificate courses in the "Leadership Clinic" from Indian Institute of Management (IIM) Kozhikode

Madhu L. Veerapaneni, a seasoned educator with 18 years of experience and a Ph.D. in Human Resource Development, is committed to empowering individuals to achieve their full potential. Her goal is to foster the development of managers who excel professionally and contribute positively to society. Dr. Veerapaneni believes that true leadership lies in nurturing the growth of others. Skilled in team building, communication, mentoring and people management, she is passionate about HR areas such as performance management and training & development and strives to create environments where individuals can thrive.

J. Prince Vijai is an Assistant Professor of Operations Management at ICFAI Business School, Hyderabad, India. He teaches graduate-level courses in Operations & Supply Chain Management, as well as Business Analytics, with an emphasis on integrating theoretical frameworks and models with applied case-based learning. His areas of research include manufacturing, service, and supply chain operations, particularly focusing on capacity, flexibility, and sustainability. His scholarly contributions, grounded in both empirical and analytical methods, have been published in leading international journals, conference proceedings, academic books, and professional magazines.

Index

A

B

C

D

E

F

G

H

I

M

O

P

S

U

V

www.ingramcontent.com/pod-product-compliance
Lightning Source LLC
LaVergne TN
LVHW062331300926
849161LV00007B/1659